Stalin's Curse

STALIN'S CURSE

*Battling for Communism in War
and Cold War*

ROBERT GELLATELY

Alfred A. Knopf

NEW YORK 2013

THIS IS A BORZOI BOOK
PUBLISHED BY ALFRED A. KNOPF

www.aaknopf.com

Library of Congress Cataloging-in-Publication Data
Gellately, Robert.
Stalin's curse : battling for communism in war and Cold War /
by Robert Gellately.
pages : maps ; cm
Includes bibliographical references and index.
ISBN 978-0-307-26915-7
1. Stalin, Joseph, 1879–1953.   2. Soviet Union—Politics and
government—1936–1953.   3. Communism—Europe—History—
20th century.   I. Title.
DK268.S8G44 2013
947.084'2092—dc23   2012028768

Front-of-jacket photograph © ullstein bild/The Granger Collection, NYC

Jacket design by Linda Huang

Manufactured in the United States of America
First Edition

To Marie

Contents

Contents

PART III: STALIN'S COLD WAR

Abbreviations and Glossary

Bolsheviks	"Majority" faction of the RSDLP, founded in 1903
Central Committee	Soviet Communist Party supreme body, elected at party congresses
Cheka (or Vecheka)	Chrezvychainaia Kommissiia (Extraordinary Commission), the original Soviet secret police, 1917–22; members of the secret police continued to be called Chekists even after 1922
Cominform	Communist Information Bureau, founded in 1947 as the successor to the Comintern
Comintern	Communist International organization, founded in 1919
GPU–OGPU	Gosudarstvennoe Politicheskoe Upravlenie (State Political Administration)–Obedinennoe Gosudarstvennoe Politicheskoe Upravlenie (Joint State Political Administration), the secret police, 1922–34
General Secretary	Stalin's title as head of the Soviet Communist Party's Central Committee, in fact, as head of government and leader of the country
Gulag	Glavnoe Upravlenie Lagerei (main camp administration), eventually in charge of Soviet concentration camps
Kremlin	A fortified series of buildings in Moscow; also, the official residence of the Soviet head of government; also, the Soviet government

kulaks	"Rich" peasants
lishentsy	Soviet people "without rights"
NEP	New Economic Policy (1921–29), introduced by Lenin
NKVD	Narodnyi Komissariat Vnutrennikh Del (People's Commissariat for Internal Affairs), the secret police; in 1934, the OGPU was reorganized into the NKVD and named GUBG NKVD
Politburo	Main committee of the Central Committee of the Soviet Communist Party
Pravda	Main newspaper of the Bolsheviks; later the semiofficial paper of the Soviet Communist Party
Sovnarkom / SNK	Council of People's Commissars, the government body established by the Russian Revolution; succeeded in 1946 by Council of Ministers
Soviet	Russian word for "council"
Stavka	Main command of the Soviet armed forces
TASS	Telegraph Agency of the Soviet Union, the official news distributor
Vozhd	Leader, equivalent to German *Führer*
Wehrmacht	German armed forces

Divisions of Poland, Germany, and Austria, 1945

Atlantic Ocean

North Sea

LATVIAN S.S.R.

Riga

LITHUANIAN S.S.R.

Kaliningrad

R.S.F.S.R.

Vilnius

Minsk

Gdansk

POLAND

BYELORUSSIAN S.S.R.

Hamburg

NETH.

U.K.

Berlin

Poznań

Warsaw

U.S.S.R.

Amsterdam

U.S.S.R.

Leipzig

Wrocław

Łodz

GERMANY

Dresden

Brussels

BELG.

Frankfurt a.M.

Prague

Kraków

UKRAINIAN S.S.R.

Lviv (Lvov)

FRANCE

France

U.S.

CZECHOSLOVAKIA

Strasbourg

France

Munich

U.S.S.R.

MOLDOVAN S.S.R.

Germany 1937

Poland 1937

U.S.

Vienna

Budapest

ROMANIA

Bern

SWITZ.

France

AUSTRIA

U.K.

HUNGARY

0

250 Miles

0

250 Km

Europe and the Soviet Union in 1945

0   500 Miles

0   500 Km

NORWAY

SWEDEN

Oslo

Stockholm

North
Sea

*Baltic
Sea*

DENMARK

Copenhagen

Kaliningrad

R.S.F.S.

IRELAND

Dublin

Hamburg

Gdansk

UNITED
KINGDOM

NETH.

U.K.

Berlin

Vistula R.

London

GERMANY

Oder R.

U.S.S.R.

Warsaw

POLAND

Atlantic

Brussels

Rhine R.

BELG.

Frankfurt a.M.

Wrocław

Ocean

France

Prague

Paris

U.S.

CZECHOSLOVAKIA

Kraków

France

Munich

U.S.S.R.

Vienna

FRANCE

Bern

AUSTRIA

Budapest

SWITZ.

France

U.S.

U.K.

HUNGARY

PORTUGAL

Marseille

ITALY

Belgrade

YUGOSLAVIA

Madrid

Lisbon

Barcelona

SPAIN

Rome

Tirana

ALBANIA

Mediterranean

Casablanca

Algiers

Tunis

Sea

MOROCCO

ALGERIA

TUNISIA

MALTA

U. S. S. R.

KAMCHTKA
PENINSULA

Amur R.

SAKHALIN
ISLAND

MONGOLIA

Khabarovsk

Harbin

KURIL ISLANDS

CHINA

Vladivostok

HOKKAIDO

Beijing

U.S.S.R.

Sapporo

Dairen

KOREA

Sea of
Japan

Hwang Ho

Seoul
U.S.
Pusan

HONSHU

Pacific
Ocean

Tokyo

JAPAN

Osaka

Nanjing

SHIKOKU

Yangtze R.

Shanghai

East
China
Sea

KYUSHU

OKINAWA

Taipei

FORMOSA

Hong Kong

Ending of the War and the
Division of Korea

0   500 Miles

0   500 Km

Stalin's Curse

Introduction

No one would have guessed it from the mug shots of one of the suspects picked up by the Russian secret police at the turn of the twentieth century. The bearded young man looked scruffy and slightly roguish, but his face revealed no obvious signs of deep-seated evil, or even anger and resentment. The police knew him as Joseph Vissariono-vich Dzhughashvili, a troublemaker, labor activist, and renegade Marx-ist, and they had arrested him several times and exiled him to the East. From there he would escape and return to the fray in his native Georgia, in the Caucasus. He was a member of the Russian Social Democratic Labor Party, and he had attracted the attention of Vladimir Lenin, leader of its Bolshevik faction. In 1912 the young firebrand adopted the nom de guerre *Stalin,* meaning "Man of Steel." He won recognition in the politi-cal struggles of the day and especially for several writings, notably on the explosive and important nationality issue in the Russian Empire.

In late 1913 the police picked him up yet again, decided they had seen more than enough, and sent him to deepest Siberia. There he would remain until early 1917, when the entire structure of the tsarist regime came tumbling down—though not because of anything that Lenin and his tiny band of followers had done. Like Stalin, most of the key Bolshe-viks were in exile as well.

The inexorable revolutionary energy in 1917 was generated by the Great War. Although in the beginning many regarded the war as a noble and patriotic affair for Imperial Russia, the years of endless deaths and sacrifice, coupled with discontent on the home front, did what several generations of dedicated rebels had been unable to do. The backlash against the war opened the floodgates of an elemental social revolution that swept away Tsar Nicholas II in February 1917 and made it possible for the Bolsheviks to return to what Lenin called "the freest country in the world." When the Provisional Government continued the war, with no more success than the tsar, the revolution struck yet again in October, this time with Lenin leading the way. Fittingly enough, Stalin became the commissar of nationalities in the new government, an important post in the multinational empire of the day.

The man who would head the Kremlin for some three decades was born in Gori, Georgia, on December 6, 1878, though he routinely gave his birth date as December 21, 1879. He may have changed the date to avoid the draft at one point, but he was always secretive about his background. Indeed, the official biography he inspired, published in millions of copies before and after the Second World War, devotes little more than a dozen lines to his family and upbringing.

When Lenin became ill in 1921 and the next year was forced to spend time away from Moscow, infighting began among the party elite to determine the successor to the beloved leader. Stalin was well placed in the committees and won supporters because of his deep commitment to Leninism, his passion for the Communist ideal, combined with realism, and a ruthlessness in politics that Machiavelli would have appreciated.

Where had he found the mission to which he devoted his life and that dominated everything? Only a week after his hero died in 1924, in a speech to the Kremlin's military school, Stalin attributed his "boundless faith" in Communism to Lenin. He pointed to Lenin's *Letter to a Comrade,* a short pamphlet written in 1902. He had received it in the mail the following year, as he lingered in one of his exiles in the East, before he entered Lenin's life. Although he told his audience in 1924 that the pamphlet had included a personal letter from its author, there had been no such message. Perhaps at the time, or on later reflection, Stalin meant that in a strange and compelling way, he felt as though Lenin's *Letter to a Comrade* had been written just for him. That was the moment of his epiphany, when he found a new faith, and looking back he recalled that the pamphlet had made "an indelible impression upon me, one that has never left me."[1]

Lenin's short "letter" reads like the outline for a modern terrorist organization, together with a sketch for a new kind of state to follow. The vision was beyond anything seen before in socialist literature. At the head of the organization, there would be a "special and very small executive group," the avant-garde leading the way to the future. Later in the Soviet Union this vanguard would be called the political bureau (or Politburo). It would include Lenin and quite remarkably also Stalin. Below the "executive group," envisioned in the pamphlet, there would be a central committee of the most talented and experienced "professional revolutionaries." Local branches would spread propaganda and establish networks, and in a preview of the future, there would be strong centralized control.

If Leninism provided the faith and the big idea, when did Stalin cross the psychological threshold of being willing to kill for it? Soon after May 1899, when he was expelled from high school, in fact a seminary, he became involved in labor politics in Georgia's capital, Tiflis, and in its second city, Batumi. He was entering a violent world, particularly after a great railway strike in August 1900. The police frequently shot at strikers and tried to infiltrate the ranks. Workers responded with savage reprisals, including maiming and murdering the staff of certain companies. Stalin's complicity in a first killing has been traced to 1902. However, here, as in several subsequent cases from the pre-1914 period, we have no direct evidence.[2] The party in the Caucasus condemned anarchism and wanton terrorism, yet it certainly did not shirk from getting rid of police spies.[3]

Until he was sent off to Siberia in 1913, Stalin "was not outstandingly different from other revolutionaries in behavior, thought, and morality."[4] When he returned from exile in 1917, he was soon thrust into a position of authority, and especially in the civil war that followed to 1921, he went through the whole range of events—as commissar, government speaker, and party journalist. He served as one of Lenin's troubleshooters, and in July 1918 he was in Tsaritsyn on a mission. It was there for the first time that he ordered executions in his capacity as a member of the new government.[5] Perhaps he had done so before, but the civil war years represented a new stage in his revolutionary career, and Tsaritsyn was special. As if to recognize that, in 1925 he allowed his comrades in government Mikhail Kalinin and Abel Yenukidze to suggest renaming that city on the Volga in his honor, as Stalingrad.

Stalin's direction of state-sponsored killing of political enemies can be traced to the civil war, through the Great Terror of the 1930s, the Second World War, and into the Cold War. A scrupulous follower of

Leninist teachings, he regarded violence as a tool that the skillful revolutionary wielded against a mighty enemy, namely the capitalists and their enablers. He killed apparently without remorse, if and when that helped him get what he wanted, though more often he used the old tsarist weapon of deporting individuals and even whole ethnic groups deemed to be "enemies." During the 1930s in particular, violence took on a momentum of its own and became counterproductive. For that reason he reined it in.

It is entirely possible that Stalin was or became a psychopath, as asserted recently by Jörg Baberowski in an account focusing mainly on the terror in the 1930s. Yet Baberowski is surely mistaken to claim that Stalin simply "liked killing" for its own sake, that the "violence was an end in itself" and bore no relation to the perpetrators' ideology or motives.[6] To the contrary, as I show, Marxist-Leninist ideology as interpreted by Stalin drove the men at the top, just as it inspired many millions more. His interpretations of the sacred texts deeply affected the country's economic, social, cultural, and foreign policies. The life of every citizen was transformed.

Stalinism was more than terror, and its ideas dominated the Soviet Union and Eastern Europe for decades to come. Stalin's influence affected other Communist regimes around the globe, such as in China. In 1949 Mao Zedong began his regime by consciously emulating the Stalinist model, and in the first three years he and his followers, according to one historian, "wrought more fundamental changes in China's social structure than had occurred in the previous 2,000 years."[7]

While the makeup of Stalin's psyche may have been set early, it took time for his more cruel propensities to be revealed. In the 1920s he became identified with making "socialism in one country," a moderate adaptation of "orthodox" Marxist-Leninist theory, which said that the revolution in Russia, to be kept alive, had to spread beyond its borders to the West. In the circumstances after Lenin's death, the Red tide ebbed everywhere else in Europe, but in Russia the "one country" approach was appealing even to militants, who now willingly turned to getting the Soviet system up and running. By the end of the decade, Stalin began attaching special urgency to what became the great national modernization project. He fostered industry, introduced the collectivization of agriculture, and sanctioned the use of terror against anyone who stood in the way. Good Bolsheviks and former allies like Nikolai Bukharin, who counseled moderation, came under suspicion, were pushed aside, and several years later met their end.

It is certainly remarkable that, regardless of their political differences, no one in the Soviet hierarchy, certainly not Stalin or even Bukharin, ever gave up on achieving Lenin's dream of bringing their great truth to the rest of the world. The Bolsheviks prided themselves on being in the vanguard of a great international socialist movement that would overcome nationalist hatreds and war. Lenin swore back in 1919 that after Communist revolutions swept over Western Europe and beyond, the Marxists would eventually establish a "World Federative Republic of Soviets," in which all states would be independent, with fraternal links to Moscow.[8] A year later Stalin thought that new Communist states of the future, like "Soviet Germany, Poland, Hungary, Finland," and so on—anticipating the success of leftist revolutions—would not be ready "to enter immediately into a federative link with Soviet Russia." He considered that "the most acceptable form of approach [for such states] would be a confederation (a union of independent states)."[9] However, they surely would become part of some sort of Red Empire eventually.

According to Lenin, wars among the capitalists were endemic, and sooner or later the new Soviet regime, already encircled by these powers, would be attacked. Stalin's variation on that theme was to press on with the great changes, avoid getting bogged down in international conflicts, and enter the battle only to win like "the laughing third man in a fight." That theory nearly led to utter disaster in mid-1941 when, thanks to the Kremlin's astonishing mistakes, Hitler's attack caught the Soviet Union by surprise and pushed it to the brink of defeat.

Even so, Stalin soon theorized that Hitler was unwittingly playing a revolutionary role. According to this updated Kremlin view, the destructiveness unleashed by the Germans would soon present the Communists with the first real opportunity since the Great War to take up anew the old Leninist imperative to carry the revolution to the world. In this book, I trace how Stalin and his comrades tried to capitalize on the intense passion and political conflicts of the war against the fascists and how, in doing so, they played a major role in bringing about the Cold War and an arms race.

Already in the 1930s, Stalin had become a dictator in everything but name and was prone to using terror as a method of rule, justifying it in the name of guarding the revolution from its internal and external enemies. At the same time, he and others fostered a leadership cult that turned him into a god. He inspired activists at home and abroad, as well as fellow travelers and sympathizers around the globe. In the wake of the Second World War and with his help, some disciples imposed Stalinist-style regimes. They varied in severity and repression, for a host of reasons I will explain. Nowhere, however, could any of these systems allow democratic freedoms to survive, so that long after Stalin was gone, many millions of people shouldered his heritage as a heavy burden and even a curse.

In this book I trace the origins of this misfortune to its incubation period, which stretched from the first days of the Second World War in 1939 to Stalin's death in 1953. I examine the central part he played in those event-filled years, when he and his followers battled for Communism in Europe and around the globe. I have taken a fresh look at the issues, using a wide variety of primary Russian documents and other sources from Eastern Europe, released since the demise of the Soviet Union, as well as German, American, and British materials.

Historians have offered a number of competing interpretations of Stalin's involvement in the Cold War, and it is worth pointing out how the analysis in this book differs from others.

The first systematic effort to explain the Soviet Union's behavior in the immediate postwar period was the highly influential account by George F. Kennan. In 1946, as the senior U.S. diplomat in Moscow, he was concerned about Washington's lack of response to Soviet aggressiveness and penned a long telegram home that attempted to show what was really going on. The "Kremlin's neurotic view of world affairs," he said, was in essence little more than the "traditional and instinctive Russian sense of insecurity" dressed in the "new guise of international Marxism." They were the same old Russians, only now their Marxist rhetoric gave them a "fig leaf" of "moral and intellectual respectability."[10] Kennan emphasized the centuries-long continuities in Russian history, played down Communist ideology, and instead pointed to the tsarist-like features of Stalin's rule and Soviet foreign policy.[11] This perspective eventually came to be dubbed the "traditionalist" school in studies of the Cold War. Kennan himself remained steadfast in his efforts to undermine the role of ideology, in favor of focusing on international strategy and power politics.[12]

It is certainly true that during all Stalin's wartime dealings with the West, he uttered not a whisper of his revolutionary theories; nor did he hint at the deep convictions that he felt separated Communists from those he labeled capitalists, imperialists, and fascists. Instead he scrupulously hid his political passions and formulated demands for the postwar settlement exclusively in the name of guarding his country's security.

Nonetheless, the "traditionalist" focus on international power politics misinterprets Stalin's ambitions. My book contests the wisdom of such an emphasis and underlines the importance of the Soviet leader's ideological convictions. As I show, Marxist-Leninist teachings informed everything in his life, from his politics to his military strategy and personal values. He saw himself as anything but an updated version of an old-style Russian tsar. For example, in 1936 and on a routine party form not meant for publication, Stalin described his "job" as "professional revolutionary and party organizer."[13] Those words reflected a certain truth, even though by that time he had been at the pinnacle of power for more than a decade and was the patron of patrons, busily constructing his own leadership cult.[14]

By the late 1950s and especially during the 1960s, American historians challenged the traditionalist approach. These "revisionists" began claiming that the East-West conflict, which by then had mushroomed into the Cold War, had arisen mainly because the Soviet Union was forced to defend itself against the aggressiveness of the United States. These writers asserted that the American pursuit of "open-door expansion" all but forced the USSR into fighting back.[15] The documents show, quite to the contrary, that Moscow made all the first moves and that if anything the West was woefully complacent until 1947 or 1948, when the die was already cast.

Although there have been several varieties of revisionism, they are united in the claim that the primary responsibility for the emergence of the Cold War rests with the United States. Disputes arising within revisionism tend to concern questions of secondary importance. For example, some claim that the Americans were not driven by economics or acquisitiveness but by "foreign policy idealism." These scholars take Washington to task for providing "the crucial impetus for the escalation" of the East-West conflict by refusing "to recognize" the validity of Soviet claims for a "security zone."[16] However, these accounts do not consider the consequences of any such concessions, nor do they ponder whether it was indeed possible to reassure Stalin. In any event, given the dozens of states along the borders of the USSR, granting his demand for such a zone would have meant forcing many millions of people to submit to domination from Moscow. And as Stalin demonstrated time and again, he did not care what the Americans theorized about his motives, so long as they did nothing to stop him from getting what he wanted.

A variation on the revisionist theme posits that the Cold War was sparked by American misperceptions of Moscow's intentions, whereupon the United States then overreacted and provoked the Soviet Union into action "in a classic case of the self-fulfilling prophecy."[17] The documents reveal, of course, that Stalin took pride in deliberately misleading the White House.

The main revisionist arguments do not hold up under examination, and here I am in agreement with Russian historians like Vladislav Zubok and Constantine Pleshakov, who rightly insist that the Kremlin was not simply reactive to the West and entertained far greater ambitions than simply securing the borders.[18]

In this book I emphasize that the Communist ideological offensive commenced in August 1939 and persisted through the war against Hitler. The Western Allies, far from being too aggressive with their partner after June 1941, were overly accommodating. President Franklin Delano Roosevelt consistently sought to understand and sympathize with the Soviet position, and he bent over backwards to ignore or downplay Stalin's horrendous methods of rule and obvious ambitions. Charles Bohlen, a Roosevelt translator, wrote that the president suffered from the "conviction that the other fellow is a 'good guy' who will respond properly and decently if you treat him right."[19] Although FDR certainly deserves full credit for keeping the USSR in the war and thus reducing the deaths of Americans in combat, he failed to recognize the fundamental ideological and moral gap that existed between the Western democracies and Soviet Communism. Instead, he emboldened Stalin.

The president's sympathies were on display during the Big Three meetings in Tehran in November 1943, when he sided with the Soviet dictator rather than with British prime minister Winston Churchill. A member of the British delegation in Tehran remarked laconically: "This Conference is over when it has only just begun. Stalin has got the President in his pocket."[20] The Soviets invariably took Roosevelt's efforts to be friendly or accommodating as demonstrations of weakness. They were quick to exploit FDR's sympathies and his condemnation of old imperialist powers like Britain.[21]

Although Churchill had sensed what the Communists were all about at the time of the Russian Revolution, during the war he came to feel squeezed between the two new world powers and at times resigned himself to thinking he had to make the best of a bad situation. His strategy, to avoid blaming Stalin personally, involved a high degree of self-deception, as when he attributed policies he found particularly abhorrent to nameless Kremlin leaders behind the scenes in Moscow. Only thus could he hold on to his "cherished belief, or illusion," that "Stalin could be trusted."[22]

Another area that sets this book apart from others pertains to how the Soviet Union exported revolution. Precisely what steps it would take had to be worked out in practice, as indeed was the case after 1917 when Moscow had to decide how to rule its multinational state. Contrary to what we might assume, neither its politicians nor its administrators saw themselves as colonial masters, much less as tsarists or Great Russian chauvinists.[23] Instead they would arrive as saviors and educators with a mission "to release" various communities and constituencies across their great land "from the disease of backwardness."[24] They did not, of course, express themselves so bluntly in public and preferred to say—at least initially—that they sought to enlighten the ignorant, to free the oppressed, and to foster their cultures and languages.

The revolutionaries had bigger dreams, centering on the creation of a Red Empire that would be a novel "anti-imperial state."[25] This "new Russia" would ride the waves of Communist revolutions that would sweep over Europe, then the rest of the world. Of course, many millions of ordinary people in Finland, the Baltic states, Ukraine, Poland, Hungary, and Germany, and not least in the former tsarist-ruled Russia, looked upon the Russian Revolution and the Communism to which it gave birth as something akin to a plague. Even in 1917 a few thoughtful sympathizers despaired as they witnessed how basic freedoms were trampled underfoot.[26] For all that, Stalin embraced the Bolshevik vision and saw chances to foster it in the wider world during and immediately after the Second World War. How far he might have carried the Red flag had he not run into opposition remains an open question.

As Hitler's ally in September 1939, Stalin began imposing Communism on eastern Poland, the Baltic states, and with less success, Finland.[27] These initial efforts were soon undone, and the Wehrmacht nearly overran Leningrad and Moscow in late 1941. Even so, Stalin remained the consummate strategic thinker. He soon perceived that the new war had the effect of leveling "old regimes" and blurring national borders. With states and societies and the international order in disarray, he had a chance to build the Red Empire that he, along with Vladimir Lenin and the Bolsheviks, had wanted at the end of the First World War.

As it happened, in 1944 and 1945 and even later, the disorder offered more opportunities to build the Red Empire than Stalin thought it prudent to exploit. Ironically, this self-proclaimed revolutionary ended up restraining some of his ardent disciples in places like Iran, Greece, Yugoslavia, Korea, and China—not because he wanted to discourage the Communists as such but out of concern not to irritate his Western Allies. For the same reason, he held back his comrades who returned to France and Italy, where an unusually favorable alignment of forces existed at war's end. The Communist parties in both countries, the backbone of the resistance and still armed to the teeth, enjoyed far more support than any others. The *Vozhd,* or Leader, sometimes also called the *Khozyain,* the Boss or Master of the Kremlin, directed them to proceed slowly. So too did he counsel Mao Zedong, who politely ignored the advice and in 1949 stormed to power.

The Soviet Union under Stalin might well have advanced the Red Empire to the shores of the English Channel, had not the United States in 1947, with the support of Great Britain, become more deeply involved in Europe. Washington, a reluctant warrior, at first simply offered generous aid through the Marshall Plan. This funding was designed to overcome the postwar social crisis gripping the Continent and to restore hope there. The money was also made available to the Soviet Union and those in its sphere of influence, but Stalin rejected it, notwithstanding the desperate situation in his own country and all of Eastern Europe. As I maintain, confronted with the offer of American aid, Stalin was forced into a corner largely of his own ideological making. Were the USSR and Soviet satellite states to receive financial support, he reasoned, it would benefit the starving, but it would have an adverse effect on the Soviet mission to bring Communism to the world. According to this cost-benefit analysis, allaying suffering in the present would only prolong the struggle for a total revolutionary solution.

In this matter as in many others, the Soviet leader kept this "truth" to himself. He was willing, actually only too happy, to face the fact that capitalists were not, and could not, be friends of the Communists. Privately, and more than once, he confided to comrades that there was little to choose among "fascist countries," whether they were Germany and Italy or the United States and Great Britain. In his eyes, all of them were fundamentally inveterate enemies, and any agreements with them were no more than short-run tactics. Stalin had been predicting a final showdown with the capitalists since the 1920s, but in 1945, with his country reeling from the conflict with Germany, the time was inopportune. Nevertheless, in the latter part of the war, he had forged ahead wherever possible, with considerable success. One moment he could be up to his neck scrambling to get the Red Army first in Berlin, or scurrying to make gains against Japan, and in the meantime he would be coaching Communist exiles in Moscow before they returned home to set up new regimes.

In 1944 or 1945 the Kremlin Boss was too shrewd to think that the Red Army could simply occupy Poland, Czechoslovakia, Bulgaria, Romania, and Hungary and then openly hoist Communist leaders into Soviet-style dictatorships. That would have set off alarm bells in Britain and the United States, from whom he wanted loans, not hostility. Therefore, and on his express orders, the native Communists parachuted into place back home were to create "national front" coalition governments. That strategy was followed all over Eastern and Central Europe, and Stalin wanted it everywhere in Asia as well. It was strictly a transition stage to quiet the fears of his Western Allies as well as the local population.

His preference was to continue the wartime alliance, to milk it for all it was worth, while at the same time planting regimes to his liking wherever the Red Army went. He stage-managed these moves and upbraided any acolytes who tried to go too fast. Although all were instructed to maintain the facade of a multiparty system, there was not the slightest chance that genuine liberal democracy would ever be permitted.

The challenge for the Soviets and those they helped into power was that for years all these countries had exhibited extreme anti-Russian and/or anti-Communist attitudes. And yet before the dust of war had settled, Stalin saw to their transformation into police states on the Soviet model.[28] He exercised a profound influence, far more hands-on than often supposed. Although he was especially cautious about getting involved in armed conflict with the West, he was always prepared to go over to the offensive, or to encourage others to do so, when the chances of success for the Communist cause looked good. As he put it succinctly to Yugoslav comrades in 1948: "You strike when you can win, and avoid the battle when you cannot. We will join the fight when conditions favor us and not when they favor the enemy."[29]

I use the term *Stalinization* to characterize this process, rather than *Sovietization,* but either concept fits the essence of how Moscow established control over what became its satellite countries.[30] Of course, Stalin put his personal stamp on the ideology and system of rule he exported, and his foreign disciples, convinced as they were that his was the winning brand, copied everything they could; even the independent-minded Yugoslavs at first begged to be instructed by advisers of all kinds from Moscow. Most of the new leaders, far from getting to know Stalin only gradually, as some historians have suggested, worked hand in glove with him.[31] They willingly went to Moscow to pay homage or to seek advice or aid from the Master as regularly as he permitted. They fell over themselves in trying to emulate the great man, while he responded to circumstances, changed the party line as needed, and enforced it on foreign comrades just as he did on those at home.

In 1947 and 1948 he called for a new wave of controls across Eastern Europe, partly as a response to the Marshall Plan, the program of aid that had also been offered to the Soviet Union. He had turned it down, then recommended and finally ordered that the leaders of the satellite states do so as well. A few muttered but then tightened the shackles on their people and saddled them with an economic system that was doomed to fail. Stalin increased Soviet defense spending at the expense of popular welfare, and in early 1951 he made a special point of demanding that Eastern European countries under Communist governments do so as well.[32]

This book also sets itself apart with respect to the attention paid to Soviet society in the postwar era, an area usually glossed over even in the "new Cold War history."[33] Such approaches would do well to focus more on the domestic scenes in the Red Empire.[34]

As for Stalin, I show that well before the shooting stopped in 1944–45, he set out to shore up his dictatorship and to straighten out the ideological wanderings that had crept into Communist theory. It was as if he were preparing the home front for the war of ideas and political principles that he was determined to pursue against the West. The image of the man and his rule in the last years of his life that I present is strikingly different from the one offered in a recent account that, by contrast, argues that the Soviet dictator "presided over a process of postwar domestic reform."[35]

What haunted him were images from the first days after the German invaders had broken through the lines in 1941. To his dismay, they had sometimes been welcomed as liberators, not just by a handful here and there but by cities, whole regions, and entire nations. As soon as the Germans were driven out, he began settling accounts with all "enemies within" in what for untold tens of thousands became a reign of terror. Multiple cases of ethnic cleansing took place in the USSR and in its sphere of influence. The wartime conferences foresaw what they euphemistically called "population transfers," which turned into living hell.

As the Red Army moved closer to Berlin, behind the lines another war against native resistance continued to be waged in the Baltic states, Poland, and Ukraine. The Soviet campaigns may have been about revenge seeking for real and imagined "treason," but at the same time they were integral to the battle for Communism and part of the crusade to bring these teachings deep into Europe. This struggle has usually been ignored in studies of the Cold War.

Hunger and the associated illnesses prevailed across the Continent and extended to the Soviet Union, where after drastic shortages during the war, a full-fledged famine in 1946–47 cost well over a million "excess deaths."[36] Why has this postwar social crisis in Eastern and Western Europe either been ignored or downplayed? There are many reasons. Some scholars have coldly assessed that the pain and suffering of those times were inevitable in the process of Europe's postwar recovery.[37] The horrors of the Third Reich and Second World War might have led some to underestimate the terrors of the aftermath. Nevertheless, in the long period since that time, historians have been slow in redressing the almost casual way in which postwar atrocities were initially treated. Several recent studies have demonstrated this point beyond doubt, including one that blames the Soviet Union for perpetrating multiple genocides.[38]

Finally I should point out that this book is not a biography of Stalin, even though he is the central character. The new documentation presents him as a curious figure, difficult to read, often brilliant, but ruthless and tyrannical. He was able to pursue numerous courses of action simultaneously and operated in such a fashion as to allow himself maximum flexibility. Like the warrior he imagined himself to be, he was adept at keeping everyone off guard. He could play the role of the jovial man of the people, down-to-earth and transparent, yet was practiced in keeping his thoughts and feelings closed off, even to his few close friends. What remains remarkable was his reserve toward ordinary people. Quite unlike Hitler, he did not crave their applause and indeed found their adoration repulsive, once saying to his daughter that every time "they open their mouths something stupid comes out!" It made him cringe. Mostly he communicated his commands and wishes through others. After the war, his few speeches were still poorly delivered, and as if he just did not care, whole years went by without his addressing the public at all.[39]

Most visitors to the Kremlin were overwhelmed, obsequious in the presence of a man who had ordered the deaths of thousands. One of his assistants later suggested that some, on first meeting the dictator, probably felt nervous because subconsciously they were intimidated at being near such a monster.[40]

For all that, Stalin impressed foreign statesmen, and most of them considered him a talented and extraordinary figure. British foreign secretary and later prime minister Anthony Eden said he would have chosen Stalin first for a team going to a conference. "He never stormed, he was seldom even irritated. By more subtle methods he got what he wanted without having seemed so obdurate."[41]

Can we possibly understand the enormity of the Communist-inspired tragedy and how it came to pass? Certainly no single individual, not even a leader more powerful than Lenin and Stalin combined, could have done it all alone. The Communist credo and its visions awakened wellsprings of enthusiasm and boundless energy and inspired untold millions of loyal followers. The original Russian revolutionaries thought they could sacrifice human rights in the short term because their goal was a future when "real freedom and justice" would prevail. They were convinced that some "external force" (including terror) was needed to enlighten their people. Once true emancipation was achieved, or so they thought, "mankind would do justice to this chiliastic dream of global revolution, and all the atrocities and crimes" that the Communists had committed "would be remembered only as passing incidents."[42] It turned out that the "final end of socialism" was always over the horizon, in a remote time and space. Still, part of what made it attractive to the true believers was that it was part of a "super-guaranteed future."[43]

Stalin was a powerful figure who identified with, symbolized, and fueled those aspirations. He and an army of Soviet standard-bearers led their own people, and then other nations, down the road to monumental failure, a man-made catastrophe that many refused to see until it imploded.[44]

PART I

THE STALINIST REVOLUTION

CHAPTER I

Making the Stalinist Revolution

Stalin was not the heir apparent when Lenin died in 1924. But within five years if not before, he was virtually the undisputed leader. A decade later he was the all-powerful dictator and creature of the Stalinist revolution, an extraordinary experiment in socialism. In his own lifetime he became a godlike figure, one to whom even the proudest comrade, wrongfully indicted by the Stalinist system, could willingly offer himself up for the cause. How was this possible? Here we will begin to put the pieces together and try to understand the emergence of Stalin, who became the Leader, Boss, or Master of the Kremlin.

IMPATIENT FOR COMMUNISM

Lenin's leadership was marked by bouts of illness, overwork, and strain, and from mid-1921 his health rapidly deteriorated, with a series of strokes beginning the following year. The question of who would take his place was uppermost in everyone's mind. Lenin was not exactly helpful in his political "testament"—two short notes he dictated to his secretary in December 1922. In those last words to his comrades, he worried about a "split" in the party and had negative things to say about all the leadership contenders. In a postscript dictated just over a week later (January 4, 1923), he said that Stalin was "too rude" and expressed the view that someone else might make a better general secretary.[1]

However, it would be a mistake to believe that Lenin wanted to exclude a bad choice for party leader and that, had he managed to get rid of Stalin, the Soviet Union would have been saved from a monster. In fact, until nearly the end, he trusted Stalin more than anyone and never mentioned removing him from the powerful Politburo or Central Committee. Stalin's "offense" was to slight Lenin's wife, Nadezhda Krupskaya, for not following doctors' orders to stop her sick husband from dictating work.

In the course of Lenin's illness, Stalin and his two weaker partners, Grigory Zinoviev and Lev Kamenev, formed an informal alliance (*troika*) in the Politburo. It was in place when Lenin died on January 24, 1924, and soon made its presence felt. In this alliance, Stalin's "ruling style," insofar as he had one, was collegial. By no means did he have everything his own way.

Arguably, the most powerful man in the country on Lenin's death was Leon Trotsky, the famed people's commissar for military affairs. However, Trotsky made careless mistakes, such as convalescing in the south and thus missing the great man's funeral. It did not matter that Stalin had misled him about the date of that event. Moreover, in early 1924 the ruling *troika* leaked old documents showing that back in 1913 Trotsky had said horrible things about Lenin.[2] Nor did Trotsky help himself when he said that the country would not accept him as leader because of his "Jewish origins."[3]

Next in line were Zinoviev and Kamenev, who were also Jewish. Their major failing was opposition to Lenin's decision to go for power in October 1917. Then there was the younger and dazzling Nikolai Bukharin, who, Lenin had thought, might not be "Marxist enough."

Although Stalin's record was mixed, his policies, which had once distanced him from many party members, were now beginning to make sense to them. He had stood almost alone in opposition to Trotsky's goal of speeding up the spread of Communist revolution. Then several such plans to foment revolution in Germany went badly wrong, and Stalin's criticism of the strategy gained traction. In the aftermath of the failed 1923 effort in Germany, the Soviet party generally moved to his side.

Along with *troika* partners Zinoviev and Kamenev, Stalin acted through the Central Committee to put mild pressure on Trotsky, who resigned early in the new year as people's commissar for military affairs. Trotsky said that he had tired of the insinuations, though by quitting he left the field to his enemies. When in due course Zinoviev and Kamenev began challenging Stalin's apparent readiness to abandon the long-standing commitment to revolution in Europe, the future dictator switched alliances and linked up with Bukharin (then only thirty-three), and the new duo soon emerged in control of the Politburo.[4]

The two friends differed on some important issues. Bukharin embraced the economic theory and political philosophy of the New Economic Policy (NEP), introduced by Lenin back in 1921, when agricultural production was down to 60 percent of its pre-1914 levels.[5] The NEP indicated that the Communists had to "retreat" because the country was in turmoil and desperation. It introduced a proportional tax on peasants, who were then allowed to sell privately any surplus that remained. This sliver of freedom gave agricultural production a boost, and by 1926 under the NEP the reforms were working. But the economy soon entered "a real, systemic crisis" because of the demands made on it.[6] Stalin came out strongly against the NEP, and in what would amount to a second Russian revolution, he advocated a planned economy based on the collectivization and modernization of agriculture. The promise was that this approach would feed the country better and also, through a "regime of the strictest economy," allow for the accumulation of surplus funds to finance industry. Ultimately, these five-year plans strove to convert the Soviet Union into an industrial and military giant.

Thus, Stalin and his supporters opted to restart the revolution that Lenin had postponed, but it took time to decide on the exact course. In his speeches and articles during 1925, Stalin began to identify himself with the "unorthodox" Marxist view that "socialism in one country" was possible.[7] As usual when he innovated, he invoked Lenin's name and liberally quoted him.[8]

At the Fourteenth Party Congress (December 1925), Stalin was solemn while giving the conclusion to his political report. Workers in capitalist countries, upon seeing the Soviet successes, he said, would gain "confidence in their own strength," and the rise in worker consciousness would be the beginning of the end of capitalism. In this scenario, as the Soviets created socialism at home, far from giving up on the international proletarian revolution, they were providing a model to inspire the workers of the world. His words were followed by thunderous applause.[9]

However, by 1927 food shortages and high unemployment demanded action. In January of the next year Stalin, Bukharin, and others in the Politburo decided on "emergency measures," a euphemism for expropriation campaigns in the countryside. Stalin directed top officials, including Anastas Mikoyan, Lazar Kaganovich, and Andrei Zhdanov—all of them his firm backers—to designated parts of the country. He went off by train to the Urals and Siberia, where agricultural deliveries to the state were down, even though the harvest was good. He learned that the peasants preferred selling to private traders, who paid more. At each stop he browbeat officials into using Article 107 of the criminal code (on withholding grain) to prosecute these kulaks (the more affluent peasants) and other "speculators."[10]

When Stalin returned to Moscow, Bukharin questioned these brutal "excesses." However, for Stalin the trip east deepened his determination to solve the agricultural problem; it convinced him more than ever that peasant cultivation of small plots had to end and that collectivization was the ultimate solution. In all his years as leader, this was his only visit to the collective farms. Mostly he knew them only as abstractions, like chess pieces to be moved around.[11]

Scarcity of food worsened in 1928 and into 1929, the result of poor harvests in some places, though the main reason was that the state offered too little in payment for grain. However, anyone who suggested giving the peasants more for their crops, as did Bukharin, was attacked as a "right deviationist," because they appeared to be leaning toward a market economy. Stalin berated Bukharin for saying the kulaks would "grow into socialism" and instead affirmed that the accumulated wealth generated by peasants on collective farms would be taken as "tribute." It would finance the industrial development of the country and the five-year plans.[12] And it did not matter in the slightest that shortly before, he had scorned precisely such an approach as exploiting the peasants.[13]

In April 1929, addressing the Central Committee, Stalin reiterated that the main idea of the first five-year plan—already being implemented—was not merely to increase production but "to guarantee the socialist sector of the economy." Now he ridiculed Bukharin's suggestion to incentivize peasants with higher prices so that they would deliver more to the state. That heresy, he believed, would raise the cost of bread in the cities; worse, it would strengthen "capitalist elements" in the countryside.

According to Stalin's theory, these "last elements" were the problem, and he postulated that as socialism grew stronger, better-off peasants like the kulaks would struggle harder than ever because no dying class in history ever gave up without a final desperate fight.[14] Bukharin thought it "strange" to point to an "inevitable law" that the more the Soviet Union advanced toward socialism, the more class warfare would intensify. Then, "at the gates of socialism, we either have to start a civil war or waste away from hunger and drop dead."[15]

Nevertheless, Stalin's arguments prevailed, and the first five-year plan was adopted at the Sixteenth Party Conference, which began on April 23, 1929. The plan called for nothing less than a second Russian revolution, encapsulated by the collectivization of agriculture, industrialization, and the transformation of culture. It set astronomical quotas, targeting agriculture to grow by 55 percent and industry by 136 percent.[16]

Obtaining these results and getting what was needed from the countryside was a massive and complex undertaking involving state agencies, the directors of factories and collective farms, workers, and peasants. Stalin expected that some or all of them would try to get around the system, and his inclination was to use force as needed.[17] Part of the revolution, therefore, would involve extending state control—which fell off dramatically outside the bigger cities.[18]

On the twelfth anniversary of the Russian Revolution in 1929— celebrated, as customary, on November 7—Stalin published a key article on the "year of the great turn" (*perelom*). Today historians call this the beginning of Stalin's revolution from above. In typically militarized language, he reminded everyone that Lenin had regarded the NEP as only a tactical "retreat," after which there would be a run-up and then "a great leap forward." The party had already launched "a *successful offensive* against the capitalist elements," the early results showed; "we are advancing rapidly along the path of industrialization—to socialism, leaving behind the age-old 'Russian' backwardness."[19] Notwithstanding this official optimism, out in the countryside the peasantry was resisting the imposition of a system worse than they had known under the tsars.[20] In 1929 the government had to resort to mass arrests, and the next year there were "disturbances" involving up to 2.4 million people. Police and brigades from the city clashed with peasants unwilling to surrender their harvests.

Moscow insisted that the resistance was led by kulaks, particularly in Ukraine, where nationalist sentiment was strong.[21] In a speech to Marxist students on December 27, Stalin announced the ominous-sounding policy of *"eliminating* the kulaks as a class." "To launch an offensive against the kulaks," he said, was to prepare and then "to strike so hard as to prevent them from again rising to their feet. That is what we Bolsheviks call a real offensive."[22]

At Stalin's urging, on January 30 in the new year, a commission led by longtime henchman Vyacheslav Molotov produced a far-reaching decree. It divided the kulaks into three categories, with appropriate punishments. The "first category" included any family of the top 3 to 5 percent of the peasants in each district. An astonishing initial execution target was 60,000 heads of these families. Quotas were also set for "category two" and "category three" kulaks, with instructions about how their land was to be taken and where they were to be sent. The strategy was like a military operation.[23] In fact, that was how chief of the secret police (OGPU) Genrikh G. Yagoda spoke of it to his paladins. He worried only about "avoiding losses" of his men.[24]

In some places no one was well off enough to be labeled a kulak. Villagers met to decide who would be sacrificed or drew lots. Some avaricious neighbors denounced as "kulaks" people whose goods, lands, or women they coveted.[25]

Families branded as kulaks lost everything and were deported to "special settlements" (*spetsposelenie*). Trains rumbled eastward for weeks and often dumped their cargo in completely uninhabitable places, resulting in starvation, disease, even cannibalism.[26] In 1930 and 1931, no less than 381,026 families, or 1.8 million people, were forced out. It is difficult to be certain about the death toll, though estimates range into the hundreds of thousands. And the process continued into the next year.[27]

FAMINE AND TERROR

The regime knew in 1931 that starvation was occurring, but when asked about the situation, Stanislav Kosior, head of the party in Ukraine, wrote to Stalin on April 26, 1932, and rejected all "rumors of famine." He said that the help already arriving would eradicate any difficulties. That statement defied the facts on the ground, especially in those parts of the Ukrainian countryside where there was open rebellion. The peasants deserted the collective farms in droves and also used violence to take back grain that had been seized. In Russia's Ivanovo Province, they did the same, and there were riots when the rations in the cities were reduced. That May, Moscow relented in the face of massive resistance. It reduced planned requisitions and, beginning in January 1933, gave peasants permission to sell surplus grains and meats, once they had met their quota targets.[28]

In the summer of 1932, Stalin was away from Moscow, and by chance we have the evidence of his frequent correspondence and instructions to Molotov and Kaganovich. In mid-June the Boss acknowledged that "despite a good harvest," Ukraine was experiencing "impoverishment and famine," and that there were problems in the Urals and Nizhny Novgorod region. Like a medieval prince, he was still convinced that the peasants were cheating or that the administrators were not ruthless enough. He called for an immediate conference of party first secretaries, who were to be told to take a more differentiated and decentralized approach, according to which districts with good crops in a region would help those with poor crops, and together they would meet their quota.[29]

Moscow sent messages that stated bluntly that no exceptions were to be made for Ukraine or anywhere else. On June 28, Molotov read aloud to party secretaries Stalin's letter, which insisted that Moscow's procurement figures had to be fulfilled. In addition, in early July Molotov and Kaganovich attended a Ukrainian Politburo meeting to convey the same demands.

Stalin was adamant that the regional party leaders were disorganized or spineless, and these demands were intended to shake them up to gather the harvest and meet target figures. However, on July 25 he wrote Kaganovich to say the situation would be different after mid-August, when it would be all right to tell the Ukrainians that many of them would get reductions to their quota. Collective farms that had done poorly would be allowed to withhold an average of 50 percent of their expected deliveries, and individual peasants could keep one-third or one-quarter of their quota.[30]

On August 7, Stalin introduced a harsh new law to stop food thefts, even of a single ear of corn or a potato. No fewer than 5,338 people were condemned to death for breaking this law in 1932 and 11,463 more the next year, though not all of these sentences were carried out.[31] His argument was that unless they made public property sacred and inviolable, as the capitalists had done with private property, the socialists would "not be able to finish off and bury the capitalist elements and individualistic, selfish habits, practices and traditions (that form the basis of theft)."[32]

By August 11, it was becoming evident to him that the harvest collection was not as good as expected, and he was especially angered by the appalling state of the Communist Party. Fifty or more district party committees in Ukraine had raised their voice against the grain quotas. Stalin called the Ukrainian party a sham and judged Stanislav Kosior, its first secretary, as not up to the job. He said that unless the Kremlin cleared up the situation there—in the party and the secret police—"we may lose Ukraine." His goal was to "transform" that republic into a "fortress of the USSR."[33]

Food-procurement brigades sent out to parts of Ukraine in December followed Stalin's orders for an attack on the "grain front." Young idealists among the activists told themselves not to give in to "debilitating pity" as they tore apart homes and stables and turned people out in the street.[34] They uncovered enough hidden stores to foster official thinking that wily peasants were hiding more. Any regional bosses who warned of the consequences were upbraided as "un-Bolshevik" in forgetting to put the "needs of the state first."[35]

More was at stake than the grain harvest—there were additional concerns about Ukrainian nationalism. Back in 1923 Stalin had drawn up a flexible nationalities policy, according to which Moscow, far from crushing the nations and hammering everyone into Russians, instead supported the "forms" of nationhood, like native languages and culture. The regime would make people feel welcome in the new empire, encouraging education and the emergence of new elites. The hard-nosed realists knew there were risks in lifting up the illiterate and helping them to work out their own national identity. But the new rulers were willing to take those risks. To be sure, their nationalities policy added the important proviso that if tribes, ethnic groups, or whole nations in the USSR resisted national directives, undermined the Communist mission, or threatened the unitary state, then they would face terror and deportation.[36] Therefore it was instructive that in December 1932, Stalin specifically changed the long-standing Soviet policy of recruiting as many Ukrainians as possible for the party and its leadership there.[37]

The Red Empire was going to become more centralized, particularly because the Soviet ruling elite had reached the conclusion that Ukrainian nationalism, which fueled resistance to collectivization, was ultimately responsible for the grain requisitions crisis.[38]

Stalin boasted at the January 1933 plenum of the Central Committee about getting 60 percent of the peasants collectivized and opening vast new areas to cultivation. Barely a whisper of concern was heard at these meetings, and the leaders of the Ukrainian Communist Party went so far as to celebrate the great victories of the five-year plan.[39] In fact, famine was already stalking the countryside, yet Moscow gave instructions that officials in Ukraine, after allowing collective farms five days to hand over "hidden stocks" to meet their quota, could confiscate seed grains to make up what was missing.

Hunger began driving peasants from the countryside. During the first five-year plan, an estimated 12 million people fled to the city, where, after careful screening, it might be possible to obtain rations.[40] On December 27, 1932, to control this tide of misery and want, the regime began issuing internal passports to city residents over sixteen years of age. Initially, the major cities, like Moscow, Leningrad, and Kharkov, were covered; in early 1933 the official reach was extended to "first priority cities" Kiev, Minsk, Rostov, and far eastern Vladivostok; and soon it included major industrial centers like Kuznetsk, Stalingrad, and Baku. The passports were introduced in phases, and there were many gaps in the official network. Nevertheless, in the first year and a half of the passport law, at least 630,000 violators were found living illegally in the cities, more people were denied the precious documents, and still other fleeing peasants decided to turn back when they heard it was hopeless.[41]

On January 22, Stalin gave orders to stop the exodus from Ukraine and the Kuban (where many Ukrainians also lived). The attempt to flee the countryside was allegedly "organized by enemies" to discredit collectivization. Police were to set up barricades and arrest and deport kulaks and "counter-revolutionary elements." They restricted the sale of railway tickets and soon extended these measures to cover hard-hit regions such as the North Caucasus and the Lower Volga. Other areas losing their population requested that Moscow impose travel restrictions to cover them as well.[42]

In spite of the undeniable evidence of famine in early 1933, Soviet authorities responded haltingly.[43] Although Moscow ordered food aid, it was "paltry" given the desperate situation and went either to the cities or to peasants who were cooperating with collectivization. To be sure, the regime had already lowered quotas from stricken regions in 1931 in Kazakhstan and several other areas. The 1932 quota for Ukraine was down from the year before and then cut another 35 percent, but this came too late to avert famine in spring 1933.[44] The Soviet government looked murderous, because it increased food exports between 1929 and 1931. Then it slowed the volume. Even so, at the height of the famine in 1933, the country was still selling abroad no less than 1,632 million tons of grain.[45]

The collectivization campaign in the countryside was almost like a war, and the fatalities resulting from violence, starvation, or famine-related disease have been estimated at between 4 and 8 million. The exact figures will never be known because deaths were not always recorded. The mortality rates of the USSR as a whole for 1930 to 1933 jumped by 83.9 percent, but those figures exclude hard-hit areas like Kazakhstan, where as many as a million people may have died. Around a million likely perished in the North Caucasus and the Black Earth regions. In Ukraine, however, mortality grew by 189.5 percent, and the figure for 1933 was triple what it had been the two previous years.[46]

Stalin shied away from inspecting the affected areas, even when he traveled south for three-month vacations in the summers of 1930, 1931, and 1932. In August the following year, by which time the worst of the famine and related diseases had passed, he went to Sochi again and en route reportedly "soaked up" everything he saw "like a sponge," including abandoned villages and obvious signs of the disaster. That was what Voroshilov, who was with him, said. Although the Boss made decisions as he went, the only one relevant to the famine was in a letter to Kaganovich telling him to see to it that by early 1934 a resettlement committee would bring in ten thousand heads of families and their households to the Kuban and Terek district (just north of Georgia), as well as fifteen thousand to twenty thousand families to the steppe in Ukraine. He added that this part of the south was always short of labor. Thus, he refused to recognize the famine and its effects in any way, just as he had done two years earlier.[47]

Recently a number of respectable historians have accused Stalin of multiple genocides, including the mass deaths from this famine in Ukraine and Kazakhstan.[48] Often what happened was that regional party bosses exaggerated their success and claimed even to be exceeding quotas. Moscow had allowed itself to believe the fables, in spite of growing evidence to the contrary, and so demanded more.

Was this intentional mass murder? Researchers have scoured the archives, but no documents have been found to substantiate the claim (expressed or implied) that Soviet leaders had motives resembling those that led to the Holocaust. While Moscow had special grievances with Ukraine, where nationalists were menacing, at no time did Stalin issue orders for people to be starved to death. He was equally heartless and would not yield to requests from elsewhere to lower the quotas. When officials in Kazakhstan begged for a reduction in grain collection because of the great suffering caused by two years of crop failure, Stalin retorted that he had better information and demanded "unconditional fulfillment."[49] If the Middle Volga complained, it was threatened with "harsh measures."[50]

At the early 1933 plenum, Stalin touted the successes on the industrial front, and using statistics "creatively," he boasted that after only four years the Soviet Union had caught up to and surpassed Russia's pre-1914 industrial output by 334 percent. The second five-year plan could afford to be more modest, aiming at a minimum of "only" 13 to 14 percent annual growth.[51] So much did he want industry that he did not shrink from inviting in American capitalists, who built whole new factory towns.[52] When there were setbacks or accidents there or anywhere else, they were blamed on spies and "wreckers." The incompetent or unlucky were already subject to show trials in May–June 1928.[53]

Given the heavy-handed, repressive approach that the Stalinist revolution adopted, a broader concentration camp system was almost inevitable. After a series of changes in 1929–30, Stalin egged on its expansion under the acronym GULAG (Glavnoe upravlenie ispravitelno-trudovykh lagerei), or Main Administration of Corrective Labor Camps.[54] A vast chain of camps and colonies was built to hold designated "enemies." In 1930 this system had 179,000 prisoners, and it grew to 510,307 in 1934; 1,196,369 in 1937; and 1,929,729 in January 1941.[55]

At the same time, an "unknown Gulag," a parallel system of special settlements (*spetsposelenie*) often overlooked by historians, was created. The settlements were carved out of the wilderness in the far north and were intended mainly for kulaks and their families caught up in the collectivization drive. It held 1.3 million prisoners in 1932 and stayed close to a million until well into the war years, when in 1942 it began to increase again.[56]

Stalin's harsh attitude did not sit well with his wife, Nadezhda Alliluyeva. She had been by his side since their time in Tsaritsyn (Stalingrad) and bore him two children. She was a good Bolshevik but found it difficult to accept the horrors of collectivization and shared her thoughts with Bukharin, who often visited. She reached the limit of her endurance during the annual festivities at the Kremlin in 1932 to celebrate the Russian Revolution. It is not clear what exactly led to her breaking point. Stalin may have flirted with another woman, "jokingly" thrown orange peels and cigarette butts at his wife, or been just his oafish self while drinking. In any case Nadya ran from the room and later that night shot herself.[57] Their daughter said that Stalin thought of his wife "as his closest and most faithful friend" and that he was crushed by her death. Perhaps so, and yet he regarded what she did as a betrayal.[58]

Thereafter the Soviet dictator lived the life of a militant revolutionary ascetic—with the exception of his overindulgence in drinking. He all but disowned his son Yakov (born 1907), from his first marriage, and eventually distanced himself from the children of his second marriage, particularly Vasily (born 1921), though he retained fond feelings for his daughter, Svetlana (born 1926).

Bereft of anyone with whom he could share human warmth, Stalin became all the more committed to the ideas that gave his life meaning. An alarm signal was struck on December 1, 1934, when Leningrad leader Sergei Kirov was assassinated. Stories circulated later that Stalin might have seen Kirov as a rival and had him killed. According to rumors from the 1960s, Stalin had been upset that 270 to 300 delegates to the Seventeenth Party Congress in 1934 had voted against his membership on the Central Committee. More recent research, however, shows that only 3 of 1,059 delegates cast a ballot against Stalin. Moreover, Kirov had no major policy differences with the Boss, remained part of the charmed inner circle, and the Kremlin had no reason to get rid of him. The assassin Leonid Nikolaev was mentally unbalanced and acted alone.[59]

Nevertheless, Stalin would use accusations of involvement in the crime to justify eliminating an ever-widening circle of real and imagined enemies. Now he arrived in Leningrad with his angel of death, Nikolai Yezhov, a longtime party member with experiences like Stalin's in the civil war. As if to show that the hand of vengeance was nigh, the police immediately executed "dozens" of prisoners in various cities, none of them remotely related to the case. Similarly innocent were the 11,095 "former people" in Leningrad itself—such as former aristocrats, tsarist officers, merchants, and clergy—who were driven out of their homes in the dead of winter.

Yezhov's greatest talent was to sense what Stalin wanted and then translate it into investigations that brought results. He was bound to come up with links between Kirov's death and "higher-ups" on Stalin's long list of doubters.[60] A purge of the Communist Party, which in fact had been envisaged before Kirov's death, thus began in mid-1935 and was officially termed a *proverka,* or verification of documents. Yezhov set off the purge and commanded it, and by year's end 9.1 percent of the members (or 177,000) were expelled when "compromising materials" were discovered.[61]

In early 1936, Stalin told Yezhov that "something did not seem right" about the Kirov investigation, which had been closed, with the lone killer caught and punished. Now the case was reopened, and the dredging went deeper; new incriminating material was then used in a show trial of the "Trotskyite-Zinovievist-Kamenevist counter-revolutionary group." The August event featured Zinoviev, Kamenev, and fourteen others—all were found guilty and executed.[62] Although the charges were farcical, many in the ruling elite believed "the defendants must be guilty of something or other, perhaps a conspiracy against Stalin."[63]

Either at Stalin's behest or on his own initiative, Yezhov also came up with networks of "right oppositionist" leaders and even discovered "deficiencies" in the work of the NKVD. He besmirched its boss, Genrikh Yagoda, at every turn and in late summer 1936, armed with files, visited Stalin at his vacation home in the south. They looked over a list of several thousand alleged Trotskyites for execution. Stalin demurred, though he saw enough to recognize Yezhov's talents and decided first to demote and ultimately to arrest Yagoda, his once-faithful executioner. On September 25, Stalin informed the Politburo that Yezhov would be the new head of the secret police, which, he complained, was already "four years behind" in its work of "exposing the Trotskyite-Zinovievite bloc."[64]

At the Central Committee plenum in December, Yezhov reported yet another conspiracy involving a "parallel anti-Soviet Trotskyite center" with ties to major figures Karl Radek, Yuri Piatakov, and fifteen additional persons.[65] A show trial was staged in January; once again all were executed. These trials were played up in the press and managed in detail, but what made them a public sensation was the apparent willingness of the accused to confess their conspiracies and crimes.[66]

This trial was merely a prelude to the Central Committee plenum in February–March 1937, after which the terror went into high gear.[67] The first item on the agenda was the case of Bukharin and Aleksei Rykov (another proponent of the NEP) and others who "deviated" to the right of the party line.

Stalin had long known about Bukharin's doubts. Traveling through Ukraine in 1930—well before the famine really struck—Bukharin had been brought to tears, having been beseeched at every train stop by "packs of children" with swollen stomachs. He wondered aloud if the whole Soviet experiment really was worth it.[68] Hardheaded ideologues knew about such empathetic comrades, but getting rid of them all at once was just not done. Stalin moved forward on the case with more care than is often assumed, and he encouraged the NKVD to wait until the Central Committee met on January 23, 1937. There Bukharin was to face a test of truth by way of a "confrontation" with his accusers. Once they all had been his close comrades, but now they voiced the most far-fetched allegations against him.[69]

Bukharin and Rykov were dragged before the high priests at the Central Committee plenum to confess to treason, wrecking, and terrorism. Bukharin was questioned and insulted by Stalin and his top paladins Mikoyan, Molotov, Kaganovich, and Voroshilov. Yezhov claimed that the accused had allied with followers of Trotsky and Zinoviev and conspired with the fascists in Germany and Japan to organize a mass uprising and seizure of power. Bukharin and Rykov were duly expelled from the party and arrested. They and nineteen others went before the third major show trial in March 1938, and all were executed.[70]

The terror, however, was only beginning, for the Stalinist revolution was about to embark on its bloodiest rampage of all. Hints of what was to come had emerged in the show trials of the more prominent characters who were tarred with the brush of treason, but no one could have guessed the scope of the unprecedented butchery that was to be visited on the country.

CHAPTER 2

Exterminating Internal Threats to Socialist Unity

W hat came to be called the Great Terror did not begin with a single order from Stalin. The terror had three interrelated sides. The first aimed mainly at political opponents, the second focused more broadly on social opposition, above all the kulaks, and the third pursued ethnic groups that might threaten inner security in the event of war. Stalin would never admit it, perhaps not even to himself, but the terror amounted to a final settling of accounts with anyone who had ever raised an eyebrow at his leadership or policies. Somewhere along the line, he concluded that his opponents would never change their minds and had to be eliminated.[1]

Recent studies have shown that the menacing international situation, the growing concern about the rise of fascism, the outbreak of the Spanish Civil War in 1936, and the increasing threat of war influenced the purges and the terror at home. Stalin was prone to claiming that ever-present "foreign threats," the "encirclement" of the country by enemy states, and the alleged presence of fifth columnists called for more repression. In the Great Terror, all of these allegations and wild speculations worked in tandem to produce the worst series of mass murders in Soviet history.[2]

STALIN'S FINAL RECKONING WITH SOCIAL AND POLITICAL OPPOSITION

Kremlin rationalizations for the terror, and especially the show trials, were printed in the press, though the stories were so far-fetched that, at this point, some people could not believe them. However, one noted and fairly representative "true believer" saw the show trials as "an expression of some far-sighted policy." He said "that on balance Stalin was right in deciding on these terrible measures in order to discredit all forms of political opposition, once and for all. We were a besieged fortress; we had to be united, knowing neither vacillation nor doubt."[3] On the other hand, one skeptic recalled thinking they were not expected to take the stories literally. "At most we accepted the fantasies in a symbolic, allegorical sense."[4]

Remarkably, the foreign press invited to the show trials generally bought into the trumped-up charges and the guilty verdicts. So did U.S. ambassador Joseph Davies, who was convinced that the conspirators, including key military leaders, had tried to carry out a coup and barely failed.[5]

In his concluding speech to the February–March 1937 Central Committee plenum, Stalin offered an older but trusted rationalization for the terror. After two decades of Soviet rule, why were there so many traitors, spies, and "wreckers with a party card"? Why had antiparty and anti-Soviet activities spread even into the top leadership? The answer, according to the Boss, was that the party had been focusing on economic construction, and blinded by its great successes, it had ignored warning signs and forgotten about the capitalist powers "encircling" the country.

Bukharin had mocked this "strange theory" to explain resistance in 1929, but Stalin and his disciples pulled it out often in the 1930s. Its main thesis was that the "further forward we move, the more success we will have, the greater fury we can expect from what remains of the defeated exploiting classes, the more intense will be the struggle they put up, the harder they will try to harm the Soviet state, and the more desperate they will become as they grasp at the last resort of the doomed." These "vestiges of the defeated classes," the "have beens," would stop at nothing, including trying to rally the "backward elements." Stalin called for vigilance against the ever-present threats, all the more dangerous for their links to foreign powers. His speeches on this theme were published in the press, issued as pamphlets for the education of the public, and even used in the indictments at the show trials.[6]

Thus it came about that Stalin began to wonder whether even the NKVD, "the avant-garde of the party," deserved the praise it received.

His new favorite Nikolai Yezhov reported on its poor leadership and led a purge of its ranks, arresting its ex-chief Genrikh Yagoda.[7]

On August 3, 1937, Stalin directed regional secretaries of the party "to organize, in each district of each region, two or three public show trials of enemies of the people—agricultural saboteurs" who supposedly had "wormed their way" into various party and state organizations in order to undermine operations. He and Molotov reinforced this directive on September 10 and again on October 2 with regard to specific kinds of "wrecking" in agriculture that should be pilloried. Already by December 10, Attorney General of the USSR Andrei Vyshinsky reported that 626 provincial show trials had been held. Although fewer would take place in 1938, there was a minimum of 5,612 convictions, resulting in at least 1,955 executions. These trials were meant to be publicized as part of the state's "pedagogical" mission, and they reveal another of the many sides of the terror.[8]

The effects of the provincial show trials and the purges varied according to the enthusiasm of the Communist bosses. Nikita Khrushchev later would play the role of the betrayed innocent, but in 1937–38 his rampage through the Moscow party was one of the bloodiest. Posted to Ukraine in early 1938, he replaced its entire leadership and had thousands arrested and "repressed." The two hundred members of the Ukrainian Central Committee were reduced to three. Between 1933 and 1939 in the USSR as a whole, 1.8 million were expelled from the party and 1 million new and more loyal members were recruited, whereby it became a more reliable Stalinist institution than ever.[9]

Stalin played a hands-on role and wanted to be informed about interrogations. At times he gave instructions regarding who should be beaten, took part in the strict wording of indictments, and even helped compose the prosecutor's final statements.[10] He pursued opponents in the Politburo and the Central Committee, which, in spite of applauding him, lost close to 70 percent of its members.[11] Nor was his supposedly beloved Georgia spared. Even before the end of 1937, Lavrenti Beria, head of the NKVD there, reported that over 12,000 had been arrested and more than half of them convicted.[12]

Also on the agenda was a purge of the armed forces. Stalin had been alerted back in 1930 that General Mikhail Tukhachevsky, one of the leaders of the Red Army, had become the favorite of "anti-Soviet elements" among the "Rightists" in the party. The general was a no-nonsense kind of person who ruffled the less gifted political appointees, and at the time Stalin had even called him a "Napoleonchik," the very charge once leveled against Trotsky.[13] However, after the secret police did a thorough check on Tukhachevsky in 1930, Stalin seemed pleased enough to drop the matter.[14] The general went on to introduce major military reforms and became a marshal of the Soviet Union. Exactly what triggered his fall in May 1937 remains in dispute.

On May 1, 1937, Tukhachevsky stood with Stalin and other dignitaries atop the Lenin Mausoleum for the annual parade. Commissar of Defense Voroshilov and Marshal Semyon Budyonny were also there. They were closer to Stalin politically and personally and had been pressing him for more than a year to cleanse the army of "enemies." The immediate background to Tukhachevsky's case was that, apart from criticizing Budyonny, he additionally began trying to push out Voroshilov. Top establishment figures did not welcome such behavior.[15] On the evening of May 1, to his cronies, Stalin mentioned wanting "to finish off" enemies in the army, even in the Kremlin. The wheels of terror began to grind, and several generals were arrested and tortured to get evidence. On May 11, Tukhachevsky was asked to resign as deputy commissar of defense, and eleven days later he was arrested, along with a handful of the high command.[16]

The sensational news made the rounds, and on June 2 Stalin spoke to a hundred assembled military leaders about an alleged "military-political" conspiracy with Nazi Germany. He called for more vigilance, and soon directives were issued to the military districts to stir things up. It all happened so fast. By June 11 a special military tribunal, not open to the public, had tried Tukhachevsky and seven other generals. The results were a foregone conclusion, given that two days before the trial Stalin had had confessions beaten out of the accused, to reveal to the Politburo. The dictator kept mumbling that it was all "incredible, but it is a fact."[17]

Just over a week later 980 senior officers and political commissars were taken into custody for being part of the "conspiracy." A Soviet general later said that "they were the flower of the officer corps, with civil war experience, and most of them were relatively young."[18] In the next two years, some 33,460 were dropped from the officer corps and nearly one-quarter of them arrested. The top command of the army and navy was decimated, with disastrous effects on the country's readiness to face an aggressor.[19]

To drive the point home, on August 15, following Stalin's orders, the NKVD issued Order 00486 calling for the arrest of the wives of all traitors and others condemned by the military tribunals.[20] They were to serve five to eight years in a correctional labor camp. Most eventually ended up in Akmolinsk, Kazakhstan, in a special "camp for the wives of traitors to the motherland," or ALZhIR. Their children were taken away, separated even from one another, and given new identities.[21]

Another side of the terror focused on Soviet society, in a process that began in the late 1920s and gradually accelerated in lockstep with Stalin's "second revolution" to deal with opposition to it. Society at large was going to be "cleansed" in a final settling of accounts with the "vestiges of defeated classes" that, he said, had been accumulating since the revolution in 1917. Stalin decided that they and their families could never be assimilated and thus that all of them would have to be eliminated, either killed immediately or sent away to the camps.

Stalin's "strange theory" held that Communism had to be defended against a whole range of "anti-Soviet elements," the "last remnants of dying classes"—such as kulaks, private dealers, former nobles, priests, and more. They were all subverting the great experiment in socialism. In early 1933 he inaugurated a campaign against "thieves and wreckers in the public economy, against hooligans and pilferers of public property."[22] He demanded "a strong and powerful dictatorship of the proletariat" that would "scatter to the winds the last remnants of the dying classes."[23] Tens of thousands were picked up, put in front of OGPU *troikas,* and sent to the camps.

By 1937 the struggle that had gone on for years reached an altogether new stage, and on July 2 Stalin composed a Politburo directive calling for radical steps against "anti-Soviet elements." The next day Yezhov instructed his officers to draw up, within five days, lists of all kulaks and criminals who had returned from exile. The first category and those deemed the "most hostile" were to be shot, once their case had been reviewed by a *troika.* The second type, while "less hostile but still dangerous," were to be sent to the Gulag for eight to ten years. The document was ready for the Politburo approval on July 30.[24]

Secret Order 00447, the "operation to repress former kulaks, criminals and other anti-Soviet elements," became a deadly instrument that reached far out into the countryside.[25] Today the document reads like a demand to exterminate the social "leftovers" that the revolution had passed by. Once and for all they were to be destroyed "in the most merciless way possible." The list began with kulaks, included the clergy and those in religious "sects," former members of armed bands or oppositional parties, bandits, and the Whites. It went on to target criminals, from cattle thieves to repeat offenders.[26] Although Lenin had composed lists like this, he wanted the people put in concentration camps. Stalin was prepared to kill nearly all of them.[27]

Given the quota thinking of the age, target figures were set. In total 79,950 were to be shot and 193,000 sent to the Gulag. *Troika* "courts" barely read dossiers of the accused, as for example when on a single day (October 9) a Leningrad *troika* sent 658 prisoners to their death. The next day in Omsk, another *troika* "sentenced" 1,301 people, of whom 937 were shot. Stalin himself chastised those who did not show sufficient zeal by getting through enough cases. Local enthusiasts met their quotas and rushed to seek permission to raise them. Ultimately Operation 00447 resulted in the "sentencing" of more than 767,000, of whom 387,000 were executed.[28]

The terror "cleansed" all aspects of the arts and sciences and was a new and even more vigorous stage of the assault on "anti-Soviet intelligentsia" that had begun in the 1920s.[29] Working-class education was encouraged, with hundreds of thousands entering postsecondary schools for the first time. A new generation of intellectuals and political leaders, people like Leonid Brezhnev—future leader of the post-Stalinist Soviet Union—rose to prominence during the 1930s. The other side of the coin was that those with the wrong social origins—such *lishentsy,* or "former" people, like former policemen, nobles, merchants, and so on—were systematically denied such opportunities. Social origins became almost as indelible as race and nearly impossible to erase. During the Great Terror tens of thousands of these "formers" were killed.[30]

LINKS REAL AND IMAGINED TO "FOREIGN ENEMIES"

The Kremlin's concern about a possible fifth column contributed to Operation 00485 against "Polish diversionist and espionage groups and organizations of the Polish Military Organization (POV)."[31] That organization had long disappeared, and now an evil eye was cast on the hundreds of thousands of Poles in the USSR. Filtering them proceeded with Yezhov's order of August 11, 1937, two days after the Politburo approved it.[32]

Stalin encouraged cleansing "the Polish espionage mud."[33] The police on the ground were more concerned about meeting their quota than about checking into espionage charges, and they trawled for suspects by looking through telephone books for Polish-sounding names. Whether such persons were Polish or not was immaterial. In total, 139,835 people were arrested, of whom 111,091 were executed. The rest were sent to the Gulag.[34]

To assert minimal control, the Kremlin insisted that its approval be given before an execution was carried out. Local officials put the briefest sketches of the doomed into albums, which began piling up in the hallways of the NKVD in Moscow. Stalin and other leaders signed the front page of hundreds of such albums, sending tens of thousands to their deaths. Some of these albums, complete with the signatures, can now be viewed online.[35] The accused never had a minute before the *troikas,* much less a day in court. By mid-September 1938, even the fiction of this "album procedure" was dropped, and new NKVD *troikas* were empowered to verify sentences and carry out executions on their own authority.[36]

The "national operations" against the Germans and Poles set the pattern for the simultaneous repression of (among others) foreign citizens or dispersed ethnic groups from Afghanistan, Bulgaria, China, Estonia, Finland, Greece, Iran, Korea, Kurdistan, Latvia, Macedonia, and Romania. These campaigns were aimed selectively at ethnic groups who were remotely considered counterrevolutionaries or "anti-Soviet elements." By the time "national operations" inside the USSR ended in 1938, they had arrested almost 350,000 people, of whom 247,157 were executed. Some 88,356 were imprisoned or sent to the Gulag. The ethnic component of the Great Terror represented an increasing part of it, estimated ultimately at around one-fifth of all the arrests and one-third of the executions.[37]

The Soviets were no doubt apprehensive that the capitalists could infiltrate the country by way of its minorities. At one time Moscow had thought that such groups with ties just over the border could be used to spread Communism. But by the mid-1930s, the Kremlin concluded that the opposite was more likely—namely, that the enemies of Communism would exploit cross-border links to ethnic groups inside the Soviet Union. Thus the authorities decided to move certain minorities into the hinterland and picked up members of such groups who lived anywhere else in the Soviet Union.

This ethnic-oriented terror accelerated quickly. For example, a campaign against the Koreans began on August 18, 1937, with a note from Stalin and Molotov calling for the deportation of 44,023 Koreans from twelve border districts. Three days later an official decree pointed to twenty-three districts, affecting 135,343 people. On September 22, the NKVD asked Moscow for the right to remove each and every Korean from the Far Eastern Region. The reasoning was that any Koreans left behind would be resentful and would become "rich soil for the Japanese to work on." In the end the entire Korean population of 171,781 was "cleansed," which is to say resettled, shipped to Kazakhstan and Uzbekistan.[38]

In a foretaste of the Cold War, the Soviet Union, by the end of the 1930s, cut itself off from the outside world and anathematized not just anti-Communist thinking but even contact with noncitizens. No less vulnerable was the Communist International, or Comintern, whose headquarters was in Moscow. Venerable leaders of the movement who had sought refuge there found themselves under attack. Some parties suffered more than others, like the Polish Communist Party, which was nearly completely annihilated. Also killed were many from the German, Austrian, Hungarian, Italian, Bulgarian, Finnish, and Baltic parties. Soviet citizens who happened to be officials in the Comintern were not spared. Thus the great international organization created by Lenin as the instrument meant to spread the gospel was itself found to be "sinning." Any "evidence" that these people had conspired against Stalin and the Soviet Union was concocted and had been beaten out of hapless victims.[39]

Some idea of the immense scale of the terror can be gathered by how many people had run-ins with the secret police (the OGPU; later the NKVD). Between 1930 and 1938, just over 3.8 million people were arrested by police bodies mainly for "counter-revolutionary crimes" or "anti-Soviet agitation." In 1937 and 1938 alone, when the terror was at wholly unprecedented levels, out of a total of 1.5 million arrested, 1.3 million received a sentence and 681,692 were executed. At the height of the terror (August 1937 to November 1938), on average 1,500 people were shot each day.[40] We should be aware that these figures are incomplete because we have only the statistics for the secret police, not for the regular police, whose arrest activities were also vast.

Stalin offered an explanation for the whole thing on November 7, 1937, the twentieth anniversary of the Russian Revolution, when he and two dozen of his cronies met for lunch at the home of Kliment Voroshilov. Also there and taking notes was Georgi Dimitrov, the Bulgarian head of the Comintern. As usual there were too many toasts, and Stalin's words followed up his earlier rationale for the terror. He gave thanks to the tsars for creating an empire all the way to Kamchatka, saying that the Bolsheviks had consolidated, united, and strengthened the state in the name of the workers and peoples:

> Anyone who tries to destroy the unity of the socialist state, who aims to separate any of its parts or nationalities from it, is an enemy, a sworn enemy of the state and of the peoples of the USSR. And we will exterminate each and every one of these enemies, whether they are old Bolsheviks or not. We will exterminate their kin and entire family. We will mercilessly exterminate anyone, who with deeds or thoughts threatens the unity of the socialist state. Here's to the extermination of all enemies, themselves and their kin![41]

A few days later he added in a private conversation that there were those "who had not really internally accepted the party line, had not stomached collectivization in particular," with its ruthlessness toward the kulaks. These forces then went underground and though "without power themselves had linked up with external enemies, promised Ukraine to the Germans, Byelorussia to the Poles, and the Far East to the Japanese." Stalin went so far as to claim that *"they had made preparations in July for an attack on the Politburo in the Kremlin.* But they lost their nerve." Thus even in private he was trying to justify the terror as defensive and supposedly necessary to avert a coup of some kind.[42]

Finally, on November 17, 1938, he brought the bloodbath to an end and stopped the nearly twenty special operations that were running more or less simultaneously. The NKVD was to straighten things out, to eliminate "shortcomings," and thereby to continue making what was called "a positive contribution to the construction of socialist society."[43] However, on a single day (December 12), he decided on the deaths of 3,167 "enemies" already "processed."[44]

After the war some of the practitioners of terror, like Kaganovich and Molotov, tried to excuse it all. Molotov said that because of the terror, there had been no enemies behind the lines during the war and no opposition afterward. He admitted that mistakes had been made and said that "Stalin was adamant on making doubly sure: spare no one, but guarantee absolute stability in the country for a long period of time—through the war and postwar years."[45] Late in life Kaganovich again agreed that there had been "errors" but dismissed any responsibility for them. He was sure that many innocent people were condemned to death, and of the "spies" whom he remembered, most, he said, were supposedly Trotskyites. Once again he tried to exculpate the regime of serious wrongdoing. He asked rhetorically: "Were there not many open enemies of socialism, of the October revolution? How many do you need? If you want to protect the revolution, Soviet power and state, then you must beat these wreckers."[46] He was still telling himself the same old Stalinist story.

The terror included a massive campaign against Germans living in the Soviet Union. On July 20, 1937, Stalin ordered the arrest of all of them working in war-related industries, and five days later NKVD chief Yezhov signed Operational Order 00439 against German "spies and wreckers." Included in the hunt were the few resident German citizens and political refugees, including Communists, though immediately targeted was also anyone with a German background and even Soviet citizens suspected of having ties with such "spies, wreckers, and terrorists."[47] The roundup ran on longer than expected, eventually condemning 55,005, of whom 41,898 (76 percent) were shot. When local police had trouble meeting their quota, as for example in the Sverdlovsk region, they still arrested 4,379 suspects, though only 122 of them were of German origin. To make up their shortfall, they grabbed Russian and Ukrainian deportees.[48]

As horrible and unwarranted as the terror was for millions, as many people and more, including prominent figures among the intellectual elite, backed Stalin and participated as the ever-watchful eyes of the system. They denounced friends and neighbors, colleagues at work, or strangers they met by chance. The net effect of the bloodletting was the thorough Stalinization of the country, with fateful long-term consequences. "New men" in their thirties took over from those in their fifties and sixties. These die-hard Stalinists in the bureaucracy and the party would go on to dominate the Soviet Union and Eastern Europe long after the dictator was gone.[49]

Although the radicalization of the terror, which had been sparked by Kirov's assassination, led to the elimination of opposition inside the ruling elite and to the establishment of Stalin's dictatorship, the man at the top was still something of a "team player." Since the late 1920s and all the way through the 1930s, he continued to meet with the paladins and to coax them along with reasoned arguments. Although the image of his running a one-man show needs to be adjusted, during these gatherings his voice undoubtedly came, in time, to count most. It remains, however, that not only Stalin but his whole team was responsible for what happened, including the terror.[50]

The dictator and his close comrades used the terror not simply to preempt opposition in circumstances of a growing threat of war, as they and some historians later claimed, but far more because the Kremlin thought such action was necessary in order to fulfill the big idea, the dream of a Communist society. That was how Bukharin also looked at it, even after the NKVD was at his door. The last time he saw his wife, he pleaded with her not to be vengeful. His great wish was for her to raise their son "a Bolshevik without fail!" Bukharin could not know that she would end up in a concentration camp or that their thirteen-month-old child, Yuri, would be sent to an orphanage.[51]

As the disgraced Bukharin awaited execution, he sought mercy and wrote to the man in the Kremlin, who was once a close friend. Perhaps the terror would indeed provide a "full guarantee" for Stalin's leadership. "For God's sake," he implored the all-powerful Master, "I wasn't born yesterday. I know all too well that *great* plans, *great* ideas, and *great* interests take precedence over everything, and I know that it would be petty of me to place the question of my own person *on a par* with the *universal-historical* tasks resting, first and foremost, on your shoulders." But if the good Stalin believed that Bukharin was simply in the way and had to be killed, "so what! If it must be so, then so be it."[52]

CHAPTER 3

War and Illusions

Soviet leaders since Lenin had held that wars among capitalist powers were inevitable. Stalin said that when the next war came among the capitalists, the Red Army would be the "last man in the fight" and reap the advantage by "tipping the scales."[1] In October 1938 he even mentioned the possibility of leading a "crusade" against the reactionary powers in order "to assist the proletariat of those countries to liberate themselves from the bourgeoisie."[2]

By March 1939 Stalin speculated about the capitalists and their hopes and aspirations. In his sketch of what the British and Americans wanted, Japan would take on China, while Germany and Italy would attack the Soviet Union. The Western powers, he fantasized, would watch these rivalries play out and see their enemies weakened, then "arrive on the scene" claiming to act in the interests of peace but "dictating conditions to the weakened belligerents."[3] Stalin was determined not to sit back passively waiting for the West to play out their rivalries or to fall in their trap.

IMPERIALIST WAR, COMMUNIST VICTORY

By every indication, the Soviet dictator saw the looming conflict and wanted to be in on the action, to help direct it to where he thought it would inevitably go. On May 3, 1939, he made Molotov his new commissar for foreign affairs, replacing the respected Maxim Litvinov, who was Jewish. This move signaled, at the very least, a readiness to open talks with Hitler. At the end of the month, the new commissar spoke on the record about resuming trade negotiations with Germany.[4] Talks were already under way with Britain and France, and until June 26 they focused mainly on economic issues. Then Politburo member Andrei Zhdanov published a short article about how efforts to reach a nonaggression treaty with Britain and France were deadlocked.[5] The Germans were right to see an opportunity and began courting the Soviet Union, all the more urgently in July and August, in view of Hitler's decision to attack Poland in early September.[6]

Stalin thought he understood Nazism and could manipulate Hitler, who was the most anti-Communist politician in the world. Indeed, as soon as Moscow dangled the bait, Berlin responded. On August 14, Hitler conveyed his desire "for serious improvement in the political relations between Germany and the Soviet Union."[7] The Kremlin's lone precondition was to bring the trade negotiations to a successful conclusion, and a large deal was signed in a matter of days.[8]

What happened next has been wrapped in controversy, but Stalin indisputably saw the coming war in more than defensive terms, for it would open political opportunities to advance the cause in the West.[9] He stated more than once that the Red Army did not exist just to protect Soviet security and that it was an instrument in the world revolution.[10]

For his part, Hitler wanted to avoid a two-front war and soon yielded to Soviet demands for a "Secret Additional Protocol," granting the USSR a sphere of influence in the Baltic states, Poland, and Bessarabia. The existence of this document has also been disputed by Russian historians and goes unmentioned even in some noteworthy Western accounts.[11] In any case, German foreign minister Joachim von Ribbentrop flew to Moscow on August 23 and signed the Non-Aggression Treaty. The two sides also agreed to work out an even more comprehensive trade agreement.[12]

Stalin's radical reversal in embracing the Nazi enemy shocked the party faithful around the globe.[13] Later on they would try to justify the treaty with Germany in strictly defense terms. It gave them time to arm and prepare, they said.[14] No doubt, mere defense of the motherland was by no means all that Stalin was mulling over. He boasted to his inner circle on September 7, 1939, that they would play off the capitalist countries against one another. "Hitler, without understanding or desiring it," he said with satisfaction, was playing a revolutionary role in "shaking and undermining the capitalist system." Stalin wanted them to fight as long and as fiercely as possible. "Under the conditions of an imperialist war," or so he wagered, "the prospect of the annihilation of slavery arises!" In order to bring that day closer, he instructed Communists around the world to foment dissent inside the warring countries.[15] Already on September 28, Moscow coerced Estonia into a treaty of mutual assistance that allowed a limited number of Soviet troops to set up army, navy, and air force bases. Similar concessions were quickly wrested from Latvia and Lithuania.

In July 1940, speaking to the Lithuanian minister of foreign affairs, Molotov laid out the strategy of using war to make Communist revolution. He explained that the USSR would provide Germany with material aid but "just enough to prevent it from accepting peace proposals." The gamble was that in due course the "hungering masses in the warring nations" would grow weary of war and rebel. Then the USSR would show up with "fresh forces, well prepared, and on the territory of Western Europe." There would follow "a decisive battle between the proletariat and the rotting bourgeoisie." Stalin had put forward these ideas many times. Molotov quoted no less an authority than Lenin and said that "a second world war will allow us to take power in the whole of Europe."[16]

The Soviets were content to give Hitler the green light for an assault on Poland because they saw ways of capitalizing on it. German forces invaded Poland on September 1, and as expected, Britain and France issued an ultimatum that two days later led them to declare war on Germany.[17] The Kremlin had wanted to coordinate with Berlin regarding plans for the attack on Poland, but given the shocking speed of the German advance, it had no time. Poland was already in the throes of defeat on September 17 when the Red Army ignobly invaded from the east.

Stalin relished finally getting into Poland, for the initial Bolshevik crusade to bring revolution to Berlin, Paris, and beyond had ended at the gates of Warsaw in August 1920. At that time Polish forces had stopped and encircled the Red Army, taken more than 100,000 prisoners, and begun driving out the invaders until an armistice was reached in October. Poland celebrated the great battle as the "Miracle on the Vistula," but now in 1939 the Red Army was back. Poland, Stalin said in early September, had "enslaved" Ukrainians, Byelorussians, and other Slavs, and when it fell, the world would have "one less bourgeois fascist state. Would it be so bad," he asked his cronies rhetorically, "if we, through the destruction of Poland, extended the socialist system to new territories and nations?"[18]

The Soviet occupation of eastern Poland lasted eighteen months before the Nazis overran it on their way to Moscow. In that short time, the Communists assaulted the very foundations of the country. The new Polish republic of 1918 had incorporated western Ukraine and western Byelorussia, which became known as the eastern borderlands. The Soviets took it back and linked the lands respectively to the Ukrainian and Byelorussian Soviet Socialist Republics. Almost as soon as they arrived, they began "cleansing" operations to arrest and deport those who were deemed enemies. The NKVD fanned the hatred that locals already harbored against the Poles. High on the hit list were landowners, those involved in administration, government, business, the military, police, and the church, all of them swept up as "hostile or socially dangerous elements" of the kind that the Soviet police had terrorized inside the USSR.[19]

NKVD boss Lavrenti Beria worked closely with Stalin on all these matters. There were three deportations, in February, April, and June 1940. The operations were meticulously organized. In February, for example, one hundred trains took away the equivalent of a large city's population in a matter of hours. Boxcars were packed with starving and uprooted people, and the voyages into the vast Soviet interior ran on for weeks.[20] The total numbers of those deported or killed remains subject to dispute, though there is no doubt about the Soviet terror. Recent studies suggest that four large deportation waves, as well as smaller individual ones, carried away between 309,000 and 327,000 Poles; the number arrested is now put at between 110,000 and 130,000. In addition, an estimated 25,000 died in captivity and 30,000 were executed.[21] Some were eventually allowed to return, but how many died in the process remains in dispute.

A recent Russian account substantiates the conclusion that wherever Soviet occupation forces went, the former Polish administration, army officers, and intellectuals "ceased to exist."[22] The occupation forces set out to make the area as "Red" as the Bolsheviks had made the Soviet

Union after 1917 by eliminating or removing the social and political elite and crushing opposition.[23]

Many Jews fled east away from the Nazis, and the Soviets also deported many. For all their harrowing experiences, flight to the USSR offered a better chance of survival than remaining in eastern Poland, which Germany took over in June 1941.

The Red Army captured 230,000 or so prisoners of war from Poland and mistreated many before shipping them to camps inside the Soviet Union. Although some were soon released, particularly those resident in eastern Poland, none of the officers were freed.[24]

Newly released documents show that decisions on the fate of these men were taken by Stalin and Beria. The two met in late February 1940 and put together a March 5 Politburo resolution to execute most of the 14,765 Polish officers and other notables held in POW camps.[25] Written in Stalin's hand across that document is his *"za"* ("in favor") followed by his penciled initials. The other signatories were K. Voroshilov, A. Mikoyan, and V. Molotov. Also to be killed were 7,300 people called members of the "bourgeois" elite, like priests, landowners, lawyers, and factory owners. The implementation was recorded in mind-numbing detail, down to the petty rewards given the killers, the numbers they shot per night, and the camp commander's final "accounting of how the prisoners' labor reduced the expense of their upkeep."[26]

The decision to execute may have followed Nikita Khrushchev and Beria's proposal of March 2 to clear the western frontier of the Soviet Union of the inhabitants of an 875-yard-wide zone along the entire border and to pick up the families of "repressed people."[27] In any case, Stalin ordered the mass executions three days later.[28]

This chapter in Red terror came to light because advancing Germans found 4,000 or so bodies in mass graves in the Katyń forest and announced it in mid-April 1943. The Nazis used this and countless other examples of Soviet atrocities to make anti-Bolshevik propaganda. The Soviets denied everything and covered up the crime for nearly a half century. In response to official questions in 1959, the then head of the KGB, Alexander Shelepin, reported to Nikita Khrushchev that in total 21,857 "persons were shot" in various camps of "former bourgeois Poland." Khrushchev wanted all the documents destroyed to continue the cover-up, but that advice was not followed.[29]

The truth finally emerged on October 14, 1992, when, after the demise of the USSR, and in President Boris Yeltsin's name, the key documents were presented to the Polish government. The Katyń graves are held up today as a symbol of the larger mass murders. The operation against the Polish officers was consistent with how the Soviets treated their own people. An NKVD defector, who was involved, said later that the murder of the Poles was "a typical operation . . . considered entirely routine and unremarkable."[30]

In the meantime German forces took Norway in April 1940, tore through the Low Countries and France in May, and won both in six weeks with apparent ease. Those victories began to undermine Stalin's conviction that a long-drawn-out war would wear down the capitalists. He decided to move on June 14, when the Germans entered Paris. Molotov extended his "warmest congratulations" to the German ambassador in Moscow and also said that the Soviet Union would soon occupy the Baltic states. Indeed, the Soviets immediately issued an ultimatum to Lithuania and two days later to Latvia and Estonia. Moscow demanded that Red Army troops be given "free passage," and they soon took the key centers.[31]

Stalin sent representatives to the capital cities of each to introduce Soviet-style rule. Indigenous political institutions were crushed and new elections called, though only Communists could run. The NKVD began arresting and executing hundreds of "anti-Soviet elements." In due course, the Baltic states were coaxed into asking to become members of the Soviet Union, a wish granted in early August.[32] These nations would never entirely accept their loss of independence and would struggle for their freedom, no matter how dark the times or slim the chances, until they finally won, half a century later.

Andrei Zhdanov, who went to Estonia, later candidly told a secret party gathering in Leningrad that Soviet policy was to take advantage of the war in order to expand. In a November 1940 speech, he quoted Stalin saying that the Bear (the historical image of Russia) had to "make the rounds to demand payment for each tree as the forester chops the wood." Zhdanov said that in the previous year that policy had "resulted in the expansion of the socialist territories of the Soviet Union" and that more gain could be expected in the future.[33]

Stalin seemed to think Red Army occupation brought happiness, since after all, he asked rhetorically, were the people not "liberated from the yoke of the landlords, capitalists and police and other scoundrels"?

Should they not be grateful that they now were situated inside the "socialist front" against the capitalists? What he wanted in all the occupied territories was to make good on the Bolshevik mission that had failed after the Russian Revolution, that is, "to substitute the pluralistic texture of the borderlands with an ideological uniformity."[34]

Nevertheless, he grew anxious about the Soviet grip on the newly incorporated areas, and Beria proposed "cleansing" them in mid-May and again in mid-June, to round up all "anti-Soviet, criminal, and socially-dangerous elements," as well as "counter-revolutionary organizations." Anyone whose past was deemed suspect was sent away or killed. The NKVD had long since worked out procedures for deporting whole families while keeping local interference to a minimum. Women and children were separated from husbands and fathers only at the railway station. The operations in the night of June 13–14 deported 12,569 from Lithuania, 16,564 from Latvia, and 6,700 from Estonia.[35] Most were the family members whose household heads had been arrested and likely already executed. All were considered dyed-in-the-wool opponents of Communism.[36] Although estimates vary, a consensus on the numbers killed, deported, or missing in the year of Soviet occupation puts the toll at 34,250 for Latvia, around 61,000 for Estonia, and 39,000 for Lithuania.[37]

Stalin also threatened Finland, and by the autumn of 1939 he had opted to invade in what he thought would be a two-week "lightning war." The attack began on November 30, but what became the Winter War dragged on for 105 days. In the midst of it, the dictator assured his circle in the Kremlin that "world revolution" would inexorably move forward, even with this slight bump in the road.[38] In March 1940, Molotov reported to a hushed meeting that 52,000 Red Army soldiers had been killed out of a total of 233,000 casualties.[39] Stalin tried to put the best spin on the disaster in a speech to the Central Committee in April. It was their army's first real war, he said. Then he gave a long list of excuses, but there was no getting around the fact that the Finns showed up the glaring weaknesses of the Soviet armed forces.

Everyone knew that Hitler was watching, and it drove Stalin to distraction when the German ambassador dared offer assistance "if we are encountering difficulties in the fight with the Finns."[40] Someone had to pay, so in May Stalin shifted responsibility for the mess in Finland onto the shoulders of People's Commissar of Defense Voroshilov, an old ally who dared blame the Great Terror for killing off the top military men. He was dismissed but remained a person of influence until his death in 1969.[41]

As the time ticked down to the clash of the two dictatorships, Hitler had every reason to hope for a quick victory, while Stalin had less room for optimism, and perhaps that was why he tried appeasement. A better course might have been to reach out to Great Britain and above all to the United States, but in Stalin's theory, the capitalists were supposed to fight among themselves, and none of them were going to rescue the USSR. He was wrong on both counts.

STALIN'S GREATEST ERROR

Hitler was long convinced that he had a mission to make war against the detested home of Communism. For years he had said that merely trading for resources was not the answer to Germany's problems, for it also needed *Lebensraum,* a vast area that the "master race" would settle and dominate. German prowess pushed the British, French, and Allied forces into hastily retreating to the English Channel near Calais and Dunkirk. France agreed to an armistice on June 22, 1940—only weeks into the fighting, leaving Stalin flabbergasted at the easy German victory and disgusted that Hitler had begun to present himself as the man who would liberate Europe from Communism.[42]

All of Europe was impressed by the German victories, and Nazism was attractive even to many people outside Germany. Prime Minister Churchill was definitely not one of them, but even he fleetingly thought some kind of peace might be an option. No matter what he said in public about "victory at all costs," it was not that simple. Back on May 26, with many troops still stranded at Dunkirk, he thought out loud about making a deal with the Nazis. The next day he said he might agree to talks, if Hitler were prepared "to make peace on the terms of the restoration of German colonies" and settle for domination over Central Europe.[43] But the wavering ended definitively on July 19, when Hitler mentioned a semiserious peace offer, to which Churchill would not deign to respond.[44] The German leader then kept postponing Operation Sea Lion, the invasion of Britain, and on September 17 he put it off indefinitely.[45]

The Battle of Britain was far from won when Hitler broke his own cardinal rule about avoiding a two-front war and on December 18, 1940, issued the directive for Operation Barbarossa, the invasion of the Soviet Union. Stalin's spies were extraordinarily well informed and had been tracking the German decision-making process intensively since June. Over the next months, they reported, with ever-growing certainty, on the attack to come. On December 29 and in follow-up notes, they confirmed Hitler's decision, which, they noted, was based on his belief that "the state of the Red Army was so low" that victory would be easy.[46] There followed a flood of reports from these spies, which were astonishingly accurate, about the coming German attack, mentioning dates, troop strength, routes of invasion, and the exact three-prong strategy, along with the respective military commanders.[47]

As Germany readied for war, it was briefly diverted from these plans and moved in a southeasterly direction toward Yugoslavia and Greece. On April 5, Stalin boldly offered the Yugoslavs a friendship and nonaggression treaty, in the hope that such a gesture would warn off Hitler.[48] Quite to the contrary, the Wehrmacht began pounding Belgrade even before the delegates in Moscow could celebrate their treaty. Rather pathetically, the Soviet Boss began worrying that holding a banquet with the Yugoslavs might be taken in Berlin to have a "brazenly provocative character." Thus, apart from the mildest protest, Stalin continued Soviet-style appeasement. He made endless gestures of goodwill, such as recognizing new puppet governments put in place by the Nazis as they conquered one country after the next.[49]

Information continued to roll in from his spies and foreign governments, including Britain and the United States.[50] One recent Russian analysis provides a table of fifty-six intelligence reports from January to June 1941, each growing more specific. By early May the sources were (correctly) giving June 20 to 22 as the exact day of the attack.[51] One said the Germans were deliberately and ostentatiously making preparations, in order to intimidate the Soviets.[52] The Red Army's general staff knew from month to month exactly where the German forces were and how they were marshaling on the border.[53]

Stalin curiously resisted drawing the obvious conclusion and at the end of May lamely told exasperated military leaders that he was "not sure" about Hitler's intentions. Not until three days before the invasion did Soviet leaders order serious efforts to camouflage military installations, tanks, and aircraft on the ground. Even those belated measures were not due to be completed for more than a month.[54] In his memoirs, Molotov tried to defend Stalin and himself by saying they had hoped to delay the inevitable attack. He does not, however, explain why they allowed the Red Army to become so exposed that it almost lost the war before it began.[55]

Later in life Red Army leaders said they had not tried hard enough to convince their leader of the country's vulnerabilities.[56] These officers admitted that Stalin's "authority was unquestioned, all believed in his infallibility," so no one dared object when he continued dismissing the mounting evidence of the impending attack.

Stalin had deceived himself in believing that the Nazis would not attack the USSR until they had finished off Britain. His prize Marxian theory was that the capitalists would fight one another first and become exhausted, after which the Soviet Union would come in for an easy victory.[57] Why did his supposed paranoia let him down when he needed it most? What did the voice within say? True, he was isolated from the "real world," but his remoteness did not hinder him from formulating astute negotiating strategies with statesmen who visited Moscow. So his distant position behind the thick walls of the Kremlin does not explain his efforts to appease Hitler.[58]

For years Stalin had, incorrectly, posited that Hitler was little more than an "agent of capitalism" who did the bidding of the industrialists and bankers. The Soviet dictator regarded the racist aspects of Nazi ideology as a jumble of irrationalities, and no doubt they were. But for all that, they drove Hitler's vision of a racial "paradise," which fueled his passion of eliminating the Jews and destroying Communism. These fantasies were conflated in the slogan Hitler chose for the invasion of the Soviet Union, a crusade against "Jewish Bolshevism." On June 22, with battles already raging, the German ambassador in Moscow passed a formal note to Molotov explaining the reasons for war. High on the list was the need to defend Germany and to stop Moscow from organizing the Communist International and "Bolshevizing" Europe.[59]

Some revisionist historians maintain that Stalin was merely biding his time and preparing an offensive of his own, which Hitler supposedly stopped with his "preventive war."[60] The sliver of evidence often used is Stalin's speech on May 5, 1941, in which he spoke to the Red Army about how it had learned from history, become stronger in the last three years, and might go on the offensive.[61] However, reading through the Soviet documents for the year leading up to June 1941, one has to be struck by the Red Army's reactive stance. On May 14, Commissar of Defense Marshal Semyon Timoshenko and Chief of the General Staff General Georgi Zhukov sent orders "of special importance" to the military commanders on the front line facing Germany to prepare a "new plan" for the defense of the western borders. They were to take a whole series of detailed defensive steps by May 20.[62]

When Stalin mentioned the option about taking to the offensive in the future, it was intended to shore up army morale in the face of Hitler's continuing successes all over Europe. The Soviet Union would bide its time and strike after the capitalist powers exhausted one another.[63]

Stalin's mistaken belief was that the Nazis were driven only by economics and a lust for booty. That led to the false conclusion that if the USSR provided essential goods—such as foodstuffs, raw materials, and oil—then a costly war would make no sense to Hitler. Indeed, under the trade treaty with Germany of February 11, 1940, the Soviets agreed to send within the year, among many things, 1 million tons of grain, 900,000 tons of fuel, 100,000 tons of cotton, 100,000 tons of chrome arrant, and 500,000 tons each of phosphate and iron ore.[64] The chairman of the German economic delegation to the Soviet Union, Karl Schnurre, said at the time that only the personal intervention of Stalin had made it possible for negotiations to succeed. In spite of all the difficulties, Schnurre was impressed by "the desire of the Soviet government to help Germany." As he saw it, the new trade agreement "means a wide open door to the East for us."[65] Indeed, already by the summer of 1940, the USSR had become the most important source of Germany's raw materials.

Nevertheless, the Soviets could not possibly provide enough to meet the inflated ambitions of some members of the German big business community and the top echelons of the armed forces and economic administration. Moreover, they would soon begin to see not opportunities but dangers in becoming too dependent on Soviet deliveries.[66] In 1940 alone, no less than 52 percent of all Soviet exports went to Germany, which was delinquent in sending manufactured goods in return, as was part of the deal. Although the treaty permitted the USSR to reduce its exports proportionally or raise prices, the Germans were surprised that no such countermeasures followed.[67]

Under the more recently renewed trade agreement of January 10,

1941, between the two countries, the Soviet Union committed to sending 2.5 million tons of grain, enough to solve Germany's food problem and, in addition, 1 million tons of fuel, 200,000 tons of manganese ore, and assorted other vital minerals. Indeed, by April "hundreds of wagons with grain, fuel, minerals, and other raw materials congested on the Soviet side of the frontier stations," held up because the German railway could not cope with it all. Stalin knew perfectly well that the deal was lopsided in favor of Germany, which was allowed to get away with inflating the prices for its manufacturing goods, without the Soviets responding in kind, either by slowing deliveries or increasing their own prices.[68]

Stalin was directly involved in these arrangements, and he must have assumed that if Germany obtained all it needed by trade, then the threat of war from Hitler would all but vanish. He failed to understand—and hence ignored all the warning signs—that ideology and economics were entwined in Hitler's foreign policy thinking and grandiose plans. In fact, the supplies delivered to Germany tended to firm up Hitler's decision to invade.[69]

Nevertheless, as late as mid-May 1941, the economic experts in the German Foreign Office thought the USSR was keeping to its treaty obligations and that any shortfalls resulted because of Germany's failure to provide sufficient rolling stock for transportation. Soviet deliveries to Germany for 1941 were going to be substantial: for example, 632,000 tons of grain, 232,000 tons of oil, 23,500 tons of cotton, 50,000 tons of manganese ore, 67,000 tons of phosphates, and so on.[70] For all that, Hitler and the German elite of big business and the military worried more about becoming reliant on Soviet trade and goodwill. They opted for war, emboldened by the thought (widely held, even in the United States), that the Red Army could be defeated in a few weeks.[71] Even "pragmatic" members of the German elite were supportive of Hitler.[72]

Some of the German concern about the trade deal was due in part to the fact that the Soviets expected in return sophisticated military and industrial technology. Private firms, the I.G. Farben conglomerate, for example, were alarmed that the Kremlin wanted access to its chemical secrets and expected the company eventually to build a complete factory to produce the materials in the Soviet Union. Farben warned the armed forces that such a project would entail giving away vital military secrets. Thus Hitler's own private reservations about long-term trade with the USSR dovetailed with those of private industry and the German military.[73]

Stalin saw the deal as adding to the might of the Soviet Union, which would be able to offer a stiff defense against a future attack and go on the offensive if the opportunity arose to add further to the burgeoning Red Empire. In the short term, he remained convinced that before Hitler attacked, he would make more demands or at the very least issue an ultimatum about another trade treaty.[74] Thus the Soviets continued faithfully shipping hundreds of thousands of tons of war matériel right up to the moment the German invasion began. Any news conflicting with Stalin's view was written off as "disinformation."

At a meeting only three days before the attack, he again ridiculed army leaders Zhukov and Timoshenko for daring to ask that troops on the borders be put on full alert. He was obsessed about avoiding "provocations."[75] Yet Soviet leaders could see for themselves that the British diplomatic mission began leaving Moscow in mid-June and that their German, Italian, and Hungarian counterparts applied on June 19 for "urgent exit visas."[76] Late that Saturday (June 21) the Politburo gathered at Stalin's dacha. Commissar Timoshenko, General Zhukov, and Chief of Operations of the General Staff Nikolai Vatutin reported that a German sergeant had deserted and warned of an attack in the morning. Stalin asked: "Isn't this defector there just to provoke us?" The most anyone could do was persuade him to notify troops along the border of a "possible surprise attack." They were to take some defensive steps before dawn but avoid "provocative actions."[77]

The German invasion began at three A.M. (Soviet time) on June 22. Word of it flooded in from all fronts to Zhukov, who had the unpleasant task of phoning Stalin. Orders were then given for a meeting at the Kremlin, where the logbook notes that military leaders and the Politburo joined him at 5:45. Stalin amazed them when he asked: "Is this not a provocation by German generals?"[78]

STALIN ALMOST DEFEATED AND THEN RESCUED

Stalin's blunder led to a tragedy of biblical proportions, for which many millions of soldiers and citizens paid with their lives. In their memoirs more than one Red Army general blamed Stalin for leaving the country open to attack. Many border units had no ammunition or live artillery shells. Chief Marshal of Artillery N. N. Voronov, who was at supreme headquarters at that time, noted that if the Germans had met an organized and strong rebuff on crossing into Soviet territory, then the Red Army almost certainly would not have sustained such appalling initial casualties.[79]

In the first week of the war "virtually all of the Soviet mechanized corps lost 90 percent of their strength."[80] Whole divisions disappeared. General Dmitri Volkogonov, writing about the first eighteen months of the war, is pained to record that the Germans took around 3 million prisoners, or a shattering 65 percent of the existing Soviet armed forces.[81]

When the harried Stalin finally admitted that the invasion was for real, he remained in his office all day and most of the next one, meeting nonstop with key figures.[82] By nine A.M. on the day of the attack, the general staff had prepared a new Supreme High Command of the Armed Forces (Stavka).[83] The fact that it had to be created in the emergency underlined again how ill prepared the country was. The following day they established a new evacuation council to move people, cultural institutions, and whole factories and their workers to the East. That was a gargantuan task in itself. Stalin had miscalculated so badly that he had no stomach for informing the nation of the attack, a job he gave to Molotov.[84] The hope was that in two or three weeks the front would be stabilized. Then the leader himself would make an appearance.[85]

Like many citizens, the top figures in the Kremlin were in disbelief at how quickly the Germans advanced. On the evening of June 29, Stalin went to the Commissariat of Defense to get answers from Timoshenko, Zhukov, and Vatutin. When he heard they had lost contact with the front in Byelorussia, he exploded at Zhukov, who left the room "sobbing like a woman," or so Mikoyan later said. He added that it was perhaps at that moment that Stalin finally realized the scope of his mistakes.[86] The next day he fled to his dacha outside Moscow.

Lavrenti Beria came up with the idea of a new State Committee of Defense (GKO) that would streamline the bureaucracy. Besides Beria, it would include Molotov, Voroshilov, and Georgi Malenkov. The four, along with Mikoyan and Nikolai Voznesensky, went to Stalin's dacha on the evening of June 30. When he saw them, he expected they were there for his arrest or at least to force him out. But when Molotov told him about the GKO, all he did was raise the question of who would be its chairman. They still thought they needed him, for even amid the crisis that started on June 22, no one had dared suggest he should be kicked out.[87]

On July 3, Stalin finally went on national radio for more than half an hour. Many were struck by the opening phrase: "Comrades! Citizens! Brothers and sisters! Men of our army and navy! I am addressing you my friends!" He underlined the gravity of the situation but admitted no mistakes, saying it would have been right for any "peace-loving country" to try the nonaggression pact. The people were told to support the troops and recognize "the immensity of the danger." He ended by calling on them "to rally round the Party of Lenin and Stalin, and round the Soviet Government for the selfless support of the Red Army and Navy, demolish the enemy, and secure victory. All the strength of the people must be used to smash the enemy. Onward to victory!"[88]

He went back to work in the Kremlin the next day and gradually assumed more authority. On July 19 he took over as commissar of defense and by August 8 allowed himself to be "appointed" as the *verkhovnyi glavnokomanduyushchii*—supreme commander of the armed forces, or Supremo. For all that, his personal dictatorship was somewhat diminished, and given the scope of the challenges of the war, real power had to be delegated to political deputies and the military.

Prime Minister Churchill was thankful that the focus of German firepower now shifted away from Britain. He announced immediately that Britain would be on the side of Russia, its old foe. He admitted that "no one has been a more consistent opponent of Communism," of which he would "unsay no word." Nevertheless Churchill vowed to "give whatever help we can" to the Soviet Union. "We shall appeal to all our friends and allies in every part of the world to take the same course."[89] Britain itself was already in dire straits and not in a position to provide the kind of aid the USSR desperately needed, so that would be left to the Americans.

Official U.S. policy on the war in Europe had reached a turning point in late 1940, when Churchill wrote of the perilous situation his country faced and its need for urgent assistance.[90] FDR responded by introducing the Lend-Lease program to get around the continuing isolationist sentiment in the country, and on January 10, 1941, Congress began deliberations on the bill. It would grant an interest-free loan for purchase of goods made in the United States. In anticipation, the president sent Harry Hopkins and Wendell Willkie to London to assist Churchill in crafting an acceptance speech assuring Americans they would not be dragged into European problems. That point was aptly conveyed by the prime minister's gem of a phrase: "Give us the tools, and we will finish the job." In spite of some congressional opposition, the legislation passed, and Roosevelt signed it on March 11.[91]

Shortly thereafter Harry Hopkins, FDR's emissary and confidant, flew to London for a meeting with Churchill. FDR also needed to know whether the Soviets could hold out, and so on July 27 Hopkins traveled on to Moscow, where he was impressed, especially when Stalin said they would be taking the fight to the Germans in the spring. He was a clever actor and was bluffing; in reality he was still looking for ways to appease Hitler. Hopkins was not in Moscow long enough to ascertain how undecided things really were, but Stalin was encouraged to hear of Roosevelt's support and then typically made exaggerated demands for arms and supplies.[92] Hopkins was well regarded in the Kremlin, so much so that some in the United States thought he was a Soviet spy, a groundless suspicion.[93]

Once he was assured by what he heard, he left and, though ill, joined Churchill aboard the *Prince of Wales* for the transatlantic voyage. They met up with FDR in scenic Placentia Bay, Newfoundland. While the prime minister wanted Roosevelt to declare war on Germany, given the American people's isolationist mood, that was out of the question. The two sent a message to Stalin offering "the very maximum of supplies that you most urgently need" and proposed a strategy meeting to be held in Moscow in the near future.[94] Stalin would wait, however, until the situation on the battlefront was more to his liking before he showed interest in any such discussions.

One product of the meeting in Newfoundland was the Atlantic Charter, issued on August 14. It represented Allied war aims and the principles of a postwar settlement. The American and British leaders said they sought no territorial aggrandizement, nor any changes that "did not accord with the freely expressed wishes of the peoples concerned." They respected "the right of all peoples to choose the form of government under which they will live" and sought to return self-government to those who had been deprived of it. They favored the economic freedoms, including freedom of the seas. Also mentioned were hopes for an enduring peace and security after the destruction of "Nazi tyranny."[95] On September 24, representatives of the Soviet Union, Belgium, Czechoslovakia, Greece, Luxembourg, the Netherlands, Norway, Poland, and the Free French signed the charter at a meeting in London. It would be mentioned often in the disputes that arose later.[96]

In spite of the offers of Western assistance, Stalin desperately tried to make peace with Germany, already in July and again in October, just as Lenin had done in 1918. Our evidence for these peace feelers is fragmentary; those involved were threatened with death if they ever leaked a word. In any event, nothing came of Stalin's efforts, serious or otherwise, because Hitler was convinced that complete victory was only moments away.[97]

In September, Stalin admitted something of the precarious situation to Roosevelt's envoy Averell Harriman and to Churchill's representative Lord Beaverbrook when they visited. The dictator taunted Beaverbrook because Britain had not opened a second front, an action that was then completely out of the question. At one stage he said the paucity of supplies they were sending "proved" they wanted his country defeated. With the talks about to fail, Stalin turned on the charm, but to frighten his guests he conceded that Hitler could have taken Moscow and that if he had done so, it "would have destroyed the nerve center of the nation." In fact, the staffs at the American and British embassies thought the talks were bound to break down. Harriman and Beaverbrook kept these doubters at arm's length while in Moscow because Roosevelt and Churchill had already decided that at all costs they had to support the Soviet Union. On October 1, when they signed the Moscow Protocol, which outlined the aid to come from the United States and Great Britain, Stalin gushed out his gratitude.[98]

The history of distrust between the United States and USSR went back to 1917, and we have no need to review that here. What changed the relationship was Hitler (appointed in January 1933), together with the rise of Japan. FDR's modest conditions for granting formal recognition of the Soviet Union had been that Moscow provide legal and religious protections to Americans in the USSR and that it cease directing the American Communist Party. On November 17, 1933, Soviet representative Maxim Litvinov signed documents in Washington that restored diplomatic relations. The immediate effects were minimal, and even trade between the two countries stagnated in the years that followed.[99]

Nevertheless, the president decided, long before America entered the war, that all possible assistance should be given to the enemies of Nazism. Once Hitler attacked the Soviet Union in June 1941, Roosevelt prepared more earnestly. Not a month later, on July 9, he instructed that a contingency plan be drawn up.

The "Victory Program" established strategic goals and laid down how they would be attained. It would take two full years to mobilize, train, and equip sufficient armed forces for war against Germany and possibly also Japan. The program called for 215 divisions (or 8.7 million men) at a cost of $150 billion. The underlying assumption was that it would be necessary to mobilize such a large force because the Soviet Union would likely be knocked out of the war before very long. The United States hoped that generous aid would keep it in the fight, and it was a pleasant surprise when the Red Army showed its mettle at Stalingrad and won there in early 1943. Although the U.S. soon scaled back the number of troops it would need to call up for service from 215 divisions to 90, the eventual cost of the war would escalate to nearly $300 billion.

Roosevelt had extended Lend-Lease to the Soviet Union on October 1, 1941. Under that federal program, the Allied nations were provided with war matériel and granted loans to pay for it at favorable rates. In making the extension, the president faced opposition from Secretary of War Henry Stimson and U.S. Army Chief of Staff George C. Marshall. Both despised the Soviet system, but FDR was right to go against their advice.[100]

On October 3 and again on November 4, Stalin wrote the president to express his "heartfelt gratitude" for the interest-free loan and the promise of war matériel. A large sum for those times, one billion dollars, was to be given under the Lend-Lease program.[101] Although the supplies barely trickled through before year's end, in those first months of the war "even bare promises were important" and provided a badly needed morale booster.[102] The economic aid itself arrived mainly after January 1943 and contributed both to the shoring up of the Soviet home front and to the great counteroffensives the Red Army mounted in the second part of the war.[103] Soviet leaders were aware that their people, not Americans, would have to do most of the dying to win the war. Nikita Khrushchev wrote in his memoirs that the United States was "using our hands and letting us shed our blood to fight Nazi Germany. They paid us so that we could keep fighting; they paid us with weapons and other matériel."[104]

Providing Lend-Lease aid to Britain and above all to the USSR may have been Roosevelt's most significant accomplishment. It saved count-less American lives, and the United States emerged from the war with victory and a booming economy. Perhaps most important of all, with-out the promise of American assistance, the Soviet Union might well have capitulated.

For Soviet citizens, what came through the press reports, official lectures, and so on was a new narrative of their country on the inter-national scene. Instead of a struggle against capitalism, the new image of the USSR was that it was "at the heart of an alliance of progressive states" in the war against the Hitlerites.[105] Be that as it may, the views of the Soviet leadership had not changed much at all. What was said represented no more than a shift in political tactics.

STALIN'S STARK DEMANDS FROM THE WEST

The initial German advance into the Soviet Union in June 1941 had looked unstoppable. People had to decide to stay or go. For the manager of a factory, when to flee became a catch-22. If he took the files and the cash and left too soon, he could be accused of treason. If he "willfully remained" and had contact with the enemy, however, he could suffer the same fate. Time to make the right decision was short.[106]

Soviet citizens, and not only just those close to the borders, knew their country was precipitously close to falling. One who made it out of Moscow after the war vividly remembered the panic there in mid-October 1941:

> Everyone was going in all directions. Nobody was punished for any crime. They broke open store windows in broad day-light. Jewish pogroms started. The arrival of the Germans was expected from hour to hour. German planes were flying over-head from street to street and no one even shot at them; the Germans weren't afraid but they waved their hats and greeted the public from the planes. They could have taken Moscow eas-ily. There was no one in command of anything.[107]

Another resident recalled that the upheaval lasted a day or two, "then there was nothing more to loot. The stores were empty."[108] Defeatists were shot out of hand, for example, on October 16, when the NKVD executed more than two hundred. Still others classified as "especially dangerous criminals" were taken from the Lubyanka prison and shot. The strong-arm tactics restored order.[109]

The Red Army fought ferociously on the outskirts of Moscow, at times within twenty miles of the Kremlin. Nevertheless, Stalin felt bold enough on November 7, the anniversary of the Russian Revolution, to hold the annual parade. He thought it would give the country a needed shot in the arm. The day before, he spoke on the radio and called the nation his "brothers and sisters." Evoking Russian patriotism, he pointed to examples of great leaders in her past. For the first time, he lauded the new link with the United States and Great Britain and said that the side "who will have the overwhelming superiority in the production of motors will win the war."[110]

Only two days after announcing the new solidarity with the Anglo-Americans, he wrote Churchill and accused them of trying to avoid discussions of the postwar settlement. He was also angry that the British had not yet agreed on mutual military assistance. Even with the Wehrmacht at the gates, Stalin already had his eye on the postwar period. Although the prime minister was offended by the tone, he soon sent Foreign Secretary Anthony Eden to iron things out.[111]

Eden and Stalin met with draft agreements in hand on December 16. Stalin wanted Germany weakened and dismembered by transferring a large slice of territory to Poland. What remained of Prussia could become an independent state but without the Rhineland, which included Germany's major industrial area. Austria would become independent again, as perhaps might Bavaria. Stalin said that all these changes would weaken Germany and make it unable to threaten war for another generation.[112] It was he who tried to persuade Eden about these steps and the need for reparations.[113]

The next day Stalin—as Eden put it—"began to show his claws" and demanded recognition of the Soviet borders of 1941. In effect, he was seeking official sanction of the USSR conquests in its war of aggression against Poland and the Baltic states. Now he proposed that, when victory came, Poland would be compensated by expanding to the west at Germany's expense. The USSR would get eastern Poland up to the Cur-

zon Line. That was the frontier proposed in vain in 1920 by British foreign secretary Curzon to divide the newly established Polish state from
revolutionary Russia. Back then Poland had been strong enough to take
land east of that line. If the USSR could get that territory, large parts of
the former Russian Empire would again be under Moscow's rule. Eden
demurred and, in a wire to Churchill at the end of the talks, summed up
the situation. Stalin wanted military agreements, "but he will not sign
until we recognize his frontiers, and we must expect continuing badgering on this issue."[114]

The recently revealed Soviet records show how Stalin meant to
mislead his allies. The dictator's passion to dismember the German
enemy was the cornerstone of the Kremlin's plan for postwar Europe,
and demanding it at every opportunity was more than mere "negotiating tactics," as some Russian historians have suggested.[115] He meant
to expand the Soviet Union and its influence as much as possible. At
the same time, being acutely aware of public opinion in the West, he
denied allegations circulating there that the USSR intended "to Bolshevize Europe."[116] During all the wartime conferences, in fact, he never
once mentioned a desire to advance Communism. Instead, he shrewdly
couched his demands exclusively in terms of Soviet "security interests."
This was his new mask, behind which he concealed his ideological and
political fixations.

Stalin went to great lengths to make it seem unreasonable that anyone would deny his demands for better security. He offered to support
British claims, should they have any, for air and naval bases in postwar
Belgium and Holland. He wondered why the British would not give
reciprocal support, when all he wanted was a return to the borders of
1941.[117]

On December 7, as the Red Army was counterattacking German
forces, the Japanese bombed Pearl Harbor. Japan had not even informed
Hitler, who would have much preferred that they had invaded the USSR
in the east and thus tied down Soviet troops.

President Roosevelt approached the Soviet ambassador on the day
following the unprovoked attack, in the hope that Stalin would join the
United States in declaring war on Japan. He was told that the Soviet
leader was in no position to do so, nor would he be until the Red Army
managed to turn back the Nazis. That was several long years away.[118]

On December 11 Hitler added to his mistakes with a grand proclamation of war against the United States and thus brought on its economic and military might without getting much in return. The next day in Moscow, *Pravda* announced that the German advance had been stopped. As if to make matters worse for Hitler, before the year was out, the U.S. and Britain affirmed their decision to defeat Germany first.[119]

CHAPTER 4

Soviet Aims and Western Concessions

The Western Allies were torn between worries about Communism and more immediate fears of Germany and Japan. Stalin knew of these concerns and tried to present the Soviet Union as an upstanding and reliable partner. Almost from the beginning of the war, he counseled resistance leaders with links to Moscow to adopt a "unity of action" with other anti-Nazi forces. They should do what they could against the occupation but avoid appearing as indigenous Communist revolutionary movements.[1] This new party line was a return to the antifascist stance propagated by the Comintern in the 1930s, which had become politically embarrassing in August 1939, when Stalin signed an alliance with Hitler.[2]

On July 7, 1941, the Comintern, now once again in its customary, more spirited operating mode, issued a special directive to foreign parties to form united or "national fronts" in countries occupied by Germany and to unify the struggle against Hitler.[3] That would also be the slogan Moscow would soon be using to sponsor new governments in the lands liberated by the Red Army.

FDR AND CHURCHILL SHED MORE RESERVATIONS ABOUT STALIN

The advance of the Germans and their allies was halted at Moscow at the end of 1941, but in the new year they renewed efforts and started to look unstoppable again. The Soviet Union wanted a new treaty of assistance, and Molotov flew to London in May 1942 to sign it. He insisted again on the USSR's 1941 borders, but the British would not agree. Then, much to everyone's surprise, Stalin changed course and told Commissar Molotov to get the treaty without an agreement on territory.[4] In his instructions to him, Stalin noted ominously that in any case frontier issues would soon be decided by force.[5]

The commissar traveled on to the United States, to get a decision about a second front in Europe and further economic assistance. At his first meeting with Roosevelt on May 29, Molotov asked the president if it was true that he was "unsympathetic" to Soviet demands for its western frontiers as of 1941. FDR "replied that indeed he did not want that question mentioned in any treaty, in view of U.S. public opinion. He believed that a proper moment should be found to raise this question, but it had not yet come." Molotov got the president's commitment or at least an expression of hope for an Allied landing in Europe in 1942, with perhaps six to ten divisions going ashore in France.

FDR confessed that these American soldiers might have to "live through another Dunkirk and lose 100,000 to 120,000 men." The operation would supposedly damage German morale, "ease the situation and raise the spirit of the Red Army." Such an outlandish statement can only be understood as a gesture to placate the abrasive Molotov. Indeed, the president confessed to his adviser Harry Hopkins that of all the people with whom he had dealings, he had never had to cope with anyone quite so difficult. According to Hopkins, the president was motivated "to spare no effort to discover the common ground which, he was sure, must somewhere exist."[6]

At eleven P.M. at the end of the first day, Hopkins took the unusual step of visiting Molotov in his room at the White House. He suggested the commissar might "draw a gloomy picture" of the Soviet situation when he next met the president, as well as Army Chief of Staff General Marshall and Commander in Chief of the Navy Admiral Ernest King. Hopkins believed a negative assessment of Soviet prospects would win over the Americans. It was peculiar that a U.S. official would be advising a foreign diplomat on how to gain advantage with his country's leaders. But it seems that Roosevelt's top adviser was convinced the Soviets were interested only in security and thought they would work with the Americans for "a world of democracy and peace." In any case, General Marshall held his ground, saying there were insufficient landing craft for an amphibious invasion in Europe. Molotov complained in his note to Stalin that "the insincerity of this reply was obvious."[7]

The commissar also turned up his nose at the president as an unredeemable capitalist and imperialist, like Churchill. When Molotov pressed FDR to open a second front, he and Stalin knew perfectly well it was impossible.[8] At a final meeting, Molotov again insisted on a direct answer to the question about a date for the second front, but Roosevelt was evasive and said only that it was under active consideration.[9]

Meanwhile, FDR and Churchill worried that Stalin might yet seek a deal with Hitler, for in July 1942 the Wehrmacht broke through into the Caucasus, heading for the big oil fields in the south. At the end of the month, Stalin finally consented to a visit from FDR's emissary Averell Harriman and Churchill himself. When they came to the Kremlin on August 12, they did not please the dictator with the news that there could be no landing in France in 1942. As if to compensate, the prime minister spoke expansively about Operation Torch, an attack in North Africa, which would begin on November 8. However, all of this left Stalin cold, muttering that it was a poor substitute for the invasion of continental Europe.[10] His spies in London had already informed him that the British War Cabinet had made its decision on July 25, so the dictator's show of surprise was purely for effect.[11]

When Stalin cast doubt on the courage of the British Army, Churchill almost stormed out. But he put country before pride and stayed, passing along the news that the Royal Air Force would bomb Germany into submission. He also mentioned the forthcoming Dieppe raid on August 19 on the French coast, but that did not placate his Soviet partner in the slightest.

The three Allied leaders agreed that Germany had to be divided to ensure postwar peace and security. At this meeting with Stalin, Churchill said he thought Prussian militarism and Nazism had to be destroyed and Germany disarmed. Stalin also wanted its military leaders exterminated and the country deprived of its main industrial center in the Ruhr.[12] One member of the British delegation, writing in his diary, compared the dictator to a python and another labeled him a criminal. Still, Churchill and Harriman came away convinced the Soviets would stay in the war.[13]

Back in the 1930s, President Roosevelt had been upset when Stalin persisted in using "Trojan Horse tactics" to help the American Communist Party and continued doing so even after U.S. diplomatic recognition of the Soviet Union in 1933. That bothered FDR, but he was no isolationist and thought he could get an understanding with Stalin. This inclination to reach agreement soon led to the president's distrust of the

State Department's hard-liners and particularly American ambassador William C. Bullitt in Moscow, who resigned in the summer of 1936. FDR took the opportunity to appoint Joseph E. Davies, who served from November of that year to June 1938. He was an old friend and political supporter and was considered "soft" on the Soviet Union. Roosevelt despised everything Hitler stood for and sending Davies was a gesture of friendship to balance things out in Europe.

When preparing for his first trip to Moscow, Davies made a point of telling everyone that he was going to be friendlier than the previous ambassador. Speaking with a Soviet newspaper reporter, he said that in the tense international situation there was room for cooperation.[14] The staff at the American embassy in Moscow instantly rejected Davies as unqualified and went so far as to consider tendering their resignations.[15] In Moscow, Davies, a lawyer by profession, attended the show trials and, remarkably, accepted their validity. He even found credible the fable that Stalin had stopped a coup "by acting with great vigor and speed."[16]

By 1939, FDR had condemned German and Soviet aggression in Poland and was sympathetic to Britain and France, but he had wanted to avoid direct involvement in the war.[17] As late as October 30, 1940—long after the fall of France in June—he assured citizens in one of his election addresses: "Your boys are not going to be sent into any foreign wars."[18] Nevertheless, in view of the grave situation Britain faced, the president soon introduced Lend-Lease aid to that country and later extended the funding to supply other nations.[19]

Somewhere along the line FDR had come to regard Nazi Germany as the greater evil, and he became ever less critical of the USSR. Charles Bohlen, the experienced Moscow diplomat who was taken into the Roosevelt White House as an interpreter and adviser, observed that FDR understood Stalin's mistrust as caused by "the neglect that Soviet Russia had suffered at the hands of other countries for years after the Revolution. What he did not understand was that Stalin's enmity was based on profound ideological convictions." Thus he did not see the moral and political chasm that separated the United States and the USSR, much less that it could never be bridged.[20]

The former American ambassador to the Soviet Union, William Bullitt, urged FDR to extend Lend-Lease to the Soviets but only in return for pledges on human rights. The president and Secretary of State Cordell Hull ruled that out, in favor of keeping the USSR in the war.[21] FDR came to think he could convert Stalin by providing plentiful aid with no strings attached and by meeting him face-to-face. The president, in communication with Ambassador Bullitt, said that he was going to follow his own "hunch" that Hopkins was right in thinking that they could work with the Soviets.

They also wanted to believe that the Soviet Union was or would soon work "toward democratic socialism." Although there had been some "rough edges" in the relationship with Moscow in the past, the White House came to think that earlier examples of the Soviets' "pathological behavior" should be overlooked or tolerated.[22] When FDR heard of the German attack on the USSR in June 1941, he must have reasoned that it was a "heaven-sent opportunity." To help keep the Red Army in the fight, the United States had extended Lend-Lease to the Soviet Union later that year with a hope and a prayer.[23]

Indeed, the Red Army held on, then carried the burden of the Allied fighting and in early 1943 won the decisive battle at Stalingrad (summer 1942–February 2, 1943), where Hitler's newly appointed Field Marshal Friedrich Paulus surrendered on January 31. Although there is controversy regarding the exact number of German and Allied troops that were surrounded—ranging from 195,000 to 290,000—there is general agreement that some 110,000 Axis troops were taken prisoner. There is no question, however, that this battle was an unmitigated disaster for Germany and represented a turning point in the war.[24] Meanwhile in North Africa, American and British forces in Operation Torch defeated the Axis powers on May 12 and took 238,243 prisoners, half of them German. It was like a second Stalingrad in the space of a few months.[25]

HELPING HIS ALLIES OVERLOOK CRIMES

President Roosevelt pressed Stalin for direct talks on four occasions during 1942 and 1943. Wanting to secure the postwar peace and win support for the United Nations, he thought his personal charisma would work if he could meet the Master of the Kremlin. That was a mistake, for the Communist leaders had long since made up their own minds. Moreover, Molotov had reported the president's efforts to be informal and scoffed at their "obvious" phoniness.[26] In the meantime, Roosevelt continued to overestimate his own abilities and, without ever having laid eyes on Stalin, confidently told Churchill he would be able to handle that man better than either the U.S. State Department or the British Foreign Office: "Stalin hates the guts of all your top people. He thinks he likes me better, and I hope he will continue to do so."[27]

The president went to great lengths to win Stalin over; in May 1943 he sent former ambassador Davies off again for talks. Rumors were circulating that a new Soviet-Nazi agreement might end the war. FDR was convinced it was essential to prevent any such outcome, even if it meant accepting the western borders that Stalin kept demanding. Davies's book about his earlier experiences had been published as *Mission to Moscow.* Not only did it whitewash everything, but it excused the Soviet invasion of Poland and Finland. A movie based on the book was even less critical. It premiered in April 1943, and Davies watched it with the president, who liked it. He wanted Davies to show it to Stalin to convince him of American sincerity. FDR remained confident that if only he could meet with Stalin alone, without the feisty Churchill around, he could get along famously with the Soviet Boss.[28]

The Kremlin was pleased enough with the Davies movie to open it for national distribution. Surely Stalin must have wondered what was behind dispatching such an apologist for Soviet crimes, but he still balked at an early meeting. Instead he asked for more deliveries through Lend-Lease and mentioned his disappointment in his allies, who, without consulting him at all, had put off opening a second front in Europe until the spring of 1944.[29]

Stalin did offer a symbolic gesture to improve his image in America: on May 22, 1943, he announced the imminent dissolution of the Comintern. (He had promised to do this for nearly a decade.) Secretary of State Hull told the public that this latest step would "promote a greater degree of trust" and contribute to the "cooperation necessary for the winning of the war and for successful postwar undertakings."[30] The British government directed the BBC to describe the end of the Comintern as "by far the most important political event of the war," for it supposedly indicated that the Soviet Communists had turned to international cooperation.[31]

The Soviet dissolution of the Comintern was also an attempt to shift attention away from the Katyń massacre. The world was astounded at revelations by the Nazis that the bodies of thousands of Polish officers had been found. Berlin broadcast the story beginning on April 13, and it made news around the globe.[32]

Surely it was not a coincidence that on April 19, not a week after the horrors about Katyń began to circulate, the Soviet Union announced new military tribunals to deal with the Nazi occupiers "and their local hirelings." The Kremlin wanted to direct the world's attention back to the crimes of the Third Reich and staged a series of show trials, the first beginning in July.[33]

In letters to FDR and Churchill in late April, Stalin denied involvement in the "monstrous crimes" against the Polish officers and claimed that the "London Poles" were allowing themselves to be used as "tools" for anti-Soviet purposes.[34] On April 25 the USSR broke off relations with the London-based Polish government. A week later Stalin decided it might be useful to dissolve the Comintern, and Moscow hurried to inform the worldwide network, including Mao Zedong, Yugoslavian boss Josip Broz Tito, and American Communist leader Earl Browder. The process began to drag, and Stalin, in a call to Dimitrov on May 20, asked him to speed things up. In an interview on May 29, carried on the front page of *The New York Times*, the Soviet dictator said that Moscow had no intention of mixing in the affairs of other countries, and he disclaimed yet again wanting to Bolshevize them. That big story succeeded in pushing the news of the murdered Poles into the background.[35]

The dissolution of the Comintern completely fooled American intelligence, never mind President Roosevelt. Thus in a May memorandum, the Office of Strategic Services (OSS)—precursor to the CIA—reported Russian voices as saying that Moscow had given up on world revolution, and it took the breakup of the Comintern as "proof" of Stalin's loyalty to his allies. In a June memo, the OSS thought it saw "fundamental changes in Russian Communism." The most important of these, it said, was Soviet rejection of the purity of Communist ideology in the name of the motherland and defense of national security. American intelligence was completely wrong, but like the British, the Americans were focused on Germany and Japan. The Soviets similarly directed attention to the common enemies but spied just as energetically on their allies. Russian historians were amazed at how completely Western intelligence services and Roosevelt accepted the significance of dissolving the Comintern.[36]

To Communists around the world, Stalin gave a rationale for this step that, he hoped, they could accept. The main reason for ending the Comintern, he said, was practical. In wartime, national parties use different tactics. Thus in Italy and Germany, he explained, there was resistance to undertake, while in Britain and the United States, comrades should support the government. Dissolving the Comintern would strengthen the national parties, which could no longer be accused of being "agents of a foreign power." In other words, the decision was tactical only. The Kremlin waited anxiously for reactions of the faithful—though the likelihood of objections was next to nil. Stalin got the unanimous agreement he sought, then on June 8 released official word of the dissolution to the press.

The whole procedure was painstaking and reflected the care Stalin took to manipulate his allies, while at the same time nurturing the international movement. Exactly four days later and leaving nothing to chance, he gathered key members of the Politiburo and Dimitrov to create the Department of International Information. It was a branch of the Soviet party's Central Committee and would direct antifascist committees, foster liaisons with foreign comrades, and so on—in other words, carry out more or less the same tasks done by the Comintern. They assigned a new leader to avoid all suspicion, but Dimitrov continued as before.[37]

When citizens heard what had happened, their opinions were mixed. Representative statements came from one man who said "it must have been a difficult decision for Stalin to take; after all, he had sworn on Lenin's tomb never to abandon the cause of world revolution. But just like his 'socialism in one country' this decision was another sign of Stalin's greatness that he could adapt himself to changed conditions."[38]

The Kremlin was in fact busy on several international fronts. Moscow was already schooling former and future leaders of the Romanian, Polish, Hungarian, Bulgarian, Czech, German, and even Italian and French Communist parties.[39] There was also a program (introduced back in late 1941) to train functionaries from among such groups as prisoners of war and defectors, who would remain devoted to Stalin, if and when they were repatriated.[40] At the same time, steps were taken to improve the image of the USSR by relaxing religious persecution. On September 4, 1943, Stalin met with the three top leaders of the Orthodox Church, promising them, out of the blue, all kinds of material support. He suggested they call a synod to select a new patriarch; none had been allowed since the death of Patriarch Tikhon in 1925. Without questioning this newfound mercy, the religious leaders were grateful and thought their synod could meet within a month. Smiling benevolently, Stalin asked whether they might be able to adopt a more "Bolshevik tempo," that is, gather sooner. Indeed, with the government's help, they met within four days.[41] All this activity was played up in the press. Churches were allowed to open again, especially in the western borderlands, which had been occupied by the Nazis.[42] No doubt there was a patriotic appeal in returning a semblance of freedom of worship, and certainly Stalin's short-lived toleration also aimed to please FDR, who had mentioned it earlier, and in that regard it worked.[43]

FIRST MEETING OF THE "BIG THREE"

Stalin agreed to meet with his allies only after his armies had more to show for their efforts and he would have a stronger hand in negotiations. Then he prepared down to the smallest detail, leaving nothing to chance, as if the meetings were an extension of the war by other means.[44] He finally assented to a leaders' conference at Tehran for November 28 to December 1, 1943, which was notably after Stalingrad. German forces were soon driven out of two-thirds of the Soviet territory they had once occupied, and in July and August 1943 at Kursk the Red Army had won the largest tank battle of the war. The massive scale of these events and sheer size of the Red Army made Stalin more willing to meet the Western leaders.

He continued worrying about the procrastination of the West in opening a front in France and did not believe the reasons for the delay. Anglo-American forces had finally landed in November 1942, not in France as he had hoped, but in distant North Africa. Although they fought ferociously there, the Germans managed to hold them back without having to pull significant numbers of troops away from the eastern front. The same was true of the Allied landings in Sicily in July 1943 and in Italy in September.

Stalin had a fear of flying, and after this flight to and from the Tehran Conference, he never flew again. He saw the event as a chance to impress Roosevelt and got off to a promising start by convincing him to stay at the Soviet mission. Perfectly in character, Stalin had all the guest rooms bugged by his secret police.

There had been a preliminary foreign ministers' conference in October in Moscow, for which he and Molotov had position papers drawn up by top foreign policy staff. The Soviet side thoroughly thought out its strategies, even the tactics to adopt, at the conference table and was better equipped and more resolute than the Western Allies for the crucial discussions that would shape the postwar world.[45] Any apparent "compromises" that resulted from the wartime meetings would be more apparent than real because Stalin had long since decided on his goals. If the West was going to stop him, it would have had to send far more troops to the battlefield, an option that FDR wished to avoid. Instead the American president preferred to let the Red Army do most of the fighting and dying, although in so doing it advanced the Soviet cause well into what would be a divided Germany.[46]

In Tehran on November 28, a Sunday afternoon, Stalin readied himself for an informal chat with Roosevelt prior to the main meeting at six p.m. Atypically, he was nervous and primed himself almost like an actor waiting for a scene to begin, carefully checking his appearance, the press of his pants and shine on his boots. He also changed his demeanor, for he became a deferential listener, giving no hint of his customary rudeness nor showing his blunt dictatorial self. Although he could be jovial, he decided in advance not to laugh at any of FDR's jokes. This approach, it turned out, cagily acted by Stalin with success, put the president off his game, for he prided himself on his good humor and comic stories.[47]

When they met, FDR spoke first and said how glad he was to be there and how long he had worked to bring them together. Stalin accepted responsibility for the delay, while reporting that he had, of course, been occupied with military matters. Then he explained the dire situation, which was made worse by the fact that the Germans had just called up fresh divisions. The news pained the president, who then changed the subject, to say that in the postwar period the American-British merchant fleet might be made available to the Soviet Union. Stalin brought up France's support of the Third Reich, criticized its exiled leader General Charles de Gaulle, and bluntly stated that he did not want the French to have an important role in the postwar world.[48]

At the first plenary session, Stalin stole the show with a description of the gargantuan scale of the fighting on the eastern front—the Red Army was throwing in 330 divisions against 260 of the enemy's.[49] He and FDR pressed Churchill to agree to an invasion through France—now called Operation Overlord. The prime minister said there would likely be sixteen British divisions and nineteen U.S. divisions.

Although there had been preparations since 1942 for a cross-Channel offensive to liberate France, nothing had come of them. At Tehran, Churchill still favored operations in the Mediterranean, which Stalin dismissed as "only diversions." Instead he wanted Overlord and a definite date. He promised that whenever it took place, the Red Army would simultaneously "undertake offensive operations, and would demonstrate by its actions the value it placed on this decision." He also wanted to know who would be in command. Roosevelt eventually named General Dwight D. Eisenhower and later telegraphed this news to Moscow.[50]

At dinner on the first evening, Stalin brought up the thorny subject of what was to happen to Nazi Germany. The Soviets, contrary to their later denials, had drawn up extensive plans for Germany's dismemberment.[51] FDR was known for wanting the same thing, but that evening he retired early because of illness. Stalin and Churchill carried on. The prime minister proposed ways of ensuring that Germany did not become a military threat again, but Stalin insistently held to his early position of moving Poland's western boundaries well into Germany, thus depriving it of land, people, and wealth. Even then he kept saying there was nothing to prevent them from uniting again. He confessed that he "was not sure" whether there should be "four, five, or six independent Germanic states," and proposed sending the matter for study to one of the committees.[52]

Even "moderates" among the Soviet leaders like Ivan Maisky were convinced that Soviet security required that Germany be weakened and in addition also undergo a "complete and thorough proletarian revolution as a result of the war, and the creation of a stable new order based on the Soviet model. The psychology of the German people that has been poisoned by fascism, has to be transformed through the fire of such a revolution and the present ruling classes in Germany must be completely exterminated." Maisky's notes in his diary from earlier in 1943 sum up what the Soviet leaders wanted to do in Germany, as well as in other countries.[53]

At Tehran the USSR played the moderates and allowed Roosevelt to harbor the illusion that he was making progress. The president felt that he was better informed about Germany than the other two, for as a young boy he had attended school there. Only recently, he said, did he feel that it should be broken into three or more independent states that would share some infrastructure. He was somewhat dissuaded from this stance by the U.S. State Department, prior to traveling to Tehran.[54] However Churchill and Stalin strongly advocated Germany's dissolution at the conference; FDR went along and moreover opted for its division into five parts.

What the Soviet leader was really after was dominant influence in that country, but he would have to bide his time before making a move in that direction, and for the moment he said only that it "should be broken up and kept broken up," not allowed any kind of federation or association. Thus he publicly favored Roosevelt's plan and held to that position until well into 1945, when he began to believe that a Communist transformation of Germany was feasible. It was with that prospect in mind that he became more inclined to keep the country in one piece.[55]

Without much prodding, the Western Allies consented to vast territorial gains for the USSR. Stalin had told the British early on that he wanted the northern part of East Prussia. He now added that it would provide his country with an ice-free port, "a small piece of German territory which he felt was deserved."[56] In the Soviet version of the minutes, however, the justification for getting this trophy was that it was "traditionally Russian."[57] It was not. Stalin wanted the far bigger prize of what had been eastern Poland up to the Curzon Line. Thus he repeated his claim to lands won as Hitler's ally in 1939. Churchill suggested that Poland "might move westward," that is, relinquish its eastern border region to the Soviet Union, and in compensation get a slice of eastern Germany. He knew that this step ignored the Atlantic Charter and the wishes of the Polish government-in-exile in London. Stalin wanted to be on the record as favoring the "restoration and strengthening of Poland," but he demanded that its borders be changed, with Moscow laying claim to a huge swath of territory. He did so in terms that resonated with many postwar historians, who tend to accept his reasoning that in view of how much the Soviet Union had suffered by invasions through Poland, its "security needs" justified expansion in all directions of the compass.[58]

Stalin made the astonishing claim that no Poles would be allowed in the area that the USSR was to take. He maligned the "London Poles" as little more than "agents of Hitler" who allegedly incited actions against "partisans" in Poland. He would help the liberated country establish more westerly borders at Germany's expense along the Oder River, but that was all.

In private Churchill warned the president that Stalin was preparing "a Communist replacement for the Polish government." A Soviet spy, Sergo Beria, the son of Stalin's chief of the secret police, who manned the recording equipment bugging their rooms, was surprised to overhear FDR level a counteraccusation at Churchill for trying to engineer an anti-Communist government. Beria recalled thinking how strange it was for the president to "put Churchill and Stalin on the same plane" and think of himself as "the arbiter between them."[59]

Roosevelt wanted to distance himself from Polish issues, which he and his advisers saw as "political dynamite" in the upcoming U.S. elections. He asked Stalin, when they were alone on December 1, to understand that he did not want his views on Poland published because of the effect it would have on the ethnic vote. The president's only question about Poland's eastern border was whether the land lost by that country to the USSR was about the same size as the land Poland would get from Germany. He wondered whether in areas of mixed population there could be "voluntary transfers." Stalin happily agreed: that was exactly what he wanted. The president tacitly accepted the Soviet arguments, even though some disagreement persisted about the exact frontier line.[60]

The concept of what was euphemistically called "population transfers" had been floated by the Polish and Czechoslovakian governments in exile in Britain almost since the first days of the war. Both suggested that selectively expelling Germans (such as known Nazis) living in their countries would help to avoid future conflicts. By mid-1941, however, they were calling for the complete expulsion of "their" Germans. In conversations with Churchill, FDR, and Stalin, the Polish and Czech officials were assured of support for the "transfers." These would become ethnic-cleansing operations, one of the most horrific features of the late war and early postwar years. Other countries followed the Polish and Czech precedents, which we will investigate in more detail in Chapter 13.[61]

Roosevelt also gave his blessing to the Soviet acquisition of Estonia, Latvia, and Lithuania. In his private meeting with Stalin on December 1, he said that those lands had in history, and again more recently, been a part of Russia. The official protocol states that he "added jokingly that when the Soviet armies re-occupied these areas, he did not intend to go to war with the Soviet Union on this point." Making matters look worse, he said that "it would be helpful for him personally, if some public declaration could be made in regard to the future elections" in those states. The Soviet leader was only too pleased to keep up appearances, though in the Russian record he insisted that a promise of letting the Baltic peoples express themselves would not mean free and unfettered elections under international supervision.[62]

The Big Three agreed to form an international organization, and Roosevelt sketched the outlines of what would eventually become the United Nations. Stalin thought it could work but shrewdly probed the depth of the president's commitment by saying that in the future the United States might have to send ground troops to trouble spots. FDR was not sure that his country would agree. In the postwar world, he said, the U.S. would consent, at most, to dispatch "planes and ships to Europe."[63]

Stalin could take these candid remarks to mean that, at least if he proceeded with reasonable caution, he could have his own way without much worry. Indeed, that was how some U.S. observers present at the talks saw the unfortunate turn of events.[64]

THE RED ARMY OPENS THE DOOR FOR COMMUNISM

At Tehran, Stalin sounded as though he trusted his allies and wanted only to get along. But his contempt for them knew no bounds. The record is full of examples, like one from March 1944, when he spoke to visiting Yugoslavian Communists. He told them not to be fooled by his cordial relationships with Roosevelt and Churchill, whom he likened to capitalist pickpockets. He warned his guests not to "frighten" the Western Allies, by which he meant "to avoid anything that might alarm them into thinking that a revolution was going on in Yugoslavia or an attempt at Communist control."[65] Stalin's political attitudes and ambitions were unchanged, despite any gestures of friendship he might make.

For now the war made its own demands, and Stalin, as commander in chief and as promised at Tehran, wanted a major strike against the Germans to coincide with Overlord, the landing in Normandy. The Soviets prepared Operation Bagration—named after a Georgian general who had fallen in the war against Napoleon. It faced numerically strong and fiercely determined Axis forces.[66]

Planning for Bagration began in March and April 1944. It was to be at the heart of a series of five coordinated offensives that would begin in the north against Finland, with the next strikes coming in phases to the far south toward Romania.[67] The operation was conceived on a grand scale, eventually involving some 2.4 million Soviet troops and more if we include the partisans, with a minimum of 140,000 in well-organized units. The Red Army aimed at achieving overwhelming numerical superiority and used 5,200 tanks, 5,300 planes, and 36,000 pieces of artillery and mortars. By comparison, the numbers for the Germans were 900 tanks, 1,350 planes, and artillery and mortars at 9,500. When the attack came, it was preceded by elaborate and successful deception.[68]

This herculean operation greatly exceeded the June 6, 1944, landings in Normandy, where 57,500 soldiers from the United States went ashore along with 75,215 British and Canadians. Soldiers from other nations soon followed. By June 30, when the first phase of that invasion ended, just over 850,000 troops had landed. Hitler's much-heralded Atlantic Wall could not hold them back, so he decided to withdraw some forces from the east to stop the advance in the west and in Italy. In that way, the Allied invasion contributed to the success of the Red Army in the east.

On March 8, Hitler ordered the creation of another line of defenses along the eastern front with "fortified positions" (feste Plätze) running from the north at Tallinn (Reval) near Leningrad, in the middle at Vitebsk, Orsha, Mogilev, Borisov, Minsk, and Bobruisk, in a line finally ending far to the south at the Black Sea west of Odessa. Eventually there were twenty-nine such fortresses. Hitler's directive stated that each was "to allow itself to be surrounded, thereby holding down the largest possible number of enemy forces," as fortresses in history had done.[69]

Bagration began after a short delay on June 22, by coincidence three years to the day since Hitler's Operation Barbarossa opened the war against the USSR. Famed Marshals Georgi Zhukov, Aleksandr Vasilevsky, and Konstantin Rokossovsky led the Red Army forward along a 350-mile-wide front that soon extended to 600 miles, often through the toughest slogging—including the almost impenetrable Pripet Marshes. The full scope of the offensive was disguised so well that the Germans were unable to figure out the direction of the attack.[70]

By chance, famed Soviet writer Vasily Grossman was in Bobruisk on June 27, just after it fell. He saw the thousands of corpses so dense that trucks and tanks had to drive over them. "A cauldron of death was boiling here," as the Red Army took its revenge, "a ruthless, terrible revenge over those who hadn't surrendered their arms and tried to break out to the west."[71] In the first two weeks, the Soviet forces destroyed not just Bobruisk but nearly all of Army Group Center, some 25 divisions and more than 300,000 men. Bagration was costlier to the Germans than Stalingrad. Soviet commanders were surprised that the enemy would not retreat, but Hitler ordered his troops to hold.

On July 8, Stalin called Zhukov back to Moscow for a conference with General Aleksei I. Antonov, the operations chief of the general staff. All agreed that Germany's final defeat was a question of time. Molotov, who was also there, suggested that Hitler would likely try to negotiate with the West. Stalin thought that Roosevelt and Churchill would not go along. Instead, he believed, they would "try to attain their political interests in Germany by setting up an obedient government, not by collusion with the Nazis who have lost the trust of the people."[72]

On July 17, Stalin put on a parade in Moscow of 57,000 captured Wehrmacht soldiers, most of them taken prisoner near Minsk, the capital of Byelorussia. The defeated and depressed marched through the streets, twenty abreast in grim silence. They took three hours to pass. By all accounts, the sight of them raised as much pity as hatred. For the most part, the men in the crowd remained silent; a few women had tears in their eyes, with one murmuring they were "like our boys, also driven to war."[73]

Beginning on August 20, the Red Army mounted yet another major offensive, toward Romania to the south. It was designed to retake Moldova (at the time, the Moldavian Soviet Republic, acquired in 1940) and to crush the German-Romanian alliance. Although its massive proportions (with 1.3 million men) came as a surprise, the troops were anything but crack divisions. Many were drafted off the streets or the fields, put in a uniform, and barely trained. In addition, there were penal (*shtraf*) units, made up of men who volunteered or were conscripted from the Gulag. These *shtrafniki* might have been sentenced for "counter-revolutionary" crimes, though many were felons, including convicted murderers. Whereas initially such men were used separately on suicide missions, by mid-1944 they could be found in regular units. Perhaps they added to the fighting spirit, but they may also have contributed to the moral erosion in the ranks.[74]

German forces were also replenished with less than fully trained personnel. More of them began to desert, and their Romanian allies were hardly fighting at all. The death toll of Wehrmacht soldiers in the summer of 1944 was staggering. German figures show that on the eastern front in June, the Red Army killed 142,079; in July 169,881; and in August 277,465. In addition, large numbers of prisoners were taken, and for these months alone, they range around 200,000. The fates of war had turned decisively against Germany and its allies. While it is true that the Red Army paid a dreadful price for this great victory, with 243,508 killed and twice as many wounded, the Soviet Union was able to replace the losses, to grow its total forces, and to equip them with more (and better) tanks and artillery.[75]

Well before the full scope of Romania's disaster became apparent, Marshal Ion Antonescu began looking for a way out, even as he assured Hitler on August 5 that he would stay the course. Instead, King Michael and assorted political groups ousted him from power on August 23. Moscow was not entirely pleased with that action because it preempted the Red Army's "liberation." They entered Bucharest only at the end of the month. One Jewish writer noted that their victory parade was met with bewilderment, alternating between "great waves of enthusiasm" and a "certain reserve." Some watchers did not appreciate the Jews who applauded, so anti-Semitism and anti-Communism persisted even after Antonescu's fall.[76]

As in most of the liberated countries, when the Romanian government collapsed and the German occupation forces were driven out, the result was a political vacuum. Regardless of popular attitudes and the little support for Communism, the Soviet Union promptly set about creating a new regime; it tried to conceal that it was in fact dominated by the Communist Party.

Meanwhile, Hungary was still in the war and determined to hold back the Reds. Dictator Admiral Miklós Horthy had been delighted to participate in the invasion of the Soviet Union. Just like Antonescu, he wanted to be part of Hitler's crusade against what they all called "Jewish Bolshevism."[77] But with Romania and Bulgaria already knocked out, Horthy had a change of heart, and in early October he sent a delegation to Moscow. There they agreed that Hungary would change sides and declare war on Germany. The deal was made on October 11, and Horthy broadcast the astounding news four days later. In response, Hitler sent Otto Skorzeny and his crew, who kidnapped Horthy's son. The Hungarian leader was then blackmailed into following Hitler's orders.

On October 18, Horthy accepted asylum in Germany after having resigned in favor of Ferenc Szálasi, leader of the fascist Iron Cross. The new leader did not want to defend Budapest as such, for as a trained general staff officer, he knew it would mean the obliteration of the city. Nevertheless, Hitler demanded that Budapest be held at all costs and on November 23 directed that no house be abandoned without a fight. Soon the siege began. It was one of the worst in the war.[78] Red Army soldiers were thrown into battle with reckless disregard for casualties; Stalin wanted to advance to the west as far and as fast as possible, and to ensure Soviet control over Budapest and Hungary.

There, as in all the other enemy countries that his armies overran, he soon set out to transform them. In order to disguise his intentions, he had each of them adopt a "national front" model, with various political parties in a coalition government. For his Western Allies, the priority was beating Hitler. That was Stalin's priority as well, but his political goals were always integral to his calculations.

CHAPTER 5

Taking Eastern Europe

Stalin always had time to think about the future of Communism. Even in the midst of the crisis in August 1941, while sitting in a Moscow air-raid shelter, he pondered the future of Poland. He told Comintern boss Georgi Dimitrov that "it would be better to create a workers' party" of some kind there, not a Communist one, because it "frightens off not only outsiders, but some who sympathize with us as well."[1] It is interesting to note how far ahead Stalin was thinking, all the more with the Germans at the gates. He and Dimitrov knew that during the Great Terror of 1937–38, the NKVD had killed off most of the exiled Polish comrades. Now, in 1941, they began fashioning a new Polish Workers' Party (PPR).

The messages sent out from Dimitrov's desk to PPR activists in Poland a year later gave them their talking points. They should underline that they stood for driving out the Nazi invaders, winning national freedom, and establishing "people's democratic power."[2] They must drop any mention of Communism and avoid creating the impression that they were "heading toward the Sovietization of Poland, which in current conditions could only play into the hands of various provocateurs and enemies of the Polish people."[3]

UPRISING IN WARSAW

During 1943, Stalin became the most powerful military and political figure in the world, and by the next year his country's armed forces could have defeated Germany by themselves; at least that was what he told his generals. Even though his Cold War political agenda was becoming more obvious, Roosevelt and Churchill repressed their worries. They wanted victory first. But in August–September 1944, they could easily have been more insistent when Stalin steadfastly rejected their appeals to support the democratically oriented resistance movement in Poland.

On July 18, 1944, the Polish Central Committee of the Communist Party in Moscow instructed its activists in the homeland to set up a national front and said that these would soon be created also "in France, Czechoslovakia, Italy, Yugoslavia, etc." The principle that Communists were to adopt, in Poland and elsewhere, came right out of Stalin's handbook. Moderation was the byword. The Poles were told that their new approach would require "compromises which will split our opponents without fundamentally altering our aim." The point was "satisfying the major demands of the masses and creating a situation favorable to our long-term plans."[4] The Polish Committee of National Liberation (PKWN) was established on July 22 in newly liberated Chełm, in the province of Lublin. It was a cover for the Communist Party, and henceforth Stalin treated it as Poland's legitimate government.[5]

The main Polish opposition to the Communists was the officially recognized Polish government-in-exile. It had been in London since 1939 and had many loyal followers who fought in their homeland against the Nazis. They were non-Communist in orientation but prepared to cooperate with the Red Army when it crossed into Poland in joint operations against the Nazis. Additionally, the Soviet Union mobilized large numbers of Poles to fight, both alongside the Red Army and as partisans.[6]

The Red Army's offensive reached the Vistula at the end of July 1944 and some of Marshal Konstantin Rokossovsky's troops got to the western bank of the river below Warsaw. A number of the mighty T-34 tanks actually broke through into one of its eastern suburbs on July 31. But then everything came to a halt.[7]

On August 1, against Stalin's wishes, the London-based Polish Home Army (Armia Krajowa) began the Warsaw Uprising. It was led by General Tadeusz Bór-Komorowski, but the motives behind the effort are still disputed. The Polish government-in-exile hoped to mobilize its troops to prevent the worst when its country was changing hands from the Nazis to the Soviets. Many, like Prime Minister Stanisław Mikołajczyk in London, wanted to reclaim Poland's prewar borders and its independence.

As far back as 1943, these "London Poles" told the British and Americans that there would be an uprising at some point in the future, but opinions among them remained divided, also about the Soviet Union. None of them, however, had any intention of fighting the Red Army.[8]

Had an uprising succeeded, politicians devoted to national independence might have come to power. Not surprisingly, Stalin refused to offer any aid, in spite of being implored by Roosevelt and Churchill; he preferred to have the Germans snuff out the resistance.[9] Since 1941, Moscow had been sending in members of the Polish Comintern to organize its own partisan movement.[10] As the Kremlin saw matters, had the Warsaw Uprising succeeded and a "bourgeois Poland" been established, it would necessarily be an "agent of imperialism."[11]

Encouraged by FDR, Prime Minister Mikołajczyk set off to Moscow on July 29 for discussions with Stalin.[12] With the fighting already under way in Warsaw, Stalin agreed to see him on August 3 at nine-thirty P.M. in the Kremlin, having let him stew a full forty-eight hours, and then sent the inflexible Molotov to soften up their guest. Stalin was even colder to a request for immediate aid, as Mikołajczyk put it, "to our men in their pitifully unequal battles with the Germans."[13] The Soviet Boss scoffed: "But you're not taking into consideration the agreement that has been reached between the Soviet Union and the Lublin Committee." Stalin never mentioned the excuse he gave his allies—that it was technically impossible to aid the resistance fighters.[14]

He toyed with Mikołajczyk, saying he had no intention of imposing a Communist regime on Poland, and asked him to talk things over with leaders of the Lublin Committee. They promptly declared that they would be pleased to have him as prime minister in a Communist-controlled government. Stalin said that anyway he doubted much of an uprising was under way in Warsaw or had the slightest chance of victory.[15]

On August 5, in response to Churchill's appeal, the Soviet leader repeated his disbelief regarding any real uprising. However, three days later, according to a recently discovered order, Marshal Zhukov reported that all units could be at the Vistula (on the eastern side of the river from the city) and ready by August 25 to move forward, link up with Polish forces, and occupy Warsaw. In his message to Moscow, he said he would await approval to proceed.[16] There is no mention of this plan even in

Zhukov's later memoirs. The report indicates that the Red Army could have done more, even if by the time they arrived, many in the resistance would already have been killed. Zhukov must have been told to stand his ground.

With the Kremlin continuing to play dumb, the British military mission in Moscow and the British embassy confirmed repeatedly that the Poles were most certainly fighting and desperately in need of arms and ammunition. Then, on August 14, the U.S. ambassador in Moscow sought permission for Anglo-American planes to land in Soviet-held territory after they had dropped supplies to the fighters.

The distance from Italy was long (815 miles or so) and involved terribly dangerous stretches of enemy territory. The Royal Air Force managed to get some supplies through during August, at the staggering cost of about one downed plane for every ton of supplies that was delivered to Warsaw. The other option was to use American bombers flying out of Britain or Italy and landing at bases in Ukraine. In this way, they were able to reach bombing targets in eastern parts of the German Reich, including Poland. Although Stalin agreed to let the bombers land and refuel after their bombing missions, he was reluctant and even hostile when Churchill or Roosevelt sought permission for flights bound for Warsaw with supplies to land in Ukraine. There is no documentation at present that permits us to determine exactly what Stalin's motives were, but there can be little doubt that he wanted nothing to do with rescuing the uprising.[17]

On August 15, Molotov informed the British ambassador that the Soviet government wished to dissociate itself from "the purely adventurist affair" in Warsaw. Henceforth, Stalin said, he would work only through the Polish Committee of National Liberation (the PKWN) in Lublin. He continued to reject requests from Roosevelt and Churchill.[18] The Soviet claim was that the material dropped "necessarily" fell into the hands of its "enemies."[19]

Stalin soon began calling the uprising an attempt by a "handful of power-seeking criminals" and decided to let the Germans finish his dirty work for him.[20] Marshal Rokossovsky would add to the mythology by saying in his memoirs that the insurgents were politically motivated and aimed to take over Warsaw before the Red Army arrived. He had been arrested in 1937 during the Great Terror and spent nearly three years in prison, and so knew what was expected when he reached the gates of

Warsaw. Zhukov came to agree with him that it was prudent to wait. Soviet troops stayed on the east bank of the Vistula until early January 1945.[21]

To this day, some Western scholars continue to suggest that, far from the Red Army "stopping" on purpose to let the Germans destroy the Polish underground, capturing Warsaw had never been in the original Soviet plans.[22] The Soviet interpretation was that the Warsaw underground, led by the Polish émigré movement in London, tried to seize power in order to prevent the Red Army from taking the capital.[23] Yet a collection of newly released Soviet documents suggests that Stalin's attitude "was not as straightforward as previously presented in Soviet literature." Although the record is still clouded, it now appears even to some Russian historians that the decision at the Vistula was not based on military considerations but was "in all likelihood taken for political reasons."[24]

Polish contemporaries knew the bitter truth: that Moscow looked at their "underground state" and the (London-based) Polish government-in-exile as standing in the way of creating a new Soviet-friendly order. The Kremlin had other arrangements in mind, and "behind the lines of the Red Army a different Polish government, appointed in Moscow, was already in office."[25]

The Warsaw Uprising, as famed Polish writer Czesław Miłosz put it, was "the revolt of the fly against two giants." It was crushed by one as the other looked on from across the river.[26] Heinrich Himmler jumped at the chance for vengeance and boasted that he would solve the Polish problem for all time.[27] The sixty-six days of hell ended when what remained of the insurgents surrendered on October 2.[28] The Polish capital, home to a million or more, was systematically reduced to rubble. Somewhere between 150,000 and 200,000 were killed, while 15,000 of the Home Army died or were missing. German losses were significant, with around 26,000 casualties.[29]

CONCEDING EASTERN EUROPE TO UNCLE JOE

Stalin's hope was to attain his political goals without risking confrontation with the West. He responded positively on September 30, 1944, when Churchill, no doubt bothered by the ongoing horror in Warsaw, asked for direct talks. Roosevelt would not be there because he was in the middle of an election, but his ambassador to the USSR, Averell Harriman, went along.[30]

What Stalin regarded as the "real" second front in the West began only on June 6, 1944, when Operation Overlord opened with the landing at Normandy. The troops were pinned along the coast and finally broke out on July 25 at Saint-Lô. Another landing, originally conceived to occur simultaneously with Overlord, hit southern France on August 15 along the Riviera. There a combination of American, Canadian, and the Free French Forces went ashore. The next day Hitler authorized the withdrawal of most of his armies from southern France, leaving only blocking units in some areas. On Friday, August 25, General Dietrich von Choltitz, the German commander in Paris, surrendered and gave up the city.[31] In Italy meanwhile the fighting had been bitter, but Rome had been freed on June 4, though the campaign in northern Italy was far from over. FDR wrote to Churchill in Moscow on October 16 to say that the campaign in Italy already had cost 200,000 Allied casualties and there was little hope of further advances there that year.[32]

Although Churchill's trip to Moscow is well known, we need to remind ourselves just how far he went in trying to satisfy Stalin. As it was, Eastern Europe was falling into Soviet hands, and his visit only confirmed it. He landed in Moscow on October 9 and, after a short rest, was whisked away to the Kremlin for talks at ten P.M. The prime minister must have been exhausted. Perhaps that explains why, in classic British understatement, one historian said that Churchill then committed "the central indiscretion" of the talks.[33]

Confounding good sense, the British prime minister tried to make a political "arrangement" for all of liberated Eastern Europe. He wondered "how it would do for you to have ninety per cent predominance in Romania, for us to have ninety per cent of the say in Greece, and go fifty-fifty about Yugoslavia?" He showed Stalin a scrap of paper on which he had scribbled the various countries and what he deemed the appropriate percentages of influence:

Romania,
    Russia 90%
    The others 10%

Greece
>   Great Britain 90%
>   (in accord with U.S.A.)
>   Russia 10%
> Yugoslavia 50-50%
> Hungary 50-50%
> Bulgaria
>   Russia 75%
>   The others 25%

Stalin glanced at it quickly and with a blue-colored pencil put a tick at the top and pushed it back to Churchill.[34] The "agreement," if it can be called that, cut the feet from under all those trying to resist Communism. The West as good as gave them up for lost, and the prime minister, who thought over what he had done, began to have doubts and suggested they burn the document.[35]

Stalin appeared nonchalant, when in fact, he took the deal very seriously. The understanding they would reach, as he likely sensed, would become a matter of great importance in the immediate postwar years.[36] The very next day Molotov began badgering Foreign Secretary Anthony Eden, who was with Churchill, to increase the Russian percentages in Bulgaria and Hungary. In both cases Soviet influence was finally bumped up to 80 percent, and in Yugoslavia to 60 percent. Stalin calculated the poor prospects of the Communists in Greece, which the British regarded as important to their Middle East interests. So he yielded there to seem conciliatory. Foreign Secretary Eden was right to say that the Soviets "had already grabbed the territory they wanted." They would continue to seek more, until the British and Americans found their political will.[37]

Roosevelt was against mapping out spheres of influence, particularly when the other two leaders met without him. Even though Averell Harriman was there to keep an eye on things, the British managed to keep this agreement from him until October 12, when he learned of it by chance. Finding Churchill in the middle of drafting a letter to Stalin to formalize the deal, Harriman said that Roosevelt would never accept it, and the prime minister left well enough alone.[38]

The agreement, such as it was, said nothing at all about the urgent question of Poland's future, and while Churchill was determined to solve this matter, he was in no position to do so. Nevertheless, he was bold enough to ask the head of Poland's government-in-exile to fly to Moscow. There, on October 13, Mikołajczyk had to face the collective opposition of Stalin, Molotov, Churchill, and Eden, who pressured him to open talks with the Lublin Committee and to accept the Curzon Line as Poland's eastern boundary. Churchill wanted to preserve "the good atmosphere" between himself and Stalin and promised the Polish leader "a nice big country," if not the one created in 1919. He said "we will see to it that for the land you lost in the east, there will be compensations in Germany, in East Prussia, and Silesia. You'll get a nice outlet to the sea, a good port in Danzig, and the priceless minerals of Silesia."

When the Polish leader held his ground, Molotov dropped the bomb: "But all this was settled at Tehran!" Looking around the table, he said, "If your memories fail you, let me recall the facts to you. We all agreed at Tehran that the Curzon line must divide Poland. You will recall that President Roosevelt agreed to this solution and strongly endorsed the line."[39] Churchill nodded. In fact FDR had not "strongly endorsed" the new boundaries; he had agreed with the principle of moving them and, where necessary, transferring populations into and out of annexed territories.

Mikołajczyk refused to go along. In a separate meeting, Churchill roared that he agreed with Stalin and would be telling Parliament just that. He flatly stated: "Our relations with Russia are much better than they have ever been. I mean to keep them that way." Mikołajczyk would not budge even after the English bulldog barked that "unless you accept the frontier you're going out of business forever! The Russians will sweep through your country, and your people will be liquidated. You're on the verge of annihilation."[40]

Then the British prime minister met with Bolesław Bierut and Edward Osóbka-Morawski, leaders in Moscow of the "Lublin Poles"— that is, the Polish Committee of National Liberation (PKWN). Anthony Eden whispered of the two, "The rat and the weasel." Bierut said firmly: "We are here to demand on behalf of Poland that Lvov shall belong to Russia." By this statement, he meant that city should go to the Ukrainian Republic of the USSR. He added: "This is the will of the Polish people." Churchill looked at Stalin while these servile remarks were being translated. The Kremlin Master flashed his amusement, but he took these issues very seriously.[41]

To the disheartened Mikołajczyk, Roosevelt later wrote with hollow words about his support for "a strong, free and independent Polish state." However, while FDR would not object to changing the borders as Stalin suggested, he still refused to commit to the "specific frontiers."[42]

Churchill told Roosevelt that he had wrested an agreement and that Stalin was willing to have the "London Poles" and the "Lublin Poles" share power in a new government led by Mikołajczyk. The truth is that Stalin offered a mere facade to help them salve their consciences. Ambassador Harriman was also quite wrong to judge that the talks had "produced a hopeful glow within the alliance" and to conclude that "with time and effort the matter could be worked out." That was precisely the impression the Kremlin wanted to convey to allay Western concerns about Communist plans for postwar Poland.[43]

At this very moment, Stalin was personally orchestrating political events there. On December 31 his "Lublin Poles" (the PKWN) declared a provisional government. The Soviet Union recognized it five days later, even though Churchill and Roosevelt specifically asked Moscow to hold off doing so until they all met. All they got was Stalin's absurd claim of being "powerless" to delay the process because on December 27 the Presidium of the Supreme Soviet had agreed to recognize the Polish government "the moment it was set up." In fact, the Presidium did exactly as he told it to do.[44]

Churchill had once opposed appeasing Hitler, but he became noticeably soft on Stalin. In his defense, it could be said that Britain was no longer the power it once was and that he was not in a position to be more forceful. However, that explanation cannot account for the affection and respect he apparently came to have for the Soviet leader. By late 1944 the otherwise sagacious prime minister indulged in the fantasy that, on a personal level, he had a good relationship with Stalin, and that their mutual respect for each other boded well for their talks. He wrote his wife to say that he had a very "nice meeting with the old Bear. I like him the more I see him. *Now* they respect us here and I am sure they wish to work with us."[45] The British leader believed, even when he wrote his memoirs years later, that Stalin had been "sincere" and that the two of them had "talked with an ease, freedom, and cordiality never before attained between our two countries."[46] He was not facing up to the facts.

THE YALTA CONFERENCE

Roosevelt and Churchill had been trying to get Stalin to the conference table since mid-1944. The Soviet leader gave various reasons for dithering and, even as late as December 15, mentioned that he would like to meet the president alone.[47] Roosevelt shared that preference, but a week later tripartite meetings were set for Yalta in the Crimea. The Big Three were to confer from February 4 to 11, 1945, in what would be their final gathering.

What did they hope to accomplish? Anyone reading the leaders' correspondence is bound to be struck by the friendly banter. They seemed to agree on most things. Only by digging deeper can we find what these leaders were really thinking.

Churchill was perhaps the least optimistic of the three. "Make no mistake" about what would happen, he said to his private secretary on January 23: "All the Balkans, except Greece, are going to be Bolshevized; and there is nothing I can do to prevent it. There is nothing I can do for poor Poland either."[48] What made his position worse was that Roosevelt was disinclined to support him. The president was at pains to avoid any appearance of being a united front with Britain, and so nothing was accomplished at preconference talks with Churchill in Malta. FDR even refused to meet him alone during their first days at Yalta, and while their concord was real enough on essentials, there were more differences than we might expect.[49]

Roosevelt poured his dwindling energies into holding the wartime alliance together and defeating Germany and Japan. When Ambassador Harriman returned from Moscow after the elections in November 1944, he found it nearly impossible to interest the president in the fate of Eastern Europe.[50] In the view of the new secretary of state, Edward Stettinius, as recorded in his diary on January 2, "to many observers it appeared that Roosevelt was pursuing a rudderless foreign policy." The president talked about the future of the Far East and China, the possibility of Pacific and African bases, and the Near East and Palestine. But he said little about postwar Europe, which was on the immediate agenda. Stettinius urged him to use the State of the Union message to make a strong foreign policy statement, but instead he offered only generalities, in a speech criticized by the press as evasive.[51]

The inaugural address was similar, and the shortest in American history. The theme was the dream of a future international order no longer filled with suspicion and mistrust. FDR did not sound at all like the image of him in revisionist literature: a cold warrior out to make the world safe for capitalism. His concern instead was his legacy, and he mistakenly concluded that he could secure it by forging a link with Stalin.

The Soviet Boss was an utterly different creature. Having experienced decades of vicious political infighting, he knew what buttons to push at meetings. He had an acute grasp of the political and military details in every European country, had worked out a long-term strategy, and was flexible in his tactics. His modus operandi at the Big Three conferences was to speak of his country's sacrifices in the war without overdoing it. His mischievousness and (mostly) pleasant manner stood in stark contrast to his fierce and bloody reputation, to the point that Roosevelt and Churchill convinced themselves it was fine to call him "Uncle Joe." They took to using that nickname behind his back and at Yalta even to his face. But he had them on a string. Stalin knew very well that Communism in theory and practice aroused their darkest foreboding, so he routinely told the story that, in everything he did, national security was the only real aim.

What was the Soviet dictator really thinking on the eve of Yalta? The contrast with Churchill and especially Roosevelt could not have been more stark. By chance we have a recently discovered record of remarks Stalin made to Communist visitors from Yugoslavia on January 28, 1945, just a week before the conference. As he saw things, the Great Depression that had gripped the West since 1929 had "manifested itself in the division of the capitalists into two factions—one *fascist,* the other *democratic.* Our alliance with the democratic faction of the capitalists came about because they also had a stake in preventing Hitler's domination; that brutal state would have driven the working class to extremes and to the overthrow of capitalism itself. At the present time we are allied with one faction against the other, but in the future we will be against the first faction of capitalists, too."[52]

This was an astonishing statement; it revealed that the ultimate war, in Stalin's view, was against his allies. His ideological convictions had not wavered from what they had been in the 1930s. In the meantime, before the final showdown, he was keeping up appearances, disciplined and above all patient. His allies, moreover, were accommodating. Churchill and FDR yielded without making much of a fuss, and even when they did, Stalin seemed to enjoy the skirmishes.

It was an article of faith among the Soviet leaders that after the war the United States would be in deep economic trouble and thus desperate for markets. This assumption played out in various ways, one of which led Molotov on January 3 to ask Ambassador Harriman for the U.S. to grant $6 billion in credits on favorable terms so that the USSR could buy American goods.[53] Molotov put the same request to Secretary Stettinius at Yalta. He brazenly made it seem as though his country would be doing the U.S. a favor: helping the capitalists solve the "inevitable" unemployment they would face after the war.[54]

When the Big Three met in early February, the Red Army was well on the way to destroying German domination of Eastern and Central Europe; it stood at the River Oder and had entered Germany itself. By contrast, the Western Allies were still struggling to overcome the Battle of the Bulge, fought into early 1945. They had not yet crossed the Rhine, which they would do only in early March.

This military situation gave the USSR an enormous psychological advantage. Everyone knew that it had carried the weight of the war and suffered infinitely more casualties than any other country.[55] On that account alone, the two Western leaders were inclined to yield to Stalin. But for good measure, the Kremlin was already busily arranging the postwar political map of the lands they had liberated.

Soviet intelligence services bugged all the facilities in advance at Yalta. They already knew that the Americans and British had no program for the postwar settlement, so the spies' mission was to develop psychological portraits of the delegates, "which were more important to Stalin than intelligence information."[56] During the conference the Soviet leader spoke with each member of his delegation, eliciting their impressions and inquiring about the positions being discussed. He was more multidimensional than often supposed and listened intently. Soviet ambassador Andrei Gromyko thought that at Yalta Stalin was at the top of his game. The diplomat wrote later that his boss had "a memory like a computer and missed nothing. During the meetings I realized more clearly than ever what exceptional abilities that man possessed."[57]

There was no agenda at Yalta, and the meetings tended to ramble. During a short conversation with Stalin on February 4, just before the main session, Roosevelt remarked that while on the way, he had been shocked by the destruction he had seen in the Crimea. Both of them admitted to having grown "more bloodthirsty" with regard to the Germans.[58]

The president led the first plenary session, though not with a strong performance. The Soviets looked bored, while the more polite British stared off into the distance. Controversial matters arose the second day as to the future occupation zones of Germany. Roosevelt still thought that Germany could be split into five or even seven parts. Churchill had wanted it separated into a north and south but now pleaded for time to think things through.

Stalin offered one of his typically forceful resolutions: (1) to accept "agreement in principle that Germany should be dismembered; (2) to charge a commission of the Foreign Ministers to work out the details; and (3) to add to the surrender terms a clause stating that Germany would be dismembered without giving any details." He thought that announcing dismemberment in advance "would facilitate acceptance by the whole German people of what was in store for them."[59]

On February 6 the foreign ministers reported their agreement with Stalin's addition to the surrender document, a point glossed over in the Soviet records.[60] Some Americans cooled about breaking up the defeated country and, like the British, began to realize that it would be in their interests to have "economically healthy democracies."[61]

Up to the present day and contrary to the evidence, respected Russian historians incorrectly assert that "it is well known that Stalin did not share the ideas of the Western Allies to dismember Germany."[62] He was actually a hawk on that score, but once again his remarks at Yalta are not included in the published Soviet record of the meeting.[63] Instead of formalizing their agreement, the leaders sent the matter to a new commission on dismembering Germany that commenced its work that March in London.[64]

The Russian minutes do not make reference to these demands, presumably because by the time they were published, Soviet aims had changed. They were now in favor of keeping Germany whole—in order, in due time, to dominate it all. Erasing part of the record, standard Stalinist practice, might help to avoid their being seen as in league with the evildoers bent on wiping the defeated country from the map.

The Allies settled on dividing Germany into three zones, with some of East Prussia going to Poland and part given outright to the Soviet Union. Discussion turned to whether France should get a zone of occupation. Stalin said that it should not and echoed his claim in 1940 that the French had "opened the gates to the enemy." However, Churchill was correct that if France was excluded and the United States was unwilling to stay in Europe "for more than two years," as FDR had said, then Britain would be alone in facing down a possibly resurgent Germany. Stalin agreed to let the French have a zone when the other two said it could be carved out of what was allocated to the United States and Britain.

Austria would also be divided into zones, although there was consensus that it should become an independent state again. Stalin was not particularly interested in exerting permanent influence there, but the Soviets would seek to extract the maximum reparations from their zone. The Americans were initially aloof about even participating in the occupation of Austria.[65]

Ambassador Ivan Maisky had drawn up a report on reparations on Stalin's orders, according to which German heavy industry would be cut by 80 percent and all factories "useful only for military purposes" removed. A Soviet-American proposal was eventually signed that foresaw a reparations bill totaling $20 billion, of which 50 percent would go to the USSR; the other countries would receive payments in accordance with their losses and their contributions to victory.[66]

Britain did not wish to set specific figures, and Churchill recalled what happened after the First World War, when the victors "indulged themselves with fantastic reparations figures." He began worrying about the specter of eighty million starving Germans and concluded that "if you wished a horse to pull a wagon," then "you would have to give it fodder." Stalin retorted that "care should be taken to see that the horse did not turn around and kick you." Roosevelt also opposed heavy reparations and said that the victors should try not "to kill the people."[67]

The president knew Maisky and afterward said to him: "Well, you surprised me with your humility, because with your huge losses and the destruction I was expecting you would ask for $50 billion." The ambassador responded that he would have been happy to seek $100 billion but knew that the Soviet people did not entertain "baseless fantasies." The matter, consigned to the Moscow Reparations Commission, was one of many issues never resolved. Nevertheless, the Soviet Union would insist on and get substantial payments in money and kind from various defeated nations.[68]

The main session on February 6 worked at establishing the United Nations, a priority for Roosevelt. Perhaps knowing how committed the president was, Stalin proved flexible. Indeed, in a speech in 1944 on the anniversary of the Russian Revolution, he had said that he wanted such an international body to maintain the postwar peace.[69] At Yalta, without much pressure, he reduced the number of additional seats he claimed in the UN on behalf of the USSR to Ukraine and Byelorussia. He was against having to "submit" to the judgment of small countries and felt that the three major victorious ones should play the dominant role. They finally agreed to the great powers' veto, which has remained in effect for the UN Security Council. A founding conference was called for San Francisco, to open on April 25, 1945.[70]

Meanwhile Yalta had to face the thorny Polish question again, and the Big Three agreed that the USSR's borders would move westward to the so-called Curzon Line. The Poles would be compensated by getting a large strip of eastern Germany and some of East Prussia. Everyone at the conference knew Stalin had the upper hand. In the last three decades, he said, German armies had attacked the USSR via Poland because that country was weak. Now, using Roosevelt's own words, he wanted to block the way with a "strong, independent and democratic Poland." What he was after, of course, was a dependent Communist dictatorship.

Stalin maintained that the Red Army was prepared to fight on against Germany, to pay in blood, in order to gain enough to compensate Poland in the west for the land it would lose to the USSR in the east. The Soviet leader disingenuously stated that it was up to the Poles to create their own government and that no one should command them to appear at the conference and be told what to do. "I am called a dictator and not a democrat," Stalin quipped, "but I have enough democratic feeling to refuse to create a Polish government without the Poles being consulted." He claimed that, in his view, the two Polish factions had to get together, and for the record he added that all he was seeking for his own country was security. As we have already seen, he was after a great deal more.[71]

In later sessions, the Big Three talked about free elections in Poland

and the status of the Polish government-in-exile. Stalin pretended to yield here and there, for example, by agreeing to include some Poles from abroad in the new government. He confided to Beria, the head of his secret police, however, that he had "not moved one inch."[72]

The "good news" was conveyed to Poland, where it was played up as a victory. The Red Army in Warsaw at the end of the month reported that the population was supposedly grateful, with many wondering how they could get a portrait of Stalin.[73]

Yalta also recognized the agreement worked out by Josip Broz Tito, president of the National Committee of Liberation of Yugoslavia with Ivan Šubašić, the prime minister of the Royal Yugoslav government. The Big Three recommended that the two leaders form a new government, which was announced out of the blue at Yalta on February 12. Tito had not even been informed about the conference and would soon enough demonstrate his independent streak. He and his followers resisted the terms dictated to their country by the Allies, not least the Soviet Union.[74]

During the session on February 7, Churchill expressed concern about all the Germans being driven out of East Prussia (he mentioned the figure of 6 million refugees) and more from other areas. Would that not cause grave problems? At their last conference in Tehran, Roosevelt had asked "whether a voluntary transfer of peoples from the mixed areas was possible."[75]

Stalin now reported that "most Germans in those areas had already run away."[76] He did not mention they had fled from the Red Army's campaign of rape, pillage, and plunder. Nor did he reveal that he had already agreed with the Czechs and others that they too could drive out "their" Germans. Churchill said he was not "afraid of the problem of transfer of populations provided that it was proportioned to the capacity of the Poles to handle it and the capability of the Germans to receive them." Such a comment revealed an appalling lack of judgment of likely matters on the ground. Already tens of thousands had been killed in these operations, and millions would eventually die.

To his credit, U.S. secretary of state Stettinius recommended that Roosevelt "oppose, as far as possible, any indiscriminate mass transfer of minorities with neighboring states." That suggestion was ignored, with tragic consequences.[77]

Stalin promised that the USSR would enter the war against Japan "two or three months" after Germany's defeat. He had stated this resolve to then U.S. secretary of state Cordell Hull in October 1943 and had assured FDR of it at Tehran.[78] In return for going to war against Japan, Stalin wanted not only territories lost to Japan before the First World War but also special rights with regard to Darien and Port Arthur and railway lines across Manchuria. He said that if he obtained such concessions, "the Soviet people would understand why they were entering the war against Japan."

These wishes were accepted, even though some impinged on China's sovereignty. FDR was sure that Chiang Kai-shek would agree though as the president knew, the Chinese leader had little say in the matter. On February 11 the Big Three signed this secret agreement, which would make the Soviet Union an Asian as well as a European power. As per Stalin's habit, all such claims were justified exclusively in terms of ensuring his country's "security interests."[79]

It is not so simple to decide who won and who lost at Yalta, which was the most important of the wartime conferences. However, it is very difficult to accept a recent study's conclusion that "in the long run it was the American president who gained most from the debate." The assertion that Roosevelt was the "winner" at Yalta and established "his reputation as an honest broker" does not hold up to scrutiny.[80]

Although Western participants and some historians have said that Yalta achieved a "compromise," Soviet ambassador Maisky was more accurate when he wrote to a colleague that their leader had determined 75 percent of the decisions. The diplomat was too tactful to add that these were all the important ones.[81]

When Roosevelt and Churchill returned from Yalta, they tried to put the best possible spin on what they had achieved. In a more sober moment, FDR privately admitted that his only hope at the conference had been to "ameliorate" Soviet control of Eastern Europe, but he had yielded to it anyway. Curiously, Churchill boasted of how proud he was to have held Stalin to the notorious "percentages" deal by which he had, in fact, conceded to the Soviet leader all he wanted. The prime minister, the champion antiappeaser in the 1930s, must have needed a strong drink after the parliamentary session on February 27 when he reported his impressions from Yalta "that Marshal Stalin and the Soviet leaders wish to live in honorable friendship and equality with the Western democracies. I also feel that their word is their bond."[82]

Churchill had long been convinced that he could deal with the

Soviet dictator. Later in the war, when he began to encounter rough patches, he assumed that Stalin must be working at the behest of power holders in Moscow. In his memoirs, Churchill recalled that, after meeting with him in October 1944 or so, he sensed that "behind the horseman sits black care." He believed that the Kremlin Boss was "not alone" and that unseen radicals were pulling the strings. Churchill mentioned to FDR that Stalin was not to blame for signs of a new stubbornness, but rather "the Soviet leaders, whoever they may be."[83] However, Stalin was fully in charge, and by no means was he bossed around by radicals inside the Politburo.

Other participants at these conferences had no doubt about who won and lost at the conference table. Foreign Secretary Eden saw Stalin more often than any other Allied statesman, and his verdict was this:

> Marshal Stalin as a negotiator was the toughest proposition of all. Indeed, after something like thirty years' experience of international conferences of one kind or another, if I had to pick a team for going into a conference room, Stalin would be my first choice. Of course the man was ruthless and of course he knew his purpose. He never wasted a word. He never stormed, he was seldom even irritated. Hooded, calm, never raising his voice, he avoided the repeated negatives of Molotov, which were so exasperating to listen to. By more subtle methods he got what he wanted without having seemed so obdurate.[84]

Alexander Cadogan, the sober permanent undersecretary of the British Foreign Office and a member of the British delegation at Yalta, observed that Stalin was "much the most impressive" of the leaders there. "He sat for the first hour and a half or so without saying a word—there was no call for him to do so. The President flapped about and the P.M. boomed, but Joe just sat taking it all in and being rather amused. When he did chip in, he never used a superfluous word, and spoke very much to the point."[85]

Stalin won not just because he was a better negotiator than the other side but because he knew what he wanted and was backed by the overwhelming force of the Red Army. He was the leader of the mightiest army in all of history, and they were headed, he believed, for world victory, however long it would take.

CHAPTER 6

The Red Army in Berlin

A t Yalta in February 1945, there were also more specialized gatherings of the Allied military leaders. Discussions here were amiable, although the Soviets were reserved. The Red Army chief of general staff, Aleksei Antonov, mentioned imminent winter and further campaigns and gave assurances that the Soviets would coordinate them with those of the Western armies when they crossed the Rhine.[1]

However, these pledges also carried indications of the underlying tensions in the "grand alliance." They came to the surface during the last months of the war. As the Red Army drove out Hitler's forces and toppled collaborationist regimes, Stalin wanted to capitalize on the political opportunities, and he prevailed on his marshals and generals to ignore all costs and get to Berlin. Not once did he express concern about the mounting casualties. For him it was a question not just of winning the war but also of outdoing the Western Allies in winning the peace.[2]

FAINT HOPES FOR QUICK VICTORY

Stalin approved the detailed military plan for taking Berlin, as worked out by Stavka and the general staff. The attack was to begin between January 15 and 20. To ensure secrecy, only Stalin and four others had the complete picture, and he personally coordinated the four army groups involved. He was hoping to knock Germany out before the Western Allies had finished in France, Belgium, and Holland.[3]

Soviet strategy envisioned taking Berlin in two stages. The first, lasting fifteen days, would be a giant offensive of two army groups that would drive straight ahead from a line along the Vistula (running through Warsaw). Their aim was to reach the Oder River, three hundred miles or so away. At the same time, two other army groups would head north to finish off East Prussia. The operations had been rehearsed, with great attention paid to deception (*maskirovka*), which the Red Army had turned into a science. After the first stage, a second would begin, with the goal of conquering the German capital in thirty days.[4]

The operational planners in the Supreme Headquarters Allied Expeditionary Forces (SHAEF) considered it feasible that the Allies would cross the Rhine between October 20 and 25, 1944. Another attack around November 25 would move through the Saarland, cross the Rhine at Mainz, and then speed northward toward the Ruhr, Germany's industrial heartland. Hitler would have to defend that with a concentration of troops, and they would be encircled.[5] Thereafter the road to Berlin would be open; all of Germany would not have to be destroyed before the Third Reich came to an end. The demarcation lines for the armies of occupation were already drawn up. Troops would move in to keep the peace, relatively few personnel would be needed, and the defeated country would be administered by "indirect rule."[6]

Hitler disrupted this line of thinking with a surprise counterattack that began on December 16. He kept telling his generals that there were political contradictions in the Allied camp and that a shock attack might cause it to collapse.

The Germans assembled 200,000 soldiers and scraped together 600 tanks, some of them taken from the eastern front. They would face 80,000 U.S. troops who had only 400 tanks. As expected, the Wehrmacht pushed the Americans back, creating a bulge in the lines, albeit one that did not break (hence the Battle of the Bulge). Barely a week into the fighting, German forces began running into stiffer resistance and out of supplies. The weather cleared on Christmas Eve, and the Allies then used their superior airpower. The next day Hitler's commander in chief in the west, General Hasso von Manteuffel, wanted to break off the action.[7]

Hitler sensed that this was his last chance and tried to restart the counterattack. On December 28 he raised the specter of Communism, telling his commanders that "a victory for our enemies must undoubtedly lead to Bolshevism in Europe."[8]

Shortly thereafter, he launched another attack to the south in Alsace, but it failed quickly. Churchill wrote to Stalin on January 6 and wondered if the Western Allies "could count on" an offensive during the month. Stalin replied that his forces had accelerated preparations and, in spite of continuing bad weather, would be ready not later than the second half of the month.[9] In fact, the Soviet offensive opened on January 12.[10]

As it happened, by January 16 the Allied armies in the west that had been pinching together around the "bulge" in the American lines finally came together. It was not possible to trap all enemy forces inside the pocket, as Eisenhower hoped, but the Battle of the Bulge was won.[11] Even so, the war was going to take longer to win than anyone had expected, and its end became entangled in politics.

On January 12 the Red Army's Vistula-Oder offensive was launched in timed sequence using nine army groups. Marshal Zhukov of the First Byelorussian Army Group was deployed in the center, with orders to take what was left of Warsaw and to head straight on for Posnań, thereafter to Berlin. Farther south, Marshal Ivan Konev commanded the First Ukrainian Army Group, and he took aim at Breslau (Wrocław). Between them they had more than 2.25 million men for what was the largest single Soviet operation in the war.

Stavka recognized that because this Warsaw-Berlin corridor was the shortest way to the German capital, it would be heavily defended. In order to stretch out Wehrmacht resources along a wider front, Marshal Rokossovsky led the Second Byelorussian Army Group north in the direction of Danzig, and General Chernyakhovski, in charge of the Third Byelorussian Army Group, set out for Königsberg in East Prussia.

Konev began, Rokossovsky went next, and one day later Zhukov and his troops roared off, with his tank armies making almost one hundred miles in the next twenty-four hours. By January 26, Zhukov was seeking Stalin's permission to continue to Berlin and soon got the go-ahead. Shortly thereafter Marshal Konev also obtained approval to strike out for Berlin. The first units of Zhukov's forces reached the Oder River by the end of the month. Troops were able to cross the frozen river, though without their artillery and tanks. On February 4 he ordered those in forward positions to dig in and seek protection from menacing aircraft attacks and sixteen days later, with Stalin in agreement, instructed them to halt.

General Vasily Chuikov, a hero in Stalingrad and one of Zhukov's best, later said that Zhukov and Stalin were too concerned about being vulnerable, that they should not have called a halt on February 20. Chuikov thought that going right for Berlin would have been feasible and would have saved weeks of war and countless lives. But Stalin, Zhukov, and Konev were more cautious, so victory would have to wait. Some of Konev's troops fought on for another week and linked up with Zhukov where the Oder and Neisse rivers meet. Then Konev also opted to dig in.[12]

The Red Army had bypassed Hitler's "fortress cities," but they continued to disrupt communication. The heavily defended strongholds like Posnań, Budapest, Danzig, Breslau, Königsberg, and Küstrin tied up the Red Army and slowed its progress. Konev agreed with Zhukov that their armies needed a "quiet period" before storming onward. They had been fighting since January 12, which was forty days and more for some of them, over distances of between 190 and 270 miles. The lines of communication were long, the ranks in the army were depleted, supplies (especially fuel) were far behind, and tanks were in need of maintenance.[13]

The decision to hold back may have been influenced by Hitler, who ordered the Stargard (Szczeciński) counterattack on February 15, to relieve Soviet pressure on Küstrin at the Oder River. Red Army leaders were surprised, though the German offensive ended after less than three days of inconclusive fighting. That SS leader Heinrich Himmler was in charge of the German side made no difference whatsoever.[14]

Marshal Zhukov recalled that on March 7 or 8 he was ordered to fly to Moscow, where Stalin told him about Yalta, his suspicions about the Allies' intentions, and his distrust of Churchill, who preferred to have a "bourgeois" (that is, a liberal democratic) government in Poland.[15] In his memoirs, General Sergei Shtemenko, deputy chief of the Red Army's general staff, writes that Germany was trying at that time to find a separate peace with the United States and Great Britain "behind the back of the Soviet Union." Given that "special historical situation we could not risk any ill-considered actions." Stavka and the general staff decided to secure the flanks because, he said, "the political and military consequences of failure in the last stage of the war might turn out to be serious or unrecoverable." What he meant was that the Western Allies were steadily advancing, and if the Red Army were to take chances and be unable to capture Berlin, then all the sacrifices would have been in vain.[16]

The Western Allies crossed the Rhine in strength only on March 7, when forces of the U.S. 9th Armored Division under General John Leonard reached the bridge at Remagen and found it largely intact. Four divisions then surged across. Eisenhower could hardly believe the good fortune, for his troops captured 300,000 prisoners, averaging 10,000 per day in the month from the end of February to the end of March.[17] The vaunted Siegfried Line of defenses was breached, and by April 1 the Rhine-Ruhr region was encircled in a pincer movement that trapped twenty-one divisions, or another 320,000 troops. That was a greater loss than the Germans had suffered at Stalingrad.[18]

SHAEF and Eisenhower came up with a strategy for the next stage, pushing toward the line Erfurt-Leipzig-Dresden (south of Berlin), with a swing farther south toward Regensburg-Linz that would cut off the area where Hitler might make a last stand. Troops would stop at the Elbe River, forty miles short of Berlin, as already agreed with the Soviets. Finally, in the north, another operation by the Western Allies would simultaneously isolate German troops in Norway and Denmark.[19]

Eisenhower was eager to accomplish these tasks as "quickly and completely" as possible and to avoid close combat in cities, where house-to-house fighting was so costly. He was criticized by Churchill and Field Marshal Sir Bernard Montgomery (and by some historians) for not attempting to set out quickly for Berlin. He and General Omar Bradley estimated that had they done so, it would have meant the deaths of at least 100,000 of their men. There was little chance of beating the Red Army to Berlin, and Eisenhower thought it "stupid" to try. Either way, there was nothing he could have done on the battlefield that would have changed the configuration of postwar Europe.[20]

In keeping with established procedures, Eisenhower sent his plan to Stalin on March 28. It was necessary to systematize communications and to determine how each side could recognize the other. Churchill had his own agenda. He thought that Eisenhower was exceeding his authority by engaging Stalin in communications that went beyond military matters. Even though the agreement reached at Yalta placed Berlin two hundred miles inside the Soviet zone, the prime minister wanted to throw everything into an all-out effort to get to Berlin before the Red Army.[21]

Eisenhower's message went to the U.S. military mission in Moscow, and Ambassador Harriman and British ambassador Archibald Clark Kerr decided to present it in person to the Kremlin. They took along General John R. Deane and his British counterpart, Admiral Ernest Archer, on March 31.[22]

The Soviets must have been alerted by someone, because even before receiving Eisenhower's plans, Stalin again called Zhukov back to Moscow, where he arrived on March 29. They met that same night and discussed strategy. The Boss said that, according to intelligence reports, the Germans were no longer putting up much resistance in the west and were shifting reinforcements to the east. He calmly asked when the Red Army would be ready for the attack on Berlin. Zhukov replied that his First Byelorussian Army Group would need "not more than two weeks." He was of the view that Marshal Konev's First Ukrainian Army Group would require about the same amount of time but that Rokossovsky's Second Byelorussian Army Group would be bogged down in the north until at least April 10. Stalin said bluntly, "Then we shall have to begin the operation without waiting for Rokossovsky."[23]

He showed Zhukov an intelligence report indicating that the Nazis had tried but failed to negotiate a separate peace with the Western Allies. Stalin doubted that Roosevelt would do such a thing, but he believed that Churchill might. Generals Shtemenko and Antonov were also given the information and concluded, like Zhukov, that there were "backstage" deals in the works to let the West beat them to Berlin.[24]

On the evening of April 1, Stalin met with his marshals, and Shtemenko read the intelligence report aloud for Konev, who had flown in the day before. He recalled that it spoke of a "U.S.-British Command under Montgomery" that was preparing to take Berlin. There was no such plan, but Stalin led them to think the worst and then turned to his two marshals to ask: "Well, who is going to take Berlin, we or the Allies?" Konev answered first, saying, "It is we who will be taking Berlin, and we shall take it before the Allies."[25] Although Marshal Rokossovsky was not there, he soon returned to Moscow and was also given to believe that the Nazis were letting the Western Allies through to Berlin, while doubling efforts to stop the Red Army.[26] Stalin spread the rumors to Soviet diplomats as well, who held the widespread conviction that the West was trying to wrest the fruits of victory from them.[27]

END OF THE ROOSEVELT ERA

Roosevelt and to a lesser extent Churchill were still under the spell cast by Stalin at Yalta, and they were surprisingly slow to believe that he would break his word by setting up thinly veiled Communist regimes in the countries liberated by the Red Army. The Foreign Office in London and the State Department in Washington clung to the idea that "other people" in the Kremlin were manipulating Stalin behind the scenes. Churchill was growing more skeptical, but he had already conceded much to Stalin that would be impossible to undo.[28]

Some high-level Nazis had indeed tried to open discussions with the West since early 1945. It was enough to confirm Stalin's conspiratorial thinking about the "capitalists." Moreover, he could take no solace from the fact that his allies had informed him about "Operation Sunrise." Since February 21, SS General Karl Wolff had sent feelers to Allen Dulles of the U.S. Office of Strategic Services (OSS). On March 8, Dulles had a short meeting with Wolff in Zurich and then informed Allied head-quarters in Caserta, Italy. Field Marshal Sir Harold Alexander, stationed there, recommended that his American deputy chief of staff, General Lyman Lemnitzer, and his British chief intelligence officer, General Terence Airey, follow up with Wolff. The SS general's braggadocio was simple. "Gentlemen," he said, "if you can be patient, I will hand you Italy on a silver platter."[29]

Word of these conversations was relayed to the British and American embassies in Moscow, where on March 12 they informed Molotov. The latter had no objections but wanted the Soviet military involved. The top U.S. brass, including General George Marshall and the Joint Chiefs of Staff, had reservations about including any Red Army officers, who might make "embarrassing demands" and kill the talks. The Western Allied leaders were transfixed by the thought of a speedy end to the fighting in Italy and perhaps even obtaining a general German surrender. Although initially Churchill had sensed that any such negotiations with the enemy would offend the Soviets, he yielded to the Americans. The whole business was badly handled and was more than enough to raise the Kremlin's suspicions. Molotov then fired off an angry note that accused the United States and Great Britain of negotiating "behind the backs" of their ally.[30] The negotiations with the Germans were fruitless and most inopportune, for the West was then vainly objecting to what the Soviets were doing in places like Poland and Romania.

Although Roosevelt and Churchill worried that the cooperative spirit of Yalta was being ignored across Eastern Europe, they were hardly in a position to hold the Kremlin to account at a time when they found themselves on the defensive about Operation Sunrise. In a note to the Soviet leader, received on March 25, FDR explained that there was no thought of a separate peace or ending the war short of unconditional surrender. They had simply made contact with "competent German military officers for a conference to discuss details of a surrender" of Italy, with the view of stopping the bloodshed. Stalin insisted this was duplicity and double-dealing.[31]

In addition, on the evening of March 31, Ambassador Harriman and Britain's Clark Kerr went to the Kremlin, this time with Eisenhower's plans showing that he had no intention of heading toward Berlin. "Ike" was now quoted as saying that Berlin "was no longer a particularly important objective." Did Stalin think that was more disinformation? Perhaps, but he replied by affirming their view that the German capital "had lost its former strategic importance." The Soviet High Command, he told Harriman and Clark Kerr, was making arrangements to send only "secondary forces" there.

That was a lie, because at that moment the Soviets were completing plans for the speediest possible conquest of Berlin. The two Western diplomats blithely judged Stalin as "calm and friendly" on the evening, but he was definitely not.[32]

Churchill complained to Eisenhower that getting Berlin should be a top priority, and he pointed out to Roosevelt, in a statement related in many Russian memoirs, that it was imperative to get there first. The Red Army would soon take Austria and Vienna, he said, and if it was then to capture Berlin, "will not their impression that they have been the overwhelming contributor to our common victory be unduly imprinted in their minds, and may this not lead into a mood which will raise grave and formidable difficulties in the future? I therefore consider that from a political standpoint we should march as far east into Germany as possible, and that should Berlin be in our grasp we should certainly take it."[33]

President Roosevelt was beginning to have doubts about Stalin and wrote him a long letter in which he mentioned his profound concern about the growing Communist dominance in Poland. FDR went so far as to say that the "present Warsaw regime would not be acceptable and would cause the people of the United States to regard the Yalta agreement as *having failed*."[34]

Instead of responding to the alarm in this letter, Stalin heated up the frictions about those secret meetings with the Nazis. On April 3 he wrote an accusatory message to Roosevelt alleging that the Germans had agreed to "open the front" to let Anglo-American troops "into the heart of Germany almost without resistance." He accused his allies of cooking up a deal that would not "help preserve and promote trust between our countries."[35]

Churchill told the president that Stalin's accusations made it imperative for the Anglo-Americans not to seem afraid and not to look like they could be "bullied into submission." He wanted to stand up to the insults. "I believe this is the best chance of saving the future."[36] FDR was angered and told Stalin that Soviet intelligence must be at fault. The Kremlin Boss would have none of it, saying that his informants were "honest and unassuming people who carry out their duties conscientiously."[37]

President Roosevelt was in the final days of his life and was discouraged by this turn of events. The last messages he wrote on April 11 went first to Churchill. He tried to minimize the "Soviet problem," which he thought would straighten itself out, and added that "we must be firm, however, and our course thus far is correct." Then he wrote a last message to Stalin, expressing the hope that future relations would not be clouded by "mutual mistrust and minor misunderstandings." However, Averill Harriman, the American ambassador in Moscow, thought the problem was far from "minor." He decided to delay passing on FDR's note in order to give the president an opportunity to rethink that part of the statement. But at one-fifteen P.M. on April 12, FDR cabled Washington from Warm Springs, Georgia, to say he wanted the original note handed over. Ten minutes or so later he died. His original message arrived at the Kremlin on April 13, but Franklin Roosevelt had passed away the day before, not living to see the end of the war.[38]

Commissar Molotov, informed of the president's death late at night on April 13, went to the American embassy in Moscow at three A.M. to convey his sympathies. Harriman reported that he had never heard the man speak so earnestly. There is no record of Stalin's reaction on first hearing of Roosevelt's sudden death. Later that day, he put on the expected show at the Kremlin and appeared "obviously deeply distressed" while shaking the U.S. ambassador's hand for what seemed an eternity. He sent his condolences to the new president, Harry Truman, and to Mrs. Eleanor Roosevelt.[39]

In his memoirs, the combative Molotov glossed over FDR's passing with scant mention. He did not think highly of American leaders, disdained the aristocratic Roosevelt's attempts to be informal with him, and looked down even more on the folksy Harry Truman. For Molotov, these presidents shared one damning attribute: they were dyed-in-the-wool capitalists and imperialists.[40]

HAMMER AND SICKLE OVER BERLIN

Back on the night of April 1, Stalin told his marshals they had to reach the Elbe River, west of Berlin, within twelve to fourteen days. By now they were all convinced that the Germans would let the Western forces through but would fight all the more tenaciously against the Red Army. That was a fantasy. What was real was the deplorable behavior of the Soviet forces and their reputation for rape, pillage, and plunder. To an extent, this passion for revenge was fueled by how brutally the Germans had acted during the invasion and occupation of the USSR. The actions of the Red Army, however, led to atrocities that went beyond all bounds and played into the Nazis' determination to stop the Bolsheviks at any cost.

Occasionally, when the Red Army briefly withdrew, people got a chance to see what was in store for them, as happened in the East Prussian village of Nemmersdorf (Mayakovskoye) in October 1944. The Wehrmacht reported that at one farm "the bodies of two naked women were nailed through their hands to both barn doors." Inside they found seventy-three more bodies. Doctors attested that all the females, even girls aged eight to twelve, had been raped—including an eighty-four-year-old woman—and "murdered in a bestial fashion."[41] The account was no invention and the abuse not reserved for German women, for a Polish report on March 19, 1945, from a nearby area told a similar story about the Red Army, with details too appalling to repeat here.[42]

What was the origin of this behavior? Part of it arose out of the ferocity of the fighting, but some of it can be traced to the Stalinist system of military justice. Red Army soldiers faced the harshest possible punishments for disobeying orders.[43] In August 1941 and again in July 1942, Stalin introduced notorious punitive measures. In the course of the war, military tribunals pronounced an astounding 158,000 death sentences. The executions were at times carried out in front of assembled troops. Military courts sent another 400,000 people to prison and forced at least 420,000 to serve in punitive units, which for these *shtrafniki,* as they were called, could amount to a death sentence. A recent Russian study concludes that no fewer than 994,000 Soviet servicemen and women were convicted by military tribunals alone, with half the sentences coming in the first two years of the war.[44]

The heavy punishments and horrifying battle experiences enraged soldiers. In addition, the new counterintelligence organization SMERSH (Smert Shpionam—"death to spies") planted agents in the armed forces and informed on anyone they deemed suspicious, a practice that undermined troop solidarity.[45] When they got to Germany or Austria, troops were stunned and outraged to find just how well the enemy lived. In places soldiers unleashed their blind fury on the homes left behind by panicking civilians. Some of them fled in such haste "that they hadn't even had time to make their beds, and now the mirrors, the dishes, the service sets, the rarest porcelain, the glass goblets, the cut-glass pitchers—all were flying to the floor." That was how one Red Army man described the first wave of hatred that boiled to the surface in his unit. He said they lashed out at everything in sight, "they took axes to armchairs, sofas, tables and stools, even baby carriages!"[46]

Military leaders sought to direct this fury into the battle against the Wehrmacht but waited until they were fully prepared before launching the attack. Marshal Zhukov would have preferred to hold off the final assault on Berlin until Rokossovsky's army group could join in, but he later wrote that the "military-political situation"—which is to say, the supposed duplicity of the Allies—made postponement impossible.[47] Meanwhile Konev's First Ukrainian Army Group approached from the less heavily fortified south. Stalin played on the rivalry of his two ambitious marshals and left it undecided which of them would take Berlin. He erased the line on the map separating the two at a point well short of the city, thus forcing the marshals to compete with each other to take it. Konev's forces would be joined by Rokossovsky's as soon as they were available.[48]

As strategist, Stalin preferred massive attacks that combined an army group that linked up with others to overwhelm the enemy. The lesson in the art of war that he never learned was that victory should be sought at the lowest cost in lives.[49] For the push to Vienna that opened on March 16, he had three-quarters of a million troops and for Berlin 2.5 million. They had 6,250 tanks and self-propelled guns, 3,200 multiple rocket launchers, 41,600 artillery pieces, and 7,500 aircraft. Zhukov himself had around half of this force at his disposal. But he overestimated his numerical advantage over the Germans, who moreover had detected the time and place of the attack.[50]

By the time Zhukov's offensive began, before dawn on April 16, the Germans had pulled back many troops from forward positions. The Red Army blasted away with everything and then switched on 140 searchlights, which did not blind the defenders as expected. Instead, the illumination of the smoke and dust made it impossible for the attackers to see ahead, and as the waves of infantry went over the top, they piled into one another. The first day of battle is caustically described by one historian as "comic opera played by five armies on a 20-mile stage."[51]

Hundreds of tanks ordered into action during the day only added to the mad tangle. They could not move freely on the flooded plain and had to travel the few roads and bridges where they were easy targets. In spite of firing over a million artillery shells, and notwithstanding endless bombing attacks from the air, Zhukov found German defenses largely intact on the Seelow Heights. Even though the German generals on the ground had held back the attack the first day, they knew the situation would deteriorate, as they had already thrown all their reserves into the fray.

Stalin, in telephone contact with the front, criticized mistakes and browbeat Zhukov, who in turn drove on with disregard for casualties. It took two full days of heavy fighting to break through the Seelow Heights, costing the lives of at least 30,000 Red Army men. The wounded lay neglected on the battlefield for hours.[52] For Stalin and his military leaders, what made conquering Berlin so vital was its political significance, a point underlined in the memoirs of the key participants.

Konev's route from the southeast moved speedily along one of the first autobahns. He had to breach several lines of defense and two rivers, the Neisse and the Spree. When reporting his progress on April 17, Stalin told him to turn his tanks to encircle Berlin. Four days later Konev's units captured the headquarters of the German Army (OKH) at Zossen and were close to Potsdam. For all that, any hope that the Red Army might be able to take Berlin on Lenin's birthday (April 22) was out of the question.

On April 25 units of the Red Army's 58th Guards Rifle Division linked up with the U.S. First Army's 69th Infantry Division at Torgau and several other places along the Elbe River. The American and Soviet troops were overjoyed, and the same day Berlin was completely encircled. Marshal Rokossovsky's Second Byelorussian Army Group finally came in from the north, pinning down the last enemy troops and ending any German hope of counterattacking Konev or Zhukov. Stalin mentioned on the radio the meeting of the troops from both sides, but he did not share their solidarity.

To bring some order to the chaos, he had reset the demarcation lines on April 22. Zhukov's and Konev's troops were already inflicting "friendly fire" casualties on each other. Stalin decided that Zhukov's soldiers would have the privilege of taking the Reichstag, the last symbol of power in the city, and they succeeded on April 30. When General V. I. Kuznetsov called Zhukov to report that the red flag was atop the building, German troops were still fighting in the upper floors and in the cellars. They surrendered only late on May 1. So much for the Allies thinking that sanity would prevail in Berlin and that there would be no need to wage war throughout the entire country.[53]

The battle as a whole, from April 16 to May 8, cost the Red Army 78,291 dead and 274,184 wounded. It seems certain that many of these casualties were needless and that the numbers could have been reduced with a more measured attack. The same was true for the Austrian-Vienna operation that ended on April 15. It cost the Soviets 32,846 dead and 106,969 wounded.[54] In the middle of the bloodbath, Stalin was in direct contact with the front, getting intelligence officers to find certain political figures, in order to begin arranging the postwar political setup.[55]

Contrary to Hitler's prediction that the Allies would fall apart, Americans and Soviets greeted each other in celebration.[56] By midnight on April 29, any chance that German troops could rescue Berlin was erased. At one P.M. the next day, Hitler had lunch with his wife and his secretaries, briefly bade farewell to those still in the bunker, and then went to his rooms, where he and his wife committed suicide.[57]

Zhukov phoned Stalin's dacha and had him awakened to tell him of Hitler's death. The dictator muttered: "That's the end of the scoundrel [*Doigralsya podlets*]. What a pity we couldn't take him alive." He told Zhukov to demand unconditional surrender and went back to bed to be rested for the annual May 1 celebrations.[58] There he announced what had happened and even mentioned that Hitler "made advances to the Allies in order to cause dissension." The war criminals would be punished and reparations paid, he said, even as he insisted that the Soviets were not against the German people as a whole. He swore that the invading forces would not "molest" the peaceful population, but such a statement was belied by what was happening on the ground.[59]

When Stalin learned that German generals had agreed to sign the unconditional surrender papers, not in Berlin in the presence of Red Army commanders but in the small French city of Rheims, he was infuriated. He phoned Zhukov and ordered him to Berlin for another ceremony, there to represent the supreme command of the Soviet forces, along with appointed Allied leaders. The document was finally signed at 12:43 A.M., May 9, 1945. That would be the Victory Day celebrated in the Soviet Union, not May 8—considered V-E Day in much of the rest of the world.[60]

Stalin broadcast the news to his people at eight P.M. Moscow time. The statement was brief and carefully calibrated. Interestingly, he portrayed the German-Soviet war not as a conflict of ideologies, Nazism versus Communism, but as part of the age-old "struggle of the Slavic peoples" against German invaders. Knowing that the world was listening, he did not say a word about Communism. The people were understandably proud, for only three years before, Hitler had threatened them with annihilation or slavery. Stalin and Communists everywhere saw the Soviet victory as a validation of the Soviet system. He now said that he did not want vengeance and would not "dismember or destroy" Germany. "Comrades," he said, "the period of war in Europe is over. The period of peaceful development has begun."[61]

CHAPTER 7

Restoring the Stalinist Dictatorship in a Broken Society

In May 1945 the Soviet dictator, fresh from the war, made two public addresses. On May 9 he announced victory in a radio speech, and three weeks later, at a reception for Red Army officers, he toasted the "Great Russian people," singling them out for praise. Both talks were short and unemotional and said little about the greater significance of the war.[1] Over the next eight months, his silence was deafening; after 1946 he spoke to the public only three times. The only chance for people to see him at all was from afar, when he appeared for parades twice a year atop the Lenin Mausoleum.[2]

Joseph Stalin was sixty-six years old at war's end and rumored to be suffering from poor health. Instead of retiring, as some close to him in Moscow might have hoped, he set out to use the political capital he had won through victory to continue his mission in his own country and to extend it across war-torn Europe and to other parts of the globe.[3] Vast sums of money were poured into military spending and soon into the Cold War. Soviet citizens paid for it all with persistent shortages of consumer goods and in the poor quality of their lives.

VICTORY FOR ONE-MAN RULE AND COMMUNISM

Stalin, the Leader or the Boss in the Kremlin, ran his vast domain like a medieval prince, conferring personally with those called to the seat of power. He was the center of a leadership cult he created. It was adorned with semireligious overtones because he recognized that the elevation of the mighty leader was useful in fulfilling the regime's "pedagogical" mission and had a place in society, which he viewed as a kind of "permanent classroom."[4] The cult reached new heights at war's end because it could be linked to Stalin's military role in leading to victory.

Behind the scenes he brushed aside the remaining institutional checks on his power and surrounded himself with a handful of men variously called the "close circle" or the "ruling group." Since the 1930s these men were usually referred to by number, such as the "quintet," and in 1945 they included, besides the dictator, Molotov, Beria, Malenkov, and Mikoyan.[5]

Nikita Khrushchev, who was later admitted to the "select group," gave a vivid portrait of Stalin's ruling style. It was to "hand out orders off the cuff. Sometimes he would listen to others if he liked what they were saying, or else he might growl at them and immediately, without consulting anyone, formulate the text of a resolution of the Central Committee or Council of Ministers [changed from Council of People's Commissars, or Sovnarkom, in March 1946] all on his own, and after that the document would be published." This was political domination by a single individual in its most extreme form. "It was completely arbitrary rule. I don't even know what to call it, but it's a fact that that's the way things were."[6]

Vyacheslav Molotov was closest to Stalin, the most recognized figure after him at home and abroad and generally regarded as nearly as important. Indeed, there were times when Churchill and others mistakenly thought he was the real leader and Stalin the front man. Anastas Mikoyan, one of the perennial survivors in the ruling elite, provides another perspective. He recalled that whenever he entered Stalin's office, Molotov was usually there—a fact supported by the record of Stalin's appointment book, which shows him present more than any other single person.[7] He sat there mostly in silence, at least according to Mikoyan, who thought Molotov was just someone the Boss wanted around to avoid giving the impression that he was deciding everything himself.[8] Molotov was not the real boss, as Churchill seemed to think; nor was his presence a mere comfort to Stalin. Even after the dictator officially demoted him later on, Molotov was kept around and frequently consulted.

Stalin had a way of dressing down those close to him, such as in November 1945, when the USSR Academy of Science elected Molotov an honorary member. As much as he might play games with Molotov and the others over drinks, he did not want anyone thinking too much of themselves.[9] The seasoned commissar was not helped when the *Daily Herald* speculated that he was the real power in the land, with Stalin ill and out of town. Some experts in the U.S. State Department thought the same. The dictator did not want any plausible heirs gaining traction and reprimanded Molotov speedily for allowing publication in Moscow of the text of a Churchill speech given in London on the anniversary of the Russian Revolution. He had only offered his respects, but for Stalin, praise from such a man encouraged "servility to foreign figures." Molotov humbly begged forgiveness and was allowed to stay. Stalin tucked the matter away in the file on "Molotov's mistakes" but would take it out again in 1949 to dismiss him.[10]

The big Communist Party events in Moscow brought together hundreds of delegates, though after the Fifteenth Congress in 1927 and Sixteenth Conference in 1929, such gatherings took place only three times in the 1930s. Stalin held only one more conference (in 1941) and a final Nineteenth Congress in 1952.[11] Even the party's Central Committee, with 138 members and candidate members in 1930, held few full meetings and during the war hardly any at all; they were called together twice in 1940 and 1941 but only once in 1944, 1946, and 1947, though twice in 1952.[12]

Since 1917 the Politburo consisted of the country's leading political lights. It had fifteen members and candidate members in 1930.[13] Until 1932 it met weekly, with additional working meetings from 1928. However, beginning in 1933 it met ever less frequently, and the real decision making became more personalized to the point where it took place in Stalin's office. In addition to hearing out those he brought in to consult, he delegated enormous power to subordinates and expected them to show initiative. Yet his remained the ultimate voice. He took a hands-on role in the most important matters, like internal security and foreign and economic policies, as well as official appointments. After the war he briefly revived the Politburo, but while it had more than symbolic significance, it was still a shadow of its former self.[14]

It was primarily also Stalin who determined how the country should interpret and remember the Second World War. Only in a February 1946 "election" speech did he outline what became the grand narrative. He said the recent war "was not only a curse" (*proklyatiye*) but was also like a "great school" that examined social systems and political regimes.

All the combatants appeared for a test "without masks and without makeup, with all their defects and merits." Victory, he proclaimed, proved several things—first of all, the superiority of the Communist social system. Far from being what enemies called a "dangerous experiment," according to Stalin, the Soviet regime turned out to be viable and was supported by the people. Second, the great multinational state, which foreigners said was artificial and could not last, "grew stronger than ever during the war." Finally, in defeating all foes, the Red Army had demonstrated it was anything but a "colossus with feet of clay," as the critics hoped. And yet the bravery of those in uniform would never have been enough to win. Taking the credit he felt was due the Kremlin, he reminded everyone that his three five-year plans—the third had been cut short by war—had transformed the country from an agrarian into an industrial and military power.[15]

Stalin's claim that the validity of Communism was proven by winning the war became the official story line. The disciples across Europe sincerely bought the story and repeated it for decades. Now he reminded voters about another Lenin axiom, namely that national security would be impossible without more heavy industry. He pledged—to loud applause from party officials present in the Bolshoi Theater for his speech—to exceed prewar production of pig iron, steel, coal, and oil in three more five-year plans.[16] In fact, already in the summer of 1945, the Central Committee had indicated that the State Planning Committee (Gosplan) was preparing a new plan.[17] For the average person, the long-suffering consumer who was accustomed to reading between the lines, the very mention of the phrase *five-year plan*—never mind three new ones—meant more sacrifices and harder work.[18]

A major drawback of one-man rule is that when the leader elevates someone whose ideas are outdated and wrong, the errors multiply and become difficult to correct. For example, Stalin backed the work of the scientist Trofim Lysenko and had done so since the 1930s. Lysenko's promise was that he would be able to revolutionize crop yields and lead an agricultural revolution. When his findings were disproven and he fought back, Stalin and later Khrushchev supported him because they were attracted by the idea of a miracle in farming that would put them ahead of the West. What made Lysenko such a menace to the scientific establishment was that he was a clever lobbyist who had Stalin's ear.

The Lysenko "affair" demonstrates how blindly Stalin could hold on to the "truths" he felt were crucial to his modernization schemes. It also shows how cruelly he could reject someone who crossed him, even if that person was someone "special" like Andrei Zhdanov.

Already prominent in the ruling elite since the late 1930s, after the war Zhdanov was elevated to greater prominence when Stalin put him in charge of straightening out the Soviet intelligentsia. Abroad he gave stern lectures to the Eastern European Communist parties as the keynote speaker at the Communist Information Bureau (Cominform) meetings in 1947 and 1948. Stalin also liked Andrei's son Yuri, a twenty-eight-year-old whom he put in charge of the Agitprop (propaganda) Science Section. The dictator thought the young Yuri a perfect match for his daughter, Svetlana, and expected they would marry in 1949. However, in 1948 it came to Yuri's attention that a number of important scientists doubted the work of none other than Lysenko, one of the dictator's favorites. The young Zhdanov gave a speech on April 10 to propaganda workers, in which he seriously criticized Lysenko, who was nearby, heard for himself, and then complained to Stalin. On May 28 the dictator, who still believed in the promise of the quack scientist, ordered the Zhdanovs, father and son, as well as others involved, to the Kremlin. Stalin was angry with Yuri but excused him because of his youth. Andrei Zhdanov, who was suffering from serious health problems, got a dressing-down. On August 31, 1948, he died in a hospital under what people believed were "mysterious circumstances."[19]

Although some thought Beria had poisoned him, medical doctor Lidia Timashuk wrote to the head of Stalin's bodyguard, General Nikolai Vlasik, and alleged that the doctors who treated Zhdanov were to blame. That information percolated through the system like slow-acting venom and, as we will see later, in 1952 culminated in a national uproar about an alleged doctors' plot to kill Soviet leaders.[20]

Stalin called for a special session of the Agricultural Academy in August 1948 to discuss Lysenko's claims and those of the geneticists. Lysenko, who had been president of the academy for ten years, filled the hall and list of speakers with his supporters. Of the fifty-six papers given at the big event, the great majority were on his side. Among other things, they said the geneticists were bourgeois and were "kowtowing to the West"—the very sin Andrei Zhdanov was ferociously fighting. That Lysenko would come out on top was a foregone conclusion, but

Stalin went through the motions of consulting the experts.[21] He had blurted out to Yuri Zhdanov that "our entire agricultural future depends on Lysenko."[22] It was simply impossible for him to take back such an endorsement. Not until years after Stalin's death would Lysenko finally be rejected and modern genetics be supported in the Soviet Union.

Another favorite among the elite who rose to the top, only to fall from grace, was Nikolai Voznesensky. He was a trained economist and had served loyally in the important position of chairman of Gosplan since 1938. Moreover, he was the author of *The War Economy of the USSR in the Great Patriotic War* (1947), which was widely reviewed and crowned with a Stalin Prize, first class. Many thought that if Zhdanov was not to be Stalin's successor, then it would be Voznesensky. Stalin, who fancied that socialist economics was his own area of special expertise, might have resented his old comrade or been concerned about him as a possible successor. The Master said he liked how the commissar expressed his opinions firmly and would not compromise with the others, though precisely such traits created enemies among the inner circle.[23]

To the extent that we can make sense of Voznesensky's fall from grace, his fateful "transgressions" began in Leningrad. There, from January 10 to 20, 1949, regional leaders on their own initiative sponsored an all-Russian wholesale fair. Although they had asked native son Voznesensky to act as patron for the event, he had declined. The organizers also had links to other national figures from the city, among them Aleksei Kuznetsov, secretary of the Central Committee. Many considered the young and good-looking Kuznetsov a star, and he also was mentioned as a possible successor to Stalin. Some senior administrators in Moscow, however, expressed mild concern that holding such a fair should have been cleared by the Council of Ministers.

Stalin heard about this and was sufficiently upset to convene a Politburo meeting on February 12 to interview the local and regional organizers of the fair. When they were condemned, Voznesensky tried to distance himself from the group by saying that he had turned down its offer to act as a "patron." Three days later Kuznetsov and his "co-conspirators" were dismissed from office. Voznesensky was given a reprimand for not informing the Central Committee either about the "antiparty" fair or the request that he act as its patron.

To make matters worse, his rivals Beria and Malenkov spread word that something was amiss in Gosplan, the agency that he led and that was in charge of planning and coordinating the economy, setting and meeting quotas. The suspicion was raised that Gosplan might be fudging the figures, when in fact growth rates were lower than expected and reported. At any rate, Stalin slowly became convinced that Voznesensky was dishonest and had "masked the real state of affairs" in the economy. That charge, on top of his association with what looked like an emerging Leningrad faction in the party, soon had fatal consequences.

On March 5, in spite of years of faithful service, Voznesensky was dismissed from his important post and soon also dropped from the Politburo. The police arrested more people and found further damning evidence until, on October 27, they took him into custody. Along with four other suspects, he was mercilessly interrogated for months, tried in secret in September 1950, and shot. Altogether, sixty-nine of the accused and 145 relatives were punished, with twenty-three of them executed, and arrests continued into 1952. This "Leningrad Affair" was unique for the postwar years in taking down a member of the Politburo. The administration of Gosplan was also purged, with many being dismissed, demoted, or transferred, rather than executed.[24]

Stalin had got it into his head that these people represented threats to his rule. The Great Terror of the 1930s might well have "unnerved" him, or he may have been "wary of embarking on a new round of bloodletting on such a scale."[25] Realistically, in the postwar years he no longer needed show trials because the climate of insecurity was already widespread and easily supplemented with press campaigns and in other ways. Moreover, police control over the country was more professionalized and extensive than it was in the 1930s, so that left Stalin free to exercise his tyranny more subtly.

Thus, even when he met the ruling group informally, the participants always had a feeling that something important was taking place. For that reason, when they were invited to his dacha, none of the elite wanted "to miss a single dinner, even when ill. It was there that everything of any importance was brought up, discussed, and sometimes conclusively decided."[26]

At the dictator's whim, he called them to discuss even crucial policy matters, without agenda, minutes, or secretaries. They usually met in the evening or at night. He might invite them to watch one of the American movies captured in Germany or elsewhere during the war. The films had no subtitles, and he loved to curse them for being so primitive. One night he commanded the USSR minister of cinematography Ivan Bolshakov to give a running translation. The poor man did not dare say he knew no English, so he improvised and imagined what the actors were saying. Stalin's cronies chuckled because they knew the truth.[27]

The custom of the all-night dinners had begun in the late 1930s, and the rituals deteriorated in the latter part of the war, when Stalin recovered from the shock of the Nazi invasion and began to sense victory. Instead of serenely basking in the limelight, the ruler reverted to teasing and insisting on never-ending toasts until guests were completely drunk. They emerged from the ordeal at dawn and then had to face work at their offices. The bizarre hours, stress, and excessive drinking had disastrous effects on their health, but that did not stop the Boss from playing childish games, like "fining" someone an extra shot of vodka if they polished off the last one too slowly. The meals sometimes degenerated into food fights. But no matter how boisterous, silly, and fun-filled these occasions, he could turn on someone in the blink of an eye. What made the man so terrifying, as one distinguished writer put it, "was that any slip in dealing with him was like mishandling a detonator: You would do it only once in your life; there was no chance to correct it."[28]

With foreign guests Stalin was more restrained though always political. Milovan Djilas, for example, on a visit with a Yugoslavian delegation just before the Allied landings in Normandy, saw that behind the banter over food and drink, Stalin was trying to intimidate them and get them to break with the West.[29]

It is also true that after the war the old man became desperate for companionship. When Khrushchev would arrive from Ukraine on business, Stalin would invite him home and keep him in Moscow until he begged permission to leave. Then all he would get was: "What's your hurry? Stay here a while. Give your comrades the opportunity of working without you." His daughter, Svetlana, was no longer nearby, for she had married (against his wishes) in 1944, and again in 1949, leaving him on his own. He had no woman friend who might have helped temper his harshness. Getting these comrades from the upper reaches of society to socialize with him, one surmises, was partly an attempt to fill the gap in his life that was otherwise devoid of human contact.[30]

A BADLY WOUNDED SOCIETY

The great victory celebrations in 1945 could not conceal a harsh reality: the Soviet Union had been bled white by the war, so badly affected that recovery would take far longer than ordinary people hoped or leaders in Moscow feared. Stalin played down the human costs that had been paid because he did not want to reveal how the war had weakened his country.

In March 1946, during an interview with *Pravda,* he mentioned in passing that the USSR had suffered 7 million deaths, which, he rightly observed, was vastly more than the combined losses of Britain and the United States.[31]

That number stuck for a long time, until the late 1980s when President Mikhail Gorbachev ordered new investigations. Studies by the Soviet General Staff then reported that 26.6 million had died in the war, 8,668,400 of them men and women in uniform. The military figures alone are astonishing, and as two British scholars have noted, if spread over four years, "Red Army losses on an average day ran at twice the Allied losses on D-Day."[32] The official Soviet statistics should be taken as a minimum. For example, the fatalities include 1.8 million Red Army prisoners who died in captivity. German statistics state, however, that there were at least 3.3 million such deaths. Some reliable Russian historians put military deaths at 10 million.[33] The "medical casualties" went up to 18,344,148, though some were "double-counted" because they were wounded more than once.[34]

If we take the more or less "official" calculation that 26.6 million people died from all causes in the Soviet Union and subtract the 8.6 million or so military deaths, the result means that 18 million or more civilians died prematurely. These figures are complicated because no precise counting was done at the time, and they have to be estimated. It is true that several million died through Stalinist wartime terror and ethnic cleansing, but they were war-related, and a net loss of people.[35] Still more almost certainly died because the government had made almost no plans for civilian needs in the event of war, and they were left to face chronic shortages and hunger.[36]

Stalin sought to compensate for the population deficit by refusing to repatriate Axis prisoners of war, the last of whom left the Soviet Union only in 1956. Of course their labors could not come close to making up for the losses.[37]

The birthrate had been falling since the 1920s, as it continues to do up to the present. There was also a gender imbalance, accentuated by the war that left 20 million more females than males.[38] In the early postwar period, that one-sidedness particularly affected rural areas, where sometimes only a handful of men returned to their village.[39]

The property damage from the war was staggering. In November 1945, Molotov announced some findings from a special investigating commission's research. He said that metropolitan areas and cultural centers, like Stalingrad, Kiev, Minsk, Smolensk, Kharkov, and many other major cities, were reduced to smoldering ruins. "The Hitlerites," as he and Stalin called them, burned or destroyed 1,710 towns and 70,000 villages. They demolished 6 million buildings and left 25 million people homeless. A total of 31,580 industrial enterprises were destroyed, cutting 60 percent of the country's metal and mine production. In the countryside, anything that could be moved was stolen, and the rest destroyed. As they retreated, the Wehrmacht methodically tore up forty thousand miles of railway track and destroyed all the stations and bridges. Molotov listed the devastation to tens of thousands of schools, libraries, hospitals, technical institutes, and universities.[40]

More recent research suggests that, if anything, he understated the damage; according to one estimate, the country lost one-quarter of its prewar physical assets.[41] The productive activity of whole generations went up in smoke, so much so that in 1945 the Soviet Union looked more like one of the defeated countries than one of the winners.

The years immediately following the war were among the most desperate in all of the twentieth century across Europe and worst of all in the Soviet Union, where poverty and want were rampant. Even at the end of 1946, young soldiers returning from war-torn Germany were shocked at how their country looked by comparison. When their train stopped at railway stations, they were beseeched by those on the platform: "Uncle, give us a little piece of bread!" The scenes were so bad in Dnepropetrovsk that the soldiers could not bear to look anymore.[42]

Some spoke of people they knew who tried to survive by eating cookies made of grass.[43] Tens of thousands of letters were sent to the authorities seeking help, like one from a town near Voronezh. "We live in frightful conditions," it said. "We have absolutely nothing, we eat only acorns, and we can scarcely drag our feet. We will die from hunger this year." From Stalingrad and villages in the area came a similar plea: "There is no bread and we do not know how we shall survive. I have sold everything to save us. There is nothing more to sell."[44] Even in places like Saratov, not occupied by the Germans and therefore relatively intact, food shortages were so bad in early 1946 that people could not redeem their ration cards for basics like bread and potatoes.[45]

The weather conspired to produce a poor harvest that year, with a drought in Ukraine and Moldova, while in Siberia late-season rains did the damage. The grain crop for 1946 was down by over 15 percent from 1945, which was itself already 2.4 times smaller than in 1940. The potato harvest in 1946 was only 69 percent of what it had been in 1940.[46]

The famine, however, resulted in part from the actions of the Communist regime, which was still playing the politics of human misery. In Moldova, for example, the government provoked the famine by grain-requisitioning techniques that aimed at alleged rich peasants in the eternal struggle against "kulaks." Just in that region in this period, at least 115,000 peasants died "from hunger and related diseases."[47]

When Stalin heard of the shortfalls in deliveries from the main agricultural areas, he was infuriated, and in October 1946, just as in the early 1930s, he sent his henchmen to the provinces to make sure that they surrendered their quotas.[48] Nikita Khrushchev reported the dire situation in Ukraine, including cases where starving people in their delirium had resorted to cannibalism. Stalin's response was predictable: "This is spinelessness! They're playing tricks on you. They're reporting this on purpose, trying to get you to pity them and make you use up reserves."[49]

The famine of 1946–47 adversely affected 100 million people, mostly in the countryside but in urban areas as well.[50] On September 16, 1946, to curtail demand for food, the regime raised prices in state stores and eleven days later took away the bread-rationing privileges of 27.5 million people who worked in rural areas, but not on farms.[51] That day also ended permission for peasants and others to grow food on minuscule private plots that had been appropriated over the years from collective farms. Now their tiny dreams of minimal economic freedom were quashed. Hunger and desperation spread in the countryside, which by and large had not been on rations in the first place. Writing to Soviet leaders and even to Stalin was a common outlet for complaints. Care had to be taken to avoid forbidden words that suggested there might be a famine, because such "slander" got people sent to the Gulag.[52]

While there was plenty of grumbling and muttering, the will to collective action was too weak and the hold of the police too strong for uprisings to develop. In response to the crisis, Stalin called a rare Central Committee meeting in February 1947. However, instead of offering relief or loosening controls, they clamped down and demanded obedience to "the peasant's first commandment," namely to make deliveries to the state and cope with what remained.[53]

For many there was too little food. However, the data are not precise on the number of "excess deaths" beyond the normal mortality rate. Even so, most historians accept that between 1 and 2 million people lost their lives through hunger and disease.[54]

The situation deteriorated further in the years 1946 to 1948, when the USSR exported 5.7 million tons of grain to new satellites Bulgaria, Romania, Poland, Czechoslovakia, and Yugoslavia and even to France and other countries. These moves were dictated by Stalin's desire to prop up new Communist regimes or to curry favor. The government also increased its grain reserves, as a hedge against an international situation that might get out of control.[55]

The reflexive popular response to the shortages was increased theft of food. In the autumn of 1946, 53,369 persons were charged with stealing bread, and nearly 75 percent of them lost their freedom.[56] It was indicative of the continuing punitive side of Stalinism that in January 1947 the regime began drawing up a new law on theft. As a draft of that measure worked its way through the bureaucracy, Stalin became involved and opted for harsher punishments for all categories of robbery. Whereas in the 1920s and 1930s the penalty for first offenders who stole "state property" was three months in jail, the new law proposed to extend it.

The mighty dictator was angered when the draft law was put before him in May 1947 and penned two new decrees, one each for the theft of personal and state property. Now he wanted a minimum sentence of three years' imprisonment for the former—with repeat offenders getting six to ten years. For those found guilty of stealing state property, the dictator demanded a minimum sentence of five years and more if the theft was part of an organized crime. When the new draft was ultimately presented for his approval, at the stroke of a pen he increased the minimum sentences yet again, adding a year or two in both cases.[57]

The law for petty theft affected poorer people, like two women whose case went to the Tomarov district court on July 16. Both were given six years in a corrective-labor camp (the Gulag) for stealing four kilograms (just over eight pounds) of potatoes from a field. That sentence was less than the minimum seven years, though it illustrates the systematic brutalization of the peasantry in the postwar years.[58] In the remainder of 1947, a half million people were sent to court under the draconian new law, so that it operated like a conveyor belt to the Gulag. On January 1, 1951, exactly 637,055 people found themselves being punished for this crime.[59] The three highest judges in the land eventually concluded that the law was too harsh and appealed to Stalin to lower the minimum punishments. He would not budge.[60]

The judicial system managed to curb the effects of the tyrant's wrath in various ways. Either the procuracy or the courts substituted lesser charges than those imposed by the decree, exempted juveniles, or spared at least some by dropping charges. Beginning in 1948, the net effect was a steady decline in the number of cases involving the theft of state and personal property.[61]

Rationing was finally repealed at the end of 1947 and the currency revalued. In some places there was a festive feeling in the air, and on the eve of the big day of the exchange, goods appeared in shops—if only for a fleeting moment.[62] Thereafter food and provisions gradually improved, though even into the 1950s consumer goods were very scarce. For example, each member of an "average worker's family" could, once a year, get either a pair of leather shoes or a pair of winter boots but not both. They could expect at most three bars of soap and in Moscow's public bathing facilities could get a proper "washing" (pomyvki) a little more than once a month. In other places public bathing was less frequent.[63]

Everyday Stalinism was largely what it had been in the 1930s, and that, for most people, was a system that has been compared to a prison/ conscript army, a strict boarding school, and a relief agency/soup kitchen.[64] Postwar propaganda was a poor substitute for a better way of life.[65]

In the country as a whole, housing was also miserable. Postwar urban rebuilding lagged behind even the modest population growth. New and rushed construction was often substandard and cluttered with every imaginable defect. By 1950 the total square footage of housing per person was still less than it had been a decade earlier, when there was already a shortage. Fewer than half of all Moscow's homes had running water and sewage disposal. In the Urals and Western Siberia, where much industry had been located in the 1930s, the feverish creation of factories was not matched by enough living quarters. Conditions in the overcrowded dormitories of mill towns sound like those of the mid-nineteenth century. In a city like Chelyabinsk, people slept in kitchens and bathrooms of homes, in recreation and toilet facilities of factories, in schools, railway cars, and garages.

Uncounted thousands had only dugouts or mud huts (*zemlyanki*). Since the 1930s, such "dwellings" were taken for granted and not just in developing areas; the Soviets gave only secondary consideration to housing for workers. A survey in 1956 of the cities, towns, and regions once occupied by the German invaders found there were still thousands living in holes in the ground and other spaces unfit for human habitation.[66]

The first waves of returning soldiers were applauded and reintegrated into society, at least if they were in one piece. Many of them became true-blue Stalinists, but some wondered about the Communist system after the relative prosperity they had seen. There were vets who criticized, and a few—fearing war with America or England—dared to say, "It was wrong not to destroy the 'allies' after the fall of Berlin."[67] Most returned to impoverishment in the countryside. Victory Day was proclaimed a holiday, until Stalin realized there was little to be gained by focusing on the past, and in 1947 he decided to drop the celebration. He discouraged his generals from writing their memoirs, partly because he preferred to saturate the public discourse with attacks on the new enemies in the Cold War.

The Soviet Union's estimated 2.75 million invalids were given humble pensions, and many had to resort to begging or hawking cigarettes at markets. By 1947 Stalin had seen enough and ordered the streets cleared of all beggars.[68]

THE GULAG

There was no better symbol of Stalin's postwar restoration of dictatorship than the Gulag. At the beginning of 1939, the combined total of prisoners in labor camps and colonies stood at 1.6 million. The number went up to 1.9 million in 1941 then fell off until 1944, when it stood at

1.1 million. Prisoners preferred volunteering to fight rather than rotting away. In 1945 the total in all the camps went back up to 1.4 million, and every year thereafter it increased until 1950, when there were 2.5 million in the system. The number was the same the next year and barely fell until 1953, when the count reached 2.4 million. In 1948 these prisoners were divided about equally into labor camps (ITL) and labor colonies (ITK), but by 1953, 70 percent were in the camps. They were distributed in 476 separate complexes containing numerous smaller camps.[69]

Female prisoners in the Gulag were always fewer in number, but their fate, movingly described by Alexander Solzhenitsyn, was far worse. In the three years 1943 to 1945, the number of women in the camps and colonies stood (respectively) at 17.3 percent; 24.9 percent; and 28.4 percent of the total.[70] These proportions were higher than usual because many men volunteered to serve and were accepted into the military. After the war, female prisoners made up between 22 percent of the total (in 1948) and 17 percent in 1951 and 1952.[71]

There was a parallel system of special camps that is usually overlooked in studies of the Gulag. In 1945 it held just over 2 million people, and the number increased until the census of January 1, 1953, when it contained no less than 2,819,776 people. Included in that figure were 885,717 children up to age sixteen. The story of these settlers (spetsposelentsy) has been investigated for the 1930s though not yet for the postwar years, when there were even more of them. Whereas before the war most were "kulaks," in the 1940s and 1950s they were mainly persecuted nationality groups, such as those from the Caucasus, the Baltic, and the Crimea. In 1953 the largest group (1.2 million) was made up of Germans.[72]

Taken together, these systems contained a captive population of more than 5 million. We can imagine how many lives were touched by this terror if we think of the relatives and friends left behind.

Solzhenitsyn, an officer in the Red Army until February 1945, when he was arrested and sentenced, told the story of the Gulag more vividly than anyone. His own offense was to criticize the regime in a private letter while on service at the front. He was then denounced and given ten years in the camps, where life was every bit as dreadful after the war as before.[73]

These institutions were by no means all in the distant east or far north. After the war prisoners worked everywhere and were impossible to overlook. Thus in the late 1940s and early 1950s, there were more than fifty Gulag divisions in the Moscow region (*oblast*). Slaves were "rented out" to work on construction sites or in factories. But no matter what the managers did, they could not make this system economically self-sufficient.

What was as bad or worse than its economic cost was that Russian historian Galina Ivanova suggests that the entire operation corrupted society. The hundreds of thousands of people employed to work in the Gulag, as guards, administrators, and managers, became used to acting like slaveholders, and many raised their children in an atmosphere dominated by the camp. Participating in that world, even witnessing it on an ongoing basis, helped to ingrain antisocial attitudes—for example, that it was perfectly acceptable to mistreat others, to cut corners, cheat, chisel, and steal. A whole way of life developed that was at odds with common decency. The Communist system, along with its inbred chronic shortages, fostered a "new Soviet man" who was in reality a far cry from the ideal any revolutionaries ever had in mind.[74]

The camps were gradually dissolved only after Stalin's death. Even before then, the Gulag was reaching a dead end. Too many prisoners became unfit because they were overexploited. The able-bodied were inefficiently used, too often with the weakest and oldest assigned to hard labor, while the barely literate and healthy could end up in the front office. For Stalin the main goal of the punitive system was not economic productivity but to terrorize the population and uphold the political system he wanted. That was why the Gulag was untouchable until he died.

At any rate, by 1947 the dictatorship and all its repressive trappings was firmly back in place, and the country was increasingly closed off to the outside world. That process was reinforced by, and became entangled in, conflicts with the West and the looming Cold War.

PART II

SHADOWS OF THE COLD WAR

CHAPTER 8

Stalin and Truman: False Starts

On April 13, 1945, Averill Harriman assured Stalin that President Truman would continue FDR's policies. The U.S. ambassador added that it would be useful for Commissar Molotov to make a courtesy call in Washington on his way to the founding meeting of the United Nations in San Francisco, scheduled for April 25. The Kremlin had been dragging its feet about participating, in spite of having been urged to go by FDR. When Harriman brought up the matter on April 13, Molotov was in the room, and though he fussed and fidgeted at the mention of such a trip to the United States, Stalin overruled him on the spot and ordered him to go.[1] The Soviet dictator was still hoping to obtain his political objectives with the cooperation of the Americans and British, and he was more than willing to try his luck with the new man in the White House.[2]

THE PRESIDENT'S FIRST ENCOUNTERS WITH THE USSR

In Washington, Harry Truman found himself thrust onto the world stage. The country was still at war in Europe and Asia, and he faced many unfamiliar problems. As a veteran of the Senate, he knew the legislative branch of government but was not well versed in foreign policy. Although he had been added to the Democratic ticket for the 1944 elections, the secretive FDR had not told him that the United States was working on an atomic bomb, much less let him in on the politics of the "grand alliance." Truman confided to his diary on the day he was sworn in: "I knew the president had a great many meetings with Churchill and Stalin. I was not familiar with any of these things and it was really something to think about but I decided the best thing to do was to go home and get as much rest as possible and face the music."[3]

The new president retained Roosevelt's entire cabinet, so contrary to Cold War legend, there was no sudden break with FDR's policies. What changed was the international situation when, within a month, Germany was defeated. Questions were now bound to arise about how to make peace in Europe, how to respond to Soviet behavior in Eastern and Central Europe, and how to end the war with Japan.

At the time, of course, Poland was "the pressing and dangerous problem" on the agenda, and on April 13 Truman wrote to Prime Minister Churchill, in response to a message of condolence, to say he wanted to do something about it.[4] The president was inclined to "get tough" with the Kremlin and had Secretary of State Stettinius ask Ambassador Harriman in Moscow to raise the Polish issue again before Molotov left on his trip to the United States.[5]

Stalin went to great lengths to allay Western suspicions regarding Soviet intentions. He prided himself on how shrewdly he had instructed foreign Communists after the Red Army liberated their countries. He met with them in Moscow before they went home and coached each and every one of them to form national front governments, made up of a coalition of parties. The reality that the Communists were dominant, however, was too obvious to ignore. Western Allied commissions in Eastern Europe sent numerous reports to that effect to Washington and London.

Once the White House was notified of Molotov's impending visit, Truman and his advisers concluded that the American government should get beyond merely exchanging pleasantries. Following up on this resolution on April 16, Truman and Churchill sent a joint message to Stalin regarding discussions under way in Moscow by a commission charged with working out a new provisional government for Poland. They asked that representatives of the Polish government-in-exile be permitted to join those discussions.[6] The backdrop for this request was that the Anglo-American leadership and Stalin accused each other of not holding to the Yalta agreements with regard to Poland, Romania, or Bulgaria. Moscow was trying to maximize the influence of Communist parties, while the West sought to protect vulnerable nations from Soviet encroachment and domination. The note hinted that further infringements would make it difficult to get Congress to grant the $6 billion loan the USSR was seeking from Washington.[7]

The new president's goal was the cautious one of keeping to agreements already made. His great fear was that he might not be up to the job and seem weak. As it was, he had no long-term plans or hidden agenda with respect to the Soviet Union, Europe, or Asia, and he wanted to get along with Moscow as much as anyone. At times he sounded terribly naïve and inclined to pursue foreign policy in absolutist terms. The overriding need of the moment was still to win the war, and he wanted the Soviet Union in it to the end, especially for the final fight against Japan.[8]

Ambassador Harriman was anxious about the meeting that he had arranged for the new president with Molotov, so he hurried back to Washington. He arrived on April 20 and went straight to the White House, where he made no effort to conceal his worst fears, saying that the Kremlin would not be satisfied until all the Eastern European countries were turned into images of the Soviet Communist regime. Using the most undiplomatic language, he offered the president a startling vision that something akin to a new "barbarian invasion of Europe" was already under way.[9]

On April 23, Commissar Molotov called at the White House to open discussions. Charles Bohlen, a Soviet expert in his own right, served as translator, as he had for Roosevelt at Tehran and Yalta. Bohlen and others in the State Department were convinced that FDR had tried too hard to get along with Stalin, with nothing to show for it.

At their second meeting, Molotov asked President Truman whether he intended to respect the treaties, agreed on by FDR, by which the Soviet Union would be given certain territories in Asia for entering the war against Japan. The president said he would fulfill those promises but wondered when the Kremlin would live up to agreements to give Eastern European countries the opportunity to establish their own democracies.

The assertive Molotov, who was usually in control of situations like this, lamely objected that the Poles had worked against the Soviet Union. When he recalled the event years later, he said he was upset by Truman's tone and responded in kind. In fact, he did no such thing.[10] Instead he tried to move the conversation back to the war with Japan, at which point Truman, whose voice had been steadily rising, broke off the conversation with the words, "That will be all, Mr. Molotov. I would appreciate it if you would transmit my views to Marshal Stalin." Bohlen remembered how he enjoyed translating those sentences. "They were probably the first sharp words uttered during the war by an American president to a high Soviet official."[11]

This relatively minor event did not "cause" the Cold War, though for years it was taken as "symbolic" of how the United States supposedly had become a "world bully" that did not understand the Soviet "obsession with a pursuit of security."[12]

Moscow's ambassador to Washington, Andrei Gromyko, was also present that day, and although the Truman-Molotov exchange was not mentioned in the official Soviet records, he later recalled his surprise that the once "kindly" Senator Truman was coming across as "harsh" and "cold" since becoming president.[13] Gromyko explained the transformation by saying the new man in the White House already had the atomic bomb and was flexing his muscles.[14] That was not the case, however, as Truman was given more details about that weapon only after, and not before, this brush with Molotov. Gromyko's misleading statement is one of many that fuel myths about the early "atomic diplomacy." It is true that the day Truman was sworn in, and in the emergency atmosphere of that moment, Secretary of War Stimson had mentioned that the United States was developing a weapon of "unbelievable destructive capacity," yet he said no more than that and left the new president "puzzled."[15]

The American memorandum of the Truman-Molotov talks struck some Soviet diplomats in Washington almost as if it were an ultimatum. Moscow was to help move the deal forward with Poland and allow non-Communists a role in government there, or else it would be difficult for the U.S. to continue its cooperation—that is, to grant the Soviet Union the aid it so badly needed.[16]

The touchy Molotov notified Stalin, who sent a stiff reply to the White House that arrived on the night of April 25. The president recalled the message as most "revealing and disquieting." The Soviet leader forcefully restated his long-held views, asserting that his country was "entitled to seek in Poland a government that would be friendly to it." As for objections that such a regime might not be representative, he pointed out what the West was supposedly doing in Belgium and Greece. He would not ask, he said, how representative those governments were.[17]

By chance also on April 25, Secretary Stimson and General Leslie Groves, the two men in charge of the Manhattan Project, visited the White House. They reported that "within four months" the United States would "in all probability have completed the most terrible weapon ever known in human history."[18] They brought with them a twenty-four-page report. The president read it and said that the enterprise sounded immense and technical. They discussed the weapon's international implications, particularly for "the Russian situation," which presumably meant its political use in regard to Soviet moves in Eastern Europe. General Groves reminded them, however, of "the dangers of over-emphasizing the power of a single bomb."[19]

On May 6, Churchill mentioned the desirability of having a Big Three conference, and Truman's first thought was to have it in the United States, perhaps in Alaska. However, Soviet expert "Chip" Bohlen said that was not a good choice. He told the president that part of the reason for the failure to carry out the Yalta agreements was the Soviet "opposition" that Stalin encountered upon his return home. So the dictator supposedly needed to be closer to home to communicate better.[20] Such fantasies as this one about resistance to Stalin should tell us just how little the Soviet regime was understood at the time in the West, even by the experts. If Stalin had appeared badly weakened in 1941, his grip on power was gradually restored and then confirmed by the great victories.

The three Allied leaders finally opted for Potsdam, just outside Berlin, but when would they meet? That is an important question because some Russian and American revisionist historians suggest that Truman wanted to postpone the conference until the experiment on the first atomic bomb succeeded, when he would have had more political clout. However, the documentation does not support that view.[21] It is also an exaggeration to claim that Truman already recognized the importance of the bomb and initiated a consistent policy based on it. As a matter of fact, he reacted haltingly to news about work on the weapon. Only on May 1 did he accept Stimson's suggestion to name an interim committee that would recommend action to him, if and when a bomb was successfully tested. Even then he did not immediately name his own representative to the committee.[22]

Churchill—who was informed about the atomic research—wanted talks with Stalin sooner rather than later, preferably in mid-June. The

Kremlin leader had already scheduled the great Victory Parade for June 24 and was content to accept Truman's suggestion for July.

Indeed, none of the Big Three leaders quite realized that a new atomic age was at hand. As for the American military establishment, the Joint Chiefs of Staff proceeded on course without taking the atomic bomb into account. On May 25, and remarkably enough without telling the president, the chiefs issued orders to subordinate commanders in the field to draw up plans for the invasion of Japan. On May 28, General Douglas MacArthur delivered the strategy (Operation Downfall). There would be a two-pronged attack, the first of which was code-named Operation Olympic and the other called Coronet. So completely was the president kept out of the picture that on June 17 he still confided in his diary that he was struggling with "the hardest decision to date," namely the question, "shall we invade Japan proper or shall we bomb and blockade." This latter approach was the ongoing one, and it was not code for the atomic bomb. The first successful A-bomb test, Trinity, was still almost a month away.[23]

The intelligence about Western atomic research in May 1945 had come to NKVD chief Beria, who reacted slowly. When Soviet scientists wrote to the Politburo (Stalin) asking to accelerate work on the bomb, they received only a muted response.[24] Caution is advised in interpreting what was in the mind of the wily Stalin, who knew more than he was prepared to divulge. His spies had informed him early on about the development of the ultimate weapon, the atomic bomb. The British had made progress in this field since 1941, as Soviet intelligence sources soon reported. By March the next year, Beria recommended setting up a committee to evaluate the information and to involve Soviet scientists. In early 1943, Molotov gave high-level authorization to proceed, but the effort was still modest.[25]

Although some Western scientists like Danish physicist Niels Bohr, who worked on the American bomb in Los Alamos, grew concerned and wanted to share the secrets of the research with the Soviets, Roosevelt and Churchill were decidedly against doing so. In September 1944 they signed an agreement to continue Anglo-American cooperation to develop "tube alloys" (code for the atomic bomb). They wanted Bohr investigated "to ensure that he is responsible for no leakage of information, particularly to the Russians."[26]

But leakage occurred, enough for Stalin to resent his allies for not sharing secrets with him. That was a curious response from someone who at that very moment had an army of spies working inside the halls of power in Washington and London. In fact, later internal U.S. investigations revealed that during the war more than two hundred Americans were spying for the Soviets. They had infiltrated all sections of FDR's administration, including the Office of Strategic Services (OSS), the forerunner of the CIA. This news came to light only in the late 1940s and early 1950s.[27]

Stalin even had top informants inside the Manhattan Project—the industrial-scale attempt to build the atomic bomb—including Klaus Fuchs, an émigré and active Communist from Germany. In Britain he became involved in atomic research and moved to New York in 1943. He and other scientists made it possible for the Kremlin, by 1945, to get "a clear general picture" of the secret project.[28] Although Soviet leaders were a long way from realizing the full potential of atomic research, they eventually produced something that was close to a copy of the U.S. bomb. Given the scale and scope of Soviet espionage, it was certainly disingenuous for Stalin to express hurt feelings that his allies did not trust him, a man notorious for trusting no one.[29]

Because of his clash with Molotov, some revisionists as well as Russian historians have pigeonholed Truman as being anti-Soviet from the start. It was true that back in June 1941 (just after the Nazi attack on the Soviet Union), Truman was quoted as making the intemperate remark: "If we see that Germany is winning we ought to help Russia and if Russia is winning we ought to help Germany, and that way let them kill as many as possible, although I don't want to see Hitler victorious under any circumstances."[30] This incautious quip was typical of the isolationist bluster of the times and was quoted in Soviet studies as being indicative of President Truman's worldview and policies.

On balance, in April 1945 Moscow saw Truman as likely less inclined to be understanding of the Soviet position than FDR had been. That was what the Soviet embassy in Washington reported.[31] To reassure the Soviets of his goodwill, the president turned for advice not to a hawk but to the best-known dove in the United States—none other than former ambassador to the Soviet Union Joseph E. Davies. On April 30, 1945, Davies was invited to the White House, where he offered his counsel.

Truman told him what he had said to Molotov and then boyishly asked how he had done, hoping for a pat on the back. The American ambassador bit his tongue and then patiently explained why it was necessary to adopt Roosevelt's old position of balancing between Stalin and Churchill "for the purpose of keeping the peace."[32]

In the weeks that followed, Truman leaned heavily on Davies, his trust in Ambassador Harriman and the State Department shaken. The president regretted the nasty exchange with Molotov and was now comforted by Davies's counsel to be nicer to Stalin.

No doubt Winston Churchill would have preferred for Truman to be forceful with the Soviets. As he contemplated the postwar scene in Europe, he grew disconcerted to learn about American plans to redeploy troops for the war against Japan. On May 12 he wrote Truman a prescient letter about the future—it sounded like his later speech about the iron curtain:

> What will be the position in a year or two, when the British and American armies have melted away and the French has not yet been formed on any major scale, when we may have a handful of divisions mostly French, and when Russia may choose to keep two or three hundred on active service?
>
> An iron curtain is drawn down upon their front. We do not know what is going on behind. There seems little doubt that the whole of the regions east of [the] line Lübeck-Trieste-Corfu will soon be completely in their hands. To this must be added the further enormous area conquered by the American armies between Eisenach and the Elbe, which will I suppose in a few weeks be occupied, when the Americans retreat, by the Russian power. All kinds of arrangements will have to be made by General Eisenhower to prevent another immense flight of the German population westward as this enormous Muscovite advance into the center of Europe takes place. And then the curtain will descend again to a very large extent if not entirely.[33]

Truman was inclined to agree, yet like Roosevelt he instinctively sought to avoid creating the impression in Moscow that he was going along too much with Churchill. The two presidents admired the British prime minister but did not want to be seen as "ganging up" on Stalin and assumed (quite wrongly) that it would be easier to get his cooperation if they could meet with him alone. They were both fortunate that Churchill persisted, because he provided both presidents with badly needed expertise and support.

Joseph Davies had advised Truman to go easy on Moscow, but not two weeks later, on May 12, the White House unceremoniously stopped shipments under the Lend-Lease program to Europe. That aid had been granted to Great Britain since March 1941 and to the Soviet Union since October of that year. According to the Lend-Lease Act, the assistance was to run until the end of the war. As that day approached, American officials discussed what should happen. Secretary Stettinius and Ambassador Harriman favored gradual reductions to pressure the Soviets into granting more democratic rights to the people in countries like Poland, Romania, and Bulgaria. However, both warned against "abrupt changes," which would "anger the Russians."

Others in the administration (like Acting Secretary of State Joseph C. Grew) said that the aid should be cut immediately, the day Germany was defeated. Although the president later denied it, at the time he went along with what turned out to be a most ill-considered decision.[34] Not only was Lend-Lease stopped short, but ships at sea laden with essential supplies, including food, even those nearing the coast of the USSR, were ordered to turn back. The outcry from Moscow left the U.S. government trying to explain that it was all a "misunderstanding."[35]

We should note that Lend-Lease was not just cut to the Soviet Union; to the horror of the White House, shipments of vitally needed food were also stopped to Britain, France, and Western Europe.[36] There was an instant backlash, and Truman hastily reversed himself, so that the aid resumed and continued until several weeks after the end of the war against Japan.

The embattled president was delighted to get another call from Davies on May 13, who again came over for talks. He generously offered to cable Stalin to smooth things out. He impressed Truman, who wondered whether it would be possible for this former ambassador to visit Moscow as his special envoy. Davies had recently been hospitalized and had to decline on health grounds. Nevertheless, he strongly advised that the way forward with the Soviet Union was to return to conciliation and cooperation, or what might more accurately be called appeasement.[37]

Ambassador Davies was not entirely out of step with the mood in America, where there was a groundswell of good feelings, especially in liberal circles, toward the Soviet Union. When Ambassador Harriman, on his trip home, spoke off the record about problems that Moscow was causing in Europe, he faced the open hostility of the press. He recalled that "their faith in the future was great and they could not believe at the time that the Russians, who had suffered so deeply in the war, would not want to live amicably with their neighbors and ourselves."[38]

It was in this context that Truman reached back to Harry Hopkins, a man known for getting on well with Stalin, to ask him to act as an envoy to Moscow. Davies, at the request of the president, then contacted the Kremlin to ask how it would respond to such a visit. He received an enthusiastic reply and, along with it, news that he had been awarded the prestigious Order of Lenin for his unstinting efforts on behalf of Soviet-American relations.[39]

Truman was hardly leading an anti-Soviet campaign; nor was he about to follow Churchill, who now favored a tougher attitude toward Stalin. In fact, he was quite tentative in the first days of his presidency and listened to those like Davies who thought the fiery British leader might rub Stalin the wrong way and make a lasting peace harder to find. When the president asked Davies to visit London on his behalf, he did not realize that sending someone known for being sympathetic to Moscow would create alarm there. Churchill was furious when Davies asked him to understand the president's wish to talk alone with Stalin before the next Big Three meeting.[40]

British foreign secretary Eden's response to Davies's visit to London was that the man was "a born appeaser and would gladly give Russia all Europe," except for Great Britain, so as to keep the United States from getting embroiled in conflict. Eden noted in his diary that Davies demonstrated "all the errors and illusions" of their own prewar prime minister Neville Chamberlain, only now Davies worked on behalf of Stalin instead of Hitler.[41]

With men like Davies and Hopkins advising him, Truman reverted to Roosevelt's approach to the Soviet Union. He would change only if and when Stalin's provocations became impossible to overlook, as indeed soon happened with a combination of events in Poland, and even more in Iran and Turkey.

STALIN'S HARD LINE IN POLAND (SPRING–SUMMER 1945)

After the beginning of 1945, the Soviet leader became slightly bolder about arranging the postwar political map of Eastern Europe. In February he told the NKVD to "eliminate the irregular situation" in Poland by tracking down the leaders of the opposition parties.[42] They were lured out of hiding by Red Army officials, who told them of the "absolute necessity and crucial importance" of talks with Soviet authorities. The army commander in the area near Warsaw personally vouched for their safety and promised to fly them to London for consultations with the exiled Polish government.

It was a lie. On March 26 and 27, the top sixteen underground political figures were arrested. The group included General Leopold Okulicki (commander in chief of the Home Army) and the deputy prime minister (of the Polish government-in-exile), Dr. Jan Stanisław Jankowski.[43] They were among the leaders of the 1944 Warsaw Uprising, who had gone over to resisting the Soviet occupation in some places after the retreat of the Nazis. Stalin wanted to remove these influential proponents of a democratic Poland.[44]

The Allies and the Polish government-in-exile asked Moscow what had happened to the missing Poles, but the Soviet vice-commissar for foreign affairs scoffed at rumors of any skullduggery. Then on April 21 the Soviet Union went ahead with its plans and signed a friendship pact with the Communist-dominated Provisional Government of Poland that tied the two countries together for twenty years. This fait accompli was presented to the world on the eve of the United Nations founding meeting in San Francisco.

At the big UN event in San Francisco on May 3, in response to yet another query from his allies, Commissar Molotov casually informed Secretary of State Stettinius and Foreign Secretary Eden that indeed the Polish leaders had been arrested and would be put on trial in Moscow. This shocking admission demonstrated what Soviet-led reconciliation meant.

Inside the State Department there was consternation, all the more so as the experts were convinced that the Soviet government was violating the Yalta agreements in Austria, Bulgaria, Hungary, Romania, Yugoslavia, and Czechoslovakia. What would happen in Germany was still up in the air, and the prognosis not good.[45]

In Moscow, Stalin directed proceedings against the captured Polish leaders. He was informed of their interrogations and worked on the indictments, just as he had for the big show trials in the 1930s. He wanted the accused put through a similar staged event in Moscow's House of Trade Unions. The defendants were charged with involvement in underground activities in the western regions of Ukraine and Byelorussia, as well as Lithuania and Poland. They were said to have organized an "illegal army" and, following orders from the émigré government in London, carried out subversive and "terrorist acts" against Soviet occupation forces.[46]

At this very moment, when the Polish leaders were being interrogated down the street, presidential envoy Harry Hopkins was confiding his concerns to Stalin about the recent deterioration in Soviet-American relations. What was happening in Poland to non-Communist political parties, he said, was indicative of how other nations in the Soviet occupation area were being treated. "American public opinion" was reacting negatively, and the president felt some changes were needed "to find a common basis to go forward."[47]

Instead of answering, Stalin had "several disturbing questions" of his own in regard to the United States. He emphasized that American attitudes to his country "had perceptibly cooled once it became obvious that Germany was defeated," and it seemed almost "as though the Americans were saying that the Russians were no longer needed." What stuck in his craw was that Lend-Lease had been ended without notice. Nor did he appreciate U.S. meddling in Polish affairs or putting France on the postwar commission that was to determine war reparations and allocate them. That "looked like an attempt to humiliate the Russians," he said, and he accused Hopkins of hiding behind American public opinion to divert attention from the real source of the objections, namely the Truman administration.[48]

Over the next several days, the weary and unwell Hopkins tried to set the record straight and break through a number of roadblocks, above all on the Polish question. Stalin would not concede a thing, and in his usual style, he said that if there were infringements on freedom of speech in Poland, then they were needed "for security reasons." If not all political parties could compete in elections there, surely, he said, that was the case as well in the United States and Britain, where the fascists were barred from participating. If the Soviet Union acted on its own instead of in concert with its allies, it was compelled to do so by circumstances.

Stalin was the master negotiator, tireless, shrewd, and with deep knowledge that he could use as needed. When he met with less prominent persons, such as Hopkins, he completely dominated them with his grasp of the issues, down to the minute details. Anyone reading his exchanges will realize immediately that it was the height of folly for Presidents Roosevelt and Truman to have dreamed of negotiating alone with him.

Hopkins ran up against Stalin's techniques at an evening session on May 30. Finally the beleaguered envoy confessed that "rightly or wrongly there was a strong feeling among the American people that the Soviet Union wished to dominate Poland." President Truman, Hopkins said, was prepared to accept that the "Lublin Poles" (that is, the Communists) would have the majority in any new provisional Polish government, but he wanted additional persons to be represented in the discussions. Appallingly, Hopkins admitted that the United States "had no interest in seeing anyone connected with the present Polish government in London involved in the new Provisional Government of Poland." Personally, he did not "believe that the British had any such ideas" either. That statement not only spelled the doom of the London Poles; it sealed the political fate of the millions they represented. In retrospect, this capitulation to the Soviet Union shows the weakness of the American stance.[49]

Little wonder that Stalin promptly agreed to have a few non-Communist Poles on the Tripartite Commission, which since February had been sitting in Moscow, working on the shape of a new Polish government and trying to broaden its democratic basis. Hopkins reported excitedly to Washington that in accepting these (insignificant) changes, Stalin was once again carrying out the Yalta agreements.[50]

Truman was positively delighted or at least relieved that he had something to show for standing up to the Soviets and calling on them to live up to their agreements. He confided in his diary on June 7, after Hopkins had returned, that the Russians had "always been our friends and I can't see why they shouldn't always be."[51]

Stalin won American support by agreeing to allow three representatives from the "London Poles" into the discussions, including the head of the Polish government-in-exile, Stanisław Mikołajczyk, who traveled to Moscow. There on June 17, the first day the Polish representatives spoke among themselves, Mikołajczyk made himself instantly unpopular by claiming that a Communist leader like Bolesław Bierut would never be accepted as president by democratic forces in their country. It did not matter what he said. A disappointed Mikołajczyk and the rest of the new government flew back to Warsaw on June 27—appropriately enough, he wrote later—on Russian transport planes. The Provisional Government of National Unity was proclaimed the next day, and though formally a coalition of parties, it was controlled by the Communists.[52]

On July 5 the United States officially recognized the new Poland, and at Truman's request, the British followed suit. Nevertheless, Stalin let the show trial of the sixteen Polish opposition leaders take its course that month. Hopkins had tried to dissuade him from that but managed only to get a feeble gesture from Stalin that the accused would be treated "leniently." Mikołajczyk again pleaded for their release before he left for Warsaw, but Molotov replied only that any "objective judge" would find the proceedings "fair." The judges sitting before General Okulicki gave him ten years in prison and Jankowski eight; neither survived their stay in custody. The others received lighter sentences.[53]

The entire episode represented another victory for the Communists. Stalin was already distributing spoils to the victors, promising Marshal Rokossovsky that he would soon be made Poland's minister of defense. This was the very leader of the Red Army who in 1944—as far as Polish non-Communists were concerned—had stood idly by on the opposite bank of the Vistula River while the Nazis finished off the Warsaw Uprising. Finally, in 1949 Rokossovsky was not only given the portfolio he coveted but was also made Poland's deputy prime minister.[54]

TURKEY AND IRAN

At the end of the war, thanks to the victories of the Red Army, Stalin set out to redraw the map of the world.[55] His underlying assumption was that the rivalries among the imperialists, especially Great Britain and the United States, would continue and would degenerate into squabbles over colonial spoils. In the meantime, the Soviet Union would, "through a mix of diplomacy and force, become a socialist world power."[56]

Although what the USSR might do in Europe was then a major concern of the West, Soviet energies also spilled over the border into

Turkey and Iran and soon into Asia. Moscow's ambitions in regard to Turkey, until 1923 the Ottoman Empire, went back generations. Most recently, in the Crimean War in the mid-nineteenth century, Britain and France had intervened to help the Turks defeat Imperial Russia. In 1936 the Montreux Convention had settled the touchy issue of the neutrality of the Dardanelles, the narrow Turkish strait where the Black Sea flows into the Mediterranean. It was agreed that this waterway would be open to Soviet warships and that Turkey could close it during wartime or if it felt threatened. As a native of Transcaucasia, Stalin was well acquainted with the political and cultural struggles in that region, and at the Tehran Conference (1943) he pleaded for revision of this treaty, which in effect kept the USSR bottled up in the Black Sea. In May 1944, partly to put pressure on Turkey and also to clarify postwar ethnic relations in the border region with that country, Moscow ordered the deportation of 183,135 Turks from the Crimea and in September a further 69,869 from Georgia.[57]

In the summer months prior to the Potsdam Conference (to meet July–August 1945), Stalin pursued a number of initiatives in Turkey, and on June 7 he instructed Molotov to press on in his discussions with the visiting Turkish ambassador.[58] The assertive commissar demanded the renunciation of the Montreux Convention. In addition, he wanted an agreement for the USSR to build military bases on the strait for its and Turkey's "joint defense." For good measure, he sought the return of disputed territories, such as Kars, Ardahan, and Turkish Armenia. The goal was to remove Turkey "as an independent player between the British Empire and the Soviet Union."[59]

Amazingly enough, the Turkish government managed to elude these high-handed tactics, and while in no position to defeat the massive Red Army, it was able to keep the Soviets at bay in 1945. Armenians hoped Stalin would encourage their repatriation from Turkish Armenia to join their brothers and sisters across the border in the USSR. However, the ethnic emotions he fostered among his own Armenians and Georgians led them to make conflicting nationalist claims to the same parts of Turkey. That December those ambitions and rumors of war fueled nationalist demonstrations in Turkey. Stalin was unwilling to push as far as some of his local paladins wanted, and in February 1946 the Kremlin, instead of invading, tried yet again to talk the Turks into submission. It was too late, for by that time the climate of world opinion was tilting decisively against Soviet ambitions. Hence Stalin's letter to Molotov on November 20 in which he said that "the time was not yet ripe" for a clash with Turkey. Thereafter, tensions on that front eased somewhat.[60]

Conditions in northern Iran looked more promising. The USSR and Iran shared a border that stretched for some 1,250 miles. Moreover, the people in the Azerbaijan Soviet Socialist Republic, with its capital in oil-rich Baku, spoke the same language as and shared the Islamic religion of their brothers and sisters across the frontier in northern Iran's Azerbaijan. At least some of those living on the Iranian side felt a kinship with their brethren and looked admiringly at life in the USSR, in spite of the terror that had torn through it over the years.

Moreover, the Red Army was physically present in Iran, because since late August 1941, and by agreement among the Allies and the Iranian government, Soviet forces occupied the northern part of that country, while the British did the same in the far larger area around Tehran and the south. They were there to keep the oil from the Germans and to secure the crucial supply lines from the West, across Iran into the Soviet Union. All parties understood that the troops would be withdrawn within six months of war's end. Britain, not the United States, exercised predominant influence in Iran, and like the Soviet Union, it sought to capitalize on the wartime situation to obtain oil concessions, in a rivalry that went back well before 1914. The United States was no less interested in the oil, and especially after it extended Lend-Lease aid to Iran in March 1942, American troops and civilians took up residence as well.

With the Western Allies preoccupied in France, where troops landed in June 1944 to defeat Germany, on September 25 that year the Soviet Union pressed its demands on Iran for a large area in the north to be set aside for Soviet-Iranian oil exploration.[61] When the Iranians dithered and held out, the secretary of the Communist Party in Soviet Azerbaijan, Mir Jafar Bagirov, approached the Kremlin and suggested that he organize separatist movements over the border into northern Iran and create a new Democratic Party there. On July 6, 1945, Stalin gave the go-ahead. The Politburo told Bagirov to establish in Tabriz (capital of Iranian Azerbaijan) "a group of responsible workers to guide the separatist movement" and to prepare elections using slogans from

Stalin's playbook. The peasants should be promised lands taken from state holdings and large landowners, and workers should be told that the new government would end unemployment and begin economic development.[62]

As it happened, Bagirov was no ordinary party functionary. Although he consciously mimicked Stalin's ruling style, he was more ostentatiously cruel, self-indulgent, and despotic. In the late 1930s he used terror to eliminate a long list of "enemies," from personal rivals, to those in the Party who questioned anything he did, to peasants who doubted the modernizing aspects of the regime or its collectivization drive. The deaths of tens of thousands were on his hands as he led a bloodstained rampage that, among other things, wiped out the cultural elite of Soviet Azerbaijan.[63]

In mid-1945 this character was peering over the border into northern Iran and no doubt relishing the prospect that a regime like his own could be established there. Iran already had a small Communist movement, led by the Tudeh, or People's, Party, and though it had some support, Stalin was cold to its call for a national revolution. He ignored it, perhaps because he thought it would be too ambitious for Communists to aim for all of Iran, an aspiration that would run up against British and American objections. Instead he limited the action to the north of the country. The Kremlin ordered the new Democratic Party of Azerbaijan (DPA), under longtime Communist activist Seyid Jafar Pishavari, to establish "friendship societies," to spread the word, and to form armed combat groups, all generously financed from Moscow.[64]

Although some historians suggest that Stalin was mainly interested in getting oil concessions, the far-reaching orders he issued sound as if he was ready to exploit the moment for all it was worth.[65] Britain and the United States were a little concerned about what Moscow was up to, and they asked for Stalin's reassurance at Potsdam in August 1945 that the Red Army would, as promised, withdraw from Iran in six months. In fact, the Kremlin promptly became more directly involved in fomenting armed insurrection in the region. Besides supplying arms and money, by early November the Soviets were sending in special operations agents to organize armed insurgents, and when Tehran ordered its army to bring order in Tabriz, the Red Army intervened. Quite apart from anything Moscow might have ordered, Pishavari showed great initiative and by

year's end had established DPA control. The USSR backed his seces-
sionist movement and also the smaller one of the Iranian Kurds, in the
short-lived Republic of Kurdistan.

To solve the continuing crisis in the north of Iran, a new prime
minister, seventy-six-year-old Ahmad Qavam al-Salana, traveled to the
Soviet capital for talks that began on February 19, 1946. Stalin and Molotov claimed to want only more self-rule for Azerbaijan and oil concessions, but in either case Moscow would be largely left to control the
area. The negotiations with Qavam carried on so long that on March
2 the deadline came and went for the withdrawal of the Red Army, as
promised most recently at Potsdam.

Instead of pulling out the 60,000 or so soldiers still in Iran, Stalin
sent in another 15,000. The U.S. vice-consul in Tabriz reported in early
March that Soviet troop movements looked more like "a full-scale combat deployment."[66] Secretary of States James F. Byrnes sent a note of
inquiry to Molotov on March 8 to ask about Soviet intentions.[67] At the
same time there were anti-Soviet demonstrations in Tehran. Within a
week Bagirov, Moscow's intermediary in northern Iran, told Pishavari
and the other leaders that the Red Army would likely be leaving soon,
even though in Tehran the government half-expected the Soviets to
march on the capital.[68] The Americans suggested that Iran take the matter to the UN, where hearings were scheduled for March 25.

On that day the Soviet news agency TASS suddenly announced that
the Red Army had begun its withdrawal on March 2 and that it would
be completed within two months.[69] For years there has been mention
of a "Truman ultimatum" to the Soviet Union to force it out, but the
most recent research has turned up no evidence.[70] The reasons behind
Stalin's about-face are still debated, and no doubt a combination of factors came into play. By early 1946 international tensions had increased
dramatically because in London and Washington some thought that the
Soviet Union was intent on moving into northern Iran and would do so
unless it met determined opposition. In March the battleship *Missouri*
was already steaming toward the eastern Mediterranean to support
Turkey's resistance to Soviet demands. The "March crisis" in northern
Iran evaporated because Stalin did not want to force the issue, particularly once the United States became more heavily involved. On March
24, Ivan Sadchikov, the new Soviet ambassador to Iran, managed to
wrest an agreement from Qavam for the creation of an Iranian-Soviet

oil company, in which most shares would go to Moscow. That concession, it was thought, might make it possible to exert political influence without pushing separatism in Azerbaijan and without continuing the confrontation with the West.[71]

Of course Stalin put a far different gloss on the exit of the Red Army. On May 8 he explained his thinking in a long letter to crestfallen Comrade Pishavari. In it he claimed that there was no revolutionary situation in the country and that if Soviet forces had stayed there, it would have "undercut the basis of our liberationist policies in Europe and Asia." If the Red Army could have remained, or so he said, why could the West not hold on where it wanted around the globe? "So we decided to pull our troops out of Iran and China, in order to grab this weapon from the hands of the British and the Americans and unleash a movement of liberation in colonies that would render our policy of liberation more justified and efficient." His advice to Pishavari was to moderate his stance, support Qavam, and win recognition for what he had been able to accomplish until then.[72]

As it happened, by December Iran's central government asserted control over the north. Stalin expressly ordered Pishavari and his comrades to cease armed resistance, Tabriz was soon captured, and the Democrats were put down violently.[73] Even the Soviet deal for oil concessions fell through in 1947, for by the end of the year the Iranian assembly (Majlis) in Tehran was confident enough to refuse its ratification. Qavam was dismissed, and the Communists (Tudeh) were forced out of the assembly.

Iran represented one of the more spectacular illustrations of what the Soviet Union apparently had in mind around its borders. Getting into northern Iran, so the thinking went, would allow the Kremlin to use it as a platform to extend influence into the rest of the country.[74] All three outside powers wanted access to the oil, but what emerged from the crisis was the growing determination of the United States to stand up to the far-reaching ambitions of Stalin and his disciples.[75]

In spite of all the issues that loomed ahead, in the summer of 1945 President Truman very much wanted the Soviet Union in the fight against Japan, and it was to secure Stalin's decision on that score that he and Prime Minister Churchill met with him at Potsdam. They also hoped to work out terms for a just and lasting peace. Certainly Stalin had long held doubts that it would be possible to attain anything of the kind. As we have seen, at the very moment the United States and Britain recognized the new Poland, he set out to establish facts on the ground in Turkey and Iran. Nevertheless, he would go to Potsdam and meet with those he regarded as inveterate "imperialist enemies" to see what could be achieved.

CHAPTER 9

Potsdam, the Bomb, and Asia

The Potsdam Conference dragged on from July 17 to August 2, 1945, and was the longest of the Allied wartime meetings. Although the leaders had every reason to celebrate victory, there was little personal warmth among them. The shame of it was that in spite of all the talking, the West largely conceded Soviet domination of Eastern Europe. Winston Churchill was there, mostly trying to prevent the worst, and when he lost the elections back home, Labour Party leader Clement Attlee arrived to take over. President Truman was in far over his head. Stalin, however, was in his element and pressed his political agenda as far as possible. For the same reason, he agreed to join the war against Japan, and the Red Army carried the mission deep into Asia.[1]

EXPECTATIONS AND SURPRISES IN POTSDAM

Potsdam brought Stalin and Truman face-to-face for the first time. The president, in his down-home style, was looking forward to meeting "Mr. Russia" and "Mr. Great Britain." He was guided by a faith that most people saw life and politics much the way he did and that such problems as arose generally came down to misunderstandings. Once people got to know one another, he reasoned, they would see that even the most complicated issues could be solved. In this way Truman's belief in personal diplomacy was every bit as firm, and perhaps as misplaced, as Roosevelt's had been.[2] Neither of them could imagine the unbridgeable gulf in experiences and expectations that divided them from Stalin and the Communist USSR.

Churchill and Truman arrived on July 15 ready to begin the next day, but Stalin was late, on purpose to inflate his importance. Truman used the time to visit Berlin. Such was Germany's defeat and utter collapse that he gave no thought to security, driving around the burned-out city with Secretary of State Byrnes in an open convertible. He wrote his wife that "this is a hell of a place—ruined, dirty, smelly, forlorn people, bedraggled, hangdog look about them."[3] He saw what he called a great world tragedy, with "old men, old women, young women, children from tots to teens carrying packs, pushing carts, pulling carts, evidently ejected by the conquerors and carrying what they could of their belongings to nowhere in particular."[4]

Stalin still thought of himself as a revolutionary, as he had done in the 1920s and 1930s. He rode to Berlin, however, in the style of the tsars. On July 2, head of the NKVD Beria reported to him that all security preparations had been made. Travel would be by train from Moscow, over a distance calculated at no less than 1,195 miles. Beria was proud to say there would be "between six and fifteen men" posted for each and every mile. He listed in loving detail all the security steps that were taken and the elaborate provisioning that would be provided on the way to and at the Big Three conference.[5]

The train station in Potsdam was cleared of people when Stalin, the military victor, arrived, much like an ancient conqueror, with no public announcements or crowds. He was out to make history and needed no applauding masses, much less to be reminded of the human suffering all around. He had not the slightest interest in touring the defeated capital. It suited his ascetic tastes to have the lush carpets and fancy furniture removed from his quarters.[6]

On July 17 he met Truman informally for a brief chat and begged forgiveness for his tardiness. He said he had been negotiating with the Chinese—which was true. What he managed on that front was to get them to accept the concessions granted the Soviet Union at Yalta. It was crucial that the Chinese agree to the Red Army's march on their country and Manchuria in the war to come against Japan. Stalin immediately pledged to Truman that the Soviet Union would enter the war in mid-August.[7]

Stalin has left little evidence of his thoughts during most of these gatherings; he wrote no diary; he never confided much to those in his delegation or let his true emotions show. Throughout, however, he conveyed a sense that the Western powers were out to rob the Soviet Union of its victory. To follow Marshal Zhukov, the Soviets were yet more cynical. Zhukov wrote in his (later uncensored) memoirs that they felt Churchill and Truman "more than ever demonstrated their desire to capitalize on the defeat of Nazi Germany to strengthen their position and dominate the world."[8]

Truman's attitude was sunny and accommodating, as can be gathered from the fact that he brought along none other than Joseph Davies, the former ambassador who favored appeasing the Soviet Union. In a letter to his wife after the first day's meetings at Potsdam, the president was pleased to have been made chairman of the conference, though he found the role tricky. "Anyway a start has been made and I've gotten what I came for—Stalin goes to war on August 15 with no strings on it." That would mean, he wrote, that "we'll end the war a year sooner now, and think of the kids who won't be killed! That is the important thing."[9] In his diary he added: "I can deal with Stalin. He is honest—but smart as hell."[10]

A new factor was about to intrude into the discussions and into world history, for the first successful atomic test took place at Alamogordo, New Mexico, on July 16 at 5:29 in the morning (1:29 afternoon time in Potsdam). A brief coded message had reached Secretary of War Stimson at 7:30 that evening, and he had rushed over to inform the president.[11] Therefore Truman knew about the success of the bomb, albeit with no details, before he first met Stalin the next day, but he did not mention it. The president, who very much looked forward to ensuring the support of the USSR in the war against Japan, did not want to say anything that might be cause for Soviet concern. The two leaders agreed that Japan would likely fold soon; the president confided to his diary that it most certainly would "when Manhattan"—that is, the atomic bomb—"appears over their homeland. I shall inform Stalin about it at opportune time."[12] Churchill, who was given the latest news by Stimson, was decidedly against sharing the information.[13]

The fifth session of the conference on July 21 has been examined minutely because at 11:35 that morning Stimson received an important memorandum. It described, with frightening exactitude, the measurable effects of the first successful full-scale atomic bomb test. The words made the horror of its destructive power somewhat imaginable. The secretary read the report aloud to Truman and Byrnes. "The president was tremendously pepped up by it" and said "it gave him an entirely new feeling of confidence."[14] Historians have pointed to these reactions and ascribed a variety of ulterior motives to the president for wanting to use the bomb, including most recently his "personal dislike of the Japanese emperor."[15] Granted, Truman viewed the bomb coldly, and numerous writers have since been troubled by that attitude.

Meanwhile events on July 21 at Potsdam continued as if nothing of great significance had happened. The conference turned to the thorny issue of Poland's western frontier; thousands of Poles already had moved into (formerly) eastern Germany. Truman observed that Yalta had agreed to the occupation of Germany by four powers, but that now "it appears another occupying government" had been given a zone. Although he concurred with Stalin on the principle of compensating Poland in the west for what it lost in the east to the Soviet Union, he objected to Germany's being sliced off in strips. How would the diminished country ever pay the reparations demanded by Stalin?

The president claimed that Poles were in effect taking over formerly German lands. He asked Stalin where the nine million or so former German residents (of the new Poland and new Czechoslovakia) were living. He knew they had either fled for their lives or been forced out. According to Churchill, Poland was claiming "vastly more territory than she gave up" in the east, and he refused to "concede that such an extravagant movement of populations should occur." All the while behind the scenes, Stalin had egged on the Poles and the Czechs to oust the hated minority. The British worried about being faced with countries in chaos.[16]

Truman thought the border question between Poland and Germany should be settled at a later peace conference. Stalin was craftier and brazenly pronounced the issue already decided. He agreed that the land "vacated" in the east was once part of Germany as it existed in 1937 (before expansion) but maintained that, since the native population had left and new inhabitants moved in, the area was now Polish.[17]

Churchill said that while the Allies had agreed to compensation for Poland, that did not give it the right "to create a catastrophic situation in Germany's food supply." Stalin's straight-faced rebuttal was that Germany could buy its food from the Poles. That remark left Truman wondering what would be left of that country, given how much it was losing in the east and with France wanting the Saar and Ruhr areas.

"The Poles," he said, "have no right to seize this territory now and take it out of the peace settlement. Are we going to maintain occupied zones until the peace or are we going to give Germany away piece-meal?"[18]

Truman closed the session on a combative note, which changed nothing: "I shall state frankly what I think. I cannot consent to the removal of formerly eastern Germany from contributing to the economy of the whole of Germany." The expulsions of the Germans, Stalin retorted, were already under way and, moreover, had the advantage of further weakening their defeated enemy. Churchill answered that nevertheless he did not want to be confronted with "a mass of starving people."[19]

At the next session and undaunted as usual in the face of criticism, Stalin returned to the question of the Polish-German border. He wanted it to follow the Oder River and the western Neisse River in the south. There had been consensus at Tehran that the frontier should extend to the Oder River, which runs north from Czechoslovakia and drains into the Baltic Sea. The River Neisse had been mentioned, but it was left unclear whether reference was being made to the Eastern (Glatzer) or Western (Lausitzer) Neisse, both of which flow north to south and drain into the Oder. Stalin wanted to shift the boundary line westward as far as possible to Germany's disadvantage, and that was what he eventually got. The difference was no mere quibble, because it meant that Germany would lose the great riches of the Silesian industrial area.

President Roosevelt and Prime Minister Churchill had already agreed in principle to give the city and district of Königsberg, East Prussia, to the Soviet Union, presumably as compensation for its suffering. They accepted Stalin's spurious claim that he needed an ice-free port. In fact, the Soviets already had three such ports, and ancient Königsberg is well inland and prone to icing. At Potsdam neither Truman nor Churchill raised objections, even though that city, the hometown of the great Immanuel Kant, was as German as Berlin, and even though handing it over violated principles enunciated in the Atlantic Charter. Nothing was said about what might have happened to the former inhabitants of the city, or of East Prussia, which would soon become part of Poland.[20] Stalin brushed aside Churchill's objections about the Polish-German border, and Truman added only that the peace conference would look into the area's "technical and ethnic details."[21]

ATOMIC BOMB AND "IRON FENCE"

The conference moved on to other questions when the Big Three returned to the table on July 24. Stalin argued that if Italy had been recognized and was on the way to being accepted into the United Nations, then the same should happen with Romania, Bulgaria, Hungary, and Finland. The president supported Churchill, who objected that, while Italy was in the process of becoming a democracy, that was not true of the states in Eastern Europe. "An iron fence has come down around them," the prime minister said, to which Stalin broke in to retort: "All fairy tales."[22]

At the end of the session, there occurred one of those rare moments where we can see history at a crossroads. Truman approached Stalin with news about the bomb. The president later recalled casually mentioning "that we had a new weapon of unusual destructive force." He described the reaction he got: "The Russian premier showed no special interest. All he said was that he was glad to hear it, and hoped we would make 'good use of it against the Japanese.' "[23] Churchill stood not five paces away, knew the exchange was potentially "momentous," and afterward, waiting outside, asked what had happened. The president replied, "He never asked a question."[24]

Another witness, Soviet ambassador Andrei Gromyko, recalled that Stalin had said only "thank you for the information." The ambassador observed in his memoirs that the president "stood there probably waiting for some other kind of response, but none came." That statement suggests Truman looked as though he expected one or more questions.[25] Secretary Byrnes remembered being "surprised" that even the next day Stalin still did not ask for additional information.[26]

We do not know how much Truman intended to reveal about the bomb, and perhaps he did not know himself. The Kremlin Boss could easily have changed his tone, pointed out how many millions of Soviets had died for the war, and demanded frank and open discussions. Even though he had some information about the bomb from his spies, at that critical juncture, however, he had nothing to say. Maybe Stalin was too much of an ideologue to admit that with the new weapon, the capitalists had regained the momentum in the war of ideas with the Soviet Union.[27] Or maybe he was shrewd enough to see a need to neutralize the advantage Truman hoped to wield. Until that moment, history seemed to be with him and the Red Army; they took full credit for stopping Hitler, reaped gains across Eastern Europe, were still making progress in Turkey and Iran, and were poised to pursue the Soviet dream in Asia.

Once Truman told him about the bomb, Stalin turned in expressionless silence and left. The Soviet dictator jumped to the conclusion that the bomb was meant to intimidate him as much as to beat Japan.[28] When he returned to his quarters, he mentioned the conversation to Molotov, who was overheard saying, "They are raising the price." Stalin replied, "Let them. We'll talk with Kurchatov and get him to speed things up."[29]

Igor Kurchatov was the head of the Soviet atomic project. It had made considerable progress itself, and by December 1944 Stalin had been persuaded to devote more resources to the project and to put it under NKVD boss Beria.[30] Did he recognize the political significance of the bomb when Truman told him about it? Probably no one really did until they saw the pictures, but he knew enough to telephone Beria and rake him over the coals, as if the NKVD were to blame that the USSR did not yet have an atomic bomb of its own.[31]

Andrei Gromyko then came in and heard Stalin say that "probably Washington and London now hope we will not soon be able to devise such a bomb. In the meantime Britain and the United States will try to take advantage of the U.S. monopoly to impose their plans on Europe and the wider world. Well, this is not going to happen!"[32]

Once the bomb was dropped on Japan, Stalin drastically accelerated the program. On August 20, having had enough time to evaluate its impact, he set up a new committee to take charge of all matters pertaining to atomic energy. Thus began the incredibly expensive nuclear arms race that persisted right up to the collapse of the Soviet Union.[33]

In January 1946 Stalin met with Kurchatov to encourage him to pull out all the stops and not spare any costs. That was at a time when the country was in desperate straits, with hunger in the air and famine around the corner. Scientists were promised the richest personal rewards.[34] By August 29, 1949, thanks partly to information supplied by spies inside the Manhattan Project, the Soviet Union succeeded in detonating a first atomic bomb. By 1950 the Central Intelligence Agency estimated that the Soviet project was employing between 330,000 and 460,000 people, from gifted scientists to Gulag slave laborers.[35]

Another significant outcome of the Potsdam Conference was the temporary settlement of the Polish-German frontier among the foreign ministers. American secretary of state James Byrnes conceded to Molotov on July 29 that the territory up to the Oder and the Western Neisse "shall be under the administration of the Polish State."[36] This was a clear win for Stalin. After supporting the concept of population "transfers" for so long, it was rather late for the West to begin expressing "moral scruples" about the movement of millions and to object that the "economic integrity" of the defeated nation was being undermined. Stalin disputed everything, but his main point was that the Germans were already gone from the eastern part of their former lands. That was a half-truth, for millions remained, and those who had fled were beginning to return. To help iron out the "fairness" issue, representatives of the new Polish government were invited to the conference, and they came with well-honed arguments.

In his diary, Truman called what Poland got nothing less than a "land grab."[37] Although the official conference communiqué stated that the "final delimitation" of the border "should await the peace settlement," no such treaty was ever drawn up or signed. Only after unification in 1990 did the reunited Germany finally accept those borders.

If Stalin had gotten his way, the outcome for Germany would have been worse again. On July 21 the Soviets had floated the idea of putting the Ruhr, the nation's industrial heartland, under the international control of the three Potsdam powers plus France. Ten days later the Kremlin Boss returned to the topic, and although he granted that they had all changed their minds about dismembering the country, he wondered aloud whether the Ruhr was "to remain part of Germany." Here was a last push to carve Germany up even further, but a subtle one. In any case, the new British foreign secretary, Ernest Bevin, said he could make no decision on the issue without the presence of the French—and they had never been invited. Truman stated as definitively as anyone could that "the Ruhr is part of Germany and is under the jurisdiction of the Control Council."[38]

If West Germany had lost control over its western industrial heartland, the economic impact certainly would have been crippling. As for the political impact, Stalin had already indicated that the Soviets were unlikely to give up any territory already in their possession. At the very least, the consequences of having the Soviet Communists in the heart of Europe would have opened any number of roadblocks to the development of democracy.

THE RED ARMY AGAINST JAPAN

When Truman went to Potsdam, he carried with him a prepared statement advising the Japanese of the hopelessness of their situation and demanding an end to the war. That document became the basis for the Potsdam Declaration, issued on July 26 by Truman, along with Prime Minister Churchill and in the name of China's head of government, Chiang Kai-shek. The declaration read: "We call upon the government of Japan to proclaim now the unconditional surrender of all Japanese armed forces, and to provide proper and adequate assurances of their good faith in such action. The alternative for Japan is prompt and utter destruction."[39]

The Americans did not consult Stalin about the declaration. They were not required to do so, since the USSR was not yet in that war. On July 29 the Soviet Boss reported ill and unable to make the day's events. Molotov, in a brief conversation with Truman, reported that Stalin thought it best for his allies to call on the Soviet Union to join the war in the Far East, and the president said he would think that over.[40] Stalin's request almost certainly stood as a rebuke. Still, Truman seemed blithely unaware that he might have upset the aging dictator. When he wrote home at the end of that day, the president joked with his wife about how he looked forward to "winding up this brawl" and going home, and he admitted candidly: "I like Stalin. He is straightforward. Knows what he wants and will compromise when he can't get it."[41]

For years historians have made a great deal of the demand for Japan's unconditional surrender. Some have contended that Truman and Byrnes insisted on it, knowing full well that the Japanese would refuse.[42] In turn, the Americans would supposedly be handed an excuse to use the atomic bomb; simultaneously, they would have the wherewithal to end the war, give the United States revenge for Pearl Harbor, and intimidate the Soviet Union.[43] There are numerous problems with that interpretation, not the least that U.S. intelligence intercepts of Japanese government communications revealed that it was not close to accepting the terms of surrender, even if the Allies were prepared to waive the issue of the emperor.[44]

More important, the demand for unconditional surrender went back to 1943 and was a cornerstone of the alliance. The slightest hint of tampering with it threw Stalin into a rage. And rage he had in the spring of 1945, when high-level SS officers had contacted the Western Allies in Bern, Switzerland, in an attempt to reach some sort of compromise peace. Suspicion of softness toward the enemy had led to Stalin's last eruption of anger at FDR.

The Soviet leader brought to Potsdam his own document that called for Japan's unconditional surrender. Although it went undelivered when his allies' declaration was issued instead, his demands were harsher and said nothing about what might happen to Japanese prisoners of war. Nor was the American position on unconditional surrender fixed from the start. Instead, inside the U.S. government in May and June, there had been some discussion about moderating the terms of surrender so as to permit the emperor to remain. These initiatives went nowhere, mainly because the Japanese government did so little to foster any hope of success.[45] Secretary Stimson belatedly suggested to Byrnes (July 16) and Truman (July 24) that the declaration mention that the emperor could remain and that the Soviets were about to enter the war. Even if this concession and threat had been in the final proposal, which they were not, the Japanese were unlikely to surrender.

In Western eyes, Stalin never appeared enthusiastic about entering the war against Japan. When in 1944 the Americans and British informed him of their planning for the final assault on Japan, he seemed to say it was fine with him if they wanted to finish off the war in the Far East on their own. The British and American missions in Moscow had been trying for a year to get joint planning sessions going, and it was the Red Army that had been slow to respond.[46] In fact, however, Soviet planning was in high gear, and Stalin did not want to inform the West.

At Potsdam he assured the Allies of Red Army cooperation, as the Soviets demanded all kinds of supplies from the West. However, he offered little in return, such as when the Americans sought permission to construct new airports in the Far East of the USSR for use against Japan. The USSR dragged its feet for so long that finally the U.S. Joint Chiefs of Staff decided on alternatives.

In April 1945, Stalin had put Marshal Aleksandr Vasilevsky in charge of operations in the Far East. Once the Red Army's battles against Hitler came to an end, the arduous task of transferring large numbers of troops began. The commanders of this effort later said they ensured not just the military preparedness of the troops but their schooling "in Soviet patriotism and proletarian internationalism."[47] By the time the vast operation was launched, more than 1.6 million Red Army troops were in position.

On June 27, after a nightlong meeting, Stalin had accepted the final strategic plan. He kept this knowledge to himself at Potsdam a month later. The goals were astoundingly bold, all the more so as they had been formulated after the costly war against Hitler. The Red Army would have to fight and move over vast distances to liberate Manchuria, take southern Sakhalin Island, launch amphibious operations against the Kurile Islands, and with luck finally land on Hokkaido Island in Japan itself. Stalin advanced the date to August 11. Moreover, while he was at Potsdam and even before his first meeting with Truman, he called Vasilevsky, in the hope they could move the date up by another ten days. He accepted that that was impossible because all the forces and supplies would not be in place, but he kept checking to see if the offensive could begin sooner.

Stalin was even more secretive than usual about the attack on Japan, not even telling Commissar of the Navy Nikolai Kuznetsov, who was with him at Potsdam, just when operations would be launched. Here was the head of Soviet naval forces, yet all he recalled was having a hunch that the war in the Far East would start soon. He heard the date for the first time when the big event was announced on the radio.[48]

Once back in Moscow, Stalin learned early in the morning of August 6 that the first atomic bomb had been dropped on Hiroshima the day before. We do not know exactly how he reacted, but he was not the sort to be emotionally "devastated" or "crushed."[49] Instead, he kept to his routine, with the attack against the Japanese going ahead more or less as planned. As might be expected, he called Vasilevsky in the east on August 7 to get him to move up the attack by two full days. Stalin did not explain the latest change.[50] When Vasilevsky called from his command post on the eve of the massive invasion to report his forces' readiness, he was told that the leader could not be disturbed and to call back later. The Generalissimo was watching a movie, a thought that gave Vasilevsky a great chuckle.[51]

On August 8 at five P.M., when Japanese ambassador Naotake Sato visited the Foreign Commissariat in Moscow to continue exploring ways of finding peace without conceding to unconditional surrender, Molotov read him a declaration of war. The Red Army attack was scheduled to begin on August 9, which in Manchuria was only an hour later. On that same day, eleven hours later still, the United States dropped an atomic bomb on Nagasaki. The following day Emperor Hirohito said he was prepared to accept the terms of surrender, with the one reservation that his role be preserved. The Western Allies quickly agreed among themselves that this was less than unconditional surrender and waited for the Soviet response.[52]

The atomic bomb forced Stalin to take steps sooner than he might have wished in order to get the maximum out of the war in the Far East. At two o'clock in the morning on August 11, Molotov called in the British and American ambassadors. He read them a statement whereby the Soviet Union associated itself with the Americans' negative response to Japan. He then added that if and when the Japanese surrendered, the Allies should agree "on the candidacy or candidacies of the Allied High Command to which the Japanese Emperor and Japanese Government are to be subordinated." Molotov thought that two Allied supreme commanders might be ideal, perhaps MacArthur and Vasilevsky.

On hearing this statement, Ambassador Harriman became "fighting mad." He pointed out that the United States had borne the brunt of the Pacific War for four years and that the Soviet Union had been in it for two days. Therefore it was unthinkable and unjust for anyone but an American to be made the supreme commander in Japan. Molotov said he would have to consult with Stalin and indeed soon called to say that the word "candidacies" should be removed from the Soviet reply.[53]

This seemingly minor war of words was of considerable importance because the Soviet Union was attempting to assert its influence on postwar Japan. On this occasion Ambassador Harriman headed off what he called another "land grab." Otherwise, the Soviets might well have tried to occupy Hokkaido and thereby extend their zone of occupation to mainland Japan.[54]

All this time the Japanese government was shockingly dilatory in ending the fighting and thereby allowed the senseless fighting to continue. The government had signaled on August 10 that it was prepared to surrender, but it was indecisive. To make matters worse, on August 12, it executed eight U.S. airmen who had been captured. Three days later it executed another eight. On the night of August 14, in the heat of hatreds that had been simmering already for years, the U.S. Army Air Forces launched a devastating thousand-bomber raid on Tokyo.[55]

On that very night young Japanese military officers, intent on carrying on the war, attempted a coup d'état. They had support in the government and the army, but key figures bowed to the emperor's will, and the revolt collapsed. The attempt itself suggests that military morale was not as broken as often assumed. Even after two atomic bombs, the continuation of American conventional bombing, Soviet entry into the war, and the Red Army's startling military successes, there were still factions in the Japanese army that were not prepared to surrender.[56]

The Soviet war against Japan must rank among the most remarkable in all of history. It began on August 9 and ended with a cease-fire of sorts after only ten days, though fighting carried on until September 3. In that short time, the Red Army's "August Storm" offensive tore through Manchuria, where it faced the Kwantung Army, considered the "most prestigious and powerful force the Japanese army fielded."[57] The attack was along a front of more than three thousand miles, so it was highly mechanized, with plenty of air and naval support. It crossed deserts, major rivers, and mountains. The Red Army put into practice the ultimate blitzkrieg, with a highly successful strategy that incorporated everything it had learned in the war against Germany.[58]

Invigorated by events in Manchuria, Marshal Vasilevsky sent troops, on August 10, to take southern Sakhalin Island, as planned, with the goal of continuing from there due south toward Japan. Five days later, Vasilevsky launched another attack through the Kurile Islands, beginning in the north and moving southwestward. These islands had been promised to the Soviet Union at Yalta. There was ambiguity, however, for it had not been specified how much of the island chain was covered by the agreement. The chain comprises more than fifty islands in all, and the last ones fade into Japanese Hokkaido. Although not everything went like clockwork for the Red Army, overall the success was remarkable.[59]

Finally, on August 15, Hirohito broadcast his acceptance of terms laid out by the Allies in the Potsdam Declaration. Inexplicably, it was only on August 18 that Japan's Imperial General Headquarters issued an order to "suspend all operational tasks and stop all hostilities." Although a cease-fire was called the next day, some Japanese troops continued fighting. The Red Army took advantage of the confusion and, often ignoring the truce, shot enemy emissaries sent out to negotiate.[60]

Stalin grew anxious when President Truman on August 15 issued General Order No. 1, which set out how the Japanese forces were to surrender, and to whom, in the entire Pacific theater. The president sent a copy to the Kremlin, with a note to the effect that the order was necessary, even though it would not "prejudice the final peace settlement."[61]

Stalin agreed and shrewdly added that at Yalta the Soviet Union was promised all the Kurile Islands and that unless the Red Army occupied part of Japan, public opinion in his country would be outraged.[62] Truman accepted the first claim, which was false, but he was adamant that the USSR would not have an occupation zone in Japan. Moreover, the president asked for an air base, for commercial reasons, on one of the Kurile Islands.[63] Stalin feigned anger and said that there would be no American base.[64] But what was really at stake was how far he was willing to push his claims. In spite of having his army and navy take all necessary steps preparatory to an invasion of Hokkaido, on August 22 he decided to call off the landing. All the same, he ordered Vasilevsky to seize the key cities of Port Arthur and Darien in Manchuria.[65]

The Red Army also advanced into Korea, which Japan had taken as a colony in 1910. Stalin ordered his troops to stop at the 38th parallel, as specified by Truman's General Order No. 1. Evidently he did so to avoid further conflict because there were no American forces on the ground there. It was also true that Moscow had only two infantry divisions in Korea, though more would soon arrive.[66]

The occupation authorities in the North and South generally created systems in their own image. The United States helped into power seventy-year-old Syngman Rhee, an American-educated exile and committed anti-Communist. The Red Army installed Kim Il Sung, who for a decade had been a member of the Chinese Communist Party. He was an established figure in the resistance against the Japanese when in 1942 he came under Soviet influence and was drafted. He emerged from the war an officer of the Red Army and a committed Stalinist. Although no one would have guessed it, the time bomb was already set for the Korean War, which would explode five years later.[67]

The Red Army carried Stalin's ambitions on its shoulders as it swept over the Kurile Islands. In spite of complaining to Truman, the Soviet forces "took back" more territory from Japan than Japan had ever seized from Imperial Russia. Although most of the fighting stopped, additional

Red Army skirmishes continued right up to September 2 and Japan's formal surrender aboard the battleship *Missouri*.[68]

Debate continues to rage over whether the atomic bombs were necessary. One Japanese study plausibly suggests that Hiroshima and Nagasaki would not have been enough, because "the Japanese military would have still argued for the continuation of the war even after the dropping of a third bomb, and even a fourth bomb."[69] On the other hand, it is necessary to disentangle the specific effects of the two bombs and the Soviet attack.[70] Stalin might have tipped the scales by ordering the Red Army into action, thereby destroying the hopes of the "peace party" in Japan that was trying to have him mediate a settlement short of unconditional surrender. The Soviet decision undermined the "war party" as well, because now the entire world was ranged against Japan.

What was Stalin attempting to gain in Asia? Opinions vary. A recent account suggests that he "was driven by geopolitical interests. Ideology or revolutionary zeal played little part in this campaign."[71] Although it was true that Stalin wanted to obtain territories lost in wars with Japan, it would be a mistake to underestimate the political and missionary aspects of the war in the Far East.

Of course it was never just "all Stalin." Millions shared his ideas, above all in the Communist Party and in the Red Army. Marshal Vasilevsky, for example, who commanded these operations against Japan, reflected what many in his country thought. He wrote with pride that "the result of the defeat of Japan created favorable conditions for the people's revolution in China, North Korea and Vietnam." He added that in August 1945, Mao Zedong was correct to say that "the Red Army came to assist the Chinese people in expelling the aggressors. This invaluable event had no parallel in Chinese history." Vasilevsky said the Soviet Red Army turned over huge stockpiles of Japanese arms to Communist Chinese forces and contributed to the coming of the revolution.[72]

Also illuminating are the views of Marshal Kirill Meretskov, commander of the First Far Eastern Army Group that invaded through Manchuria and went on to Korea. His remarks were representative of those who condemned the United States for starting the Cold War.[73] According to Meretskov, the bomb was meant mainly to intimidate the Soviet Union "and the world," and its use showed that "the U.S. elite was already considering the establishment of its world domination."[74]

As Meretskov's testimony suggests, the Red Army embodied Stalin's view of the world and the ideology he propounded. In September, the Soviet dictator spoke in celebration of the great victory. He emphasized how they had put down Japan, another fascist-imperialist power that was comparable to Nazi Germany, spoke of righting past wrongs done by Japan, and looked to the future. As in all his messages and speeches at war's end, he said nothing whatsoever about any political ambitions, much less about wanting to foster revolution or to spread the Communist faith, for such revelations would have been completely out of character. Even in a moment of glory, he guarded against disclosing his agenda to the world at large.[75]

Stalin weighed the risks that his policies might alarm the United States and Great Britain. Even though he wanted the Red Army to be part of the occupation of Japan, he deferred when such action seemed to be too upsetting to his allies. For the same reason, he signed a Sino-Soviet Treaty of Friendship and Mutual Assistance with the Kuomintang (KMT) leader Chiang Kai-shek (Jiang Jieshi) on August 14, a step regarded by Communist Mao Zedong as a betrayal. The Chinese Communist Party had been founded in 1921 under the auspices of Moscow and the Comintern. Nevertheless, Stalin preferred to work with the KMT as a partner, considering it the major power, able to defeat the warlords, unify the country, and thereby "unintentionally" prepare China for Communism.[76] While convinced that the Chinese Communists were not ready militarily or politically to enter the contest for power, Stalin by no means gave up his vision of their eventual revolution, which in fact would arrive far sooner than he anticipated.[77]

In the meantime the USSR exploited the labor of between 1.6 and 1.7 million Japanese prisoners of war. It put these men to work in factories and on construction sites until they were too sick to continue.[78] Their repatriation was dragged out for years, and 300,000 are still unaccounted for. Prisoners were subjected to years of "re-education" and forced to learn Communist doctrine.[79]

The Red crusade in Asia was taken up by indigenous revolutionaries, many of whose leaders had spent time in Moscow and experienced Stalin's influence at first hand. These political movements and the cultures in which they flourished were so diverse that they eluded control from a single center. They took their own bloody paths to realizing the dreams of the millennium, often helped along by funding and advice from Moscow.

Closer to home, Stalin's immediate postwar agenda was to settle accounts with all those who had sided with the Hitlerite invaders or wavered in their loyalties. This retribution was not just revenge seeking but was deemed necessary to secure the home front of the motherland, as Soviet forces crossed the western border, heading for Berlin and carrying the Red cause with them as far as possible.

CHAPTER 10

Soviet Retribution and Postwar Trials

Soviet Communist leaders were convinced, more than ever after their great victory at Stalingrad in early 1943, that it would soon be possible to grow the Red Empire over the USSR's prewar borders. To be sure, Stalin found it disconcerting that large numbers of his own troops had not shown staying power early in the war and had been taken prisoner. In addition, some civilians and whole ethnic groups had collaborated with the German occupation. As Soviet forces began chasing out the invaders and setting their sights on Berlin, the dictator was determined to settle accounts with all these "enemies within" as a necessary prerequisite to the Red Army's campaign that would bring Communism deep into Europe. Soviet retribution became bloodier than anywhere else, and for millions of people it constituted a grim chapter in the coming Cold War, usually overlooked in studies of the East-West conflict.

As it happened, the Soviet decision to deal with collaborators and turncoats dovetailed with Western concerns, going back to 1942, about atrocities committed behind the lines by the German invaders and their allies. The exiled Polish and Czech governments had pressed the United States and Great Britain to warn the Germans of retribution in hopes of deterring further mayhem against the civilian population. As the evidence of Nazi mass crimes began to leak out, however, word also spread of Soviet misdeeds. Pressured by this flood of revelations, Stalin ultimately went along, and yet the political aims of Soviet retribution bore little resemblance to what Roosevelt and Churchill had in mind.

SOVIET AND ALLIED PROSECUTION OF WAR CRIMES

In June 1942, on a visit to Washington, Prime Minister Churchill had mentioned his desire to set up an Allied commission to deal with atrocities. Following up on these remarks, Harry Hopkins, under FDR's direction, composed a memorandum that became the basis of Churchill's proposal to the British War Cabinet on July 1 to create a United Nations (that is, an Allied) commission that would collect material on the crimes and the perpetrators. The British called for input from all the exiled governments in London. On July 30 representatives of these governments also went to FDR with a long list of German misdeeds. In response, on August 21 the president issued a vaguely worded warning to the Axis powers that he intended "to make appropriate use" of all evidence of the "barbaric crimes of the invaders, in Europe and Asia," in "courts of law." Great Britain did not, however, want a repeat of the failed efforts that had been made after the First World War to bring to court those who were accused of war crimes.

The British House of Lords now suggested the Allies proceed by creating a fact-finding commission and asked Foreign Secretary Eden to sound out all relevant governments. On October 3 he set out to do just that. President Roosevelt's response had insisted on strong language, and on October 7 the British and Americans announced they were establishing a United Nations War Crimes Commission. Although in a joint statement they said their intention was to mete out "just and sure punishment" to the "ringleaders responsible for the organized murder of thousands of innocent persons," it was not clear what the UN commission would do beyond fact-finding.[1]

Eden received no response from the Soviet Union or China. Instead, on October 14, the Kremlin issued a detailed statement about the "monstrous atrocities" being perpetrated by the invaders, and on November 2 it announced its own Extraordinary State Commission for the Establishment and Investigation of the Crimes of the Fascist German Invaders and Their Accomplices (Chrezvychainaia gosudarstsvennaia komissiia, or ChGK). This new body, whose workings were soon fine-tuned by Stalin, was led by prominent public persons and intellectuals. Interestingly, its reports were intended mainly to influence the politics in Allied countries and less for use in the Soviet Union.[2]

On December 17 the United States, Britain, and the USSR, along with nine European exile governments, condemned German authorities for "now carrying into effect Hitler's oft-repeated intention to exterminate the Jewish people in Europe." The announcement reaffirmed the Allied resolve "to insure that those responsible for these crimes shall not escape retribution."[3]

As we have seen, in 1943 the reality of wartime massacres entered the public domain in April when the Nazis began publishing evidence they found of the mass graves of Polish officers at Katyń. The Soviet atrocities commission (ChGK) was still getting organized, but the political ramifications of Katyń and the need for an urgent response energized it.[4]

When the stories were published on April 13, Propaganda Minister Joseph Goebbels in Berlin was delighted at the resonance the findings had in Germany and abroad.[5] Only six days later the pressure to counterbalance the news about Katyń could be seen in a new Soviet edict, again checked through by Stalin, that promised harsher punishments for Nazi "criminals and their local hirelings." In May the Germans came across more mass graves, this time nearly 10,000 corpses in Vinnytsia (Ukraine), and in the following months publicized those as well.[6] It was generally accepted in the West that these mass murders were indeed the work of the Soviet secret police, though in the wartime circumstances the atrocities were quietly overlooked or put aside.

Moscow's April decree on war crimes stipulated that the accused would face a public court-martial, with punishment either by public hanging or banishment and tsarist-style hard labor (*katorga*) for fifteen to twenty years.[7] Three trials followed in Krasnodar, Mariupol, and Krasnodon. Most of the accused were Soviet citizens, but a total of forty-six Germans were also indicted, twelve of whom were eventually executed.[8]

On July 14 the first of these events opened in Krasnodar. The eleven accused Soviets faced a show trial of the kind well practiced in the 1930s. Thus the "legal" task of the proceedings was to demonstrate guilt and apportion punishment. Eight of the eleven were sentenced to execution, and a crowd estimated at 30,000 gathered for the hanging.[9] Stalin's edict stated that "the corpses were to be left on the gallows for several days."

In December 1943 another such event was staged in Kharkov (today

Kharkiv, Ukraine). The case was noteworthy for indicting three Germans as well as one local collaborator. The four accused were clearly "small fry" (two lower-ranking officers and a corporal) chosen to represent branches of the occupation, along with one Russian accomplice. The trial followed the usual script, complete with the overeager confessions of the accused. According to the verdict, they were responsible for shooting, hanging, or poisoning in gas vans no fewer than "30,000 peaceful and completely innocent citizens."[10] There was silence on the fact that most of the victims of these atrocities were Jews.

The Kharkov trial itself was widely publicized, complete with a full-length documentary film, *The Trial Goes On,* which revealed the stark evidence of mass murder. The public execution of the guilty in the town's square was watched by a cheering crowd of 50,000.[11] Washington and London were disquieted, though not because of legal scruples about the trials. Rather they were worried about how Hitler might retaliate against their own POWs in German hands. The United States and Britain did not ask that such events be stopped, and Moscow said they would continue, but in fact there were no more until after the war.[12]

The Soviets also drew criticism for refusing to sign on to the UN War Crimes Commission, officially in existence since October 20, 1943. However, the foreign ministers achieved a degree of concord at the tripartite conference held in Moscow at about the same time (October 19–30). That meeting issued the Moscow Declaration, in the name of Britain, the United States, and the Soviet Union, as well as thirty-two other nations. The signatories sternly warned Germany that when the armistice arrived, the accused offenders "will be brought back to the scene of their crimes and judged on the spot by the peoples whom they have outraged."[13]

Stalin, Roosevelt, and Churchill were unresolved about what to do with the top leaders, though the Soviet dictator briefly broached the topic at the Tehran Conference in late 1943. The Big Three leaned toward summary executions. Stalin suggested over dinner on November 29 that unless effective means were adopted, Germany would rise again in fifteen or twenty years. Then he suggested that such an event could be preempted if the Allies "physically executed" 50,000 or perhaps 100,000 leaders of the German armed forces. He also thought that the victorious powers should retain control over the "strategic points in the world and if Germany moved a muscle she could be rapidly stopped."

Roosevelt, somewhat taken aback by the scale of the executions proposed by Stalin, jokingly wondered whether the number might be set at "49,000 or more." FDR's son Elliott, who was there that evening, joked about raising the number to 49,500.[14]

Churchill objected vigorously to "the cold-blooded execution of soldiers who had fought for their country." He felt that anyone charged with "barbarous acts" should be judged according to the Moscow Declaration that all three leaders had just signed. Although the record does not mention it, Churchill was so upset that evening that he got up to leave, but was chased down by a jovial Stalin, who said that he was only joking. The prime minister returned to the table but later recalled thinking that the dictator was testing the waters.[15]

In early 1945 at Yalta, FDR, in private conversation with Stalin, brought up the topic of dealing with war criminals and asked him whether "he would again propose a toast to the execution of 50,000 officers of the German army." The Soviet leader ducked the question, because by then he had changed his mind about executions and wanted a major show trial of the kind his minions had already perfected.[16]

In any event, after Yalta the decision about the major war criminals was given to the foreign secretaries to consider, and deeper discussions of the legal implications continued within and among the three administrations. They agreed on holding major war criminals responsible before an international military tribunal, but the principal remaining difference was that Moscow wanted show trials to demonstrate the "self-evident guilt" of the accused and to apportion punishment. Nevertheless, the Americans and British succeeded in getting a process that was consistent with their legal traditions, in which the accused was regarded as innocent until proven guilty. The long negotiations culminated on August 8, 1945, when Allied representatives signed the charter for an international military tribunal. The trials of selected major war criminals went ahead at the Nuremberg Military Tribunal later that year, with more to follow.[17]

The Soviet Union tried on its own a total of 55,000 lesser-known Germans and Austrians accused of war crimes and found 25,921 of them guilty. Caution is advised about these numbers; we do not know how many suspect persons were shot out of hand or died in custody.[18] Only eighteen cases involving 224 defendants were tried in public. Most of the accused were prisoners of war. In addition, inside the POW camps thousands of enemy "wreckers" were tried and convicted, with the last of them leaving the USSR only in 1956.

RETRIBUTION AGAINST SOVIET COLLABORATORS

There were savage acts of retribution all across Europe as it was liberated from the Nazis and Fascists. What happened in the Soviet Union was both bloodier and far more sweeping than anywhere else. Right from the start of the war in 1941, the regime had introduced martial law to impose order in areas in or near the fighting. Military tribunals and courts-martial could try members of the armed forces and ordinary citizens individually or collectively and could banish anyone deemed "socially dangerous" or suspect on any grounds. Most accused Soviet citizens were charged under the Criminal Code, Article 58–1a on "counter-revolutionary activity," with the latter term given a wide definition. The accused were allowed no more than a single day to prepare a defense and had no right of appeal. During the next year the situation on the battlefront worsened, so that on June 24, 1942, a new decree sharpened punishments by threatening family members of anyone found guilty of working for the Germans. They could be sentenced to a minimum of five years' hard labor. As the Red Army pushed occupation forces out of the USSR that year, an estimated 16,000 Soviet citizens went before tribunals on charges of "betraying the motherland."[19]

Between 1941 and 1954, a total of 333,065 "civilian collaborators" were charged under Article 58–1a of the Criminal Code and another 36,065 under an April 1943 decree. These accused included mainly those involved in the administration or police, but not the million or so men who Russian scholars estimate donned the uniform of the invaders, either because they volunteered in order to strike at the Soviet system, or because, as POWs, they were all but forced to sign on with the Wehrmacht.

Elsewhere in Europe, the nature and extent of the postwar retribution varied greatly. In some countries the purge was initially bloody, as it was in France with around 9,000 summary executions, but then it subsided. In Norway fewer were killed, but a higher proportion of the population was adversely affected in some way.[20] Strangely enough, and even if prosecutions outside Europe are included, far more non-German collaborators were tried than Germans and Austrians who went to court on war-related charges—a total of 329,159, with 96,798 of them found guilty.[21]

Soviet tribunals during the war found a relatively "modest" 5 percent guilty and executed. That number fell to one percent or so when peace came. These figures from the Central Procurator's Office do not reflect the whole story; some years are missing, and additional trials were held before other judicial bodies. Evidence shows that not just select individuals but whole villages were executed for supporting the invaders.[22]

Inside the Soviet Union, as the Germans were driven out, the incoming NKVD arrested tens of thousands, variously described as spies, saboteurs, German supporters, or "gangs." Although not all of them went to court, the experience of NKVD custody and questioning was punishment in itself.[23] Beria reported to Stalin at the end of 1943 that as the Red Army went through, special units had "cleaned up" behind the lines and, for that year alone, had detained 582,515 uniformed persons, and in addition 349,034 civilians. They ranged from deserters to "gangsters and marauders," or those without proper papers. Thousands more died in armed struggles.[24]

Moscow had been infuriated when in 1941 major cities had been overrun and occupied by the Germans. Even worse, from the Kremlin's perspective, some local officials of the Communist Party disobeyed orders to get out, and some not only collaborated with the occupation but ostentatiously burned their membership cards. Although it is impossible to say exactly how many collaborated, the numbers were vast. The regime publicized its determination to pursue as many as possible.

How communities responded to the collaborators in the postwar period varied from place to place. In Rostov, a key city on the Don River, the Party had ordered all its members to leave when the Germans approached, but many stayed. The city reported to Moscow that in the period ending in September 1945, 11,429 party members had failed to evacuate, and 7,124 were expelled on various grounds. When it came to professionals who stayed, the authorities were circumspect. For example, close to 90 percent of the higher education administration and nearly 50 percent of the teachers remained behind German lines, and it was as bad or worse among other branches of the civil service. Although party officials recommended that they be thrown out, there were few qualified candidates to replace them. Moreover, and in spite of the anticollaborator rhetoric, one of Rostov's Communist first secretaries said in May 1946 that many leaders were inclined to hold on to collaborators who "are afraid and are thus very agreeable, quiet, and always trying to please their boss."[25]

How much the treatment of collaborators varied can be seen in the Donbas (Ukraine), where one woman felt the immediate sting of Soviet retribution when she was liberated. She said that the Red Army "did not return with a feeling of guilt toward the population," whom they had let down in the war, "but as judges." Girls and women suspected of sleeping with the enemy were immediate targets. In Kramatorsk and other cities in Ukraine, for example, the NKVD not only shot women for fraternizing with the Germans but killed children born of the relationships as well. There were all kinds of summary executions, and no records have been found detailing how many there were.[26] Even some of the virtuous were chastised, like a woman who convinced the Germans not to take all the provisions from her village. If they had done so, the children and the weak would have starved. The NKVD interrogator came down hard on her for not letting the invaders take everything because "then the people would have hardened their attitudes."[27]

In another village the story was similar. One letter that made it through the censor from a wife to her husband at the front told of how the locals had fed the hungry Red Army troops when they arrived. She was shocked that they hanged the village elder, "because he served the Germans, they said. But it was his own village people he served; he helped the orphans. But they paid no heed. They came with a half-tonner, grabbed him, and took him away. No matter how the people tried to stand up for him, it did no good." All around back home, so the letter continued, it was a horror story. People were being tracked down in the woods. "So you see we are living in great fear now. You never know which will kill you first, our troops or the hunger."[28]

Soviet retribution punished not only suspected collaborators but also their families, whose only hope was to prove to a tribunal that they had aided the Soviet forces or resisted in some way. Otherwise, those living in the dwelling at the time of the alleged crime, or collaborative act, were subject to deportation for a period of five years.[29]

Later in life Molotov was asked why, since the 1930s, the regime had adopted the practice of "isolating" (which is to say, deporting) the family members of those who were "repressed." He thought the reasons were self-evident. If steps had not been taken, he said, these people "would have fostered complaints and contributed to a general demoralization. Those are facts."[30]

It was in keeping with such an approach that Beria wrote to Stalin on August 18, 1944, about the small Caucasus spa towns Pyatigorsk, Kislovodsk, Zheleznovodsk, and Essentuki in the Stavropol district. Still living there, he said, were "the families of active German collaborators and traitors who have been convicted or voluntarily departed with the Nazi occupiers." He wanted permission for the NKVD "to purge these cities by relocating 850 family members." All would be sent to Novosibirsk by the beginning of September. Given this kind of thinking and procedure, it would mean that the number of people who became caught up in the Soviet retribution was likely far greater than usually reported.[31]

REPATRIATING SOVIET POWS AND CIVILIANS

The ruthlessness of Soviet retribution in all aspects of life was evident in Stalin's attitude toward officers of the Red Army who had "allowed" themselves to be taken prisoner. He branded them as traitors, and according to the notorious Order 00270, generals and other officials, including those in the NKVD, were subject to the death penalty. Even their relatives could be imprisoned, and Stalin made no exception when it came to his own family. When his son Yakov was captured, his wife was arrested; she was released two years later, only after Stalin was satisfied that his son had not betrayed the motherland.[32]

The Germans treated Soviet POWs worse than animals, and an appalling 3.3 million "died in captivity," while others were exploited until the war ended.[33] In addition, when invaders arrived, they forced or recruited millions of Soviet civilian workers for jobs in the Third Reich. As of August 1944, there were 2.1 million such *Ostarbeiter*, or eastern workers (out of a grand total of 5.7 million from all over Europe) on site inside Germany.[34] For Stalin, these workers were as treacherous as Red Army soldiers who had "allowed themselves" to be encircled and captured.

Of great symbolic importance was the mythic figure of General Andrei A. Vlasov, a highly decorated Red Army commander: a veteran officer serving since the civil war, holder of the prestigious Order of Lenin, and a member of the Communist Party. Captured by the Wehrmacht in July 1942, he soon revealed his anti-Stalinist sentiments, and some Germans hoped to use him to spearhead a Russian liberation movement. The top Nazi brass had their doubts, though by early 1945 they allowed Vlasov to form two divisions mostly from Soviet POWs. The Red Army captured him near Prague on May 12 with some of his troops and sent him to Moscow. On August 2, 1946, newspapers announced that he and eleven others had been found guilty of espionage and terrorist activity and executed. In Soviet parlance, accusing someone of being a Vlasovite was even worse than calling them a fascist.[35]

Soviet citizens fighting for Hitler, however, constituted a larger problem than just the two divisions of Vlasovites, a fact that became evident to the Western Allies after the Normandy landings in mid-1944. As they began capturing more prisoners, some were identified as "Russians" who had served in the Wehrmacht, the Waffen-SS, or other branches. Indeed, many "foreigners" (*Ausländer*) fought in some capacity on Germany's side, but it is impossible to say exactly how many, since inflated numbers are often given. As a rule, however, Hitler and Himmler did not welcome Slavs in the ranks. Most non-Germans in the Wehrmacht came from Western Europe—such as the Netherlands and Belgium, Alsace and Lorraine, or the Baltic states.[36]

According to the Geneva Conventions, the uniforms soldiers wore at the time of their capture determined the country to which they should be repatriated. Britain thought otherwise, and already on July 17, 1944, the War Cabinet decided, at Moscow's request, that it would send back all Soviet citizens captured as German soldiers, even if such POWs faced severe treatment or execution.[37] Foreign Secretary Eden reinforced the point in an August memorandum to Churchill, in which he noted that the men were caught firing on Allied troops, so there was no room for sentimentality. When Churchill and Eden traveled to Moscow in October to discuss the postwar settlement, they also worked out the notorious "percentages deal" on spheres of influence. After dinner at the British embassy, Stalin unexpectedly mentioned Soviet prisoners (in German uniform) who were in British camps. He wanted them back, and Eden, while agreeing, used the moment to ask for help to facilitate the return of British POWs found in German camps. The Kremlin Boss was pleased to do so, and to assuage any British pangs of conscience, he said that even though some of those Soviets might be "rascals," they would not be harshly treated.[38] In fact, they were doomed.

In Britain, when Soviet POWs learned they were to be repatriated, some despaired, and a few took their own lives. In the months ahead, suicide would become a common response. All resistance and protests were ignored, and by October 31, only weeks after Churchill and Eden returned from Moscow, the first transport left Britain for Murmansk. In total during the war, 10,000 of these soldiers traveled back on British ships to an uncertain future in the USSR.[39]

In the United States, partly because it wanted to follow the Geneva Conventions, the fate of Soviet citizens who had fought for Hitler was more complex. German prisoners taken in North Africa, and later in the landings in France, were sent to the United States. By year's end American camps already held 400,000 German POWs, around one percent of whom were regarded as "Russian."[40]

The American and British military missions in Moscow approached the Red Army General Staff on June 11, 1944, to discuss the POWs but received little cooperation. The Americans went ahead and gave their "Russian" prisoners the clumsy label "German prisoners of Soviet origin."[41] The United States adopted the procedure of asking all POWs what citizenship they claimed and did so without informing them of possible consequences. By December, Secretary of State Hull formalized this "claimant policy."[42]

In the early autumn, Andrei Gromyko, the Soviet ambassador in Washington, began to raise questions about these "Russian" prisoners, once stories about them had appeared in the press. The ambassador told the State Department that such POWs had not really fought for the Wehrmacht. He maintained that they had worked behind the lines as drivers or doctors or had been coerced into going along. The assumption underlying this official position was that no one raised in the Soviet Union could possibly oppose Stalin and Communism. The Americans found it convenient to accept this fiction.

Even though General Eisenhower would have preferred that such POWs volunteer to be repatriated, he was prepared to follow the British example. The U.S. Joint Chiefs of Staff agreed, and President Roosevelt was also persuaded. By December 1944 the Americans began sending POWs back to the Soviet Union. Included were also persons described as having "Slavic names who disclaim Soviet nationality." For example, in early 1945 a group of 1,100 were turned over to Soviet authorities on the west coast for a return voyage to the motherland that they did not want.[43] Thus well before the Yalta Conference (February 1945), the

Western Allies were returning Soviet prisoners in German uniform to the USSR.

At Yalta, General John R. Deane, the head of the U.S. military mission in Moscow, was assigned to work with the Soviet military on a proposal to deal with the exchange of liberated POWs and civilians. The general was not optimistic about Soviet cooperation, for he had waited a full six months to get a response to his request for a meeting. The Red Army, in the meantime, had prepared an agreement and presented it for Deane's signature at Yalta. It formalized existing practices, according to which "the contracting parties shall, wherever necessary, use all practicable means to ensure" the evacuation of each country's nationals and send them home.[44]

Although the agreement made no specific mention of compulsory repatriation, it was implied. And in practice, both the United States and Great Britain were already acting as if they were obliged to return all uniformed or civilian citizens of the Soviet Union—with the exception of important defectors. No thought was given to granting political asylum. The British outdid themselves by turning over "White Russian" émigrés—that is, anti-Bolsheviks who had fought Lenin and Co. and had never been Soviet citizens at all.[45]

Ambassador Averell Harriman recalled that at the time they were concerned about the estimated 75,000 British and American POWs whom the Soviets might soon liberate from German camps: "We had no idea that hundreds of thousands of the Soviet citizens would refuse because they had reason to suspect they would be sent to their deaths or to Beria's prison camps. That knowledge came later."[46] In fact, the Americans and British knew what would likely happen, and Soviet POWs certainly suspected the worst. U.S. newspapers reported on their protests and suicides at the prospect of being sent back to the USSR.[47]

For all the cooperation Moscow received with the repatriation of the millions of Soviet POWs and civilians, it was both slow and disorganized in handling liberated American POWs. Some of them waited around in Poland, where ordinary people gave them "the kindest treatment" and shared the little food they had. Several miraculously hitchhiked all the way to Moscow and made it to the American embassy.[48] Becoming ever more aware of the chaos facing the liberated POWs, General Deane and Ambassador Harriman asked the president to intervene. On March 3, FDR cabled Stalin asking permission for U.S. planes to fly in medical supplies to compatriots stranded east of Soviet lines and to evacuate the sick. He received a polite but firm no. Such flights were allegedly not needed; the men were in good care.[49]

The president was given contrary information and tried again on March 17. This time the Kremlin Boss noted that, whereas Americans in the care of the Red Army were being well looked after, the same could not be said of Soviet prisoners in American camps—they "were subjected to unfair treatment and unlawful inconveniences up to beating as it was reported to the American Government more than once." The upshot was that the United States was not permitted to pick up its liberated prisoners, some of whom were shipped in boxcars hundreds of miles south to Odessa and generally neglected. General Deane asked for permission to visit Poland to see for himself but was refused.[50]

He observed that, when the two sides worked as allies, the Soviets were invariably mistrustful, bureaucratic, and uncooperative. "During the entire course of the reciprocal repatriation program," Deane writes, "the Soviet authorities, including Stalin, Molotov, and others, poured forth a continuous stream of accusations regarding the treatment which Soviet citizens were receiving at the hands of the United States forces which had liberated them. In almost all cases these accusations were proved false and were admitted to be unfounded by Soviet representatives."[51]

Stalin's accusations bewildered and saddened FDR. Harriman realized that the Soviets were playing politics with the POW matter and on March 24 advised standing up to them. Stalin and Molotov, he said, were clearly lying about the good treatment accorded American servicemen, and something had to be done about it. Harriman urged the president and secretary of state to complain about the situation immediately.[52] This time the president said nothing, though we should note that he was terribly weakened physically and had only a little over a week to live.

Between 1944 and 1949, a total of 5.45 million Soviet citizens from all countries—including POWs and civilians—were repatriated to the Soviet Union, whether they wanted to be or not. Some tried to travel home on their own, but the Kremlin's aim was to process them all through "filtration camps" where specially trained NKVD personnel interrogated them.[53] Having to endure the long and horrific process was bad, with the outcome uncertain.

Various figures are cited in the literature as to the fate of all these men and women, though without reference to archival or other reliable sources.[54] However, a more thorough recent investigation concludes that three million, or 57 percent, of all repatriates suffered some form of additional "repression," including being sent to the Gulag, subjected to forced labor, remobilized into the armed forces, or executed.[55] We know more about the 1.8 million POWs who went through the harrowing experience of filtration camps, and in total only 300,000 (16.7 percent) were "sent home" and presumably spared further punishment. Another 300,000 or so were "given over to the NKVD," while about the same number had to serve in a labor battalion. The remaining 900,000 had to reenlist in the army, and while being compelled to do so might not sound like "repression," such soldiers were given the most dangerous duties and dirtiest jobs. They and the repatriates carried a stigma and were also subject to special police actions in the late 1940s and again in 1951.[56] Moreover, "even those not mobilized or subjected to criminal penalties suffered discrimination thereafter, in many cases to the end of their lives."[57]

TRANSFORMING MURDERED JEWS INTO ORDINARY NAZI VICTIMS

In the course of the postwar Soviet trials, mention of what the Germans had done to the Jews was sometimes made. The Krasnodar case involved members of SS Sonderkommando 10a. Charges included "executing arrests, going on military searches and expeditions against the partisans and peaceful Soviet citizens, and exterminating Soviet citizens by hanging, mass shootings, and use of poison gases." The prosecution brought out the systematic nature of these murders but neglected to mention the cardinal fact that the overwhelming majority of the victims were Jews.[58]

Did Stalin suppress the news about the Holocaust? The dictator's latent anti-Semitism seemed to emerge increasingly during the war. From the outset of the German invasion, he was aware that Jews were being singled out for murder, but he said nothing about it. In his lengthy message of November 6, 1941, on the twenty-fourth anniversary of the Russian Revolution, he quoted Hitler as saying that to establish the new German Reich they would "above all things force out and exterminate the Slavonic nations—the Russians, Poles, Czechs, Slovaks, Bulgarians,

Ukrainians, Byelorussians." Stalin made no mention of the many dire threats Hitler issued against the Jews. The Soviet leader denounced the "Hitlerite party" as "a Party of medieval reaction and Black-Hundred pogroms." Otherwise in this speech nothing more was said about what was happening to the Jews. Remarkably enough, this sparse mention of "pogroms" was the last time Stalin even came close to saying anything about the fate of the Jews publicly during the entire war, in spite of how well informed Soviet authorities were of what the Germans were doing.[59]

Commissar Molotov sent four notes to foreign countries between 1941 and 1943, reporting the terrible crimes and atrocities committed by the occupation forces in the Soviet Union. In only one of these did he allude to how the Germans were killing "unarmed defenseless Jewish working people."[60] The emphasis in all four notes, which were also published in the Soviet press, was invariably to underline Nazi victimization of "Soviet citizens," Red Army prisoners of war, and the deportation of Soviet people to slave labor in Germany. Most commonly, the Kremlin highlighted Nazi eradication policies but without mentioning the Jews or any other nationality.[61]

On December 17, 1942, the World Jewish Congress finally succeeded in getting the United States, Great Britain, and exiled European governments to issue a denunciation of the "extermination of the Jewish population of Europe."[62] Moscow signed on as well but the next day provided a clarification that there were similar murderous plans for "a considerable part of the civilian population in German-occupied territories, innocent people of different nationalities, different social status, various convictions and beliefs, people of all ages."[63] The Soviets were not alone in backtracking from the specificity and scope of the crimes against the Jews. A *New York Times* front-page story in early 1943 spoke about the possible fate of "some peoples" to come. In fact, the mass murder was well under way.[64]

Stalin set the party line on May 1, when he said that Soviet citizens were being deported to Germany for enslavement and were victims of "extermination by the Hitlerite beasts." On November 6 he made reference to the murder of "hundreds of thousands of our peaceful people."[65] Remarkably, that was one of the very last times he said anything at all about the victims of Nazism. An exception came during a March 1946 interview, when he estimated the total number of all Soviet deaths in the war. He gave it as 7 million, when it was more than three times larger than that.[66]

During the war, Soviet newspapers provided enough information for anyone to find out more of the truth about the Jews.[67] Even if it was not official policy to bury the stories, they tended to fade from sight.

Using the pre-1939 borders of the USSR, an estimated 1 million Soviet Jews lost their lives during the war. They are counted among the total of all civilians and members of the armed forces killed in the war. An additional number of Soviet Jews died in Stalin's labor camps and prisons; millions of other citizens of the USSR were also killed or perished at the hands of Soviet authorities.[68]

A glaring example of the Soviet suppression of information about the specific suffering of the Jews pertained to the murder of 33,000 of Kiev's Jews in September 1941 at Babi Yar.[69] The Soviet atrocities commission (ChGK) reported (correctly) that its investigation showed that in reprisal for sabotage in Kiev, the Germans had "called all Jews together, brought them to Babi Yar, and killed them there." Stalin changed the story to read that "thousands of peaceful Soviet citizens" had been murdered. The trial of fifteen accused killers for Babi Yar in January 1946 heard testimony about a Himmler order to exterminate all the Jews, but in the prosecutor's closing summary, the phrase was changed to an order to kill "Soviet citizens, Ukrainians."[70] Thousands of people jammed the square for the public hanging of the twelve Germans who were convicted.

The Soviet government sought to track Nazi crimes during the war and used the Jewish Anti-Fascist Committee (JAFC), as one of five established in February 1942, to collect material for publication in the West that would foster support for the Soviet Union. Closely watched by the Kremlin, the committee included notable Jewish figures like the writers Ilya Ehrenburg and Vasily Grossman. They wrote occasional pieces on the fate of the Jews, but they wanted to do more, as the Red Army began uncovering the extent of the mass murder. The JAFC decided, with the strong support of prominent American Jews, to collect eyewitness testimony and publish it in English as *The Black Book*. Ehrenburg, Grossman, and others were heavily involved and opted also for a Russian edition. Then, in 1947 when the completed book was already in production, Soviet authorities stopped the presses and ordered the printing plates destroyed.

Gregory Alexandrov, the head of the Propaganda and Agitation Department, reported to Andrei Zhdanov on February 3, 1947, that anyone reading the book would be "misled" into thinking "that the Germans looted and destroyed only the Jews." The study conveyed the false impression "that the Germans fought against the Soviet Union only to destroy the Jews." It was shameful, he thought, to report that the Jews in mixed marriages were killed and that their non-Jewish spouses were often spared, or that Jews who concealed their identity as Russians or Ukrainians were not executed. Alexandrov was particularly upset that Grossman's introduction claimed that killing Jews was a Nazi priority, a contention later shown by historians to be true. The Soviet authorities concluded that the *Black Book* contained "serious political mistakes" and should not be published. The influential editors appealed to highly respected Solomon Mikhoels to intercede, but with no luck.[71] Nevertheless, a manuscript of the book survived and was smuggled out and given to Ehrenburg's daughter in January 1992. The first uncensored Russian edition finally appeared in 1993.[72]

In the battle over the memory and significance of the war, Stalin and his experts opted to erase any notion of a "distinct Jewish catastrophe" and to emphasize instead the universal suffering of the Soviet people. There was no room for commentary on what happened to any particular nation and certainly not the Jews.[73] Until 1948 it was still possible to mention their murder at least in the indictments of war criminals in the Soviet Union, but from that point on, Stalin's orders were that there be only silence.[74] That year the JAFC was dissolved, Stalin had Mikhoels murdered, and key members of the committee were arrested, as official anti-Semitism accelerated.[75]

Those who served on the Soviet atrocity commission (ChGK) did not need much prodding as to what crimes should be uncovered and publicized. Jews are mentioned in some of their reports, but nearly always the victims are referred to as Soviet citizens. Russian historian Marina Sorokina notes that the commissioners "understood perfectly well what the authorities expected." For example, writer Aleksei Tolstoy, one of its prominent members, said that from June to August 1943 he "personally established" what happened in Stavropol under the Nazis. In fact, the NKVD investigated and wrote the report, which is still in the files, and relates that the entire Jewish population had been slaughtered. In Tolstoy's version, however, the victims are called "Soviet people," "Soviet children," and "Soviet citizens."

The attitude of the commission was that the documents and their accuracy could be left for the future. In the here and now of the times, their leaders in Moscow needed "detailed material that lends itself to more general conclusions," in order to promote Soviet claims in the international arena.[76]

The silence on the persecution of the Jews is particularly disturbing in that so much of the Holocaust played out inside the Soviet Union and involved its citizens directly. There was plenty of evidence of Soviet citizens who collaborated specifically in the mass murder of the Jews. On July 25, 1941, Heinrich Himmler ordered the creation of "additional protective units from the ethnic groups suitable to us" into what became police auxiliary forces, or *Schutzmannschaften*. By late 1941, 33,000 had volunteered, many of them from the Soviet Union. Using conscription as well, the Germans recruited ten times that number within the year.[77]

Anti-Semitism persisted in the Soviet Union after the Germans were driven out, even in areas that had seen massive pogroms and that, like Kiev, had witnessed mass murder. Indeed, for Ukraine as a whole, the Soviet authorities reported in September 1944 that following its liberation, there were "severe anti-Semitic manifestations on the part of local population in almost all cities." These included isolated physical attacks and verbal abuse. The Soviet government was well informed about the persistence of anti-Semitism, but getting citizens to face up to what had happened to the Jews was the furthest thing from Stalin's mind.[78]

Why this initiative by Stalin, leader of a major power who formerly did not stand out as particularly anti-Jewish? In the first instance, Stalin's motives for suppressing the news about the "final solution" were likely connected to military and political concerns. Soviet authorities were aware that the Nazi crusade against "Jewish Bolshevism" hit a responsive chord among many citizens already opposed to the Jews and Communism. In order to mobilize the country behind Stalin, in defense of the motherland, the regime emphasized the message that the Nazis were out to exterminate or enslave all Ukrainians, Russians, and other Slavic peoples.

However, this explanation does not account for the acceleration of Soviet anti-Semitism in the postwar period. My hypothesis is that Stalin,

the supreme commander and Nazi-slayer, saw himself in competition
with the persecuted Jews. Not for decades would the world community
come to terms with the catastrophic dimensions of the Holocaust, but
Stalin already sensed that the plight of the Jews would gain increasing
attention and could achieve significance well beyond anything he had
envisioned. The persecution of the Jewish people had the potential to
become *the* cause on the world stage. And Stalin, so shrewdly sensitive
to the faintest trace of deviance, within and without the Soviet Union,
felt that he had to stamp out any memory of a victimized Jewish people.
More than any other group, they were a threat to the very identity of his
idealized "Soviet citizens."[79]

CHAPTER 11

Soviet Retribution and Ethnic Groups

During the civil war after the Russian Revolution, Stalin saw for himself that some of the ethnic groups in the Soviet south hated everything about Communism. When Hitler's invading forces arrived in 1941, some of the same groups collaborated. Stalin determined that, as soon as the Germans were driven out, he would punish them. He did not learn this approach from Hitler. Rather, he built on Russian traditions and the pattern he had established in the 1930s of deporting entire "suspect" peoples. After the Second World War, the scale of such operations grew exponentially and soon spilled over to the "recovered territories" of the Baltic states and western Ukraine.

Historians of the Cold War usually overlook what happened in the Baltic states, the Caucasus, and the Crimea. This tendency in the literature is unfortunate, since it was precisely in those regions that Stalinization showed its true face at war's end. The retributive operations were part of the larger process of reestablishing the Soviet dictatorship and securing its hold on the people, in anticipation of the coming struggle outside Soviet borders.

THE USSR'S GERMAN MINORITY

When war broke out in 1941, there were only a few German passport holders in the USSR and they were interned. However, there was a large German minority of 1.4 million who were Soviet citizens and had lived in Russia for decades, even centuries. Stalin was not the only leader to have some doubts about their loyalty, but on August 3 his anger was sparked when the military informed him that "residents of a German village" on the southern front greeted the invaders with bread and salt and that a few shot at the retreating Red Army. The Soviet military wanted steps taken because there were other German villages near the fighting. Since the reports came at the time of the invaders' early victories, Stalin lashed out and told NKVD chief Beria "to get rid of the lot."[1]

Beginning on August 27, a series of orders were issued to deal with the "tens of thousands of spies and saboteurs" among the *Povolzhskie Nemtsy*, the long-settled Germans on the Volga. The rationalization was simple: If subversive acts were to take place among these people, then the government would have to take steps that could well lead to "mass bloodshed."[2] Rather than take that risk, the Supreme Soviet (in fact, Stalin) decided it would be better to "resettle without exception" all Germans of the Volga region, estimated at 479,841 people, as well as all those living in the Saratov and Stalingrad areas.[3]

The NKVD sent in 14,000 troops, and tribunals drew up lists of those to be evicted from their homes. Detailed accounts were taken of their property, and people were given the impression they would be compensated at their destinations. German women married to non-Germans were granted a privileged status and exempted. After a final house search, each family was brought to the railway depot, where the male heads were separated. The operation went off without a hitch. The unfortunates endured a trip east that took weeks, and as usual the reception areas were completely overwhelmed. No one knows how many died in this process, though the distinctive culture and way of life of the Volga Germans, along with their Autonomous Socialist Republic, was obliterated.[4]

Soon anyone with even a tenuous link to German ethnicity, no matter where they lived, was sent to Siberia or Kazakhstan. There they were employed in new labor armies, in which death rates were even higher than those in the Gulag's special settlements. The final tally of German ethnics deported reached 1,209,430, which was close to every last one.[5]

As for German prisoners of war, Stalin decided as early as September 1939 that their labor would be exploited. More than four million of them went through more than five hundred camps or worked on mass construction, and though some were released soon after the war ended, many were retained and forced to slave until they were no longer "usable." Their mortality rate in captivity has been estimated by Russian scholars at 15 percent, which may be low, but still translates into 600,000 deaths.[6]

These POWs were not simply destined by Stalin to serve as slave labor. He also saw to their ideological reeducation in "antifascism." His underlings proudly reported to him the millions of POWs who were indoctrinated, so that when they made it home, they would proselytize the Communist faith.[7]

As the Red Army pushed back the invaders across Eastern Europe, the NKVD also arrested *Volksdeutsche,* that is, persons who had put themselves on a list claiming to be "ethnic Germans" to win favorable treatment.[8] The new regimes soon created in Eastern Europe after the Nazis were driven out needed no special urging from the Kremlin to go all out against these people.

SOVIET-STYLE ETHNIC CLEANSING

Although we are used to thinking about ethnic cleansing as an invention of the twentieth century, it was "discovered" earlier. In Russia, for example, in the wake of its defeat in the Crimean War in 1856, tsarist forces deported tens of thousands of Muslim Tatars, supposedly for siding with Turkey. At the same time, Russia tried to subjugate the mountainous Caucasus and the Muslims there. In 1856 Dmitri Alekseevich Miliutin was sent to the region as chief of staff and after two years proposed to Tsar Alexander II that they remove all the mountain tribes and settle Russians in their place. The tsar agreed, and "demographic warfare" ensued. One of the Russian generals said its aim was to produce "a finality of result as had never previously been seen." When Miliutin became minister of war, he preferred "voluntary resettlement" and even proposed helping the Muslims leave for the Ottoman Empire.

The military men on the spot, however, thought that "it was necessary to exterminate a significant portion" to make the others surrender. In the following two decades, the Caucasus lost an estimated 2 million people; some were deported, while others fled to the Ottoman Empire. Many tens of thousands died in the process.[9]

In the 1930s, Stalin built on that kind of thinking, and as the Second World War ended, he applied it to some of the same areas that had been occupied by Hitler's army. When the German invaders first came, people wanted to lash out at the Soviet system and hoped to gain a measure of independence.[10] Aleksandr Nekrich, later a well-known historian, was in the Crimea when the Tatars were deported in 1944; he recalled how the official Soviet mind and rumor combined to "conclude" that all of them had collaborated with the Nazis.[11] The official reason for punishing certain ethnic groups was "betrayal of the motherland," exactly the same terminology used to name individual collaborators.[12]

The Soviet variety of ethnic cleansing was an ideological drive to level cultural and ethnic identities that were perceived as standing for actual or potential resistance to the motherland.[13] The plan called for the smaller ethnic groups to be uprooted from their traditional communities and "dispersed among the collective farms with Russian, Kazakh, Uzbek, and Kyrgyz populations."[14] The expectation was that the evicted people were to be assimilated, as the more dominant languages and cultures took their course and erased the identities of the outsiders.

One of the first groups to be targeted was the Karachays, a Turkic Islamic people living between the Black and Caspian seas. The accusation was that "most" Karachays had "treacherously joined" the Germans against Soviet rule. One survivor later admitted that "our people" were "100 percent for liberation from the Bolsheviks and the Russians."[15] Instead of achieving liberation, most of them disappeared—even the names of villages, roads, rivers, and mountains were changed to expunge traces of their existence. The deportation took place in a single day, on November 2, 1943. Ismail Baichorov, a decorated Red Army officer who was at home because he had been wounded, was told by the NKVD that he and his entire family were going "to be moved" and had a half-hour to prepare.[16]

In short order, a total of 69,267 men, women, and children were shipped out. Their autonomous region had already been dissolved as of October 12, and in a pattern following the fate of the Volga Germans, the territory was redistributed among their neighbors.[17]

The Kalmyks, a Mongolian Buddhist people from the Lower Volga region, had resisted Communism, and some had joined the "White" counterrevolutionary armies after the Russian Revolution. These nomadic cattle herders were wholly unsuited to the collective farming that the Soviet system tried to impose. Some Kalmyks had welcomed the German invaders, who allowed for the dissolution of the collectives, but after the Battle of Stalingrad ended in early 1943, the invaders were driven out.[18]

Initially Soviet retribution entailed a purge of the responsible members of the party and administration, like those who stayed behind in the Kalmyk Autonomous Soviet Socialist Republic (ASSR) during the occupation. Soon, however, Moscow decided to deport all the Kalmyks for collaborating with the Germans, including the thousands who were fighting in the Red Army.[19] Virtually all were forced out of the services and deported as well. Ivan Serov, the deputy head of the NKVD, supervised the main operation, which ran for four days (December 27–30) during which the police picked up 26,359 families or 93,139 persons. Beria told Stalin that the main action was carried out without "excesses" or "incidents." In fact the winter took its toll, and hundreds died in transit on disease-ridden trains.[20]

To look at the Kalmyks as one example among many of what happened, we can see the difficulties they faced, given that their culture could not be adapted to the severe climate in the east. After a year the authorities reported that one-third of the Kalmyks could not work because they had no shoes or proper clothing. Few spoke Russian, which made matters worse. Those stuck on collective farms, where even the locals could hardly feed themselves, received practically nothing in compensation for their work. Any who labored in factories were ill at ease with modern heavy machinery and improperly paid and fed. It was officially "expected" that in Siberia thousands would die within months of their arrival. Survivors lived in mud huts or in holes in the ground. In 1946 the police wrote from Novosibirsk province that the Kalmyks were still living in unsuitable buildings like "barns, baths and some even in huts made of tree branches."[21]

CHECHEVITSA

The Chechen-Ingush in the North Caucasus never had a chance to collaborate, because German invaders did not reach them. Nevertheless, they were accused of treason behind the lines.[22] They were converts to Islam, and as far back as 1827, some of them had declared a jihad against the Russian government. Their popular image was of a group impossible to control, and the prejudicial saying went that if drafted into the

Red Army, they would not serve, and when given weapons, they would run for the hills. In fact, like other Soviet Muslims, their service record was not uniformly negative. Nor were they alone among the nations in the USSR in their dislike for Communism and general unwillingness to fight for it. With the approach of the Germans, some certainly commenced an anti-Soviet insurgency, along with other Caucasian minorities.[23]

Between 1940 and 1944, according to its report, the special counterbanditry branch of the NKVD tracked down 197 "organized bands" with 4,532 "guerrillas" among Chechen and Ingush nationalists. Of them, 657 were killed, 2,762 were captured, and 1,113 were persuaded to surrender.[24]

By late 1943 Soviet authorities began preparing a *Chechevitsa*, a roundup and complete deportation of all the peoples of the North Caucasus. It would be punishment for collaboration and a solution to this ethnic problem "once and for all." After passing through Beria's apparatus, the appalling decision was approved on January 31, 1944. The charge was "betrayal of the Motherland in the time of the Patriotic war," with an additional accusation tacked on: that over the years they had participated in "armed raids" and banditry against the Soviet state and its citizens. The authorities began the process by registering the population and devising a detailed, militarylike strategy.

Beria traveled to Grozny to supervise the operation, given its "importance." The security forces mustered 100,000 troops for an attack initially aimed to pick up no fewer than half a million people. As he explained in his note to Stalin on February 17, the scale was such that "it was decided to conduct operations for eight days, with the first three to collect 300,000 people from all lowland, foothill, and some mountain settlements. In the next four days the evictions will take place in the mountains to get the remaining 150,000." He expected resistance, so Russian, Ossetian, and other residents were mobilized to assist by watching the fields and livestock after the deportations took place.[25]

The "cleansing" began in the night of February 23–24 and lasted for weeks. Outdoing their quota, the NKVD captured and sent east an astonishing 478,479 people, with more to follow.[26] The security forces were given license to finish off those who could not travel. In Khaibakh hundreds were lured into resting in a barn, which was then set aflame; those who tried to escape were shot. Magomed Gayev (born in 1931) recalled that the "elderly, ill and weak and also those who took care of them were sent to the stable. I saw how the stable was set on fire. A thick smoke rose to the sky. Even over a great distance we could understand that something terrible happened in the village." In other areas people were shut inside mosques, which were then torched. Hospital patients who could not be moved were killed as a matter of course, as were often children and others unfit for the journey ahead.[27]

Stalin wrote to congratulate the NKVD for the "successful fulfillment of state tasks in the North Caucasus."[28] He admitted that there might have been "abuses," but as always he preferred to exceed quotas rather than to fall short. In a note to Stalin on July 9, 1944, Beria gave the final tally of the Chechen-Ingush as nearly a half million people, though his figures have a typically phony exactitude.[29] Standard operating procedure was to erase all place-names, and change them into either Russian or another language, thus to make the disappearance total.[30]

One survivor of the ordeal heading east recalled: "In 'cattle cars' filled to overflowing without light or water, we traveled for almost a month to our destination. Typhus was having a heyday. There was no medicine. During the short stops at lonely, uninhabited stations we buried our dead near the train." Murad Nashkoyev, a Chechen journalist, had similar experiences. He recently spoke of his trip and said that when they arrived in Kazakhstan, "the ground was frozen hard, and we thought we would all die. It was the German exiles who helped us to survive—they had already been there for several years."[31]

Some adjusted better than others, though the conditions were invariably bleak and the reception by the indigenous population anything but comradely. Those groups with unsavory reputations found it particularly difficult, as did the Chechens. One such woman recalled that entire families went for months "with swollen bellies, searching for animal carcasses in the steppe." A Chechen farm worker in Kazakhstan stated that he had "worked as a cattle herder for twenty-five years. In all this time I never once humiliated my animals like they humiliated us. The *komendanty* [local authorities] and collective farm chairmen told us straight out that we were to be the lowest of the low, without rights."[32]

What about the suddenly emptied lands back home? Almost as much misery and death was caused by the forced resettlement of the "cleansed" areas. What did outsiders know about the special forms of farming, animal husbandry, or wine growing there? According to oral testimonies, the people in the resettled lands were reduced through mortality by as much as one-quarter in the first two years, when sickness and epidemics tore into their midst.[33]

A separate but related operation targeted the Balkars (a Muslim people with Turkic language), also living in the North Caucasus. On February 24, 1944, Beria proposed to Stalin that they all be banished. Their lands had been briefly occupied by the Germans, who initially mistook them for Jews and murdered them.[34] As soon as the Wehrmacht was driven out, the Balkars were accused of having joined "German organized bands to fight against Soviet power." There is little information on their fate, save that a total of 37,044 people were counted in the east, minus 562 who died in transit. As usual, every effort was made to obliterate all evidence that the Balkars had ever existed in their former homeland.[35]

CRIMEA AND GEORGIA

When the Soviets liberated Crimea from the invaders, Stalin apparently decided to remove all offending or potentially hostile "foreigners." In their place he wanted Russians or Ukrainians—not unlike the tsar many years before. The area was not threatened by Turkey, as Stalin and Beria claimed, and in fact they dreamed of possible offensive operations against that country. Were there to be such a war, so the Kremlin ruminated, "their" Muslims might cause difficulties. Indeed, as we have seen, the Soviets went to the brink of war with Turkey in 1946 and were aggressive in Iran.[36]

The largest of the Turkic people targeted were the Crimean Tatars, who were Sunni Muslims. Stalin alleged that "many" of them had "betrayed the Motherland." They deserted the Red Army, he charged, joined the enemy, attacked Soviet partisans, and "actively participated in 'Tatar National Committees,' organized by the German intelligence organs." He also accused them of trying to separate the Crimea from the USSR. In a letter of May 10, 1944, Beria presented the Boss with a plan to deal with between 140,000 and 160,000 people, and the next day orders were given for their banishment, to be completed by June 1. The operation began two days early, when Red Army and NKVD troops surrounded the villages and seized everything. The people were given receipts for what was taken and money to pay for the trip to Uzbekistan, where they would supposedly live as "special settlers."[37]

A sense of how these operations descended on victims is conveyed by Isaak Kobylyanskiy, a Jewish officer on regular duty in the Red Army who happened to be in the Crimea in mid-May 1944. At nine in the morning he and four others were having breakfast in the courtyard of a home owned by a Tatar, Rakhim by name. A truck drew up with a sergeant of the NKVD in fresh uniform. He read out the family's names and declared: "According to government decree, you and your family are to be resettled. You have fifteen minutes to prepare." Rakhim's wife began crying uncontrollably. Of course, resistance was hopeless, and within minutes they were gone. The kerosene stove used to prepare breakfast still hissed away.[38]

The next day, as Kobylyanskiy and the Red Army began the long march out of the Crimea, they passed near another Tatar village. It was completely deserted—the people had apparently been removed the previous morning. The houses were still unlocked, and the eating utensils lay undisturbed on the tables. In several cases, rising dough in a pan had overflowed and fallen on the floor. "The entire village," he recalled, "resounded with wild howls from abandoned, suffering cows, which had not been milked for two days."[39]

Tenzila Ibraimova remembered that she was seized in the village of Adzhiatman in Freidorfskii district on May 18:

The deportation was carried out with great brutality. At 3:00 in the morning, when the children were fast asleep, the soldiers came in and demanded that we gather ourselves together and leave in five minutes. We were not allowed to take any food or other things with us. We were treated so rudely that we thought we were going to be taken out and shot. Having been driven out of the village we were held for twenty-four hours without food; we were starving but were not allowed to go fetch something to eat from home. The crying of the hungry children became continuous. My husband was fighting at the front, and I had the three children.

Finally we were put on trucks and driven to Yevpatoria. There we were crowded like cattle into freight cars full to overflowing. The trains carried us for twenty-four days until we reached the station at Zerabulak in Samarkand region, from which we were shipped to the Pravda kolkhoz in Khatyrchinskii district.[40]

The operations did not go smoothly. People destined for Uzbekistan ended up in Siberia or the Altai region. Beria reported daily, stating that by May 20, a total of 180,014 (later revised upward) had been caught, from the Kremlin's perspective, all without "incidents." In fact more than 20,000 people died in transit east.[41] To add to the misery, the sullied reputation of the deportees and their "guilt" as enemies of the people preceded them, so they were received at their destinations with hostility and hatred. They were never given work appropriate to their skills and instead were often put up in barracks next to factories and told what to do. The real aim was to wipe out their social identity and entire way of life.[42]

The NKVD boss, who liked to observe the process firsthand, reminded Stalin in May 1944 that there were still more "anti-Soviet elements" in the Crimea, namely the Bulgarians, Greeks, and Armenians who had cooperated with the Germans or had family ties to foreign states. Their turn came on July 1, when the authorities reported that through June they had deported 15,040 Greeks, 12,422 Bulgarians, 9,620 Armenians, an assorted group of 1,119 Germans, Italians and others, and finally 3,642 "foreigners." The total number eventually reached 66,000. All were said either to have been involved in anti-Soviet activity during the German occupation or to have family ties to foreign states.[43]

Muslims on the Turkish-Soviet border in Georgia also were subject to deportations. It was suspected that Turks, Kurds, and Khemshins who lived there might give aid to Turkey, a "potential aggressor," so Stalin and Beria decided these people would have to go as well. Beginning on November 17, 1944, every man, woman, and child was rounded up, a total of 92,307 individuals. No consideration was given to those who were card-carrying members of the Communist Party or had otherwise shown their loyalty. What counted was that they were Muslims with actual or potential ties to "foreigners." It took eleven days in a typically brutal operation to collect and ship them to distant lands in the east.[44]

The mortality rates of the ethnic groups deported from the Caucasus and Crimea between 1944 and 1950 was just over 25 percent. The

Kalmyks' mortality was at that average, but the Chechens' was worse again, at 33.2 percent. The first years were the most difficult, but the death rates even after that paralleled those of prisoners in the Gulag.[45]

The correspondence to and from Moscow about the unfortunates conveys the air of rationality in tune with the lofty ideals of the country's social experiment. And yet the retribution and revenge were emotional and vicious, striking innocent and guilty alike.

RETRIBUTION IN THE "RECOVERED" BALTIC STATES

Ivan Serov and Bogdan Kobulov, Beria's top NKVD deputies, who worked together to sort out the Caucasus and Crimea, went into action behind the lines of the Red Army as it moved west.

The Soviet offensive to drive the Germans out of the Baltic states began on September 14, 1944. The sheer scale of the action dwarfs the justly famous landings earlier that year in Normandy. The Red Army used roughly ten times as many troops (900,000 in all) against Hitler's Army Group North in Estonia, Latvia, and Lithuania. Even with a two-to-one Soviet advantage, it was tough slogging. Stalin insisted they batter their way through heavily defended positions, instead of trying to go around them, and so they took unnecessarily heavy losses. They captured the Latvian capital, Riga, on October 13 and drove thirty German divisions back to the northern tip of Lithuania (the Courland peninsula), where they were isolated. The battle for the Baltic states was won.[46]

Earlier in 1939 when the Red Army arrived there, Stalin had intended the permanent incorporation of these "recovered territories" into the USSR. Hitler had other ideas and in 1941 drove the Communists out. By 1944 on their return, the Kremlin had developed strategies to transform all three into Soviet republics run directly by the Politburo in Moscow.[47]

The Baltic peoples did not greet the Red Army as liberators. The new occupiers carried out executions of suspected collaborators, "spies," politicians, civil servants, leaders of political parties, and assorted others, including some landowners branded as kulaks. We do not know exactly how many were killed. The Soviet arrival in Latvia was called "the time of chaos," when arrests and killings were the norm. The NKVD built "filtration camps," and tens of thousands went through them, to be checked for their political and social past.[48]

To the Red Army, locals were enemies or Nazi collaborators who deserved to be punished. One wounded air force pilot on his way home and traveling through Latvia in 1944 said that he would have loved to bomb "every house" because "they are traitors." Such attitudes were also reflected in the behavior of the occupation forces. Thus the NKVD reported from Lithuania in 1945 that "many officers, sergeants and privates routinely drink, plunder and kill citizens." The Estonian Communist Party said the same and was helpless to do anything, all the more as it needed the presence of the Red Army to stay in power.[49]

Moscow created special institutions to control each of the republics, with Stalin directly involved until autumn 1944.[50] Soviet influence was confirmed physically by having Russians dominate the police and central administrations. In early 1945 they made up one-third or more of the central committees and the memberships of the Communist parties of the Baltic states. Trusted people with Baltic origins, who were Communists and who had lived for years in the Soviet Union, moved home and into privileged positions, as did demobilized Red Army soldiers.[51]

The NKVD measured success in terms of "liquidations"—those killed or arrested or who surrendered. In 1944 they numbered 7,504 in Lithuania, 1,075 in Latvia, and 1,394 in Estonia. The next year was by far the worst, and Lithuanian losses jumped to 40,541, in Latvia they went up to 7,016, and in Estonia to 5,671.[52]

There were attempts by the Baltic states to resist the invaders with movements going back for years, commonly called the Forest Brethren. Their latest hope was that the West would change its mind about the Soviet Union and might even go to war, a hope soon shared by other peoples once they were forced to live under Communism. By the summer of 1945 those expectations were gone, but young men like Edgar Ranniste, one of the Forest Brethren in Virumaa County, Estonia, carried on anyway. He recalled telling his men that their situation would get worse that autumn: "I think that whoever wants to continue hiding must stay alone or in a small group. Those of you who want to leave the forest, go ahead, but don't start informing on those of us who stay. Don't betray our positions as the price of your freedom. I personally have decided to remain loyal to the Republic of Estonia and not to subordinate myself to the terrorist government of Stalin, who has occupied our homeland." He was soon discovered and deported to Siberia, though he survived the ordeal.[53]

A sure sign that the resistance was fading were the falling number of people caught in the Soviet net. In Lithuania those "liquidated" in 1946 declined from the previous year by almost 75 percent to 8,228. In Latvia they went down to 4,218, and in Estonia they dropped by more than half to 2,085. Thus the struggle gradually petered out, although it continued in some places into the 1950s, when small groups fought on.[54]

The Soviet interpretation of the resistance to the occupation was that "kulaks" were behind it all. It was they who supposedly led the struggle and incited the *bedniaks* (the poorest peasants) and *seredniaks* (literally, middle peasants, the second poorest) to join the fray. To deal with this situation, the authorities determined that a way had to be found to undermine the solidarity among the peasantry. Hence they adopted the policy of redistributing the lands of all those who had fled with the Germans. The Soviets favored the middle-range peasants at the expense of kulaks, who were harassed and gradually squeezed out. The USSR pursued this approach between 1944 and 1948, even though the resulting tiny and fragmented farms led to an overall decline in agricultural productivity. Once the insurgency was put down and the people were left with no one to fight for them, the Soviets would take the land back. Indeed, on May 21, 1947, the Politburo—in fact Stalin—issued secret orders to begin preparations for collectivization in the three countries, regardless of what local Communists thought.[55]

In lockstep with that process, the Soviet Council of Ministers decided on May 18, 1948, that the time was right for deportations of those who opposed them. Operation *Vesna* (Spring) was designed as a sudden assault on Lithuania and those described as "bandits, kulaks and their families." The "total to be evicted" was preset at 12,134 families, or 48,000 people. The roundup began in May and exceeded the quota. The first official reports from the camps to which the deportees had been sent described poor housing and unhygienic conditions, with resulting cases of typhus and dysentery. If they made it through the first years, they survived, but the elderly did not last long.[56]

An even bigger sweep of all three countries was initiated on January 29, 1949, when Stalin signed Soviet government Order No. 390-138ss, code-named *Priboy* (Surf). Those designated for "eternal settlement" (*vechnoe poseleniye*) in the east included "all kulaks, bandits and their accomplices, illegal nationalists," and all their families. There were quotas: 8,500 families or 25,500 people in Lithuania; 13,000 families or 39,000

people in Latvia; and 7,500 families or 22,000 people in Estonia. The brutal action began simultaneously on March 25 and included anyone out
of favor with the police. Among the total of 94,779 people who ended
up in the mix were 2,850 "elderly infirm people," 146 "invalids," and 185
children without any families.[57] In the years to come, there would be
more deportations, though none on this scale.

Stalin was relentless. He would brook no objection, nor tolerate any
excuse. No matter what anyone said or did, by the time he died in 1953,
the farms in all three states were almost totally collectivized.

The Kremlin imposed its will in every imaginable way, right down
to deciding which individual Communists got onto the *nomenklatura,*
the special list for the ruling elite that brought great privileges to the
few. In time the Baltic peoples adjusted as best they could; their liberation would have to wait until the Soviet Union dissolved.

UKRAINE AND EASTERN POLAND

Soviet retribution in the area variously called western Ukraine/eastern
Poland became entangled in the civil war raging there. Although the
Ukrainian and Polish underground shared a common enemy—namely
Soviet Communism—the few efforts they made to unify their struggle
came to nothing, and they clashed. There were also bloody conflicts
within the Ukrainian resistance movement, all of which worked to Moscow's advantage.

When the Nazis invaded to the east in 1941, Ukraine initially greeted
them warmly, showing its thin support for Communism. But what was
to happen when the Germans were driven out? It would have been
impossible for Moscow to try each and every collaborator because the
elites in the civil service, the judiciary, and the economy—"essentially
the entire existing order"—had accommodated itself to life under
Nazism. One internal assessment from 1944 for Vinnytsia (in western
Ukraine) stated that "almost 99 percent of the population hates the Bolsheviks and view them with hostility." The Soviets opted for show trials
of a "few" bad apples, overlooked the rest, and then conducted a determined counterinsurgency operation.[58]

The main opponent was the underground Organization of Ukrainian Nationalists (OUN), which had been established after the First

World War, when the area was made part of Poland. When the Germans invaded in 1941, the OUN saw an opportunity for Ukrainian independence, but it went down the road to collaboration and participation in the Holocaust. In 1943 the OUN created a separate military branch (the UPA) that killed between 40,000 and 60,000 Poles in Volhynia, western Ukraine.[59] The Polish Home Army fought back.

Stalin was determined to end this strife, based on his newly acquired conviction that homogenized states inside and outside the USSR would be easier to rule. So on September 9, 1944, he worked out an "agreement" with the Polish government-in-waiting (the PKNW) to accept the transfer of all the Poles out of Ukraine, Byelorussia, and Lithuania. In return Ukrainians living in the "new Poland" would be moved east into the USSR. What they were permitted to take with them was set down in detail, and it was far more generous than what was allowed to those deported out of the Caucasus.[60]

These were supposed to be "voluntary transfers," when in fact they were forced deportations. The Soviets ran into immediate opposition from the UPA and soon faced a genuine insurgency. In 1944 the UPA killed 3,202 Soviet occupiers—mostly NKVD, police, and militia, as well as an additional 904 "Soviet activists," presumably advisers and administrators. The insurgents killed another 2,539 of the enforcers in 1945, along with 823 Soviet "activists." In 1946, as a sign of the guerrillas' dwindling fortunes, their "kill" rate was down to 1,441 members of the occupation forces and 347 advisers.[61] The UPA slaughtered twice and three times as many civilians, including Ukrainians, as often happens in a civil war. The conflict became vicious—the UPA spared no one, including children, who were sometimes executed in public for the "misdeeds" of their absent fathers, under suspicion of having answered the forced Soviet draft.

Later, when surviving members of the UPA looked back, they thought of 1944–45 as the time when the "Red Broom" swept through village and home, terrorized the inhabitants, and established a network of informers.[62] In 1944 the NKVD "liquidated" (that is, killed), arrested, or forced the surrender of 123,782 people. The next year was worse when the toll was 129,016, and if in 1946 it fell to 29,480, by that time the resistance was all but eliminated there, as in the Baltic states. The NKVD also deported eastward a steady stream of suspected culprits,

their relatives and their supporters, variously labeled "bandit accomplices" or kulaks. Most were sent away between 1944 and 1946, their
total reaching 203,662 by 1955.[63]

The western Ukrainians, having lived outside the Soviet Union,
with their own religious life and customs, had not experienced collectivization. However, they knew all about it and dreaded it, and for
that reason Moscow waited until the guerrilla movement was defeated
before the process began. In 1947–48 the Soviets levied heavy taxes on
the kulaks or demanded delivery of so much that it was impossible to
satisfy. Maria Pyskir, a young woman with a newborn, living in Hranky,
Ukraine, when the collectivization began, recalled that people were
browbeaten into joining the farms and that sometimes "the authorities
would descend unannounced on a village and take away the heads of
household for questioning and conversion."[64]

In the meantime Stalin got rid of the Poles who lived in the region,
even though they had been there for generations. By October 1946, the
Soviets uprooted and sent to Poland from Ukraine a total of 272,544 Polish families, or 789,982 people of all ages.[65] From Byelorussia they forced
out 72,511 families, or a total of 231,152. The new Communist-dominated
government in Poland consigned many to its recently acquired western
border region. In exchange, the Poles uprooted and sent 122,454 Ukrainian families, or 482,109 people, to the Soviet Ukraine. These were the
main deportations, though more followed in one direction or another.[66]

The displaced began voyages into the unknown, full of foreboding
and already traumatized by what they had gone through. The travel
was a prolonged nightmare, and the overloaded communication systems broke down. Thousands of Poles waited around railway stations
in appalling conditions for weeks to travel west, while equal numbers
of Ukrainians were stuck in similar hell on their way east. The UPA or
the Soviet police harassed Poles into leaving, and whole villages were
burned to the ground. The trains carrying them were given specific destinations, but often the freight cars were unloaded anywhere at all in the
"new Poland." It was worse in those areas that were still populated by
ethnic Germans, who had not yet been driven out. In Poland's collective
memory, the "transfers" of the Poles are regarded to this day as "expulsions." The social fabric was weakened when so many were torn from
their moorings, and they were left prone to anxiety and race hate.[67]

Similar and sometimes worse things happened in Poland to force the Ukrainians to go east. Many preferred living anywhere but in the Soviet Union. In 1947 the remaining Ukrainians who tried to stay were subjected to an all-out military campaign. Little wonder they supported or collaborated with the UPA in the struggle. Nevertheless, by January 1947 the insurgency was largely at an end, with thousands who once dared resist dispersed across either Poland or Ukraine.[68]

The vast scale of the Soviet retribution was aimed at punishing alleged past and present misbehavior of individuals or whole nations and cleansing the new lands to the west of all enemies in preparation for their "rejoining" the Soviet Union. Counterinsurgency operations "were accompanied by thorough ideological and socio-economic measures."[69] From Stalin's perspective, moreover, the country as a whole had to be readied for the looming struggle with the West, and it was also high time to straighten out any ideological wanderings and "false consciousness" that had crept into people's heads during the war.

CHAPTER 12

Reaffirming Communist Ideology

The cataclysmic events of wartime rattled the Soviet dictatorship and opened more space for people to think for themselves. In October 1944 the police secretly recorded novelist Sergei Golubov reflecting on the newfound freedom that came with earlier setbacks: "When we had military defeats, the authorities lost their head a little, people wandered where they wanted ideologically, and no one took any interest in us."[1] Moreover, temptations to deviate from the Soviet path were plentiful for the millions of soldiers and others who had experienced the allures of the West for themselves.[2] One Red Army officer, a party member in good standing, later recounted his feelings upon crossing the border heading west. He realized that everything he had been taught "about conditions of life outside Russia, also about the history of the Communist Party, was false."[3]

However, already in 1944 people sensed that the fist would come down again. "Now that we are winning," Golubov said that year, the powers that be "are recovering and the old ideology has resurfaced."[4] Even before the shooting stopped, Stalin began restoring his rule with a full-fledged campaign on the ideological front.

PATCHING THE IDEOLOGICAL FRONT

Stalin assigned Andrei Zhdanov the job of getting Communist thinking back on course.[5] He called Zhdanov from Leningrad full time in December 1945, bringing him immediately into the ruling group, which expanded to a "sextet." The years 1946 to 1948 are often dubbed the *Zhdanovchina* (Zhdanov era) to suggest that he dominated the assault on the arts and sciences. We now know, however, that the label is inappropriate because Stalin was behind the whole thing, initiating and directing it. Still, for a period of just over two years, his protégé was amazingly active both inside the Soviet Union and in the international Communist movement.[6]

On April 18, 1946, Zhdanov observed in a meeting of the Central Committee that their leader had raised questions about literature, movies, plays, and the arts and believed that the agitprop (propaganda) section needed improved criticism from "the best people on matters of ideology."[7] He was appalled that poems were being published about what it was like to visit devastated "hero-cities" like Sevastopol, without mentioning its defenders and bringing out the popular political implications.[8]

The minister explained the mission to a young man he was trying to recruit. Stalin's strategy, he said, was to restore the economy and raise its levels of production. In order to accomplish that, the party had to do more and better ideological work among the people. The "plans of the imperialists" had failed on the battlefield, so now they were pursuing an ideological offensive and catching the Soviet Union unprepared. An "apolitical, non-ideological sentiment" supposedly pervaded the intelligentsia, and it had become servile to the West. For these misguided souls, he said, everything was "Ah, the West!" "Ah, democracy!" "Now there's real literature for you!"[9]

On another occasion, Zhdanov pointed to the ideological and political role that the arts had to play in the Soviet Union. He said that Leninism "starts from the premise" that literature should not be apolitical. There was no place for "art for art's sake," and novels, poems, plays, and all the rest had to take a leading part in forming the new society. As an illustration he quoted Stalin's famous dictum that "writers are the engineers of the human soul." For Zhdanov, the implication was that all of them had an "enormous educational responsibility" to train youth and to elevate popular consciousness.

At a time when the country faced so many national and international challenges, why would Stalin and the Central Committee bother with the finer points of poetry, literary criticism, novels, plays, music, and movies? That was the question Zhdanov posed. His answer was that it was essential "to bring the ideological front into line with all other sectors of our work." To his chagrin, he noted serious failings in those who looked to fashionable "modern, bourgeois writers in America and Western Europe" who were trying to attract "the attention of the progressive strata" in the USSR. The West wanted to entice Soviet writers "into a groove of cheap meaningless art and literature, dealing with gangsters and show-girls and glorifying the adulterer and the adventures of crooks and gamblers." Fully in tune with the Master, he preached a return to socialist realist art that taught "morally and politically" sound values.[10]

As for Stalin, even though he was busy hammering together a new empire and facing growing resistance from the United States, he still found more than enough time to get involved in the details of the arts. Nothing was too small to ignore. For example, he considered the abstruse literary journals of singular importance, and on August 9, 1946, he met editors from several of them. He and Zhdanov wanted explanations for decisions to publish this or that work by a non-Soviet author or by a writer out of favor with the regime. Stalin queried Boris Likharev, editor of the journal Leningrad: "Is it worthy of a Soviet man to walk on tiptoe in front of foreign countries? This is how you cultivate servile feelings, this is a great sin." Likharev's meek response was that indeed they had published some translated works. Stalin replied sternly: "By doing this you are instilling a taste of excessive respect for foreigners. You're instilling the feeling that we are second-rate people and there the people are first-rate, which is wrong. You are the pupils, they are the teacher. In its very essence, this is wrong."[11]

Such journals needed staff changes and more appropriate editorial policies. They had opened their pages to writers like the humorist and satirist Mikhail Zoshchenko, who liked to poke fun at everyday foibles. Also singled out for censure was the poet Anna Akhmatova. Neither she nor Zoshchenko was an oppositional writer; nevertheless, both were viewed as sending mixed messages, and it was now deemed a political mistake to give them a forum, which would only result in "ideological disarray and disorder." An August 14 resolution of the Organization Bureau (Orgburo) stated that the supervising personnel and editors had "forgotten Leninism's thesis that our journals, whether scholarly or artistic, cannot be apolitical." The state and party simply could not permit youth to be educated "in a spirit of indifference to Soviet policy."[12] More Central Committee actions followed, played up in the press, like an August 26 report about a resolution aimed at the theater and another on September 4 directed at the movies. The whole range of creative artists was attacked for its "servility and slavishness before Western culture." Even children's magazines were not overlooked.[13]

A book of poems by Akhmatova awaiting distribution was immediately destroyed (though copies survived), and in September she and Zoshchenko were dropped from the Union of Soviet Writers. That meant the end of their writer's ration cards and the near impossibility of getting anything published. She had been attacked earlier by Stalin and arrested in 1937, as was her son, who was swallowed up in the camps for years. Her revenge is her poetry, especially *Requiem,* written between 1935 and 1961 in response to her son's incarceration and disappearance. It is an act of witness and one of the most moving condemnations of dictatorship in all of literature. The poem shows the agony of those left wondering about their loved ones—sent away "without right of correspondence." Sometimes that phrase was a euphemism for execution, but no one knew for sure. The relatives and friends on the outside went on searching. This aspect of the terror was often overlooked, but it went on tormenting people for years.[14]

The Kremlin Boss took to holding his own hearings—or interrogations—of the country's cultural elite. In early 1947 he hauled in Sergei Eisenstein, famous for directing the movie *Ivan the Terrible.* During the war Stalin had thought that he found a kindred spirit in that tsar, the most brutal in all Russian history. Even during the leanest days of the struggle, he decided that he wanted a big film made about his historical soul mate, and he named Eisenstein to make it.[15] The dictator personally approved what was to be a three-part epic. He commissioned the work, edited the screenplay, and did not quibble about its expensive production in 1943, complete with music by the renowned Alexander Prokofiev. When the first part of the trilogy was shown in 1944, it earned the dictator's rave reviews. His disappointment was all the greater after the war, however, when he previewed part two, saying it was "some kind of nightmare!"[16]

Late in the evening on February 26, 1947, Eisenstein and leading man Nikolai Cherkasov were called to the Kremlin, where Stalin, Molotov, and Zhdanov took turns grilling them. The two outsiders agreed between themselves beforehand that their only hope was not to argue back. Stalin's first criticism was that the film showed Ivan to be "indecisive, like Hamlet. Everyone suggests to him what should be done, but he cannot make a decision." The Master was surprisingly old-fashioned, saying that the movie "did not show historical figures correctly in their period. So, for instance, in the first part, it is wrong that Ivan the Terrible spent so long kissing his wife. That was not tolerated in those times."[17]

Judging from indications in this conversation, Stalin had come to see in the tsar something akin to an alter ego. For example, he admitted to Eisenstein: "Ivan was very cruel. You can show that he was cruel, but you have to show why it was necessary to be cruel." One of Ivan's mistakes, as depicted in the movie, was his inability to have done with his enemies. He "would execute someone and then spend a long time repenting and praying. God interfered with him there. He should have been even more decisive." Was that how Stalin saw himself and wanted to be characterized, as a ruler who was cruel but also just? As a real reformer more determined than the "best" of the tsars? As one who was decisive because he knew he was dispensing justice?

The aged dictator asked Eisenstein several times how his film was going to end. Being only too aware of how little time he might have left in life, he agonized about it and told the director not to rush. He subtly hinted that another moviemaker had taken eleven years to complete a project. One difficulty was that the second part of Ivan's reign degenerated and ended in military defeats and weakness. So the latter part of the movie was bound to disappoint, unless the director could be coaxed into adjusting the script.[18]

In the end Eisenstein adopted delaying tactics. He said, although not to the dictator: "I do not have the right to distort historical truth or to retreat from my creative credo." He died within the year of natural causes at the age of fifty, and his uncut movie miraculously appeared in Soviet theaters a decade later.[19]

One of Stalin's final comments to Eisenstein indicates that his anti-Western mood was in full bloom. Ivan, he said, "was more a national tsar, more prudent, he never allowed foreign influence into Russia, whereas Peter [the Great] opened the gates to Europe and let in too many foreigners."[20] He disliked Peter for starting Russians' tradition of measuring themselves against the West and feeling that they were "minors, inadequate, not quite one-hundred percent."[21] In Stalin's playbook, Europe stood for the doomed path of capitalism and bourgeois greed, whereas Russian nationalism uniquely signified the triumph of the proletariat and the force for good in the world.[22]

Running concurrently with the Stalinist campaign in movies and literature were others, including one that began in April 1947 against the publication of pornographic and fascist materials. That was used as a pretext to weed out libraries and use censorship more extensively. Further hints, instructions, and reprimands were soon doled out against philosophers, historians, poets, novelists, and musicians.[23]

In January 1948 the country's leading musical composers, including Prokofiev and Dmitri Shostakovich, were subjected to three days of hearings before the Central Committee. They were eventually condemned with a resolution published in *Pravda* that denounced their transgression: they had lost their organic ties to the people and wrongfully written music and operas meant to appeal to the modern bourgeois taste in Europe and America.[24]

The new society could have no "modern" music, with its atonalities and dissonances, only work that "strikes a chord in the human spirit." Zhdanov insisted that Soviet composers had to reflect their society and protect it "against penetration by elements of bourgeois decay." In a memorable address, he said, without blinking an eye, that the USSR had become "the true custodian of the musical culture of mankind just as she is in all other fields." Composers had to be on the alert that "alien bourgeois influences from abroad" would try to muster "what remains of the capitalist outlook in the minds of some Soviet intellectuals in frivolous and crazy attempts to replace the treasures of Soviet musical culture by the pitiful tatters of modern bourgeois art."[25]

ERECTING A WALL AGAINST WESTERN INFLUENCES

Comrade "scientist" Stalin also delved into more abstruse academic matters. He set the ideological "line" or decided on the "proper approach" in branches of learning as diverse as physics, genetics, physiology, economics, philosophy, and linguistics. Scholars could settle none of the major controversies in these disciplines, some of them highly technical, without reference to his statements or demands. He was convinced that he knew best, even when confronted by serious questioners humbly suggesting he might be wrong.[26]

An example of how the strident anti-Western tone crept into science concerns the cancer research of Nina Kliueva and Grigorii Roskin, a husband-and-wife team. They attracted the attention of American cancer patients, who in early 1946 wrote for information to the new U.S. ambassador in Moscow, Walter Bedell Smith. He contacted the minister of Soviet public health, Georgi Miterev, who arranged for Smith to visit with the Kliueva-Roskin team in late June. Smith was impressed, offered support, and was pleased to hear that Dr. Vasily Parin, head of the Soviet Academy of Medical Sciences, would be traveling to the United States and would report there on the cancer project. Smith's visit in turn encouraged the Soviet authorities to fund the K-R project more generously.

Parin traveled to New York in October. He took a sample of the K-R serum and a manuscript of the couple's book that they wanted translated and published. Parin continued to fret about security and was reluctant to give the materials to the Americans without complete clearance from the Kremlin. He asked for Molotov's opinion on November 7, when their paths crossed on separate missions in the United States. The foreign minister, being no risk taker, asked officials in Moscow to check with Stalin. The messages did not reach the Soviet leader, who was in the south; a junior official finally approved the exchange. Dr. Parin returned to New York later still, heard the news, and on November 24 gave the cancer serum and book manuscript to the Americans. Alas two days later another telegram arrived from Moscow, this time from the "Seven"—that is, the Politburo—telling him not to hand over anything.[27]

The K-R case ran along two tracks, one of reward and the other of punishment. Zhdanov was concerned about the willingness of the cancer researchers to share their ideas with foreigners. True, the health authorities had cleared them. Nonetheless, in late November he consulted with others in the Politburo and organized an investigative commission. If Zhdanov pressed hard down this line, the doctors would almost certainly be punished.

However, at the same time, the Soviet bureaucracy continued to push in the direction already sanctified by Stalin himself, and so officials supported the two researchers by offering still more generous funding. Crowning those efforts on December 26, the dictator personally signed a resolution "to assist" their work. Indeed, with his blessing, Nina Kliueva was "nominated" to be elected to the Supreme Soviet and won her seat. Fatefully, on February 17, 1947, the two tracks in the patronage system (reward/punish) seemed to cross when the happy medical couple was invited to the Kremlin to meet the Master. He spoke with them and posed a few questions. He gave no hint of a threat. In fact, he praised their book. They were then nominated for a Stalin Prize, something that could happen only with his approval. On May 1 the honors kept rolling in, and the two scientists found themselves atop the Lenin Mausoleum to witness the ceremonial parade.

All the while Zhdanov pursued his investigation. On January 28, the day after his return from vacation, he called in Kliueva for a less-than-friendly talk. He and others also questioned the officials involved and forwarded these materials to Stalin. By February 17, the Boss was sufficiently troubled to bring the Politburo together, the only time for the entire year, specifically to discuss the K-R business. Ill winds were blowing, for that very same day the Voice of America just happened to broadcast its first anti-Communist program to the USSR.

Kliueva and Roskin were invited to the Politburo meeting. They arrived, no doubt thinking they were to be praised, and to some extent they were. However, matters were more complicated, for immediately following the meeting, the officials in the public health ministry were dismissed, and the unfortunate Dr. Parin was arrested for passing over those materials in New York. Stalin remained surprisingly ambivalent about whether to reward or punish the medical duo. They were still in good graces and on the patronage track, and less than a week afterward they reached the lofty heights on the Lenin Mausoleum. Then came the tipping point, as Zhdanov finally had enough evidence to accuse them of "anti-state and anti-patriotic acts abusive of their honor and integrity as Soviet scientists and citizens."[28]

Zhdanov had Stalin's backing to hold Kliueva and Roskin to account before a Court of Honor. These institutions harked back to an earlier time, but on March 28, 1947, on the orders of the Politburo, they were established in the ministries of health, trade, and finance. In order "to educate employees," the courts, composed of five to seven persons, were to judge those accused of "anti-patriotic, anti-government and anti-social" behavior.[29] In June the accused K-R couple went on trial in front of eight hundred colleagues, and as was expected, they confessed. Insofar as the three-day ordeal was scripted by Zhdanov, with a nod and a wink from the Kremlin, the event was reminiscent of the 1930s show trials.[30] This time the dictator was satisfied to let the guilty be "reprimanded" and shamed, rather than demanding their execution or banishment. Maybe he was thinking that something might still come of their research. An interesting new touch was that the Communist Party sent out a twenty-five-page brochure detailing the "K-R affair." It went to party committees all over the country to bring their attention to the regrettable "slavishness and servility to the West" that existed among the intelligentsia in general and scientists in particular.[31]

Ambassador Smith recalled the K-R case as an example "of the jealousy with which the Soviet Union guards the accomplishments of its scientists and the extent to which it eschews collaboration with the West, even in those fields which have no military or industrial implication, but which, on the contrary, would only be for the benefit of mankind."[32]

More than jealousy was involved in the K-R case, because Stalin was in the midst of erecting a wall against the outside world. He pushed the antiforeign attitude to the point that on February 15, 1947, the Supreme Soviet outlawed marriage with foreign aliens, even if the prospective spouse was from another socialist country.[33] This measure was simply announced in the press, without explanation. The few Russians who married foreigners had been allowed exit visas from time to time, and that practice was now stopped as well. Robert Tucker, an American historian living in Moscow, was unable to leave with his Russian wife until after Stalin's death, when the rule was repealed. Professor Tucker went on to write a classic biography of the leader that pointed to the dictator's psychological problems. According to Tucker, Stalin coped with the knowledge that there existed "anti-Stalin feelings," even in the party, by suspecting that no matter how much critics pretended to be loyal, they were in his view "enemies of the *party's* cause." Yet it was he who wore a mask and was "two-faced." While "always telling people to be modest," and deporting himself "in public as simple and unassuming," the Soviet dictator "concealed an arrogant inner picture of himself as a paragon of revolutionary statesmanship."[34]

In any event, Stalin's antiforeign campaign continued on June 9, 1947, when the Supreme Soviet decreed that in future anyone disclosing state secrets would be sent to a Gulag concentration camp for ten to fifteen years. This measure dealt with information conveyed by a slip of the tongue or through negligence and covered practically all fields of human endeavor. It did not replace the laws against intentionally passing information to the enemy, which was still treated as treason or espionage and punished accordingly.[35] After it became law, *Glavlit*, the official literary censorship board, wrote editors repeatedly to tighten vigilance of scientific, technical, and economic issues.[36]

Denunciations from all over the country rained down on the authorities about aberrant "cosmopolitan" and anti-Soviet behavior in all the arts and sciences, including charges that even "many mathematicians" adored foreign "idols." In late 1947 reports from Minister of State Security Viktor Abakumov stated that "antiforeign materials" had been found in international, especially American, scientific and technical journals. These had not been subject to censorship, and such exemptions were promptly withdrawn by order of the Politburo.[37]

In May, Stalin commissioned the noted writer Konstantin Simonov to compose a play that turned out to be *Alien Shadow,* about the two K-R scientists whose deeds exposed the submissiveness of the intelligentsia to the West. Actually it was Simonov who suggested in a meeting with Stalin that the affair would make an interesting play. Simonov's own story reveals that the Soviet patronage system was a house with many rooms. He was troubled when a new book he had submitted was held up because the dictator had reservations about it. Simonov said in his memoirs that he was an "avid admirer" of Stalin, wanted desperately to please, and had agreed to do the script about the scientists. The dictator made "suggestions," and Simonov liked and followed them in how the drama ended.

The political lesson of the play was to show the selfishness of the scientists and to emphasize the benevolence of the government in letting them continue their work. It was a propaganda success and won a Stalin Prize. Looking back years later, the author was not proud of how easily he had gone along with the campaign, which at times was ugly. Nevertheless, he was not entirely opposed to stamping out the spirit of cosmopolitanism and self-deprecation in the Soviet Union.[38]

Cosmopolitan became a term of abuse. Whereas once it had been praiseworthy to be called a citizen of the world, the term was now identified with "servility to the West," that is, with abetting American imperialism and its long-term goal of imposing Anglo-American culture on the world.

The anticosmopolitanism campaign intensified during 1948 and peaked after publication in *Pravda,* on January 28, 1949, of a notorious article "on an anti-patriotic group of theater critics." It pilloried Jews for not being sufficiently appreciative of (officially condoned) plays that were supposed to educate and elevate popular consciousness. "At a time when we are faced with acute problems," the article complained, "and standing against rootless [*besrodnii*] cosmopolitanism, against manifestations of bourgeois influences alien to the people, these critics do not find anything better to do than to discredit the most progressive events in our literature."[39] All of them were eventually expelled from the party and the writers' union, as were numerous other critics who happened also to be Jewish.

Although the anticosmopolitanism campaign did not end in mass executions, people were arrested, tortured, and shot. Mostly, however, the regime used "administrative" measures, and selected individuals lost their jobs. The entire campaign was part of the larger struggle to get the intellectual establishment back on track and firmly supportive of Soviet Communism. It also sealed off foreign contacts and influences, as the Stalinists created their version of the iron curtain.

As we will see in Chapter 20, Soviet anti-Semitism became more pronounced in the last years of Stalin's life, and though he was the first to recognize the new Israeli state in 1948, he soon changed his mind and then fostered official anti-Semitism as never before.

STALIN AS IDEOLOGIST IN CHIEF OF INTERNATIONAL COMMUNISM

Stalin's postwar campaign on the ideological front brought him rich dividends. Millions, including most of the intelligentsia, came to admire his accomplishments and learning, even to associate him with their own ever-deeper love of country. Hence there emerged a pronounced and deeper Stalin worship.

Many thought that with the USSR's hard-won victory in the war, their country had finally caught up with the West. They had been proud that the Red Army had stood in Berlin in May 1945, in advance of the Americans and the British. But then in August they had been shattered when the atomic bombs dropped on Hiroshima and Nagasaki showed the USSR to be behind after all. Some people, feeling personally vulnerable again, took solace in Stalin's calm equanimity and in the long silences in which he projected fearlessness before the Americans.

Russian historians go so far as to suggest that in the postwar period, the Soviet leadership formed a new compact with the country. The people stood together with the Kremlin, rolled up their sleeves, and sacrificed so that their country could achieve atomic parity. According to that view, in the eyes of the people, the first successful testing of the Soviet atomic bomb on August 29, 1949, vindicated Stalin and represented a moral triumph over the West.[40]

Although Marxism played down the role of the "great man" in history in favor of impersonal economic and social forces, Stalin knew it was politically useful for the people to be encouraged to see him as a "great man," "father of the peoples," and so on. As a good Marxist, his attitude was ambivalent about his own cult, but he thought it was necessary. And in his view, if something was necessary, it was also just.

The dictator edited a *Short Biography*, published in 1947, that sang his own praises. He went through it carefully to mark where the admiration needed brushing up. For example, he inserted the sentence: "Although he performed his task as leader of the party and the people with consummate skill and enjoyed the unreserved support of the entire Soviet people, Stalin never allowed his work to be marred by the slightest hint of vanity, conceit or self-adulation." At another place he added: "Comrade Stalin's genius enabled him to divine the enemy's plans and defeat them. The battles in which Comrade Stalin directed the Soviet armies are brilliant examples of operational military skill."

Stalin was also mythologized in a popular movie, *The Unforgettable Year 1919*. A perfect example of socialist realism, it shows the gallant Stalin, side by side with the revered Lenin, in the Russian Civil War. However, the epitome of the adulation showered on Stalin came on his official birthday in 1949. Plays were staged about episodes in his life, and so many gifts arrived from admirers at home and around the world that a special museum was created to display them all. For over a year *Pravda*, the country's most important newspaper, under the headline "The Stream of Greetings," carried long lists of individuals and organizations who conveyed their best wishes to the great man.[41]

Stalin was not just the head of government—he prided himself first and foremost as a theoretician, an ideologist. Already in 1924 he had delivered and published a series of lectures, *Problems of Leninism*. That slim volume, in which he distilled the lessons taught by Lenin, became a textbook for those in higher education. It sold more than seventeen million copies. He used the concept of the vanguard more than three dozen times, along with quotations and aphorisms, to make his key point that the relatively small group of Bolsheviks had captured and exercised power. Other countries should follow their example![42]

The dictator's literary ambitions became still more evident at the time of the Great Terror in 1937, when he concluded that there was a need for a handbook on the history and "lessons" of the party's rise.[43] The volume, which would serve in the postwar period as a handbook for would-be dictators elsewhere, set out "to highlight state-building—particularly Russian state-building"—and rehabilitate at least some of the tsars, like Peter the Great.[44] The finished product had to have broad appeal and eventually was published as *The History of the Communist Party of the Soviet Union (Bolsheviks): Short Course.* Between 1938 and 1953 no fewer than 42.8 million copies were printed.[45] Although he was in effect editor in chief and went over the text innumerable times, Stalin did not claim authorship. Instead he was featured prominently, and his wise words were frequently cited—more than a dozen times for the period before 1914.[46]

The *Short Course* was meant to be a political primer for the Soviet Union, and every educated person had to pass exams based on it. No doubt the textbook helped socialize generations to the appeals of Stalinism. It was translated into sixty-seven languages and turned Communists around the world into Stalinists.[47] It instilled in them his hatred for the "double-dealer" (*dvurushnik*), and it spelled out how constant vigilance was needed. That message was taken to heart especially in the developing countries, like China, Vietnam, and Cambodia, where it was used as part of political and ideological Stalinization.[48]

The recently uncovered documentation shows that Stalin played a key role and wore many hats. He was the decider, the ideologist in chief, a patron and "oracle," a father figure and "friend of the people," but also a taskmaster, judge, and jury. As we will now see, ultimately, he became a new kind of emperor—one who issued decrees in the name of Communist ideals.[49]

PART III

STALIN'S COLD WAR

CHAPTER 13

New Communist Regimes
in Poland and Czechoslovakia

C ommunist dictatorships were built in two stages in Eastern Europe. In the first, running from the late war years until 1946–47, Stalin and his advisers worked with indigenous politicians who set up "national front" governments. In a second phase, "people's republics" emerged that, notwithstanding their labels, were one-party Communist dictatorships under the rule of Moscow.[1]

For Stalin, an early, complex, and especially significant strategic concern was Poland. There he faced long-standing hatreds of all things Russian and popular hostility to Communism. By contrast, more people in Czechoslovakia were positively disposed to the Soviet Union and still felt the sting of betrayal over the West's 1938 surrender to Hitler. Some support for the Czech Communist Party, which went back to the 1930s, remained. The two countries had in common their liberation by the Red Army and the Communist-backed popular fury aimed at their large German minorities. Although both countries took somewhat different paths, both ended up, like the others in Eastern Europe, more or less as Stalin wanted.

RISE OF COMMUNISM IN POLAND

The Polish Committee of National Liberation (PKWN) was officially proclaimed on July 22, 1944, in Chełm, in the province of Lublin, just after the arrival of the Red Army. As we saw in Chapter 5, this thinly veiled Communist organization was the vehicle Stalin used to establish a regime to his liking.[2] Although Poland was not even part of the notorious "percentages agreement" to which Churchill had given his assent in October, the prime minister more or less acknowledged that Poland belonged to the Soviet sphere of influence. Stalin blithely told Prime Minister Stanisław Mikołajczyk of the "London Poles" not to worry: "Communism does not fit the Poles. They are too individualistic, too nationalistic. Poland's future economy should be based on private enterprise. Poland will be a capitalistic state."[3]

Already in November, intellectuals were encouraged to join new Polish-Soviet Friendship societies, the aim of which was to cultivate ties among "fraternal Slavic peoples" and to make those bonds a source of "material and cultural prosperity."[4] The organizations had the difficult task of inventing a tradition of Polish-Russian friendship.[5] Out in the countryside, the PKWN and the Soviet forces were hunting down the opposition.[6]

In the night of December 31, 1944, the PKWN proclaimed itself the new Polish Provisional Government, which came into being the next day. The president, Bolesław Bierut, was a longtime Communist functionary who had lived in Moscow for years; the prime minister, Edvard Osóbka-Morawski, was head of the Polish Socialist Party (PPS). The key figure, however, was the deputy prime minister, Władysław Gomułka, first secretary of the Polish Workers' Party (PPR or Communist Party).[7] The Soviet Union formally recognized the new government almost immediately.

On April 21, 1945, Stalin took time from the Battle for Berlin to sign a "treaty of friendship" with the provisional government. It was publicized the next day, on Lenin's birthday, and so in a way it achieved the Bolsheviks' old dream that had been cut short in 1920 at the gates of Warsaw.[8]

As a gesture to Western concerns, Stalin invited members of the Polish government-in-exile, headed by Mikołajczyk, for talks that began on June 16. They were even given four of the twenty-one ministries in a "united" Provisional Government of National Unity, announced on June 28—Mikołajczyk was made a second deputy prime minister. This flimsy window dressing was enough for the United States and Great Britain to extend formal recognition to the new government on July 5.

In early 1945, with only 30,000 members in the PPR, Stalin was anxious lest the activities of the new regime spark local resistance. He told Communist leaders in no uncertain terms to avoid being overly ambitious. In response, the Polish government, backed up by the Red Army on the ground, confiscated the property of "only" 10,000 landowners and around 13,000 or so larger estates and parceled it out to curry favor. In those days, that kind of restraint apparently passed for moderation.[9]

The Red Army was unruly, a fact bemoaned by Soviet political officers in the field, who seemed helpless to stop the rape, pillage, and plunder, especially in the new western regions.[10] In spite of it all, on balance most Poles concluded that the Reds were not as bad as the Third Reich had been.[11] Moreover, army engineers chalked up positive accomplishments and helped to reconstruct cities, dams, bridges, and roads.[12] In addition, there was a steady flow of Soviet advisers, and in March 1945 the Kremlin had sent an economic mission of forty or so experts to assist in restoring the infrastructure and getting the economy going again.[13]

Stalin invited Polish leaders to Moscow to keep them on the right path, at times once a month, and impressed them with lavish receptions. Polish party chief Gomułka was a hard-bitten character who had been arrested in the 1930s. He had escaped and been shot but had stayed in Poland to battle the Germans. For Gomułka, what stood out in his November 1945 meeting in the Kremlin was Stalin's sovereign control and intimate knowledge of Polish politics, society, and the economy. Although the Boss was still hoping for a $6 billion loan from the United States, he was not at all worried that the Americans might be upset by the land confiscation and nationalization of industry that was going on in Poland. He encouraged the Poles to push ahead, telling them that Czech president Beneš was already doing such things.[14]

As the Poles set up their administration, Moscow gave more advice. Practically the first thing they did was to create a secret police based on the Soviet model. A new Ministry of Public Security opened for business on January 1, 1945, the first day of the new regime. It was run by longtime Communist Stanisław Radkiewicz. The department of security, Bezpieka (officially Bezpieczeństwo), was constructed by Polish officers trained at the Soviets' NKVD school in Kuybyshev, with the continuing aid of more than a thousand Soviet advisers. In 1945 the secret police already had 23,718 national and local officials equipped with nearly unchecked powers.[15]

The first Polish concentration camps took over the already existing facilities at Auschwitz and Majdanek, as well as at Sikawa (formerly Dachsgrube, a subcamp of Auschwitz) and Jaworzno. In short order, there were more than a hundred of them.[16] The camps had three functions, namely to hold German men, women, and children prior to deportation; to serve as places of punishment (for crimes committed under the occupation); and to operate as work camps "renting out" prisoners to industry and agriculture. They also held German POWs who were forced to work. Many camps had more than 1,000 inmates and a few, like Jaworzno, close to 50,000 at its high point in May 1945. Polish studies describe what happened in the camps "as a role reversal," with the winners trying to outdo what the Germans had done. Following the Soviet model, German prisoners were exploited until they were useless and then sent home.[17]

Stalin thought the Polish Communists should push for early elections, but they knew their limits and opted to test the waters by holding a referendum on June 30, 1946. Citizens were asked three questions: whether the "principles" of nationalizing industry and land reform should be adopted; whether the new western borders should be accepted; and whether the Senate should be abolished. By then the security services, along with the army and citizens' militia, put together and mobilized a force of 250,000 to influence the outcome for the Communists. When all else failed, they tore up opposition ballots.[18] In spite of such voter fraud, Polish Socialist Party (PPS) leaders visiting Stalin in August said that only 28 percent of the voters were behind the government.[19] The PPS wanted him to act as a "referee" and bring about a Socialist-Communist alliance.[20]

After much preparation, the first elections were called for January 19, 1947. Stalin had lost interest in keeping Mikołajczyk in the mix because this deputy prime minister had unforgivably demanded an international commission to ensure fair balloting.[21] Gomułka, of the misleadingly named Democratic Bloc—a coalition of parties led by the Communists—charged that Mikołajczyk was a "proxy" sent by Winston Churchill "to become the Polish Führer."[22]

The Democratic Bloc won a prearranged massive majority, getting just over 80 percent of the vote and 327 seats out of 372. The results were fraudulent, but people were already used to mocking the initials of the PPR (the Communists) by reading them not as Polska Partia Robotnicza (Polish Workers' Party) but as Płatne Pachołki Rosji, or the Paid Servants of Russia.[23] Mikołajczyk's Peasant Party came in a distant second with just twenty-four seats, while the "others" got twenty-one.

The regime stage-managed the election to propagate the myth that it was founded with the backing of the people.[24] The PPR kept the presidency while upholding the appearance of "plurality" by not taking the premiership, which it gave to Józef Cyrankiewicz of the Socialist Party (PPS).

These were desperate times all over Eastern Europe, and Stalin, anxious to ensure the success of the political mission he had set himself, had to find a way of providing food aid to Poland. And he did, even though he could do so only by taking from the already dreadfully needy citizens of the USSR, who were themselves suffering through a famine.[25]

For the time being, the PPR was content with five positions in a cabinet of twenty-four, but they included the crucial ones, of security, the economy, and education. Politics now changed and became more like a series of stage-managed rituals. Political opposition was weakened without a leader like Mikołajczyk, who in October felt he had no choice but to flee.[26] The story of Communism in Poland was by no means prewritten, and it would turn out that Władysław Gomułka had ideas of his own of a "Polish road to socialism."[27] That Stalinism would emerge at the end, however, was no longer really in doubt.

CZECHOSLOVAKIA'S PASSAGE FROM ONE EMPIRE INTO ANOTHER

During the war, Dr. Edvard Beneš had been president of the exiled Czechoslovakian government in London. A trained philosopher and later a professor at the renowned Charles University in Prague, he was a nationalist and dedicated anti-Communist. Since 1940, Beneš had been working on a political program for his country's rebirth, the centerpiece of which was the expulsion of most of its large German minority.[28] Convinced that the key to postwar peace in Europe was to solve "disruptive" minority problems, he advocated population transfers "on a very large scale."[29] Such arguments helped persuade the British War Cabinet in July 1942 to adopt the "general principle of the transfer of German minorities in Central and Southeastern Europe back to Germany after the war."[30] Beneš went to Washington in May 1943, secured Roosevelt's agreement, and basked in the applause on an American speaking tour.[31]

The Czech president knew perfectly well that he would need Soviet support, as in all likelihood the Red Army would be directly involved in liberating his country. In addition, the Soviet Union would almost certainly be more supportive of pushing the German minority to the west. Thus he flew to Moscow and met with Stalin and Molotov between December 13 and 20 and signed a treaty of friendship. He told Molotov of the West's reservations about "the extent of the punishment" to be meted out to the Germans in the formerly Czech Sudetenland. On December 18, Stalin gave his approval for their expulsion and for sending hundreds of thousands of Czech Magyars back to Hungary as well. Overflowing with good wishes, he urged Czechoslovakia to get closer to the USSR. He even proposed that the Czechs make small territorial demands on Poland, in order that the resulting Soviet-Czech border would become "as long as possible."[32]

The Czech record of the conversations shows that it was Beneš who offered Moscow the services of his new government. He said that the new Czech regime would "speak and act in a fashion agreeable" to the Soviet government on all major foreign policy decisions and that he wanted "the policies of the two nations to be coordinated from this time onwards."[33] Without lifting a finger, Stalin was handed a "friendship treaty" that all but delivered Czechoslovakia to the Soviet sphere of influence and opened the door for the Communists to assume a leading role. No wonder Stalin used this treaty as an example of how to regularize postwar relationships between the Soviet Union and other countries in Europe.

In Moscow, Czech Communist leader Klement Gottwald was elated when he heard about these events. However, the head of the officially abolished, but nonetheless active, Communist International (Comintern), Georgi Dimitrov, believed that Beneš was setting a trap for them by encouraging their radicalism in the hopes that the Czech people would be appalled and repulsed by Communism. Thus Dimitrov advised Gottwald and the Czech Communists to proceed cautiously and, further, to insist that the new Czech government be formed by a coalition of parties.[34] Gottwald was a colorful figure, born in 1896 to an unmarried mother in dire poverty. A militant for years, he fled to Moscow during the war and, in consultation with the Soviets, developed plans for postwar Czechoslovakia.

During another stay in Moscow in March 1945, Beneš and Foreign Minister Jan Masaryk spoke with Molotov and received "confirmation of a positive attitude of the Soviet government" for their plans to evict the German population. The president thought that he could outmaneuver his Czech political opponents by leading the country's campaign of retribution and renewal, but he was about to find out otherwise.[35] Before the Czech delegation, including Beneš and Gottwald, left for their temporary headquarters in liberated Košice, Stalin hosted a banquet and in a toast to them played his most important card. He offered a solid commitment "to resist the German danger" in the future and gave his assurance that "the Soviet Union will never interfere in the internal affairs" of its allies. That statement was taken to heart by the Czechs and especially by Beneš, who perhaps somewhat naïvely then put aside earlier worries about Stalin's revolutionary aims in Europe.[36]

When Beneš returned to Prague in May 1945, it was with a Moscow-approved coalition government led by Prime Minister Zdeněk Fierlinger, a Social Democrat with strong sympathies for Communism. The Kremlin saw Fierlinger as a perfect choice to head the "National Front"; he was politically aligned with Moscow in every important respect, yet his Social Democratic credentials would serve to hide from worried voters the extent of the Communist penetration into their homeland. The Czech-Moscow deliberations also produced a cabinet that included seven Communists, some holding such key posts as the ministries of the interior and of information. According to one insider at the time, the "real head of the government was Klement Gottwald," the deputy prime minister and head of the Communist Party.[37]

To some extent, events in the streets overtook the political process: on May 5, 1945, factions hoping to grab power before the Soviets arrived mounted an uprising in Prague. This attempt, similar to the action taken by the Poles in Warsaw in August 1944, lasted until the Red Army entered five days later.[38] Enthusiastic crowds welcomed the liberators— until Soviet troops began to indulge themselves. No one was safe, least of all German women in the internment camps. Among the tales of horror was one about an unfortunate who was "raped until she died and was left where she lay."[39]

At the same time, some of Prague's citizens, themselves reveling in this hatred, led German women through the streets, beat them, forced them to perform punishing exercises, and savagely shaved their heads. They whipped the women until their clothes were in shreds or they were stark naked and shoeless. Adding to the abject humiliation, red ink or oil was then poured over their heads, all to the savage merriment of the mob.[40]

Part of what was called "wild retribution" was deliberately fostered by Czech leaders who, like Beneš, thought that revolution and vigilante justice would consume their German enemies. In a speech on May 12, he declared that they could not risk another war in ten or twenty years, and he held the Germans collectively guilty for the crimes of Nazism: "We have said to ourselves that we must liquidate the German problem out of the Republic." By his decree on May 19, the government took over the property of those individuals and organizations deemed "unreliable."[41]

All political parties demanded the expulsions, though at first the Communists tried to protect German resisters to Nazism. That effort did not last long. They then took steps, with mixed success, to channel the raging masses by issuing various calls, such as to establish work camps, where Germans would be forced to make good the damages they had caused.[42]

Sexual violence became the order of the day in the Prague football stadium, where some 10,000 Germans were held for days. One man and his family entered there on May 16 and left on June 3; he saw that the women (and likely also his wife) paid the heaviest price. They were dragged away each night or just raped among the prisoners, either by Czech guards or by Red Army soldiers.[43]

As these crimes were being perpetrated, the Communist minister of education on May 29 boasted of being able to "purify" Prague and the surrounding areas of Germans. He said the people had a great helper in the Red Army, and the alternatives were clear: "We must decide either for the East or the West."[44]

Czechoslovakia's liberation was followed by so many arrests of Nazis, collaborators, POWs, and then ethnic Germans, that, like Poland, it also resorted to using former Nazi concentration camps, Theresienstadt, for example. As of May 1945, the western part of the country (Bohemia and Moravia) had some 500 "camps"—carrying various labels—and Slovakia had many as well. At that time in greater Prague, up to 25,000 people were interned in forty or so different places, from schools and prisons to the football stadium. By mid-June they were centralized, with three of the Czech camps holding more than 20,000 each, and one at Tábor that contained 40,000 people.[45]

The first concentration camps hosted the horror and mistreatment unto death. People were executed through beating, hanging, and lethal injection. By the beginning of September, there were at least 10,000 children in the camps under the age of fourteen. Research has been unable to determine the total number of deaths in these camps, but by all accounts it was considerable.[46]

In the meantime, when Stalin met with Czech prime minister Fierlinger on June 28 to solidify Soviet-Czech friendship, they ironed out further population questions. They signed a deal about Carpatho-Ukraine, a small territory that Czechoslovakia had obtained as part of the peace settlement in 1919. It was now ceded to the Soviet Socialist Republic of Ukraine. Population exchanges would be allowed, and the inhabitants would be free to become either Soviet or Czech citizens. It was in this context that Stalin told his Czech guests that they should deport their Germans. "We won't disturb you," he said, "throw them out."[47] The Czech army proceeded to leave truckloads of desperate and starving women, older people, and children, in the Soviet zone of Germany without notice, to fend for themselves. Soviet occupation authorities complained to Moscow but to no avail.[48]

Stalin and his Czech and Polish comrades wanted to move out as many Germans as possible before the upcoming Potsdam Conference. So force the issue they did, for in the first or "wild" period of the expulsions, a total estimated at 400,000 were driven from Poland and 450,000 from Czechoslovakia.[49] The radicals who participated in these expulsions were often enticed by promises that they would get the lands and properties of the dispossessed.[50]

CZECH COMMUNISTS SOLIDIFY THEIR HOLD ON POWER

At the first elections on May 26, 1946, the Communists emerged as the big winners, with 40.2 percent of the vote in Czech lands and just over 31 percent nationwide. Non-Communists were shocked at the results but admitted that the elections were relatively free and not stolen, as they were elsewhere in Eastern Europe. A strong pro-Soviet mood prevailed in the country, which felt betrayed by the West over the 1938 deal that gave them away to Hitler at the notorious Munich Conference. Now the Communists were by far the best-organized and largest party, with a membership growing from 28,485, at war's end, to more than one million by the time of the first elections.[51] The idealists among the joiners thought things could be different and better here than in Russia. More advanced Czechoslovakia, "with an intelligent, well-educated population," they thought, could avoid all the mistakes made in the Soviet Union, and "we would leap over a whole epoch." Moreover, material considerations led some to seek the party card as a necessary credential in the competition to become managers or custodians of nationalized properties of evicted Germans or Czechs who had fled.[52]

Their new leader, Klement Gottwald, who became prime minister, was intent on securing their hold on power and delighted to play by rules set in Moscow. Revolution rolled across the country, fueled by a desire to conquer the past and run through "the wide-open gates of the millennium."[53] Czech politicians, who acted without being pressured by the Kremlin, led the surge toward a more collectivist future, carried along by ideas shared by Communists, Social Democrats, and members of other parties. A land reform in May confiscated large tracts of property, and in July the state nationalized the banks and large industry. The Communists, surprised at winning such hearty support, reported to Moscow that they had made breakthroughs among the workers and even in the countryside.[54]

Regardless of such backing, the Czech Communists and their Soviet advisers assumed that control of the security apparatus would be crucial to getting and holding power. The Communist minister of the interior, Václav Nosek, set out to centralize and control Czechoslovakia's security apparatus and its secret police—the State Security StB (Státní bezpečnost).[55] Although after the elections of 1946, the minority parties persisted in trying to limit Communist control of the StB and other branches of the security system, neither Gottwald nor Rudolf Slánský, the general secretary of the Czech Communist Party, would hear of such a thing. With remarkable speed, they succeeded in having party comrades appointed to key security positions all over the country. They used materials gathered from all sources, including incarcerated Nazi police, to blacken the names of political opponents.[56]

The new regime gained considerable popular support by driving out the German minority. In the 1946 elections, people who moved into formerly German-dominated regions of Czechoslovakia voted overwhelmingly for the Communists, especially in what used to be the Sudetenland. There the party got three-quarters of the ballots.[57] Moreover, the new regime won both legitimacy and gratitude from the new residents, who were more deeply tied to and dependent on the state. A similar pattern of reliance on, and solidarity with, the government can be discerned for the Poles who moved into parts of their new country that had formerly been German.[58]

The Czechoslovakians wanted still more ethnic cleansing and yearned to get rid of their Hungarian minority, which exceeded 400,000 people. Given those numbers in the southern part of Slovakia, the operation would have been another brutal one. Stalin initially told the Czech leaders he would support such a "transfer," but the idea was gradually dropped because of objections from the Hungarian government, as well as Soviet officials on the spot.[59]

The big news on the national scene in 1946 was that Czechoslovakia would be taking its own "special path" to socialism and would not have to follow the Soviet model. Prime Minister Gottwald made this announcement after meeting with Stalin in September. The coalition government soon convened and agreed unanimously on a two-year plan. That measure did not go far enough for the Communists, and in January 1947 they proclaimed their intention to win an absolute majority in the next elections. Even so, their opponents were unable to form a unified front to stop this looming threat to their existence.[60]

WINNING SUPPORT THROUGH ETHNIC CLEANSING IN POLAND

When Władysław Sikorski, president of Poland's government-in-exile, went to Moscow in late 1941, Stalin took him aside and offered German lands in the west as compensation for what Poland would lose in the east. In a speech back in London, Sikorski promised his people protection from the "German horde that for centuries had pressed to the east." His government would obtain secure borders, and it would grant full legal equality to all—with the exception of the ethnic Germans.[61]

Churchill shared some of Stalin's ideas on "transferring" populations. As early as December 1940, the prime minister mused in private that certain "exchanges of population would have to take place."[62] He was transfixed by the allure of the 1923 Lausanne Treaty, which had ended the bitter conflict between Turkey and Greece. It mandated an exchange of populations from the contested regions. The process resulted in tens of thousands of deaths and the enduring misery of the resettlers on both sides. Nevertheless, Churchill and others in the anti-Hitler coalition overlooked the costs and pointed to the benefits. As he had put it in a speech to the British House of Commons on December 15, 1944, expelling the minorities would mean there would "be no mixture of the populations to cause endless trouble."[63]

Given such attitudes in the West, which were matched and outdone in Moscow, the Polish government had a green light to proceed with the expulsion of those Germans who stubbornly refused to flee on their own. At a February 1945 sitting of the Central Committee of the Polish Communist Party, First Secretary Władysław Gomułka declared that all forces in society had to focus on "removing completely the Germans from historically Polish lands." In May he told the party's Central Committee "that if we don't Polonize the formerly German areas, then we will have no basis to take what they [the Allies] don't want to give us. We have to work out all the details of a plan for the resettlement action. We will have to provide the means. Extending the country to the West and a land reform binds the nation to the system." He said that unless they managed to move Poles into the new western parts, the administration would fall into the hands of the Red Army, and the Germans who had fled might be allowed to return. Gomułka said they had to throw out all the Germans to create a country built on a national, and not on a multinational, basis. Stalin most certainly approved, and indeed the Soviets were already evicting their own "Poles and Jews" from former eastern Poland. Many of those people were encouraged to move to the new west of Poland.[64]

Polish officials, in cooperation with the Soviet Union, took over those liberated areas in eastern Germany. In the spring of 1945, the British and Americans objected that they should not take such far-reaching steps until after a peace conference. Molotov answered that they were only entrusting the administration of the areas to the Poles "as a matter of convenience," and since nearly all the Germans had left, the Poles had become the "basic population."[65]

For Gomułka, the link between driving out the Germans and winning support for Communism was self-evident. He told the party's Central Committee that it had to station guards at the new borders and "throw out the Germans, and for any that remain we must create such conditions that they do not want to stay."[66]

In June, Polish authorities were alarmed to learn that some Germans who had been driven out were beginning to return, unhindered by the Red Army, which was unable to cope with the influx of refugees into its occupation zone in Germany. Warsaw wanted the returnees stopped and ordered expulsions, initially along the new border up to a distance of 18.6 miles. The orders, like those issued to the Polish 5th Infantry Division on June 21, were prefaced with the statement that "a great day in Polish history has arrived: the expulsion of the Germanic vermin."[67] An army report expressed mild "surprise" at the "ever greater increase" in the number of rapes committed by soldiers. It mentioned the "development of a psychosis as to the legitimacy of rape as an act of retaliation" against German women.[68]

A sense of the hatred of those days was conveyed in a Polish order in June; it stated that Germans were "to be permitted to take only enough food with them so that on their crossing the River Oder, there is *nothing left.*"[69] The Communist regime reaped the political gains, even when it meant the area's economy would be adversely affected and take longer to recover.[70] For example, at the beginning of June, the population of Breslau (Wrocław) swelled to 200,000, counting only 15,000 Poles. If all the Germans were driven out, what would happen to the city? Across wide swaths of Silesia, there were no Poles whatsoever.[71]

To replace the Germans, Poles were brought in from elsewhere. One such person was Teresa Postrzewska, who had once lived in Poland's east. The Soviets forced her out of her homeland, and she had hoped to live in Warsaw, but given the complete desolation of that city, she continued west, then received government aid, along with a new and bigger farm. For her, ethnic cleansing made it possible to have a new home, though because she was little used to the land, she remained dependent on the state.[72]

The Red Army's excesses made matters worse for Poland and also partly undermined Stalin's project of winning people over to Communism. Soldiers ran amok and destroyed property senselessly. One Polish report from early May from the rich Silesian area noted that the war had left many urban areas untouched and that the real destruction came after the fighting when the Red Army burned down 60 to 70 percent of the cities in drunken revelries. Factories not destroyed were disassembled and sent back to the Soviet Union in such numbers that Polish authorities feared the worst. Looking to the future, they said: "We will likely take over only naked walls."[73] The Poles were sickened and revolted by the Red Army's campaign of rape, which left behind venereal diseases of epidemic proportions.[74]

At Potsdam in mid-1945, the Western Allies showed some, but not much, concern for what was happening. Indeed its official declaration recognized that "the transfer to Germany of German populations" out of Poland, Czechoslovakia, and Hungary "will have to be undertaken." These "transfers" were supposed to take place "in an orderly and humane manner," but nothing was done to make that happen.[75]

The "sanctioned phase" of the expulsions after Potsdam was no more humane than the first. The condition of Germans who survived the trip from Poland or Czechoslovakia—many dying in the cattle cars—became such a scandal that on August 27, just back in the House of Commons from Potsdam, Churchill expressed his uneasiness at the "tragedy" taking place. Until a few weeks before, he had favored these transfers. Only on November 20 did the Allied Control Council in Germany put forward a systematic plan to resettle Germans from the east and negotiations with the occupation powers begin.[76]

Gomułka visited Moscow that November and brought Stalin the news that Marshal Zhukov, head of the Soviet zone of occupation in Germany, would not accept any more deportees. Stalin brushed that information aside, along with Churchill's belated objections, and said simply: "You should create such conditions for the Germans that they want to escape themselves. Keep only the ones you need."[77]

If some reservations were voiced in the West, most were sympathetic to the "need" for the expulsions. The main complaint from the Western Allies was that starving and propertyless people were being transported to an occupied Germany that was already short of all the essentials.[78]

The Polish government became fanatical in its efforts to stamp out the smallest sign that Germans had once dwelled in the "recovered territories." For example, in late 1946 and early 1947, new strictures were decreed to erase any sign of the German language. Fines were levied on anyone heard speaking it, even in private, or found using it in letters with acquaintances. In October 1947 new committees were created to seek out the last vestiges of the hated script in cemeteries, on roadside crosses, on household dishes, and even on ashtrays.[79]

In spite of this official fanaticism, people found ways of quietly resisting, as can be seen in Silesia. Government instructions for "de-Germanization" (*odniemczenie*) called for erasing the culture and history of all things Germanic as quickly and completely as possible.[80] The last "resettlement" train, carrying 32 persons, left Silesia on January 18, 1951. The ethnic cleansing, begun six years before, had finally ended, and 211,000 persons from that region were gone. According to Polish sources, "at least 22,000" families had been torn apart. What appalled the authorities was to learn in 1952 that 80,000 citizens there still gave "German" as their nationality in their personal passports, so the regime continued its efforts.

BLEMISHES ON VICTORY

Polish and Czech historians insisted for many years that the "resettlement" of the Germans was "necessary" and a "justified act of defense" to avoid being swallowed up by their neighbor. Often Western historians echoed the triumphalism by claiming the ethnic cleansing was needed for postwar "stability." Anyone who disagreed was denigrated as an apologist for the racist process that the Germans started during the war.

Czesław Miłosz, one of Poland's most gifted writers and a disappointed patriot, recalled what it was like after the war:

> The entire country was gripped by a single emotion: hatred. Peasants, receiving land, hated; workers and office employees, joining the Party, hated; socialists, participating nominally in the government, hated; writers, endeavoring to get their manuscripts published, hated. This was not their government; it owed its existence to an alien army. The nuptial bed prepared for the wedding of the government with the nation was decked with national symbols and flags, but from beneath that bed protruded the boots of an NKVD agent.[81]

This description fits practically every country in Eastern Europe at that time. Ilya Ehrenburg, who traveled the area, was struck by how the bile of racism spilled over into the postwar period. He saw fistfights between Hungarians and Romanians, and Italians cursing at Slovenes. In Bucharest, Jews told him that people yelled at them, "Too bad Hitler didn't get you!" In the Sudetenland he saw Czechs force Germans to wear white armbands as a sign of humiliation, and he became extremely upset that Czechoslovakia was adopting fascist methods supposedly to fight fascism.[82]

All across Eastern Europe, the Germans were driven out. By 1950, 12 to 15 million had fled or were expelled, with most resettled in divided Germany.[83] No consensus exists on how many perished, but common estimates range between 1.71 and 2.8 million.[84] However, one historian of the Wehrmacht maintains that while scholars tend to underestimate how many Germans were killed in uniform, they overestimate the numbers who died through the expulsions, a figure he puts at between 500,000 and 600,000.[85]

The anti-Semitism that had flourished virulently in Germany, and that was all over Central and Eastern Europe during the war years, did not dissolve overnight, and it sometimes even flared into violence. The cry of "down with the Żydokomuna" or "Jewish Communism" was still heard in parts of Poland. It was reinforced by ancient religious myths that culminated in pogroms in Kraków in August 1945, in which several Jews were killed. In Kielce almost exactly a year later, another 42 people were murdered and others wounded.[86] The NKVD reported to Beria that in the period from January to mid-September 1945, 291 Jews were killed on Polish territory. The literature indicates that there were more.[87]

Jan Gross suggests that the Polish regime gained favor by never demanding anything like the restitution of property confiscated from the Jews during the Holocaust.[88] For many Jews, the violence and hatred became unbearable, and they emigrated.

As a matter of record, 90 percent of the Jewish community in Poland had been murdered in the Second World War. Most of those who survived had either sought refuge or had been deported east by the Soviets. Between 1944 and 1946, a total of 780,000 persons were repatriated to Poland, and they included 137,000 Jews. During roughly the

Tsarist police photographs of Joseph Stalin taken after his arrest in Baku, Azerbaijan, March 1908. In early November he was sent to Siberia, from where he escaped, as he had before, to be rearrested and exiled again. Finally in June 1913 he was sent to Turukhansk in northern Siberia.

Stalin (right) photographed in 1935 with Communist Party official Nikita Khrushchev and members of the Communist Young Pioneers. Khrushchev would emerge as the first of Stalin's heirs.

Outside the Soviet embassy during the Tehran Conference, 1943. From left, American general George C. Marshall, shaking hands with British ambassador to the USSR Archibald Clark Kerr; Harry Hopkins; a Soviet interpreter; Joseph Stalin; Commissar Vyacheslav Molotov; and Marshal Kliment Voroshilov.

President Harry Truman and Stalin at the Potsdam Conference in July/August 1945. To Truman's right, with his hand on the rail, is Secretary of State James Byrnes. On Stalin's left is Commissar Molotov. Leaning over Truman's left shoulder is Charles Bohlen, presidential translator and adviser.

President Franklin Delano Roosevelt (right), leaving New Year's Day services in Alexandria, Virginia, with British Prime Minister Winston Churchill, January 1, 1942.

A ceremonial meeting at the border between the Soviet and British sectors near the Brandenburg Gate in defeated Berlin in 1945. British field marshal Bernard L. Montgomery, with his back to the camera and shaking hands with Marshal Georgi Zhukov, with Marshal Konstantin Rokossovsky saluting on the right.

The celebration of Stalin's seventieth birthday in Moscow, December 1949, brought together most of the leaders of the Communist world. From left: Mao Zedong, Walter Ulbricht, Stalin, and Nikita Khrushchev.

An oversized and godlike image of the Soviet leader in an event at Moscow's Bolshoi Theater, 1951. This was one of many examples of Stalin's popular deification.

The 1952 poster says "Glory to the great Stalin—the architect of Communism!" Such titles had been used since the 1930s. In the background is one of the seven "tall buildings." Stalin remarked to Nikita Khrushchev after 1945, "We won the war and are recognized as victors the world over. What will happen if visitors walk around Moscow and find no skyscrapers? They will make unfavorable comparisons with capitalist cities."

At the Seventh World Congress of the Communist International in Moscow, 1935, with several persons who gained prominence after the war. Left to right, front row: Georgi Dimitrov (Bulgaria), Palmiro Togliatti (Italy), Wilhelm Florin (Germany), Wang Ming (China); back row: Otto Kuusinen (Finland), Klement Gottwald (Czechoslovakia), Wilhelm Pieck (Germany), and Dmitry Manuilsky (Ukraine).

A meeting of the Yugoslav Communist Partisan guerrilla leadership at Vis, Yugoslavia, in 1944: Josip Tito is in the middle and his next in command, Edvard Kardelj, is to his immediate left; on Tito's right is secret police boss Aleksandar Ranković. Milovan Djilas is on the far right.

above: Communist leaders of Hungary, from left to right: Mátyás Rákosi, first secretary of the party (1945–56) and deputy prime minister until 1952, then prime minister to 1953. In the center is Ernö Gerö, prime minister (July 18, 1956–October 25, 1956); and on the right Imre Nagy, prime minister (1953–1955, briefly also 1956).

center: Władysław Gomułka, first secretary of the Polish Communist Party, arrested in 1951 as part of purges that swept Eastern Europe. He was released, rehabilitated, and, in 1956, made first secretary again. He ruled "with an iron fist" until 1970.

at left: The newly appointed Czechoslovakian cabinet under Communist leader Prime Minister Klement Gottwald (right). Following a coup in February 1948, Deputy Prime Minister Antonín Zápotocký is signing papers, and to the left is President Edvard Beneš, who would resign and die in June, and be succeeded by Gottwald.

Romanian leaders in 1950, from left to right: Prime Minister Petru Groza; Gheor-ghe Gheorghiu-Dej, general secretary of the Communist Party; Ana Pauker, minister of foreign affairs; Vasile Luca, vice premier; Teohari Georgescu, minis-ter of the interior; and propaganda chief Iosif Chişinevschi.

Berliners watching the arrival and departure of planes after the beginning of the blockade in mid-1948, as the Cold War unfolded. The picture conveys a sense of how people were enthralled because, just over three years after Hitler's death, Western bombers were flying to their rescue, bearing the necessities of life.

same time, 140,000 Jews left for Palestine, and the Jewish community in Poland faded away almost completely.[89]

Officially the Polish Communists were opposed to all forms of prejudice and anti-Semitism. However, when Władysław Gomułka spoke with and wrote to Stalin in December 1948, he offered a negative opinion about the Jews in his own movement, some of whom did "not feel tied by any bonds to the Polish nation or therefore to the working class." There was evidence, he said, that the Jews in senior positions of the party and state provoked "bitterness and discontent" among the population. He accepted some of the blame himself and went so far as to say that in the future the party should cut or at least "limit the increase in the number of Jewish comrades" in its higher echelons, as well as in the state bureaucracy.[90] Gomułka had recently been removed as general secretary and was under threat of being purged and arrested. Perhaps he hoped to appeal to Stalin's prejudices, which were growing ever more obvious during this period. None of it helped, and Gomułka was to be forced out.

Facing up to all that happened in the wake of the war in Eastern Europe has been difficult. Only after the revolutions of 1989 did questioning the grand narrative about the "need" for ethnic cleansing really begin. Newly elected Czech president Václav Havel cast doubt on the morality of those actions, above all the assignment of collective guilt to all Germans. Johann Wolfgang Brügel, like Havel one of the Czech dissidents in the 1970s, said that "from the denial of basic civil rights to almost one-quarter of the population, to the confiscation of all rights of the entire population is a comparatively small step." Another writer felt the experiences of the Nazi occupation "brought to power forces that accommodated the totalitarian methods, symbols, speech, thought, codes, and slogans" and that they "prepared the ground for the validation of the Communists in Czechoslovak society."[91]

Polish historian Krystyna Kersten says that, one way or another, the deportation of the Germans "encouraged many Poles" who "might otherwise have been negatively disposed" to Communism to go along. Uprooted Polish settlers in the west lost their cultural points of reference and came to see themselves in terms of a Polish national identity along the lines set in the Cold War.[92] Moreover, like Czechoslovakia, Poland made itself hostage to the Soviet Union, because only the Red

Army had sufficient clout to enforce the territorial and ethnic changes, which were not recognized in law by the West until 1989–90.[93]

At the very least, the means used by the Polish and Czech Communists to get into power led both countries away from creating a civil society that fostered values like tolerance, pluralism, civility, openness, self-determination, responsibility, and solidarity.[94]

CHAPTER 14

The Pattern of Dictatorships: Bulgaria, Romania, and Hungary

Bulgaria, Romania, and Hungary, though very different in their traditions and histories, were anti-Communist in their values from the 1930s into the Second World War. Nevertheless, under Soviet tutelage all three created Stalinist-style dictatorships and police states. It happened astonishingly fast. By 1946 the Communists had consolidated their power in coalition governments and already had the upper hand. Although there were still shocks and adjustments to come, the essentials put in place in a few months held for the next fifty years.[1]

In each of these three countries, the Communists faced varying amounts of opposition from the people, and in line with Stalinist policies, they adjusted their strategies to fit conditions on the ground. Moscow judged that Bulgaria, for example, had too many hotheads among its local Communists and instructed them to place their zealotry on hold for fear of inflaming the opposition parties. For their part, Romania and especially Hungary were both heavily anti-Communist nations. Here Stalin's approach was more cautious still. Some democratic-leaning Hungarians, initially unreceptive to the Communists, even began to think that it might be possible to work together in some sort of coalition government.

But on Moscow's rules, any such relaxation of pressure on the local population was always considered a tactical measure and thus temporary. Sooner or later, and in each of the countries, the Communists, under the direction of their Soviet Boss or on their own, would judge exactly when the moment was right to use dictatorial methods and terror. Crushing political freedom, they shackled their nations with economic systems that proved to be inefficient and required a rigid authoritarianism to sustain.

BULGARIA

Churchill and Stalin had agreed, in the percentages deal, that the Soviet Union would get 90/10 share of influence in Romania, 75/25 in Bulgaria, and 50/50 in Hungary. After Molotov haggled the next day with Foreign Secretary Eden, the Soviets bumped up their percentages in Hungary and Bulgaria to 80/20. Even if such bargaining could not be binding, it sent an unmistakable message that Stalin took to heart.

Bulgaria's fate was decided mainly in Moscow in discussions between Stalin and Georgi Dimitrov, a veteran revolutionary who had attained a degree of fame in Nazi Germany when he was arrested and tried for his alleged part in burning down the Reichstag in February 1933. The Soviets had arranged an exchange for him, and he returned to Moscow, where he continued as head of the Comintern. His goal, in the war years and afterward, was to get Communists into power around the globe and especially in his native Bulgaria.

Thus, when Marshal Zhukov flew back to Moscow on August 23, 1944, to work out plans for the coming military campaign, Dimitrov swore to him that he and his countrymen would all greet the Red Army in the Slavic tradition with bread and salt. In Sofia on September 2, however, a pro-Western group took over and sought an armistice with Britain and the United States. For Stalin, that was completely out of the question and three days later the Soviet Union declared war on Bulgaria. At midmorning on September 8, the Red Army crossed the border, and the shooting, to the extent there was much at all, was over by 9 P.M. the next day.[2]

The first Soviet representatives in Sofia were officers of SMERSH, in charge of tracking anti-Soviet activities, espionage, and traitors. They wanted the files of the Bulgarian secret police, with the lists of opponents. Soviet agents helped to revamp the Security Service (Darjhavna sigurnost), which had roots going back to the 1920s. It was transformed into the dreaded DS, which haunted the country for more than a half century. In addition, Communist partisans and former political prisoners formed a People's Militia (Narodna Militsiya). One of its leaders was Todor Zhivkov, a hard-liner from an impoverished background who went on to become dictator from the mid-1950s until forced out by the reforms sweeping Eastern Europe in 1989.[3]

With the support of characters like Zhivkov and the Soviet advisers, the Bulgarian Fatherland Front carried out a coup early on September 9. As per Stalin's advice, the government had only three or four Communists—to be sure, they were given the key ministries of the interior and justice. They cleansed the administrative system, police, army, mayors, and so on of all "antinational elements." Local Communists set out to settle scores, and one study estimates that they killed 3,000 to 4,000 people.[4] Recently, however, two historians put the death toll far higher. Marietta Stankova suggests it was "not less than 20,000," while Ekaterina Nikova maintains that between 25,000 to 30,000 "were killed or disappeared" during the first ten days of the takeover.[5]

The scale of the bloodshed was staggering and somewhat out of character in Bulgaria, with its generally easygoing political culture. When Soviet writer Ilya Ehrenburg visited after the war, he was struck by how civilized, reserved, and educated the people were. There was no milk, however, and one look at the children told him they were in poor condition.[6] Bulgaria had a tradition of religious toleration, so that along with the Christian Eastern Orthodox, it had significant Muslim, Catholic, and Jewish minorities among its prewar population of 6.6 million. Into the Second World War, it was ruled by a generally benevolent King Boris, notwithstanding the fact that it had a fascist government and became one of Hitler's allies. Yet it would not declare war on the Soviet Union and thus afterward was spared the kind of damage inflicted on its neighbors.

The last thing Stalin wanted there was a full-scale revolution, which might unleash a civil war. His preference was for a stable country, willing and able to marshal its army in the war still raging to the west. On September 11 and 24, Dimitrov sent long telegrams to the Communist Party's Central Committee in Sofia, telling them in no uncertain terms to work with their partners in the Fatherland Front. They were instructed to avoid any appearance of introducing Communism, for a mere hint of such a thing would be used by enemies. Moreover there had to be "regular people's courts, not lynch justice." As he put it, "We must speak and act not as run-of-the-mill and irresponsible provincial agitators, but as befits sober, real Bolshevik politicians and statesmen."[7]

In October, Soviet officials reinforced the point about adopting "legal means," and a new people's court began. Between November 1944 and April 1945, no fewer than 11,122 defendants were tried, and 2,730 were sentenced to death; 1,516 of the latter were executed. The verdicts of the major personages were announced only after checking with Dimitrov.[8] Between 1944 and 1962, tens of thousands were sent to one of the country's eighty-eight concentration camps.[9]

These actions blighted the reputation of Communism. Still, the party grew rapidly, for already in January 1945 it had 250,000 members, with a youth wing of 400,000. The whole country was mobilized, and Bulgaria had more activists, as a percentage of the population, than Poland or even Czechoslovakia.[10]

Communist leaders were summoned to Moscow for consultations with Stalin in early 1945 and, along with visiting Yugoslavs, met at his country dacha. He told them in so many words that the Soviet Union's alliance with the capitalists was a temporary expedient. For now, they should be cautious and maintain some "ideological flexibility."[11]

Local radicals did not agree with the "moderate" approach advocated by émigrés in Moscow. The U.S. Office of Strategic Services reported that the zealots were impatient and would try to make their country either into an independent Soviet republic or to integrate it into the Soviet Union.[12] They called for elections to show their strength, and one was set for August.

Calling out the vote in such times is unpredictable, especially when people of conscience and courage, such as Nikola Petkov, one of the leaders of the opposition, take casting a ballot seriously. He even spoke about needing international supervision to ensure a fair process. During the war Petkov had tried to stop the deportations of the Jews from (then Bulgarian) Macedonia and Thrace. In May 1943 he was among a group of notables who wrote to King Boris, beseeching him to intercede. They said that the "mass deportation of Bulgarian citizens who enjoy the same rights as all others and who are guilty of no crime, has been condemned by the great majority of Bulgarians and aroused their compassion." Although these and other appeals failed, nearly all of the 50,000 native-born Bulgarian Jews survived the war, and that must be to the credit of their fellow citizens.[13]

In the summer of 1945 at the Potsdam Conference, Stalin tried to coax the Allies into recognizing the new regimes in Bulgaria and Romania. Truman would not hear of it without proper elections. At the very least, opposition parties should be allowed to run, and to that end the Americans and British used nonrecognition to apply pressure. As the clock ticked down to the election scheduled for August 26, the Allies pointed to flagrant abuses and the terror used against non-Communist candidates. With a mere thirty-six hours to go, the Soviet representative on the Allied Control Council in Sofia postponed the voting, obviously with Stalin's permission, but without consulting the Bulgarian government.[14]

In August 1945, Stalin was deeply involved in the last hectic phase of the Soviet Union's war against Japan, but he made time for Bulgaria. He received one of the Communist delegations and instructed them to make sure that the new government had the appearance of legitimacy. He told them not to be afraid of a little opposition. "You can allow some other parties to exist outside the Fatherland Front," he admonished, and "you can hold the elections in mid-October."[15]

Petkov had been encouraged by the news that filtered out of the Potsdam Conference that summer about even moderate Western support. His opposition to the fascist wartime government had brought him into temporary alliance with the Communists, and now he wanted genuine democracy—not what the Soviets had in mind. The Allies were finally insisting on proper elections, rescheduled to November 18, and again he took heart. Unfortunately, he and others overestimated the commitment of the West, for police-state methods continued to be used to intimidate the opposition. Petkov's secretary, for example, was arrested and died in custody. Against this background, the opposition decided to boycott the elections.

Stalin, disgruntled by the events, moved into action and on November 4 dispatched Georgi Dimitrov to Sofia. The legendary figure did not return with a sense of joy or vindication but rather harbored old grievances and acted more like an imperial envoy sent from Moscow than a native son. He was outfitted with his own Soviet guard and sealed off in a grand house, with the outer walls topped by barbed wire and searchlights. He had a direct line to the Kremlin, so that Stalin could keep things moving along. To no one's surprise, the Communists "won" the elections, getting (as part of the Fatherland Front) no less than 88 percent of the votes.[16]

The results were so outlandish that the American and British foreign ministers raised the matter at their December meeting in Moscow with Molotov. They asked the Soviets to ensure that the Bulgarian government was broadened to include opposition party members.[17] Stalin, putting them off, said it would be undemocratic to meddle with the results of another country's elections. Later that day he called Dimitrov to ask him to "include one or two ministers from the opposition. Give them some kind of meaningless tasks. Obviously we are not talking here about Petkov. Someone else who is not too popular can be found."[18]

On January 7, 1946, the Bulgarian prime minister and some members of his cabinet (also a single opposition figure, but not Petkov) went to Moscow for consultations. That night they went straight to the Kremlin to hear the dictator say he would "allow" building a new government only if it included two members of the opposition. He raked them over the coals, then offered a fig leaf of mercy by saying he was willing to reduce the costs he demanded for the Red Army's occupation of their country. The Bulgarians were shocked by the entire event.[19] Even so, the Communists renewed their campaign in Bulgaria against opposition parties, almost certainly with Soviet permission. They already controlled the police and the courts, and new laws expanded their powers to arrest or detain practically anyone.

Dimitrov went to Moscow in June 1946 to get the dictator's approval for a referendum on the monarchy and to call elections for a Grand National Assembly that would draw up a constitution. Stalin wanted him to keep the Fatherland Front together and told him exactly the percentage of votes that the Communists and all the other parties should get. The balloting would be rigged to make his prediction come true.[20]

In mid-August, Dimitrov was in Moscow again to look after his failing health. He met with Stalin and his circle on September 2, and among other things they spoke about a new Bulgarian constitution, yet to be written. The Boss was convinced they needed a people's republic with a parliamentary system. He said they should "avoid frightening" the social strata that did "not belong to the working class" and make the constitution sound less radical than the one in Yugoslavia. As a self-proclaimed constitutional expert, he generously offered to read the first draft when it was ready.

The Kremlin dictator was quite candid about the future of the Communist Party in Bulgaria and revealed in passing what all the Eastern European revolutions were about. He said that the Bulgarians should found something like the British Labour Party, "a people's party," and give a home to both workers and peasants. They should not simply copy the Bolshevik model of revolution, not seek an immediate dictatorship of the proletariat and the elimination of all political opposition. Instead, they should adopt different methods and "mask" the party's Communist character for the time being.[21]

The referendum went ahead later that month, and 96 percent voted in favor of abolishing the monarchy. The election to the Grand National Assembly in October 1946 went just as Stalin ordered. The Fatherland Front got 366 deputies, of whom 265 were Communists, while the opposition Agrarians led by Petkov managed only 28 percent of the vote and 99 deputies. Appropriately enough, Dimitrov became the prime minister.[22]

The Americans and British tried to have the Soviets ensure freedom of the press, noninterference in the vote, and release of political prisoners, but their efforts got nowhere.[23] The Allies finally ratified a peace treaty with Bulgaria in mid-1947, an act that was as good as recognizing the new government. It did not moderate the regime. In August police arrested the defiant Nikola Petkov, right in the National Assembly. Colleagues who tried to stop it were brutally beaten and their party soon dissolved.

In September, Petkov was put through a show trial and sentenced to death. The Anglo-Americans demanded that the verdict be overturned, but this response had the opposite effect, since Dimitrov became convinced that it was important to act all the more swiftly. To his way of thinking, a delay would only encourage further outside interference. Petkov was hanged on September 23, 1947, and with that the opposition lost heart.[24]

ROMANIA

The Communist Party in Romania was insignificant, with only eighty members in the capital Bucharest at war's end, and no more than a thousand in the whole country, with a population (in 1947) of 15.9 million. Ilya Ehrenburg's impression was that Romania was a land of strong contrasts. In the modern capital, he saw oxen driven by the poorest peasants blocking fancy limousines. Intellectuals in sidewalk cafés discussed novels by James Joyce or the poems of Comte de Lautréamont, but outside Bucharest he found people living in the most primitive conditions.[25]

If the nation had been given a free choice in 1940 and 1941 between Nazi Germany and the Soviet Union, it would have opted for Hitler. It certainly backed the fascist leader Marshal Ion Antonescu, whose dream was the ethnic homogenization of the country through deportations. For the Jews, the operation meant mass murder. But by mid-1944, with the Red Army approaching, the *Conducător* (Leader), as Antonescu was called, could see that his time on the world stage was drawing to a close.[26]

Stalin began anticipating what would follow. In Moscow, on June 20, 1944, he created a National Democratic Bloc with the intention of using it to get Romanian Communists into power. That scheme was interrupted on August 23, when military leaders, in the name of King Michael, toppled the fascists. The new government opted to throw in with the Allies, to break its alliance, and to declare war on Germany. These steps surprised Stalin and Molotov, so that when Soviet troops entered Bucharest on August 31, they could not simply overthrow the government, nor could they immediately set about engineering a new one.

By that October, however, under Moscow's watchful eye, a more stable National Democratic Front government was formed by the Communist Party, the Social Democrats, and two other groups. The Romanian Communists decided that their party's leadership should not go to Ana Pauker, the "obvious" candidate, a brilliant strategist and politician and among the best of the exiled leaders in Moscow during the war. Instead, they opted for Gheorghe Gheorghiu-Dej, an "ethnic Romanian" who, as a former railway worker, also had impeccable proletarian roots. Pauker, they held, could act as the real power behind the scenes for a time. However, partly or perhaps mainly because Pauker was Jewish, she came into conflict with Stalin.[27]

On or before January 4, 1945, the Kremlin dictator summoned the Romanian Communist leaders to Moscow for two weeks of consultations. This was just prior to the crucial Yalta Conference. Bringing in the Romanians at such a time indicates that, notwithstanding the pleasantries he was exchanging with Roosevelt, he was busily advancing the Communist cause. Now he instructed the Romanian guests to avoid setting off alarm bells among the bourgeoisie at home; they should not "bring up nationalizing at present." Reforms were to be modest, even in the countryside, where lands such as those left behind by the émigrés could be redistributed. Such a step would win support and make it possible for the Communists to "work toward a national-democratic front."[28] Stalin confirmed that Gheorghiu-Dej would be the party's general secretary and not Pauker, who was Jewish and had "bourgeois" origins. For her part, she was terribly worried about being summoned to Moscow and half feared she would never emerge from the meeting in the dreary Central Committee building.[29]

Back in Bucharest, there was social turmoil and demonstrations on February 24. Political killings resulted: whether the Communists or die-hard fascists were the perpetrators remained unclear.[30] Three days later Stalin's henchman Andrei Vyshinsky arrived. Capitalizing on the unrest, the Red Army occupied government facilities and pressured King Michael into dismissing the government led by General Nicolae Rădescu. Finally on March 6 the king agreed to hand the premiership to Petru Groza, a peculiar character who in his dapper clothes and top hat did not look like the leader of a political party calling itself the Ploughmen's Front. Vyshinsky insisted on Groza, who was notably not a member of the Communist Party but was sympathetic to the cause. The new National Democratic Front government that emerged had Communists getting the ministries of internal affairs, justice, and communications, all crucial for the eventual takeover. A fellow traveler was in charge of propaganda.[31]

In a bid to gain support, on the day before Groza's appointment, the government confiscated the lands of war criminals and of those who had fought against the Allies or fled for political reasons. Also seized was the property of absentee landlords and those who possessed more than fifty hectares—the latter were compensated. Most of the spoils were redistributed to the poorest peasants. Production fell almost immediately, and soon desperate shortages and famine arose in a place the Soviets viewed as one of "milk and honey," where they could always find badly needed foodstuffs.[32]

On March 7 a delegation of Soviet specialists met with Pauker and four of her comrades. According to a report by the fledgling OSS, the team came with a ten-point political plan that the government would follow for the next three years to transform it into a one-party dictatorship. Using a refurbished secret police, they were to eliminate political opposition, one way or another.[33]

That evening the fifteen members of the Central Committee of the Romanian Communist Party met to map out specifics. Pauker expressed confidence that the national front strategy would help gain support, although she felt that they had to make themselves more visible and recruit members, as indeed soon happened. She also said that the Communists had to repress the "reactionary" segments of society and not allow "people on the street who will become active enemies," perhaps even put them in camps. The Party would have to make strenuous efforts to win over the population at large, organize the workers, and reach out to the countryside with land reforms.[34]

The same day Groza announced that there would be a purge of the fascists from public life, and that meant getting rid of anyone standing in the way. In April two people's courts were established, and Communist minister of justice Lucrețiu Pătrășcanu, recently returned from the Soviet Union, appointed public prosecutors, most of them members of the party, to examine the cases of 2,700 persons. About half were indicted and 668 were found guilty, mostly in absentia because they had fled. In total, 48 people were sentenced to death, but only four of them were executed. Groza mentioned offhandedly in May 1945 that 90,000 people were under arrest. Something on the order of one thousand magistrates were forced out and replaced by more politically reliable candidates. By the end of 1945, an estimated 50,000 to 60,000 government workers had been dismissed, and beyond that threats were used to gain people's support for the regime.[35]

On June 28, 1946, the tribunals were disbanded. Their verdicts had been mild, especially given the extent of the previous regime's crimes—which included the wartime mass murder of Jews. According to a recent commission's report, between 280,000 and 380,000 Romanian and Ukrainian Jews from "territories under Romanian administration" had been killed during the Holocaust.[36] Half or even less of the Jewish community survived.

The Kremlin had long since decided that the only way the Romanian Communists would get into power seamlessly was through elections that could be held up to the West as beyond reproach. However, the majority of the people still hated the Soviet Union and had little taste for Communism. Moreover, the Red Army's occupation of the country led to inevitable crimes against the population, which partly undermined the Stalinist political mission. Additionally, the factions in the Romanian Communist Party sometimes worked at cross purposes.

In spite of everything, when Gheorghiu-Dej visited the Soviet capital in April 1946, he was bold enough to assure Molotov that in the next elections he and his allies would certainly get 70 to 75 percent of the vote. The party was badly in need of funding, however, and to ensure the results, Molotov provided $200,000.[37]

The Romanian Communists then formed a Bloc of Democratic Parties (BPD), another of the grand alliances of the Left. The first elections were finally held on November 19. By that time everything possible had been put in the way of a free expression of opinion. Although rumor had it that the vote ran against the Communists, the official tally (published after checking with Moscow) gave the Bloc 349 seats, or 70 percent of the vote. Gheorghiu-Dej had promised Stalin that they would get close to those figures. The opposition parties combined ended up with only 65 seats, a result no one believed. Recent research suggests that non-Communist parties likely obtained 70 percent of the ballots.[38]

This lack of popular backing made local Communists that much more dependent on the Soviet Union. In Romania during 1947, the governing officials eliminated one political party after the next, until December 30, when the king was forced to abdicate, and the Communists proclaimed the Romanian People's Republic.[39]

Looming over it all was the notorious Securitate, or security police, which arrested hundreds of people. The organization had been created in the 1930s and during the war had been used against the Jews. With the emergence of the Groza government, the Communists took it over. Soviet agents or others schooled in the Soviet Union ran its operations, modeling the Romanian setup on what they knew best. In August 1948, Gheorghe Pintilie moved from a position on the Communist Party's Central Committee to reorganize the Securitate. He formulated its broader mission, as defined by its statute, as "to defend the democratic achievements and to protect the security of the People's Republic of Romania from enemies at home or abroad."[40]

In real terms, the mission called for keeping the Communist regime in power and crushing opposition. Pintilie was born in a Romanian part of the Russian Empire in 1902. He had fought in the Red Army during the civil war, was later recruited by the Soviet secret police, and worked for the Romanian revolution on Moscow's behalf. Along with two assistants who were also Soviet agents, he fashioned a service modeled on the NKVD, and the practices of the Securitate were every bit as brutal.[41]

From the outset, the regime created its own concentration camp system, which spread across the country like a cancer. Recent Romanian reports point to tens of thousands dragged through these dens of horror and count as many as 230 different camps. Thousands were arrested on the eve of the elections in 1946, and the waves of arrests continued for years. The Romanian Communists strove to be "more orthodox than the Kremlin," as the saying went; they kept their concentration camps operating long after Stalin died and the Soviets had dismantled the Gulag.[42]

The government kept up its efforts to get Romanians to embrace Communism. One of the benign ways was to orchestrate a leadership cult for Stalin. Although some citizens found collectivizing agriculture and nationalizing industry hard to swallow and felt keenly the loss of freedom, the government found it easy to acknowledge Stalin as a paternal figure who stood for progress, peace, and humanity. The regime took great care to foster that image in Romania, which culminated on his official seventieth birthday festivities in 1949 with conferences, celebrations in the public squares, and adulation in all the newspapers.[43]

HUNGARY

The Hungarians may have been more bitterly opposed to Communism and the Soviet Union than the Romanians, but like them they were liberated and occupied by the Red Army. According to the percentages deal, Churchill offered Stalin only a 50/50 split of influence in Hungary. After Molotov got through wrangling with Secretary Eden the following day, the British caved in to 80/20 shares. This outlandish horse trading was a symptom of the times, and though Stalin smiled and Churchill felt awkward, the Kremlin never failed to bring up that agreement. It was their "proof" that the British accepted the rightfulness of Soviet domination.[44]

The best known of the Hungarian Communists was Mátyás Rákosi, one of the leading activists in the 1920s, whom the fascists imprisoned until the Soviet Union negotiated his exchange in 1940. When he returned to Moscow, Stalin personally chose him as the leader of the tiny corps that remained of the party. Stalin's anti-Semitism was not yet showing; five of the six top figures among the Hungarian Communists—including Rákosi—were Jewish.

The painful transition to peace began on October 5, 1944, in Moscow, when a Hungarian military delegation arrived on behalf of Admiral Miklós Horthy, who in mid-1941 had been delighted to join Hitler's crusade against "Jewish Bolshevism." By the autumn of 1944, however, the Red Army was at the gates of Budapest. On October 11, Hitler pushed Horthy out in favor of Ferenc Szálasi, leader of the fascist Iron Cross, whose fanatics then fought on in the capital alongside Hungarian troops and the Wehrmacht.[45]

Meanwhile in Moscow, Rákosi and several other émigrés joined the Hungarian delegation for meetings between December 1 and 5 with Molotov and occasionally also Stalin. They opted to create a National Independence Front, a grand coalition that included Socialists, Smallholders, Communists, and National Peasants. Most of them would receive two portfolios in the Provisional Government that took office in Debrecen on December 22. Stalin liked the program, and just as he had counseled the Romanians and Bulgarians, he told the Hungarians "to underline more strongly the defense of private property and the preservation and development of private enterprise." He wanted "more flexible formulas" with "nothing scary" in them. That would be the first stage, as elsewhere in the east. "Once you gain strength," he said, "you may press on" with the Communist agenda.[46]

On December 27 the new assembly met and "elected" a new government, giving it a gloss of legitimacy. The cabinet had only two Communists, but there were others who concealed their affiliation, most notably Ferenc Erdei, the first minister of internal affairs.[47] The immediate problem was feeding the population and restoring the economy. That task was difficult because the Red Army plundered everything it could find, and in addition the USSR used specially organized squads to carry out systematic robberies of "trophies," valuables of all kinds, and did not stop at breaking into banks and carting away the spoils before shocked onlookers. All of this added to the desperate situation of the people, who were put on thin rations.[48]

Fierce battles continued to rage in Budapest, and Stalin ordered more soldiers thrown into the fray. The Red Army took dreadful casualties—sometimes so foolishly that the defenders were aghast as one senseless attack after another was launched and overwhelmed. All together the Soviets sustained 80,026 killed and 240,056 wounded in the siege of Budapest and associated operations, making it one of the costliest in the war.[49] When triumph came on February 13, 1945, General Rodion Malinovsky, commander of the Second Ukrainian Army Group, turned the city over to his men, who left a trail of rape, pillage, and plunder on such a scale as to defy the imagination.

Hungarian Communists complained bitterly. For example, the party in Kőbánya, a Budapest suburb, wrote Soviet authorities that the "longed-for liberation" had led instead to the town's senseless destruction. Soldiers exhibited "an outbreak of rampant, demented hatred. Mothers were raped by drunken soldiers in front of their children and husbands. Girls as young as 12 were dragged from their fathers and mothers to be violated by 10 to 15 soldiers and often infected with venereal diseases. After the first group came others." Even the obvious victims of the former regime, the Jews, were not immune to being mistreated and robbed.[50]

Stalin shrugged off all complaints about the Red Army, and the occupation set about performing the tasks he assigned. One of his pet projects for all of Eastern Europe was to introduce land reform, at first usually on a modest scale. Molotov told Kliment Voroshilov, Soviet head of the Allied Control Commission in Budapest, that land redistribution would "concentrate the democratic social strata, particularly the peasants." Voroshilov called in members of the government and said such a step might win over Hungarian troops still fighting against the Red Army.

On March 17, once the Peasant's Party and the Communists mapped out the whole process, the sweeping decrees were announced.[51] Small, medium, and large landowners lost their properties. Regardless of promises, no compensation was ever paid. Lands were passed over to 642,000 families, but the confiscations did not win much support, and as in Romania, they failed to produce any more food.

That June in Moscow, Rákosi sounded optimistic in conversations with Dimitrov. The Communists already had 200,000 party members, and in his view, they would likely have been doing still better were it not for the continuing Red Army "excesses." If these could be stopped, food supplies improved, and the Hungarian POWs returned, then the future would be bright.[52] It was taking time to get all that done. Behind the scenes, Soviet occupation authorities worked at getting "reactionaries and right-wingers" out of the administration.[53]

Retribution in Hungary had wings of its own and took several forms. Evidently there was no lynching. The police interned around 40,000 people, and denazification commissions purged 62,000 public servants.[54] A special feature was the institution of people's courts; the first of twenty-four such judicial novelties began in January 1945. They tried and executed the major figures of the former regime in the autumn. In total, the courts handled 58,629 cases and sentenced 477 to their death, though only 189 were executed.[55]

In addition, Communists were in control of the secret police in Budapest, where Gábor Péter was in charge from January 1945. Alhough he had a rival in András Tőmpe, a partisan leader recently returned from the Soviet Union with ambitions of his own, they worked in tandem at Andrássy Street 60, the former headquarters of the fascist Iron Cross, and carried on the tradition of terror.

In the summer the Communists and Socialists convinced themselves that their support was growing and wanted elections to prove it. Voroshilov, a key Soviet official in Budapest, was not so sure but acquiesced. On October 7 there would be a round of municipal elections, because the Left felt it was strongest in the cities and hoped to build on successes there in the subsequent national vote. The Communists and Social Democrats ran as the United Workers' Front and did well to get 42.7 percent of the ballots in Budapest. However, the Smallholders secured outright victory there with 50.4 percent. The Hungarian comrades said that the Soviets should have agreed to more radical social reforms. On the other hand, Voroshilov explained to Moscow that Rákosi and company had been overconfident and had not put any positive proposals to the electorate.[56]

From the Communists' perspective, the results of the national elections held a month later were even worse. Instead of joining in a grand bloc, the Smallholders insisted that they all run separately. Voroshilov pressured them to issue a preelection manifesto that said there would be a coalition government, regardless of the results. The Kremlin was upset when he failed to get a Bulgarian-style joint campaign.[57]

The November 7 national election was the freest there would be for many decades and likely reflected public opinion. Once again the Smallholders were the winners, with 57 percent, the Social Democrats obtained 17.4 percent, the Communists trailed with a miserable 16.9 percent, and splinter parties picked up the rest.[58]

The results showed a decisive rejection of Communism, and the

Kremlin went into damage control. It denied the Smallholders' claim to the Interior Ministry, which had jurisdiction over the police. Molotov had Voroshilov arrange for Communist László Rajk to get that post and to have two deputy prime ministers appointed. One was a Social Democrat loyal to Moscow and the other a Smallholder who was secretly a member of the Communist Party. Rajk named Communist Gábor Péter to head the secret police, so that in sum they were perfectly situated to crush opposition. These postelection manipulations mostly nullified the results. Nevertheless, the Smallholders' leader, Zoltán Tildy, was president, and Ferenc Nagy from the same party was prime minister, with a majority in parliament and likely supported by most people in the country.[59]

Communists regarded the vote against them as tangled up in "wrong thinking" and "false consciousness" that they would have to undo, and starting early in the new year, they orchestrated demonstrations around the country to "cleanse" government offices. Sometimes these actions got out of hand and led to mob lynching or backfired into anti-Communist riots, as in February 1946 in the mining town of Ozd. The violence was touched off by the mysterious murder of a Communist leader who was known for being anti-Semitic. Crowds of workers demonstrated, but against the Communists and the Jews. In other towns in May and June, stories circulated about supposed Jewish religious practices, and as in Ozd, the Jews' property was attacked. The unrest culminated in pogroms that killed two and wounded more in Karcag.

Some of the anti-Semitism was stoked by none other than Rákosi, a curious business for someone who was Jewish. Apparently he wanted to link the black marketers, a source of popular discontent, to the Jews and gain support for the cause. He went to Miskolc in July, and an enraged crowd stormed the police station and lynched a Communist police lieutenant who was Jewish—yet another sign of the anti-Semitism that still simmered barely below the surface all over Eastern Europe.[60]

When Rákosi met Stalin on April 1, 1946, to try to get better terms in the coming peace negotiations, he made little progress. Either as a reaction to Winston Churchill's "iron curtain" speech of March 5 at Fulton, Missouri, or using it as a pretext to do what he already intended, Stalin began thinking out loud that all the Communist satellites should eliminate opposition parties. No record of his meeting with the Hungarian leader has been found, and we know about it only because when Rákosi returned home, he mentioned it to a few insiders. Stalin apparently also spoke about creating some kind of organization to replace the defunct Comintern.[61]

In due course that summer, Communist interior minister Rajk struck a blow against a pluralist society by banning hundreds of organizations. In October the regime created a new Hungarian State Security Department, or ÁVO (Államvédelmi Osztálya), out of the already existing political police working in Budapest.[62] The new organization followed the Soviet model and was led by Péter. Mere mention of his name was enough to strike fear in people's hearts. Athough the organization changed its name slightly in December 1948 to ÁVH (Államvédelmi Hatóság), or State Security Authority, it was common especially for English speakers to keep calling it "the Avoh."[63]

It hardly bears repeating that Stalin was committed to Communist success in Hungary and the eventual establishment there of a "people's democracy." Given circumstances on the ground, the Communist takeover of Hungary was always a question of timing: would it happen right away, along with Bulgaria and Romania, or later on, when the situation would be more conducive to Soviet action? The latter option also carried the benefit of allaying the concerns of the Anglo-Americans, who, from Stalin's perspective, were forever sniffing around for something to worry about.

There is evidence that well into 1946 the Soviet dictator was ruminating that, all in all, it might be advisable to have Hungary remain a bourgeois-style democracy for a while longer.[64] The country as a whole had strong anti-Communist feelings, and the British and Americans were breathing down his neck; thus delaying a Communist takeover in Hungary could calm fears all round. Delay, according to this reasoning, would make the Soviets less encumbered with the Allies and more in a position to devote their energies to Bulgaria and Romania.

Such considerations explain why Stalin was not overly eager to spend much time receiving Rákosi in the Kremlin. Between 1944 and 1948, while Communists from other Eastern European countries visited dozens of times, he was there only on four occasions.[65] Of course, as things in Hungary began to heat up, and as their local leader set to work, Communist prospects for that country improved.

Rákosi went about the business of eliminating the opposition in stages, using what he later famously called "salami tactics," cutting off one slice at a time. The Communists fabricated charges against twenty-two Smallholder deputies and had them expelled from parliament. More anti-Communist conspiracies were discovered, several hundred individuals were prosecuted by the people's court, and a few were executed. The pinnacle of the attack on the Smallholders came on February 25, 1947, when the Soviets—not the Hungarians—arrested Béla Kovács, who was general secretary of the party and a member of parliament. He was not executed but removed from the scene and neutralized. These events were mentioned in the American president's speech before Congress on March 12, in which, as we will see in Chapter 15, he announced what came to be called the Truman Doctrine.

According to Rákosi's memoirs, it was in May that the decisive impulse came from Moscow to create a "people's democracy." The Soviet representative in Budapest revealed supposedly "incriminating material" about Prime Minister Ferenc Nagy, who was outside the country at the time and decided not to return. New elections were called for August 31, and this time the Communists ran as partners in a grand bloc, which won 60.9 percent of the vote.[66] Nevertheless, even with intimidation and manipulation of the results, the Communists were unable to manufacture majority support. It would take a few more twists of the screws to lock the country down and all but compel it to fall in behind the one-party dictatorship.

Stalin and his comrades also had ideas about the future of Communism in the Balkans along the Mediterranean coast. However, the geography is rugged there, as are the people, and they soon showed the limits of the Kremlin's reach.

CHAPTER 15

Communism in
Yugoslavia, Albania, and Greece

F ar to the south and west of Moscow, indigenous Communist resistance movements struggled against the Nazi invaders. Yugoslavia and Albania did not owe their liberation to the Red Army, but such was the attraction of Stalin as leader, and so prized were the "accomplishments" he represented, that the two new regimes engaged in what can only be called "self-Stalinization." Greece did not fit this pattern. The Communists there had long since become a force to be reckoned with; they were embroiled in bitter, continuing, and often violent feuds with oppositional political forces; and they stood out in that they managed to provoke Churchill into a serious effort to save Greece from falling into the arms of the Soviets. The Greek Communists, it has to be said, did feel a kinship with the "great man" in the Kremlin. At the same time, they had a unique identity forged in their own bloody conflict and did not yield easily to direction of the kind Stalin was offering. In the context in which they found themselves, his "go slowly and don't worry the Allies" mandate must have seemed very much out of place.

COMMUNIST VICTORY IN YUGOSLAVIA

Hitler's forces had attacked Yugoslavia in 1941 and left its army demoralized. He took some of the territory for Germany, gave some of the rest to his allies—Bulgaria, Hungary, and Italy—and allowed a new client state to arise in Croatia. It had been easy for the invaders to declare victory but something else entirely to deal with the resistance that followed. Moscow assumed that Josip Broz Tito, the Communist leader, would take charge, and indeed on November 26 and 27, 1942, he and his men formed the Anti-Fascist Council of the People's Liberation of Yugoslavia (or AVNOJ) at Bihać in liberated Bosnia.

Tito was a charismatic figure who combined the determination of a hard-bitten guerrilla fighter with a taste for the good life. He fought in the First World War on the side of Austria-Hungary and was captured and sent to Russia, where he learned about Bolshevism and became a Red Guard. In 1920 he returned to Yugoslavia and was active in the Communist movement until imprisoned. When released in the early 1930s, he emigrated and eventually represented his country at the Comintern (1935–36) in Moscow. He was well acquainted with Kremlin intrigues, was wily enough to survive the Great Terror, and managed to get Stalin's blessing to become general secretary of the Yugoslav party. Even so, like his comrades, Tito had a strong independent streak and was more difficult to control than any of Stalin's foreign disciples.

The major problem in Yugoslavia, with a population of 16.4 million in 1939, was its multiple divisions along ethnic-religious lines; the Serbians made up 38.8 percent, the Croatians, 23.8 percent, and another six groups accounted for the rest.[1] Tito's Partisans came mostly, though not exclusively, from Serbia. Among competitors were the Chetniks, headed by Dragoljub (or Draža) Mihailović, whose aim was to create a greater Serbia based on traditionalist principles. Also important was Ante Pavelić, fascist leader of the fearsome Ustaša, who hated Communism and strove to build a greater Croatia. A civil war erupted among these factions, which led to horrendous atrocities and fostered lasting bitterness.

From the beginning, Tito instinctively looked to Moscow for aid and was disappointed to be told to make do with what he could scrounge from the invaders. At the end of January 1943, he struck a note of desperation when he wrote the Kremlin with another plea to help his people who, though starving themselves, were giving their last crumb to his fighters.[2] Toward the end of the year, the situation improved, even though in November the Chetniks, now formalizing their bond to the Germans, could secure better supplies. That development induced the Western Allies to put aside their political reservations and begin supplying Tito's Partisans, whom they already saw as the likely future rulers.

At the second session of AVNOJ, meeting from November 21 to 29, 1943, in Jajce, Bosnia, the Partisans declared a kind of provisional government, without informing Stalin because they anticipated he would have told them to wait. They wanted bold action. When the Boss found out, he reacted with what the Yugoslavs called "exaggerated care for the feelings of his Western Allies."[3] They also decided to elevate Tito with the title of Marshal, to give the "masses" an identity symbol. They did this in a spontaneous shower of tears and ecstasy. Tito was still modest enough to blush but soon got over it, for he was a man "inclined to personal power," and to say his lofty position went to his head would be an understatement.[4] When the British asked Stalin what part he was playing in this business, he stonewalled and said it was strictly an internal matter. In fact, the Soviets were deeply involved, provided some aid, and the USSR continued its "Radio Free Yugoslavia" propaganda broadcasts.[5]

The Partisans modeled everything possible on the Soviet Union and, on Stalin's birthday, formed the First Proletarian Brigade as the armed wing of the Communist Party of Yugoslavia. They proudly emblazoned their uniforms with stars like those worn by the Red Army and even celebrated traditional Soviet holidays. Tito traveled to Moscow for a face-to-face meeting with Stalin in the week of September 21 to 28, 1944. They agreed that the Red Army would help in the liberation of Belgrade, which finally happened on October 20.[6]

During his stay in Moscow, Tito did not bow and scrape, but Stalin thought the moment right to give him instructions about the future, as he was doing with the Communists all across Europe. Accordingly, Yugoslavia was supposed to follow the "national front" pattern—that is, the Communists should share power with "bourgeois" politicians for the time being. Tito did not appreciate that advice and would not hear of bringing back King Peter as head of state. That stance earned the dictator's notorious remark "You need not restore him forever. Take him back temporarily, and then you can slip a knife into his back at a suitable moment."[7]

Tito found discussions with Dimitrov more congenial. The two speedily mapped out what might be a federation of the South Slavs to include Bulgaria, Macedonia, Serbia, Croatia, Montenegro, and Slovenia. Stalin continued to fret about possible British objections, and he was put off when Tito would not do as instructed.[8] Shortly thereafter, in October, Churchill visited Moscow and notoriously "offered" Stalin a 50/50 share, soon to be bumped up to 60/40, of influence in Yugoslavia.

At that very moment, Tito was already well on the way to victory, and under no circumstances would he have permitted the British or anyone else to land troops there to claim a slice of the pie.

The Yugoslavs who met with Stalin in later months continued resisting his demand to set up the monarchy again. It would confuse the people about who was in charge. Stalin considered King Peter of Yugoslavia and King Michael of Romania as temporary figureheads, to be used for show and then discarded. The Yugoslavs disagreed. They regarded their monarch as completely unacceptable, compromised as he was by his involvement with the Chetniks, the wartime atrocities, and Serbian domination.[9]

The war against Germany and the civil war went into a last phase in spring 1945. But no matter how pressing those events, Tito took time for another long visit to Moscow, staying there from April 5 to 20. No protocols have been found of his conversations with Stalin, but we know they discussed the details of the new government and how far west the Partisans ought to pursue their retreating enemies. Stalin was genuinely pleased that the Communists won in Yugoslavia, for victory there dramatically increased the likelihood of similar success in Greece. Moreover, the Kremlin apparently nurtured the hope of a great socialist Balkan federation, which in turn would continue the process of making "world revolution."[10] Thus he seemed ready to agree that Yugoslavia should create some kind of federation with other new Communist regimes in the region, such as Bulgaria and perhaps Albania. He was strategic enough, however, not to rush things and risk upsetting his Western Allies.

A small but telling incident occurred at one of the receptions in April, when Stalin, champagne glass in hand, turned abruptly to the man serving them and asked him to join in the toast. One of the Yugoslavs noted: "The waiter became embarrassed, but when Stalin uttered the words: 'What, you won't drink to Soviet-Yugoslav friendship?' he obediently took the glass and drank it bottoms up. There was something demagogic, even grotesque, about the entire scene, but everyone looked upon it with beatific smiles, as an expression of Stalin's regard for the common people and his closeness to them."[11]

Tito's territorial ambitions on this occasion again upset some in Moscow, just as they had the last time he was there. Even Dimitrov, who was usually on his side, scratched in his diary how Tito completely "underestimated the complexity of the situation," was "too arrogant and conceited," and suffered from symptoms of "dizziness with the success." Stalin had used the latter phrase to describe those who got out of hand and did not follow the party line in the campaign against the kulaks in the early 1930s.[12]

Once back home, Tito pushed ahead anyway, and the Partisans went in two directions. First they headed west for Trieste, an Italian city that, were they to take and hold it, would give Yugoslavia a major port on the Adriatic. They entered there in triumph on May 1, after which Tito made repeated demands on the West to recognize the conquest, including the hinterland, as the seventh republic of Yugoslavia. On May 15 the Western Allies gave him an ultimatum to leave. Tito gradually withdrew, but his claims to the area and to parts of Austria continued long afterward. When the Yugoslav Communists remembered these events later, they recalled that Stalin had failed to back them up.[13]

The second major Partisan drive was even bigger. On May 8, 1945, a formidable Partisan army (estimated at 800,000) took Zagreb, heading through Slovenia toward Klagenfurt in Austria. They were in hot pursuit of 100,000 to 200,000 enemy soldiers, police, and dependents trying to escape. Most were Croatians or Slovenes, and there were also some Serbians and Muslims. Tito issued an order to "annihilate" all who could be caught, and they were chased to the northwest. The Partisans persisted until May 21, when an exasperated Allied Combined Chiefs of Staff authorized Field Marshal Alexander, with help as needed from Eisenhower, to ready Allied troops to intervene. The war in Europe, after all, was officially over.

Partisan forces were still facing around 18,500 Chetniks, Ustaša, and Slovenian home guards cornered with their backs to Austria, who decided to surrender to the British, thinking or hoping they would be sent by train to Italy.[14] Instead, the British turned them over to the Partisans, who executed them, as they did opponents they themselves found.[15] How many were shot in this period at war's end remains in dispute. Croatian and other writers estimate that 60,000, and perhaps as many as 90,000, were executed within a matter of days.[16] According to a member of one of the special "extermination companies," the killers were treated like heroes and given rewards such as gold watches.[17]

Yugoslavia followed the pattern, established in Poland and Czechoslovakia, of using the expropriated property of ethnic Germans to win support for the new Communist regime. Already on November 21, 1944, the presidency of the Anti-Fascist Council of the People's Liberation of Yugoslavia—that is, Tito's de facto provisional government—ordered the seizure of all assets of Germans and persons of "German ethnicity." The only exception was for those who fought for the Partisans. The others were held to be "collectively guilty" for the crimes of Nazism, and roughly one quarter-million people were interned; the lucky ones had already fled.[18] The Communists used "the rich and fertile land of Vojvodina" to entice new families from Montenegro and Bosnia and to compensate "people from poor mountainous regions devastated by war."[19]

The ethnic cleansing that followed had all the characteristics that it had elsewhere in Europe at that time: mistreatment, rape, murder, forced work, internment camps, and deportations. Some of these villages were in what locals called Danube-Swabia, where ethnic Germans had lived for centuries. In all of Yugoslavia, as many as 50,000 of these people may have died in the camps, and 15,000 more were killed by Partisans.[20]

Even before the war ended, the Yugoslav Communists volunteered to subordinate themselves to Moscow. They pleaded to be shown what was expected and asked how to shape their new state, economy, culture, and the arts. They sought out Soviet advisers to set up the police and on their own sent their teachers, lawyers, agronomists, and others to the Soviet Union to be instructed.[21] As one of their leaders put it, the regime became "the most militant, the most doctrinaire, and the most pro-Soviet" of them all, so much so that at the time the Western press called it "Satellite Number One."[22]

The Yugoslavs also enacted measures that sounded as though they were inspired by Stalin's terror in the 1930s. For example, in September 1945 a new law "on crimes against the people and the state" condemned any deviation from the party line as "national treason." Complex and explosive ethnic issues were declared "solved." By the end of 1945, the party began to purge its own "internal opposition."[23]

Elections on November 11, 1945, were preceded by police terror against the opposition, barring its candidates from standing. Trying to follow Stalin's dictates, they put forward Popular Front candidates who were in fact usually Communists or fellow travelers. Together they took 81.5 percent of the vote. Tito might have won even had the vote been free, but he "wanted an overwhelming majority," because—so ran the thinking inside the party—if the opposition won much support, it might "have been legalized and become a permanent factor of political life."[24] In conversations with Soviet representatives in early 1946, Tito and his close comrade Edvard Kardelj said they controlled every meaningful organization and planned to close down the last non-Communist parties.[25] A short time later Kardelj proudly reported to Moscow that Yugoslavia had already nationalized 90 percent of its industry.[26]

He admitted frankly to the new People's Assembly in December 1945 that "democratic rights are not something absolutely valid for all times."[27] They established Soviet-style domination, and as far back as May 1944 they created their own secret police, the Department for the Protection of the People (Odjeljenje za zaštitu naroda, or OZNa). It was led by Aleksandar Ranković with the assistance of NKVD advisers. Beginning that September, following the example of all the Eastern Europeans, Yugoslav police officials and others were sent to the Soviet Union to be "schooled."[28]

The civil war left a heritage of brutality, and numerous atrocities continued. Executions became so common that Tito supposedly remarked back in mid-1945 that "nobody is afraid of death any more." That June he told a meeting that OZNa "is an organ of security which has sprung from the people. If it strikes fear into the bones of some of those gentry abroad, that is not our fault. But certainly I think it an advantage if OZNa strikes fear into those who do not like the new Yugoslavia."[29]

Ranković created a network of informers, as was the pattern in other "people's democracies." The "enemies" were thought to be everywhere and mass arrests routine. OZNa kept the population permanently under watch, tracking their every move and noting their reliability on detailed conduct sheets.[30] The retribution carried on into 1946 with countless small and several large trials. Historians have estimated that in 1945–46 between 100,000 and 250,000 Yugoslavs were killed either through mass executions or in the new concentration camp system.[31] There is no doubt about the extent of the deadly settling of accounts, as evidence exists in many forms.[32]

Some Yugoslav historians deny the scale of the killing and then in the same breath call Tito's Croatian or Serbian opponents "quislings" or traitors who would have killed all the Communists if they had had the chance. One such account admits that "the annihilation of most quisling troops captured at the end of the war—which is a fact—was an act of mass terror and brutal political surgery."[33]

Captain Frank Waddams, the British liaison officer to Tito's Partisans during the war, saw the abuses himself. When he returned to England in 1946, he talked about "the all-powerful OZNa," which was, he thought, "responsible for the murder of thousands of Yugoslavs, for the maltreatment in concentration camps of thousands more and for the permanent terror in which the vast bulk of the population lives."[34] Not much changed when the secret police got a new name, UDNa (Administration for State Security). It was still headed by Ranković, and concentration camps became a fixture of the regime.[35] The harrowing tales told of the notorious Goli Otok camp on an island in the Adriatic, created in 1949 for "Stalinists" who opposed Tito, read like something out of the Third Reich or Stalin's Gulag.[36]

Ranković admitted some things about the repression in the camps, and these were reported in the press.[37] In spite of the great deal that was known about the terror, it did not stop the West from being charmed by Tito and bending over backwards to overlook the fact that this regime was brutally crushing civil and legal rights.[38]

The British representatives in Belgrade at war's end misleadingly reported to London that Tito "puts Yugoslavia first and his subordinates put communism first," and that it was the latter who pushed the terror. U.S. ambassador Richard Patterson told President Truman a similar half-truth on a brief return to Washington in August 1945. He claimed to be "good friends" with the leader; the two had already made plans to go hunting together. The ambassador thought Tito was certainly a "thorough Communist" but intelligent, and he jovially suggested to the president that they might "bring him back to America for a month of indoctrination."[39]

Yugoslavia became the most Stalinized country in all of Eastern Europe. Later on, when Stalin attempted to exert still more control there, it was also the first to break from his grasp. Part of the reason for the split was Tito's ambitions toward neighbors like Albania.

THE ALBANIAN STALINISTS

Albania is a tiny country that in 1944 had a population of only 1.1 million, a majority of them Muslim. The land is squeezed between combative Yugoslavia to the north and spirited Greece to the south. The Albanian "working class," in the sense of industrial employment, was estimated at around 15,000 in the 1930s. Illiteracy was the norm, and the life expectancy of males forty-two.[40] The country was so poor that when Ilya Ehrenburg visited in 1945, he was shocked to see the army march past in bare feet.[41]

Wealthier and more powerful neighbors coveted Albania, and already in the 1920s it was dominated by Fascist Italy. Hitler's successes in the 1930s prodded Mussolini into believing that victory came to the bold, and on March 25, 1939, he issued an ultimatum to Albania. It could either accept shelter as Italy's protectorate or face invasion, which in any case soon followed. The Albanian army was defeated quickly, and the king fled to London. Thereafter, Mussolini became more ambitious, and on October 28, 1940, he ordered the invasion of Greece. Here the Italians ran into stout resistance and in short order were fought to a standstill. That left Hitler feeling that he had little choice but to invade both Albania and Greece in early 1941, even though those military operations would take valuable time and resources away from the planned attack on the Soviet Union. However, in the meantime, Italy was able to consolidate its hold over Albania.

In November 1941, Tito sent advisers to help establish a new Albanian Communist Party. It had perhaps seventy members and several hundred sympathizers. Enver Hoxha emerged as the leader, a reasonably well-educated person, having studied at Montpellier University in France. Rumor had it that, while there, he had written for the Communist Party's prestigious newspaper, *L'Humanité,* though all efforts to find any such articles have come up empty. Nevertheless, it was in France that he began to believe that Stalinism was the way of the future.[42]

The first directives to the small Albanian party arrived from Moscow in December 1942, with orders to create a broad people's front of all patriots and to attack the German and Italian occupations. Tito's Partisans helped, but resistance only got up and running in mid-1943. They soon created an Anti-Fascist Committee for National Liberation, similar to the one in Yugoslavia.

Frictions also emerged, at least according to Hoxha's memoirs, because the imperious Yugoslavs sought to direct not only Albania's military effort but its Communist movement, ultimately to incorporate Albania and make it Yugoslavia's seventh republic. Hoxha drank deeply from Moscow's cup of inspiration and became one of the most ardent Stalinists.[43] He recognized that having friends in the Kremlin was helpful for a small country with such a powerful and ambitious neighbor.

The Albanian Anti-Fascist Committee of National Liberation elected Hoxha as president of a provisional government in May 1944, and he was confirmed in October as national president. The Communists here could claim that they had liberated their country on their own; in bitter fighting the next month, they drove the Germans from the capital, Tirana. In elections on December 2, 1945, the Albanian Democratic Front—a disguised Communist Party—took 93 percent of the vote. The new assembly transformed the country into a people's republic early in the new year.[44] They already had a secret police, the Directorate of Security (Sigurimi), created on March 20, 1943, which became one of the most fearsome in the Balkans.[45] It invaded the private sphere with spies and informers and used labor camps to "reeducate" the politically wayward.

Tito had already let it be known in January 1945 that he wanted to incorporate not only Albania but Greek Macedonia, as well as parts of Hungary, Austria, Romania, and Bulgaria. To the Kremlin, these aims appeared overambitious and "unreasonable."[46] When Yugoslav representatives pressed for Stalin's agreement, all they got was his sage remark that if they continued, they would find themselves "at loggerheads with Romania, Hungary and Greece" and would have to "do battle with the whole world; such a situation would be absurd."[47]

For the time being at least, the Kremlin was content to seek control of Albania by issuing orders and directives through Yugoslavia.[48] When one of the top Yugoslav politicians, Milovan Djilas, visited the Albanian capital in May 1945, he was impressed by what the Italians had constructed during the occupation. He was there to formalize diplomatic relations and found Hoxha, the thirty-five-year-old leader, eager to learn.

Djilas was unsettled by Hoxha's habit of breaking into "a sudden and strangely cruel smile." Behind the man's Europeanized exterior, there "loomed a personality bent on its own course, turned in on itself, and inaccessible." The Yugoslav leaders regarded him as suffering from intellectualism and also as a petit-bourgeois—he opened a tobacco shop when times were tough at the start of the Italian occupation. Djilas recalled hearing later that Hoxha eventually turned modest, "except in matters involving power and ideology. But those were different times. We imitated the Russians in management; the Albanians imitated us in management and autocratic luxury."[49]

Tito let his ambitions show on May 27, 1945, just over a month after his return from his long visit in Moscow. In a meeting, he expressed his dissatisfaction that his country was being held back from expanding its borders. He was not at all pleased that Stalin was calling the shots on that score; nor was he happy that Dimitrov was having second thoughts about Yugoslavia's absorbing of Bulgaria as the seventh republic. Tito was denied support from Moscow for his claims to Carinthia (in Austria) and Venezia Giulia (in Italy). There had been a just war, Tito said, "but we now seek a just conclusion. Our goal is that everyone be the master in his own house." He came close to putting the Soviet Union in the same category as the Western Allies for denying the Yugoslavs what he saw as rightly theirs, and he swore that the Yugoslavs "would not be dependent on anyone ever again, regardless of what has been written and talked about."[50]

Stalin was incensed at Tito's intemperance and willingness to risk war with the West so soon after the conclusion of the major hostilities. The Kremlin Boss wanted to calm things down, so he instructed his man on the spot in Belgrade to tell Tito in no uncertain terms that, if he were to mount another such verbal assault against the Soviet Union, "we would be compelled to respond openly in the press and disavow him."[51]

In May 1946, Albania and Yugoslavia signed a close economic treaty that might have led to "socialist integration," were it not for the political conflict that soon arose between them. The Albanians began complaining to Moscow that Tito's embrace was smothering them. Hoxha had wanted for some time to visit the home of Communism and to put his case to the Kremlin Leader, but only in July 1947 was permission granted. Stalin was briefed in detail well in advance on the problems facing Communism in Albania.[52] The Party there had grown to 12,361 members by that March, and Hoxha and his second in command, Koçi Xoxe, sought Stalin's approval and blessing.[53] Hoxha was a convert, a true believer, and completely committed to Stalinism.[54] While he was in Moscow, he met with Zhdanov to finalize the party's structure and organization. He also solicited advisers to help bring members back home up to scratch on ideological questions.[55]

The Albanians fell over themselves to become perfect students of all that the Soviet Union had to teach. They believed that by embracing Stalin, they had found not only the font of wisdom and truth but a patron and father-figure who would protect them from Tito.

GREECE BETWEEN EAST AND WEST

Tito's enthusiasm for Sovietization, which went beyond what Moscow deemed prudent, included giving assistance to the Greek Communist Party (KKE), whose roots went back to 1918. The Bolshevik faith had flourished in the 1920s and 1930s among the Greek refugees forcibly "transferred" from Turkey. Thousands had been dropped onto the quays in harbors and ended up crammed into public buildings and churches or stuck in camps and prone to disease. This was the "population transfer" that Churchill, and to a lesser extent Roosevelt, pointed to as the example worth following after 1945. It had been a disaster that bred resentment, and many on the Central Committee of the KKE had been among those refugees.

Nikos Zachariadis, general secretary of the KKE between 1934 and 1952, was born in Asia Minor, became attracted to Bolshevism, went to Russia, and fought in the Civil War. After training in the Soviet Union, he returned to Greece, where in 1936, on orders from Moscow, he was made head of the party. He promptly Stalinized and unified it to run in elections that year, but it collected a meager 5 percent of the vote. That was enough for the government to stick Zachariadis in prison, where the Nazis found him upon their arrival in 1941. They shipped him to the Dachau concentration camp, where he spent years and somehow miraculously survived.

In the meantime, George Siantos took over the KKE. In October 1941 the party announced the creation of the National Liberation Front (EAM), through which it reached out to the people suffering under Italian or German occupation. EAM also established the Greek People's Liberation Army (ELAS), which grew slowly. The resistance movement was politically fragmented, with EAM as the most important component, and ELAS was the largest armed group. Together they gained a substantial following among the population, radicalized by the war. However, the people were divided about what was to be done, and the insurgents reflected these sentiments. The Communists were uncertain about whether they should seek power directly or follow orders from Stalin in the summer of 1944 to form a "national front" with other parties. The Kremlin insisted on "moderation" and sent advisers to ensure that the KKE kept to the script.[56]

The German invasion in 1941 had shocked the fragile food market and brought famine. Warned of the dire situation, the Axis powers sent in some aid but not nearly enough. The death toll would have been worse had it not been for the efforts of the American Greek War Relief Association and others. As it was, an estimated 250,000 to 450,000 deaths resulted in the period May 1941 to April 1943, significant losses in the small population of 7.3 million as of 1940.[57]

When the occupation ended in 1944, it left behind desolation, bitterness, and political turmoil. On October 18, a pronounced anti-Communist regime of the prewar establishment, led by George Papandreou and backed by British troops, took over in Athens. Although his cabinet included members of the EAM, that front was soon troubled by his determination to disband ELAS, its military wing, which would have left EAM vulnerable to attacks from the radical Right. To pressure the government, EAM members resigned from it on December 2, then promptly called a general strike. There followed on the first Sunday of the month a large protest march in Athens, with people carrying international flags and occasionally chanting "Long live Roosevelt!" or "Long live Stalin!" Emotions ran high, and the crowd became threatening. The police panicked, opened fire, and soon lost control of the streets. Over the next several days, the police who were caught were tortured to death or literally torn limb from limb.

Thus began the *Dekemvriana*, the December Uprising. In the middle of the month, ELAS went all out against British troops in a dirty war, which at times was so horrific as to defy the imagination. Suffice it to say that the instrument of choice among the executioners was the ax. Brutality grew to a level that can only be called hysterical madness.[58]

Churchill was determined that Greece was not going to fall to the Communists and, along with Foreign Secretary Eden, flew to Athens on Christmas Day 1944. They wanted a settlement and soon sent in an estimated 75,000 troops. This was precisely when the KKE began asking Stalin for help.[59] He turned them down and on January 10, 1945, muttered to Dimitrov that they should have stayed in the government and not started fighting.[60] For Stalin, this uprising was most inopportune, coming as it did on the eve of the Yalta Conference, where he wanted to calm concerns about Communist revolution. If the KKE had succeeded, Britain would certainly have considered it a breach of the "percentages deal" that Churchill was obviously taking seriously.[61] U.S. ambassador Lincoln MacVeagh kept President Roosevelt informed and was pleased to say that at least there were no signs that the Soviet Union was behind the Communists.[62]

On February 12 the Greek government and KKE negotiated an agreement to stop the fighting and to hold a referendum within a year to resolve constitutional issues. Instead of social peace, a right-wing backlash followed. Some of it was carried out by the 12,000 or so members of the Security Battalions, who were newly released from prison, where they had been serving time for collaborating with the Germans. Now anyone suspected of having links with Communism became the object of their semiofficial violence. Tens of thousands were sent to prison.[63]

In January 1946, when a Greek delegation in Moscow told of the continuing attacks and the likelihood of armed conflict, they were still cautioned to go slow. The Greek Communists had all along been of two minds about whether to adopt violence and seek power or to participate in government, as Moscow wanted. The KKE decided to boycott the elections held in March. They perhaps sensed that they were in for a drubbing, since they had been blamed for the earlier atrocities. The conservative-royalist victory at the polls led to still more state-sponsored repression. Stalin showed his displeasure with the KKE by not answering its pleas for help. However, when Nikos Zachariadis visited Belgrade in March–April, Tito received him warmly and promised assistance. Zachariadis then went to Bulgaria, where he hoped for the same, but as might have been expected, Dimitrov followed the Kremlin line and tried to dampen his enthusiasm for insurrection.[64] Throughout 1946 violence was rampant in Greece, and that October Tito began sending Zachariadis army units and war matériel. Although Greek Communist forces were not large and support for their efforts limited, the insurgency was disruptive and assistance to the government was becoming costly for Britain to sustain.

The United States had not anticipated getting involved in Greece. On Friday, February 21, 1947, however, the British ambassador in Washington delivered an important note. Undersecretary of State Dean Acheson read it first and was shocked to learn that as of March 31, Britain would be unable to continue its aid to Greece and Turkey.[65] The British economy was in crisis, the population still on wartime rations. The winter was one of the harshest on record, snow and ice stopped industries and jammed roads, and as many as six million people were unable to work for weather-related or other reasons. Under the circumstances, Britain had to prepare for its imminent departure from Greece and Turkey, whose needs were so great.

Acheson immediately ordered the European and Near Eastern experts to work out the political and military implications of the British pullout, including the importance of an independent Greece and Turkey for Western Europe. Specific recommendations had to be readied by early Monday, when the recently named secretary of state George C. Marshall would return to Washington.

The Truman administration was not in a strong political position to handle this emergency. The honeymoon with the president was long over, and his approval ratings had fallen to 32 percent. The Democrats had done poorly in the 1946 elections, losing control of the House and Senate for the first time in fourteen years.

Marshall met Acheson on February 24 and wanted to know what would happen if the United States did nothing. If American military forces were needed, for how long and at what cost? It was assumed that Congress would have to grant funding and authority, and that meant the new congressional leaders would have to be persuaded.

President Truman was far from the cold warrior he is often depicted as being. Almost exactly one year earlier, on March 5, 1946, former prime minister Churchill, at the invitation of the president, gave an address at Westminster College in Fulton, Missouri. The press hated the talk and among other things called Churchill a warmonger. Legendary columnist Walter Lippmann said that the "iron curtain" speech was an "almost catastrophic blunder." Truman disavowed the remarks as soon as possible. Far from having made up his mind to fight Stalin, he wrote the dictator to say that "he still held out hope for better relations" and even invited him to the United States to deliver a rebuttal to Churchill.[66]

Former U.S. ambassador Joseph Davies rushed to the White House to calm the waters. By the time Truman gave his Army Day speech on April 6, delivered from Chicago and broadcast on national radio, he sounded conciliatory. Although he pointed to areas of concern around the globe, none were linked to the Soviet Union. One of the few times

that the USSR was mentioned was in connection with Korea. The
president stated that the United States was "even now working with
our Soviet Allies and with the Korean leadership to create a provisional
democratic government."[67]

Now it was a year later, in March 1947, and when Britain notified the
United States that it would soon have to pull out of Greece, Truman
still proceeded cautiously. The State Department put together a case
for assistance, and a congressional delegation was invited to the White
House to hear it. They were not impressed by Truman and Marshall,
but Dean Acheson's worst-case scenario was persuasive. Not only was
Greece under Communist threat, the secretary declared, but so too was
Western Europe. Later he recalled saying that "the Soviet Union was
playing one of the greatest gambles in history at minimal cost. It did
not need to win all the possibilities" because "even one or two offered
immense gains."[68]

On March 12 the president gave a moderate speech to a joint session of Congress. Making no mention of the Soviet Union, much less
Stalin, he said that the Yalta agreements had been broken in Eastern
Europe and that "the peoples of a number of countries" had "recently
had totalitarian regimes forced upon them." He did not say that the
United States would have to contain Communism. For many, however,
he said as much, even though he put the issue quite differently:

> At the present moment in world history nearly every nation
> must choose between alternative ways of life. The choice is too
> often not a free one. One way of life is based upon the will of the
> majority, and is distinguished by free institutions, representative
> government, free elections, guarantee of individual liberty, free-
> dom of speech and religion, and freedom from political oppres-
> sion. The second way of life is based upon the will of a minority
> forcibly imposed upon the majority. It relies upon terror and
> oppression, a controlled press and radio; fixed elections, and
> the suppression of personal freedoms. I believe that it must be
> the policy of the United States to support free peoples who are
> resisting attempted subjugation by armed minorities or by out-
> side pressures. I believe that we must assist free peoples to work
> out their own destinies in their own way. I believe that our help

should be primarily through economic and financial aid which is essential to economic stability and orderly political processes.

The substance of these remarks was soon called the Truman Doctrine, though he did not use such a concept, and the administration never tired of saying that the intention was not to support any and all movements or governments trying to resist Communism. The president's thesis was that "misery and want" give rise to "totalitarian regimes," which "spread and grow in the evil soil of poverty and strife. They reach their full growth when the hope of a people for a better life has died. We must keep that hope alive." To that end, he asked for the funds to help Greece and Turkey. Both sides of the House heartily applauded his remarks, even if some had serious doubts about such a policy.[69]

In April 1947, Greek Communist leader Zachariadis drew up plans for an armed struggle. The next month he met with Stalin, who only reluctantly agreed to provide aid because Greece was still not a Soviet priority.[70] The dictator changed his mind somewhat in the course of the next months, though not because of anything President Truman had said. Newly released Russian documents show that in September Stalin instructed Zhdanov and Molotov to fulfill the Greek requests for arms, but to be sure of procuring them from outside the Soviet Union to disguise any links.[71]

On December 23–24, the Greek Communists declared a Provisional Democratic Government and soon opened a major offensive. The aim was to take the north, make Salonika the capital, and hope for speedy recognition from Moscow and the regional Communist regimes.

On February 10, 1948, as we have seen, Stalin got into a heated debate with visiting Yugoslav and Bulgarian delegations on whether the two Balkan neighbors should form a federation. Then the question of aiding the Greek Communists came up for discussion, and Stalin became unusually revealing of his postwar revolutionary strategy. He said that of course he wanted to support the Partisans in Greece. However, if their chance of achieving a successful insurgency was small, then, as in any other country, the armed conflict should be postponed. What was needed at all times was a "sober analysis of the forces involved." He told his Balkan guests: "You are not bound by some 'categorical imperative' " to aid revolutionaries at any cost. "You strike when you can win and avoid the battle when you cannot. We will join the fight when conditions favor us and not when they favor the enemy."[72]

Thus, lacking the necessary forces or a navy in the Mediterranean, the Soviet Union was bound to remain circumspect about the Greek revolutionaries and would have Yugoslav and Bulgarian comrades follow that lead. Stalin acknowledged the new U.S. engagement to some extent in March 1948, when he advised the KKE leadership to yield. Zachariadis agreed, but the Greek government wanted to finish off the Communists, and the civil war dragged into 1949. After years of political instability and turmoil, in 1967 a colonels' coup d'état imposed a right-wing dictatorship. Only after it was toppled in 1974 did real democracy finally arrive in its ancient home.

CHAPTER 16

The Passing of the Communist Moment in Western Europe

Stalin's restraint in Greece came from the fact that he was simultaneously operating on so many fronts. He was quietly pressing forward into the very heart of Western Europe, where in the first postwar years, the prospects for Communist takeovers looked better than any time since the end of the First World War. Not only did Communist parties have deep roots in Western Europe, but Communists had played leading roles in the resistance and could ride the wave of popular fury against Nazism, Fascism, and the collaborators. The Left was resurgent, the Right was discredited or silent, and people flooded to the ranks of the Communist parties. The prospects for Soviet influence appeared even stronger, given that the new governments faced enormous problems, even in providing enough food and fuel to meet immediate needs.

Stalin had thought that the war would open unprecedented political opportunities, and planning had begun early. Among other career diplomats, Maxim Litvinov and Ivan Maisky formulated specific proposals. Taking their cue from the Kremlin, however, they did not envision the expansion of the USSR through the incorporation of new territories.

SOVIET PLANS FOR WESTERN EUROPE

On January 11, 1944, Maisky sent Molotov a detailed outline for the "postwar order." Although he was commonly regarded as a "moderate," Maisky was a Stalinist, and even though he had spent a great deal of time in the West, he did not hold their democracies in high regard. He visualized "proletarian revolutions" in postwar Eastern Europe and anticipated inevitable tensions with the United States, which he thought would build a postwar empire of a "new kind." Instead of taking over countries outright, as empires of old had done, the United States would seek their "financial-economic annexation." He was apparently blind to the fact that, with his own blessing, the Soviet Union was also becoming a new-style empire. It would be somehow more righteous, based on fraternally shared Communist ideas, and involve mutual security arrangements, but all would be firmly under Moscow's political and ideological control.[1]

Maisky advised negotiating loans via Lend-Lease as soon as possible, when "the Americans and the English were still hypnotized by the war." Moscow would get a better deal now, he reasoned, because with the return of peace, the "basic merchant psychology" of the Anglo-Americans would take over again. It did not seem to occur to him that, by making his own calculations, he was following this same merchant psychology. He went on to advise that staying out of the Japanese war would "save us losses in men and matériel." The Soviet Union should let the United States and Great Britain take the heavy casualties, which "would also cool down a little the imperialistic zeal of the USA for the postwar period. At the same time that would be our *revanche* for the tardiness of the Anglo-Americans" in opening a second front in Europe, as Stalin had demanded so often.[2]

Ambassador Maisky also headed a "special commission for compensation of the damage inflicted on the USSR by Hitlerite Germany and its allies." In July his preliminary report called for Germany and its allies to pay between $70 and $75 billion in reparations—very large sums for those times. To afford them, the country's living standards would be cut in half, in comparison to the 1930s. The implications would be dramatic: "Everything that Germany possesses 'above the minimum necessary to survive,' has to contribute to the reparations fund for compensating the allied nations, in the first instance the USSR for its losses." Germany could meet part of these costs by conscripted labor. If around five million Germans were drafted each year, then in ten years they would pay off $35 to $40 billion. Thus "reparations through labor" (*reparatsii trudom*) would cover half of what was due. That approach had the additional advantage of paralyzing Germany's economy, since of course millions of men and women would be condemned to years of slavery.[3]

In 1944 the United States and Great Britain flirted with imposing a similarly harsh peace. The plan, identified with Secretary of the Treasury Henry Morgenthau, Jr., would have changed Germany into a nation that was "primarily agricultural and pastoral in its character."[4] The Soviet ambassador in the United States got all the details over dinner from Morgenthau himself and passed on the information to Moscow.[5]

Among others in Roosevelt's cabinet, Secretary of War Henry Stimson was outraged at the Morgenthau plan and that September sent the president a withering critique. A nation such as Germany, he said, could not "be reduced to a peasant level" without providing the breeding ground for another war. He noted that "sound thinking" suggested that prosperity in one part of the world helped to create it in others, and that the same was true about poverty. However, "enforced poverty is even worse, for it destroys the spirit not only of the victim but debases the victor. It would be just such a crime as the Germans themselves hoped to perpetrate upon their victims—it would be a crime against civilization itself." For Stimson, the drastic measures proposed were "an open confession of the bankruptcy of hope for a reasonable economic and political settlement of the causes of war."[6]

Although Roosevelt, Churchill, and their successors ultimately rejected a punitive peace, Stalin did not, and the Soviets later publicized Morgenthau's idea to run down the Anglo-Americans in the eyes of Germans.

Ambassador Maisky thought the Soviet Union had no direct interests at stake in Western Europe. The Boss, however, had grander ideas, as had Maurice Thorez, the leader of the French Communist Party (PCF), in for talks on November 19, 1944. Backed by Molotov and Beria, Stalin's "advice" to Thorez was that the PCF should keep a low profile and forge links with other parties in a "Left bloc." The Soviet dictator believed that French Communism was not strong enough to achieve power on its own and needed allies in a national front. Otherwise it risked being destroyed.[7]

Thorez had been one of the key leaders of the PCF since the late 1920s, and he was associated with the Popular Front government formed in 1936. At that time there was genuine all-party concern to stop Hitler, but even then it was Stalin who "suggested" forming broadly based coalition governments.[8] As we have seen, beginning in 1944, as the Wehrmacht was pushed back in Eastern Europe, he recommended creating similar "fronts" there, as Trojan horses that concealed the dominant position of the Communists.[9]

COMMUNISM IN FRANCE REACHES AN IMPASSE

Maurice Thorez arrived home unannounced in November 1944, a week after meeting Stalin, and immediately counseled restraint, the adoption of a parliamentary route to power, and the creation of a mass party. In an important report to the French Central Committee meetings on January 21–23, 1945, he urged the dissolution of the "irregular armed groups" and counseled local committees of liberation to work with and support the state's existing administration and not try to replace it. Stalin underestimated the mood of the times. The PCF had played a major role in the resistance, was well organized, and had momentum on its side. In 1944–45 the party grew and at one point in 1945 claimed to be a million strong, making it one of the largest Communist parties in Europe outside the Soviet Union.[10]

Many in France had been disgusted by French collaboration with the German occupation, and they greeted liberation with jubilation mixed with bloody retribution, the most brutal in all of Western Europe. The purge, or *épuration*, executed an estimated 10,800 people without trial, 5,234 of them during the liberation. Rumor was that the numbers were far higher. Official tribunals later sentenced close to 7,000 to death; fewer than 800 of the verdicts were carried out. Women who slept with the enemy were publicly shamed in disgusting rituals common across Europe. The courts prosecuted 32,000 people, but by the 1950s most had been released or amnestied. The civil service was purged of 11,343 or so.[11] Anyone wanting to look behind these dry figures should see the stunning documentary by Marcel Ophuls, *The Sorrow and the Pity*, which focuses mainly on one locality and shows how France was divided against itself after liberation.

Maurice Thorez tried repeatedly but still failed to create a new popular front with the Socialists (SFIO). Some who feared such a "Left bloc" created a Christian-democratic-leaning Popular Republican Party (MRP). In October 1945, in an election for a constituent assembly, the PCF won 26.1 percent of the vote and the SFIO 25.6 percent. The Socialists would be the weaker partner in any bloc and wanted no part of one. Besides, they feared France might slip into becoming a "people's democracy" similar to those in Eastern Europe. The upshot was a divided Left, coalition governments, and instability.[12]

After eight days of wrangling, the new assembly elected General Charles de Gaulle as president. According to his own account, the parties were unwilling to work with him, and on January 20, 1946, he resigned abruptly. He wrongly expected that the shock would make politicians see the light; he would wait more than a decade to become president again. Meanwhile, by April 1947, he was involved with the new Rally of the French People (RPF), with the aim of mobilizing the nation for unity and reform. He shunned the embrace of either Moscow or Washington.[13]

In June 1946 elections to another constituent assembly, the two leftist parties lost the support of the majority. The nation reverted to its "normal" voting traditions. The MRP came in first with 28.2 percent of the vote, and the PCF held its constituency and obtained 26.4 percent, while the SFIO fell to 21.3 percent. In the November elections to the National Assembly, the PCF was the frontrunner with 28.8 percent of the vote, the MRP took 26.3 percent, and the SFIO dropped to 18.1 percent.

This result surprised the Kremlin as well as the French Communists, whose leader Maurice Thorez had made a brief trip to Moscow in September. At that time he was told that while the current international situation favored the Soviet Union, the Kremlin was not prepared for war, needed to gain time, and hence had to discourage the French comrades from trying to seize power—even though the PCF was in a position to do so. The Kremlin considered that such a step might precipitate a conflict that the USSR could not win, so the advice was to go more slowly. However, with the positive electoral results for the PCF in November, Moscow now thought that Thorez should go all out to form a government, as he was entitled to do as head of the strongest party. Thereby he would succeed in following Stalin's original order of getting into power via the ballot box. All the greater then was Thorez's disappointment in being unable to cobble together a coalition. Instead the Communists were symbolically stopped by the Socialist Léon Blum, seventy-four years old, who came out of retirement.

On November 16 he formed a government coalition of five parties and, six weeks later, on January 1, 1947, in an attempt to stem inflation, introduced a compulsory 5 percent price cut. This effort solved nothing: people increasingly felt that the government was fumbling and incoherent.[14]

Economics expert Jean Monnet developed a plan for recovery and modernization, and it was accepted by the assembly on January 14, 1947. But the problem was how to finance it, meet government debt, and pay for imports. French officials had been traveling to Washington to seek assistance, and U.S. ambassador Jefferson Caffery strongly favored providing food and coal to help them cope. The black market flourished, and people suffered. In May the bread ration was fixed at 250 grams per day, and in August it was reduced to levels lower than those during the German occupation. That September riots broke out in cities over shortages of bread and sugar.[15]

The Communists employed a two-pronged strategy. In the first place, they would participate in government to gain respectability while at the same time being obstructionist. Second, they would support extraparliamentary opposition and strikes that made economic recovery difficult. They knew France desperately needed U.S. loans, yet they attacked the government for trying to get them. Thorez could not stand in the way of more jobs, and so he backed Monnet, but then he also supported the strikers.

The turning point came on May 4, when Prime Minister Paul Ramadier called the Communists' bluff by asking for a vote of confidence on the government's social and economic policy. The PCF had to vote against it, even though Thorez and four other Communists were in the cabinet. The next day Ramadier cleared the cabinet of its PCF members. Since that time no Communist has served as a minister in a French government.

Some historians suggest that U.S. ambassador Caffery made the provision of U.S. assistance to France dependent on keeping the PCF out. The documents, however, do not support that contention, though Caffery might well have given broad hints of what Washington wanted.[16]

The ambassador's communications with the State Department reveal that he liked the new coalition government and admired Ramadier's courage in steering between the extremists on the Left and Right. "If a really strong democratic France is to be established," he reported on May 12, "such a coalition is not only desirable but in fact offers the best chance of success. Furthermore, its component elements are oriented toward us through mutual belief in the new basic conception of liberty and human decency and through deep fear and distrust of ruthless Soviet imperialism."[17]

On June 5, when Secretary of State George C. Marshall announced the intention of the United States to fund a recovery plan for Europe, his remarks were very general.[18] The Truman administration was divided on the details and faced a Congress with newly elected, more fiscally conservative Republican majorities in both houses. Since the war the United States had already given $3 billion in aid and lent Great Britain another $3.25 billion. Negotiating the costly Marshall Plan might be difficult.

What would happen in the meantime to France, where the scent of crisis was already in the air? That summer, when the Soviet Union nudged the Communists in Eastern Europe to consolidate their hold on power, many non-Communists in France turned to General de Gaulle, who opposed the PCF on nationalist grounds. The new Gaullist RPF successfully ran in the municipal elections that October.[19] Then in December the U.S. Congress, responding to what the president called the "crisis in Western Europe," passed an interim aid package of $522 million.[20] These grants were to buy American food and fuel for Europe, particularly France, Italy, and Austria, but it was still going to be tough slogging to get the more ambitious and expensive Marshall Plan accepted by the American people and through Congress.

ITALIAN COMMUNISM IN PERMANENT OPPOSITION

Palmiro Togliatti, the exiled general secretary of the Italian Communist Party (PCI), who had been living mostly in the USSR since the late 1920s, was preparing to return home in March 1944, when he was called to the Kremlin. Stalin's instructions were that he should cooperate with all anti-Fascists and get the Italian people behind the still-raging war against Germany. The Soviet dictator's preference was for a strong Italy. The British did not share his view, he said, because it would interfere with their Mediterranean plans.[21]

Shortly after his arrival in Italy, Togliatti reported that there was a groundswell of support for Communism and that Moscow's image was far more positive than Washington's or London's. The PCI, with a membership that would swell to over 1.7 million by the end of 1945, was taking an active part in the gruesome acts of revenge against the Fascists. In early 1945 alone, between 5,000 and 8,000 were killed in "wild" retributions. Special courts tried up to 30,000 people; perhaps 1,000 were sentenced to death, although with few executed.[22]

The Allies had not formulated postwar plans because the "focus had always been to force Italy out of the war, then force the Germans out of Italy—and worry about peace afterwards."[23] The peninsula had been partly liberated back in 1943 when it switched sides and overthrew Mussolini. At war's end the country was in a shambles, and people tried to cope in any way possible. Food shortages grew worse than under the Germans, shady dealings were rampant, and black-marketeering common. According to a survey for 1945–46, widespread malnutrition led to the spread of diseases like tuberculosis and malaria.[24] Even after the United Nations Relief and Rehabilitation Administration (UNRRA, created in 1943) later stepped in, frequent food riots continued.

Italy was overwhelmingly Catholic, and the religious factor represented a major obstacle that the Communists never entirely overcame. In November 1945, Christian Democratic leader Alcide De Gasperi formed a government and, in the elections to a constituent assembly in June 1946, won 35 percent of the vote. Like the French Left, the Italian Left was divided. The PCI did well to obtain 18.9 percent, while the rival Socialists (PSI) gained slightly more. In a plebiscite held at the same time, the nation voted in favor of a republic. The politics of the PCI would be marred by coalition governments that formed and dissolved sometimes in a matter of months. De Gasperi offered the Communists several key posts, including the ministry of justice (which went to Togliatti) and the ministry of finance.

The desperate times favored the PCI in local elections, and it did well at the expense of De Gasperi's Christian Democrats. In January 1947 the prime minister traveled to Washington, where he was received in an atmosphere of concern about the Italian Communists.[25]

The PCI, by 1947 with over two million members, pursued the same strategies as did the Communists in France. It would participate in government to appear a viable alternative to the Christian Democrats, but it would use obstructionist tactics to make the country's leaders look unsteady. Indeed, Communists' support of strikers slowed economic recovery and eroded the legitimacy of the government. De Gasperi hesitated to call new national elections because he worried that he might not win without solid promises of substantial American aid. He received such assurances, resigned, formed a new cabinet without Communists, and called for new elections, to take place in the autumn.

Although some Italian and American historians have long claimed that President Truman and Secretary Marshall pressured De Gasperi into eliminating Communists from his new cabinet, the evidence is thin. In a letter of May 14, 1947, Italian ambassador Alberto Tarchiani in Washington informed his prime minister about a frank discussion that he had had with Truman. The American president left it to the Italians to make the decision about their own best interests and said that, while the preferred option would be a government without Communists, he appreciated "the difficulties" of attaining such a goal. There would not be a problem as long as "the Communist presence was sufficiently diluted."[26]

On May 16, Ambassador Tarchiani met Secretary Marshall and painted a dark picture of his country's poverty, the massive funding behind the PCI, and the gloomy outlook for the coming elections. It was Tarchiani who stated that it was "highly important that Italy should not fall under Communism." He also suggested that, if the Communists did not win the election, they might try a coup. If that were to happen, he said, the Italian government would not be able to cope and might want to call on U.S. troops for help. The problem was that those forces were due to be withdrawn. Marshall agreed to look into the matter and promised to see what he could do.[27] By that time a Special Procedures Group in the CIA "spread money to various Italian centrist parties" to redress some of the imbalance, and such operations were no doubt used elsewhere as well.[28]

To add spice to the mix, former U.S. undersecretary of state Sumner Welles, who was visiting Italy, suggested in a radio interview (correctly) that the PCI was supported by the Soviet Union and (also true) that it had a large cache of arms. The implication was that the Communists were intent on revolution. Communist boss Togliatti, responding with a vitriolic attack, seemed to confirm such suspicions. At any rate, De Gasperi decided that he would point to "American demands" as a pretext to exclude the Communists from the new government announced on May 31. Stalin was infuriated, all the more so since only weeks before the Communists in France had also been dropped from the cabinet.[29]

For the 1948 elections, the Italian Communists joined a united Left, which obtained 31 percent of the vote. The Christian Democrats did far better and took 48.5 percent. For the next generation, the PCI was stuck at just over 20 percent of popular support and was more or less permanently excluded from government.[30] When the Marshall Plan finally came along, Togliatti denounced it heartily, but it was the American support that helped to turn things around in Italy.

The Soviet Union could not compete on the aid front, though it generously funded the PCI. In late 1947, when visiting Italian Communists had asked Stalin for $600,000 to cover propaganda costs, the Boss was ready to hand it over, then and there, in two large sacks. It was eventually delivered in a more seemly fashion.[31] From 1948 onward, Moscow organized systematic contributions and pressed Communists who were in power in Europe, and eventually also China, to pitch in. On January 17, 1950, the Soviet Politburo created a special fund. It donated 40 to 50 percent, and the other Communist countries gave 8 to 10 percent each. In 1950 just over $2 million went to Communists in Austria, France, Finland, and Italy. As the amounts went up, contributors complained, so the USSR gradually assumed a larger share. The flow of money continued into the 1970s, a part of the Stalin legacy rarely acknowledged.[32]

The pattern in Italy and France can also be seen in neighboring Belgium. The Communist Party there had some support at war's end and joined the first coalition governments, which came and went quickly. By early 1947 the party claimed to have 100,000 members, had won 23 seats in the most recent elections out of 202 deputies, and had four members in the cabinet. However, in order to bring more stability to the government, the majority parties wanted them out. Premier Camille Huysmans insisted on increasing coal prices and thus raising the cost of living, maneuving the Communists into rejecting the proposal. They resigned in protest on March 12. As with their French and Italian comrades, it would be their last time in government.[33]

COMMUNISM IN OCCUPIED GERMANY

Soviet occupation policy was laden with a major contradiction in Germany and Austria, as indeed it was all across Eastern Europe. On the one hand, the Kremlin wanted to champion Communism and win over the people. At the same time, it was determined to collect reparations, which in turn alienated possible supporters. Already in mid-1945, to mention but one example, in its zone in Germany, the USSR introduced a modest land reform to please landless and poor peasants, just as it had done elsewhere.[34] However, simultaneously Soviet authorities pressed on with dismantling factories—including some needed locally to process fertilizer and thus to make the new farms productive. German Communists who dared ask their leaders to intercede in this "exceptional" case were shouted down.[35]

On June 5, 1945, the four military commanders of the victorious powers, the United States, Great Britain, the Soviet Union, and France, signed a "declaration regarding the defeat of Germany and the assumption of supreme governmental authority."[36] Each of the four commanders in chief of the occupying powers was to have "supreme authority" in their zone and "also jointly, in matters affecting Germany as a whole" as members of the Allied Control Council (ACC). The latter was also responsible for governing divided "Greater Berlin." Decisions of the ACC had to be unanimous to ensure "uniformity of action" in each of the zones. In effect, that stipulation meant that each of the four had veto power and could hold up everything.[37]

The next day in Moscow the Council of People's Commissars—in fact, Stalin—decided to set up the Soviet Military Administration of Germany (SMAD). Order No. 1 on June 9 put Marshal Georgi Zhukov in charge. The military commander and war hero announced that the task of the new body included supervising the surrender, administering the Soviet zone, and implementing Allied decisions.[38]

The Soviets were first off the mark on the political front because they had a well-tuned agenda and almost immediately allowed political parties to organize. The Americans permitted some district-level activities in August, the British followed suit in September, and the French in December.[39]

General Eisenhower remained supreme commander of the Allied Expeditionary Forces from his headquarters. In April he delegated General Lucius D. Clay as deputy military governor. Field Marshal Sir Bernard Montgomery initially ran the British zone, and General Jean de Lattre de Tassigny the French.[40]

In October 1945 the U.S. finally created the Office of the Military Government, United States, or OMGUS, the equivalent to the SMAD. Occupation guidelines were formulated as Directive JCS 1067, which had been worked out by the U.S. Joint Chiefs of Staff and signed by President Roosevelt on March 23, 1945. The orders bluntly stated that "Germany will not be occupied for the purpose of liberation but as a defeated enemy nation. Your aim is not oppression," the directive cautioned, but to realize "certain important Allied objectives. In the con-

duct of your occupation and administration you should be just but firm
and aloof. You will strongly discourage fraternization with the German
officials and population."[41] The War and Navy departments went so far
as to insist on separate toilets for German and American staff in the
buildings of the Military Government.[42]

The declaration issued at the end of the Potsdam Conference
in August 1945 confirmed the agreement of the Big Three as to "the
political and economic principles of a coordinated Allied policy toward
defeated Germany during the period of Allied control." The stated
intention was not "to destroy or enslave" the people but to give them
"the opportunity to prepare for the eventual reconstruction of their life
on a democratic and peaceful basis."

Although the specific aims included disarmament, demilitarization,
and denazification, each occupying power pursued them differently.
Dealing with Nazism and all its expressions was complex, given that so
many millions of Germans were involved. American efforts took on the
dimensions of a moral crusade, the French were not as rigorous, and
the British less again. Soviet occupation policy was going to be used,
as in Eastern Europe, to extract reparations where possible, to enhance
Moscow's political control, and to assist local Communists.[43]

The three leaders at Potsdam noted with approval their separate
decision to prosecute all Nazi war criminals. Germany's own legal,
educational, and political systems had to be transformed, the economy
decentralized and controlled, and its industrial capacity and production
strictly limited. The vanquished nation lost much territory, and along with
its allies, it was expected to pay reparations. The lion's share was to go
to the Soviet Union, which would be permitted to dismantle and take
industrial capital equipment (like whole fertilizer factories) not only from
its own zone but, after negotiations, also from the three Western zones.
President Truman said the United States wanted no reparations at all.[44]

Since 1919 Communism had been a major factor in German politics.
Some good citizens found it menacing and were pleased when Hitler
dissolved the Communist Party and sent many of its leaders to concentration camps. Some Communists had found refuge in Moscow while
they prepared for their return, and on April 30, 1945, three "initiative
groups" were sent home. The first of them, led by Walter Ulbricht,
headed for Berlin; the other two went to different parts of the Soviet
zone. Their task was to reorganize the party and to advise Red Army

leaders on whom to appoint to "antifascist" slots in local and regional administrations. On May 26 Moscow gave the go-ahead for trade unions and a few anti-Nazi political parties to start up.[45]

Stalin called the leaders of the three "initiative groups" back to Moscow, and on June 4 he, Molotov, and Zhdanov met with them. Also present was Wilhelm Pieck, who like Ulbricht was a veteran Communist. To escape Hitler's persecution, he had spent almost a decade in Moscow, where his loyalty to Stalin had been unswerving.

The Kremlin appointment book shows that they met for a total of seven hours, and though no Soviet records survive, we have Pieck's notes from their meeting. Stalin's "advice" was similar to much he gave all other returnees, with the notable variation in this case to tell their people that the West had wanted to dismember Germany. At this point in time, he was beginning to think a divided Germany would likely emerge, and he told them to fight it. Their party should bring together not just workers but all the gainfully employed, including peasants and intellectuals.

How did the Kremlin Boss visualize the struggle ahead? The German Communists' first duty was to fight fascism and to complete a bourgeois revolution that would finally break the "power of the land-holding nobility and eliminate the remnants of feudalism." These words became themes that ran through the history of East Germany for decades. He then approved the list of appointments to the leading organs of the German party, including to its major publications.[46]

Over the next few days, the Germans met with Georgi Dimitrov to work out a manifesto, to be announced when they arrived home. On June 7 they visited the Kremlin for four hours. They wanted to impose a Soviet-style regime, but Stalin preferred that they form a bloc or coalition with other antifascist parties. In one of his favorite refrains, he even warned them "not to speak so glowingly about the Soviet Union."[47] In follow-up talks, Dimitrov advised against nationalizing property. Such steps would have to be carefully prepared so as not to alarm the farmers. It would be wiser to underline the intention of confiscating only properties of the "feudal" Junker class.[48]

Stalin had hoped to unify the Communists and Socialists into one party, but he briefly changed his mind and instructed Pieck to restart the old Communist Party (KPD). The Soviets then encouraged longtime Communist rivals, like the Social Democratic Party (SPD), and even some old bourgeois parties, to get organized again, in an attempt to re-create at least the illusion of political plurality. Stalin's plan was a familiar one: when the full political spectrum of parties was up and running, then an antifascist bloc or national front would emerge, and just as everywhere else, it would be dominated by the Communists.[49]

The "action program" announced by the KPD on June 11 incorporated Stalin's ideas. The goal was to establish "an anti-fascist, democratic regime"—a parliamentary republic that would ensure individual rights, including the right to private property. Among themselves, the Communists admitted that all this was for show, and they made sure that reliable comrades got the jobs in local police forces and administration.[50]

In December, KPD leader Anton Ackermann boasted that in the Soviet zone they could already count 300,000 members.[51] He was given the green light to write about "the German route to Socialism," as that concept was understood in Eastern Europe.[52] This statement found support because it meant that not everything would be dictated from Moscow.

On February 6, 1946, when Ulbricht went to Moscow, Stalin told him that in spite of difficulties in the Western zones, he still favored a united Germany. He wanted the KPD to play the nationalist card and to use the unification question to advantage. At this very time he was concerned because the Communist parties in Hungary and Austria, both still under Soviet occupation, had experienced recent and startling electoral setbacks.[53] To avert that, and changing his mind yet again, he told Ulbricht to arrange for a fusion of the KPD with the Social Democratic Party (SPD). Moreover, Stalin ordered that all signs of Communism be removed from the banners. Instead there would be a Socialist Unity Party (SED). He wanted all negotiations completed in time for an announcement on May 1, the traditional workers' holiday.[54]

On April 21 the leaders founded the new SED, and in early May they called on all "German Social Democrats and Communists" to link together across the country.[55] However, by August they had to admit that the attempt to attract other members was getting nowhere.[56] Even in the Soviet zone, an estimated 10 percent of the Communists refused to join the SED, and the majority of the SPD, many of them suspicious about Moscow's aims, would not hear of calls for unity.[57]

Stalin's plan was to prevent the reemergence of capitalism and at the same time to take over the property of the large landowners. This effort, he reminded Ulbricht, would eventually culminate in Communism. That would not happen overnight and could not be left to "spontaneous" confiscations, whereby grassroots workers' committees took over factories whose owners had been Nazis or had fled to the West. In October, SMAD officially confiscated the properties of the German state, of former "fascists," and of the Nazi Party.[58]

In order to give a semblance of legality to "the popular will," the SED in consultation with Soviet authorities held a referendum. They were cautious enough to restrict the voting to Saxony, known for being "red," and just before the voting, the Soviets arranged for 1,900 smaller businesses to be returned to their rightful owners.[59]

In the referendum held on the last day of June 1946, people were asked whether enterprises of "Nazi and War Criminals" already seized by Soviet authorities should be transferred to the German administration. No less than 77.7 percent answered "Yes!" But not all included in this number were voting for Communism. The Soviets themselves recognized that some people went along because they feared that if the referendum failed, "there would be a sharpening of the occupation regime, sinking of food rations, and so on." A SMAD report noted with consternation the evidence that a "substantial part" of the working class continued to exhibit "an underdeveloped class consciousness."[60] That was typical Communist "newspeak" for implying that workers were befuddled because they dared have ideas of their own.[61]

In the other occupation zones between January and June 1946, the Western Allies allowed elections in stages, beginning at the local, then provincial, and finally at the zonal level. The Communists participated and did poorly, in some places not making it into the double digits. The Soviets let elections proceed in their zone on October 20, 1946, but in spite of efforts to manipulate the outcome, the results were not as good as they wanted. In the five elections to provincial parliaments (*Landtagswahlen*), the SED won on average 47.6 percent of the vote and could not win a majority in any of them.[62]

The results of elections held the same day across the rest of the country were worse. The Christian Democratic Union (CDU) averaged 34.5 percent of the vote, followed by the SPD with 23 percent. The SED garnered a mere 16.8 percent, and the KPD, where it still ran independently, got only 4.8 percent.[63] In Berlin, where elections were under "quadripartite inspection teams" of the occupying powers and likely reflected actual opinions, the SED received only 19.8 percent of the vote. U.S.

deputy military governor Clay thought that those results "must have stunned the Soviet authorities and made them realize that their hope of gaining Germany by normal political methods was futile." Unquestionably, he added, those elections caused them to change tactics.[64]

When it came to Germany's neighbor Austria, the stakes were not as high. That country had been incorporated into Germany in 1938 and had generally welcomed being brought "home to the Reich." Nevertheless, during the war the Allies declared that Austria was in effect the first victim of Hitler's aggression and that, when peace came, the country's independence would be restored. Its borders would be returned to what they had been before the "conquest."

On April 13, 1945, Vienna was liberated by the Red Army, and Soviet occupation authorities recruited veteran Social Democrat Karl Renner to lead a provisional government and to declare a new republic on April 27. Moscow soon dispatched members of the Austrian Communist Party (KPÖ), like veteran activists Johann Koplenig, Friedl Fürnberg, and Ernst Fischer. Communists obtained the ministries of the interior and education in the new government and hoped to create a "true people's democracy." However, in elections held in November, they were decisively rejected and managed to get only 5.4 percent of the vote.[65]

The Soviet occupation forces, through their deplorable behavior, did not help the Red cause, and their insistence on collecting immediate reparations caused further grief. The United States, on the other hand, tried with increasing determination to mitigate the growing desperation faced by the people. In April 1946, UNRRA took over responsibility for feeding the country, and beginning early in the new year, the United States began to provide substantial assistance, soon through what would become the Marshall Plan.[66]

Stalin was flexible but hopeful about a Red future for Austria, perhaps more than has been suggested by those who claim he had never wanted or intended to turn that country into a "people's democracy."[67] The Soviet Union continued to supply advice and generous funding for the Communists there—in 1953 around $530,000, a considerable sum for the time—and only slightly less than that provided to the French party. If the KPÖ had been able to mobilize the electorate, then the Kremlin might have been willing to risk more. After the elections in 1949, in which the party barely obtained 5 percent of the vote, the lone Communist was dropped from the government.[68] By that time, whatever distant hopes the Soviets might have had for Austria and Western Europe were on the wane.

The Kremlin dictator was intent on making the most of the peace treaty negotiations, but the victors argued among themselves about what the losers would pay. Stalin was decidedly against the recovery of capitalism in Germany and advocated the harshest terms, including a four-power division of its industrial heartland in the Ruhr, a resource-rich area also important to France, Belgium, and the Netherlands. With a Soviet foothold in the Ruhr, so this thinking went, Germany would be permanently incapacitated.

The United States and Great Britain opposed the Soviet Union in Germany. Much of the slogging was done by U.S. secretary of state James Byrnes, a man with little international experience and one notorious for working on his own. In a sense, he "won" against the better-prepared Molotov, because in Western Europe, in free elections, people decided for themselves that they wanted liberal democracy, not Communism.

The peace treaties were to be negotiated by the Council of Foreign Ministers, which was created at the Potsdam Conference. It met every three months in sessions that went on for days and weeks. Secretary Byrnes had been upbeat when he left for the first round in London in September 1945, but discussions bogged down, thanks mainly to Molotov, the nightmare at the negotiating table. The gatherings were like a war of attrition that ground away at Secretary Byrnes and his British counterpart, Ernest Bevin, both of whom developed health problems.[69] Molotov questioned everything, from lofty political principles down to the tiniest details, and he did so again when the foreign ministers met in Moscow from December 16 to 26. A keen observer noted that Molotov was in his element, his "eyes flashing with satisfaction and confidence" as he glanced around the table. Ruthless and incisive, he "had the look of a passionate poker player who knows that he has a royal flush and is about to call the last of his opponents. He was the only one who was clearly enjoying every minute of the proceedings."[70]

Byrnes spoke with Stalin over dinner on Christmas Eve and sought to assure him that the United States would not retreat to isolationism, that it would stay in Europe and join the other three powers to keep

Germany demilitarized and thus allay Soviet fears of another invasion. Stalin called it the best proposal he had heard and hoped that Byrnes would fight for it.[71]

In 1946 there were two sets of meetings in Paris, the first from April 25 to May 16. French foreign minister Georges Bidault was eager to discuss Germany because his country aimed to get reparations, perhaps part of the Ruhr, and access to the Saarland. Molotov's goal was to have the occupation of Germany last as long as possible, get a four-power division of the Ruhr, and receive the oft-mentioned $10 billion in reparations.[72]

However, the welfare of the people in occupied Germany was worsening, and the United States and Great Britain felt increasingly forced to do something. Since November 1945, millions more destitute ethnic German refugees had been flooding in from the east, and to make matters worse, the USSR was insisting on immediate reparations in their zone of occupation and demanding all it could get from the Western zones. On May 3, 1946, after more fruitless discussions on the Allied Control Council in Germany, the U.S. deputy military governor announced a halt to further deliveries of reparations from the American zone.[73]

At the next session of the Council of Foreign Ministers, in Paris (June 15–July 12), Molotov, in a speech prepared in close consultation with Stalin, rejected U.S. proposals to keep Germany disarmed and demilitarized. Although the Soviets, and also France, wanted a four-power administration of the Ruhr, Molotov suggested that the West wanted to separate the natural-resource-rich Ruhr from Germany. His key admission on July 10, however, was that it would be years before a German government could ever exist, and only then would it be possible to work out a peace treaty.[74]

On a related matter, Foreign Secretary Bevin said Britain could not continue financing its zone, and he proposed more interzonal cooperation, to which Molotov gave a firm no.[75] Byrnes was annoyed that Molotov kept presenting himself as defending Germany against the vengeful Americans. Of course, Byrnes recognized that Molotov was making a clever political appeal to Germans, who still feared the vengeance of the Morgenthau Plan. He said that the United States was far from wanting Germany's division and was prepared to "join with any other occupying government or governments for the treatment of our respective zones as an economic unit." It had become untenable to continue administering Germany "in four air-tight compartments."[76]

On July 11 Byrnes invited "all his colleagues," including the Soviets, to join in an effort to merge the zones; something had to be done to deal with the country's growing economic chaos. Britain agreed the next day, while the Soviet Union and France hesitated. On December 2 the British and Americans announced their odd-sounding German "Bizonia," which became operational on New Year's Day.[77]

The Council of Foreign Ministers meeting in New York (November 4–December 12, 1946) finalized peace treaties with most of the former Axis powers, though no progress was made on Germany. When Byrnes resigned for health reasons shortly afterward, President Truman named a replacement in General George C. Marshall. The new secretary of state flew to Moscow to take up where Byrnes left off at the next gathering of the foreign ministers, scheduled for March 10 to April 24.

The Soviets kept demanding immediate reparations, also from the Western zones. However, the level of production and subsistence there was already so low that the only way they could have been paid, as French foreign minister Bidault admitted, was for the United States "to increase its aid and subsidies to Western Germany." In effect, the United States would send funds or goods in the front door and the Soviets would shovel them out the back, with the Germans just as badly off and sinking into chronic dependency.[78]

Bidault recalled that Stalin was only too willing to cooperate with France when it came to dividing the Ruhr area into four zones, after which what had happened in Berlin would be repeated. The Soviets "would have looted their section," encouraged all the workers to revolt, and production would have fallen drastically. That was how Bidault saw things, and he knew perfectly well that France would still not be getting access to the coal it desired; the U.S. would have had to persist in subsidizing the area, while in the meantime the reach of the Soviet Union would have been extended as far to the west as the Rhine.

Marshall realized that this arrangement was a losing proposition and could not agree to it. He found Molotov every bit as obstructionist as had Byrnes. What should the United States do? By common consent, the so-called Truman Doctrine was not taken seriously, and the foreign ministers were getting nowhere. Marshall decided a new response was needed, but he was unsure what that should be. Not just Germany but all of Europe was in a mess, with no end in sight.[79]

CHAPTER 17

Stalin's Choices
and the Future of Europe

In his most optimistic moments, Stalin had envisioned Sovietization, "stretched out" over time, of all the European states, even those far to the West.[1] He had been especially interested in making progress in France and Italy, which had strong Communist constituencies. However, the inability of their Moscow-oriented parties to move ahead did nothing but presage political stalemate. The voting majorities in European democracies were making their voices heard, and they did not want their nations run by Communists. The West gradually found good reason to step in and help. Indeed, President Truman seemed ready to take the lead. However, while he made several attempts to identify himself as a friend of democratic Europe, he was not quite able to hit the right note. Everything changed when the president, in a stroke of genius or good luck, named General George C. Marshall as his secretary of state.

STALIN'S OFFENSIVE AND TRUMAN'S REACTIONS

As we saw earlier, Truman first met Molotov in 1945. Wanting to avoid appearing weak, he asked the commissar just when the Soviet Union was going to start living up to its agreements. His question, with its sharp tone, was magnified into an international incident, and he soon beat a hasty retreat. The pattern repeated itself in 1946. The president quietly encouraged Churchill's "iron curtain" speech, then disavowed it when journalists accused the prime minister of warmongering. In March 1947 the president sounded ready to challenge the Soviets with the Truman Doctrine, but no one took him seriously, least of all the Kremlin.

In 1945, when he led the country to victory, Truman was popular; a year later his approval ratings fell to 32 percent. He was trying to play tough with Moscow, but the message was not working. In the congressional elections in 1946, he heeded the advice of Democrats and made no campaign appearances. The Republicans won both houses by claiming, among other things, that the president, far from being hard on Communism, was actually too soft. Chastised by the election results, Truman kept a low profile and left for a vacation in Florida. On his return, he was almost resigned to being a one-term president and to doing the best job possible in the meantime.

In his State of the Union address in January 1947, however, the president had big positives to report. The nation was at peace and wealthier than ever, and it had full employment. He promised policies to improve the quality of life, to keep a balanced budget, and to establish international economic cooperation.[2] Not many presidents before or since could deliver such a welcome message.

Truman also gave his administration a new face or two. Among them was General Marshall, who had become U.S. Army chief of staff on the day the war broke out in 1939 and held the position until victory.[3] Marshall was so revered in Washington that when Truman named him as secretary of state Republican Senate leader Arthur Vandenberg waived the rules on appointments. In his case, there were no hearings; he was confirmed by unanimous vote the same day. That expression of confidence added to Marshall's stature and conveyed the impression that the Truman administration might do great things after all.[4]

Marshall's first direct experience in dealing with the Soviet Union as secretary of state was at the Council of Foreign Ministers meeting in Moscow, scheduled to begin on March 10, 1947. He prudently waited to see how things were going before requesting a courtesy call at the Kremlin. On April 18, Stalin, who seemed relaxed, received him. No one could have guessed that the dictator's country was desperately struggling to cope with war damages and in the midst of a famine. He advised Marshall not to be discouraged by the lack of progress in the talks and to think of them as a long battle in which combatants fight until they are exhausted and finally ready to compromise.[5]

The "compromise," need it be said, would be in favor of the more determined combatant, the one who could hold out longer. Stalin clearly saw himself as having what it took to outlast any opponent. Was that not what he was doing at that very moment? As Marshall could see for himself, the West more or less stood idly by as the Soviet dictator put Communists into power across Eastern Europe. Also in Moscow with Marshall was the British foreign secretary Ernest Bevin, a longtime Labor politician. He sensed, rightly, that the "Russians" were waiting for the Americans to lose interest and give in or go home. He also knew that all of Europe was in desperate condition, with no end in sight.[6]

Indeed, hunger was everywhere on the continent. Britain was still on wartime rations and in June 1947, for the first time in its history, had to ration bread. Italy and France were not doing much better, and Germany was worse again. Eastern Europe got by only because the Kremlin sent some food, but the USSR had its own drought and harvest failure in 1946, then a famine that took more than one million lives.[7]

The French foreign minister Georges Bidault noticed the signs of social distress on his way to Moscow for the talks. Bidault had been a Catholic teacher who played a leading role in the resistance and helped found the MRP. He had been to Moscow before, but this time he traveled by rail. Two things struck him about the trip:

> The first was that, going from West to East, the train went slower and slower with each country we crossed and the second was that people's faces got progressively sadder and more expressionless as we journeyed towards the East. Germany was still in ruins and I wondered how its cities, particularly Berlin, would ever be rebuilt. All that was left of German factories were a few vast chimney stacks still standing here and there. East Germany was already perceptibly sadder than West Germany. Poland, where Warsaw was not yet rebuilt, was sadder than East Germany. And Russia was saddest of all.[8]

On March 4, 1947, just before leaving for Moscow, Bidault had signed the Dunkirk Treaty with Great Britain. Although he hoped to avoid a breach between East and West, he recalled that "every exhausting and fruitless conference with the Soviet Union made me less certain of success."[9] The Anglo-French alliance was symbolic; it showed that concerns about the Soviet Union were not merely a figment of Washington's imagination. Stalin had taken half the Continent already, and the other half felt deeply threatened. Europe was thus seriously divided, well before there was any mention of a Marshall Plan.[10]

Charles Bohlen, the veteran State Department expert who had translated for President Roosevelt at the wartime conferences, went with the new secretary to Moscow. Bohlen recalled that Marshall was taken aback when Stalin, seemingly indifferent to what was going on in Germany, appeared to think that "the best way to advance Soviet interests was to let matters drift." Bohlen was particularly struck that "all the way back to Washington Marshall talked of the importance of finding some initiative to prevent the complete breakdown of Western Europe."[11]

On April 28 the secretary of state gave a radio report on his trip, mentioned Stalin's assurances about future cooperation, and said something had to be done and soon. "We cannot ignore the factor of time involved here. The recovery of Europe has been far slower than had been expected. Disintegrating forces are becoming evident. The patient is sinking while the doctors deliberate. So I believe that action cannot await compromise through exhaustion. New issues arise daily. Whatever action is possible to meet these pressing problems must be taken without delay."[12]

The next day he called in George Kennan, one of the State Department's Russian experts and asked him to build a Policy Planning Staff. Its task was to figure out what the United States had to do in order to turn things around in Europe, and Marshall wanted a concise plan within two weeks.[13]

Kennan delivered a brief report on May 23. It said that the root of the crisis was not Communist activity but the disruption of the economy brought on by the war. Although Kennan acknowledged that Communism was gaining, he also said that a recovery program had to aim at undoing "the economic maladjustment that makes European society vulnerable to exploitation by any and all totalitarian movements." Ultimately, the crisis could only be addressed by a plan developed by the Europeans. The United States should give only its "friendly support." Although Kennan believed the Soviets might try to stall things, they still should be included in any program.[14]

Others in the State Department, such as Dean Acheson and Will Clayton, put forward broadly similar proposals for Marshall to consider.[15] Then he put Bohlen and Kennan to work, independently, on a speech no longer than ten minutes that he would give at Harvard University on the recovery program.

Marshall's address to the Harvard convocation on June 5 began by stating that, while most of them likely knew about the visible destruction in Europe, perhaps they did not realize that its entire economic structure was dislocated. The crux of the problem was that Europe needed more food and fuel than it could pay for. If the problem was not solved, he said, demoralization would surely set in and disturbances would grow. His mildly phrased proposal was that if Europeans could come up with an international, cooperative plan for recovery, then the United States would be willing to offer "friendly advice" in drafting the program and provide "later support."[16]

There was no "Marshall Plan" in the sense that the United States presented a thick document like one of Stalin's five-year plans, setting out production targets and quotas and all the rest. In his speech at Harvard, Marshall stated in no uncertain terms that "our policy is not directed against any country or doctrine but against hunger, poverty, desperation and chaos." A new approach was needed, and "it would be neither fitting nor efficacious for this Government to undertake to draw up unilaterally a program designed to place Europe on its feet economically. This is the business of the Europeans."

Marshall was serious about including Eastern Europe. Those who knew him said "he deplored the emotional anti-Russian attitude in the country and kept emphasizing the necessity to talk and write about Europe in terms of economics instead of ideologies."[17] Of course he recognized that if "the Russians" agreed to go along with any recovery program, then it would be more difficult to get Congress to fund it. Nevertheless, to Marshall and Kennan it was self-evident that any offer of aid had to include the Soviet Union and all of Eastern Europe.[18]

Stalin saw things differently. In his view, the United States and Great Britain, the two major capitalist powers to survive the war, had been pleased to defeat their main competitors in Italy, Germany, and Japan and intended to keep them down to control prices and dominate the globe. That was his message in January 1947 to visiting German Communist leaders. He also predicted that the United States would fail: "The Americans believe that they alone will be able to deal with the world market. That is an illusion. They will not be able to cope with it."[19]

He was quite wrong to suppose the United States would be against the recovery of Europe, and he did not anticipate such generous assistance. The American offer to the Soviet Union confronted Stalin with a momentous choice.

Britain's foreign secretary Bevin heard the first report about Marshall's Harvard speech on his bedside radio in early June and realized its potential at once. When he and French foreign minister Bidault spoke of it later, they said "it was like a life-line to sinking men. It seemed to bring hope where there was none. The generosity of it was beyond our belief."[20]

Bevin promised Washington a speedy response and contacted Bidault; they called for a meeting on June 27 to discuss the next step. During the interim Marshall reiterated that by "European" recovery he definitely included the Soviet Union. According to the report of U.S. ambassador Jefferson Caffery, the British thought that Soviet participation would "complicate things," as did the French. However, on June 19, and because Marshall was quite emphatic, they extended an invitation to the Soviet Union.[21]

To this day, some Russian historians maintain that the United States, Britain, and France were playing a "double game," inviting Soviet participation while hoping they would not accept. Supposedly, the West had "decided everything in advance."[22] In fact, the plan had yet to be written. Moreover, even had it been already drawn up, and even if, as Soviet spies reported, a few or many bureaucrats in Washington, London, or Paris "hoped" the Russians would turn it down, the decision was still Stalin's to make.[23]

Why should the Soviet leader not concede that the war had been much worse than he had at first let on? Why not remind the West of the bitter truth that the Soviets had paid with far more blood than anyone else for victory over Hitler? Millions upon millions of its citizens had been killed and the country devastated. Why not ask for help?

Alas, Stalin was caught in the trap of his own theories. He and his followers had created a system that regarded economic data almost like state secrets. It did not help matters that Soviet diplomats and spies added to their leader's doubts. Thus Ambassador Nikolai Novikov wrote from

Washington that the underlying goal of the recovery plan was to hinder Europe's "democratization"—a code word for stopping Communism.[24]

The Soviet leadership approached international relations as a zero-sum game. If the United States was going to gain in some way in Europe, then the USSR would have to lose. That thinking became integral to Cold War psychology and incredibly difficult to overcome.[25] With the Marshall Plan, the game had changed. The U.S. secretary had left a way for destitute Soviet citizens to be winners too, along with those in the West.

Of course, it is also true that the Marshall Plan, in addressing the economic causes of Europe's problems, would have the effect of reducing the potential sources of Communist support. Although Bevin and Bidault indicated, at least privately, that they neither wanted nor expected Soviet participation in the program, the two men were not completely out of step with the mood of the U.S. government. Some historians overstate the case by concluding that the State Department's insistence on treating Europe "as one common economic area" and on getting a coordinated response to the American proposal was the equivalent of excluding the USSR.[26]

Stalin had many misgivings about the June talks scheduled in Paris, but he dispatched Molotov, who was accompanied by a delegation of close to a hundred. The unusually large number of representatives was a symbol of strength, a visual display of Communist solidarity. It hardly shows, as has been supposed, that the Soviets were "still moderate." They were not there as a team that would participate, take notes, and make suggestions.[27]

At the first session on Friday, June 27, the hosts Bevin and Bidault opened by saying that a larger meeting was to be called and that specialized committees would examine the requests of each country and coordinate them. The goal was to develop a European-wide program that would be presented to the United States for financial support.

The instruction to Molotov was to find out how much money the Americans were prepared to give and to make sure that there would be no interference in the internal affairs of recipients.[28] At the first session he wondered aloud what was in the American plan—supposing "it" was largely finished. Bevin and Bidault confessed that all they knew was what they had read in Marshall's speech. It gave no specifics and asked only that the Europeans put forward a joint plan. Bevin and Bidault likely had spoken with U.S. officials, and they all may well have hoped to stop Communism, but that was beside the point. The "plan" was not yet even a work in progress, and the Soviets could have hammered out a deal.

Stalin had it in his power to stop the drift toward Cold War then and there. Contrary to what some historians have suggested, he had choices. All he had to do was be prepared to say how the money would be spent. The all-powerful Stalin had no worries about political objections back home. The hindrances stopping him were entirely of his own creation. He was unable to imagine revealing economic "secrets" that, incidentally, democracies routinely publish.

By the second day, Molotov had time to consult with the Kremlin and came out strongly against any coordinated plan. He suggested again that they compile a list of each country's needs and find out how much the United States would pay and whether Congress would approve it. Bevin and Bidault repeated that the plan had to be coordinated. It soon became obvious to all present that Molotov was "dragging his feet."[29]

When they convened on Monday, June 30, he again condemned the concept of a joint plan and added that the British and French were contemplating a new organization to intervene in "subordinated states." The discussion made no progress, and by July 2 Molotov did little more than warn that, if they proceeded, they would "split Europe into two groups of states." With that he marched out.[30]

The East-West division that Molotov described had developed since the war, largely because of the steps taken by the Soviet Union. After the war, Western Europe was in no position to do anything, and in the United States the overwhelming urge was a retreat to isolationism. By rejecting the Marshall Plan, the Soviets in effect flung open the doors to the Cold War.

Historians are rightly reluctant to apportion "war guilt." We should not conclude, however, that both sides were equally responsible for the Cold War.[31] Marshall was dealing with an economic problem in a Europe devastated by war and famine. The aid that the United States offered was available to all nations, independently of their political commitments. Granted, the American planners hoped to lure Soviet satellites and to loosen Moscow's grip on them, while Stalin was just as determined to resist. He wanted a Communist transformation of Europe that would eventually extend to other lands.[32]

Marshall was fighting poverty, while Stalin was faced with a choice between the impoverishment of his own people, the pursuit of his political agenda, and no doubt also Soviet security interests as he defined them. Western Europeans did not share his vision of the future, as became apparent in the early postwar period, when France and Italy, despite widespread misery, were already saying no to Communist pressure. Stalin could see that wherever he looked in Western Europe, his hopes for a Red future could not stand up to the will of the people, as demonstrated in fair elections, and it would certainly be doomed if there were economic recovery. He opted for his political mission and gave thumbs down to American aid.

It was overwhelmingly Stalin's actions that led to the Cold War. The Moscow dictator was willing to bide his time and to let Western Europe stagnate and fester. If the United States had turned away, those who condemn it for offering the Marshall Plan would blame it—and rightly so—for doing nothing to put an end to the suffering and starvation in war-torn Europe.[33]

Years later when Molotov looked back, he was completely unrepentant. His only argument was the spurious one that if some Western writers were saying that he made a mistake in rejecting the American aid, then he must have done the right thing. Still blinded by his ideology, he insisted that "the imperialists" were out to turn all of Europe into something like dependent colonies.[34]

The British and French forged ahead with the Conference on European Reconstruction that began in Paris on July 12, 1947. They invited twenty-two countries, including all those in Eastern Europe and Turkey, but not the USSR. Spain was excluded because of its fascist government. Germany was represented by its occupying powers. Fourteen Western countries accepted the invitation, and together they created a new Conference for European Economic Cooperation and took the first step toward a European community. Notwithstanding numerous complications and sincere concerns, in the end they reached an agreement.

Their two-volume *General Report* was published on September 22. The Truman administration then faced the daunting task of getting the very costly package called the European Recovery Program (ERP) through a Republican-dominated Congress. In his congressional testimony in January 1948, Marshall estimated the total expenditure at between $15.1 and $17.8 billion, of which $6.8 billion would be needed for the first fifteen months. The United States would provide outright grants for European countries to buy the essentials needed to get their factories and farms up and running.

The secretary of state went on the road to sell the ERP. Frankly, it helped his cause that the Communists at that time were asserting themselves in Eastern Europe and that in February 1948 there was a coup in Czechoslovakia. It all added such urgency to passing the bill that many Republicans came out in favor of it, most notably Senator Arthur Vandenberg. He said to those who would cut the cost of the package: "There is no sense throwing a fifteen-foot rope to a man drowning twenty feet from shore." President Truman signed the bill on April 1, 1948, and in its first fiscal year it would absorb more than 10 percent of the federal budget.[35]

Secretary Marshall hoped to avoid having the ERP appear as if it were just a measure to stop Communism. That impression emerged anyway during the long legislative process, which was overtaken by emotions whipped up by fears about the Communists at home and events in Europe.

Since that time, debates have raged about the economic impact of the ERP, and some historians have insisted that its miraculous effects have been wildly exaggerated.[36] A more sober evaluation suggests that the ERP made it possible for Europe to solve the catch-22 problem it faced: it had to export in order to pay for imports, but it could not produce anything to export until it imported materials and machinery.[37] The aim of the ERP, to get Europe back on its feet in four years, was reached because, once the vicious circle had been broken, Europe already had the prerequisites for sustained economic growth.

There was American altruism in the plan and also economic interest. Then, again, when is altruism never mixed with self-interest? It does nobody any good to have trading partners who are desperate and starving. We should also recall that the American economy in the postwar period was at full employment, and domestic demand could have been further stimulated without the investments attached to foreign aid. Nor was it in the interest of the U.S. government to have misery become a permanent condition in Europe or anywhere else. Stalin could explain this behavior only with the theory that the Americans were out to "enslave" them all.

Partly because Stalin cut the Soviet Union out of the Marshall Plan, its economy fell behind Western Europe's and never caught up. Ordinary people in the Soviet Union and its satellites paid the price. Their standard of living and life expectancy was, and remained, persistently lower than that of their neighbors, with contrasts between West and East growing more obvious with every passing year. Communists in Western Europe never again put in a serious bid for political power.

SECURING THE COMMUNIST FORTRESS

For years Stalin told foreign Communists to avoid ostentatiously copying the Soviet Union. However, while each nation was advised to take its "own road" to socialism, he never seriously doubted that all roads would be under the Kremlin's direction and that they all had the same destination, Communism. Up until 1946 or 1947, the question of how closely the satellite states would be tied to Soviet imperatives rarely came up. Faithful comrades everywhere certainly felt an allegiance to Moscow, and some assumed that, while sharing the Communist dream, they would have a degree of independence. Perhaps even Stalin had not thought through the place of the Soviet Union in the Red Empire beyond the borders of the USSR.

The first indication that he envisaged more vigorous control from Moscow came in Germany, where the Soviet zone already was ruled directly from the Kremlin. Wolfgang Leonhard, a former exile in Moscow and a true believer for decades, noted that a month after the disastrous 1946 autumn elections, the notion of taking a German "road to socialism" began to be subtly discouraged. An SED insider, he recalled that in contrast to the year before, the speeches of the leaders in Moscow, given on the Soviet National Day (November 7), were published verbatim: no fine-tuning for locals. The German-born Leonhard, having lived in Moscow as a schoolboy since the 1930s, had returned home with the Walter Ulbricht group. Mischa Wolf, a close friend, told him in August 1947 that "higher authorities" had decided it was time to forget about a special path to socialism. Wolf said the party program would soon be rewritten, as indeed it was. The Soviet impositions and complete lack of concern for local hopes and dreams eventually led to Leonhard's disillusionment with the Moscow variety of Communism, and he moved to Yugoslavia.[38]

Conformity with Stalin's will among the Eastern Europeans varied according to circumstances, as in Romania, where a "fake pluralism" persisted during the Petru Groza government (March 1945–December 1947). In fact the Communists were in a dominant position, and as they began to feel safe from Western eyes, they set about establishing a Stalinist regime. In August 1947 the most important opposition parties were dissolved. Iuliu Maniu, the leader of the historic National Peasant Party, was arrested in October. After a show trial for conspiring with the Americans and British, he was given a life term and died in prison. On December 30 King Michael was forced from the throne, and Romania became a people's republic.[39] Thereafter, internal threats were taken care of by the secret police, and the Romanians were saddled with Communism for generations.

The Bulgarian Communists went from a tiny prewar minority to victory as part of the Fatherland Front, admittedly in rigged elections to the Grand National Assembly in October 1946.[40] As we saw in Chapter 14, the nail in the coffin of political freedom came when Nikola Petkov, the leader of the Agrarians and a symbol of continuing resistance, was unceremoniously dragged from the National Assembly in August 1947 and put on trial. Stalin quickly agreed with the death sentence, and Petkov was executed on September 23. That happened one day after Western Europeans finished their recovery plan, to be submitted to the United States for Marshall Plan funding. The two events symbolized the starkly contrasting futures of Eastern and Western Europe.[41]

In Hungary the Communists were completely dependent on Moscow, and yet they still had high hopes of participating in the Marshall Plan meetings. Their leader, Mátyás Rákosi, had a tough time finding popular support, and in the elections of November 7, 1945, the Communists were trounced by the Smallholders Party, which won an outright majority. In early 1947, with instructions from Moscow, the secret police traced an alleged antigovernment conspiracy to the Smallholders' leader, Béla Kovács, who was arrested by Soviet military police on February 25. In May the Soviet secret police (MGB) revealed that it had wrested incriminating information from Kovács and others about Prime Minister Ferenc Nagy. He was vacationing abroad and decided not to return. On May 21, Molotov advised Rákosi "to switch to more emphasis on class struggle" and to move away from national unity government.[42]

With new national elections scheduled for August, the Hungarian Communists almost certainly would have preferred to be among the recipients of U.S. recovery funding, and yet they had to reject it. József Révai, one of the hard-line Stalinists who had been socialized during the war in Moscow, responded to the invitation to attend the event in Paris by saying that it would be impossible to participate in such an "anti-Soviet" endeavor.[43] In the Hungarian elections, the Communists obtained only 22 percent of the vote, no doubt partly because they were blamed for missing out on American assistance.[44] By December, when party boss Rákosi was convalescing in a hospital near Moscow, he developed a plan, in consultation with Stalin, for the complete transformation of Hungary along Soviet lines, and that followed in 1948 without much resistance.[45]

In Czechoslovakia the situation was more awkward. When Communist Party leader Klement Gottwald met with Stalin in autumn 1946, he was told it was perfectly acceptable to pursue the "Czechoslovak path to socialism."[46] The Czech party had more than a million members and won enough support at the polls to form a government with the Socialists.

On July 4, 1947, when the Americans and British called on Czech foreign minister Jan Masaryk to invite him to Paris for the Marshall Plan meetings, he accepted immediately, a decision the government discussed and unanimously endorsed. The next day the Soviet Central Committee wrote Prime Minister Gottwald to inform him that the USSR would not be in Paris, but the Czechs, and other countries like Poland, could go ahead. They should disrupt the meeting and then walk out to give the Americans a rebuff. The Kremlin at first wanted to play a double game and then on July 6 issued new instructions to Soviet representatives in Warsaw, Prague, Bucharest, Sofia, Belgrade, Budapest, Tirana, and Helsinki. They were to tell the Communist Party leaders not to reply to the invitation for several days, and because the USSR was not going to Paris, they should not go either.[47] Finally on July 7 the Kremlin ordered all of them to refuse the invitation outright and said that they could give their own reasons for doing so.[48]

The Czech Communist Party faced a dilemma, as did the Poles, for both were part of coalition governments. Gottwald told the Soviet representative they could not follow Stalin's orders because the rest of the government would not support them. When Stalin heard, he was infuriated and ordered them to Moscow at once. A delegation consisting, among others, of Gottwald, Foreign Minister Masaryk, and Minister of

Justice Prokop Drtina went there and on July 9 met twice with Stalin and Molotov.

The extraordinary conversations, recorded by the Soviets and the Czechs, show how Stalin crushed Czechoslovakian hopes. Masaryk and Drtina explained that their country's imports and exports were 60 percent dependent on the West and that because of that fact, they had agreed to attend the Paris meetings. Drtina said that if they did not participate in the Marshall Plan, the Czech standard of living would be adversely affected. Of course, they certainly did not wish to offend their Soviet ally.

Stalin judged that subjectively they might feel friendly toward his country, but objectively their acts revealed the opposite. The "real aim" of the Marshall Plan, he asserted, was "to create a western bloc and isolate the Soviet Union." Therefore he would regard their going to Paris "as a break in the front of the Slav states and as an act specifically aimed at the USSR." All he offered as compensation was more trade with the Soviet Union. The delegation obsequiously asked for his help to formulate a rejection to the British and French that did not offend him in any way. Dismissively, he told them to get in touch with the Bulgarians, who had already turned down the invitation. At the end of the little chat, he emphatically reminded them to send their refusal to Paris "immediately."[49]

When the weary travelers returned to Prague, they closeted with the government all day on July 11, then rescinded their acceptance of the invitation. Jan Masaryk told his friends about the ghastly experience: "I went to Moscow as the Foreign Minister of an independent sovereign state. I returned as a lackey of the Soviet Government."[50]

After this turn of events, even the Czech Communists, who perhaps had believed they could bring about socialism their own way, knew what was really expected. They might have thought they were linked to Soviet Communism by comradeship and shared ideas, but after their appearance as supplicants in Stalin's court, they could hardly doubt that theirs was a master-slave relationship.[51]

On July 11 the U.S. ambassador in Moscow, Walter Bedell Smith, wrote Secretary Marshall to express alarm at Soviet actions. Smith, a senior army general who had served under Marshall and Dwight Eisenhower, said that he regarded the Kremlin's act of forcing the Czechs to back out as "nothing less than a declaration of war by the Soviet

Union on the immediate issue of the control of Europe." The Kremlin believed it could win such a contest with the food and resources under its command, or at least that was what Smith thought. He said that never before had Moscow been "so firm in handling its satellites."[52]

The Communist boss of Poland, Władysław Gomułka, was convinced that a "Polish road to socialism" was possible, and Stalin initially encouraged him. By the time the Poles got around to holding elections in January 1947, the Soviet dictator was no longer as interested in keeping up appearances.[53]

The issue of American aid became a test for Poland. After Molotov walked out of the Paris meetings in a huff, he wrote party leaders in Warsaw on July 5 to say that the Soviet Union would not be attending the Marshall Plan meetings, but that it would be "desirable" for "friendly countries" to go along, be obstructive, and then march out. As of July 7, Polish leaders were telling U.S. authorities they were interested and wanted to hear more "about the scope of the plan."[54] As of two P.M. on July 9, the president of Poland informed the new U.S. ambassador, Stanton Griffis, that they would certainly be in Paris. Seven hours later the foreign minister called the ambassador back to say that Poland had rescinded its acceptance. Griffis reported that the Poles wanted to go but were "overruled by higher authority."[55]

And so it was that the Soviet empire took on more formal appearances, much to the chagrin of at least some of Stalin's faithful disciples.

CHAPTER 18

Stalinist Failures:
Yugoslavia and Germany

At the pinnacle of Soviet power in the postwar years, the ruling process was highly personalized, with an almost feudal character. Stalin knew and met with the key people both from the USSR and from the countries in the Soviet sphere of influence. Communists from abroad sought and sometimes all but begged for his permission to make trips to Moscow or to visit him on vacation. Between 1944 and 1952 his Kremlin visitors' book recorded no less than 140 meetings with Eastern European leaders. In addition, he had as many or more semiofficial gatherings at one of his dachas outside Moscow or in the south. Invitations were selective and usually prized. The most frequent visitors in the Kremlin were the Poles (59 times), but the East Germans were there on 11 occasions. At these events, just as during his international conferences, he could be rude, gruff, and intimidating, or he could be quiet and charming, changing his persona as the context demanded.[1]

In this period Stalin's thinking about how to rule the Communist parties across Europe was gradually taking shape. The image that emerged was that of a single transnational party that covered the globe. The various branches, all sensitive to conditions on the ground, would culminate in a single headquarters based in Moscow and run from the Kremlin.[2] However, it proved not to be so simple to control Communists who became leaders of their own countries, and while the self-proclaimed Master might lay down ideological-political dogma from Moscow, enforcing it was a delicate matter.

VISITS AND PRIVILEGES

Foreign disciples who made it to Moscow tended to view Stalin as the Kremlin oracle dispensing wisdom. Interlocutors were spellbound by his knowledge, overwhelmed by the simplicity of his lifestyle, and impressed by the quiet manner of this "friend of the people."[3]

The Boss took it for granted that foreign Communists would see him in person on important issues. His preferred role was that of a patron who tempted foreign clients with shows of opulence and lavish vacations. Communists from abroad came to expect the best and loved to be spoiled. The top ranks of the Polish party, for example, took time away from state making in September 1946 for sumptuous family vacations in Livadia, near Yalta on the Black Sea. The Soviets flew them in and welcomed them with a buffet of cold appetizers, fruit, and soft drinks. An honor guard escorted them to roomy and posh accommodations. This locale was where the Big Three had once met. Nothing was spared, especially when it came to provisions; "perishable produce, delicacies and drinks" were brought in daily by plane from distant Moscow.[4]

Communist leaders rationalized their privileges to themselves as necessary to ensure their well-being, to help them do the best possible job of looking after their nations. That was precisely the explanation offered by the ruling pigs in George Orwell's famed allegory *Animal Farm,* which was written in 1943, before any of these events occurred. The story was inspired by what the English writer saw as he fought alongside the Reds in the Spanish Civil War in 1936–37 and by what he had read about the Soviet Union.[5]

Like Orwell's pigs, Stalin's clients were self-centered and demanding. Indeed, Stalin could not continue to manage all of them on an individual basis and concluded that some kind of international organization might provide a better means of exerting control. As far back as April 1945 he had mentioned to Tito the idea of creating a new international organization, and he hinted to other visitors from time to time that Tito wanted something vaguely resembling the old Communist International, but he invariably added that any such body was no more than a remote possibility. In March 1946 he mentioned the topic to Hungarian party boss Mátyás Rákosi, and he brought it up several times in May and

June, when Yugoslavs and Bulgarians, looking for Soviet economic assistance, came to visit.[6] One evening and seemingly out of the blue, Stalin began running down the old Comintern. He embarrassed its former head Georgi Dimitrov, who was present, then coaxed him into saying that it would be useful to create a new International and, further, that it might be led by Tito. No one dared to take the bait.

The events that had rocked the Communist world, like the setbacks in France and Italy, as well as the evidence of centrifugal nationalist forces that might tear the movement asunder, made the need for a "unifying ideological message" all the more urgent.[7] In late spring 1947, Stalin pressed the idea of an international body on Poland's independent-minded Władysław Gomułka by saying that the goals of this Communist Information Bureau (or Cominform) would be to publish an informational journal and that Polish and other comrades would edit it. At the end of July, he helped Gomułka draw up a list of invitees for a conference that included the Communist parties of Yugoslavia, Czechoslovakia, Bulgaria, Hungary, Romania, France, and Italy. Stalin was determined to establish a center to coordinate the activities of the Communist parties. Those invited were given no agenda, though he left them with the impression that they would exchange information and set up some kind of journal. Officially the Poles were the hosts of a top-secret gathering in the isolated winter resort town of Szklarska Poręba.[8]

The event opened on September 22. The speeches of Soviet representatives Georgi Malenkov and Andrei Zhdanov showed that from Moscow's perspective, the Cold War had arrived. Malenkov repeated Stalin's theory that the "general crisis" of capitalism had led to the last war and that, with the elimination of its competitors, the United States had gone over to an expansionism that "aimed at establishing its domination of the world."

According to Malenkov, the Soviet Union and Eastern Europe had set themselves the task of "undermining imperialism" and "securing a democratic peace." The period of rivalry with the United States would be long, and the Soviet Union would always be ready to support "its really loyal allies." Since the end of the Comintern in 1943, however, the links between the Soviet Communist Party and the others had not been "adequate or satisfactory." In words coming straight from Stalin,

Malenkov stated that at a time when the United States was using aid as a disguise to enslave Europe, "we must take definite steps" to cooperate more closely.[9]

Andrei Zhdanov, the front man in Stalin's ideological battle against all deviations from the party line at home, gave the keynote address on the second day. His militant message was that the imperialist United States, Britain, and France had "hoped" that Germany and Japan would weaken or even defeat the Soviet Union in the last war. That did not happen, he said, and in the aftermath there arose "two camps"; one was "the imperialist and anti-democratic camp"—namely, the Americans and their allies—and the other the Communist or "anti-imperialist and democratic camp." The latter's mainstay was the "USSR and the countries of new democracy." Zhdanov claimed that whereas the Truman Doctrine had tried to terrorize the Communists into submission, the Marshall Plan set out "to seduce" and blind with promises of aid. The Soviet Union had refused to participate because if it had gone along, it would have given the program a veneer of legitimacy and thereby made it easier for the United States to entice the Eastern Europeans into the trap called the "economic restoration of Europe with American aid."

Zhdanov admitted that the days of the old Comintern were over. It had been correct to dissolve it in 1943, though wrong for some comrades to conclude that all links among the parties had been liquidated. Now more than ever there was "need for consultation and voluntary coordination of action between different parties." The absence of connections could lead to more "serious mistakes."[10]

The Soviets then inveigled the Yugoslavs present to attack the errors of the French and Italian parties, both of which had been eased out of government only months before. Milovan Djilas and Edvard Kardelj assaulted them in turn. Their main point was that "parliamentary illusions" had led both parties into believing they could attain power via the ballot box.[11] Actually that was what Stalin had instructed them to do, but he and the Yugoslavs now thought otherwise. The French and Italians were virtually ordered to engage in more revolutionary tactics. Indeed, both tried that on their return home, to no avail, because the great majority had already turned their backs on Communism.

The meeting also addressed the related issue of national variations on the "road to socialism." It turned out that nearly everyone outside the Soviet Union believed that their nation was special and could go its own way. For Stalin, that thinking was no longer acceptable, but he picked a curious host for this event in Władysław Gomułka, whose opening remarks shockingly pointed with pride to "the Polish peaceful road to social changes and the Polish revolution."[12] Glossing over the terror and intimidation the Communists had used in Poland, he claimed that the revolution there had been legal and bloodless. Apart from being inaccurate, he was now wildly out of step with the Kremlin. The theory of the national roads to socialism had been superseded.

Gomułka's days were numbered because he was against the "excessive standardization" imposed by the Soviet Union. The assault on the opposition Polish Labor Party (PSL) was under way even as he was speaking at the founding meeting of the Cominform in September 1947. Only a month later the elimination of the opposition in Poland began in earnest when the deputy prime minister and PSL leader Stanisław Mikołajczyk was warned of imminent arrest and fled the country. Whereas formerly Stalin had tolerated national variations and coalition governments, he soon supported radical followers in Poland who would oust Gomułka in mid-1948 for being on the wrong side of the party line. By the end of the year, the last opposition party was gone, and the Communists had a complete monopoly.[13] The same was more or less true all over Eastern Europe.

STALIN'S FAILURE WITH YUGOSLAVIA

Yugoslavia was becoming a problem in the perception of Soviet leaders, and it was partly because of that country that Stalin pushed for the Cominform. Although Yugoslavia backed the new organization, Tito did not attend the big founding event. Instead he sent along Milovan Djilas and Edvard Kardelj as representatives. Behind Tito's hail-fellow-well-met personality and his tolerance, even his fostering of ostentatious wealth, at least for party leaders, he represented Communist and revolutionary aims. He also had territorial ambitions to create a larger federation than the one over which he ruled. In January 1945, Yugoslavs visiting Moscow mentioned their nation's interests in Albania, parts of Greece, Hungary, Austria, Romania, and Bulgaria. Although at the time the West tended to blame the Soviet Union for Tito's ambitions, Stalin was strongly inclined to rein in the Yugoslavs. He regarded their visions of linking up with their Balkan neighbors as absurd, and worried that coming out with such widespread territorial demands might jeopardize his delicate postwar relationship with the West.[14]

Tito visited Moscow in May 1946 in search of assistance. His Yugoslav party was radical, and within six months it had nationalized 90 percent of the country's industry. However, the country was poor and the economy underdeveloped.[15] He felt that U.S. aid, if he could get it, would come with a demand for "political concessions"—presumably gestures to liberal democracy. Tito mentioned forming a Yugoslav federation with Albania, something, he said, its leader, Enver Hoxha, also favored. Stalin did not respond directly, though he wondered why Hoxha kept asking to visit Moscow for discussions, if there were no issues.[16]

When another group of Yugoslav dignitaries led by Milovan Djilas visited in December 1947, the subject of Albania came up again, and Stalin said that some comrades there were apparently opposed to unification with Yugoslavia. Djilas wanted to clarify a point, when Stalin broke in: "We have no special interest in Albania. We agree that Yugoslavia swallow Albania."[17]

Djilas was appalled at the crudity, making it sound like Yugoslavia was imperialistic. He said that they did not want to "swallow" Albania and instead sought to work out friendly relations. Molotov retorted: "But that is swallowing." What staggered Djilas was that Stalin, as he spoke, put his fingers to his lips to mimic eating a morsel of food. And then he repeated: "Yes, yes, swallowing. But we agree you ought to swallow Albania—the sooner the better." And then he gestured again with his fingers as if eating the tiny country.[18] He was playing at imperial games, and what bothered him most was that Yugoslavia and Albania might form a federation without consulting him.

When the Yugoslavs sought economic aid from Moscow, they found they were not going to get anything for free—not even the return of property that had been stolen from their country during the war and that had ended up in the USSR. Anastas Mikoyan, one of the main Soviet negotiators, told a Yugoslav delegation bluntly: "Trade is trade; I am not engaged in making gifts but in carrying out trade."[19] Thus, when the Soviets formed joint-stock companies with their allies, at least so the Yugoslavs said, they invariably drove a hard bargain, tried to get monopolies, and hived off the profits. Subsequent negotiations on the trade front revealed that Moscow wanted to import raw materials from Yugoslavia, sell that nation manufactured goods in return, and transform it into a dependent colony, just as later the Kremlin would attempt to do with Communist China.[20]

In early 1948, Tito proposed sending a division of his troops into Albania, supposedly to protect it from an attack by Greece. Stalin was angry and grew apoplectic when Bulgarian leader and onetime close comrade Dimitrov, on his own initiative, proposed creating a Balkan federation that might eventually include Bulgaria, Yugoslavia, Hungary, Czechoslovakia, Romania, Poland, and perhaps even Greece. At the time Dimitrov was in Bucharest on a friendly visit and became speculative when answering a reporter's question. He had not only acted without getting the Kremlin's blessing, but the broad federation he suggested made no mention of the USSR.

In Moscow, *Pravda* immediately published the official objections, and Stalin commanded Yugoslav and Bulgarian leaders to the seat of power. He met with them on February 10, 1948. Once again it was expected that Tito make an appearance, but rightly fearing for his life, he sent his comrades instead.[21] Molotov began the discussions calmly by saying that it was unacceptable for Dimitrov to put forward and sign a treaty of unification between Bulgaria and Yugoslavia and others, such as Greece, without informing the Soviet Union. Then Stalin, who could sit still no longer, began the attack. He was not going to tolerate the "people's democracies" developing relations among themselves as they pleased. The aging and ill Dimitrov tried to defend himself by saying that Bulgaria was in economic difficulty and had to learn to collaborate more closely with its neighbors. Although he had once been head of the Comintern, now he was the leader of his own country and had responsibilities.

Stalin put the worst possible spin on Dimitrov's motives: "You wanted to shine with originality. It is completely wrong, for such a federation is inconceivable. What historic ties are there between Bulgaria and Romania? None!" And he pressed on with his attack, as Dimitrov humbly submitted, "We are learning our way in foreign politics." The Boss scoffed at how the Bulgarian leader "bandied words like a woman of the streets!" "Learning," he roared. "You have been in politics for fifty years, and you talk about learning!" The issue was not about correcting this or that error. There was only one right way, one correct conception of what was to be done, and that was Stalin's. Anyone who differed was wrong.

The brutal side of the Master was showing, the majesty gone. There stood the imperial ruler threatening his vassals. He said that the proposed union was stupid, mistaken, and worst of all, even "anti-Marxist." He browbeat Dimitrov as if he were an errant schoolboy, telling him "you rushed headlong" trying "to astound the world, as if you were still secretary of the Comintern. You and the Yugoslavs don't let anyone know what you are doing and we have to find out about it in the street!"[22]

Then and there he proposed several other federations, insisting that one could be cemented the next day between Yugoslavia and Bulgaria and perhaps both with Albania. That was at least the third time he had changed his mind on this topic. The Yugoslavs were convinced he wanted to weaken them by linking their country to Bulgaria. They said nothing and stayed over in Moscow for several days, until Edvard Kardelj was awakened at three o'clock one morning and driven to the Kremlin. Molotov thrust a document in front of him and said nothing more than "Sign this!" It was one of the friendship treaties Moscow had worked out with its satellites like Poland and Czechoslovakia.[23]

What upset Stalin was that these disciples were not following what he deemed the "normal procedures" of consulting him. However, his emotional outburst showed that he sensed the fragility of the Red Empire in which he had invested such energies to build. Indeed, it was crumbling before the cement dried.[24]

A month did not pass before Tito and his comrades rejected the federation with Bulgaria because they considered that the Kremlin wanted to use it to undermine Yugoslavia's route to socialism. They then committed more sins, by pressing Albania to accept a merger and to allow in troops. Tito also provided aid to the Communists in Greece, when the USSR was inclined to more caution there.

Thereupon Stalin began a paper war against Tito in Belgrade. He launched the first missile on March 18 as a letter from the Soviet Central Committee—hand-delivered to Tito by an NKVD officer, to intimidate him. It contained a long catalog of Yugoslavia's alleged unfriendliness to the USSR. To make the point, Moscow withdrew all Soviet civilian and military advisers. The Yugoslav Central Committee asked for an open explanation of what was wrong, and on March 27 they got a block-buster response. The Soviet party (Stalin) doubted the legality of Tito's regime, branded its Marxism as opportunism and revisionism, and ended by comparing Tito to the discredited Nikolai Bukharin and even Leon Trotsky. For good measure, he accused the Yugoslavs of regarding the USSR as an imperialist power, as if it were the United States.[25]

Stalin then raised the stakes, though not by threatening boycotts or invasion. Rather he decided to do battle in the arena of Communist ideology and to capitalize on his position at the commanding heights of the Marxist movement.

THE SPLIT WITH YUGOSLAVIA AND ITS AFTEREFFECTS

To deliver a judgment on Tito, the Kremlin mobilized the parties in the Cominform for another session in 1948 and tried to entice the Yugoslavs into attending. Their two top spokesmen, Milovan Djilas and Edvard Kardelj, had been stars at the last such gathering, but in the year since then Stalin's attitude toward them had changed. Now they politely declined his invitation. On May 22 a Stalin-Molotov note ordered their appearance. The missive stated categorically that "every Party is obliged to give an account of itself" to the Cominform. Refusal to do so would be considered "breaking away from the united socialist front of the people's democracies with the Soviet Union" and "treason to the cause of international solidarity of the working people."[26]

The second Cominform conference, from June 19 to 23, 1948, dealt with this charge of "treason." Andrei Zhdanov, again the keynote speaker, went through all the allegations, great and small, theoretical and practical. The Yugoslav Communist leaders, so went one of the most serious charges, identified the foreign policy of the Soviet Union with that of the imperialist powers "and behave toward the USSR in the same way that they behave toward bourgeois states." Zhdanov accused them of leaving the Marxist-Leninist road and turning into some kind of "nationalist-kulak party," based on the view that peasants provided "the soundest foundation of the Yugoslav state." Of course, Lenin had said that only the working class could play such a leading role. In addition, Zhdanov ridiculed the Yugoslavs for denying that the class struggle became more acute in the period of transition from capitalism to socialism, as Stalin had been saying since the 1920s. Instead of following that doctrine, he said, Tito and his comrades were claiming that capitalism could grow peacefully into socialism.

Zhdanov specifically condemned Yugoslav leaders Tito, Kardelj,

Djilas, and Aleksandar Ranković, head of the secret police. Stalin's front man, and therefore the Boss himself, believed that within the Yugoslav party there were many who remained true to Marxism-Leninism and to the idea of a united socialist front. The Soviet strategy was to connect with these "sound elements" and to work with them to stage a revolt against the Yugoslav leaders who would not change their ways.[27]

Almost nothing was said about the Marshall Plan, which was front-page news at the time. Instead the Stalinists focused primarily on Yugoslavia's ideological mistakes and its "nationalist deviations." Zhdanov claimed to be protecting and fostering the "international solidarity of the working class," when in fact he was out to impose rigid ideological uniformity and subordination to the USSR.

Contrary to Stalin's wishes, the Yugoslav party did not turn on Tito and the other accused. So Stalin expelled the entire party from the Cominform, a step filled with significance. With that blow, he destroyed the solid Communist front that had existed since 1917. That Yugoslavia was the object of this castigation was ironic: Tito and his comrades had taken Stalinization further and faster than anywhere else, falling over themselves trying to mimic the Soviet model. Even after they were ostracized, they became more Stalinist in the sense that they increased the terror and purged those they now labeled as "Cominformists," that is, believers in Stalin's dictates through the Cominform. Tito soon had thousands of them arrested and sent to special concentration camps, the most notorious being Goli Otok, a desolate island in the Adriatic.

Svetozar Stojanović, once persecuted by Tito, was right to say that the essence of the Yugoslav Communist Party "was the same both when it obsequiously followed Stalin and when it wrenched itself free from his coattails!"[28] Tito's repressions were known in the West, and occasional stories appeared in the New York press. For example, Ranković reported in the 1950s that 11,130 "Cominformists" had been arrested in 1948 and that 4,089 of them were still in custody.[29]

After Moscow cast out Yugoslavia and the dust had settled, Tito led the country gradually away from economic Stalinism. The system of collective farms was not working, and in October 1950 he was compelled to ask Washington for assistance to deal with a disastrous crop failure. President Truman agreed to help and obtained congressional approval to provide $50 million in emergency food relief. Western contact and trade never turned Yugoslavia into a democracy, but at the dawn of the Cold War, it looked like a slightly more humane alternative to full-fledged Stalinism.

After the split with Yugoslavia, Stalin inspired or ordered purges across Eastern Europe, as we will see in Chapter 20. The political situation in Germany was more complex and precarious because there the East-West confrontation was immediate, dangerous, and full of implications for the emerging Cold War.

THE POLITICAL BATTLE FOR GERMANY

In 1947–48 the course of German history reached a turning point. That country had once been the economic powerhouse of Europe, and American officials argued that its three Western zones should be included in the Marshall Plan. Eventually funds were provided primarily as loans, while countries like France and Britain received more money and outright grants.[30]

Germans were living with a barter economy and a black market, and the absence of a proper currency was a major obstacle to be overcome before the country could even start down the road to recovery. The four occupation powers did not agree on the problem, much less on finding a cure. Once again, on November 23, 1947, the Council of Foreign Ministers, meeting in London, could not decide on any kind of economic plan for Germany. Secretary Marshall's proposal that they adjourn "indefinitely" came as a surprise to Molotov, who would have been prepared to talk almost indefinitely. The Soviet Union failed to understand that the United States and Britain were greatly concerned about the lack of Soviet cooperation in feeding the Germans, a factor the West increasingly regarded as a humanitarian disaster in the making. In the face of stonewalling by the USSR, Marshall and British foreign secretary Bevin instructed their officials in Germany to try yet again to convince their Soviet counterparts to accept a common economic plan. However, they allowed for the possibility that, in the event of failure, the United States and Britain would introduce new money into the two zones.[31]

Stalin remained convinced that it was possible to win the political struggle for Germany and feasible to press the Western Allies into leaving occupied Berlin. In late 1947 the Soviets quietly began preparing a new currency for Germany. In the meantime, on March 15, 1948, the dictator met with his specialists on Germany, along with Molotov, Zhdanov, Beria, and others. They decided to put pressure on the West by slowly tightening the transit arteries to Berlin, which was located well inside the Soviet zone and in need of a steady flow of goods to survive. By prior agreement among the victors, the Western Allies were permitted to use only designated highways, railway lines, and canals to get to Berlin. In mid-March, Red Army officers began random inspections and slowed all traffic in both directions to a crawl.[32]

When Stalin met a German delegation led by Wilhelm Pieck of the SED on March 26, he still had not decided to force the issue. Pieck boasted of the SED's political successes back home but noted that in Berlin it faced particularly powerful counterpropaganda. When he said he would be happy to see the day the Allies were driven out, Stalin chimed in, "Let's combine forces and perhaps we'll succeed." Saying nothing more on the topic, they moved on to other matters.[33]

Nevertheless, an East-West showdown would soon break out over the thorny issue of a new currency for Germany. In mid-May 1948 a special commission led by Molotov worked out implementation measures to exchange the old marks for new. However, not until July or even August could the printing of the banknotes be completed.[34] At the same time the United States and Britain, having exhausted all attempts to work with the Soviets in March, decided to move ahead, and they had the new money ready by June 1. After a short delay, France finally agreed to join the other two zones, and together on June 17 they informed Soviet authorities of their decision to introduce a new currency three days later.[35]

This relatively simple step sparked the story of the German "economic miracle," that overnight food and other goods appeared in stores out of nowhere. In fact, German recovery took more time and effort, but issuing the new currency began the restoration of hope.

The Soviets' apparent "shock" was meant to reinforce the impression that they were reacting defensively. Their newspapers reported stories about the Western powers' duplicity and asserted that they and their German accomplices had never really wanted a common currency, that only the USSR favored a "complete Germany."[36] In truth, the Soviets had preferred not to issue the new money first because they were reluctant to run the risk of being blamed for the division of the country.

Moscow wanted to appear as the champion of unity, a line Stalin had been working for years.

The Soviets threatened further measures against the use of the new currency in Berlin. Already in April they had stopped regular passenger trains as they moved to and from the city, and on June 24 all rail traffic was halted "for technical reasons." By August 4 a blockade of all land routes and waterways was in place.[37] For Stalin, none of this was supposed to have happened. He had envisioned more discussions until the Western powers yielded. Instead the "capitalists" began what turned into the heroic Berlin Airlift, usually dated June 24, 1948, to May 12, 1949. The planes of the Royal Air Force and U.S. Air Force, with pilots also from Canada, Australia, New Zealand, and South Africa, flew in everything that a city of two million or so needed.

The Berlin Blockade became one of Stalin's worst nightmares. According to U.S. ambassador Robert Murphy, who was there, the really surprising effect of the airlift was that "the American people, for the first time in their history, formed a virtual alliance with the German people." Only a few years before, such an outcome would have been unthinkable.[38]

On March 9, 1949, Molotov became a scapegoat for this failure and others and was dismissed from his position as minister of foreign affairs.[39] He was replaced by his deputy Andrei Vyshinsky, an able diplomat, who was notorious for his role as a prosecutor in the great show trials of the 1930s. Molotov was kept around and also blamed when the three Western zones formed the Federal Republic of Germany (FRG) on May 23, 1949. Moscow lamely responded with the foundation of the German Democratic Republic (GDR) on October 7. Both countries would remain on the front lines of the Cold War until the Berlin Wall (built in 1961) finally collapsed in 1989. Most Germans on both sides adapted with resignation and equanimity to the division of their country.

It was the Berlin Airlift in 1948–49 that brought the Cold War out into the open. The Soviet Union had sent a horrific signal to the world, and overnight the Stalinist regime more than ever was seen as a major threat to freedom. At the same time the United States came to be portrayed as the white knight—at least in the eyes of non-Communists. One observer who lived through the period writes that until the Soviet blockade of Berlin, Western powers had understood their task in Germany to be to prevent it from becoming a danger again. That changed as the Berliners' willingness to fight for their freedom impressed them.[40]

The Soviet actions over Berlin shook most Western Europeans' sense of security. Shortly thereafter the Benelux countries, as well as Denmark, Norway, and Italy, opted to join the North Atlantic alliance, which was being negotiated precisely during the Berlin Airlift. The treaty, signed on April 4, 1949, amounted to a commitment by the United States to defend Western Europe. In June 1950, when the Communists invaded South Korea, the picture emerged of the Soviet Union as the enemy of freedom. This entire turn of events was exactly what the Soviet leaders had hoped to avoid.

In order to recover and to throw the West onto the defensive, Stalin and his comrades redoubled their efforts to present the Soviet Union as leading a great struggle for peace. Ever alert to possibilities for extending the world Communist base, they found it especially opportune to reach out to the Germans in the new GDR and to welcome them as allies and comrades. Stalin proclaimed that together they would make it impossible for the "world imperialists" to enslave Europe or to bring about another war there.[41]

An extension of this tactic involved a complex double game by which the Soviets would make it look as though their steps in Germany were reactions to Western aggression. The ploy apparently began in February 1951, when Walter Ulbricht, the general secretary of the SED, mentioned to Soviet officials that it would be politically useful for Moscow to propose Germany's reunification and its conversion into a neutral zone. The Anglo-Americans and French would reject that suggestion, it was believed, because it would involve moving Western defenses out of Germany.

The Kremlin saw promise in Ulbricht's proposal, then refined it extensively. The scenario began to unfold when on September 15 the prime minister of the GDR, Otto Grotewohl, sent a proposal to Chancellor Konrad Adenauer of the FRG to hold all-German "free elections" to a new institution empowered to negotiate a peace settlement with the four occupation powers. Although Adenauer asked him repeatedly for clarification on the electoral procedures, Grotewohl was evasive and rejected the counterproposal to have the United Nations supervise any balloting.

Then on February 13, 1952, after close consultations with Stalin, the

East German leaders wrote to the four occupation powers to ask that they expedite the conclusion of a peace treaty and withdraw all troops. As expected, only Moscow responded. On March 10 a note in Stalin's name was sent to the three other powers to ask that they hold a peace conference. In addition, the countries that had participated in the war against Germany would be invited. To guide the discussions, Stalin included his own "Principles for a German Peace Treaty." As we now know, these principles had been formulated like a series of chess moves to ensure that the West would inevitably reject them.[42]

Behind the apparent simplicity of the note lay a mountain of complications—not least, the history of Western frustrations since 1945 in trying to negotiate peace with the USSR. Although Stalin said that a united Germany would eventually be created, he gave no hint of how it would happen. Clearly the already existing Federal Republic of Germany would have to be dissolved. The then-reunited country would, however, not participate in the peace conference and would have to accept what the victors decided. The note said that the new Germany would also have to renounce all coalitions or military alliances that might be directed at any of its former enemy states. As a consequence of that stipulation, Germany would not be able to join NATO. It was precisely that prospect that bothered Stalin most.

His note was published to add political pressure on the West and to make the expected negative response by the three occupation powers look unreasonable. The rejection would have all the more traction in that the proposal was designed to appeal to a wide audience, especially in Germany.

The Western Allies consulted among themselves and came up with a counterproposal. Britain's Anthony Eden suggested that the foreign ministers try to find out if the Kremlin was serious, and they agreed to focus on the elections to the all-German parliament. The reply, crafted by U.S. secretary of state Dean Acheson, said that the Western Allies accepted the desirability of a peace treaty and that its conclusion would require the formation of a government that expressed the will of the people. In order to be certain that the elections to an all-German parliament were proper, a UN commission would be asked to investigate all of Germany to ensure that the necessary facilities existed. Would the Soviet Union permit the UN to undertake this mission in its zone? There were other issues, but the most important one was that the Soviet note had not indicated the international status of the new Germany. The Western Allies maintained that the country should determine its own foreign policy, including entering into associations "compatible with the principles and purposes of the UN"

On March 25, 1952, this carefully worded reply was handed to Foreign Minister Andrei Vyshinsky in Moscow. By prior agreement, the Americans, British, and French decided their notes would be identical, to avoid any unnecessary complications.[43]

Any all-German election, monitored by the UN to ensure fairness, would of course show evidence of the country's overwhelmingly anti-Communist majority. Stalin would never accept such a process. Although he sent more notes, the initiative got nowhere. Nevertheless, he got plenty of political "credit" in some quarters, then proceeded as he had originally intended. The GDR was going to be rearmed and integrated into the Soviet defense system, and he had made enough noise about peace and German unification to make it appear that his East German allies were acting defensively.[44]

On April 1, when Stalin met for talks with SED leaders Pieck, Ulbricht, and Otto Grotewohl, he mostly listened to their questions and gave cryptic answers. However, when they reconvened on April 7, he did most of the talking and spelled out the future for them. To their surprise they were informed that chances for a united Germany were as good as gone, because no matter what they proposed on a peace treaty the Western powers would never leave. The United States, he said, claimed to need an army in Europe for defense against the USSR, whereas their real motive for setting up a military base there was "to keep Europe in its grasp." Western Germany would be drawn into NATO, and the demarcation lines of the zones in Germany would become borders. Therefore the SED would need to organize a new state, construct a strong barrier to the West, and build up the armed forces. He also advised them to take only small steps on the road to socialism. The SED would have to "mask" its intentions. They should leave their "kulaks alone for the time being" and not "shout about socialism," policies that, he said, had already helped them in their efforts "not to scare the middle class of West Germany."[45]

The final question put to Stalin by the visitors came from Otto Grotewohl, who wondered whether the SED should change its policy of calling for German unification, given that the country was now more clearly divided than ever. Stalin answered: "Propaganda for the unity of Germany should be continued. It has great importance for influencing the people in Western Germany. Now it is a weapon in your hands that, under no circumstances, should you put down. We also will continue to make proposals regarding German unity in order to expose the [policies of] the Americans."[46]

Stalin was in the last year of his life, and as we will see, he seemed to grow more irrational and unpredictable on the domestic front. In foreign policy, however, he could still appear as the reasoned oracle and power broker. The sagacious advice he offered in loving detail to the German visitors about how to construct socialism was immediately translated into policies when they returned home. And yet his elevated tone and lofty position could not conceal the stark reality that his efforts to spread the Red Empire into Western Europe had reached their limits. The momentum that had once been behind Communism, and which had made its advance seem inevitable, was lost and never regained. In addition, the failure to keep Yugoslavia in the Eastern camp showed that the Kremlin had been unable to maintain control over even all the self-declared Communist regimes.

In Asia somewhat similar developments unfolded at the same time as these setbacks in Europe. The Soviet Union had become a major Asian power at the end of the Second World War, and there were excellent prospects of spreading the faith into Asia, far better than Stalin could imagine. Yet he would bungle his chances, miscalculate the options, and create a situation that culminated in the Korean War. It is to that story we now turn.

CHAPTER 19

Looking at Asia from the Kremlin

In 1945 the Allies divided the Korean peninsula along the 38th parallel. Soviet authorities in the North briefly adopted the "national front" strategy of rule by a coalition of parties. However, in February 1946, they fostered a new Provisional People's Committee, the kernel of which was to become the North Korean state. Kim Il Sung, a former Red Army officer, was installed as committee chairman, and in spite of a lack of popular support, he and his tiny band of followers outpaced their European comrades in introducing Communism and created the first "people's democracy" in Asia.[1]

South of the 38th parallel, the United States put in power Syngman Rhee, who, after the elections in 1948, formed the new Republic of Korea (ROK). In the North, Kim soon followed by founding the Democratic People's Republic of Korea. Although by December the Soviet military had departed, it left behind thousands of advisers. U.S. forces were supposed to evacuate as well but delayed until June 1949 because of concerns that the ROK would be vulnerable to attack.

Stalin was deeply involved, anxious about Asia in general and China in particular. He instructed Soviet advisers and diplomats to send their correspondence directly to his desk in the Kremlin. Ivan Kovalev, the USSR's chief envoy to China, recalled that the Boss wanted to handle even the most parochial matters himself. As early as May 1948, the two were in conversation about aiding the Chinese revolution.

Stalin told Kovalev of the immense importance he attached to giving "the new China all possible assistance. If socialism is victorious in China and our countries follow a single path, then the victory of socialism in the world will be virtually guaranteed. Nothing will threaten us."

Given that ideological perspective, the question became how to develop mutual cooperation. In July 1949, Kovalev was present at a Soviet Politburo meeting, along with a top Chinese visitor, Liu Shaoqi. Stalin, glorying in the role of the father figure, lauded their growing success, while warning them of the dangers of becoming too arrogant. The "revolutionary movement had shifted from the West to the East," he said, and "the Chinese Communists had to assume a position of leadership among the peoples of Eastern Asia."[2]

In October 1949, Mao Zedong led the Communists to victory in China and brought one-quarter of the world's population into the Red brotherhood. North Korea, which shared a border with the USSR, was well situated to follow; it had been liberated by the Red Army in 1945 and occupied by the Soviets for a time. With support for Communism growing across Asia, what should happen in Korea was a question that was bound to arise in the Kremlin. Indeed, Stalin came to be tempted by the prospect of an easy victory.

STALIN AND ASIAN COMMUNISTS

Although Stalin was pleased with the Communist infiltration into Asia, he worried that it might create unwanted attention from the West. He had counseled Mao to slow things down in China and to disguise the Communist takeover. The Chinese brushed that advice aside, seized power, and on October 1, 1949, proclaimed the establishment of the People's Republic of China. Afterward they continued to look to Moscow for leadership, and Stalin personally ensured that the USSR was the first among the Communist nations officially to recognize the new government. But he did not consider it necessary to send a personal note of congratulations to Mao, who took this neglect as a "slight."[3] What the new China then desperately needed was funding and experts to help transform the country into an industrial and military power.

For months Mao had been pleading for an invitation to Moscow, and he finally got one for Stalin's official seventieth birthday on December 21, 1949. The Boss received him five days before the big day and was reserved, while Mao was prepared to bow and scrape before the leader in the Kremlin, determined to do what was "best for the common cause" of Communism.[4] He also expressed his keen interest in meeting the other Communist "heroes" who were in Moscow. Stalin, donning his imperial mask, had other ideas and put him on ice in an isolated dacha well outside town.[5] On January 22 they discussed a new treaty between the two countries, and in a show of respect for Stalin's authority, Mao suggested that the agreement stipulate China's obligation to "consult" the Soviet Union in international affairs.[6]

Mao asked the Main Master (*glavnyi khozyain*), as he often called Stalin, to recommend an editor who was educated in Marxism to help him prepare his articles and speeches for publication and to keep "any theoretical mistakes from creeping in." In the heady world of Communist ideology, this small gesture represented a bow of recognition to Stalin's dominance.[7]

On February 14, 1950, the two signed the Sino-Soviet Treaty of Friendship, Alliance, and Mutual Assistance. The USSR granted a loan of $300 million and in return asked to retain exclusive access to the "industrial, financial, and commercial" activities in the huge provinces of Manchuria and Xinjiang. The Kremlin insisted, moreover, that Soviet citizens in China be exempted from local law. Those terms bothered Mao, who for years had said that such demands were the essence of imperialism.[8]

Also at this time other Asian leaders sought out Stalin's support. Kim Il Sung wrote to him proposing a military effort to unite North and South Korea, and in March 1949 he traveled to Moscow.[9] However, at that very moment the Soviet Union was involved in the increasingly embarrassing Berlin Blockade, so that Stalin was certain to be cool about supporting an adventure in Korea. When Kim proposed an invasion, the Boss advised against it, saying it would be a violation of the agreement between the USSR and the United States on the question of the 38th parallel. Although the talks were mainly about economic aid, Stalin was also curious about the military forces on the ground in North and South Korea, with the imminent departure of the last American troops. In May, Kim visited Mao, who also said that attacking the South would give a bad impression politically. China would not be able to help because at that time it was still trying to win its own war with the Nationalists.[10]

Kim Il Sung was a living example of center-periphery relations in the Soviet empire, whereby the periphery to some extent drives the decision making at the center. On January 17, 1950, and back in Pyongyang, he met with Soviet ambassador T. F. Shtykov and Chinese representatives.

He mentioned issues that he knew would be reported to Moscow and would play on Stalin's great weakness: his need to be seen as the unrivaled leader of the Communist world. Kim said that China's revolution had just succeeded and that Korea was next. Of course he could not undertake such a mission if the Soviet leader were opposed to it. Kim called himself "a communist, a disciplined person," for whom an order from Stalin was law.[11]

In Vietnam, Ho Chi Minh had done so well that on January 30, 1950, the USSR formally recognized the new government in Hanoi.[12] Ho knew Moscow from the 1920s and was now flown there to meet up with the victorious Mao, who was at the time in the Soviet capital, and they traveled home together. Although Stalin was prepared to make polite gestures to Vietnam, and might have been inclined to do more, he was reluctant to provide the military and other aid requested by Ho. As he had already told Chinese comrades visiting in the summer of 1949, he wanted "to leave the leadership role in the revolutionary movements in Asia" to them. Nevertheless, "he claimed the right to determine the shape of the People's Republic of China's relations with the United States and the West."[13]

The international Communist movement appeared to be making some headway, in spite of the stalemate in Germany, and Stalin now judged that the timing was right to pick up the pace in Korea. On the same day in January 1950 that the USSR recognized Vietnam, the Kremlin Boss sent more encouraging words to Kim Il Sung in Korea. Stalin said that "such a large matter in regard to South Korea"—that is, its invasion—required a "large preparation." Nevertheless, he was "ready to help him in this matter" and would be pleased to receive him for further discussions. That invitation was in fact an agreement to back North Korea's ambitious plans.[14] Even though Mao was in Moscow, Stalin said nothing to him about this key decision, evidently still not trusting the Chinese leader to follow his lead. Stalin had already twice refused Mao's request, made most recently during his visit to Moscow in late 1949, for Soviet support for an invasion of Taiwan to unite China. After that the Kremlin leader likely assumed that Mao would not go along with the Soviet decision to back North Korea's plans unless presented with certain facts on the ground.[15]

Kim was in Moscow from March 30 to April 25, 1950. He sounded more certain than ever that the United States would not interfere because, he now thought, he had good reason to hope that the two Communist giants would back the North. He boasted that tens of thousands of sympathizers would arise in the South and side with the invaders. Stalin allowed himself to be convinced by these thin arguments.[16] The main reason he reconsidered giving Kim the green light in Korea was, he said, the recent success of the Chinese revolution and its new alliance with the USSR. This development also had an important psychological effect, for it "proved the strength of the Asian revolutionaries, and showed the weakness of Asian reactionaries and their mentors in the West, in America."

He told Kim, however, that the USSR "was not ready to get involved in Korean affairs directly, especially if Americans did venture to send troops." The two leaders went over the strategy of the attack in detail, with Stalin emphasizing the need for speed. Kim's bold prediction was that "the war will be won in three days." The "Americans won't have time to prepare," and by the time they realized what was happening, he said with assurance, "all the Korean people will be enthusiastically supporting the new government."[17]

Kim then flew straight to Beijing and met with Mao on May 15. Again the Chinese leader was concerned that the Americans might intervene, but he went along partly because Stalin was on board. On his return home, Kim had discussions with Soviet ambassador Shtykov. On May 29 they agreed that the attack would take place June 8–10. Shtykov as usual notified the Kremlin to be certain he was cleared, and Stalin gave his immediate approval. North Korea, after a delay of just over two weeks, launched the invasion.[18]

STALIN AND THE KOREAN WAR

On Sunday, June 25, 1950, John Muccio, the U.S. ambassador in Seoul, reported that, as of six A.M. that day, North Korean infantry, tanks, and amphibious units had crossed the 38th parallel in an "all out offensive." The message, received in Washington on Saturday, June 24, at 9:26 P.M., set off a flurry of activity.[19] Secretary of State Dean Acheson, in consultation with President Truman, decided on the basis of that message to present a resolution to the UN Security Council. A note from U.S. ambassador Alan Kirk in Moscow arrived at 9:59 A.M. on June 25; he stated flatly that the invasion was a "clear-cut Soviet challenge" and threat "to our leadership of the free world against Soviet Communist aggression" and should be given a "firm answer."[20]

The UN Security Council condemned the breach of the peace and called on the North Koreans to withdraw. The resolution was adopted by a vote of nine in favor and one abstention (Yugoslavia). Notably absent was the USSR, for with its veto it could have stopped this process dead in its tracks. However, since January the Soviets had been boycotting the UN to protest the nonrecognition of China.

Before the Security Council met that Sunday, Yakov Malik, the Soviet ambassador to the UN, cabled Moscow to ask for instructions. Stalin then phoned Andrei Gromyko, a veteran diplomat and deputy minister of foreign affairs. Gromyko said that the ministry had prepared a statement about Korea and that Malik should be at the UN to veto any action proposed.[21]

Later on Gromyko recalled that Stalin never let his emotions rule him—except in this one case. This statement is belied by Stalin's determination that Malik would be absent from the Security Council when it met again on Tuesday, June 27. The Soviet ambassador was not there to stop a UN resolution that called on members to "furnish such assistance to the Republic of Korea as may be necessary to repel the armed attack and to restore international peace and security in the area." The Truman administration decided to send troops. They would fight under American command but fly the UN flag. Gromyko had warned about this turn of events, and even so Malik was still not at the Security Council on July 7 and 31 to veto the resolutions supporting armed intervention.[22]

For years historians thought that Stalin made a "mistake," was "ham-fisted," "stupid" or "stubborn," to keep his ambassador away from the UN. In fact, the Soviet leader acted with cold rationality, for as we have just seen, he had planned the war in Korea and explicitly gave his approval for the attack.

He wanted war, but certainly not one that involved the USSR directly. The conflict officially would be waged by the North Koreans against the United Nations, and if there were complications, also by the Chinese. More than two dozen nations contributed to the UN forces, but more than half the troops came from the United States. The Soviet goal was to get the Americans "entangled" in hostilities that would "squander" their "military prestige and moral authority." That was what

Stalin said in an August 27 note to one of his Eastern European com-rades, and he also admitted that the USSR had deliberately abstained from attending the Security Council meetings. The longer the struggle in Korea lasted, the better, he thought, because it "would distract the United States from Europe," where a third world war would be "post-poned" and there would be "time to consolidate socialism."[23] Granted, the USSR had some economic and security interests in Korea and in China, but for Stalin, as nearly always, the decisive factors were politics and ideology.[24]

The northern invaders drove the defenders relentlessly back into the South until by August they clung to defensive positions in front of the port city of Pusan. It looked like they were about to be pushed into the sea. However, the UN still had complete control of the air and every day landed more supplies and fresh troops. There would be no speedy victory for the invaders and no revolutionary uprising in the South.

General Douglas MacArthur opted for a Hollywood-style counter-attack, a daring amphibious assault well up the western shore of the peninsula and two hundred miles from Pusan. On September 15, despite not having a beach for an easy landing, 70,000 troops began going ashore at Inchon and took the city in a day. Within two weeks, they cut off the North Korean forces stuck in the South. MacArthur favored a "hot pursuit" of enemy troops who fled back over the 38th parallel, and everyone in Washington agreed. The new mission was to destroy the North Korean armed forces, but under no circumstances to track them down if it meant crossing the border into either neighboring China or the USSR.[25]

On September 29, Kim and South Korean Communist leader Pak Hon-yong wrote to Stalin and pleaded for Soviet support to counter the efforts of "hostile forces" about to cross the 38th parallel into North Korea. "Dear Comrade Stalin," the note stated, "we are determined to overcome all the difficulties facing us so that Korea will not be a colony and a military springboard of the U.S. imperialists. We will fight for the independence, democracy and happiness of our people to the last drop of blood."[26] Already in July, the Kremlin leader had mentioned the likely need for the Chinese to send troops into the area to help out, and now in October he asked Mao to send five or six divisions immediately to cover the retreat.[27] The Chinese leader decided that it was his turn to play politics and gave the startling answer: "Having thought this over thoroughly, we now consider that such actions may entail extremely serious consequences," including war with the United States.[28]

Stalin admitted in a hair-raising reply that even though the Americans were not yet ready for "a big war," they could be drawn in. That would cause the USSR to follow and, because of its assistance pact, China as well. In other words, World War III was a possibility. "Should we fear this? In my opinion, we should not, because together we will be stronger than the USA and England, while the other European capitalist states, without Germany which is unable to provide any assistance to the United States now, do not present a serious military force."[29]

Mao agreed to send up to nine divisions, even though he said he lacked sufficient air cover and artillery and pleaded for Soviet assistance. His preference was to have a four-to-one advantage in human forces and a three-to-one superiority in technical equipment. The Chinese troops would prepare and be sent in "after some time." His strategy was "to give the Americans a chance to advance deeper to the North."[30]

That did not sound like a particularly firm commitment, and on October 12, Stalin ordered Kim to begin retreating. The very next day, however, Mao wrote to say that "regardless of the insufficient armament of the Chinese troops," they would "render military assistance to the Korean comrades."[31] On October 18, when the Chinese Politburo conferred about the decision, Mao showed it a cable from Stalin: "The Old Man" (*starik*)—that is, Stalin—said "we have to act," and no one dared speak against it.[32]

Stalin and especially Mao disguised their decisive roles so well that generations of historians claimed that China was merely reactive and entered the battle only to defend its physical security after the UN forces crossed the 38th parallel.[33] The war was blamed on the United States and South Korea. In fact, the USSR had given Kim Il Sung the green light to invade the South as far back as January 1950.[34] The USSR would provide essential war matériel under the table. Mao and the Chinese began preparations to get involved in August, more than a month before the Inchon landing and UN counterattack. The goal was to go beyond merely defending the North Korean border, to win a glorious victory by driving UN forces off the Korean peninsula. Without Soviet aid, the Chinese and North Korean troops would have been unable to continue their fight. What bothered Mao and Prime Minister Zhou Enlai was that the USSR insisted on payment for the supplies. In Chinese eyes, the Soviets' "stinginess" showed them up as not "genuine Communist internationalists," and such behavior served to heighten Mao's sense of moral superiority.[35]

After MacArthur's daring and successful attack at Inchon in September 1950, the UN forces marshaled at the 38th parallel and readied their advance. Although the United States did not want to escalate the war, Washington aimed to negotiate from a position of strength. General MacArthur was champing at the bit and yearned to conduct an "end-the-war" offensive.

What he did not know was that China had decided to capitalize on the crisis in Korea. Mao was using anti-American slogans to mobilize support for his new regime, and although he dithered about getting air cover and arms before committing, he never doubted that Red Chinese troops were going to North Korea. He hoped that success in the war would energize his drive to consolidate Communism in China, and in fact, during the conflict, nationwide propaganda campaigns penetrated "almost every area of Chinese society." They also sought to make the Chinese model of revolution the one adopted by other Asian leaders like Ho Chi Minh and Pol Pot in Cambodia.[36]

UN forces crossed the 38th parallel on October 1, but in the meantime a Chinese "volunteer" army secretly entered North Korea and, on October 25, opened a successful counter-strike. On November 24, when the UN hit back, it was ambushed by 300,000 Chinese troops who operated on the theory that decisiveness in the first battle would rout the enemy.[37]

Stalin was delighted by the progress of the battle. During the first week in December, he wrote to Premier Zhou Enlai that the Chinese "successes gladden not only me and my comrades in the leadership, but also all Soviet people. Allow me to greet from the soul you and your friends in the leadership, the People's Liberation Army of China and the entire Chinese people in connection with these enormous successes in their struggle against the American troops."[38] He encouraged them to fight on: "We think that the time has not arrived for China to show all its cards, while Seoul is still not liberated."

Word of this new Communist success on the battlefield hit Washington hard because it was so unexpected. The public mood was not helped by Truman's incautious remarks at a news conference that the option of using an atomic bomb was on the table. Finally on December 15, at the urging of George Marshall, now secretary of defense, the president declared a state of national emergency, something that had not happened in the United States during two world wars. The country appeared to be heading for World War III, especially with MacArthur ready to use Nationalist Chinese forces and to drop forty atomic bombs on China. The general made other statements that were at variance with government policy, and for a while, he got away with such challenges to presidential power. Their effect was to make Truman look weak, and that, to say the least, did not bode well for U.S. relations with China.

It might have been possible to open negotiations at the end of 1950. However, with the Chinese forces winning or even just holding their own, Mao was looking strong. On December 31, with Stalin's complete support, he ordered another offensive, in spite of warnings from his military that more troops were needed. The attack began on January 3, overran Seoul within a week, and gave the Communists another victory to celebrate. Mao was greedy for more and brushed aside a remarkably generous cease-fire offer put forward by UN representatives on January 11, according to which all foreign troops would be withdrawn from Korea. A four-power meeting of the United States, Britain, the Soviet Union, and China would then negotiate the Korean crisis, and beyond that all outstanding Far East issues, including Taiwan. Mao turned it down and stoked Chinese nationalism, hoping to use an even greater victory to win over more people for Communism.[39]

The Communist leaders were pleased with the initial success of their renewed offensive. Toward the end of January 1951, however, UN forces stopped the assault from the North and began pushing it back. It was too little to save Truman's presidency, and on March 29, discouraged by the war and nagged by the show of popular support for MacArthur, he announced he would not run for reelection. On April 11 he finally fired MacArthur, an action that provoked howls of protest from the American public. When the general returned home, he was treated like a hero and played it for all it was worth. He gave a farewell address to a joint meeting of Congress and received a bigger ticker-tape parade in New York than the one given Dwight Eisenhower in 1945. The tide had really turned against Truman and the Democrats, but U.S. politics did not matter much in Korea, where war continued to rage. Eisenhower and the Republicans would sweep the elections in 1952.

During the war, Stalin was in frequent telegraphic contact with Mao, sometimes several times a day, and he was asked to consider military matters right down to the tactical level. Then he had to answer numerous political questions from Beijing, for example, about the demands that should be made in negotiations for a cease-fire and on delicate POW issues. Additionally, the Chinese sent him endless requests for arms. When the war degenerated into a stalemate once again in May 1951, Mao wanted to continue anyway.

The brutality of Stalin's logic comes across in a June 5 letter of support for Mao's decision. "The war in Korea should not be speeded up," he said, "since a drawn out war, in the first place, gives the possibility to the Chinese troops to study contemporary warfare on the field of battle and in the second place shakes up the Truman regime in America and harms the military prestige of the Anglo-American troops." The Kremlin Boss recommended another short, hard blow at the enemy to give a boost to the sagging morale of the Chinese and Korean troops.[40]

In August and September 1952, Mao sent Zhou Enlai to Moscow for still more in-depth discussions. He was there to pursue their goal of making China independent in defense and transforming it into a military superpower. Stalin preferred to send finished parts that would be assembled in China. That relationship would keep the Chinese in a position of dependence, and in any case they wanted more than the Soviet Union could deliver. Zhou said that China's five-year plan would devote more than one-third of the budget to the military. Stalin was taken aback by what he considered to be this "very unbalanced" ratio of civil and military spending. It was, he thought, more tilted to supplying the military than the Soviet Union's budget had been during the Second World War.[41]

While in Moscow, Zhou said that since May 1951 the military situation on the ground had been stable. The conflict had changed from a war of movement to one of position, with each side heavily dug in. The Chinese thought that the struggle should continue. If Stalin agreed, what exactly would he recommend? "Mao Zedong is right," was his answer, "this war is getting on America's nerves." He added, in one of his deliberately icy statements, that "the North Koreans have lost nothing, except for casualties that they suffered during the war." The struggle had revealed "America's weakness," and even with the help of more than twenty countries in the UN, it was bound to fail. The Soviet

Union would provide the Koreans with the supplies to carry on. Zhou noted that China was playing "the vanguard role in this war" and that if it succeeded, "then the USA will not be able to unleash a third world war at all."

That remark led Stalin into a long reflection that shows his thinking at the time. The Americans were not to be feared and were not capable "of waging a large-scale war at all, especially after the Korean War." The Germans, he said, "conquered France in 20 days. It's been already two years, and the USA has still not subdued little Korea. What kind of strength is that? America's primary weapons are stockings, cigarettes, and other merchandise," Stalin joked. "They want to subjugate the world, yet they cannot subdue little Korea. No, Americans don't know how to fight." Instead they were "pinning their hopes on the atom bomb and air power. But one cannot win a war with that. One needs infantry, and they don't have much infantry; the infantry they do have is weak. They are fighting with little Korea, and already people are weeping in the USA. What will happen if they start a large-scale war? Then, perhaps, everyone will weep."[42]

Nevertheless, Stalin counseled the Chinese that if they bombed South Korea from the air, they should not use planes with their own markings. That is, they should keep up the illusion that only volunteers from China were fighting in Korea and that China itself was not involved in the war. Zhou said that negotiations in Panmunjom would continue to seek an armistice on favorable terms, while at the same time the Chinese government was preparing for the conflict to continue for two years or longer.

Mao aimed at victory in Korea and thereby to elevate China's status in the international Communist movement. In a last meeting with Stalin on September 19, 1952, Zhou Enlai tried with no luck to broach this delicate topic. As it happened, Stalin had called the Nineteenth Party Congress of the Soviet Communist Party for October 5–14 in Moscow, and representatives of all the foreign parties were invited. Zhou asked if it would be appropriate for the Chinese to talk about party matters with the Indonesians who were coming. The real issue concerned the extent to which the Chinese should be admitted to the Communist inner circle in Asia. Stalin's view was that it was "too early to tell yet." That was as good as saying he was still thinking it over and had yet to decide whether to favor China. He did not neglect to add that the Indian comrades had arrived and asked for "help in determining the party policy." Stalin thought he had to do so, even though he was busy. Then Zhou wondered about the Japanese and, in reply, got only the opaque remark "that older brothers cannot refuse their younger brothers." Would Stalin discuss party matters with the Chinese? The Master replied that it would depend if they brought it up, but at that point he began to sound more like a cagey medieval prince than a modern Communist leader. For whatever reason, he was not yet ready to give Mao the recognition he craved.[43]

Even if Stalin might be prepared to delegate some matters to regional centers, he had no intention of yielding his leadership of the worldwide movement to anyone.[44] Nor did he want another independent thinker like Tito. It was perhaps to take Mao down a peg or two that he decided to treat the visiting Liu Shaoqi, one of Mao's potential rivals, with exaggerated respect.[45] This was a characteristic Stalinist strategy of reminding even the most powerful emissaries of their proper place in the world of Communism.

THE ARMS RACE

The Korean War was not resolved in Stalin's lifetime, and its ripple effects lasted far longer. An armistice signed on July 27, 1953, at Panmunjom left Korea divided exactly as before.

It is difficult to overestimate the psychological impact of that war on the United States, magnified by the first successful test of the Soviet atomic bomb (code-named "First Lightning") on August 29, 1949, at the Semipalatinsk 21 site in Kazakhstan. The United States found out about it (dubbing it "Joe-1") by tracking the winds and testing for radioactivity. President Truman announced on September 23 that there had been "an atomic explosion" but said nothing about a bomb. Molotov issued an opaque statement asserting that there had been some "blasting work" and, incidentally, that the existence of the atomic bomb had long since ceased to be a secret.[46] Insofar as U.S. ambassador Kirk in Moscow could gauge Soviet public opinion, he reported in October that after the test, people felt slightly less under threat, had a greater sense of security, and took pride in the accomplishment.[47]

Russian historian V. L. Malkov has observed that the USSR was still far behind the United States and had no delivery system for the new weapon. By remaining silent at the time about having a bomb, he writes, Stalin meant to demonstrate that "nothing unusual had happened" and that in the game of "catch up and overtake," Soviet science and economics had been able to shoulder the task. Moscow wanted to cure Washington of thinking that it had absolute technological superiority.[48]

News of the Soviet bomb came not long after the clash over Berlin and just before the October victory of the Communists in China. Together these events made the American government feel vulnerable and threatened. The Democrats, who had been keen on cutting the defense budget, suddenly reversed themselves. At a cabinet meeting on July 14, 1950, and not long after the outbreak of the war in Korea, Truman learned that the USSR was capable of military actions in several places around the globe and that the United States would have insufficient military power to do much about it. The president and Congress soon agreed to double the size of the armed forces. Spending for defense and international security went from $17.7 billion in fiscal year 1950 to a total of $140 billion for fiscal years 1951 and 1952. The new top priority was to establish an industrial base to create the tanks, aircraft, and matériel needed "to wage global war."[49]

In early 1951 the president authorized a crash program to build a superweapon. The United States detonated a thermonuclear device in the South Pacific on November 1, 1952. Although the USSR had benefited from information gained from its spies to copy the A-bomb, the Soviets developed their own approach to the superbomb. Beria was again the politician in charge, and by August 12, 1953, they successfully replicated the American experiment. The United States was able to build a deliverable H-bomb by March 1, 1954, and less than a year later, on November 22, 1955, the USSR dropped its first H-bomb.[50]

Some historians have suggested that Truman missed an opportunity to stop the arms race when he accepted recommendations to carry on research for the superbomb. Their supposition is that Stalin might have been impressed and refrained as well. Andrei Sakharov, who helped develop the Soviet bomb and later became a dissident, did not agree with such conjectures. He believed that Stalin would more likely have considered unilateral American restraint as a trick or sign of weakness.[51] Once the infernal "logic" of the arms race existed, it was difficult to reverse.

Americans were not the only ones who were worrying about Soviet intentions. In March 1948, Britain, France, Belgium, Luxembourg, and the Netherlands formed a defensive alliance. On April 4, 1949, at the end of the struggle over Berlin, they were joined by Canada, Portugal, Italy, Norway, Denmark, and Iceland, together with the United States, to sign the North Atlantic Treaty. NATO was created as a defensive alliance to provide protection from the Soviet Union.

Russian historians balefully note that even before their country had recovered from the Second World War, Stalin dragged them into the Cold War over Berlin and Korea. Beyond that struggle, he decided as far as possible to match U.S. defense spending. Soviet outlays for that purpose doubled between 1948 and 1953.

Stalin also called a summit of the Eastern European Communist party leaders and their defense ministers for January 9–12, 1951. Although the Russian records of what was said remain closed, over the years at least a half dozen of those in attendance published their accounts. Stalin told them that the Korean War provided "favorable conditions" by tying down U.S. forces and that gave them three or four years to modernize and grow their armed forces. Underlying the "urgent need to coordinate military and organizational activities," he said that the people's democracies had to expand their armed forces into a three-million-strong army that was "combat ready" and backed by substantial reserves. Each nation was given target figures, which all the participants said were too great for their shaky economies to meet. Poland, for example, would have to double its military expenditures. Former Red Army marshal Konstantin Rokossovsky, one of Stalin's favorites during the war and now Polish minister of defense, was shocked at the scale of the expansion being demanded.[52]

The Soviet Union would not pay for this military buildup. Each country had to shift financing away from consumer goods and agriculture to defense and heavy industry. Dyed-in-the-wool Stalinists like Mátyás Rákosi agreed with Stalin and did everything possible to meet and exceed the quota of troops set for Hungary. That meant ordinary people suffered substantial declines in their already-low standard of living.[53] The same was true for all the other countries, as it was for the USSR. In Stalin's last two years, Soviet armed forces almost doubled, from 2.9 million or so, up to 5.6 million.[54]

Moving forward on the Kremlin's political and international agenda in the early 1950s, Soviet military advisers "carried out preparatory work for the unification of the armies of Eastern Europe into a single military-political bloc." Thus they paved the way for the creation of the Warsaw Pact Treaty Organization in 1955.

In China after Korea, Mao proclaimed a great victory because his army had fought the capitalist West to a standstill. The Korean War allowed him to consolidate Communist control and also to promote the new China's image in the world.[55] During that war, more than a third of China's budget was devoted to defense needs. In December 1952, Mao asked for still more deliveries of military goods in preparation for an expected UN attack. He wanted such large quantities that Stalin felt it was beyond the capability of the Soviet Union to supply them all.[56]

The Chinese persisted in their demands. They were especially interested in getting the atomic bomb and kept putting pressure on Stalin to provide the secrets, but to no avail. In 1956, however, Nikita Khrushchev, the new man in the Kremlin, consented to Soviet cooperation with China's development of its nuclear energy program for peaceful purposes. He hoped thereby to win over Mao and gain his support in the post-Stalin power struggle. In spite of a breakdown in Sino-Soviet relations and after a long struggle, on October 16, 1964, the Chinese had their first atomic bomb test.[57]

The results of the Korean War on the ground, in terms of population dislocation and death, were catastrophic. The full toll will never be known. Some estimates of the number of Koreans killed—most of them civilians—run into the millions. Although the Chinese used three million men in the war and claimed that 152,000 were killed, Soviet sources put the death figure at a million.[58] The Soviet Union was barely involved in the fighting and registered a total of 315 deaths, most of them attached to the air force.[59] Secretary of State Acheson reported that the United States suffered 33,600 killed in action and a casualty total of 142,000.[60] Other nations fought in Korea for the UN, of whose forces 3,063 were killed, including 1,263 from the British Commonwealth: Australia, Britain, Canada, and New Zealand.[61] The United States could have learned from the war to avoid another entanglement looming on the horizon in Vietnam.[62]

Kim Il Sung emerged from the war fortified in power. He created a personality cult that in its sheer idolatry easily topped those of Stalin and Mao, and he combined Communism with various Korean religious traditions. The version of Stalinism he adopted was more rigid than the original, and in time Kim would suspect both the post-Stalinist Soviet Union and China of not being Communist enough. Before he died in 1994, he groomed his son Kim Jong Il as his successor. The deprivation and poverty of the people, especially when compared to prosperous South Korea, was caused in no small part because father and son devoted vast sums to defense spending.[63]

CHAPTER 20

New Waves of Stalinization

Stalin had once favored a "national" approach to Communism, albeit one under the direction of the Kremlin. This way of seeing things, however, allowed for a degree of flexibility that could undermine Moscow's authority. As the Soviet empire firmed up its grip on Eastern Europe, opportunities were opened up for disciples on the periphery to settle scores with opponents and, for example, without specific instructions from Moscow, to push the churches out of the schools and to nationalize education. Still, in the changing international climate, especially following the break with Tito and Yugoslavia in 1948, the possibility that other European followers might also embark on a "special path" to socialism struck a note of alarm to Stalin's ears.

At the very moment the Soviet dictator was tightening the screws on the Red Empire, he was venting his own phobias, most notably his anti-Semitism, which had simmered beneath the surface since the war, both in the USSR and elsewhere in Eastern Europe. Now it became more prominent and, in varying degrees, entangled in the Stalinization process that marked the last years of the dictator's rule.

STALINISTS' FLIRTATION WITH ANTI-SEMITISM

The USSR, in May 1948, was the first country to recognize the new state of Israel de jure. The Kremlin hoped to make political inroads in the Middle East, and Stalin encouraged the Eastern Europeans to follow suit. From the Soviet perspective, however, it was not a happy turn of events that Israel almost immediately looked to the United States for solidarity and support. Even more threatening was the powerful symbolic significance of a Jewish homeland. The very existence of the new Israel sparked the nationalist sentiment of Soviet Jews.[1]

Stalin's stated position—as well as long-standing official Soviet policy—on anti-Semitism was indicated as far back as 1931, when the Jewish News Agency in the United States asked his opinion about it. He said that such prejudice was completely inappropriate for the Communist movement because its updated version "acted like a lightning rod for the exploiters, absorbing the blows aimed at capitalism by the workers. Anti-Semitism is dangerous for the working people, a false path that leads them astray and into the jungle." He insisted that blaming the Jews was "an extreme form of chauvinism" and "the most dangerous vestige of cannibalism."[2]

Nevertheless, the clear-cut condemnation of anti-Semitism began to change and, as we noted in Chapter 10, Soviet authorities played down the victimization of the Jews at the hands of the Nazis and did not tolerate any attempt by organizations or individuals to sanctify the memory of the Holocaust. Stalin and his henchmen then became concerned that their own Jewish population was becoming too "nationalistic." Mikhail Suslov, of the foreign affairs department of the Central Committee, wrote Molotov on January 7, 1947, to explain that steps had to be taken against the Jewish Anti-Fascist Committee (JAFC): "With the end of the war the activities of the Committee are becoming more nationalist, Zionist, it objectively contributes to strengthening the Jewish reactionary bourgeois-nationalist movement abroad and triggers nationalist, Zionist sentiment among the Jewish population of the USSR."[3]

However, the JAFC had a heroic past and could not simply be erased as if it had never existed. Founded in April 1942, its membership list reads like a *Who's Who* of the Jews in the country. Its stated and laudable goal was "to mobilize the Jewish masses of all countries for the active struggle against fascism and to obtain the greatest possible support for the Soviet Union and the Red Army, which is carrying the heaviest burden in the struggle."[4] The committee president was the director of the Yiddish theater, Solomon Mikhoels, a famed holder of the Lenin Prize. Among other services, he and others traveled to the United States, England, and Canada in 1943, visiting dozens of cities to raise funds and support for the Soviet cause.

Their sympathetic reception led Mikhoels and the JAFC to hope that a homeland for the Jews could be found in the Soviet Crimea. In the summer of 1946, Mikhoels contacted Molotov's Jewish wife, Polina Zhemchuzhina and asked her to intercede with higher authorities. When she could offer no encouragement, he thought an appeal to Stalin's daughter might work, for she had married Grigori Morozov, who was Jewish. However, before any meeting took place with Svetlana, their marriage failed, largely because of her father's displeasure at the Jewish identity of his son-in-law. The background story was that unless she left Morozov, Stalin would have him arrested.[5]

By this time Mikhoels and the JAFC were in the cross hairs of the Minister of State Security Viktor Abakumov, who tarred the unfortunate man with an assortment of accusations, the worst of which was involvement in an American-Zionist plot. The minister alleged that Mikhoels, on his trip to the United States during the war, spoke to "intelligence sources." For that reason, and perhaps also because Mikhoels tried to obtain access to his daughter, Stalin decided to have him killed and ordered security officials to stage an accident, as happened in Minsk on January 12, 1948.[6]

Mikhoels was given a burial, with full honors as a smokescreen. When the dust finally settled, the Politburo decided on November 20 to dissolve the JAFC, alleging that "the facts show that this Committee is the center of anti-Soviet propaganda and regularly provides information to the anti-Soviet foreign intelligence agencies." Its newspaper was closed, and all its files were seized.[7]

Also "repressed" was Solomon Lozovsky, a Jewish member of the Communist Party Central Committee. His long and distinguished career went back to the 1905 Bolshevik conference in Tammerfors, Finland, where he had met Lenin and Stalin. Lozovsky was involved with the JAFC and arrested in January 1949 on Stalin's orders. He was expelled from the party on the charge of conspiring with the JAFC, which "recently turned into a spy organization of Jewish nationalists." Its aim was to create "a Jewish state in Crimea," allegedly as part of a plan of "American capitalist interests." The innocent seventy-year-old Lozovsky was pressured to confess, but he stood firm.

Another side of the Soviet anticosmopolitanism campaign was the adoption of anti-Zionism. Soviet Jews embraced the idea of the new Israel and joyously showed their feelings on September 3, 1948, when Golda Myerson (later Meir, eventually prime minister of Israel) came to Moscow as an envoy. She was celebrated by crowds and when she appeared at a synagogue, the streets overflowed outside. Such a blatant demonstration of "bourgeois nationalism" would, in Stalin's view of the world, ignite among the Soviet Jews the very centrifugal forces he was trying to control in the Soviet empire.[8]

Anyone who openly favored Israel or applauded the accomplishments of Jewish intellectuals came under suspicion. Even Konstantin Simonov, a man well placed in Stalin's regime, was accused of keeping the wrong company. He responded with a scathing speech to a meeting in Moscow of playwrights and critics, part of which was printed in *Pravda* on February 28, 1949:

> The harmful activity of cosmopolitanism cannot be reduced only to the sphere of art and science, but it also has political implications. The propaganda of bourgeois cosmopolitanism now aids the world reactionaries and those who want a new war. Cosmopolitanism is the imperialists' policy and at the same time it seeks to weaken patriotism and afterwards to deliver the people to the American monopolies. Cosmopolitanism in art aims to deprive people of pride in their national roots and to run down their national pride, at which point they can be sold as slaves to American imperialism.[9]

The campaign against cosmopolitanism focused on the intellectual elite in general, and because the Jews were heavily represented members, the purges had strong anti-Semitic overtones. Although Simonov said he was not anti-Semitic, as editor of the influential journal *Novi Mir* (New World), he soon fired all the Jewish writers, some of them close friends. Initially, even the famed writer Ilya Ehrenburg was silenced. He was Jewish, and in February 1949 his works suddenly stopped being printed. Instead of waiting for the ax to fall, he wrote Stalin to ask what fate awaited him. The dictator had been pleased with Ehrenburg's wartime articles that had whipped up hatred against the Germans, and he was impressed when, at the dawning of the Cold War, Ehrenburg turned his guns against the United States. By April he was allowed to travel to the World Peace Conference in Paris, so he was back in good graces again.[10]

The anticosmopolitanism campaign featured a flood of notes to the authorities from all kinds of people with suggestions to make the system more watchful, like one hand-delivered to the Kremlin that provided a motto: "Vigilance must be everywhere!" These letters frequently exaggerated the shortcomings of this writer or that professor. Taken as a whole, the atmosphere that was created closed off the Soviet Union more than ever to new ideas, criticism, and the outside world. Although the files of all those attacked for "Jewish bourgeois nationalism" are still closed, estimates are that fifty people were executed out of the five hundred or so arrests, more than enough to send a chill through the country.[11]

POLAND, ALBANIA, HUNGARY, ROMANIA

At the time Stalin was cracking down on "Jewish nationalism," he began to rethink his relatively flexible theory that each of the Eastern European countries could take their own road to socialism. The breakaway of Yugoslavia and the creation of Israel in 1948 he saw as forceful examples of the need to centralize power and to assert more control from Moscow. The responses of Communist leaders on the periphery varied; while some dragged their feet before dutifully following orders, others capitalized on Soviet demands and channeled their terror against homegrown enemies.

During Stalin's conversations with Polish head of government Bolesław Bierut in August 1948, they agreed that General Secretary Władysław Gomułka, the champion of a Polish "road to socialism," had to be removed from the party's leadership. In Stalin's eyes, Gomułka was or could become a Polish Tito. Although he and more than a hundred party officials were subsequently arrested, no large-scale purge or great show trial followed. Other areas of potential opposition, especially the Catholic Church, were scrutinized, and arrests were numerous, though by the early 1950s the authorities had backed off.[12]

At the end of 1948, a Polish United Workers' Party (PZPR) resulted from the forced unification of the Communist (PPR) and Socialist (PPS) parties, which by and large ruled the country until 1989. Everyday surveillance, a secret police with files on millions of people, and thinly veiled terror became the norm. Just why Stalin did not insist on a show trial remains unexplained. As it was, the years between 1944 and

1956 were filled with another round of terror; no fewer than 243,066 people were arrested, though the estimates run up to between 350,000 and 400,000.[13]

At the same time the head of state security, Stanisław Radkiewicz, "recruited" 200,000 or more informers. He admitted that the object was not merely to collect information but to degrade people, to break their morale. In addition, the Polish army had its own network of informers in every district of the country. The army became one of the mainstays of the government, and annually it recruited, trained, and propagandized tens of thousands for two-year periods of indoctrination.[14]

When Stalin died in 1953, the Communist regime in Poland had the country well under control. Although the dictator's successors made it possible for the resilient Gomułka, who survived prison, to get back into power in 1956, he brought little relief for the Polish people, who had to endure decades more of Communist rule.

In Albania, Enver Hoxha had consolidated his position even before the big blowup with Tito. In 1946, and under the country's new constitution, the thirty-five-year-old Hoxha combined the offices of prime minister, foreign and defense minister, commander of the armed forces, along with the post of general secretary of the Communist Party. He had visited Stalin in July 1947 and, veritably overwhelmed to be in the presence of the Great Man, allowed his adulation to flow freely. He wanted nothing more than to be instructed on how to create a Stalinist system in Albania. Back home the party had consolidated its hold on power through a series of attacks on organized religion, the tiny intellectual opposition, and what remained of the pillars of the old society. He soon adopted a cult to Stalin that transformed the Soviet dictator into the guarantor of the country's independence.[15]

Hoxha's only rival to total power was a faction inside the Communist Party led by Koçi Xoxe, a man with notably pro-Yugoslav tendencies. Stalin had not yet made up his mind about what should happen to Albania and had not invited them to the founding meeting of the Cominform in September. Xoxe was making headway inside the Albanian party and was on the verge of displacing Hoxha, until June 1948, when Moscow broke with Yugoslavia and the situation changed. It went without saying that Hoxha would side with Stalin, so that the faction around Xoxe was in danger of being purged. Indeed, after the Albanian leader returned from a visit to the Kremlin in March–April 1949, Xoxe was arrested, tried in secret, and executed in June. The purge continued into 1950–51, and anyone remotely suspected of pro-Yugoslav sympathies—a considerable number, it turned out—was ousted.

The Albanians took every possible step to follow the Stalinist model, including the widespread use of terror, so much so that the tiny country became notorious for its repressive practices. Between 1945 and 1956, in a country with a population of around 2 million, some 80,000 political arrests were made.[16]

When Hoxha last visited the Kremlin in April 1951, Stalin was pleased. "You have done well," he said. Caution was still very much advised because the enemy "will even try to worm his way into the Party, indeed into its Central Committee, but his attempts are uncovered and defeated through high vigilance and a resolute stand." Hoxha knew what to do—he had already purged the party and eliminated the basic freedoms. He remained a Stalinist long after Stalin was gone, and in fact he eventually fought with Nikita Khrushchev until the new Soviet leader in frustration broke diplomatic relations with Albania in 1961.[17]

Hungary was a bigger and tougher nut to crack, and it was far more difficult to impose Communism there. Party boss Mátyás Rákosi wanted to take on the churches, particularly Catholic cardinal József Mindszenty, who angered the regime by being both passionately anti-Communist and a firm believer in denominational education. By January 10, 1948, Rákosi announced a veritable all-out attack. "We must not allow the impossible situation to continue," he said, "in which the majority of the enemies of the people hide behind the cassocks of priests, in particular of the Catholic Church." Nevertheless, the regime proceeded cautiously until June, when it nationalized the schools. There was a backlash, and popular protest was even greater than when the state collectivized the land. The arrest of Mindszenty in December was inevitable, as was his show trial, after which he was incarcerated until freed during the Hungarian Revolution in 1956. He became a worldwide symbol of what was wrong with Communism and went into exile.[18]

The church struggle in Hungary reveals once again that the Stalinization of these years had native roots. Moscow never issued any orders to battle the churches, so that the Hungarian events suggest that in the center-versus-periphery debate over the creation of the Stalinist system, this case has to be credited to the periphery. Of course it was also true that the signals from Moscow about eliminating freedom were impossible not to hear.

The Hungarian Communists were no less determined to show solidarity with the Kremlin's desires for a purge of the party ranks, and they soon narrowed their focus to Minister of the Interior László Rajk. No doubt from the Kremlin's perspective, it helped Rákosi to pillory the Jewish Rajk, the latter a faithful Communist since the 1930s who had fought in the Spanish Civil War and later in the resistance and did not seek exile in Moscow during the war. Rajk was arrested in May 1949 and finally charged after Rákosi returned from talks with Stalin, who personally went over the indictments.[19] That Rákosi, who was also Jewish, managed to stay in the good graces suggests that Stalin's anti-Semitism was not race-based as such but more political and tactical.

Rajk and several other mostly midlevel officials were put on trial in September. The object was to link them to Tito and the Western "imperialists." They were accused of treason, tarnished as Trotskyites and "nationalists," and said to be working for American intelligence. It did not matter that Rajk had done nothing of the kind. Although Mátyás Rákosi was ruthless, he thought the court's seven death sentences were harsh and proposed to Stalin that along with Rajk, perhaps it would suffice to execute only two more. The Boss magnanimously agreed.[20] Hundreds of other "Rajkists" were arrested and, in groups of up to a dozen, tried in secret. Others were consigned to the camps without even a semblance of a trial.[21] Stalinization then steamed full speed ahead, with his name attached to public places and streets and his birthday turned into a national holiday. One of the propagandists said, "We have to keep alive and strengthen" love and loyalty "towards our teacher, Comrade Stalin." Anyone wavering "a tenth of a millimeter" from supporting him and the USSR would cease being a true Communist.[22]

The terror drastically affected the small country with a population of around 10 million. Between 1945 and 1950 alone, 59,429 persons had to face trials before people's courts, and in the same period somewhere between 20,000 and 40,000 were interned without trials. For the period 1948 to 1953, some 1.3 million people were hauled before various tribunals. Of those, a staggering 695,623 were found guilty and received punishments ranging from losing their job to paying with their lives. When a Hungarian delegation was called to the Kremlin in June 1953 and met with Soviet leaders, they were reproached by none other than Secret Police boss Beria for going overboard. He wanted to know how it was possible for such a small country to subject so many to legal proceedings in the last two or three years. He said there was a "virtual wave of oppression" that had turned "honest people into traitors."[23]

For sixteen-year-old George Konrád, the year 1949 in Hungary marked the end of "the brief period of normal civil life that followed the Germans' collapse." Looking back, he said facetiously that after Rajk and his associates were tried and executed, "the only people not yet arrested were the ones whose trials the authorities had lacked time to arrange. They were scheduled for the following year."[24] And yet other Hungarian Jews like the young János Kornai were completely blind to these harsh realities, shielded—or so he recalled—by his blind faith in Marxism-Leninism and the conviction that the Communist Party "embodied true ideas, pure morals, and service to humanity." At the time it never crossed his mind that "the admiration and respect" he felt for Stalin and Rákosi might be called a "cult of personality."[25]

Charles Gati, who was also there, is right to remind us that the numbers tell only part of the terror. Two points stood out for him: "More than anything else the totalitarian era in Hungarian history was marked by an immense gap between popular hatred of the Communist regime and professed solidarity with it and between conditions of anxiety and the officially proclaimed euphoria about the new world order."[26]

The Russian documents show Rákosi's persistence in trying to get Soviet leaders to trigger proceedings even beyond his own borders and against Communists all over Eastern Europe. He returned repeatedly to the theme of "enemies" who had entrenched themselves in the leadership of various countries, and he was disconcerted when foreign comrades did not follow up on his leads.[27] Eventually he provided the Kremlin with a list of 526 "persons of interest" that had emerged from the investigations in Hungary, and he kept on informing Soviet authorities in many more communications.[28]

A Bulgarian version of the Rajk event was supposed to take place earlier, though it was modest in comparison, mainly because Communist leader Georgi Dimitrov and his close comrade Traicho Kostov already had killed tens of thousands of would-be opponents. Stalin knew Kostov, the general secretary of the Bulgarian Communist Party (1944–45) and deputy prime minister (1946–49). He was a man so committed to the cause that when he was under fierce interrogation by Bulgarian police in 1924, he had jumped from a window on the fourth floor, willing to fall to his death lest he betray comrades. If his legs were broken and back deformed, his spirit was not. Indeed, after 1945, when Soviet occupation authorities wanted to collect information on the Bulgarian economy, Kostov resisted. On December 6, 1948, when he visited Moscow, Stalin dressed him down and threatened him: "This is exactly how our conflict with Tito began!"[29]

Early in the new year, Soviet officials in Sofia sent Stalin a lengthy and damning report on the political mood in Bulgaria. Although the people loved the USSR, many thought they could follow their "special path" to socialism and did not want or need much from Moscow. Kostov was said to be the worst of the Communist leaders and "not to be trusted." The report claimed that, under the guise of caring for Dimitrov's health, Kostov tried to get him out of the country for extended periods and then inserted "his own people" in key places. The Soviets lauded Dimitrov for being cooperative, but certainly not Kostov; in short, the report confirmed Stalin's judgment that here was a Tito in the making.[30]

In March 1949 the Bulgarian Central Committee removed Kostov from the government for reasons that could have been dictated by Stalin. They focused on his "nationalism" and claimed that he had sown the seeds of distrust between the USSR and Bulgarian governments. By the summer he was expelled from the party, and preparations were made for a show trial. In the meantime Dimitrov was taken ill and flown to Moscow for treatment. Had he been healthier, he likely would have led the attack, for he read the relevant documents from his sickbed and on May 10 recommended proceeding against the man he hatefully called "an intellectual individualist and a ruthless careerist."[31] Dimitrov himself died in Moscow on July 2, and if for years there were rumors he was murdered, in fact, his utterly slavish loyalty to Stalin was such that it is more likely that he died of natural causes.[32]

Along with Kostov, two hundred more arrests followed, from whom they picked ten for a big show trial staged between December 7 and 14, 1949. It was broadcast on radio, and the entire process was directed from Moscow. During the proceedings, rallies and meetings were organized nationally. The crowds howled out their hatred and screamed for Kostov's death. When the court verdict was reached, and he was hanged, some people danced with joy, or at least made a public show of their hatred for the man, in order to prove they were team players, could be trusted, and should be rewarded.

Between 1948 and 1953, 100,000 members of the Communist Party were closely examined by the authorities. In addition, each year two to six thousand or more people were arrested "on political grounds," and usually between 60 and 80 were executed. In the same period, there were campaigns against representatives of the various religions. The famed tolerance of the Bulgarian people was being ignored in favor of a Stalinist-style regime.[33]

A young man who lived next door to Kostov remembered all the "enemy mania" of the times. Georgi Markov witnessed how people gave in to the temptation to curse and to blame and to hate. Even in the 1970s, he urged the truth on his people: "Let us not lie to ourselves today by conveniently blaming Stalin for everything. The tragic truth is that Stalin was not alone, that Stalin would not even have existed if it had not been for the little Stalins, the thousands upon thousands of his followers, nameless criminals."[34] Markov himself was forced into exile and assassinated in 1978.

In Romania, the purge of the party, likely sparked by Yugoslavia's break with Moscow, began in November 1948 and ran until May 1950. It removed 192,000 members as "exploiting and hostile elements." A separate purge of "nationalist" leaders and suspected Tito supporters focused especially on Lucrețiu Pătrășcanu, who wanted to pursue a Romanian "road to socialism." He had been an activist as far back as the 1930s, had been jailed during the war, and later had served as minister of justice. By all accounts, he was a gifted intellectual who was resented by the party's general secretary, Gheorghe Gheorghiu-Dej. Worse still, he had awakened Stalin's suspicions.

At the Cominform meetings in 1949, Gheorghiu-Dej said that his country also had "imperialist agents" just like Hungary's Rajk, and he mentioned the already imprisoned Pătrășcanu. From December 1949 to January 1950, another fifty-one people were also picked up and interrogated, but without getting much out of them. Just as in similar cases in the other satellite countries, the Romanians asked Moscow to send torture specialists. The regime wanted enough material for a sensational show trial and ultimately staged one from April 6 to 13, 1954. Pătrăşcanu and one other person were executed, while the rest were given long prison terms.[35]

Gheorghiu-Dej capitalized on Soviet orders to flush out "enemies."[36] He used anti-Zionism to eliminate one of his main rivals: Ana Pauker, who was arrested on February 18, 1953. She had been a faithful servant of the party for years, someone of note and stature. Although she and her non-Jewish allies were said to be connected to "the international Jewish plot," the Romanian authorities purged her not simply in the name of ethnic "purification," because her successor at the Ministry of External Affairs was Simion Bughici, who was also Jewish.[37]

After Stalin's death, Pauker was released, and though her career was over, her love for Communism was not. In mid-1956 a party commission questioned her, and what she said at one point should remind us of the power and meaning of Stalin's model for the true believers: "If a Soviet official told me something, it was the gospel for me. That's how I was brought up. I'm telling you that things got to the point that anything Soviet was considered wonderful. If they had told me that the USSR needed it, I would have done it. A mistake, no doubt, but I would have done it. If they had told me to throw myself into the fire, I would have done so."[38]

In Romania, as in all the countries dominated by the Communists, it is difficult to put together the exact number of victims of Staliniza-tion. One 1950s document from the Ministry of the Interior states that for the period 1948–1953, police arrested 60,428 people on various politi-cal grounds, ranging from defaming the regime, to spreading forbidden leaflets, to "enemy religious activity." Of these, 24,826 were arrested in 1952 at the high point of the mania unleashed since 1948. For the remain-der of the 1950s the Securitate picked up between two and six thou-sand "enemies" per year. Quite apart from this political repression, the regime backed up its forced collectivization of agriculture in the three years following the land reform of March 1949, with the arrest of more than 80,000 peasants.[39]

Gheorghiu-Dej ended up with complete control of the party and continued the Stalinization of the country until his death on March 19, 1965. He was succeeded by Nicolae Ceauşescu, who ruled as one of the most repressive dictators in Eastern Europe until the regime collapsed in 1989.

MORE STALINIZATION IN CZECHOSLOVAKIA AND GERMANY

Hungary's boss Rákosi was particularly exercised about the supposed pervasive infiltration of "spies" in neighboring Czechoslovakia and complained to his Soviet advisers that Czech prime minister and soon-to-be president Klement Gottwald did not take him seriously enough.[40] In fact, the Prague coup on February 25, 1948 pushed all non-Communists from government, and there soon followed the arrest of most opposition leaders. Show trials of democratic and Socialist notables were held in Slovakia and Moravia in 1948, and these culminated in a May–June 1950 big event in Prague that featured thirteen leaders, including a Socialist member of parliament, Dr. Milada Horáková, a woman who had fought in the resistance, been captured by the Gestapo, and spent years in a Nazi concentration camp. She was part of the first real show trial in the country, minutely organized by Soviet specialists and given enormous publicity. Ultimately, she was executed on June 27, 1950. Three codefendants suffered the same fate, and the rest were given lengthy prison terms. In December the regime staged a trial of "Vatican agents" to run down church dignitaries. Hundreds of trials followed, and thousands were sentenced. Already in mid-1950, more than one-third of the 32,638 prisoners in Czechoslovakia were locked up for "political" crimes.[41]

Back in September 1948, Stalin had informed Gottwald in Moscow that his party was infested with Western spies and that he should clean its ranks.[42] On September 3 of the next year, the ever-watchful Mátyás Rákosi wrote Gottwald to report that his police had discovered spies in Hungary and that there were even more of them in Czechoslovakia, and he gave names. Gottwald thought these claims were sheer fantasy, but very soon he and Rudolf Slánský, the general secretary of the Communist Party, wrote Moscow to ask for police specialists familiar with the Rajk case in Hungary.[43]

Major arrests began in November, and some evidence pointed to Slánský who, conveniently enough, was also Jewish. In November 1949, still unsullied, he spoke as the Czech representative to the Cominform meeting in Bucharest and mentioned how "helpful" the Rajk trial had been in exposing Anglo-American spies. "Heightened vigilance" was needed, he said, as was the "timely elimination of elements that are unreliable, alien, and hostile to the Party."[44] He could not have imagined that his own head was already on the block.

Although initially the Czech secret police (StB) and their Soviet helpers thought that there was a conspiracy directed against Slánský, by late summer 1951 they began to conclude that he was part of the plot. In fact, each month from October 1950 to August 1951, one or two major figures were arrested, including cabinet ministers, top StB, and other officials.[45]

On July 24, 1951, Stalin subtly let Gottwald know that he had seen the materials collected by his specialists on Slánský and that after some deliberation, he had concluded the man could not remain as the general secretary of the party.[46] The Czechs moved too slowly for Stalin, and on November 14 he dispatched Anastas Mikoyan to Prague with orders for President Gottwald to have Slánský arrested. Gottwald dragged his feet for nine days until another message from Moscow arrived, and he agreed. Slánský was picked up and so were 220 others, among them some of the most prominent politicians in the country, including Foreign Minister Vladimír Clementis.[47] It was no accident that many of them were Jews, who could be accused of being "bourgeois Zionist nationalists," a charge that fit Stalin's own imagined "others" of the time.[48]

What he had in mind for Czechoslovakia was a grand show trial that would be orchestrated by his specialists on the spot. Under interrogation, Slánský admitted to making mistakes, but he obstinately rejected the charge that he was a Zionist. When the jailers screamed that he had staffed the party with Jews, he replied: "The point is not that they were Jews, the point is that they were in the resistance."[49] Those who failed to see this, he said, were racists. He was tough, though prolonged torture finally broke him, and he gave them enough to proceed. He was featured along with thirteen others in an event that lasted a week beginning on November 20, 1952.

The "monster trial" was rehearsed and also broadcast on radio for propaganda purposes. The prosecuting team paid attention to language and wording. Should the accused be called a "conspiratorial Zionist espionage group" or worse? Ultimately the prosecutors opted for the prosaic "anti-state conspiratorial center led by R. Slánský." Eleven of the fourteen defendants were Jews, but how to refer to them? In the Soviet Union, the accused would be characterized as having "Jewish nationality," but in Prague officials decided on the absurd mixture of

"Czech nationality, Jewish origin." That the accused were Jews, how-ever, was mentioned often, and it went without saying that all would be found guilty. Eleven were executed, and the other three were given life sentences.[50]

The show trials were only part of the more wide-ranging repressions of various kinds between 1948 and 1954. For that period alone, an esti-mated 90,000 citizens were prosecuted for "political crimes"; more than 22,000 were sent to labor camps; and over 10,000 soldiers or conscripts forced into special construction battalions. From 1950 to 1953 various "special actions" of the police and security officials picked up thousands of "anti-state elements," "kulaks," as well as bishops, priests, monks, and nuns of the Roman and Greek Catholic churches. The 247,404 pri-vate craft firms were, by a law enacted in 1950, forced out of business and a decade later were all but gone, so that nothing of the old society went untouched, including the nation's sense of independence. This was Stalinist terror in its Czechoslovak setting. It left a legacy of mis-trust and fear that undermined public faith in politics and haunted the country long after March 1953, when both Stalin and Gottwald died.[51]

In neighboring Germany, at least in the eastern part, leaders of the newly created German Democratic Republic (GDR) did not miss out on the enemy mania. By the time leaders Wilhelm Pieck and Otto Grotewohl met with Stalin on April 1, 1952, they had already purged the Socialist Unity Party (SED) of 317,000 members, roughly one-fifth of the total number.[52] Pieck desired holding "open trials" of the saboteurs and Western spies, and Stalin agreed.[53]

Six names of prominent SED leaders had come to light in August 1950, thanks to information from the Rajk affair in Hungary. The most senior politically was Paul Merker, a veteran and member of the Polit-buro as far back as 1926. Although he was not Jewish, the others were, and the SED prepared "a German Slánský" trial with a distinctly anti-Zionist tone. Although Merker was finally arrested only on December 3, 1952, the plans for a big event never materialized. Instead a few trials were held in secret after Stalin's death, and they resulted in no executions.

As George Hodos, who went through the ordeal himself in con-nection with the Rajk trial in Hungary, has said, the show trials were the "propaganda arm of political terror." Their aim was "to person-alize an abstract political enemy, to place it in the dock in flesh and blood and, with the aid of a perverted system of justice, to transform abstract political-ideological differences into easily intelligible common crimes."[54]

If East Germany did not have to suffer through a series of show trials, other layers of terror reached into every neighborhood, household, and family. The Ministry for State Security was founded on February 8, 1950, with its officials usually referred to as the Stasi, short for Staatssicherheit (state security). Soviet occupation authorities had established a secret police almost as soon as they arrived, and like those everywhere in Eastern Europe, it was modeled on Cheka. It grew like a cancer, until a month before the Berlin Wall came down on November 9, 1989, when the Stasi had 91,015 full-time employees and 174,000 informants. Translated into everyday life, that number meant that for every fifty citizens, one person worked for the Stasi. It became notorious both for its size and the scope of its activities.[55]

Part of the reason the SED did not proceed with show trials was that the process was overtaken by social turmoil. Back in April 1952, when the East German leaders visited Stalin, he warned them to go slow with their "kulaks," and to proceed modestly in organizing collective farms. He agreed they should firm up the border and recruit more guards, and after the SED bosses returned home, on May 26, they all but sealed the country off from the outside world. Yet they wanted to do more and prevailed on Stalin in July for permission to embark on what they called "the construction of the fundamentals of socialism." Their eschatological vision of a new, better world haunted every step they then took, from forcing small farmers into collectives, to confiscating the properties of private businesses. Following the Stalinist model, their new five-year plan emphasized heavy industry over consumer goods. Early in 1953, and in response to what was called "ideologial laxness," the SED regime imposed new higher quotas on the people and a "strict economy."[56]

Soviet officials, as well as some German ones, grew alarmed at the sheer volume of the arrests that soon resulted. In May 1953 Beria expressed dismay at East Berlin's ham-handed methods and the large numbers fleeing the country because of its social policies.[57] By June 2 the Soviet Council of Ministers called SED leaders to Moscow and told them in no uncertain terms to deal with "the serious dissatisfaction" and "mass flight of residents," that is, to reverse course. They were instructed to cease the radical drive to socialism and restore a semblance of legal rights.[58]

Whatever fitful efforts were made in East Germany by the SED, they failed to stem the immediate tide of unrest that began erupting during the second week of June 1953. There were similar rumbles of discontent at this time also in Czechoslovakia, Romania, Hungary, and Bulgaria, though these were soon contained.[59] In East Berlin and the GDR, however, popular defiance culminated in a mass uprising on June 17. Soviet and East German officials were shocked at the scale of the events, which (Soviet documents said) affected 270 or so towns and as many as 157,000 strikers and 335,000 demonstrators.[60] Although one *Pravda* reporter confided in a note to his editor that the outburst was not all that significant and likely organized by the West, the uprising became the biggest protest against Stalinization since the war and was put down only by declaring martial law.[61]

The Soviet Council of Ministers brought in the leaders of most of the Communist parties during June and July. The message was like that given the Hungarians on June 13: they had made bad judgments—admittedly sometimes following mistaken orders from Moscow, in fact Stalin, and they all needed to take a "new course" that was less likely to spark popular unrest. The Hungarian boss Rákosi, however, was held responsible for most of the errors in his country, where the situation was getting out of control. As Beria put it, "If the great Stalin made mistakes, Comrade Rákosi can admit that he made mistakes too." At another meeting on June 16, the Hungarians were given specific directives, and while Rákosi was permitted to keep control of the party, he was replaced as prime minister by Imre Nagy, a longtime Communist known to be more moderate.[62] Moscow expected Nagy to act in character and what he did with relatively small concessions was to "lift the lid off the pot" and let out steam.[63] The effort worked for a time, though not enough to avert the eruption of the Hungarian revolution in October 1956, savagely repressed by direct Red Army intervention to underline the country's vassal status.

It turned out that Moscow was not really interested in backing reformers, and in one country after the next the "new course" set after Stalin's death was soon derailed.[64] With the Cold War already well under way, and the Korean War continuing, U.S. policy on the front lines in Germany and Berlin during the June events in 1953 was cautious to the point of appearing "impotent."[65] Given the rapid intervention of Soviet troops, any action by the West to support the German protesters in 1953 would have been unrealistic. The SED regime faced a mass of discontent, and yet regardless of what it conceded, it "could not keep up with the shifting complexity of its populace, which required ever more personalized cajoling and coercion."[66] In the wake of the uprising East German officials began to build anew a Soviet-style state and resorted to fostering the Stasi. On August 13, 1961, in order to stop the mass flight from the country, they constructed the Berlin Wall.

It was then that the sense of powerlessness really hit families like Joachim Gauck's. The Wall forced them and all East Germans to adjust, and yet they had to go on living, so if they could not travel to neighboring Denmark anymore for an ice cream, they convinced themselves that their own was better anyway. Looking back in his recently published memoirs, Gauck said: "That was how we often declared the abnormal to be the normal, in order not to be overwhelmed from pain, fury and rage."[67]

But what kind of system had to lock all its citizens in? During the existence of the Wall up to November 9, 1989, a mere 16,348 managed to escape, while tens of thousands were arrested and hundreds were shot for attempting to do so.[68] We can gain some insight into the process that produced the GDR through the massive documentation relating to and collected by the Stasi. These materials are held at the new institution established when the Wall came down in 1989 and subsequently led by Joachim Gauck.

Gauck, a Protestant minister, had his first experience with the secret police when he was six years old. His father, Joachim Gauck Sr., went to visit his mother on her birthday on June 27, 1951; she had just turned seventy-one. Gauck Jr. remembered the date, because that day his father disappeared or, as the expression went, he was "picked up" (*abgeholt*). No one would say where he was, what he had done, or even if he was still alive. Gauck Sr. was a works inspector at the Rostock shipyard, and a former boss had written to him from West Berlin with an invitation to visit. Gauck never responded, and yet the police heard something and put him before a military tribunal that gave him twenty-five years for "espionage." He received another twenty-five for "anti-Soviet activities," because after they searched his home they found a technical journal published in the West.

"The charges were arbitrary," said Gauck Jr., "and followed the principle: If we already have the person, we'll soon find a crime." Without permitting a word to his family, the authorities shipped his father to deepest Siberia. He was fortunate to survive and was released on October 19, 1955, as part of the "thaw" following Stalin's death.[69] If the elder Gauck could have foreseen the future, he would not have believed that one day his son would become the president of a free and united Germany, as indeed happened when Joachim Gauck took the oath of office on March 23, 2012.

CHAPTER 21

Stalin's Last Will and Testament

Stalin saw himself as having a unique place in the lineage of Marx and Lenin, and he believed that he had something valuable to contribute to humankind. From his privileged position in the movement of world history, so went the direction of his thinking, he could make way for future Stalins who would continue to work for the elimination of capitalism. The ascetic dictator and former theology student, uninterested in the pleasures of the flesh, apart from notorious drinking bouts with his guests, was transfixed on the big question of a final reconciliation in this earthly world. Having found his mission in life, his thoughts on a last will and testament were necessarily political.

This rational side of Stalin, his analytic intelligence, so attuned to strategy and calculation, deeply impressed the intellectuals and professors charged with ironing out the details of a great book he wanted to pass on to those who would follow in his footsteps. At the same time, Stalin's personality had a ruthlessly irrational side, one that latched onto conspiracies, rumors, wild speculations, and spy manias. Among his phobias, as we have seen, was anti-Semitism, which to some extent he let loose as he solidified his grip on the Eastern European satellites.

Not only did Stalin never resolve these contradictory sides of his nature, but at the end of his life, there were disturbing signs that the strong, irrational urges were getting the upper hand.

THE POLITICAL TESTAMENT

Stalin began the project of setting down his political testament decades before, in the 1930s. At that time he saw to the production of *The History of the Communist Party of the Soviet Union (Bolsheviks): Short Course.* It was meant to teach political lessons and appreciation for the great accomplishment of getting into power, creating the dictatorship of the proletariat, and establishing the Soviet Union. In 1937, in the midst of the Great Terror, Stalin commissioned companion volumes on economics, one an introductory textbook and the other an advanced version. A team of authors set to work and sent him something like fourteen or fifteen drafts over the years. He scrupulously read and edited each one, ultimately finding all of them inadequate.

Somewhere along the way he came to regard a book on economics as his magnum opus, a treatise that would outdo both Marx, who tended to be abstract and philosophical, and even Lenin, who knew how to seize power but had died after only a few years. Stalin ruled far longer, introduced the new system, and one way or another managed to get it going. The book he wanted would detail his accomplishments and serve as a catechism, a textbook and font of wisdom for future generations on how to establish and run a Stalinist economy. Such a work would reveal "scientific socialism" in action and its superiority to capitalism as an economic system.

Although this book would represent his political testament, the economists who slaved on it had a tall order to fill. In 1950 he finally approved an initial text.[1] This submission would be used as a starting point for more intensive work by top party officials and experts. On February 22 he appointed a special commission led by Secretary to the Central Committee Georgi Malenkov and gave them a month to make revisions. The results disappointed him, so he added new people and set them up in style in Maxim Gorky's house. The team, inspired by the surroundings and with Stalin's confidence, worked fiendishly. He was at their disposal and met with them as needed, and they later admitted that they were overwhelmed by the depth of his knowledge. Discussions continued.

In November 1951 the revised text was taken up by a conference with 247 experts, whose comments filled three large volumes. The Master studied all this material and in early 1952 wrote lengthy "remarks" on it. Then on February 15 he had the team of authors, the Politburo, and more than a dozen leading economists discuss the textbook and his remarks. In all of Soviet history, no book or study ever received anything close to as much scholarly and political attention before publication.[2]

Stalin devoted so much time and energy to this project because the finished book would convey the lessons of Stalinist economics as codified into a textbook, accessible to all and less than six hundred pages long. It would be the Stalinist bible. Marx had laid out the principles of socialism, Lenin had provided a theory of revolution, and the new textbook would show the world that Stalin was the genius who got it all up and running. The book would reveal, he declared, "how we escaped from the bondage of capitalism; how we transformed the economy along socialist lines; how we won the friendship of the peasantry; and converted what was until recently a poor and weak country into a rich and powerful one."[3]

Although he was emphatic—just like Marx and Lenin—about wanting a "scientific" and "objective" book, he gave the authors politically charged instructions and met with them to ensure that they kept to the "correct" political line.

The only way they could produce a "rational," as opposed to a political, account of Stalinist economics was to ignore a host of monumental facts. For starters, they all knew that to the extent that the Soviet Union had attained economic success at all, it was because of its resort to the overwhelming use of violence and force. To break away from "capitalist slavery," the Soviets had killed off or intimidated the industrialists and the bourgeoisie. To win the peasants' "friendship," Stalin had mounted a sustained war against them; the regime shot or exiled the kulaks—the keenest and most economically efficient peasants. That war in the countryside led to disastrous famines in the early 1930s and again after World War II. To explain what collective farms were and why the peasants "loved them," as Stalin said, the authors would have to overlook the compulsion that had been needed to make them function. Even then their productivity paled in comparison to that of capitalist American or Canadian farmers. Stalin knew little about the countryside, let alone how agriculture worked—he visited farms exactly once (in 1928) and at best had only general ideas about the agricultural system.[4]

In order to convert the country from military weakness to strength, the regime poured vast sums into five-year plans and heavy industry at the expense of consumers and society at large, with the result that in terms of housing space and real wages, most people were materially worse off in 1952 than they had been back in lean 1928, before the five-year plans began. Even in basics like hourly wages measured in terms of food, workers in the United States were over three times better off in 1928 than their Soviet counterparts at that time, and well over five times better off in 1951–52.[5]

When the writers of Stalin's economics textbook huddled with him in February 1952, he was in high spirits, liked the way things were going, and gave them yet another year to finish the job. They would use his remarks and suggestions as a guide. The finished product was due in March 1953, but he died before reading it. The text, finally published in 1954, was allowed to fade into obscurity.

Alongside this rational if exaggerated effort to codify his "lessons," Stalin simultaneously pursued patently absurd leads, such as one alleging that Jewish doctors had already killed several prominent Soviet leaders and even sought to kill the great dictator himself.

THE DOCTORS' PLOT

The predisposition to conspiracy thinking, present among the socialist elite almost from the birth of Marxism in the nineteenth century and shared by Stalin during his long career, became more pronounced in the last years of his life. The secret police, during their investigation of the Jewish Anti-Fascist Committee (JAFC) in the late 1940s, unearthed information that led on November 18, 1950, to the arrest of a certain Dr. Yakov Etinger. Viktor Abakumov, head of State Security (MGB, formerly NKVD), halted Etinger's questioning because the suspect was in poor health. However, Mikhail Ryumin, an enthusiastic member of a special investigative branch, continued to grill Etinger who, aged sixty-four and suffering heart problems, died suddenly on March 2, 1951. After several months passed, Ryumin began to feel threatened by his immediate superiors and opted to write Stalin. Dr. Etinger, he alleged, had confessed that back in 1945, when treating top Soviet leader Alexandr Shcherbakov, that he had "shortened" the man's life. Ryumin claimed that in spite of the likelihood of solving that crime, his boss Abakumov had ordered him to shelve the case and had Etinger transferred to the notorious Lefortovo prison, where he died in a damp cell of natural causes.[6]

Stalin was already upset with Abakumov for not completing the case against the JAFC, and on July 4, 1951, the head of State Security was relieved of his duties. A committee led by Malenkov and Beria checked

Ryumin's allegations, and sensing what Stalin expected of them, they arrived at far-reaching conclusions. They alleged that indeed "among physicians there was a conspiratorial group" who were "intending through medical treatment to shorten the life of leaders of the party and the government." They also claimed that Abakumov had hindered the investigation, so that he and others in the MGB should be dismissed and the Etinger file taken up.[7] In addition, on July 11 Stalin ordered a special police inquiry on former patients and all doctors who had worked at the Kremlin medical center. Included among the police investigators was Mikhail Ryumin, who was soon put in charge of the JAFC case. On August 10, Stalin began his last vacation and stayed away from Moscow for four and a half months.

In the meantime, Ryumin tortured more information out of suspects to feed Stalin's appetite for conspiracies and succeeded enough to be promoted to deputy minister of state security on October 19. The Kremlin Boss ended his holiday on December 22, and on his return he spoke with top MGB officials and threatened them with dire consequences unless they got results. In January 1952 the cross-examination of those involved in the JAFC file resumed, and the case was finalized on March 31. A report was sent to Stalin within the week containing Ryumin's recommendation for punishment—execution for all but one of the main culprits.[8]

A closed trial before three military judges—notably not a show trial for the public—took place between May 8 and July 18, with the result a foregone conclusion. The main theme in the indictments was that "Jewish nationalists" had spied for the United States. They wanted to establish a homeland for the Jews in the Crimea and would thereby open the door into the USSR for the Americans. The JAFC members were accused of promoting a special status for the Jews, and the *Black Book on the Holocaust in the Soviet Union* was mentioned as evidence on that charge. The most important defendant, Solomon Lozovsky, formerly a distinguished veteran of the Communist Party Central Committee, was sentenced and finally shot on August 12, along with twelve others. An additional 110 people were given varying sentences for "crimes" ranging from supporting Zionism to espionage and nationalism.[9]

In the course of uncovering and concluding the JAFC conspiracy, the police found or invented more secret schemes. For Stalin, the most important concerned the physicians. By the end of 1952, his special team investigating the "wrecker doctors" confirmed that indeed the late Dr. Etinger was responsible for the death of Alexandr Shcherbakov. Moreover, so the report went, Andrei Zhdanov's heart condition might have been misdiagnosed. Arrests of more than twenty-five doctors culminated on November 4, when no less a figure than Dr. Vladimir Vinogradov, Stalin's own physician, was taken into custody.

The dictator grew emotionally involved and reminded his enforcers of the tradition of police torture dating from Lenin and Dzerzhinsky. They were told not to be so timid: "You work like waiters in white gloves. If you want to be Chekists, take off your gloves."[10] One way or another, he got evidence to present to a special meeting of the Central Committee that sat from December 1 to 4. After deliberations it concluded that indeed there was a plot involving two former administrators of the Kremlin hospital, four doctors that included Vinogradov, as well as two "Jewish nationals" and Dr. Etinger. All supposedly worked for the Anglo-American intelligence services and were implicated in the deaths of Zhdanov and Shcherbakov, incidents, it was asserted, that the MGB leadership should have known about and prevented.[11]

Off the record at the meeting, Stalin sounded a note reminiscent of the Great Terror: "The more we progress, the more enemies will try to harm us. Under the influence of great successes, there has been complacency, gullibility, arrogance." He had used almost the identical words in 1937. Now, however, he was particularly aggravated by the Soviet Jews who did not want to assimilate. "Every Jewish nationalist," he asserted, "is an agent of the American intelligence. Jewish nationalists think that the U.S. (where you can become rich, bourgeois, and so on) saved their nation. They feel obliged to the Americans. Among the doctors are many Jewish-nationalists."[12]

Stalin was triumphant, but no matter how strongly he felt, he avoided making public charges. Given the widespread anti-Semitic feeling in parts of the Soviet Union, if he had done so, it would not have been difficult to mobilize pogroms. The wily dictator, however, liked to keep his followers guessing. And in any event, he was temperamentally ill disposed even to staged popular violence, which could easily take on a momentum of its own. Thus it came to pass that Stalin introduced official anti-Semitism into the Soviet Union, the country that had once prided itself on its ideology of emancipation.

The story of a "doctors' plot" finally made the news in mid-January,

1953, when *Pravda* ran a story headlined: "The Arrest of a Group of Wrecker-Doctors" (*vrachei-vreditelii*). The paper mentioned all their names and noted that "most of the terrorist group" had ties to an "international Jewish bourgeois nationalist" organization that was "guided by American intelligence services." Its goal was to kill the leading Soviet politicians. These "monsters in a human face" were not only linked to the deaths of Zhdanov and Shcherbakov, the story said; they also had threatened leading military officers. More charges were mentioned. The Jews and Zionists, it was claimed, had "exposed themselves as agents of American imperialism and enemies of the Soviet state." TASS and the newspapers carried similar articles, heightened suspicions about the Jews, and called for their exclusion from various institutions, newspapers, and factories.[13]

Officially condoned anti-Semitism, not open violence, spread, and Lev Kopelev, a prisoner in a special camp near Moscow, heard civilian employees whispering among themselves: "Beaten up at school . . . Pushed from a bus . . . Beaten almost to death . . . They say they gave shots in the hospital that infected people with syphilis . . . Hanged himself . . . Thrown out of the institute." Some prisoners were appalled, and one said, "This is just like Hitler." A few rejoiced that the Jews had been "tripped up" and caught.[14]

Although the doctors' case never went to trial, some historians have suggested that it was intended as a prelude to the mass deportation of the Jews.[15] At the time there were widespread rumors that they would all be deported, just like the Chechens, the Crimean Tatars, the Balkars, and all the others. There were whispers that the regime would build a city of camps somewhere in Siberia and that the doctors might even be publicly executed in Red Square.[16] However, in spite of an exhaustive hunt through the archives for documentation in the 1950s, and again since the 1990s, no evidence has come to light that a mass deportation was in the works.[17]

Nevertheless, the negative stories, and the proclivity to believe whatever the state said, had a chilling social effect. Irina Dubrovina, who lived in St. Petersburg in January 1953, remembered that she was waiting in the lab with top chemistry students for a job placement when the radio blared out news of the Doctors' Plot: "We simply stopped breathing. Among us the Jews were the very best students. The very best, whom we treated as equals." Suddenly they were all wreckers and murderers—at least that was what they heard. Then the students parted "without saying a word to each other. That's how well we were all trained, that ideology—it was necessary to say nothing about anything. We understood everything." How could it be true? "We had been raised to believe that all nationalities were the same, that we were internationalists, that we welcome everyone." She and a few others tried a mild protest that got nowhere, and for that act of disobedience, she ended up with a teaching position in the remote mountains of Chechnya.[18]

That story illustrates one of the insidious ways in which official anti-Semitism spread. Alexander Yakovlev remembered those times as well. He was only twenty-eight, a member of the party and working in Yaroslavl, a city about 160 miles northeast of Moscow. In early 1953 he was superintendent for schools and higher education. He was summoned by Comrade Shkiryatov, the chairman of the Party Control Commission, its main repressive body, and he was told to bring along his list of personnel. Shkiryatov had a letter of denunciation claiming that Yakovlev did not understand Kremlin policy on cosmopolitanism and had therefore failed to promote it. For his incompetence, he "would have to be punished." As he left the office, he limped, and when Shkiryatov asked about the problem and learned that it was the result of a war injury, he changed his mind. Yakovlev knew he was lucky to escape, but realized that another victim would have to be found to take his place.[19]

Yakovlev later became the chair of Russia's Presidential Commission for the Rehabilitation of Victims of Political Repression. His foundation has published numerous volumes of documents on Stalin's dictatorship. It is his educated opinion that indeed in February 1953, "preparations for mass deportation of Jews from Moscow and other major industrial centers to the northern and eastern regions" had begun. With Stalin's death, "a new bloodbath was averted."[20]

Stalin allowed the anti-Semitic mania to creep into his own family. During the war his seventeen-year-old daughter, Svetlana, had a flirtatious relationship with the fascinating Alexei Kapler, twice her age, a known womanizer, married, and also Jewish. Stalin was offended on all counts, and Kapler was lucky to escape with his life. Then Svetlana fell hard for Beria's son Sergo, though that relationship did not last. In 1944 she met Grigori Morozov, who was Jewish. Although her father did not approve, he did not stand in the way of their marriage. However, he never gave them his blessing and refused to meet his new son-in-law, let alone allow the couple to remain in the Kremlin, and he forced their separation in 1947. The marriage became intolerable to Stalin when he learned that JAFC leader Mikhoels and others hoped to gain access to political influence by using the Stalin family connection. Morosov was whisked away, as were other Stalin relatives. At the end of 1948, Stalin told Sventlana that they all worked for a "Zionist center." The Zionists "threw that first husband your way," he said, and the older generation of Jews was teaching Zionism to the young.[21]

As part of the investigation of the JAFC, the police collected evidence on Molotov's Jewish wife, Polina Zhemchuzhina. Stalin had read out her dossier at a Politburo gathering in late 1948. It was filled with lies about her sexual exploits that had been extorted from others already in custody. She was a notable person with a successful career, and Stalin had made her a commissar for fisheries in 1939. Once she had prided herself as the best-dressed woman in the USSR, and now she was damned.[22] The Boss demanded that the Politburo expel her from the party and that the couple divorce. The noblest interpretation of the couple's obedience to his command was that Molotov wanted to save her and that she agreed in the hope that the family would be spared.[23]

Commissar Molotov provides an alternative view in his memoirs, which paints the two of them as totally dedicated to the cause. When Polina heard what Stalin had said, she supposedly turned to her husband and without complaint remarked: "If it is necessary for the Party, then we divorce." She was arrested, imprisoned for a year, and sent to the camps for three more. Molotov initially abstained from voting for her expulsion from the party, but soon in a note to Stalin, he admitted his political mistake, favored throwing her out, and expressed remorse for not preventing her from forging links "with anti-Soviet Jewish nationalists."[24] After she was sent away, he apparently made little or no effort to find out where she was. This episode bespeaks the cowardice of the man whose name has become synonymous with subservience and brutality. In regard to his wife, his conscience could be assuaged by the friendly gesture of Beria, who took to whispering in his ear at meetings: "She is alive, alive!"

Molotov's reminiscences reek of self-deception and offer glimpses of a servant mentality trying to justify a brutal regime and his own complicity in it. It is hard to accept the account he gives of Polina's return from the camps. The first thing on her mind, he claims, was the leader's welfare. Not aware that Stalin had died, she wanted to know how he was doing. Molotov writes as if he needed to clear his wife's good name, and it seems hardly to have occurred to him that she was an innocent victim. But perhaps it did, and the thought of her innocence made him try harder to convince not just others but himself that it was all for the greater good. He recalled, after Polina passed away, that she had never cursed Stalin and that she had chastised others if they spoke ill of him: she was a "genuine Bolshevik, a real Soviet person."[25]

Even "sensible people" like Konstantin Simonov became entangled in the latest conspiracy mania. He readily adopted a strong anticosmopolitan stance, which pleased Stalin, and in 1950, as a reward, he put the writer in charge of one of the country's top literary newspapers, the *Literaturnaia Gazeta.* It was "expected" that he would continue his vigilance, and indeed Simonov dismissed all the Jews right away—for their "poor work and political mistakes." Then he was elevated to the Central Committee, where he heard Stalin's last speeches and wondered about the remarks on the Jews. But in his own life he was unrelenting, and on March 24, 1953, he came up with a list of Jewish writers who should be purged from the Union of Soviet Writers, in effect ending their careers. His letter, written two weeks after the dictator died, would have been given a stamp of approval by Stalin.[26]

Yuri Slezkine, whose own family experienced this upheaval, observes that for the Jews, with their expulsions from the party and the loss of their jobs, the slanderous charges meant that the dreams and hopes that many of them had associated with the Soviet belief system were over. "The great alliance between the Jewish Revolution and Communism was coming to an end as a result of the new crusade against Jewish Communists. What Hitler could not accomplish, Stalin did, and as Stalin did, so did his representatives in other places."[27]

LAST PARTY CONGRESS

Behind his drive to uncover the "truth" about the Jews and his hope to finish his book, Stalin seemed to sense the imminence of death. That was also why he called the Nineteenth Party Congress, which opened on October 5, 1952, the first time it had met in thirteen years. More than 1,300 delegates and Communist leaders from around the world gathered at the Great Kremlin Palace. Just days before, in *Pravda,* Stalin had published his brief account of "The Economic Problems of Socialism in the USSR." These were his "remarks" on the economics book, and he let it be known that they represented his political report to the meeting.

Although during the congress he was on stage some of the time, he said nothing until October 14, the last day. When he approached the microphone, he was greeted with thunderous applause, more God than man. He did not make the slightest effort at oratory, but that was of no account: he was the Master, the Boss, the fearsome Leader, the terror-ist, and the emperor all rolled into one. The audience, bonding with the great man, was spellbound before he said anything and clung to every syllable once he began. It was as if, so one of them recalled, each word was a "lofty revelation, great Marxist truth, a pearl of wisdom about the present and a prediction for the future."[28]

They were a privileged group, this audience, masters themselves, powerful, identifying with the Kremlin in the grand battle for the future. In a few short minutes, Stalin reminded them that the Bolsheviks, the "shock brigade" of world revolution, had succeeded against the odds. Their victory had made it easier for the next "shock brigades" to win in Eastern Europe and China, and so it would go until judgment day. The class struggle was becoming "simpler" against the capitalist bourgeoisie, which had dropped the last trace of its liberalism. It now defended the rights of the "exploiting minority," not those of the "exploited major-ity." Given those trends, he concluded, there was "every reason to count on the success and victory" of Communism all over the world.[29]

In his "remarks" published on the eve of the congress, he went more deeply into the problem. He contended that the capitalist countries had advanced by trying to "strangle" those that did not go along with the Marshall Plan. The Soviet Union and the "people's democracies" in Europe and China, he claimed, were able to succeed on their own and in fact were eliminating global markets and securing scarce resources. As he saw things, capitalist rivals would have to compete more fiercely among themselves for what was left and would end up making war on one another. The class struggle would heat up within those states as a prelude to the final showdown with Communism, just as he had said all along. Granted, there was a peace movement, but it would never be strong enough to stem the tide of the great fight to come.

According to this view, the United States and its capitalist lackeys had tried to seduce the Communists into taking part in the Marshall

Plan, in an effort to beef up their own flagging economies. But the final battle could be delayed only so long. In the end, he was convinced, the only way to be rid of war was to eliminate its cause—capitalism. Stalin's faith in the inevitable ideological clash and war with the capitalists remained unshaken.[30]

He brought up again his favorite theory on the general crisis of capitalism, which was both economic and political. The first stage of the crisis had led to the First World War and made the Russian Revolution possible, the second stage had led to the last war, and the ultimate battle was at hand. On one side there would be "the ever-increasing decay of the world capitalist system" and on the other "the growing economic power of the countries that have fallen away from capitalism—the USSR, China and the other People's Democracies." To his great satisfaction, the theory and the predictions he made in the late 1920s now looked more valid than ever.[31]

Anyone who thought Stalin's energy might be flagging could see otherwise two days later in Sverdlov Hall. On October 16, in an address to the Central Committee, he spoke without notes for an hour or more and was often in a rage. He demanded the expansion of the party executive, just as Lenin had done at the end of his life.[32] A new Central Committee would have 125 members, increased by over two-thirds from the previous one. He dissolved the Orgburo and enlarged the Politburo from 9 members and 2 candidates into a "Presidium" of 25 members and 11 candidates.[33]

The part of the speech to the Central Committee that Konstantin Simonov remembered was Stalin's solemn pronouncement that "it was approaching the time when others would have to continue the work he had done." The "difficult struggle with the capitalist camp was ahead and the most dangerous thing in this struggle was not to flinch, to be scared, to retreat, to capitulate." As usual he did not talk about himself and instead reminded them of Lenin's fearlessness.[34]

Everyone in the hall was then startled when he turned to threaten the Communist veterans. Pointing to Molotov, Kaganovich, Voroshilov, and Mikoyan—all of them to a greater or lesser extent already out of favor—he said that they should be relieved of their duties. Here he was also following in Lenin's footsteps. In fact, whenever Stalin thought aloud about possible heirs, he ran them all down, and in their presence he would demean or insult each one to show how undeserving they were.[35] That day in Sverdlov Hall, the Master singled out Molotov for an especially fierce drubbing, blamed him for several mistakes and—along with his wife, Polina, then serving time in a camp—for conspiring to create a Jewish homeland in the Crimea. Stalin said that no sooner did the Politburo make a decision than Molotov informed his spouse and her friends, and they were not to be trusted. These remarks puzzled many and revealed that Stalin was sinking ever more deeply into a manic preoccupation with conspiracies.[36]

There were also signs that he was preparing for another war. That was the impression recollected by Lieutenant General N. N. Ostroumov, one of the deputy chiefs of the air force staff. In the spring of 1952 Stalin ordered no fewer than one hundred new tactical bomber divisions, a massive buildup whose purpose the experts could not figure out.[37]

Before he had a chance to act on his growing phobias against the West or the Jews or his own comrades, he died in circumstances that are still subject to controversy. New documents have recently turned up, but there will never be enough information to quiet doubters who insist that Beria or someone involved in a plot may have poisoned Stalin. On Saturday, February 28, he hosted a dinner at his dacha in Kuntsevo, and his guests Beria, Malenkov, Khrushchev, and Bulganin stayed until around four early Sunday morning. The guards grew anxious during the day, waited until special mail arrived at around ten P.M. to intrude, and found him collapsed and semiconscious. Instead of calling for a medical team, they phoned the politicians, who arrived in the early morning of March 2. Everyone hesitated to send for doctors, perhaps half afraid that Stalin, who seemed fast asleep, should awaken to find physicians there. The Doctors' Plot was in full swing at the time, and he might suspect his followers of wanting to kill him. Emergency help was finally requested, and a medical team arrived at seven A.M., when it was already too late. He had suffered a cerebral hemorrhage with loss of consciousness, speech, and paralysis of the right arm and leg.

REACTIONS TO STALIN'S DEATH

A recently discovered document in the Russian archives provides some details about Stalin's final days. With the exception of several "short moments" on March 3, he never regained consciousness and died on March 5, 1953, at 9:50 P.M.[38]

According to Dr. Alexander Myasnikov, one of those called to treat Stalin and one of the specialists who performed the autopsy on March 6, there was evidence of stomach hemorrhaging "caused by hypertension." They also discovered that the dictator suffered from "strong sclerosis of the cerebral arteries," which had developed over the last several years. Among the symptoms of this thickening and hardening of the arteries in the brain, Myasnikov mentioned, were disorders of the nervous system, which might help explain some of the dictator's behavior in the last years of life, when he grew more suspicious than ever.[39] On the other hand, as late as the previous October, Stalin had been perfectly capable of delivering a lengthy speech without notes to the Central Committee. When India's ambassador K. P. Menon and Dr. Saiffudin Kitchlu had met with the Soviet leader back on February 16, in what would be his last contact with foreigners, they found him in top form. Their lengthy discussion covered the whole range of international problems, and Stalin had all the facts at his fingertips.[40]

His daughter, Svetlana, was by his side at the end, "when he suddenly lifted his left hand as though he were pointing to something above and bringing down a curse on us all." She recalled that the years leading up to her father's death were difficult—and not just for her: "The whole country was gasping for air. It was unbearable for everybody."[41] Although it is generally accepted that the country was torn by grief over Stalin's death, the picture that has come down to us is multidimensional.

In the camps of the Gulag, the response was mixed. Some women "diligently wailed for the deceased," some men wanted to donate money for a wreath, and still others heard the news "in tomb-like silence." Prisoners and guards were confused, and no one knew what to expect.[42]

Officials at the American embassy in Moscow watched events closely and kept Washington informed up to the minute. Jacob Beam, who was monitoring the situation, noted that it was only on March 4 at two A.M. that the first official medical bulletin was issued. In the morning, citizens went their usual way, though longer lines than usual queued at newspaper stands.[43] The death was announced only on March 6, and while Beam observed "some" weeping, it seemed to him that people were "subdued" and that fewer than might be expected gathered in Red Square: "The general impression in Moscow at this point is a surprising lack of response to this morning's news of Stalin's death and contrasts with American and British reactions to the deaths of President Roosevelt and King George."[44] Two days later Beam reported that there was a long line to see the coffin in the Hall of Columns, with "little evidence of extreme grief." Moreover, "one American who was [in Moscow] at the time of President Roosevelt's death" was of the opinion that there had been more "active grief" in the Soviet capital on that occasion.[45]

What impressed Harrison Salisbury of *The New York Times* was the emotional restraint of the people's reactions. When the authorities opened the doors for viewing the body early on March 6, he wrote, tens of thousands moved forward to see it almost as if they were stunned or in shock. Determined to control any signs of "disorders or panic," the government sealed off the inner city with lines of trucks and tanks and thus slowed the endless stream heading toward the center.[46]

Nevertheless, people from all walks of life flooded downtown Moscow, filling the streets up to a hundred miles away as they made their way on foot to catch a glimpse of the fallen Master. Some traveled by train from far away, and as the masses converged, a mortal crush resulted in hundreds of deaths in Moscow and in Stalin's own Georgia. These fatalities went unreported in the press, perhaps because the regime did not want to reveal such evident chaos.[47]

According to most memoirs from those times, there was widespread emotional turmoil—more than one person described it as the death of God. No doubt motives for such responses were mixed, for when Evgenia Semyonovna Ginzburg heard the reports, she collapsed into sobbing, "not for the monumental historical tragedy alone, but most of all for myself. What this man had done to me, to my spirit, to my children, to my mother."[48] Lev Kopelev and his wife, Raisa Orlova, in spite of being persecuted for their beliefs and in camps at the time, were nonetheless grief-stricken when they heard the news.[49]

The public demonstrations of sorrow, whatever else they were, constituted ritualized political acts. They were expected, in a sense commanded, which of course does not mean that there was no sincere sorrow.[50] Funeral meetings were held at every factory and collective farm in the country, and there were deep outpourings of emotion. Some villages left nothing to chance, and in some places local authorities gathered everyone and ordered firmly: "Our dear beloved leader has died, you should all cry." When they went home and behind closed doors, it was a different matter: "Praise to God! Satan has croaked!"[51] Evidence from isolated cases prosecuted at the time indicates that a minority of the population cheered Stalin's death, cursed him, burned his pictures, and tore down his statues. Many were denounced for "anti-Soviet agitation" and some of the offenders were prosecuted and given stiff sentences.[52]

It happened that at this very time Alexander Solzhenitsyn finished his term as a political prisoner in the Gulag. On March 2, although technically "free," he found himself under armed escort to Kazakhstan and more than 1,300 miles southeast of Moscow. He had served his time for an errant remark and mild political criticism. Now he was told that he would have to live in "perpetual exile" and never be allowed back into Russia. The penalty for leaving his place of exile would be severe: twenty years imprisonment and hard labor. By March 3, Solzhenitsyn reached the small Kazakh town of Kok-Terek. Compared to the north that he had left behind, it was warm, and he was grateful to be allowed to sleep outside a jail in a haystack. Three days later the news of Stalin's passing was broadcast on the radio.

The Russian schoolteachers and other women sobbed uncontrollably and cried: "What is to become of us now?" Solzhenitsyn wanted to yell: "Nothing will become of you now! Your fathers will not be shot! Your husbands-to-be will not be jailed! And you will never be stigmatized as relatives of prisoners!" He wanted to dance a jig but dared not.[53]

What changes were to be expected now that Stalin was gone? According to Charles Bohlen, the soon-to-be U.S. ambassador to the USSR, the mystique of the man's name, his association with Lenin, and his connection to the original Russian Revolution had helped to impose Soviet rule in Eastern Europe and to a lesser extent in China. Within a week of Stalin's death, Bohlen thought it fruitful to open dialogue with Mao Zedong in an effort to end the Korean War, because while Mao "might have been willing to play the part of the younger brother to Stalin," he was unlikely to do so with those now in the Kremlin.[54]

It took until July for the endless negotiations in Korea to yield a cease-fire agreement. More than half a century later, the border between North and South remains as hot as Stalin left it.

Across Eastern Europe, reactions to the Leader's death were varied. In Bulgaria, playwright Georgi Markov recalled, "It had been drilled into us for years on end from all sides that Stalin was the wisest, the most courageous, the greatest man on earth." Eventually, "we, like the propaganda, had accepted unquestionably that he could not fall ill, let alone die." One of Markov's workmates in the carpentry shop said: "Stalin cannot die, do you understand! Even if he dies, we will resuscitate him, and though he is seventy-three now, he can start over, perhaps at thirty, what do you say!"[55]

The ruling Communist elites across Eastern Europe saw Stalin's death as a calamity. He had been their parties' protector and greatest supporter, "the very embodiment of their highest dreams, the hero they had come to revere, the symbol of their vigor, passion, and boundless enthusiasm."[56] They all endorsed the Soviet model and a noncapitalist, collectivist future and, like Stalin, used this great "final goal" of social-ism as justification for the sacrifice of individual rights and the com-mission of the most terrible crimes. Although by the time he died, Stalin had this part of the Red Empire firmly under control, he dared not make any real attempt to realize the early Bolshevik vision of turn-ing the states of Central and Eastern Europe into republics within the USSR.[57] Such a move would have provoked a backlash and would have created more tensions in the expanded Soviet Union than even Stalin might have managed. He was content to bind them to Moscow with treaties of friendship and mutual cooperation. The embrace would endure for close to fifty years.

Epilogue

The USSR in the immediate postwar years exhibited enormous energy, having gained confidence and territory by winning the Second World War. Not only did the Red Empire reclaim "lost territories" such as the Baltic states and western Ukraine, but Stalin saw to it that regimes based on Communism, and more or less taking orders from Moscow, were established all the way to Berlin. There were barely missed opportunities to plant the Red flag in parts of Iran and Turkey, perhaps also in Greece, Italy, and France. The door to Germany was opened, and to Asia as well. If the West had left Stalin and his entourage to their own devices, there is no telling how far the Communist cause might have advanced.

At the same time, the fundamental flaws in the foundation of the Red Empire were already showing. Stalin's heavy-handed methods alienated true believers in Yugoslavia, and he sowed seeds of discord in China. Although the Soviet Union was unquestionably a superpower, it had underlying economic weaknesses that became more apparent over time. Worse still, Stalinism was unable to tolerate freedom of thought and expression and so could not tap the full energies and involvement of the people.

Stalin's heirs, lacking his iron will and revolutionary militancy, papered over these basic faults. If the Soviet system became less totalitarian than it had been in its bloodiest days, it remained a Communist dictatorship. Those who governed from the Kremlin continued to believe that Communism was the wave of the future. Although they faced a structurally different world in the Cold War they had inherited from Stalin, none of them had the slightest intention of loosening their grip on the Red Empire.

Indeed, the new Soviet leaders carried on Stalin's foreign policy, refused to be seen as "soft" on the West, and innovated insofar as they made a more concerted effort to reach out to the third world than Stalin had done. His rigid Marxism decreed that every society had to pass through the modern or bourgeois stage of economic development before the social situation would be ripe for a Soviet-style revolution. He had counseled Mao and the Chinese Communists to slow down, even after their revolution succeeded in 1949. Elsewhere around the globe, Stalin was prepared to give moderate encouragement to revolutionary movements, yet he saw their main role as siding with the Soviet Union in the Cold War.

Two months after Stalin's death, Moscow agreed to increase and sustain substantial aid to China. "It was a massive attempt at stamping Soviet socialism in China—in every department of every ministry, in every large factory, in every city, army, or university there were Soviet advisors, specialists, or experts" to help China's modernization.[1] Thus, even without Stalin, the Cold War continued, more or less along the same track. In time the USSR ran up more defense costs than it could sustain, the Red Empire in Eastern Europe never paid for itself, and additionally client states like Vietnam and Cuba drained away billions each year.[2]

The immediate need at home, after Stalin's sudden departure, was to carry on the business of governing, and on March 8, 1953, a new collective leadership was formed, with Georgi Malenkov in charge of the government and the party, Molotov in foreign affairs, Beria in security, and Bulganin in control of the army. By a strange irony, it was Beria, Stalin's blood-spattered enforcer, who took the first steps to make the regime appear less brutal. Already on March 6 he shuffled the security apparatus and began the process of handing over the vast Gulag system to the Justice Ministry.[3]

On March 26 he sent the Presidium an amnesty proposal that was, without intending it, an astonishing condemnation of Stalinism. Beria said there were 2,526,402 prisoners in work camps and colonies. Of them, 221,435 were regarded as the "most dangerous state criminals" (spies, terrorists, Trotskyites, nationalists, etc.), and they were not going anywhere. He wanted to free some of the others, namely those sentenced to serve less than five years, offenders younger than eighteen, pregnant women, and women with children under the age of ten. In total around one million prisoners would be released.[4]

The first news of the changes afoot was published in *Pravda* on April 4. Under the still-misleading headline "Soviet Socialist Law Is Inviolable," it reported a review of the Doctors' Plot. It turned out that the arrests were "without legal foundation" and that testimony had been obtained by "means not permitted under Soviet law." The physicians were released and errant police officials blamed for it all.[5]

Beria's rivals for power did not applaud his efforts to moderate the Stalinist system. A group headed by Khrushchev had him arrested on June 26, and he was later tried and executed. The release of the Gulag prisoners continued mainly because, as everyone in the Kremlin knew, the camps were becoming too costly and a political liability to the regime. Still, the USSR continued to be almost as repressive as it had ever been.

Those remaining in the camps, overlooked by the amnesty or excluded, like political prisoners, found the conditions more intolerable than ever, and during the spring of 1953, protests, strikes, and even rebellions involved tens of thousands of prisoners. The authorities fought back with armed troops and tanks and in some places killed hundreds.[6] This resistance, coupled with the unprofitability of the camps, induced the release of still more prisoners. They would wait expectantly for months, only to be abruptly told that they would be leaving within hours and were left to find their way home. Many died along the way, in desperation committed suicide, or engaged in a criminal act in order to be rearrested. Most were physically or psychologically maimed and found it difficult to adjust to life on the outside.[7]

Nikita Khrushchev's famous speech to the Twentieth Party Congress on February 24, 1956, sent tremors through the entire Communist movement because he addressed the "cult of personality" and some of the crimes of the Stalinist era. Above all, Khrushchev wanted to rescue Communism, to explain away "excesses," and return to mythologized "Leninist principles." Remarkably enough, far from distancing himself and the regime from Stalin's ideas, policies, and practices, he defended the dead leader's use of forced collectivization, the war on the kulaks, and even lauded him for destroying Trotsky. Khrushchev actually ridiculed what he labeled Nikolai Bukharin's "cotton-dress industrialization," with its promise of more consumer goods. Instead he praised Stalin's five-year plans, without which, according to Khrushchev, "we would not now have a powerful heavy industry, we would not have collective farms, and find ourselves disarmed and weak in a capitalist encirclement."[8]

In his speech, Khrushchev mentioned in passing that after reviewing the evidence of some particularly egregious cases of legal abuse, the Military Collegium of the Supreme Court had conferred *reabilitatsiya,* or "rehabilitation," on 7,679 persons.[9] This "exoneration" was defined initially as "revision of all legal consequences of a judgment pertaining to a person who was unlawfully prosecuted." The proviso was that this individual was innocent of some or all the charges, in which case they might receive full or partial exoneration, as well as restoration of their reputation and civil rights. Some obtained compensation, such as the return of lost property or pensions, while others took up again their position in the bureaucracy. For all too many, however, exoneration came posthumously.[10]

To put the small number of those "rehabilitated" in some perspective, we need to recall the vast scale of the victims, for whom Stalin's curse had immediate personal consequences: between 1929 and 1953, an estimated 18 million people were sent to the Gulag of the camps and colonies.[11]

For those who survived the ordeal, obtaining the official "certificate of rehabilitation" was both complicated and frustrating.[12] Some wanted the official paper in order to get back their Party card, to obtain the benefits that went with it. Others had personal reasons or acted on behalf of a deceased relative. A total of 612,000 rehabilitations were granted between 1953 and 1957, but then the numbers dropped off, and they fell to almost nothing after 1962. Indications of the continuing pain felt by those who experienced the terror could be seen in the Soviet Union to the end of its days. Between 1987 and 1989, under Mikhail Gorbachev, close to 840,000 individuals were exonerated. Russia since 1991 has a new and improved federal law, and between 1992 and 1997 the government received 4 million applications for rehabilitation and granted around 1.5 million of them.[13]

What generated so many millions of arrests and sentences in the first place? The motor was Stalin's ideology, part of which asserted that "the country was full of covert enemies posing as loyal citizens—assassins, saboteurs, and traitors—who were conspiring to destroy the Soviet system and betray the nation to foreign powers."[14] It was assumed anyone arrested on remotely political grounds must have been involved with like-minded others, and information about these supposed coconspirators was tortured out of the unfortunates in custody. In this process, Soviet citizens were denied the presumption of innocence.

The Stalinist regime also sent whole nations into banishment "for eternity," between 1929 and 1953, a total of more than 6 million people. The rehabilitation of those who survived took a long series of decrees, which began in 1954 by lifting restrictions. Although their property was not restored, groups like the Karachays, Kalmyks, Chechens, Ingushetians, and Balkars eventually went back to their former homelands, in a process that lasted more than three decades. The Crimean Tatars, Volga Germans, and others have had even longer to fight for their rights. The resettlement of these evicted people led to disharmony, a situation that continues to this day.[15]

More generally, the post-Stalin Soviet Union found it impossible to live with freedom of speech. Even after Khrushchev denounced Stalin's abuses in February 1956, that September Boris Pasternak was told that he would not be able to publish *Doctor Zhivago,* a novel that belongs among the best in all of literature. Pasternak tried to convince himself that the regime could not indefinitely postpone freedom of expression. However, Konstantin Simonov and a group of editors wrote him to warn that publishing the book "was out of the question" because the author believed that "the October Revolution, the Civil War and related subsequent social changes" had brought the people "nothing but misery." The editors detailed their objections in a thirty-five-page letter that pointed out all Pasternak's "political mistakes."[16]

In spite of everything, the *Doctor Zhivago* manuscript found its way to Italy in 1957. The Communists there tried to prevent publication of the book, but it appeared anyway, and soon also in France. It became a best seller, and in 1958 the author was nominated for a Nobel Prize in Literature. Meanwhile back in the USSR, the Union of Soviet Writers held hearings to attack Pasternak. One Moscow writer said: "Get out of the country, Mr. Pasternak. We don't want to breathe the same air as you." Others called him a "traitor," "warmonger," "agent of imperialism," and worse. The Pasternak case was one of many that indicate how little the Soviet system had changed after Stalin.

Khrushchev came under attack from hard-liners who thought him too soft in general and could not forgive what they saw as his mismanagement of the 1962 Cuban crisis. He also pursued dubious economic policies and harebrained schemes. Finally in October the next year, he was deposed by a group led by the colorless Leonid Brezhnev, who held on to power for eighteen long years until he died in 1982. The only person he wanted to rehabilitate was Stalin, and indeed the fallen leader officially came back into fashion for a time.

In sum, after Stalin died, the course that the Soviet Union would take for almost forty years was firmly in place. Soviet leaders and ruling elites continued to articulate their position very much along the lines he set, until the entire edifice of the once-mighty Red Empire came crashing down.[17]

THE SOCIAL COSTS OF STALINISM

The brilliant future promised by Communism, for which generations struggled and sacrificed, failed to appear. How big a price did the Soviet people and those in the satellites pay for the social experiment that was conducted with them and at their expense? In terms of the loss of life through repression and execution, impossibly high numbers have been given. However, Alexander Yakovlev, chair of Russia's Presidential Commission in charge of looking into the matter, took a more sober approach. In his report given in February 2000, he concluded that the deaths that resulted inside the USSR were "comparable to the losses suffered during the Great Patriotic War." That would put them in the range of 25 million, a staggering figure.[18]

According to Yakovlev, Lenin and Stalin had, in effect, led a war against their own people that was as destructive of human life as the Second World War. It should be noted that those like Yakovlev, who calculated the figures, had dutifully served in the war and once had believed in the faith. He had been a member of the party since 1943, became head of its propaganda department in 1969, and was made secretary of the Central Committee in 1986. The following year, he joined the Politburo, and as a Gorbachev supporter, he helped lead the reform movement until the Soviet Union collapsed in 1991. Today an organization he founded makes available to scholars a wide range of formerly classified documents, many of them used in this study.

It is impossible to calculate what 20 or 25 million people might have accomplished, but we can provide at least some measurement of the impact of the experiment in socialism on the economy. One way is to use the statistics of the Organization for Economic Co-operation and Development in Paris. Angus N. Maddison, one of its economists, calculated the gross domestic product (GDP), or the value of everything a country produces in a year, and then divided that figure by the total population to get the GDP per capita, which is a reasonable measure of "economic prosperity." Stalin himself insisted that the GDP was the ultimate test for any economy.

Finding all the numbers going back into the past is not as easy as it sounds because many governments misreported so much. With all due caution, however, using Maddison's figures, we can trace increases and decreases in prosperity over time and compare and contrast nations.

Thus tsarist Russia on the eve of the First World War was the poorest of the advanced countries in Europe, measured in terms of GDP per capita. However, it was rich compared to the rest of the world. The tragedy of Soviet history is that no matter what the Kremlin did, regardless of how grand its plans and how many people it sacrificed to fulfill them, the USSR was unable to match Western European prosperity levels over the entire period from the Russian Revolution up to 1989. The gap between the USSR and the so-called European offshoots—the United States, Canada, Australia, and New Zealand—widened yearly from 1917 until 1940, and thereafter the gap increased even more rapidly.[19]

Even though the Soviet Union eventually attained reasonable growth rates after the Second World War, the countries that lost the war did better. For example, Japan was less prosperous than Russia in 1913, and yet by 1970 the Asian giant had recovered and moved ahead of the USSR, and by 1989 its GDP per capita was 2.5 times larger. Postwar Western Europe, including war-ravaged Germany, easily outpaced the Soviet Union and by 1989 was further ahead of it than Japan.

Stalin's disciples in other countries—either on his orders or their own initiative—led crusades that were nearly as destructive as his. Each of those lands is coming to grips with the past and all the victims, as well as trying to build for a better future.[20] The economies of Eastern Europe have been slow to recover since 1990, and with the notable exception of Poland and Hungary, the GDP per capita in all of them actually fell during their first years of freedom.[21]

More recently attempts have been made to assess the elusive "quality of life" in the nations of the world. One effort, published in 2005, included nine variables in the calculation, such as each country's measurable health (calculated by life expectancy in years), its family life (by looking at divorce rates), and so on, to quantify community life, climate, job security, political freedom, political stability and security, and gender equality. The numbers were then tallied up.

The resulting rankings varied when compared to the calculation of GDP per capita. The United States, for example, came in second for its GDP per capita but fell to thirteenth on the quality of life scale; the U.K. placed thirteenth in "prosperity" but dropped to twenty-ninth for its quality of life. Nearly all the top thirty quality of life slots were Western European countries or European offshoots like Australia, New Zealand, the United States, and Canada. The only former Communist country to make it into this select group was Slovenia (at number twenty-seven). Although in 2005 Russia's GDP per capita ranked fifty-fifth, its quality of life plunged to 105; Belarus ended up at 100; and Ukraine at 98. These results were only slightly better than some of the worst-off third-world countries. Of all the former Soviet satellites, the only ones in the top fifty on the quality of life scale were the Czech Republic (at 34); Hungary (at 37); Slovakia (at 45); and Poland (at 48). This is not to say that everything is just fine in the United States, the United Kingdom, or Western Europe, because we can find ample data to show that too many people in those countries do not enjoy a decent quality of life.[22]

From beginning to end, all the Communist countries suffered from a deficit of legitimacy, because the great majority of their populations faced enduring scarcities and limited opportunities. Official attempts to compensate by propaganda rituals and refurbishing the official ideology "ran up against cognitive dissonance, the gap between promise and reality."[23] The trade-off between accepting restrictions on basic freedoms and political rights, in return for the state provision of material benefits, began to fail so badly that most people grew demoralized and others disobedient. The economies of all the Communist countries did not completely fail, but to the very end, they never created a modern consumer-oriented market.[24]

When the Communist systems finally collapsed, great expectations arose that the self-liberated countries would introduce liberal democracy. It turns out that political cultures, authoritarian traditions, and command economies do not change as quickly as regimes. In several former Soviet republics, as well as in Russia, many long for another Stalin, and periodically his image is refurbished. Vladimir Putin, the former and now again president of the Russian Federation, embodies the ambivalent feelings of his country toward its Stalinist past. On the one hand, he has been hard on the political opposition and made a farce out of freedom of the press, but on the other hand, in 2007 he visited a former NKVD killing field near Moscow, then met with Alexander Solzhenitsyn, regarded by many as an icon of the Soviet victims. When the famed author died the next year, the Putin government remarkably made *The Gulag Archipelago* "mandatory reading" in schools. On top of that, in 2010 Prime Minister Putin invited his Polish counterpart to commemorate the Polish officers murdered at Katyń, the symbol of Stalinist crimes against foreign countries.[25]

The struggle between the anti-Stalinists and the Stalinists is still going on in Russia and, to a greater or lesser extent, also in the former Soviet Union and its satellite countries. Given the trends in the world, the anti-Stalinists will most likely prevail. We need to keep in mind that it took the Soviet Union three-quarters of a century or so to dig itself into a hole, and with varying amounts of coercion and encouragement from Moscow, other nations followed the Red flag into the abyss. It is going to take time to get out of it. Even now there are signs that the worst may be behind them and grounds for hope that they will ultimately triumph over Stalin's curse.

Acknowledgments

I began research for this book with the generous support of the Alexander von Humboldt–Foundation. At that time I was serving as the Strassler Professor in Holocaust History at Clark University. My present academic home at Florida State University has provided a congenial research environment, and I am thankful for the encouragement offered by Joe Travis and Joe McElrath and by my colleagues in the history department. I have benefited immensely from exchanges with many of the students I have met here and elsewhere.

Norman Naimark and Paul Gregory invited me to one of their summer research workshops at Stanford's Hoover Institution, dealing with recently released documents from the Russian archives. The experience, including the seminars and discussions with international colleagues, was especially helpful. Jonathan Brent answered questions and led me to Yale University Press's Stalin Digital Archive. Also invaluable is the virtual archive of the Cold War International History Project in Washington. In Russia the Alexander Yakovlev archive makes tens of thousands of documents available online. Many Russian sites offer online the entire works of nearly all the major figures, such as Lenin http://politazbuka.ru/biblioteka/marksizm/562-lenin-vladimir-polnoe -sobranie-sochineniy-5-izdanie.html and the sixteen volumes of Stalin's collected works: http://grachev62.narod.ru/stalin/t1/cont_1.htm.

Special thanks go to Andrew Wylie and James Pullen, to my editors Andrew Miller and Matthew Cotton, and to the four anonymous referees who made excellent suggestions for improving the book. I am extremely grateful to Erik van Ree and Mark Harrison, who were unfailing in their generosity in answering questions and providing certain documents. Many others gave advice, answered questions, or helped me in other ways at various stages of the project. These include Jörg Baberowski, Amir Weiner, Robert Service, Lynne Viola, Paul Hagenloh, David Shearer, Jeffrey Burds, Michael Ellman, Peter Krafft, Timothy Colton, Steven Wheatcroft, Tanja Penter, Simon Sebag Montefiore, Vladimir Tismăneanu, Jan Behrends, Yuri Slezkine, Donald Rayfield, Chen Jian, Simon Ertz, Orlando Figes, Robert Argenbright, Yoram Gorlizki, Ingo Haar, and Dieter Pohl.

Words cannot convey my deepest gratitude to Marie Fleming, to whom I dedicate the book. Without her encouragement and her moral and intellectual support at every turn, the book would never have been completed.

Abbreviations in Notes

APRF	Arkhiv Presidenta Rossiiskoi Federatsii (Archive of the President of the Russian Federation)
AVPRF	Arkhiv Vneshnei Politiki Rossiiskoi Federatsii (Foreign Policy Archive of the Russian Federation), Moscow
BAB	Bundesarchiv Berlin (German Federal Archives)
CWIHP	Cold War International History Project, Washington, D.C.
DGFP	*Documents on German Foreign Policy, 1918–1945, Series D* (Washington, D.C.)
DRZW	*Das Deutsche Reich und der Zweite Weltkrieg* (Stuttgart, 1979ff.)
FRUS	*Foreign Relations of the United States* (Washington, D.C.)
GARF	Gosudarstvennyi Arkhiv Rossiiskoi Federatsii (State Archives of the Russian Federation), Moscow
HIA	Hoover Institution Archives, Stanford, California
HP	Harvard Project on the Soviet Social System, Russian Research Center, Cambridge, Mass.

Lenin, *Polnoe sobranie sochinenii*	V. I. Lenin, *Polnoe Sobranie Sochinenii* (Moscow, 1959ff.), the complete collected works in Russian
NA	U.S. National Archives, Washington, D.C.
PRO	Public Record Office, London
RGASPI	Rossiiskii gosudarvstvennyi arkhiv sotsialno-politicheskoi istorii (Russian State Archive of Social and Political History), Moscow
SDFP	*Soviet Documents on Foreign Policy,* ed. Jane Degras (New York, 1978)
Stalin Correspondence	*Correspondence Between the Chairman of the Council of Ministers of the USSR and the Presidents of the USA and the Prime Ministers of Great Britain During the Great Patriotic War* (Moscow, 1957)
Stalin, *Sochineniia*	J. V. Stalin, *Sochineniia* (Moscow, 1952ff.), the complete collected works in Russian

Notes

Note on Russian dates used in the text: Prior to February 1918, Russia used the Julian calendar (or "Old Style"), which was twelve days behind the Western calendar in the nineteenth century and thirteen days behind it in the twentieth century. January 31, 1918, was the last day of the Julian calendar in Russia, with the next day becoming February 14.

INTRODUCTION

1. Speech, Jan. 28, 1924, in Stalin, *Sochineniia*, 6:53. It was issued illegally in Siberia in June 1903 and published in 1904. Lenin, *Polnoe sobranie sochinenii*, 7:5–25.

2. The classic study, analyzing all the evidence, is Simon Sebag Montefiore, *Young Stalin* (New York, 2007), 90–91, 113, 151, 163, 210–11.

3. See Erik van Ree, "Reluctant Terrorists? Transcaucasian Social-Democracy, 1901–1908," *Europe-Asia Studies* (2008), 127–54.

4. Donald Rayfield, *Stalin and His Hangmen: The Tyrant and Those Who Killed for Him* (New York, 2004), 44.

5. K. E. Voroshilov, *Stalin i krasnaya armiya* (Moscow, 1939), 11–12, cites the account of an "enemy," Colonel Nosovich, *Donskaia volna* (Feb. 3, 1919); V. L. Goncharov, *Vozvyshenie Stalina: oborona Tsaritsyna* (Moscow, 2010).

6. Jörg Baberowski, *Verbrannte Erde: Stalins Herrschaft der Gewalt* (Munich, 2012), 15–16, 29, 109, 131, 307.

7. Maurice Meisner, *Mao's China and After: A History of the People's Republic*, 3rd ed. (New York, 1999), 103; more generally see Vladimir Tismaneanu, *The Devil in History: Communism, Fascism, and Some Lessons of the Twentieth Century* (Berkeley, Calif., 2012).

8. For his speech to the Third International, Mar. 6, 1919, see Lenin, *Polnoe sobranie sochinenii*, 37:515–20; for the national revolutions, see Geoffrey Hosking, *The Russians in the Soviet Union* (Cambridge, Mass., 2006), 70–89; Robert Service, *Russia: Experiment with a People* (Cambridge, Mass., 2003), 30–44.

9. Quoted in Erik van Ree, *The Political Thought of Joseph Stalin: A Study in Twentieth-Century Revolutionary Patriotism* (New York, 2002), 209.

10. Kennan to Secretary of State, Feb. 22, 1946, in *FRUS, 1946, Eastern Europe; the Soviet Union*, 6:696–709; reprinted as X, "The Sources of Soviet Conduct," *Foreign Affairs* (July 1947), 566–82. For a recent reiteration of Stalin as heir to the tsars, see Marc Trachtenberg, *A Constructed Peace: The Making of the European Settlement* (Princeton, N.J., 1999), 19.

11. Peter Novick, *That Noble Dream: The "Objectivity Question" and the American Historical Association* (Chicago, 1988), 445–57.

12. See the instructive Louis Menand, "Getting Real: George F. Kennan's Cold War," *New Yorker* (Nov. 14, 2011), 76–83.

13. HIA, Russian Subject Collection, Box 13, Folder 11.

14. See Jan Plamper, *The Stalin Cult: A Study in the Alchemy of Power* (New Haven, Conn., 2012), 29–74.

15. See William A. Williams, *The Tragedy of American Diplomacy* (New York, 1959), 206–7. For more recent variations, see Walter LaFeber, *America, Russia, and the Cold War, 1945–2002*, 9th ed. (Boston, 2002), 22; and Campbell Craig and Sergey Radchenko, *The Atomic Bomb and the Origins of the Cold War* (New Haven, Conn., 2008), xv.

16. Wilfred Loth, *The Division of the World, 1941–1955* (New York, 1988), 306–7.

17. See Geoffrey Roberts, *Stalin's Wars: From World War to Cold War, 1939–1953* (New Haven, Conn., 2006), 253. For the same argument, see Loth, *Division of the World*, 171, 308.

18. See Vladislav Zubok and Constantine Pleshakov, *Inside the Kremlin's Cold War: From Stalin to Khrushchev* (Cambridge, Mass., 1996); and Vladislav M. Zubok, *A Failed Empire: The Soviet Union in the Cold War from Stalin to Gorbachev* (Chapel Hill, N.C., 2007).

19. Charles E. Bohlen, *Witness to History, 1929–1969* (New York, 1973), 210.

20. Field-Marshal Sir Alan Brooke, quoted in David Dilks, ed., *The Diaries of Sir Alexander Cadogan, 1938–1945* (New York, 1972), 582.

21. Robert A. Nisbet, *Roosevelt and Stalin: The Failed Courtship* (Washington, D.C, 1988). For a magisterial survey, see Jonathan Haslam, *Russia's Cold War: From the October Revolution to the Fall of the Wall* (New Haven, Conn., 2011).

22. David Reynolds, *In Command of History: Churchill Fighting and Writing the Second World War* (London, 2004), 486.

23. Odd Arne Westad, *The Global Cold War: Third World Interventions and the Making of Our Times* (New York, 2005), 48.

24. Jörg Baberowski and Anselm Doering-Manteuffel, "The Quest for Order and the Pursuit of Terror: National Socialist Germany and the Stalinist Soviet Union as Multiethnic Empires," in Michael Geyer and Sheila Fitzpatrick, eds., *Beyond Totalitarianism: Stalinism and Nazism Compared* (New York, 2009), 204.

25. Ronald Grigor Suny and Terry Martin, eds., *A State of Nations: Empire and Nation-Making in the Age of Lenin and Stalin* (New York, 2001), 8; and Terry Martin, *The Affirmative Action Empire: Nations and Nationalism in the Soviet Union, 1923–1939* (Ithaca, N.Y., 2001). Also useful is Yuri Slezkine, "The USSR as a Communal Apartment, or How a Socialist State Promoted Ethnic Particularism," *Slavic Review* (1994), 414–52.

26. Maxim Gorky, *Untimely Thoughts: Essays on Revolution, Culture, and the Bolsheviks, 1917–1918* (New Haven, Conn., 1995).

27. Jan Gross, *Revolution from Abroad: The Soviet Conquest of Poland's Western Ukraine and Western Belorussia* (Princeton, N.J., 2002).

28. For a Russian perspective, see T. V. Volokitina et al., *Moskva i Vostochnaia Evropa: stanovlenie politicheskikh rezhimov sovetskogo tipa, 1949–1953: ocherki istorii* (Moscow, 2002), 1–30, and L. Y. Gibiansky, "Problemii Vostochnoi Evropii i nachalo formiprovania miprovania sovetskogo bloka," in N. I. Egorova and A. O. Chubarian, eds., *Kholodnaia voina, 1945–1963 gg.: Istoricheskaia retrospektiva. Sbornik statei* (Moscow, 2003), 104–31.

29. V. K. Volkov and L. Ia. Gibianskii, "Na poroge pervogo raskola v sotsialisticheskom lagere: Peregovori rykovodiashikh deiatelei SSSR, Bolgarii i Iogoslavii 1948 r.," *Istoricheskii arkhiv* (1997), 92–123.

30. Balázs Apor, Péter Apor, and E. A. Rees, eds., *The Sovietization of Eastern Europe: New Perspectives on the Postwar Period* (Washington, D.C., 2008).

31. John Lewis Gaddis, *We Now Know: Rethinking Cold War History* (New York, 1997), 33.

32. See, e.g., Moscow meeting, Jan. 9–12, 1951, in N. I. Egorova, "Voenno-politicheskaya integratsia stran Zapada i reaktsiya SSSR (1947–1953)," in Egorova and Chubarian, *Kholodnaia voina*, 200–2.

33. Gaddis, *We Now Know*, 281–95.

34. For an overview, see Caroline Kennedy-Pope, *The Origins of the Cold War* (London, 2007).

35. Roberts, *Stalin's Wars*, xii.

36. V. F. Zima, *Golod v SSSR 1946–1947 godov: Proiskhozdenie i posledstviia* (Moscow, 1996), 179.

37. See the evidence cited in Tony Judt, *Postwar: A History of Europe Since 1945* (New York, 2005), 89.

38. Timothy Snyder, *Bloodlands: Europe Between Hitler and Stalin* (New York, 2010), and Norman M. Naimark, *Stalin's Genocides* (Princeton, N.J., 2010).

39. The best recent biographies are Simon Sebag Montefiore, *Stalin: The Court of the Red Tsar* (New York, 2004); Robert Service, *Stalin: A Biography* (London, 2004); and Hiroaki Kuromiya, *Stalin* (New York, 2005). The classic Russian account is Dmitri Volkogonov, *Triumf i tragediya. Politichesky portret J. V. Stalina*, 2 vols. (Moscow, 1989).

40. Valentin M. Berezhkov, *Kak ya stal perevodchikom Stalin* (Moscow, 1993), 312.

41. Anthony Eden, *The Reckoning: The Memoirs of Anthony Eden, Earl of Avon* (Boston, 1965), 595. For a similar view, see W. Averell Harriman and Elie Abel, *Special Envoy to Churchill and Stalin, 1941–1946* (New York, 1975), 536.

42. Vladimir Tismăneanu, "Diabolical Pedagogy and the (Il)logic of Stalinism in Eastern Europe," in Vladimir Tismăneanu, ed., *Stalinism Revisited: The Establishment of Communist Regimes in East-Central Europe* (New York, 2009), 46.

43. Alexander Yakovlev, *The Fate of Marxism in Russia* (New Haven, Conn., 1993), 191–92.

44. For an interesting perspective, see Stephen Kotkin, *Uncivil Society: 1989 and the Implosion of the Communist Establishment* (New York, 2009).

CHAPTER I. MAKING THE STALINIST REVOLUTION

1. Lenin, *Polnoe sobranie sochinenii*, 45:343–48.

2. For an insider's account, see Boris Bazhanov, *Vospominaniia byvshevgo sekretaria Stalina* (Paris, 1980), chaps. 2 and 3.

3. Robert Service, *Trotsky: A Biography* (Cambridge, Mass., 2009), 307–12.

4. Ibid., 326–27.

5. Stephen F. Cohen, *Bukharin and the Bolshevik Revolution: A Political Biography, 1888–1938* (New York, 1974), 228.

6. Mark Harrison, "Why Did NEP Fail?," *Economics of Planning* (1980), 57–67; Paul R. Gregory, *The Political Economy of Stalinism: Evidence from the Soviet Secret Archives* (New York, 2004), 29.

7. Erik van Ree, "Socialism in One Country Before Stalin: German Origins," *Journal of Political Ideologies* (2010), 143–59.

8. Letter, Jan. 25, 1925, in Stalin, *Sochineniia*, 7:15–18.

9. *XIV sezd vsesoiuznoi kommunisticheskoi partii (b). 18–31 dekabria 1925 g.: stenograficheskii otchet* (Moscow, 1926), 55.

10. Stalin speeches, Jan. 1928, in Stalin, *Sochineniia*, 11:1–9.

11. For the reports, see Lynne Viola et al., eds., *The War Against the Peasantry, 1927–1930: The Tragedy of the Soviet Countryside* (New Haven, Conn., 2005), 69–75.

12. Speech, Plenum of the CPSU, July 9, 1928, in Stalin, *Sochineniia*, 11:158–59.

13. Robert V. Daniels, ed., *A Documentary History of Communism in Russia: From Lenin to Gorbachev* (Hanover, N.H., 1993), 139–41.

14. CC plenum, Apr. 16–23, 1929, in Stalin, *Sochineniia*, 12:31–38.

15. Bukharin at Apr. 1929 plenum, quoted in Anna Larina, *This I Cannot Forget: The Memoirs of Nikolai Bukharin's Widow* (New York, 1994), 290.

16. Alec Nove, *An Economic History of the USSR*, rev. ed. (London, 1990), 137.

17. Stalin to Molotov, Aug. 10, 1929, in *Pisma I. V. Stalina V.M. Molotovu, 1925–1936 gg.: Sbornik dokumentov* (Moscow, 1995), 141–43.

18. Jörg Baberowski, *Der Rote Terror: Die Geschichte des Stalinismus* (Munich, 2003), 58–61.

19. Stalin, *Sochineniia*, 12:118–35.

20. Moshe Lewin, *Russian Peasants and Soviet Power: A Study of Collectivization* (New York, 1968), 241.

21. Viola et al., *War Against the Peasantry*, 367–69.

22. Stalin, *Sochineniia*, 12:166–67.

23. Politburo decree, Jan. 30, 1930, in Viola et al., *War Against the Peasantry*, 228–34.

24. Yagoda memorandum, Jan. 24, 1930, ibid., 237–38.

25. Orlando Figes, *The Whisperers: Private Life in Stalin's Russia* (London, 2007), 86–87.

26. Nicolas Werth, *Cannibal Island: Death in a Siberian Gulag* (Princeton, N.J., 2007).

27. Lynne Viola, *The Unknown Gulag: The Lost World of Stalin's Special Settlements* (New York, 2007), 196, table 2.

28. Oleg W. Chlewnjuk (a.k.a. Oleg V. Khlevnyuk), *Das Politbüro: Mechanismen der Macht in der Sowjetunion der dreissiger Jahre* (Hamburg, 1998), 84–90.

29. Stalin to Kaganovich, June 18, 1932, in O. V. Khlevniuk et al., eds., *Stalin i Kaganovich perepiska 1931–1936 gg.* (Moscow, 2001), 179–80.

30. Stalin to Kaganovich, July 25, 1932, ibid., 244–45.

31. GARF, f. 9474, op. 1, d. 76, l, 118; d. 83, l, 5; Law (Aug. 7, 1932).

32. Stalin to Kaganovich and Molotov, prior to July 24, 1932, in Khlevniuk et al., *Stalin i Kaganovich perepiska*, 240–41.

33. Stalin to Kaganovich, ibid., 273–74.

34. Lev Kopelev, *The Education of a True Believer* (New York, 1980), 235.

35. Nicolas Werth, "The Great Ukrainian Famine of 1932-33," Online Encyclopedia of Mass Violence, http://www.massviolence.org/The-1932-1933-Great-Famine-in-Ukraine.

36. Terry Martin, *The Affirmative Action Empire: Nations and Nationalism in the Soviet Union, 1923–1939* (Ithaca, N.Y., 2001), 9–10; Jörg Baberowski, *Der Feind ist überall: Stalinismus im Kaukasus* (Munich, 2003), 184–214.

37. Martin, *Affirmative Action Empire*, 302–8.

38. Jörg Baberowski and Anselm Doering-Manteuffel, "The Quest for Order and the Pursuit of Terror: National Socialist Germany and the Stalinist Soviet Union as Multiethnic Empires," in Michael Geyer and Sheila Fitzpatrick, eds., *Beyond Totalitarianism: Stalinism and Nazism Compared* (New York, 2009), 209–12.

39. Stalin, *Sochineniia*, 13:161–215.

40. Sheila Fitzpatrick, *Stalin's Peasants: Resistance and Survival in the Russian Village After Collectivization* (New York, 1994), 82.

41. Paul Hagenloh, *Stalin's Police: Public Order and Mass Repression in the USSR, 1926–1941* (Baltimore, 2009), 131; David R. Shearer, *Policing Stalin's Socialism: Repression and Social Order in the Soviet Union, 1924–1953* (New Haven, Conn., 2009), 21, 192–200, 256; and Gijs Kessler, "The Passport System and State Control over Population Flows in the Soviet Union, 1932–1940," in *Cahiers du Monde russe* (Apr.–Dec. 2001), 483–84.

42. Letter from Stalingrad regional party secretary, Feb. 16, 1933, APRF, f. 3, op. 30, d. 189, l. 34.

43. R. W. Davies and Stephen G. Wheatcroft, *The Years of Hunger: Soviet Agriculture, 1931–1933* (New York, 2004), 411.

44. R. W. Davies, "Making Economic Policy," in Paul R. Gregory, ed., *Behind the Facade of Stalin's Command Economy: Evidence from the Soviet State and Party Archives* (Stanford, Calif., 2001), 70–71.

45. In 1929 the USSR exported 178 million tons; in 1930, the figure jumped to 4,764 million; and in 1931, to 5,056 million. See R. W. Davies, Mark Harrison, and S. G. Wheatcroft, eds., *The Economic Transformation of the Soviet Union, 1913–1945* (Cambridge, Mass., 1994), 316, table 48.

46. Figures are from Stephen Wheatcroft, "More Light on the Scale of Repression and Excess Mortality in the Soviet Union in the 1930s," in J. Arch Getty and Roberta T. Manning, eds., *Stalinist Terror: New Perspectives* (New York, 1993), 283, table 14.2. Robert Conquest, *Harvest of Sorrow: Soviet Collectivization and the Terror-Famine* (New York, 1986), suggests that five million died in Ukraine, not four million (306). See also Nicolas Werth, "A State Against Its People: Violence, Repression, and Terror in the Soviet Union," in Stéphane Courtois et al., *The Black Book of Communism* (Cambridge, Mass., 1999), 167.

47. Stalin to Kaganovich, Aug. 27, 1933, in *Stalin i Kaganovich perepiska*, 315–16; also K. E. Voroshilov to A. S. Yenukidze, Aug. 27, 1933, in A. V. Kvashonkin, et al., eds., *Sovetskoe rukovodstvo: Perepiska 1928–1941 g.* (Moscow, 1999), 249–52.

48. Norman M. Naimark, *Stalin's Genocides* (Princeton, N.J., 2010), 70–79; and Timothy Snyder, *Bloodlands: Europe Between Hitler and Stalin* (New York, 2010), 42–46. See also Halyna Hryn, ed., *Hunger by Design: The Great Ukrainian Famine and Its Soviet Context* (Cambridge, Mass., 2008). For a critique, see Yana Pitner, "Mass Murder or Massive Incompetence," *H-Russia* (Oct. 2010), http://www.h-net.org/reviews/showrev.php?id=30622.

49. Letter to Stalin, Jan. 28, 1931, and his response, Feb. 1, 1931, APRF, f. 3, op. 40, d. 77, l. 24–26. See the documentary record provided by V. V. Kondrashin, ed., *Golod v SSSR: 1929–1934* (Moscow, 2011–12), 2 vols.

50. Stalin-Molotov letter to First Secretary Middle Volga, Nov. 28, 1931, APRF, f. 3, op. 40, d. 79, l. 150.

51. Stalin, *Sochineniia*, 13:177–88.

52. The classic study is Stephen Kotkin, *Magnetic Mountain: Stalinism as a Civilization* (Berkeley, Calif., 1995).

53. Hiroaki Kuromiya, *Freedom and Terror in the Donbas: A Ukrainian-Russian Borderland, 1870s–1990s* (Cambridge, U.K., 1998), 119–50; and Arkady Vaksberg, *Stalin's Prosecutor: The Life of Andrei Vyshinsky* (New York, 1990), 42–45.

54. Doc. 3 in N. V. Petrov, ed., *Istoriia stalinskogo Gulaga* (Moscow, 2004), 2:58–59; Oleg V. Khlevniuk, *The History of the Gulag: From Collectivization to the Great Terror* (New Haven, Conn., 2004), 9–12.

55. Doc. 32 in A. B. Bezborodov and V. M. Khrustalev, eds., *Istoria stalinskogo Gulaga* (Moscow, 2004), 4:110; V. N. Zemskov, "GULAG (Istoriko-sotsiologicheskii aspekt)," *Sotsiologicheskii issledovaniya* (1991), no. 6, 10–27; no. 7, 3–16.

56. Doc. 211 in T. V. Tsarevskaia-Diakina, ed., *Istoria stalinskogo Gulaga* (Moscow, 2004), 5:707–8.

57. Larina, *This I Cannot Forget*, 133–47; Robert Service, *Stalin: A Biography* (London, 2004), 288–98; Simon Sebag Montefiore, *Stalin: The Court of the Red Tsar* (New York, 2004), 5–22.

58. Svetlana Alliluyeva, *Dvadtsat pisem k drugu* (New York, 1967), 116–34.

59. See the exhaustive archival research by Matthew E. Lenoe, *The Kirov Murder and Soviet History* (New Haven, Conn., 2010), 128, 141, 611.

60. J. Arch Getty and Oleg V. Naumov, *Yezhov: The Rise of Stalin's "Iron Fist"* (New Haven, Conn., 2008), 139.

61. J. Arch Getty and Oleg V. Naumov, eds., *The Road to Terror: Stalin and the Self-Destruction of the Bolsheviks, 1932–1939* (New Haven, Conn., 1999), 198, also n3.

62. Marc Jansen and Nikita Petrov, *Stalin's Loyal Executioner: People's Commissar Nikolai Ezhov* (Stanford, Calif., 2002), 46; Stalin to Kaganovich, Aug. 23, 1936, in Khlevniuk et al., eds., *Stalin i Kaganovich perepiska*, 642–43.

63. Larina, *This I Cannot Forget*, 283.

64. Stalin and Zhdanov to Kaganovich, Molotov, and Politburo, Sept. 25, 1936, in Khlevniuk et al., eds., *Stalin i Kaganovich perepiska*, 682–83; Getty and Naumov, *Stalin's Iron Fist*, 204; Jansen and Petrov, *Stalin's Loyal Executioner*, 57.

65. Indictment, Jan. 5, 1937, APRF, f. 3, op. 24, d. 269, l. 38–58.

66. Instructions, Jan. 22, 1937, APRF, f. 3, op. 24, d. 274, l. 72–74. See also Donald Rayfield, *Stalin and His Hangmen: The Tyrant and Those Who Killed for Him* (New York, 2004), 279, 315–20; and William Chase, "Stalin as Producer: The Moscow Show Trials and the Production of Mortal Threats," in Sarah Davies and James Harris, eds., *Stalin: A New History* (Cambridge, Mass., 2005), 226–48.

67. Karl Schlögel, *Terror und Traum: Moskau 1937* (Frankfurt am Main, 2010), 239–66.

68. Larina, *This I Cannot Forget*, 127.

69. Ibid., 313–16.

70. Schlögel, *Terror und Traum*, 258–59; transcripts in Getty and Naumov, *Road to Terror*, 364–419.

CHAPTER 2. EXTERMINATING INTERNAL THREATS TO SOCIALIST UNITY

1. Stalin's remarks, Nov. 7, 1937, in Georgi Dimitrov, *Dnevnik: mart 1933—fevruari 1949: izbrano* (Sofia, 2003), 60–62.

2. See Oleg W. Chlewnjuk (a.k.a. Oleg V. Khlevnyuk), *Das Politbüro: Mechanismen der Macht in der Sowjetunion der dreissiger Jahre* (Hamburg, 1998), 246–69. For emphasis on Stalin as a "degenerative psychotic," see Donald Rayfield, *Stalin and His Hangmen: The Tyrant and Those Who Killed for Him* (New York, 2004), 293–339.

3. Lev Kopelev, *To Be Preserved Forever* (New York, 1977), 92.

4. Victor A. Kravchenko, *I Chose Freedom* (1946; New Brunswick, N.J., 2002), 282.

5. Joseph Davies, *Mission to Moscow* (New York, 1941), 269–70; Stephen F. Cohen, *Bukharin and the Bolshevik Revolution: A Political Biography, 1888–1938* (New York, 1974), 374–81.

6. Speech, Jan. 7, 1933, in Stalin, *Sochineniia*, 13:210–11; speech, Mar. 3, 1937, ibid., 14:161.

7. APRF, f. 3, op. 58, d. 6, l. 30–31.

8. For Stalin's initiating order, see doc. 163 in J. Arch Getty and Oleg V. Naumov, eds., *The Road to Terror: Stalin and the Self-Destruction of the Bolsheviks, 1932–1939* (New Haven, Conn., 1999), 457. The records, including the Vyshinsky report, Dec. 17, analyzed in Nicolas Werth, "Les 'petits procès exemplaires' en URSS durant la Grande Terreur (1937–1938)," *Vingtième Siècle. Revue d'histoire*, No. 86 (Apr.–June, 2005), 5–23.

9. William Taubman, *Khrushchev, the Man and His Era* (New York, 2003), 99–122. Robert C. Tucker, *Stalin in Power: The Revolution from Above, 1928–1941* (New York, 1990), 528.

10. Order, Sept. 13, 1937, APRF, f. 3, op. 24, d. 321, l. 68–69, See Jörg Baberowski, *Der Rote Terror: Die Geschichte des Stalinismus* (Munich, 2003), 135–208.

11. Evan Mawdsley and Stephen White, *The Soviet Elite from Lenin to Gorbachev: The Central Committee and Its Members, 1917–1991* (Oxford, U.K., 2000), 74–76.

12. Beria to Stalin, Oct. 30, 1937, APRF, f. 3, op. 58, d. 212, l. 137–39.

13. Anna Larina, *This I Cannot Forget: The Memoirs of Nikolai Bukharin's Widow* (New York, 1994), 198.

14. Stalin to Molotov, Oct. 23, 1930, in L. Kosheleva, et al., eds., *Pisma J. V. Stalina V.M. Molotovu, 1925–1936 gg. Sbornik dokumentov* (Moscow, 1995), 231.

15. That was the conclusion of KGB insider Pavel Sudoplatov and Anatoli Sudoplatov in *Special Tasks: The Memoirs of an Unwanted Witness—A Soviet Spymaster* (New York, 1994), chap. 5.

16. Vladimir Z. Rogovin, *1937* (Moscow, 1996), 344–51.

17. Speech, RGASPI, f. 558, op. 11, d. 1120, l. 28–57; Simon Sebag Montefiore, *Stalin: The Court of the Red Tsar* (New York, 2004), 222–25.

18. Dmitri Volkogonov, *Triumf i tragediya. Politichesky portret J. V. Stalina* (Moscow, 1989), 1:2:276–77.

19. Marc Jansen and Nikita Petrov, *Stalin's Loyal Executioner: People's Commissar Nikolai Ezhov* (Stanford, Calif., 2002), 70; Sebag Montefiore, *Stalin*, 225–27; David M. Glantz, *Stumbling Colossus: The Red Army on the Eve of World War* (Lawrence, Kansas, 1998), 30–31.

20. Note, June 19, 1937, APRF, f. 3, op. 24, d. 309, l. 131–31.

21. Special report Beria and Yezhov, Oct. 14, 1938, APRF, f. 3, op. 24, d. 366, l. 78–79.

22. RGASPI, f. 17, op. 2, d. 514, l. 14–17; Stalin, *Sochineniia*, 13:207, 210 (Jan. 7, 1933).

23. Jan. 7, 1933, in Stalin, *Sochineniia*, 13:207, 210.

24. For a quantitative study tracing the effects, see Evgenii V. Kodin, *Repressirovannaia rossiiskaia provintsiia: Smolenshchina, 1917–1955 gg.* (Moscow, 2011), 8–31.

25. APRF, f. 3, op. 58, d. 212, l. 55–78; also V. P. Danilov, R. T. Manning, and L. Viola, eds., *Tragediia Sovetskoi derevni: Kollektivizatsiia i raskulachivanie: Dokumeny i materialy* (Moscow, 1999–2006), 5:1:319.

26. Doc. 58 in S. V. Mironenko and N. Werth, eds., *Istoriia stalinskogo Gulaga* (Moscow, 2004), 1:268–75.

27. Doc. 24 in Richard Pipes, ed., *The Unknown Lenin: From the Secret Archive* (New Haven, Conn., 1996), 50.

28. Rolf Binner and Marc Junge, "Wie der Terror 'Gross' wurde: Massenmord und Lagerhaft nach Befehl 00447," in *Cahiers du Monde Russe* (2001), 557–614; and by the same authors, *Kak Terror stal bolshim: Sekretnyi prikaz Nr. 00447 i tekhnologiia ego ispolneniia* (Moscow, 2003).

29. Doc. 7, April 23, 1932, and doc. 9, May 7, in Andrei Artizov and Oleg Naumov, eds., *Vlast i khudozhestvennaia intelligentsia: Dokumenty TsK RKP(b)-VKP(b), VChK-OGPU-NKVD o kulturnoi politike, 1917–1953* (Moscow, 1953), 172–76.

30. Golfo Alexopoulos, *Stalin's Outcasts: Aliens, Citizens, and the Soviet State, 1926–1936* (Ithaca, N.Y., 2003).

31. Chlewnjuk (a.k.a. Khlevnyuk), *Das Politbüro*, 246–302.

32. Doc. 59 in Mironenko and Werth, eds., *Istoriia stalinskogo Gulaga*, 1:275–77.

33. Doc. 60, ibid., 277–81; Jansen and Petrov, *Stalin's Loyal Executioner*, 96–97.

34. Nikita Petrov and Arsenii Roginskii, "The 'Polish Operation' of the NKVD, 1937–8," in Barry McLoughlin and Kevin McDermott, eds., *Stalin's Terror: High Politics and Mass Repression in the Soviet Union* (New York, 2003), 168–69; Nicolas Werth, "The Mechanism of a Mass Crime: The Great Terror in the Soviet Union, 1937–1938," in Robert Gellately and Ben Kiernan, eds., *The Specter of Genocide: Mass Murder in Historical Perspective* (Cambridge, U.K., 2003), 237.

35. The Russian link to Stalin's "lists" is http://stalin.memo.ru/spiski/index.htm.

36. Jansen and Petrov, *Stalin's Loyal Executioner*, 99.

37. Ibid.; see also Terry Martin, *The Affirmative Action Empire: Nations and Nationalism in the Soviet Union, 1923–1939* (Ithaca, N.Y., 2001), 338.

38. Martin, *Affirmative Action Empire*, 333–34.
39. For individuals caught in the trap (docs. 47–66), see William J. Chase, ed., *Enemies Within the Gates: The Comintern and the Stalinist Repression, 1934–1939* (New Haven, Conn., 2001), 328–403.
40. Doc. 223 in Mironenko and Werth, *Istoriia stalinskogo Gulaga*, 1:609. See also Oleg V. Khlevniuk, *The History of the Gulag: From Collectivization to the Great Terror* (New Haven, Conn., 2004), 165–66. Nicolas Werth, "Les 'Opérations de Masse' de la 'Grande Terreur' en URSS (1937–1938)," *Bulletin de l'Institut d'histoire du temps présent* (2006), 6–167.
41. Dimitrov, *Dnevnik*, 60–61.
42. Meeting, Nov. 11, 1937, ibid., 165–66; emphasis in the original.
43. APRF, f. 3, op. 58, d. 6, l. 92–96.
44. Baberowski, *Der Rote Terror*, 174.
45. Feliks Ivanovich Chuev and Vyacheslav Molotov, *Sto sorok besed s Molotovym: iz dnevnika F. Chueva* (Moscow, 1991), 321, 416, 428.
46. Kaganovich interview, May 6, 1991, in Georgii A. Kumanev, *Govoriat stalinskie narkomy: Vstrechi, besedy, interviu, dokumenty* (Smolensk, 2005), 103–4; and Lazar M. Kaganovich, *Pamiatnye zapiski: Rabochego, kommunista-bolshevika, profsoiuznogo, partinogo i sovetsko-gosudarstvennogo rabotnika* (Moscow, 1996), 482–86.
47. Doc. 57 in Mironenko and Werth, *Istoriia stalinskogo Gulaga*, 1:267–68.
48. Werth, "Mechanism of a Mass Crime," 232, 235.
49. See the statistics in Vadim Z. Rogovin, *Partiia rasstreliannykh* (Moscow, 1997), 243–47.
50. Stephen G. Wheatcroft, "From Team-Stalin to Degenerate Tyranny," in E. A. Rees, ed., *The Nature of Stalin's Dictatorship: The Politburo, 1924–1953* (New York, 2004), 79–106.
51. Mother and son reunited in 1956 after a separation of nineteen years. Larina, *This I Cannot Forget*, 334.
52. Bukharin to Stalin, Dec. 10, 1937, in J. Arch Getty and Oleg V. Naumov, eds., *The Road to Terror: Stalin and the Self-Destruction of the Bolsheviks, 1932–1939* (New Haven, Conn., 1999), 556–60.

CHAPTER 3. WAR AND ILLUSIONS

1. Speech to Central Committee plenum, Jan. 19, 1925, in Stalin, *Sochineniia*, 7:14. See also Andreas Hillgruber, *Deutschlands Rolle in der Vorgeschichte der beiden Weltkriege*, 2nd ed. (Göttingen, 1979), 97.
2. Speech, Oct. 1, 1938, in N. N. Maslov, "I. V. Stalin o 'Kratkom kurse istorii VKP (b),' " *Istoricheskii arkhiv*, no. 5 (1995), 13.
3. Speech, Mar. 10, 1939, in Stalin, *Sochineniia*, vol. 14, 296–97.
4. *Izvestia*, June 1, 1939.
5. *Pravda*, June 29, 1939, in SDFP, 3:352–54.
6. Derek Watson, *Molotov: A Biography* (New York, 2005), 166–69.
7. Received in Moscow Aug. 15, see SDFP, 3:356–57; DGFP, Series D, 5:62–64.
8. RGASPI, f. 558, op. 11, d. 296, doc. 1 ff. Deal signed Aug. 19, in DGFP, Series D, vol. 5.
9. A Stalin speech, supposedly given to the Politburo on August 19 and revealing offensive intentions, was published in France at the end of November and turned up later in a special Moscow archive. Most Western historians insist it is a forgery. Osoby archive SSSR, f. 7, op. 1, d. 1223. See T. Bushueva, "Proklinaya—Poprobuite ponyat," *Novy Mir* 12 (1994), 232–33. A translation is printed in Albert L. Weeks, *Stalin's Other War: Soviet Grand Strategy, 1939–1941* (New York, 2002), 171–74. A vigorous refutation is S. Z. Sluch, " 'Rech' Stalina, kotoroi ne bylo," *Otchestvennaya Istoriya* (2004).

10. F. I. Firsov, "Arkhivy Kominterna i vneshniaia politika SSSR v 1939–1941 gg.," in *Novaia i noveishaiia istoriaiia* (6), 12–35; also diary entry for Jan. 21, 1940, in Georgi Dimitrov, *Dnevnik: mart 1933—fevruari 1949: izbrano* (Sofia, 2003), 84.

11. A. A. Kungurov, *Sekretnye protokoly ili kto poddelal pakt Molotova-Ribbentropa* (Moscow, 2009). AVPRF, f. 06, op. 1, l. 8, d. 77, l. 4, Sept. 28, 1939.

12. Mikhail I. Meltiukhov, *Upushchennyi shans Stalina: skhvatka za Evropu, 1939–1941 gg.: dokumenty, fakty, suzhdeniia* (Moscow, 2000), 79–82; Joachim von Ribbentrop, *Zwischen London und Moskau: Erinnerungen und letzte Aufzeichnungen* (Leoni am Starnberger See, 1953), 178–85; *DGFP*, Series D, 5:427–29.

13. Nikita S. Khrushchev, *Memoirs*, vol. 1, *Commissar* (University Park, Pa., 2004), 226.

14. Geoffrey Roberts, *The Soviet Union and the Origins of the Second World War: Russo-German Relations and the Road to War, 1933–1941* (London, 1995), 100.

15. Stalin's remarks in Dimitrov, *Dnevnik*, 79.

16. Quoted in Erik van Ree, *The Political Thought of Joseph Stalin: A Study in Twentieth-Century Revolutionary Patriotism* (New York, 2002), 227.

17. Docs. 228 and 229 in *DGFP*, 7:245–47.

18. Dimitrov, *Dnevnik*, 79–80

19. Docs. 103 to 107 in S. V. Mironenko and N. Werth, eds., *Istoriia stalinskogo Gulaga* (Moscow, 2004), 1:389–95; Norman Davies, *God's Playground: A History of Poland, 1795 to the Present* (Oxford, U.K., 1981), 2:448; David R. Marples, *Stalinism in Ukraine in the 1940s* (New York, 1992), 24–41.

20. See personal accounts in Tadeuz Piotrowski, ed., *The Polish Deportees of World War II: Recollections of Removal to the Soviet Union and Dispersal Throughout the World* (London, 2004).

21. Jan Gross, *Revolution from Abroad: The Soviet Conquest of Poland's Western Ukraine and Western Belorussia* (Princeton, N.J., 2002), 194. Timothy Snyder, *Bloodlands: Europe between Hitler and Stalin* (New York, 2010), 151.

22. Pavel Polian, *Ne po svoyey vole. Istoriya i geografiya prinuditel'nykh migratsii v SSSR* (Moscow, 2001), 98.

23. Gross, *Revolution from Abroad*, 229; Andrzej Paczkowski, "Poland, the 'Enemy Nation,' " in Stéphane Courtois et al., *The Black Book of Communism* (Cambridge, Mass., 1999), 372.

24. For background, see George Sanford, *Katyń and the Soviet Massacre of 1940: Truth, Justice and Memory* (New York, 2005), 35–62.

25. A. A. Chernobaev, ed., *Na prieme u Stalina: Tetradi (zhurnaly) zapisei lits, priniatykh I. V. Stalinym, 1924–1953* (Moscow, 2008), 292.

26. Doc. 216 in Natalia S. Lebedeva and Wojciech Materski et al., eds., *Katyń: Plenniki neobiavlennoi voiny* (Moscow, 1999), 384–90.

27. No mention of Khrushchev's role is made in either his memoirs or in his son Sergei's biography. The recent study, William Taubman, *Khrushchev, the Man and His Era* (New York, 2003), mentions that a colleague (Ivan Serov) was involved with Katyn´ (133–46, 370).

28. Doc. 208 in Lebedeva and Materski et al., *Katyń*, 375–78.

29. Doc. 227, Mar. 3, 1959, ibid., 563–64.

30. A. I. Romanov, *Nights Are Longest There: A Memoir of the Soviet Secret Service* (Boston, 1972), 136–37; Michael Parrish, *The Lesser Terror: Soviet State Security, 1939–1953* (Westport, Conn., 1996), 54–57.

31. Doc. 10 in A. N. Yakovlev et al., eds., *1941 god: Dokumenty* (Moscow, 1998), 1:29–30; *Pravda*, June 16 and 17, 1940; Watson, *Molotov*, 181.

32. Doc. 76 in Yakovlev et al., *1941 god: Dokumenty*, 1:150–52.

33. Quoted in Aleksandr M. Nekrich, *Pariahs, Partners, Predators: German-Soviet Relations, 1922–1941* (New York, 1997), 230.

34. Speech to the Central Committee, Sept. 1940, in I. P. Senokosov, ed., *Surovaia drama naroda: uchenie i publitsisty o priode stalinizma* (Moscow, 1989), 503. Alexander V. Prusin, *The Lands Between: Conflict in the East European Borderlands, 1870–1992* (Oxford, U.K., 2010), 147.

35. These higher figures are in Elena Zubkova, *Pribaltika i Kreml, 1940–1953* (Moscow, 2008), 127.

36. Docs. 107 and 108, May 16, 1941, and doc. 112, June 17, in Mironenko and Werth, *Istoriia stalinskogo Gulaga*, 1:394–400; 404–5.

37. Alexandras Shtomas, "The Baltic States as Soviet Republics: Tensions and Contradictions," in *Totalitarianism and the Prospects for World Order: Closing the Door on the Twentieth Century*, ed. Robert Faulkner and Daniel J. Mahoney (Oxford, U.K., 2003), 207. Those statistics are accepted by Valdis O. Lumans, *Latvia in World War II* (New York, 2006), 138. I. Joseph Vizulis, *Nations Under Duress: The Baltic States* (New York, 1985), 102–4, for different figures.

38. Entry for Jan. 21, 1940, in Dimitrov, *Dnevnik*, 84.

39. Figures, Mar. 27, 1940, ibid., 85.

40. Stalin's remarks are quoted in Khrushchev, *Memoirs*, 1:251–52.

41. Doc. 6, Apr. 17, 1940, in K. M. Anderson et al., eds., *"Zimniaia voina": rabota nad oshibkami (aprel–mai 1940 g.): Materiali kommissii Glavnogo voennogo soveta Krasnoi Armii* (Moscow, 2004), 31–42; William R. Trotter, *Frozen Hell: The Russo-Finnish War of 1939–40* (Chapel Hill, N.C., 1991), 16–22.

42. Khrushchev, *Memoirs*, 1:266.

43. Quoted in John Lukacs, *Five Days in London: May 1940* (New Haven, Conn., 2001), 151.

44. David Reynolds, *In Command of History: Churchill Fighting and Writing the Second World War* (London, 2004), 169–70.

45. Klaus Hildebrand, *Das vergangene Reich: Deutsche Aussenpolitik von Bismarck bis Hitler* (Berlin, 1999), 836–48; John Lukacs, *The Last European War: September 1939–December 1941* (New Haven, Conn., 2001), 98–99.

46. Doc. 6.28, Sept. 29, 1940; doc. 6.50, Dec. 29, 1940; and doc. 7.1, Jan. 4, 1941, in Viktor Gavrilov, ed., *Voennaya razvedka informiruet*, http://www.alexanderyakovlev.org/fond/issues-doc/1001634.

47. Georgi K. Zhukov, *Vospominaniya i razmyshleniya* (Moscow, 2002), 1:255–56; doc. 289 in Yakovlev et al., *1941 god: Dokumenty*, 1:683.

48. Docs. 368 and 369, in Yakovlev et al., *1941 god: Dokumenty*, 2:47–48.

49. *SDFP*, 3:484–85. Stalin is quoted in Gabriel Gorodetsky, *Grand Delusion: Stalin and the German Invasion of Russia* (New Haven, Conn., 1999), 151.

50. Ambassador L. A. Steinhardt's confidential discussion with Deputy Foreign Commissar Lozovsky, Apr. 15, 1941, doc. 388 in Yakovlev et al., *1941 god: Dokumenty*, 2:81–82; Andrei I. Yeremenko, *V nachale voiny* (Moscow, 1965), 46; Lew Besymenski, *Stalin und Hitler: Das Pokerspiel der Diktatoren* (Berlin, 2002), 416.

51. Vladimir Lota, *Sekretnyi front generalnogo shtaba. Kniga o voennoi razvedke 1940–1942* (Moscow, 2005), 220–34.

52. Doc. 377, Apr. 11, 1941, in Yakovlev et al., *1941 god: Dokumenty*, 2:60–61.

53. See, e.g., doc. 7.4, Feb. 12, 1941, and following, in Gavrilov, *Voennaya razvedka informiruet*, http://www.alexanderyakovlev.org/fond/issues-doc/1001644.

54. Doc. 575 in Yakovlev et al., *1941 god: Dokumenty*, 2:387–88; Stalin quoted in Gorodetsky, *Grand Delusion*, 225.

55. Felix I. Chuev, *Molotov: Poluderzhavnyi vlastelin* (Moscow, 2000), 28–38.

56. See, e.g., Zhukov, *Vospominaniya i razmyshleniya,* 1:229–30.

57. Ibid., 1:246–55.

58. V. K. Volkov, *Uzlovye problemy noveishei istorii stran Tsentralnoi i Iugo-Vostochnoi Evropy,* rev. and expanded as *Stalin wollte ein anderes Europa: Moskaus Aussenpolitik 1940 bis 1968 und die Folgen, eine Dokumentation,* Harald Neubert, ed. (Berlin, 2003), 79–80; Besymenski, *Stalin und Hitler,* 417–18.

59. Ribbentrop to Schulenburg, June 21, doc. 600 in Yakovlev et al., *1941 god: Dokumenty,* 2:418–20.

60. The classic case was put by Viktor Suvorov, *Der Eisbrecher: Hitler in Stalins Kalkül* (Stuttgart, 1989). For a recent and selective reading of (military) documentation, see Bogdan Musial, *Kampfplatz Deutschland: Stalins Kriegspläne gegen den Westen* (Berlin, 2008).

61. Speech, doc. 437 in Yakovlev et al., *1941 god: Dokumenty,* 2:158–62.

62. Directive, doc. 468, ibid., 2:201–9; also Alexander M. Vasilevsky, *Delo vsei zhizni* (Moscow, 1978), 105; and Dmitri Volkogonov, *Sem voshdei* (Moscow, 1999), 1:212–13.

63. See, e.g., directives from the Main Political Department of the Red Army (beginning June), doc. 512, in Yakovlev et al., *1941 god: Dokumenty,* 2:301–3.

64. Heinrich Schwendemann, "German-Soviet Economic Relations at the Time of the Hitler-Stalin Pact 1939–1941," *Cahiers du Monde russe* (1995), 165.

65. Schnurre memorandum, Feb. 26, 1940, doc. 636 in *DGFP,* 8:814–17.

66. *DRZW,* 4:166.

67. S. Z. Sluch, "Sovetsko-germanskii otnossyeniya v sentyabre-dekabre 1939 goda i vopros o vstuplenii SSSR vo vtoryio mirovyio voiny," *Otechestvennaya Istoriya* 5 (2000), 10–27.

68. Mikoyan to Stalin and Molotov, Mar. 11, 1941, doc. 317 in Yakovlev et al., *1941 god: Dokumenty,* 1:760–64.

69. *DRZW,* 4:166–67.

70. Schnurre memorandum, doc. 471 in Yakovlev et al., *1941 god: Dokumenty,* 2:212–13.

71. Rolf-Dieter Müller, "Von der Wirtschaftsallianz zum kolonialen Ausbeutungskrieg," in *DRZW,* 4:98–189.

72. Adam Tooze, *Wages of Destruction: The Making and Breaking of the Nazi Economy* (New York, 2006), 422–25.

73. Müller, "Wirtschaftsallianz," 109–11.

74. Gorodetsky, *Grand Delusion,* 184–94.

75. Zhukov, *Vospominaniya i razmyshleniya,* 1:239–40; Vasilevsky, *Delo vsei zhizni,* 107–8; also remarks quoted in Gorodetsky, *Grand Delusion,* 299.

76. Docs. 74 and 75 in V. K. Vinogradov et al., *Sekrety Gitlera na stole u Stalina: razvedka i konstrrazvedka o podgotovke gemanskoi agressii protive SSSR, mart-jiun 1941 g.: Dokumenty iz Tsentralnogo arkhiva FSB Rossii* (Moscow 1995), 166–69.

77. Doc. 605 in Yakovlev et al., eds., *1941 god: Dokumenty,* 2:423. See also Mikoyan interview in Georgii A. Kumanev, *Govoriat stalinskie narkomy: Vstrechi, besedy, interviu, dokumenty* (Smolensk, 2005), 58–59; and Anastas I. Mikoyan, *Tak bylo: Razmyshleniya o minushem* (Moscow, 1999), chaps. 30–31.

78. Chernobaev, *Na prieme u Stalina,* 337; Zhukov, *Vospominaniya i razmyshleniya,* 1:265–66.

79. Nikolai N. Voronov, *Na sluzhbe voennoi* (Moscow, 1963), 171–74.

80. David M. Glantz and Jonathan M. House, *When Titans Clashed: How the Red Army Stopped Hitler* (Lawrence, Kansas, 1995), 51.

81. Volkogonov, *Triumf i tragediya,* 2:1:192–93.

82. Chernobaev, *Na prieme u Stalina,* 337–38.

83. Yuri A. Gorkov, *Kreml, stavka, genshtab* (Tver, 1995), 86.

84. Feliks Ivanovich Chuev and Vyacheslav Molotov, *Sto sorok besed s Molotovym: iz dnevnika F. Chueva* (Moscow, 1991), 44–45.

85. Volkogonov, *Triumf i tragediya*, 2:1:156–7.

86. Mikoyan interview in Kumanev, *Govoriat stalinskie narkomy*, 61–62; Zhukov, *Vospominaniya i razmyshleniya*, 1:287–88.

87. Mikoyan and Voznesensky were added to the GKO on Feb. 3, 1942. Mikoyan, *Tak bylo: Razmyshleniya o minushem*, chap. 31; doc. 654 in Yakovlev et al., *1941 god: Dokumenty*, 2:496–500.

88. Stalin, *Sochineniia*, 15:56–61.

89. Winston S. Churchill, *The Grand Alliance* (Boston, 1950), 372.

90. Churchill to Roosevelt, Dec. 7, 1940, in Warren F. Kimball, ed., *Churchill and Roosevelt: The Complete Correspondence* (Princeton, N.J., 1984), 1:102–9.

91. David M. Kennedy, *Freedom from Fear: The American People in Depression and War, 1929–1945* (New York, 1999), 471.

92. Record of Conversation, July 30, 1941, in *Sovetsko-Amerikanskie otnosheniya vo vremya Velikoi Otechestvennoie Voiny, 1941–1945* (Moscow, 1984), 1:80–82.

93. Christopher Andrew and Oleg Gordievsky, *KGB: The Inside Story of Its Foreign Operations from Lenin to Gorbachev* (London, 1990), 235–36.

94. Roosevelt and Churchill to Stalin, received Aug. 15, 1941, in *Stalin Correspondence*, 1:17–18.

95. Roosevelt and Churchill, joint statement, Aug. 14, 1941, in *FRUS, 1941. The Soviet Union*, 1:367–69.

96. Kennedy, *Freedom from Fear*, 496.

97. Doc. 651 in Yakovlev et al., *1941 god: Dokumenty*, 2:487–88. Further documents are cited in Volkogonov, *Triumf i tragediya*, 2:1:172–73; also Pavel Sudoplatov and Anatoli Sudoplatov, *Special Tasks: The Memoirs of an Unwanted Witness—A Soviet Spymaster* (New York, 1994), 145; and Khrushchev, *Memoirs*, 1:358. For additional evidence and doubts about Stalin's efforts to seek peace, see Chris Bellamy, *Absolute War: Soviet Russia in the Second World War* (New York, 2007), 221–22.

98. W. Averell Harriman, *America and Russia in a Changing World: A Half Century of Personal Observation* (Garden City, N.Y., 1971), 23.

99. Cordell Hull, *Memoirs* (New York, 1948), 1:292–307; Jean Edward Smith, *FDR* (New York, 2007), 342–43.

100. Kennedy, *Freedom from Fear*, 485, 631.

101. Stalin to Roosevelt, Oct. 3 and Nov. 4, 1941, in *Stalin Correspondence*, 2:13, 15.

102. Evan Mawdsley, *Thunder in the East: The Nazi-Soviet War, 1941–1945* (London, 2005), 192; Bellamy, *Absolute War*, 421.

103. Mawdsley, *Thunder in the East*, 193.

104. Khrushchev, *Memoirs*, 1:638–39.

105. Timothy Johnston, *Being Soviet: Identity, Rumour, and Everyday Life Under Stalin, 1939–1953* (Oxford, U.K., 2011), 48–49.

106. Rebecca Manley, *To the Tashkent Station: Evacuation and Survival in the Soviet Union at War* (Ithaca, N.Y., 2009), 76.

107. HP 387, pp. 10, 21–23, 42–45, 80–81, 94–95, 97–99.

108. HP 144, pp. 2–3.

109. Rodric Braithwaite, *Moscow 1941: A City and Its People at War* (New York, 2006), 233–34.

110. Speech, Nov. 6, 1941, published the next day in *Pravda*. For background, see Andrew Nagorski, *The Greatest Battle: Stalin, Hitler, and the Desperate Struggle for Moscow That Changed the Course of World War II* (New York, 2007), 217–42.

111. Ivan M. Maisky, *Vospominanya sovetskogo diplomata, 1925–1945 gg* (Moscow, 1980), 536–38; Stalin to Churchill, Nov. 8, 1941, in *Stalin Correspondence*, 1:33–34.

112. PRO: PREM, 4/30/8; Anthony Eden, *The Reckoning: The Memoirs of Anthony Eden, Earl of Avon* (Boston, 1965), 335.

113. See doc. 11 and, for the original Soviet demands, doc. 12, in G. P. Kynin and Jochen Laufer, eds., *SSSR i germanskii vopros, 1941–1949: dokumenty iz arkhiva vneshnei politiki Rossiiskoi Federastsii* (Moscow, 1996), 1:124–35; Maisky, *Vospominanya sovetskogo diplomata*, 538–39.

114. Eden, *Reckoning*, 352; David Dilks, ed., *The Diaries of Sir Alexander Cadogan, 1938–1945* (New York, 1972), 422–23.

115. A. M. Filitov, "SSSR i germanskii vopros: povortotnye punkty," in N. I. Egorova and A. O. Chubarian, eds., *Kholodnaia voina, 1945–1963 gg.: Istoricheskaia retrospektiva. Sbornik statei* (Moscow, 2003), 224–25. For an early demand, see Molotov's report of Stalin's opinion in note to Maisky, Nov. 21, 1941, doc. 7 in Kynin and Laufer, *SSSR i germanskii vopros*, 1:118–19.

116. Additional Soviet minutes, Dec. 18, 1941, doc. 8 in Oleg. A. Rzheshevsky, ed., *War and Diplomacy: The Making of the Grand Alliance. Documents from Stalin's Archives* (Amsterdam, 1996), 38.

117. Doc. 7, December 17, ibid., 31.

118. Litvinov to Molotov, Molotov to Litvinov, Dec. 8–11, 1941, in *Sovetsko-Amerikanskie otnoseheniya*, 1:143–44.

119. This decision was taken at the Arcadia conference in Washington that met from Dec. 22, 1941, to Jan. 14, 1942.

CHAPTER 4. SOVIET AIMS AND WESTERN CONCESSIONS

1. See, e.g., Stalin to Tito, Feb. 1942, in Vladimir Dedijer, *Tito Speaks: His Self-Portrait and Struggle with Stalin* (London, 1953), 178; Alfred J. Rieber, *Stalin and the French Communist Party, 1941–1947* (New York, 1962), 26–33.

2. For the background, see Dimitrov to Stalin, July 1 and Oct. 6, 1934, and Stalin to Dimitrov, Oct. 25, 1934, in Alexander Dallin and F. I. Firsov, eds., *Dimitrov and Stalin, 1934–1943: Letters from the Soviet Archives* (New Haven, Conn., 2000), 13–22.

3. Entries for July 6 and 7 in Georgi Dimitrov, *Dnevnik: mart 1933—fevruari 1949: izbrano* (Sofia, 2003), 121–22.

4. Felix I. Chuev, *Molotov: Poluderzhavnyii vlastelin* (Moscow, 2000), 73–74.

5. Stalin to Molotov, May 24, 1942, doc. 38 in Oleg A. Rzheshevsky, ed., *War and Diplomacy: The Making of the Grand Alliance. Documents from Stalin's Archives* (Amsterdam, 1996), 122.

6. Doc. 70, ibid., 176–79; Robert E. Sherwood, *Roosevelt and Hopkins: An Intimate History*, rev. ed. (New York, 1950), 557–61.

7. Docs. 97 and 98 in *Sovetsko-Amerikanskie otnoseheniya vo vremya Velikoi Otechestvennoie Voiny, 1941–1945* (Moscow, 1984), 1:179–80; late-night visit, doc. 98, 1:179–81.

8. Chuev, *Molotov*, 70–71, 82.

9. Doc. 100 in *Sovetsko-Amerikanskie otnoseheniya*, 1:187–91; Sherwood, *Roosevelt and Hopkins*, 575.

10. Winston S. Churchill, *The Hinge of Fate* (Boston, 1950), 472–502; Martin Gilbert, *Churchill: A Life* (New York, 1991), 726–29; W. Averell Harriman and Elie Abel, *Special Envoy to Churchill and Stalin, 1941–1946* (New York, 1975), 159.

11. Doc. 1041, Resident to GKO, Aug. 4, 1942, in S. V. Stepashin, ed., *Organy gosudarstvennoi bezopasnosti SSSR v Velikoi Otechestvennoi voyne. Soborník dokumentov* (Moscow, 2003), 3:2:115.

12. Doc. 29, Aug. 16, 1942, in G. P. Kynin and Jochen Laufer, eds., *SSSR i germanskii vopros, 1941–1949: dokumenty iz arkhiva vneshnei politiki Rossiiskoi Federastsii* (Moscow, 1996), 1:165–67.

13. David Dilks, ed., *The Diaries of Sir Alexander Cadogan, 1938–1945* (New York, 1972), 472–74; Martin Kitchen, *British Policy Towards the Soviet Union During the Second World War* (London, 1986), 132–40.

14. TASS reporter's letter to Commissariat of Foreign Affairs, Dec. 22, 1936, in AVPRF, f. 0129, op. 20, p. 133a, d. 393, l. 50.

15. George F. Kennan, *Memoirs, 1925–1950* (Boston, 1967), 82–83.

16. Entries for Mar. 6–8, 1938, in Joseph E. Davies, *Mission to Moscow* (New York, 1941), 235–46.

17. Warren F. Kimball, *The Juggler: Franklin Roosevelt as Wartime Statesman* (Princeton, N.J., 1991), 30–31.

18. William C. Bullitt, "How We Won the War and Lost the Peace," *Life*, Aug. 30, 1948, 88.

19. David M. Kennedy, *Freedom from Fear: The American People in Depression and War, 1929–1945* (New York, 1999), 465–76.

20. Charles E. Bohlen, *Witness to History, 1929–1969* (New York, 1973), 211.

21. Cordell Hull, *Memoirs* (New York, 1948), 2:1273–74.

22. Dennis J. Dunn, *Caught Between Roosevelt and Stalin: America's Ambassadors to Moscow* (Lexington, Ky., 1998), 263.

23. Kennedy, *Freedom from Fear*, 483–84.

24. Antony Beevor, *Stalingrad: The Fateful Siege: 1942–1943* (New York, 1999), 439–40. John Erickson, *The Road to Stalingrad: Stalin's War with Germany* (New Haven, Conn., 1975), 47–49.

25. Jeremy Noakes and Geoffrey Pridham, eds., *Nazism, 1919–1945*, vol. 3, *Foreign Policy, War and Racial Extermination* (Exeter, U.K., 1995), 3:846–48.

26. Molotov to Stalin, June 7, 1942, doc. 99, in Rzheshevsky, *War and Diplomacy*, 226.

27. FDR to Churchill, Mar. 18, 1942, in Warren F. Kimball, ed., *Churchill and Roosevelt: The Complete Correspondence* (Princeton, N.J., 1984), 1:421.

28. Roosevelt to Stalin, May 5, 1943, in *Stalin Correspondence*, 2:63–64; Todd Bennett, "Culture, Power, and *Mission to Moscow*: Film and Soviet-American Relations During World War II," *Journal of American History* (2001), 489–518.

29. Stalin to Roosevelt, May 26 and June 11, 1943, in *Stalin Correspondence*, 2:66, 70–71.

30. Hull, *Memoirs*, 2:1252; *New York Times*, May 25, 1943.

31. Quoted in David Reynolds, *From World War to Cold War: Churchill, Roosevelt, and the International History of the 1940s* (Oxford, U.K., 2006), 245.

32. Entry for Apr. 14–28, 1943, in Elke Fröhlich et al., eds., *Die Tagebücher von Joseph Goebbels* (Munich, 1993), 2:8:101–78.

33. *New York Times*, July 14, 16, 19, 1945.

34. Stalin to Roosevelt, Apr. 21 and 29, in *Stalin Correspondence*, 2:61–62.

35. For the meetings May 8–20, see Dimitrov, *Dnevnik*, 179–83; *New York Times* (May 29, 1943).

36. V. K. Volkov, *Uzlovye problemy noveishei istorii stran Tsentralnoi i Iugo-Vostochnoi Evropy*, rev. and expanded as *Stalin wollte ein anderes Europa: Moskaus Aussenpolitik 1940 bis 1968 und die Folgen, eine Dokumentation*, Harald Neubert, ed. (Berlin, 2003), 148–49.

37. Entries for May 20–June 12, 1943, in Dimitrov, *Dnevnik*, 182–89; Mark Kramer, "The Role of the CPSU International Department in Soviet Foreign Relations and National Security Policy," *Soviet Studies* (1990), 429–46.

38. Alexander Werth, *Russia at War, 1941–1945* (1964; New York, 1984), 672–73.

39. François Furet, *The Passing of an Illusion: The Idea of Communism in the Twentieth Century* (Chicago, 1999), 346.

40. Gerhard Wettig, *Stalin and the Cold War in Europe: The Emergence and Development of East-West Conflict, 1939–1953* (Lanham, Md., 2008), 25–26.

41. GARF, f. 6991, op. 1, d. 1, l. 1–10.

42. Steven Merritt Miner, *Stalin's Holy War: Religion, Nationalism, and Alliance Politics, 1941–1945* (Chapel Hill, N.C., 2003), 123, 136–40.

43. Ibid., 123–40; Robert Dallek, *Franklin D. Roosevelt and American Foreign Policy, 1932–1945* (New York, 1979), vii.

44. Hull, *Memoirs*, 2:1247–64.

45. Docs. 60–77 in Kynin and Laufer, eds., *SSSR i germanskii vopros, 1941–1949*, 1:177–240.

46. Jochen Laufer, *Pax Sovietica: Stalin, die Westmächte und die deutsche Frage, 1941–1945* (Cologne, 2009), 361–64.

47. Harriman and Abel, *Special Envoy*, 256–83.

48. Bohlen minutes, in *FRUS, The Conferences at Cairo and Tehran, 1943*, 483–86; Bohlen, *Witness to History*, 139–43. Though he was not the translator at the first meeting, see also Valintin M. Berezhkov, *Kak ya stal perevodchikom Stalin* (Moscow, 1993), 251–59.

49. *Sovetskii Soyuz na mezhdunarodnykh konferentsiyakh perioda Velikoi Otechestvennoi Voiny, 1941–1945 gg.: Sbornik dokumentov: t. 2 Tegeranskaya konferentsiya rukovoditelei trekh soyuznykh derzhav—SSSR, SShA i Velikobritanii* (Moscow, 1984), 85–86, henceforth *Tegeranskaya konferentsiya.*

50. Ibid., 115–17; *FRUS, Cairo and Tehran*, dinner, 538–39; luncheon meeting, Nov. 30, 565–68; Roosevelt to Stalin, telegram, Dec. 6, 819.

51. For the suggestion that Stalin did not want dismemberment, see Andrei A. Gromyko, *Pamiatnoe* (Moscow, 1990), 1:215.

52. *Tegeranskaya konferentsiya*, 146–50; *FRUS, Cairo and Tehran*, 600.

53. Diary entry for Jan. 5, 1943, cited in Jochen Laufer, "Stalins Friedensziele und die Kontinuität der sowjetischen Deutschlandpolitik 1941–1953," in Jürgen Zarusky, ed., *Stalin und die Deutschen: Neue Beiträge der Forschung* (Munich, 2006), 142.

54. For Hull's meeting in the White House, Oct. 4–5, 1943, see Hull, *Memoirs*, 2:1265.

55. *Tegeranskaya konferentsiya*, 148–50; *FRUS, Cairo and Tehran*, 600–4, 847.

56. *FRUS, Cairo and Tehran*, 598–605.

57. *Tegeranskaya konferentsiya*, 150.

58. Ibid., 147–48; *FRUS, Cairo and Tehran*, 510–12; Winston S. Churchill, *Closing the Ring* (Boston, 1953), 362; Anthony Eden, *The Reckoning: The Memoirs of Anthony Eden, Earl of Avon* (Boston, 1965), 495–96; Valentin M. Berezhkov, *Stranitsy diplomaticheskoi istorii* (Moscow 1987), 287–88, 520–21.

59. Sergo Beria, *Beria, My Father: Inside Stalin's Kremlin* (London, 2001), 94.

60. *Tegeranskaya konferentsiya*, 148–49; *FRUS, Cairo and Tehran*, 594–96, 600; Bohlen, *Witness to History*, 151.

61. See, e.g., Francis Dostál Raška, *The Czechoslovak Exile Government in London and the Sudeten German Issue* (Prague, 2002), 44, 51.

62. *Tegeranskaya konferentsiya*, 151–52; *FRUS, Cairo and Tehran*, 594–95.

63. *Tegeranskaya konferentsiya*, 104–5; *FRUS, Cairo and Tehran*, 531.

64. Bohlen, *Witness to History*, 153.

65. On the visit in March 1944, see Milovan Djilas, *Conversations with Stalin* (New York, 1962), 73.

66. Steven J. Zaloga, *Bagration 1944: The Destruction of Army Group Center* (Westport, Conn., 2004), 42–84.

67. Alexander M. Vasilevsky, *Delo vsei zhizni* (Moscow, 1978), 398–417; Georgi K. Zhukov, *Vospominaniya i razmyshleniya* (Moscow, 2002), 2:224–30.

68. Chris Bellamy, *Absolute War: Soviet Russia in the Second World War* (New York, 2007), 612–13; Evan Mawdsley, *Thunder in the East: The Nazi-Soviet War, 1941–1945* (London, 2005),

303; and David M. Glantz and Jonathan House, *When Titans Clashed: How the Red Army Stopped Hitler* (Lawrence, Kansas, 1995), 196.

69.　Walter Hubatsch, ed., *Hitlers Weisungen für die Kriegsführung, 1939–1945. Dokumente des Oberkommandos der Wehrmacht* (Munich, 1965), 281–85.

70.　John Erickson, *The Road to Berlin: Stalin's War with Germany* (New Haven, Conn., 1983), 202–24.

71.　See Antony Beevor and Luba Vinogradova, eds., *A Writer at War: Vasily Grossman with the Red Army, 1941–1945* (New York, 2005), 273–74.

72.　Zhukov, *Vospominaniya i razmyshleniya*, 2:233.

73.　Remark overheard by Werth, *Russia at War*, 863. See also Erickson, *Road to Berlin*, 228–29.

74.　Catherine Merridale, *Ivan's War: Life and Death in the Red Army, 1939–1945* (New York, 2006), 278–81.

75.　For German casualties, see table 59, Rüdiger Overmans, *Deutsche militärische Verluste im Zweiten Weltkrieg* (Munich, 2004), 277; convenient Soviet figures are in Glantz and House, *When Titans Clashed*, 214–15.

76.　Entries for Aug. 29–31, 1944, in Mihail Sebastian, *Journal, 1935–1944* (Chicago, 2000), 608–10.

77.　Doc. 614 in *DGFP*, 12:996–1006; and doc. 667 in *DGFP*, 13:1077–78. See also *DRZW*, 4:360.

78.　Krisztián Ungváry, *The Siege of Budapest: 100 Days in World War II* (New Haven, Conn., 2005), 40–43.

CHAPTER 5. TAKING EASTERN EUROPE

1.　Entry for Aug. 27, 1941, in Georgi Dimitrov, *Tagebücher 1933–1943* (Berlin, 2000), 1:419.

2.　Entries for May 16, 1942, and Mar. 2, 1943, ibid., 516–17, 657–58.

3.　Entry for Feb. 25, 1944, in Ivo Banac, ed., *The Diary of Georgi Dimitrov, 1933–1949* (New Haven, Conn., 2003), 299.

4.　Doc. 17 in Antony Polonsky and Boleslaw Drukier, eds., *The Beginnings of Communist Rule in Poland* (London, 1980), 230–32.

5.　Krystyna Kersten, *The Establishment of Communist Rule in Poland, 1943–1948* (Berkeley, Calif., 1991), 63–65.

6.　*Russkii Arkhiv: Velikaya Otechestvennaya Voina: T 14 (3-1): SSSR i Polsha* (Moscow, 1994), 105, henceforth *SSSR i Polsha*.

7.　Konstantine K. Rokossovsky, *Soldatskii dolg* (Moscow, 1988), 274–75; Norman Davies, *Rising '44: The Battle for Warsaw* (New York, 2003), 165.

8.　Davies, *Rising '44*, 204–9.

9.　Marek Jan Chodakiewicz, "The Warsaw Rising, 1944: Perception and Reality" (2004), http://www.warsawuprising.com/doc/chodakiewicz1.pdf.

10.　Docs. 14 and 15, Feb. 29, 1944, in *SSSR i Polsha*, 130–32.

11.　Felix I. Chuev, *Molotov: Poluderzhavnyii vlastelin* (Moscow, 2000), 89.

12.　Stanisław Mikołajczyk, *The Rape of Poland: Pattern of Soviet Aggression* (New York, 1948), 69.

13.　Doc. 13 in *SSSR i Polsha*, 206–7.

14.　Minutes in T. V. Volokitina et al., eds., *Sovetskii faktor v Vostochnoi Evrope, 1944–1953* (Moscow, 1999), 1:67–74; also Mikołajczyk, *Rape of Poland*, 72–73.

15.　Volokitina et al., *Sovetskii faktor*, 1:84–87; Mikołajczyk, *Rape of Poland*, 77–79.

16.　Doc. 29 in *SSSR i Polsha*, 218–20.

17.　Davies, *Rising '44*, 307–15.

18. Docs. 37 and 39, in *SSSR: Polsha*, 230–33; Stalin-Roosevelt-Churchill letters, Aug. 16–22, in *Stalin Correspondence*, 1:257–58.

19. Doc. 4, Nov. 22, 1944, in *SSSR i Polsha*, 182–84.

20. John Erickson, *The Road to Berlin: Stalin's War with Germany* (New Haven, Conn., 1983), 285.

21. Rokossovsky, *Soldatskii dolg*, 274–83; Georgi K. Zhukov, *Vospominaniya i razmyshleniya* (Moscow, 2002), 2:250–52; Richard Wolff, "Rokossovsky," in Harold Shukman, ed., *Stalin's Generals* (New York, 1993), 177–96, here 191.

22. For a "refutation" of the "conventional" view in the West that Stalin was to blame, see Richard Overy, *Russia's War* (New York, 1998), 247–49.

23. *SSSR i Polsha*, 191–92.

24. Here I agree with the compilers of *SSSR i Polsha*, 193–94.

25. Czesław Miłosz, *The Captive Mind* (New York, 1951), 96.

26. Ibid.

27. Bradley F. Smith and Agnes F. Peterson, eds., *Heinrich Himmler Geheimreden 1933 bis 1945* (Frankfurt am Main, 1974), 242.

28. Davies, *Rising '44*, 433–34.

29. Józef Garliński, *Poland in the Second World War* (London, 1985), 293–94.

30. Stalin to Churchill, in *Stalin Correspondence*, 1:258–59.

31. Dwight D. Eisenhower, *Crusade in Europe* (Garden City, N.Y., 1948), 291–97; *The Complete War Memoirs of Charles de Gaulle* (New York, 1972), 646.

32. Roosevelt to Churchill, Oct. 16. 1944, in Warren F. Kimball, ed., *Churchill and Roosevelt: The Complete Correspondence* (Princeton, N.J., 1984), 3:356–58.

33. Roy Jenkins, *Churchill, a Biography* (New York, 2001), 759.

34. Winston S. Churchill, *Triumph and Tragedy* (Boston, 1953), 226–28; Anthony Eden, *The Reckoning: The Memoirs of Anthony Eden, Earl of Avon* (Boston, 1965), 559–50.

35. Churchill to his cabinet, Oct. 14, 1944, in *Triumph and Tragedy*, 233–35.

36. Valentin M. Berezhkov, *Stranitsy diplomaticheskoi istorii* (Moscow, 1987), 477–82.

37. Eden, *Reckoning*, 557; Derek Watson, *Molotov: A Biography* (New York, 2005), 215; Geoffrey Roberts, *Stalin's Wars: From World War to Cold War, 1939–1953* (New Haven, Conn., 2006), 217–25.

38. W. Averell Harriman and Elie Abel, *Special Envoy to Churchill and Stalin, 1941–1946* (New York, 1975), 358.

39. Mikołajczyk, *Rape of Poland*, 95–96; Harriman and Abel, *Special Envoy*, 359–60.

40. Mikołajczyk, *Rape of Poland*, 98; for the British record, see Jenkins, *Churchill*, 762.

41. Eden, *Reckoning*, 563; Churchill, *Triumph and Tragedy*, 235, 237–38.

42. Mikołajczyk, *Rape of Poland*, 103–4.

43. For the exchange of letters among Roosevelt, Churchill, and Stalin, see *FRUS, Conferences at Malta and Yalta*, 206–12.

44. Roosevelt to Stalin, Dec. 16, 1944; Stalin to Roosevelt, Dec. 27, ibid., 217–18, 221–23; Kersten, *Establishment of Communist Rule in Poland*, 104–10.

45. Churchill to Clementine, Oct. 13, 1944, cited in David Reynolds, *Summits: Six Meetings That Shaped the Twentieth Century* (New York, 2007), 114.

46. Churchill, *Triumph and Tragedy*, 238.

47. Harriman to Roosevelt, Dec. 14, 1944, in *FRUS, Conferences at Malta and Yalta*, 20.

48. Quoted in Reynolds, *Summits*, 134.

49. Eden, *Reckoning*, 592; Jenkins, *Churchill*, 773–79.

50. Harriman and Abel, *Special Envoy*, 367–72.

51. Thomas M. Campbell and George C. Herring, eds., *The Diaries of Edward R. Stettinius, Jr.* (New York, 1975), 210–14.

52. Entry for Jan. 28, 1945, in Georgi Dimitrov, *Dnevnik: mart 1933–fevruari 1949: izbrano* (Sofia, 2003), 240–41.

53. Harriman to Secretary of State, Jan. 4, 1945, in *FRUS, 1945. Europe*, 5:942–44.

54. Edward R. Stettinius, Jr., *Roosevelt and the Russians: The Yalta Conference* (Garden City, N.Y., 1949), 119–20; Charles E. Bohlen, *Witness to History, 1929–1969* (New York, 1973), 186–87.

55. See Berezhkov, *Stranitsy diplomaticheskoi istorii*, 504–5.

56. Pavel Sudoplatov and Anatoli Sudoplatov, *Special Tasks: The Memoirs of an Unwanted Witness—A Soviet Spymaster* (New York, 1994), 226.

57. Andrei A. Gromyko, *Pamiatnoe* (Moscow, 1990), 1:224.

58. *Sovetskii Soyuz na mezhdunarodnykh konferentsiyakh perioda Velikoi Otechestvennoi Voiny, 1941–1945 gg.: Sbornik dokumentov: T. 4 Krymskaya konferentsiya rukovoditelei trekh soyuznykh derzhav—SSSR, SShA i Velikobritanii* (Moscow, 1979), 50–53, henceforth, *Krymskaya konferentsiya*.

59. Feb. 5, 1945, in *FRUS, Conferences at Malta and Yalta, 1945*, 615.

60. *Krymskaya konferentsiya*, 87.

61. Stettinius, *Roosevelt and the Russians*, 136–37, 162–63; Eden, *Reckoning*, 596–97; Peter Graf Kielmansegg, *Nach der Katastrophe: Eine Geschichte des geteilten Deutschland* (Berlin, 2000), 17–18.

62. V. K. Volkov, *Uzlovye problemy noveishei istorii stran Tsentralnoi i Iugo-Vostochnoi Evropy*, rev. and expanded as *Stalin wollte ein anderes Europa: Moskaus Aussenpolitik 1940 bis 1968 und die Folgen, eine Dokumentation*, Harald Neubert, ed. (Berlin, 2003), 166.

63. *Krymskaya konferentsiya*, 69–70; *FRUS, Conferences at Malta and Yalta*, 615; Berezhkov, *Stranitsy diplomaticheskoi istorii*, 510–11.

64. Doc. 144, Feb. 15, 1944, in G. P. Kynin and Jochen Laufer, eds., *SSSR i germanskii vopros, 1941–1949: dokumenty iz arkhiva vneshnei politiki Rossiiskoi Federastsii* (Moscow, 1996), 1:606–8.

65. Molotov to Stalin, Feb. 12, 1944, doc. 88, ibid., 409–17.

66. *Krymskaya konferentsiya*, 71–74; *FRUS, Conferences at Malta and Yalta*, 620–21, 630–32, 982–83.

67. *Krymskaya konferentsiya*, 78–82; *FRUS, Conferences at Malta and Yalta*, 621–24.

68. Ivan M. Maisky, *Vospominanya sovetskogo diplomata, 1925–1945 gg* (Moscow, 1980), 655–56; his full report is doc. 1 in Volokitina et al., *Sovetskii faktor*, 1:22–48.

69. Speech, Nov. 6, 1944, in Stalin, *Sochineniia*, 2:15, 192–203.

70. *Krymskaya konferentsiya*, 88–96; *FRUS, Conferences at Malta and Yalta*, 589–90, 660–67, 976.

71. *Krymskaya konferentsiya*, 98–103; *FRUS, Conferences at Malta and Yalta*, 669–70.

72. Sergo Beria, *Beria, My Father: Inside Stalin's Kremlin* (London, 2001), 106.

73. Doc. 56, Feb. 21, 1945, in *SSSR i Polsha*, 411–12.

74. *FRUS, Conferences at Malta and Yalta*, 251–54, 980–81.

75. *FRUS, Conferences at Cairo and Tehran*, 600.

76. *Krymskaya konferentsiya*, 127; *FRUS, Conferences at Malta and Yalta*, 717.

77. Memo, Feb. 4, in *FRUS, Conferences at Malta and Yalta*, 568.

78. Hull, *Memoirs*, vol. 2:1309; *FRUS, Conferences at Cairo and Tehran*, 489.

79. *Krymskaya konferentsiya*, 139–43; *FRUS, Conferences at Malta and Yalta*, 766–71; agreement on Soviet entry, 984.

80. S. M. Plokhy, *Yalta: The Price of Peace* (New York, 2010), 101.

81. Ivan Mikhailovich Maisky, *Izbrannaya perepiska s rossiiskimi korrespondentami* (Moscow, 2005), vol. 2:161, doc. 550.

82. See the convincing account in Reynolds, *Summits*, 145, 148; Jenkins, *Churchill*, 778–80.

83. Churchill to Roosevelt, Apr. 5, 1945, in Kimball, *Churchill and Roosevelt: Complete Correspondence,* 3:613.
84. Eden, *Reckoning,* 595.
85. Cadogan to his wife, Feb. 8, in David Dilks, ed., *The Diaries of Sir Alexander Cadogan, 1938–1945* (New York, 1972), 706.

CHAPTER 6. THE RED ARMY IN BERLIN

1. See the map in S. M. Shtemenko, *Generalnyi shtab v gody voiny: ot Stalingrada do Berlina* (Moscow, 2005), 1:366–67; Meetings, Feb. 5 and 6, in *FRUS, Conferences of Malta and Yalta 1945,* 606–7, 646.
2. Dmitri Volkogonov, *Triumf i tragediya. Politichesky portret J. V. Stalina v 2 knigakh* (Moscow, 1996), 2:359–60.
3. Georgi K. Zhukov, *Vospominaniya i razmyshleniya* (Moscow, 2002), 2:261; docs. 260–77, in *Russkii Arkhiv: Velikaya Otechestvennaya Voina: T. 16 (5-4): Stavka VGK: Dokumenty i materially 1944–1945* (Moscow, 1999), 177–87.
4. Shtemenko, *Generalnyi shtab,* 1:360–62; Zhukov, *Vospominaniya i razmyshleniya,* 2:254–64.
5. Klaus-Dietmar Henke, *Die amerikanische Besetzung Deutschlands* (Munich, 1995), 98–99, citing Joseph R. Storr, *U.S. Military Government in Germany: The Planning Stage* (Karlsruhe, 1947), 50.
6. *DRZW,* 10:1:278–79; Henke, *Die amerikanische Besetzung Deutschlands,* 98–99; Earl F. Ziemke, *The U.S. Army in the Occupation of Germany, 1944–1946* (Washington, D.C., 1975), 59.
7. Walter Warlimont, *Im Hauptquartier der deutschen Wehrmacht 1939–1945* (Frankfurt am Main, 1962), 518–21.
8. Helmut Heiber and David M. Glantz, eds., *Hitler and His Generals: Military Conferences, 1942–1945* (New York, 2002), 554–68; also Warlimont, *Hauptquartier,* 522–24.
9. For the letters, see *Stalin Correspondence,* 1:296.
10. See Geoffrey Roberts, *Stalin's Wars: From World War to Cold War, 1939–1953* (New York, 2006), 256–57; Konstantine K. Rokossovsky, *Soldatskii dolg* (Moscow, 1988), 294–96.
11. Dwight D. Eisenhower, *Crusade in Europe* (Garden City, N.Y., 1948), 342–65.
12. Vasily I. Chuikov, *Konets tretevo reikha* (Moscow, 1973), 286–88. For the critique, see Zhukov, *Vospominaniya i razmyshleniya,* 2:273–80; also I. S. Konev, *Sorok piatyi* (Moscow, 1970), 72–73; Evan Mawdsley, *Thunder in the East: The Nazi-Soviet War, 1941–1945* (London, 2005), 367–68.
13. Konev, *Sorok piatyi,* 55–56.
14. Zhukov's note, in *DRZW,* 10:1:529. The operation is also referred to as Sonnenwende (Solstice); see Earl F. Ziemke, *Stalingrad to Berlin: The German Defeat in the East* (New York, 1996), 445–48.
15. Zhukov, *Vospominaniya i razmyshleniya,* 2:283–84.
16. Shtemenko, *Generalnyi shtab,* 1:376.
17. Eisenhower, *Crusade in Europe,* 378–81; Henke, *Die amerikanische Besetzung Deutschlands,* 343–77.
18. Eisenhower, *Crusade in Europe,* 406, gives 325,000; Henke, *Die amerikanische Besetzung Deutschlands,* 400.
19. John Erickson, *The Road to Berlin: Stalin's War with Germany* (New Haven, Conn., 1983), 528.
20. Eisenhower, *Crusade in Europe,* 396–99; Max Hastings, *Armageddon: The Battle for Germany, 1944–1945* (New York, 2004), 422–25.

21. Eisenhower to U.S. Military Mission in Moscow, Mar. 28, in Eisenhower, *Crusade in Europe*, 398–99.

22. Marshall to Eisenhower, Mar. 29, in *Crusade in Europe*, 506n23.

23. Zhukov, *Vospominaniya i razmyshleniya*, 2:290–91; and Chris Bellamy, *Absolute War: Soviet Russia in the Second World War* (New York, 2007), 649–50. For Soviet sources, see Roberts, *Stalin's Wars*, 261 and n19.

24. Shtemenko, *Generalnyi shtab*, 1:381–85; Zhukov, *Vospominaniya i razmyshleniya*, 2:291.

25. Konev, *Sorok piatyi*, 87–89; Zhukov, *Vospominaniya i razmyshleniya*, 2:291–92.

26. Rokossovsky, *Soldatskii dolg*, 338–39.

27. Nikolai V. Novikov, *Vospominanya diplomata: zapiski, 1938–1947* (Moscow, 1989), 286–88.

28. David Reynolds, *Summits: Six Meetings That Shaped the Twentieth Century* (New York, 2007), 149–52.

29. Jochen von Lang, *Top Nazi: SS General Karl Wolff, the Man Between Hitler and Himmler* (New York, 2005), 274.

30. Peter R. Black, *Ernst Kaltenbrunner: Ideological Soldier of the Third Reich* (Princeton, N.J., 1984), 243; Bradley F. Smith and Elena Agarossi, *Operation Sunrise: The Secret Surrender* (New York, 1979), 86–93, 103–7.

31. Roosevelt to Stalin, Mar. 24, and Stalin's answer, Mar. 29, in *Stalin Correspondence*, 2:188–91.

32. W. Averell Harriman and Elie Abel, *Special Envoy to Churchill and Stalin, 1941–1946* (New York, 1975), 435.

33. Churchill to Roosevelt, Apr. 1, in Francis L. Lowenheim et al., eds., *Churchill and Roosevelt, Secret Wartime Correspondence* (New York, 1975), 696–99. Churchill to Eisenhower, Mar. 31, ibid., 697, n1.

34. Roosevelt to Stalin, Mar. 31, in Susan Butler, ed., *My Dear Mr. Stalin: The Complete Correspondence Between Franklin D. Roosevelt and Joseph V. Stalin* (New Haven, Conn., 2005), 311.

35. Stalin to Roosevelt, Apr. 3, in *Stalin Correspondence*, 2:195–96.

36. Churchill to FDR, Apr. 5, in Lowenheim et al., *Churchill and Roosevelt, Secret Wartime Correspondence*, 704–5.

37. Valentin M. Berezhkov, *Stranitsy diplomaticheskoi istorii* (Moscow 1987), 537–46; Roosevelt to Stalin, Apr. 5, and Stalin to Roosevelt, Apr. 7, in *Stalin Correspondence*, 2:196–99.

38. Roosevelt to Churchill and Stalin, Apr. 11, in Warren F. Kimball, ed., *Churchill and Roosevelt: The Complete Correspondence* (Princeton, N.J., 1984), 3:629–30; Harriman and Abel, *Special Envoy*, 439–40.

39. *Pravda*, Apr. 13, 1945.

40. Felix I. Chuev, *Molotov: Poluderzhavnyii vlastelin* (Moscow, 2000), 93.

41. Report cited in *DRZW*, 10:2:583.

42. Report Olsztyn/Allenstein, doc. 233 in Włodzimierz Borodziej and Hans Lemberg, eds., *Die Deutschen östlich von Oder und Neisse 1945–1950: Dokumente aus polnischen Archiven*, vol. 1, *Zentrale Behörden, Wojewodschaft Allenstein* (Marburg, 2000), 481–83.

43. Roger R. Reese, *Stalin's Reluctant Soldiers: A Social History of the Red Army, 1925–1941* (Lawrence, Kansas, 1996), 63–69.

44. Alexander N. Yakovlev, *A Century of Violence in Soviet Russia* (New Haven, Conn., 2002), 174.

45. Catherine Merridale, *Ivan's War: Life and Death in the Red Army, 1939–1945* (New York, 2006), 231–32.

46. Boris Gorbachevsky, *Through the Maelstrom: A Red Army Soldier's War on the Eastern Front, 1942–1945* (Lawrence, Kansas, 2008), 359–60.

47. Zhukov, *Vospominaniya i razmyshleniya*, 2:293.

48. Shtemenko, *Generalnyi shtab*, 1:383–85; Zhukov, *Vospominaniya i razmyshleniya*, 2:307–8; docs. 330–37, *Russkii Arkhiv: Velikaya Otechestvennaya Voina: T. 16 (5-4): Stavka VGK: Dokumenty i materialy*, 219–24; DRZW, 10:1:626–27; Erickson, *Road to Berlin*, 533; Bellamy, *Absolute War*, 651.

49. Zhukov, *Vospominaniya i razmyshleniya*, 2:255–56.

50. *DRZW*, 10:1:628.

51. Ziemke, *Stalingrad to Berlin*, 474.

52. Hastings, *Armageddon: The Battle for Germany*, 468.

53. Zhukov, *Vospominaniya i razmyshleniya*, 2:318–20; Chuikov, *Konets tretevo reikha*, 290–92.

54. G. F. Krivosheev, *Rossiia i SSSR v voinakh XX veka: poteri vooruzhennykh sil: statisticheskoe issledovanie* (Moscow, 2001), chap. 5 tables.

55. Shtemenko, *Generalnyi shtab*, vol. 2, chap. 10; also Stefan Karner et al., eds., *Die Rote Armee in Österreich: Sowjetische Besatzung 1945–1955: Dokumente* (Vienna, 2005), 87–121.

56. Joachim Fest, *Der Untergang: Hitler und das Ende des Dritten Reiches* (Berlin, 2002), 105.

57. Anton Joachimsthalter, *Hitlers Ende: Legenden und Dokumente* (Berlin, 2004), 185–200; Traudl Junge, *Bis zur letzten Stunde: Hitlers Sekretärin erzählt ihr Leben* (Munich, 2002), 203.

58. Zhukov, *Vospominaniya i razmyshleniya*, 2:324.

59. Order, in Stalin, *Sochineniia*, 15:218–21.

60. Zhukov, *Vospominaniya i razmyshleniya*, 2:329–30.

61. Stalin, *Sochineniia*, 15:223–24.

CHAPTER 7. RESTORING THE STALINIST DICTATORSHIP
IN A BROKEN SOCIETY

1. Stalin, *Sochineniia*, 15:223–24, 228–29.

2. Ilya Ehrenburg, *Liudi, gody, zhizn: vospominaniia, v trekh tomakh* (Moscow, 2005), vol. 3, part 23.

3. Odd Arne Westad, *The Global Cold War: Third World Interventions and the Making of Our Times* (New York, 2005), 58.

4. E. A. Rees, "Leader Cults: Varieties, Preconditions and Functions," in Balázs Apor, Jan C. Behrends, Polly Jones, and E. A. Rees, eds., *The Leader Cult in Communist Dictatorships: Stalin and the Eastern Bloc* (New York, 2004), 14.

5. Entry for Dec. 16, 1936, in Georgi Dimitrov, *Dnevnik: mart 1933–fevruari 1949: izbrano* (Sofia, 2003), 53; Yoram Gorlizki and Oleg Khlevniuk, *Cold Peace: Stalin and the Soviet Ruling Circle, 1945–1953* (New York, 2004), 46–47.

6. Nikita S. Khrushchev, *Memoirs*, vol. 2, *Reformer* (University Park, Pa., 2006), 33.

7. A. A. Chernobaev, ed., *Na prieme u Stalina: Tetradi (zhurnaly) zapisei lits, priniatykh I. V. Stalinym, 1924–1953* (Moscow, 2008).

8. Mikoyan interviews in Georgii A. Kumanev, *Govoriat stalinskie narkomy: Vstrechi, besedy, interviu, dokumenty* (Smolensk, 2005), 61.

9. Vladimir O. Pechatnov, " 'The Allies Are Pressing on You to Break Your Will.' Foreign Policy Correspondence Between Stalin and Molotov and Other Politburo Members, September 1945–Dec. 1946," CWIHP Working Paper no. 26 (1999), 23–24.

10. Kumanev, *Govoriat stalinskie narkomy*, 69; Gorlizki and Khlevniuk, *Cold Peace*, 20–23; Alexander O. Chubarian and Vladimir O. Pechatnov, "Molotov 'the Liberal': Stalin's 1945 Criticism of His Deputy," in *Cold War History* (2000), 129–40.

11. *Spravochnik po istorii kommunisticheskoi partii i Sovetskogo Soiuza 1898–1991*, at http://www.knowbysight.info/2_KPSS/07178.asp.

12. Evan Mawdsley and Stephen White, *The Soviet Elite from Lenin to Gorbachev: The Central Committee and Its Members, 1917–1991* (Oxford, U.K., 2000), 128, table 3.7.

13. *Spravochnik po istorii kommunisticheskoi partii i Sovetskogo Soiuza 1898–1991*, http://www .knowbysight.info/2_KPSS/07177.asp. The site also contains the list of all members and their biographies.

14. E. A. Rees, "Stalin as Leader, 1924–1937: From Oligarch to Dictator," in E. A. Rees, ed., *The Nature of Stalin's Dictatorship: The Politburo, 1924–1953* (New York, 2004), 19–58.

15. Speech, Feb. 9, 1946, in Stalin, *Sochineniia*, 3:16, 6–11.

16. Lazar M. Kaganovich, *Pamiatnye zapiski: Rabochego, kommunista-bolshevika, profsoi-uznogo, partinogo i sovetsko-gosudarstvennogo rabotnika* (Moscow, 1996), 536–38.

17. *Pravda*, Aug. 19, 1945.

18. Hiroaki Kuromiya, *Freedom and Terror in the Donbas: A Ukrainian-Russian Borderland, 1870s–1990s* (Cambridge, U.K., 1998), 303.

19. Dmitrii T. Shepilov, *Neprimknushii* (Moscow, 2001), 127–36; Ethan Pollock, *Stalin and the Soviet Science Wars* (Princeton, N.J., 2006), 41–55.

20. Jonathan Brent and Vladimir P. Naumov, *Stalin's Last Crime: The Plot Against the Jewish Doctors, 1948–53* (New York, 2003), 49.

21. Pollock, *Stalin and the Soviet Science Wars*, 56–71.

22. Shepilov, *Neprimknushii*, chap. 6, 130.

23. Konstantin M. Simonov, *Glazami cheloveka moego pokoleniia* (Moscow, 1990), 160–61.

24. Another 69 accused and 145 relatives were either executed or given lengthy terms, and hundreds languished in jail. See Gorlizki and Khlevniuk, *Cold Peace*, 79–87, and Simon Sebag Montefiore, *Stalin: The Court of the Red Tsar* (New York, 2004), 592–94. For later rehabilitation, see doc. 84, Dec. 10, 1953, S. N. Kruglov and I. A. Serov; and doc. 168, May 6, 1954, R. A. Rudenko, http://www.alexanderyakovlev.org/db-docs/pages/5/searchstr =Реабилитапия&topicId=0

25. Gorlizki and Khlevniuk, *Cold Peace*, 5.

26. Shepilov, *Neprimknushii*, 93.

27. Khrushchev, *Memoirs*, 2:115.

28. Aleksander Solzhenitsyn, *In the First Circle* (New York, 2009), 130.

29. Milovan Djilas, *Conversations with Stalin* (New York, 1962), 82.

30. Nikita S. Khrushchev, *Memoirs*, vol. 1: *Commissar* (University Park, Pa., 2004), 288–91.

31. March 14, in Stalin, *Sochineniia*, 16:25–30.

32. John Barber and Mark Harrison, "Patriotic War, 1941–1945," in Ronald Grigor Suny, ed., *The Cambridge History of Russia* (Cambridge, U.K., 2006), 3:225.

33. Dmitri Volkogonov, *Triumf i tragediya. Politichesky portret J. V. Stalina* (Moscow, 1989), 2:2:26–27.

34. G. F. Krivosheev et. al., *Rossiya i SSSR v voinakh XX veka. Poteri vooruzhennykh sil: Statis-ticheskoe issledovanie* (Moscow, 2001), 229–37, table 120; also John Erickson, "Soviet War Losses: Calculations and Controversies," in John Erickson and David Dilks, eds., *Barbarossa: The Axis and the Allies* (Edinburgh, 1994), 255–77.

35. See Michael Ellman and S. Maksudov, "Soviet Deaths in the Great Patriotic War: A Note," *Europe-Asia Studies* (1994), 671–80; Mark Harrison, "Counting Soviet Deaths in the Great Patriotic War: Comment," *Europe-Asia Studies* (2003), 939–44.

36. See William Moskoff, *The Bread of Affliction: The Food Supply in the USSR During World War II* (New York, 1990), 236–39.

37. M. M. Zagorulko, ed., *Voennoplennye v SSSR 1939–1956: dokumenty i materialy* (Moscow, 2000), 25–59.

38. S. G. Wheatcroft and R. W. Davies, "Population," in R.W. Davies, Mark Harrison, and

S. G. Wheatcroft, eds., *The Economic Transformation of the Soviet Union, 1913–1945* (Cambridge, U.K., 1994), 78.

39. Kees Boterbloem, *Life and Death Under Stalin: Kalinin Province, 1945–1953* (Montreal and Kingston, 1999), 54.

40. *Pravda*, Nov. 6, 1945; and N. A. Voznesenskii, *Voennaia ekonomika SSSR v period Otechestvennoi voiny* (Moscow, 1947), 157–66.

41. Mark Harrison, *Accounting for War: Soviet Production, Employment, and the Defense Burden, 1940–1945* (New York, 2002), 164–65.

42. HP, Schedule A, vol. 17, case 332, male, 24, Ukrainian, no occupation.

43. HP, Schedule A, vol. 28, case 541, male, 25, Great Russian (prewar: student, then army).

44. Letters cited in Elena Zubkova, *Russia After the War: Hopes, Illusions, and Disappointments, 1945–1957* (New York, 1998), 48–49.

45. Donald Filtzer, *Soviet Workers and Late Stalinism: Labour and the Restoration of the Stalinist System After World War II* (New York, 2002), 45–46.

46. V. F. Zima, *Golod v SSSR 1946–1947 godov: proiskhozdenie i posledstviia* (Moscow, 1996), 20.

47. Charles King, *The Moldovans: Romania, Russia, and the Politics of Culture* (Stanford, Calif., 1999), 96.

48. Jonathan Harris, *The Split in Stalin's Secretariat, 1939–1948* (Lanham, Md., 2008), III.

49. Khrushchev, *Memoirs*, 2:7.

50. I. Y. Zelenin, *Agrarnaya politika N. S. Khrushcheva i selskoye khozyaistvo* (Moscow, 2001), 27.

51. Filtzer, *Soviet Workers*, 52, table 2.2.

52. See, e.g., woman's case from Ukraine in 1946, doc. 217 in S. S. Vilensky et al., eds., *Deti Gulaga 1918–1956* (Moscow, 2002), 376.

53. For a local perspective, see Boterbloem, *Life and Death Under Stalin*, 211–12; and Alec Nove, *An Economic History of the USSR*, new ed. (London, 1990), 289–90.

54. Zima, *Golod v SSSR 1946–1947 godov*, puts the deaths at two million (179). Michael Ellman, "The 1947 Soviet Famine and the Entitlement Approach to Famine," in *Cambridge Journal of Economics* (2000), suggests a range of 1 to 1.5 million (603–30).

55. Zima, *Golod v SSSR 1946–1947 godov*, 149.

56. Zubkova, *Russia After the War*, 49.

57. Peter H. Solomon, *Soviet Criminal Justice Under Stalin* (Cambridge, U.K., 1996), 411–13.

58. Galina Mikhailovna Ivanova, *Istoriia GULAGa, 1918–1958: sotsialno-ekonomicheskii i politiko-pravovoi aspekty* (Moscow, 2006), 279–80.

59. V. N. Zemskov, "GULAG (Istoriko-sotsiologicheskii aspekt)," *Sotsiologicheskii issledovaniya* (1991), table 6, 10–27; table 7, 3–16.

60. Paul R. Gregory, *Lenin's Brain and Other Tales from the Secret Soviet Archives* (Stanford, Calif., 2008), 99–102.

61. Yoram Gorlizki, "Rules, Incentives and Soviet Campaign Justice After World War II," *Europe-Asia Studies* (1999), 1245–65.

62. Zubkova, *Russia After the War*, 54–55.

63. Also for what follows, see Filtzer, *Soviet Workers*, 77–116; and his "Standard of Living Versus Quality of Life: Struggling with the Urban Environment in Russia During the Early Years of Post-War Reconstruction," in Juliane Fürst, ed., *Late Stalinist Russia: Society Between Reconstruction and Reinvention* (London, 2006), 81–102.

64. Sheila Fitzpatrick, *Everyday Stalinism: Ordinary Life in Extraordinary Times: Soviet Russia in the 1930s* (Oxford, U.K., 1999), 226–27.

65. Timothy Johnston, *Being Soviet: Identity, Rumour, and Everyday Life Under Stalin, 1939–1953* (Oxford, U.K., 2011), 167–208.

66. For the 1930s, see Victor A. Kravchenko, *I Chose Freedom: The Personal and Political Life of a Soviet Official* (New York, 1946), 324–25; for 1956, Zubkova, *Russia After the War*, 102–3; Judith Pallot and Tatyana Nefedova, *Russia's Unknown Agriculture: Household Production in Post-Socialist Russia* (Oxford, U.K., 2007), 7.

67. Mark Edele, "More Than Just Stalinists: The Political Senitments of Victors, 1945–1953," in Fürst, ed., *Late Stalinist Russia*, 172.

68. See Nina Tumarkin, *The Living and the Dead: The Rise and Fall of the Cult of World War II in Russia* (New York, 1994), 103–5; Catherine Merridale, *Ivan's War: Life and Death in the Red Army, 1939–1945* (New York, 2006), 336–71.

69. The figures are for January 1 of each year. See V. N. Zemskov, "Arkhipelag Gulag: glazami pisatelya i statistika," *Argumenty i fakty* (1989), 6–7; A. B. Bezborodov and V. M. Khrustalev, eds., *Istoriia stalinskogo Gulaga* (Moscow, 2004), 4:109.

70. Zemskov, "GULAG (Istoriko-sotsiologicheskii aspekt)," *Sotsiologicheskii issledovaniya* (1991), no. 6, 10–27; no. 7, 3–16. See also Edwin Bacon, *The Gulag at War: Stalin's Forced Labor System in the Light of the Archives* (New York, 1994), 151.

71. See Anne Applebaum, *Gulag: A History* (New York, 2003), 311.

72. Doc. 211 in T. V. Tsarevskaia-Diakina, ed., *Istoria stalinskogo Gulaga* (Moscow, 2004), 5:707–8; Lynne Viola, *The Unknown Gulag: The Lost World of Stalin's Special Settlements* (New York, 2007).

73. Aleksander Solzhenitsyn, *The Gulag Archipelago, 1918–1956*, 3 vols. (New York, 1973).

74. Ivanova, *Istoriia GULAGa*, 388–89.

CHAPTER 8. STALIN AND TRUMAN: FALSE STARTS

1. Meeting, Apr. 13, 1945, doc. 219 in *Sovetsko-Amerikanskie otnoseheniya vo vremya Velikoi Otechestvennoie Voiny, 1941–1945* (Moscow, 1984), 2:356–59; *FRUS, 1945*, 5:825–29.

2. V. O. Pechatnov, "Ot siouza—k vrazde: Sovetsko-amerikanske otnoshenia v 1945–1946 gg," in N. I. Egorova and A. O. Chubarian, eds., *Kholodnaia voina, 1945–1963 gg.: Istoricheskaia retrospektiva. Sbornik statei* (Moscow, 2003), 21–35.

3. Robert H. Ferrell, ed., *Off the Record: The Private Papers of Harry S. Truman* (New York, 1980), 16.

4. *FRUS, 1945*, 5,:211.

5. For the exchange, see ibid., 5:213–25.

6. Truman and Churchill to Stalin, received Apr. 18, 1945, in *Stalin Correspondence*, 2:204–5.

7. Bohlen to Stettinius, in *FRUS, 1945*, 5:832–38.

8. David McCullough, *Truman* (New York, 1992), 486.

9. W. Averell Harriman and Elie Abel, *Special Envoy to Churchill and Stalin, 1941–1946* (New York, 1975), 447–50.

10. Felix I. Chuev, *Molotov: Poluderzhavnyii vlastelin* (Moscow, 2000), 93.

11. Charles E. Bohlen, *Witness to History, 1929–1969* (New York, 1973), 213; *FRUS, 1945*, 5:219–21; Thomas M. Campbell and George C. Herring, eds., *The Diaries of Edward R. Stettinius, Jr., 1943–1946* (New York, 1946), 328–29.

12. See the classic study by Daniel Yergin: *Shattered Peace: The Origins of the Cold War and the National Security State* (Cambridge, Mass., 1977), 83, 181.

13. Doc. 226 in *Sovetsko-Amerikanskie otnoseheniya vo vremya Velikoi Otechestvennoie Voiny*, 2:367–69.

14. Andrei A. Gromyko, *Pamiatnoe* (Moscow, 1990), 1:257–58.

15. Harry S. Truman, *Memoirs*, vol. 1, *Year of Decisions* (Garden City, N.Y., 1955), 10.

16. Nikolai V. Novikov, *Vospominanya diplomata: zapiski, 1938–1947* (Moscow, 1989), 289–91.

17. Stalin to Truman, Apr. 24, 1945, in *Stalin Correspondence*, 2:208–9; Truman, *Memoirs*, 1:85–86.

18. Henry Stimson, Diary, entry for Apr. 25, 1945, Library of Congress, microfilm; Truman, *Memoirs*, 1:87.

19. NA, RG 200, Papers of General Leslie R. Groves, Correspondence 1941–1970, Box 3, F.

20. Truman, Grew, Harriman, and Bohlen, conversation, May 15, 1945, in FRUS, *The Conference of Berlin (Potsdam Conference)*, 1:13, henceforth FRUS, *Potsdam Conference*.

21. See, e.g., Tsuyoshi Hasegawa, *Racing the Enemy: Stalin, Truman, and the Surrender of Japan* (Cambridge, Mass., 2005), 78; Gar Alperovitz, *The Decision to Use the Atomic Bomb and the Architecture of an American Myth* (New York, 1995), 138–54. See also Soviet accounts; Dimitri Volkogonov, *Stalin: Triumf i tragediya. Politichesky portret v 2 knigakh* (Moscow, 1996), 2:409, Gromyko, *Pamiatnoe*, 1:270.

22. Richard Rhodes, *The Making of the Atomic Bomb* (New York, 1986), 628–29.

23. Richard B. Frank, *Downfall: The End of the Imperial Japanese Empire* (New York, 1999), 117, 132.

24. David Holloway, *Stalin and the Bomb* (New Haven, Conn., 1994), 114–15.

25. Ibid., 72–88; Chuev, *Molotov*, 96.

26. Aide-memoire, Sept. 19, 1944, in FRUS, *Conference at Quebec, 1944*, 492–93.

27. Christopher Andrew, *Defend the Realm: The Authorized History of MI5* (New York, 2009), 368.

28. Holloway, *Stalin and the Bomb*, 105.

29. Gromyko, *Pamiatnoe*, 1:274.

30. See *New York Times*, June 24, for a story by Turner Catledge and another by Arthur Krock, the latter noting that Truman's remark was not to be taken seriously.

31. Gromyko, Apr. 21, 1945, doc. 224 in *Sovetsko-Amerikanski otnosheniya vo vremya Velikoi Otechestvennoie Voiny, 1941–1945*, 2:364–67.

32. Wilson D. Miscamble, *From Roosevelt to Truman: Potsdam, Hiroshima, and the Cold War* (New York, 2007), 137.

33. Churchill to Truman, in FRUS, *Potsdam Conference*, 1:9.

34. Campbell and Herring, eds., *Diaries of Stettinius*, 357–58; Truman, *Memoirs*, 1:227–28.

35. Telegram from Novikov, to Commissariat for Foreign Affairs, May 12–13, 1945, doc. 250 in *Sovetsko-Amerikanski otnosheniya vo vremya Velikoi Otechestvennoie Voiny, 1941–1945*, 2:388–91. For a revisionist interpretation of this misstep, see Yergin, *Shattered Peace*, 83–100.

36. For a nuanced account, see Miscamble, *Roosevelt to Truman*, 87–135.

37. Davies diary and Davies journal (May 13), Joseph E. Davies Papers, Library of Congress, Box 16.

38. Harriman and Abel, *Special Envoy*, 457.

39. Davies to Stalin, via Molotov, May 14; Molotov to Davies, May 20; and Davies to Truman, May 22, in Joseph E. Davies Papers, Library of Congress, Boxes 16 and 17.

40. Miscamble, *Roosevelt to Truman*, 148–53.

41. Diary entry for May 29, 1945, in Anthony Eden, *The Reckoning: The Memoirs of Anthony Eden, Earl of Avon* (Boston, 1965), 624.

42. Ivan Serov, report to Stalin, Mar. 22, in GARF, f. 9401, op. 2, d. 94, l. 122–26.

43. Doc. 42, Apr. 6, in *Russkii Arkhiv: Velikaya Otechestvennaya Voina: T 14 (3-1): SSSR i Polsha* (Moscow, 1994), 478–79, hereafter *SSSR I Polsha*.

44. Beria to Stalin, May 11, APRF, f. 3, op. 58, d. 277, l. 92–101.

45. Arthur Bliss Lane, *I Saw Poland Betrayed: An American Ambassador Reports to the American People* (New York, 1948), 108.

46. Beria to Stalin, May 31, APRF, f. 3, op. 58, d. 277, l. 141–142; also RGASPI, f. 17, op. 162, d. 37, l. 144.

47. Hopkins meeting, May 26, 1945, in *FRUS, Potsdam Conference*, 1:27.

48. Ibid., 1:29, 32–33.

49. *FRUS, 1945*, 5:301–6.

50. Hopkins to Truman, May 30, ibid., 5:307.

51. Ferrell, *Off the Record*, 44.

52. Stanisław Mikołajczyk, *The Rape of Poland: Pattern of Soviet Aggression* (New York, 1948), 111–30.

53. Docs. 43–45, June 19–21, in *SSSR i Polsha*, 479–86.

54. Rokossovsky whispered this news at Potsdam to Commissar Kuznetsov. See N. G. Kuznetsov, *Kursom k pobede* (Moscow, 2000), 500.

55. Jamil Hasanli, *Stalin and the Turkish Crisis of the Cold War, 1945–1953* (Plymouth, U.K., 2011), 379.

56. Odd Arne Westad, *The Global Cold War: Third World Interventions and the Making of Our Times* (New York, 2005), 58.

57. Hasanli, *Stalin and the Turkish Crisis*, 381.

58. Jonathan Haslam, *Russia's Cold War: From the October Revolution to the Fall of the Wall* (New Haven, Conn., 2011), 47–48.

59. Vladislav M. Zubok, *A Failed Empire: The Soviet Union in the Cold War from Stalin to Gorbachev* (Chapel Hill, N.C., 2007), 39–40.

60. Stalin to Molotov, Nov. 20, 1946, quoted in Vladimir O. Pechatnov, " 'The Allies Are Pressing on You to Break Your Will.' Foreign Policy Correspondence Between Stalin and Molotov and Other Politburo Members, Sept. 1945–Dec. 1946," CWIHP Working Paper no. 26 (1999), 22.

61. Jamil Hasanli, *At the Dawn of the Cold War: The Soviet-American Crisis over Iranian Azerbaijan, 1941–1946* (Cambridge, Mass., 2006), 48–50.

62. CWIHP archive, 1945–46 Iranian Crisis, CPSU Politburo to Central Committee, Communist Party of Azerbaijan, July 6, 1945.

63. Jörg Baberowski, *Der Feind ist überall: Stalinismus im Kaukasus* (Munich, 2003), 791–830.

64. Hasanali, *Dawn of Cold War*, 70.

65. Zubok, *Failed Empire*, 41.

66. Allan Bullock, *Ernest Bevin, Foreign Secretary, 1945–1951* (London, 1983), 236.

67. Byrnes to Kennan, Mar. 8, 1946, in *FRUS, 1946*, 7:348.

68. Hasanli, *Dawn of Cold War*, 234.

69. Ibid., 244.

70. Ibid., 239–42.

71. Bullock, *Bevin*, 237.

72. Stalin to Pishavari, cited in Natalia Egorova, " 'Iranskii krisis,' 1945–1946 gg: vzglyad iz rossiiskikh arkhivov," *Novaiia i noveishaiia istoriia* (May–June 1994), 41.

73. Hasanli, *Dawn of Cold War*, 370.

74. Louise L'Estrange Fawcett, *Iran and the Cold War: The Azerbaijan Crisis of 1946* (Cambridge, U.K., 1992), 179.

75. *FRUS, 1946*, 7:816; *FRUS, 1945*, 1:1017–18; William Taubman, *Stalin's American Policy: From Entente to Détente to Cold War* (New York, 1982), 149–50.

CHAPTER 9. POTSDAM, THE BOMB, AND ASIA

1. See T. V. Volokitina et al., *Moskva i Vostochnaia Evropa: stanovlenie politicheskikh rezhimov sovetskogo tipa, 1949–1953: ocherki istorii* (Moscow, 2002), 27–41. See also T. V. Volokitina et

al., *Narodnaja demokratija: Mif ili realnost? Obchchestvenno-politicheskie processy v Vostoch-noi Evrope: 1944–1948 gg.* (Moscow, 1993), 314.

2. David McCullough, *Truman* (New York, 1992), 409.

3. Truman to Bess, July 20, in Robert H. Ferrell, ed., *Dear Bess: The Letters from Harry to Bess Truman, 1910–1959* (New York, 1983), 520.

4. Robert H. Ferrell, ed., *Off the Record: The Private Papers of Harry S. Truman* (New York, 1980), 50–53.

5. Dimitri Volkogonov, *Stalin: Triumf i tragediya. Politichesky portret v 2 knigakh* (Moscow, 1996), 2:410–11.

6. Georgi K. Zhukov, *Vospominaniya i razmyshleniya* (Moscow, 2002), 2:368.

7. *Sovetskii Soiuz na mezhdunarodnykh konferentsiiakh perioda Velikoi otechestvennoi voiny 1941–1945 gg.: Berlinskaia (Potsdamskaia) Konferentsiia: Sbornik dokumentov* (Moscow, 1984), 6:39–41, henceforth *Potsdamskaia Konferentsiia; FRUS, Potsdam Conference*, 2:44–45.

8. Zhukov, *Vospominaniya i razmyshleniya*, 2:368–69.

9. Truman to Bess, July 18, 1945, in Ferrell, *Dear Bess*, 519.

10. Ferrell, *Off the Record*, 53.

11. George L. Harrison to Stimson, July 16, 1945, doc. 1304 in *FRUS, Potsdam Conference*, 2:1360.

12. Ferrell, *Off the Record*, 53–54.

13. Henry Stimson, Diary, July 17, 1945, Library of Congress, microfilm.

14. Ibid., July 21, 1945; also cited in *FRUS, Potsdam Conference*, 2:1361. The Groves report is doc. 1305, 2:1361–70.

15. Sean L. Malloy, *Atomic Tragedy: Henry L. Stimson and the Decision to Use the Bomb Against Japan* (New York, 2008), 130.

16. *Potsdamskaia Konferentsiia*, 114–15; *FRUS, Potsdam Conference*, 2:210–19.

17. *Potsdamskaia Konferentsiia*, 114; *FRUS, Potsdam Conference*, 2:210.

18. *Potsdamskaia Konferentsiia*, 115–16; *FRUS, Potsdam Conference*, 2:220–21.

19. Remarks to plenary session, July 21, 1945, *Potsdamskaia Konferentsiia*, 115–20; *FRUS, Potsdam Conference*, 2:214.

20. George F. Kennan, *Memoirs, 1925–1950* (Boston, 1967), 263–65.

21. Meeting of July 23, in *Potsdamskaia Konferentsiia*, 153; *FRUS, Potsdam Conference*, 2:305, 314.

22. *Potsdamskaia Konferentsiia*, 172–73; *FRUS, Potsdam Conference*, 2:362.

23. Harry S. Truman, *Memoirs*, vol. 1, *Year of Decisions* (Garden City, N.Y., 1955), 416.

24. Winston S. Churchill, *Triumph and Tragedy* (Boston, 1953), 669–70.

25. Andrei A. Gromyko, *Pamiatnoe* (Moscow, 1990), 1:272.

26. James F. Byrnes, *Speaking Frankly* (New York, 1947), 263.

27. A. I. Ioirysh, I. D. Morokhov, and S. K. Ivanov, *A-Bomba* (Moscow, 1980), 234–37.

28. Felix I. Chuev, *Molotov: Poluderzhavnyii vlastelin* (Moscow, 2000), 98–99.

29. Zhukov, *Vospominaniya i razmyshleniya*, 2:374–75.

30. See G. A. Goncharov and L. D. Riabev, "O Sozdanii pervoi otechestvennoi atomnoi bomby," http://wsyachina.narod.ru/history/rds.

31. Vladimir M. Chikov and Gary Kern, *Okhota za atomnoi bomboi: Dosye KGB No. 13676* (Moscow, 2001), 250–52.

32. Gromyko, *Pamiatnoe*, 1:277.

33. L. D. Riabev, ed., *Atomnyi proekt SSSR. Dokumenty i materialy. Tom II, Atomnaia bomba 1945–1954, kniga 1* (Moscow, 1999), 11–13; David Holloway, "Jockeying for Position in the Postwar World: Soviet Entry into the War with Japan in August 1945," in Tsuyoshi Hasegawa, ed., *The End of the War in the Pacific* (Stanford, Calif., 2007), 185.

34. Stalin-Kurchstov conversation, Jan. 25, 1946, in CWIHP, *Bulletin* (Fall 1994), 5.

35. David Holloway, *Stalin and the Bomb* (New Haven, Conn., 1994), 172–223.

36. Doc. 1152 in *FRUS, Potsdam Conference*, 2:480, 1150–51.

37. Entry for July 25, 1945, in Ferrell, *Off the Record*, 56.

38. Remarks, July 31, 1945, in *Potsdamskaia Konferentsiia*, 244–45; *FRUS, Potsdam Conference*, 2:522, 536.

39. *FRUS, Potsdam Conference*, 2:1474–76.

40. Ibid., 2:476.

41. Letter, July 29, 1945, in Ferrell, *Dear Bess*, 522.

42. For a review of the literature, see Barton J. Bernstein, "Introducing the Interpretive Problems of Japan's 1945 Surrender: A Historiographical Essay on Recent Literature in the West," in Hasegawa, *End of the War in Pacific*, 11–64.

43. Tsuyoshi Hasegawa, "The Soviet Factor in Ending the Pacific War: From the Neutrality Pact to Soviet Entry into the War in August 1945," in Hasegawa, *End of the War in Pacific*, 202. For a concise refutation of the theory that the bomb was aimed mainly to intimidate the Soviets, see Campbell Craig and Sergey Radchenko, *The Atomic Bomb and the Origins of the Cold War* (New Haven, Conn., 2008), 81–86.

44. For discussion and further reading, see the online H-Diplo Roundtable discussion of Hasegawa's *Racing the Enemy*, here the remarks of Barton J. Bernstein, http://www.h-net.org/~diplo/roundtables/PDF/Roundtable-XIII-30.pdf.

45. Frank, *Downfall*, 214–39.

46. John R. Deane, *The Strange Alliance: The Story of Our Efforts at Wartime Co-operation with Russia* (New York, 1947), 267–85.

47. Alexander M. Vasilevsky, *Delo vsei zhisni* (Moscow, 1978), 518.

48. Kuznetsov, *Kursom k pobede*, 510–11.

49. Hasegawa, "Soviet Factor," in Hasegawa, *End of the War in Pacific*, 221–22.

50. Directive in V. A. Zolotarev, ed., *Sovetsko-iaponskaia voina 1945 goda: istoriia voennopoliticheskogo-protivoborstva dvukh derzhav v 30–40e gody: Dokumenty i materially v 2 t.* (Moscow, 1997), vol. 18 (7–1), 341.

51. Vasilevsky, *Delo vsei zhisni*, 523.

52. Tsuyoshi Hasegawa, *Racing the Enemy: Stalin, Truman, and the Surrender of Japan* (Cambridge, Mass., 2005), 217–26; Holloway, "Jockeying for Position," in Hasegawa, *End of the War in Pacific*, 175–78.

53. Deane, *Strange Alliance*, 278–79; W. Averell Harriman and Elie Abel, *Special Envoy to Churchill and Stalin, 1941–1946* (New York, 1975), 498–500.

54. Harriman and Abel, *Special Envoy*, 501.

55. Wesley Frank Craven and James Lea Cate, eds., *The Army Air Forces in World War II* (Washington, D.C., 1953), 5:732–33, cited in John W. Dower, *War Without Mercy: Race and Power in the Pacific War* (New York, 1986), 300–1.

56. Hasegawa, *Racing the Enemy*, 241–48.

57. David M. Glantz, *The Soviet Strategic Offensive in Manchuria, 1945: "August Storm"* (London, 2003), 60.

58. Zolotarev, *Sovetsko-iaponskaia voina*, vol. 18 (7-1), 343–48.

59. Hasegawa, *Racing the Enemy*, 256, 259.

60. Ibid., 252–55.

61. For the order and accompanying note, see *FRUS, 1945*, 6:658–60.

62. Stalin to Truman, Aug. 16, 1945, ibid., 667–68.

63. Truman to Stalin, Aug. 18, 1945, ibid., 670.

64. Stalin to Truman, Aug. 22, 1945, ibid., 687–88.

65. Directive in Zolotarev, *Sovetsko-iaponskaia voina*, vol. 18 (7-2), 43.

66. Erik van Ree, *Socialism in One Zone: Stalin's Policy in Korea, 1945–1947* (Oxford, U.K., 1989),

62–67; Holloway, "Jockeying for Position," in Hasegawa, *End of the War in Pacific*, 180–81; Hasegawa, *Racing the Enemy*, 268–70.

67. *Voina v Koree, 1950–1953* (Moscow, 2003), 3–6. For a general account, see David Halberstam, *The Coldest Winter: America and the Korean War* (New York, 2007), 47–81.

68. Hasegawa, *Racing the Enemy*, 280–85.

69. Tsuyoshi Hasegawa, "The Atomic Bombs and the Soviet Invasion: Which Was More Important in Japan's Decision to Surrender?" in Hasegawa, *End of the War in Pacific*, 143. For evidence of the military's will to fight on after August 15, see Toshikazu Kase, *Journey to the Missouri*, David N. Rowe, ed. (New Haven, Conn., 1950), 258–65.

70. Sumio Hatano, "The Atomic Bomb and Soviet Entry into the War: Of Equal Importance," in Hasegawa, *End of the War in Pacific*, 112.

71. Hasegawa, *Racing the Enemy*, 288.

72. Vasilevsky, *Delo vsei zhisni*, 535.

73. For a similar assertion, by a commander of the attack through Mongolia, see I. A. Pliev, *Cherez Gobi i Khingan* (Moscow, 1965), 49.

74. K. A. Meretskov, *Na sluzhbe narodu* (Moscow, 1968), 449; for similar argumentation, see Chuev, *Molotov*, 98–99.

75. Stalin, *Sochineniia*, 15:212–15.

76. Dieter Heinzig, *The Soviet Union and Communist China, 1945–1950: The Arduous Road to the Alliance* (New York, 2004), 4.

77. Chen Jian, *Mao's China and the Cold War* (Chapel Hill, N.C., 2001), 26–32.

78. M. M. Zagorulko, ed., *Voennoplennye v SSSR 1939–1956: dokumenty i materialy* (Moscow, 2000), 10, 25–59.

79. John Dower, *Embracing Defeat: Japan in the Wake of World War II* (New York, 1999), 51–52n27, 570.

CHAPTER 10. SOVIET RETRIBUTION AND POSTWAR TRIALS

1. U.S. Department of State, Oct. 7, 1942, in Report of Robert H. Jackson, *International Conference on Military Trials* (London, 1945), 9; Arieh J. Kochavi, *Prelude to Nuremberg: Allied War Crimes Policy and the Question of Punishment* (Chapel Hill, N.C., 1998), 28–35.

2. Marina Sorokina, "People and Procedures: Toward a History of the Investigation of Nazi Crimes in the USSR," *Kritika: Explorations in Russian and Eurasian History* (2005), 801; *FRUS, 1942. Europe*, 3:473.

3. U.S. Department of State, Dec. 17, 1942, in Jackson, *International Conference on Military Trials*, 9–10.

4. Sorokina, "People and Procedures," 824–25.

5. Entries for Apr. 14–28, 1943, in Elke Fröhlich et al., eds., *Die Tagebücher von Joseph Goebbels* (Munich, 1993), 2; 8:101–78.

6. Wendy Lower, *Nazi Empire-Building and the Holocaust in Ukraine* (Chapel Hill, N.C., 2005), 194–97; Anthony Dragan, *Vinnytsia: A Forgotten Holocaust* (Jersey City, N.J., 1986), 11.

7. Sergey Kudryashov and Vanessa Voisin, "The Early Stages of 'Legal Purges' in Soviet Russia (1941–1945)," in *Cahiers du Monde russe* (2008), 263–96, and more generally Amir Weiner, *Making Sense of War: The Second World War and the Fate of the Bolshevik Revolution* (Princeton, N.J., 2001).

8. Ilya Bourtman, "'Blood for Blood, Death for Death': The Soviet Military Tribunal in Krasnodar, 1943," *Holocaust and Genocide Studies* (2008), 248; Tanja Penter, "Local Collab-

orators on Trial: Soviet War Crimes Trials Under Stalin (1943–1953)," *Cahiers du Monde russe* (2008), 357.

9. *New York Times*, July 19, 1943.

10. The trial was held Dec. 15–18. See *Nazi Crimes in Ukraine 1941–1944, Documents and Materials* (Kiev, 1987), 279–83.

11. W. Averell Harriman to Cordell Hull, Dec. 16, 20, 22, and 31, 1943, in *FRUS, The British Commonwealth, Eastern Europe, the Far East* (1943), 3:846–51; also *New York Times*, Dec. 20, 1943.

12. Kochavi, *Prelude to Nuremberg*, 73.

13. *FRUS, 1943, General*, 1:768–69.

14. *Sovetskii Soyuz na mezhdunarodnykh konferentsiyakh perioda Velikoi Otechestvennoi Voiny, 1941–1945 gg.: Sbornik dokumentov: T. 2 Tegeranskaya konferentsiya rukovoditelei trekh soyuznykh derzhav—SSSR, SShA i Velikobritanii* (Moscow: 1984), xxx; *FRUS, The Conferences at Cairo and Tehran*, (1943), 553–54; Michael Beschloss, *The Conquerors: Roosevelt, Truman and the Destruction of Hitler's Germany, 1941–1945* (New York, 2002), 27.

15. Winston Churchill, *Closing the Ring* (Boston, Mass., 1951), 374.

16. Feb. 4, 1945, in *Sovetskii Soyuz na mezhdunarodnykh konferentsiyakh perioda Velikoi Otechestvennoi Voiny, 1941–1945 gg.: Sbornik dokumentov: T. 4 Krymskaya konferentsiya rukovoditelei trekh soyuznykh derzhav—SSSR, SShA i Velikobritanii* (Moscow, 1979), xxx; *FRUS, Malta and Yalta* (1945), 571.

17. Kochavi, *Prelude to Nuremberg*, 224.

18. Norbert Frei, ed., *Transnationale Vergangenheitspolitik: Der Umgang mit deutschen Kriegsverbrechern in Europa nach dem Zweiten Weltkrieg* (Göttingen, 2006), 31–32, table 1.

19. Bourtman, " 'Blood for Blood, Death for Death,' " 248.

20. For overviews, see Tony Judt, *Postwar: A History of Europe Since 1945* (New York, 2005), 41–50; Jean-Pierre Rioux, *The Fourth Republic, 1944–1958* (Cambridge, U.K., 1987), 32; and István Deák, Jan T. Gross, and Tony Judt, eds., *The Politics of Retribution in Europe: World War II and Its Aftermath* (Princeton, N.J., 2000), 4.

21. Frei, *Transnationale Vergangenheitspolitik*, 32.

22. B. N. Kovalev, *Kollaboratsionizm v Rossii v 1941–1945 gg.: tipy i formy* (Moscow, 2009), 5–20; A. E. Epifanov, *Otvetstvennost za voennye prestupleniia, sovershennye na territorii SSSR v period Velikoi Otechestvennoi Voiny: istoriko-pravovoie aspekt* (Moscow, 2001), 382; Kudryashov and Voisin, "Early Stages of 'Legal Purges,' " 266–67. For slightly different numbers, see Penter, "Local Collaborators on Trial," 356.

23. See, e.g. Merkulov to Stalin, Mar. 19, 1943, in APRF, f. 3, op. 58, d. 207, l. 159–75.

24. Beria to Stalin, Jan. 8, 1944, in GARF, f. 9401, op. 2, d. 64, l. 9–13.

25. Jeffrey W. Jones, " 'Every Family Has Its Freak' ": Perceptions of Collaboration in Occupied Soviet Russia, 1943–1948," *Slavic Review* (2005), 755.

26. Hiroki Kuromiya, *Freedom and Terror in the Donbas: A Ukrainian-Russian Borderland, 1870s–1990s* (Cambridge, U.K., 1998), 298.

27. Marius Broekmeyer, *Stalin, the Russians, and Their War, 1941–1945* (Madison, Wisc., 1999), 180–81.

28. Ibid., 208.

29. Decision GKO, June 24, 1942, in APRF, f. 3, op. 57, d. 59, l. 67.

30. Felix I. Chuev, *Molotov: Poluderzhavnyi vlastelin* (Moscow, 2000), 453–54.

31. GARF, f. 9401, op. 2, d. 66, l. 232.

32. Simon Sebag Montefiore, *Stalin: The Court of the Red Tsar* (New York, 2004), 379–80.

33. Christian Streit, *Keine Kameraden: Die Wehrmacht und die sowjetischen Kriegsgefangenen, 1941–1945* (Stuttgart, 1978), 244, 247.

34. Ulrich Herbert, *Fremdarbeiter: Politik und Praxis des "Ausländer-Einsatzes" in der Kriegswirtschaft des Dritten Reiches* (Berlin, 1986), 271, table 42.

35. Catherine Andreyev, *Vlasov and the Russian Liberation Movement: Soviet Reality and Émigré Theories* (Cambridge, U.K., 1987), 7–10, 72–79.

36. The standard work, also on incorrect numbers, is Rüdiger Overmans, *Deutsche militärische Verluste im Zweiten Weltkrieg* (Munich, 2004), 161–63, 229.

37. Ulrike Goeken-Haidl, *Der Weg zurück: Die Repatriierung sowjetischer Zwangsarbeiter und Kriegsgefangener während und nach dem Zweiten Weltkrieg* (Essen, 2006), 77–78.

38. Anthony Eden, *The Reckoning: The Memoirs of Anthony Eden, Earl of Avon* (Boston, 1965), 560–61.

39. S. M. Plokhy, *Yalta: The Price of Peace* (New York, 2010), 300.

40. Jason Kendall Moore, "Between Expediency and Principle: U.S. Repatriation Policy Toward Russian Nationals, 1944–1949," *Diplomatic History* (2000), 386.

41. Goeken-Haidl, *Der Weg zurück*, 89–93; John R. Deane, *The Strange Alliance: The Story of Our Efforts at Wartime Co-operation with Russia* (New York, 1947), 183–84.

42. Moore, "Between Expediency and Principle," 384.

43. Stettinius to Harriman, Jan. 3, 1945, in *FRUS, Conferences at Malta and Yalta*, 416.

44. *Sovetskii Soyuz na mezhdunarodnykh konferentsiyakh perioda Velikoi Otechestvennoi Voiny, 1941–1945 gg.: Sbornik dokumentov: T. 4 Krymskaya konferentsiya rukovoditelei trekh soyuznykh derzhav—SSSR, SShA i Velikobritanii* (Moscow, 1979), 210–11; *FRUS, Conferences at Malta and Yalta*, 985–87.

45. Mikhail Heller and Aleksandr M. Nekrich, *Utopia in Power: The History of the Soviet Union from 1917 to the Present* (New York, 1986), 451.

46. W. Averell Harriman and Elie Abel, *Special Envoy to Churchill and Stalin 1941–1946* (New York, 1975), 416–17; David Reynolds, *Summits: Six Meetings That Shaped the Twentieth Century* (New York, 2007), 141.

47. See the front-page story "Russians Captured with Nazis Riot at Fort Dix: 3 Commit Suicide," *New York Times*, June 30, 1945.

48. The story is told in Deane, *Strange Alliance*, 190–94.

49. Roosevelt to Stalin, Mar. 3, 1945, and Stalin to Roosevelt, Mar. 5, 1945, in *Stalin Correspondence*, 2:184–85.

50. Stalin to Roosevelt, Mar. 22, 1945, ibid., 2:186–87; Harriman and Abel, *Special Envoy*, 419–23.

51. Deane, *Strange Alliance*, 200.

52. Harriman to Roosevelt, Mar. 24, 1945, and Harriman to Secretary of State, Apr. 2, 1945, in *FRUS, 1945, Europe*, 1084–88.

53. Goeken-Haidl, *Der Weg zurück*, 545–50.

54. See the oft-cited statistics in Richard Overy, *Russia's War* (New York, 1997), 303.

55. Goeken-Haidl, *Der Weg zurück*, 549.

56. Mark Edele, *Soviet Veterans of the Second World War: A Popular Movement in an Authoritarian Society, 1941–1991* (Oxford, U.K., 2008), 102–18.

57. Geoffrey Hosking, *Rulers and Victims: The Russians in the Soviet Union* (Cambridge, Mass., 2006), 217.

58. Alexander Victor Prusin, " 'Fascist Criminals to the Gallows!': The Holocaust and Soviet War Crimes Trials, Dec. 1945–February 1946," *Holocaust and Genocide Studies* (2003), 6; Bourtman, " 'Blood for Blood, Death for Death,' " 251, 257.

59. Stalin, *Sochineniia*, 15:71–83.

60. Molotov's Jan. 6 report in *Pravda*, Jan. 7, 1942.

61. Ibid., Apr. 28, 1942, May 11, 1943.

62. U.S. Department of State, Dec. 17, 1942, in Report of Jackson, *International Conference on Military Trials*, 3–17.

63. *Pravda*, Dec. 18 and 19, 1942. For a detailed study, see Karel C. Berkhoff, " 'Total Annihilation of the Jewish Population': The Holocaust in the Soviet Media, 1941–45," *Kritika: Explorations in Russian and Eurasian History* (2009), 61–105.

64. See the declaration and story, Jan. 18, 1943, in Laurel Leff, *Buried by The Times: The Holocaust and America's Most Important Newspaper* (New York, 2005), 159–62.

65. Stalin, *Sochineniia*, 15:162–74.

66. Mar. 14, ibid., 16:25–30.

67. Berkhoff, " 'Total Annihilation of the Jewish Population,' " 93.

68. Sergei Maksudov, "The Jewish Population Losses of the USSR from the Holocaust: A Demographic Approach," in Lucjan Dobroszycki and Jeffrey S. Gurock, eds., *The Holocaust in the Soviet Union: Studies and Sources of the Destruction of the Jews in Nazi-Occupied Territories of the USSR, 1941–1945* (London, 1993), 212.

69. For this story and analysis of the Holocaust, see Robert Gellately, *Lenin, Stalin, and Hitler: The Age of Social Catastrophe* (New York, 2007), 413–68.

70. Andreas Hilger, " 'Die Gerechtigkeit nehme ihren Lauf': Die Bestrafung deutscher Kriegs- und Gewaltverbrecher in der Sowjetunion und der SBZ/DDR," in Frei, *Transnationale Vergangenheitspolitik*, 183.

71. Doc. 33 in D. G. Nadzhafov and Z. S. Belousova, eds., *Stalin i kosmopolitizm: dokumenty Agitpropa TSK KPSS, 1945–1953* (Moscow, 2005).

72. Josuha Rubenstein and Ilya Altman, eds., *The Unknown Black Book: The Holocaust in the German-Occupied Soviet Territories* (Bloomington, Ind., 2008), xix–xxxix.

73. Amir Weiner, "When Memory Counts: War, Genocide, and Postwar Soviet Jewry," in Weiner, ed., *Landscaping the Human Garden: Twentieth-Century Population Management in a Comparative Framework* (Stanford, Calif., 2003), 167–88.

74. Manfred Zeidler, "Der Minsker Kriegsverbrecherprozess vom Januar 1946: Kritische Anmerkungen zu einem sowjetischen Schauprozess gegen deutsche Kriegsgefangene," *Vierteljahrshefte für Zeitgeschichte* (2004), 226.

75. G. V. Kostyrchenko, *Tainaia politikika Stalina: Vlast i antisemitizm* (Moscow, 2001), 388–94.

76. Sorokina, "People and Procedures," 829–30.

77. Christopher R. Browning, *The Origins of the Final Solution: The Evolution of Nazi Jewish Policy, September 1939–March 1942* (Lincoln, Neb., 2004), 274–75.

78. Frank Grüner, "Did Anti-Jewish Mass Violence Exist in the Soviet Union? Anti-Semitism and Collective Violence in the USSR During the War and Post War Years," *Journal of Genocide Research* (2009), 361.

79. See Yitzhak Arad, *The Holocaust in the Soviet Union* (Lincoln, Neb., 2009), 543–44.

CHAPTER 11. SOVIET RETRIBUTION AND ETHNIC GROUPS

1. Pavel Polian, *Ne po svoyey vole. Istoriya i geografiya prinuditel'nykh migratsii v SSSR* (Moscow, 2001), 105.

2. Docs. 134 to 149 in S. V. Mironenko and N. Werth, eds., *Istoria stalinskogo Gulaga* (Moscow, 2004), 1:455–75.

3. Beria to Stalin, in APRF, f. 3, op. 58, d. 178, l. 6–9.

4. Fred C. Koch, *The Volga Germans in Russia and the Americas, from 1763 to the Present* (London, 1977), 284–85. On the lost culture, see Gerd Stricker, ed., *Deutsche Geschichte im Osten Europas: Russland* (Berlin, 1997).

5. Polian, *Ne po svoyey vole,* 105–16; Nicolas Werth, "A State Against Its People: Violence, Repression, and Terror in the Soviet Union," in Stéphane Courtois et al., *The Black Book of Communism* (Cambridge, U.K., 1999), 218; J. Otto Pohl, *Ethnic Cleansing in the USSR, 1937–1949* (Westport, Conn., 1999), 54.

6. M. M. Zagorulko, ed., *Voennoplennye v SSSR 1939–1956: dokumenty i materialy* (Moscow, 2000), 10, 25–59; for figures on German POW deaths in the USSR (363,000), see Rüdiger Overmans, *Deutsche militärische Verluste im Zweiten Weltkrieg* (Munich, 2004), 286.

7. Kruglov report to USSR government, May 24, 1950, doc. 9.1, in Zagorulko, *Voennoplennye v SSSR,* 916–20.

8. Notification, Dec. 28, 1943, APRF, f. 3, op. 58, d. 178, l. 73–76.

9. Peter Holquist, "To Count, to Extract, and to Exterminate: Population Statistics and Population Politics in Late Imperial and Soviet Russia," in Ronald Grigor Suny and Terry Martin, eds., *A State of Nations: Empire and Nation-Building in the Age of Lenin and Stalin* (New York, 2001), 116–19; Charles King, *The Ghost of Freedom: A History of the Caucasus* (New York, 2008), 94–96.

10. Jörg Baberowski, *Der Feind ist überall: Stalinismus im Kaukasus* (Munich, 2003), 553–632.

11. Aleksandr M. Nekrich, *The Punished Peoples: The Deportation and Tragic Fate of Soviet Minorities at the End of the Second World War* (New York, 1978), 25.

12. Alexander Statiev, "The Nature of Anti-Soviet Armed Resistance, 1942–44: The North Caucasus, the Kalmyk Autonomous Republic, and Crimea," *Kritika: Explorations in Russian and Eurasian History* (2005), 285–318.

13. Terry Martin, "The Origins of Soviet Ethnic Cleansing," *Journal of Modern History* (1998), 824–25.

14. Doc. 3.189 in N. L. Pobol and P. M. Polian, eds., *Stalinskie Deportatsii* (Moscow, 2005), 546.

15. HP, Schedule B, vol. 7, case 89; see also case 354; Polian, *Ne po svoyey vole,* 116.

16. Svetlana Alieva, ed., *Tak eto bylo: natsionalye repressii v SSSR 1919–1952 gody* (Moscow, 1993), 1:312.

17. Mironenko and Werth, *Istoria stalinskogo Gulaga,* 1:476–77.

18. Merkulov to Stalin, in APRF, f. 3, op. 58, d. 207, l. 159–75.

19. Statiev, "Anti-Soviet Armed Resistance," 305.

20. Beria to Stalin, Jan. 3, 1944, in GARF, f. 9401, op. 2, d. 64, l. 1. For their story in the oral testimony of a Kalmyk, see HP, Schedule B, vol. 7, case 23; Pohl, *Ethnic Cleansing,* 61–69; Mironenko and Werth, *Istoria stalinskogo Gulaga,* 1:477–80.

21. Alexander Statiev, "Soviet Ethnic Deportations: Intent Versus Outcome," *Journal of Genocide Research* (2009), 250.

22. Mironenko and Werth, *Istoria stalinskogo Gulaga,* 1:491–92.

23. HP, Schedule A, vol. 22, case 434, male, 54, Chechen, laborer; also case 81. See also Norman M. Naimark, *Fires of Hatred: Ethnic Cleansing in Twentieth-Century Europe* (Princeton, N.J., 2001), 94.

24. Jeffrey Burds, "The Soviet War Against 'Fifth Columnists': The Case of Chechnya," *Journal of Contemporary History* (2007), 305–6.

25. See GARF, f. 9401, op. 2, d. 64, l. 167–68; Polian, *Ne po svoyey vole,* 122.

26. Beria to Stalin. Feb. 29, 1944, in GARF, f. 9401, op. 2, d. 64, l. 161.

27. Quoted with other witnesses in Lyoma Usmanov, "The 1944 Deportation," *Chechen Times,* Feb. 13, 2004. See also Yo'av Karny, *Highlanders: A Journey to the Caucasus in Quest of Memory* (New York, 2000), 227; Amir Weiner, *Making Sense of War: The Second World War and the Fate of the Bolshevik Revolution* (Princeton, N.J., 2001), 151.

28. Quoted in Anatol Lieven, *Chechnya: Tombstone of Russian Power* (New Haven, Conn., 1998), 319.

29. For various numbers in this range, see Naimark, *Fires of Hatred*, 220n63.

30. Ibid., 98–99. For lower numbers, see N. F. Bugai, *Iosif Vissarionovich Stalin—Lavrentyu Berii: ikh nado deportirovat* (Moscow, 1992), 102n.

31. Quoted in Amy Knight, *Beria: Stalin's First Lieutenant* (Princeton, N.J., 1993), 127; and in Lieven, *Chechnya*, 320.

32. Quoted in Michaela Pohl, "From the Chechen People: Anti-Soviet Protest, 1944–1946," *Chechen Times*, Mar. 13, 2004.

33. Polian, *Ne po svoyey vole*, 131–35.

34. HP, Schedule A, vol. 13, case 159, 4.

35. Polian, *Ne po svoyey vole*, 125; Pohl, *Ethnic Cleansing*, 74–77, 87–92.

36. Natalia I. Egorova, "The 'Iran Crisis' of 1945–46: A View from the Russian Archives," CWIHP Working Paper no. 15 (Washington, D.C., 1996), 1–25; Bryan Glyn Williams, "Hidden Ethnocide in the Soviet Muslim Borderlands: The Ethnic Cleansing of the Crimean Tatars," *Journal of Genocide Research* (2002), 357–73.

37. Stalin order, May 11, 1944, in Mironenko and Werth, *Istoriia stalinskogo Gulaga*, 1:499–500.

38. Isaak Kobylyanskiy, *From Stalingrad to Pillau: A Red Army Artillery Officer Remembers the Great Patriotic War* (Lawrence, Kansas, 2008), 115–17.

39. Naimark, *Fires of Hatred*, 102.

40. Nekrich, *The Punished Peoples*, 111.

41. The correspondence is in Mironenko and Werth, *Istoriia stalinskogo Gulaga*, 1:495–500. See also Polian, *Ne po svoyey vole*, 126; Pohl, *Ethnic Cleansing*, 115.

42. Alieva, *Tak eto bylo*, 3:93.

43. Mironenko and Werth, *Istoria stalinskogo Gulaga*, 1:503–6; Polian, *Ne po svoyey vole*, 128.

44. Polian, *Ne po svoyey vole*, 127–29; Pohl, *Ethnic Cleansing*, 121, 132.

45. Statiev, "Soviet Ethnic Deportations," 248, table 3.

46. John Erickson, *The Road to Berlin: Stalin's War with Germany* (New Haven, Conn., 1983), 411–22.

47. Elena Zubkova, *Pribaltika i Kreml* (Moscow, 2008), 128–44.

48. See Valdis O. Lumans, *Latvia in World War II* (New York, 2006), 376–77.

49. Alexander Statiev, *The Soviet Counterinsurgency in the Western Borderlands* (Cambridge, U.K., 2010), 276–77; Mart Laar, *War in the Woods: Estonia's Struggle for Survival, 1945–1956* (Washington, D.C., 1992), 46–50.

50. Zubkova, *Pribaltika i Kreml*, 141–42.

51. Statiev, *Soviet Counterinsurgency*, 186–87.

52. Zubkova, *Pribaltika i Kreml*, 234, table 4.3.

53. Testimony in Laar, *War in the Woods*, 75–76.

54. Zukova, *Pribaltika i Kreml*, 234, table 4.3. Some variations in the statistics can be found in Statiev, *Soviet Counterinsurgency*, 110, table 4.4, also 190.

55. Statiev, *Soviet Counterinsurgency*, 156–58.

56. Docs. 177 and 178 in Mironenko and Werth, *Istoriia stalinskogo Gulaga*, 1:513–15.

57. I. M. Vladimirtsev and A. I. Kokurin, eds., *NKVD—MVD SSSR v borbe s banditizmom i vooruzhennym natsionalisticheskim podpolem na Zapadnoi Ukraine, v Zapadnoi Belorussii i Pribaltike (1939–1956): sbornik dokumentov* (Moscow, 2008), 371–72.

58. Weiner, *Making Sense of War*, 130–35.

59. Timothy Snyder, *The Reconstruction of Nations: Poland, Ukraine, Lithuania, Belarus, 1569–1999* (New Haven, Conn., 2005), 170.

60. Docs. 1–3, Sept. 17–22, 1944, in Stanisław Ciesielski, ed., *Umsiedlung der Polen aus den ehemaligen polnischen Ostgebieten nach Polen in den Jahren 1944–1947* (Marburg, 2006), 76–96.

61. Calculated from Statiev, *Soviet Counterinsurgency*, 125, table 4.10.

62. Maria Savchyn Pyskir, *Thousands of Roads: A Memoir of a Young Woman's Life in the Ukrainian Underground During and After World War II* (Jefferson, N.C., 2001), 38–39.

63. Statiev, *Soviet Counterinsurgency*, 110, table 4.4, also 190.

64. Pyshir, *Thousands of Roads*, 108–9.

65. For impressions, see Zygmunt Klukowski, *Red Shadow: A Physician's Memoir of the Soviet Occupation of Eastern Poland, 1944–1956* (Jefferson, N.C., 1997).

66. Kruglov to Stalin, Beria, and others, Oct. 31, 1946, doc. 127, in Vladimirtsev and Kokurin, *NKVD—MVD SSSR v borbe s banditizmom*, 365–67.

67. Krystyna Kersten, "Forced Migration and the Transformation of Polish Society in the Postwar Period," in Philipp Ther and Ana Siljak, eds., *Redrawing Nations: Ethnic Cleansing in East-Central Europe, 1944–1948* (Oxford, U.K., 2001), 75–86.

68. Timothy Snyder, *Bloodlands: Europe Between Hitler and Stalin* (New York, 2010), 328; Weiner, *Making Sense of War*, 173; Orest Subtelny, "Expulsion, Resettlement, Civil Strife: The Fate of Poland's Ukrainians, 1944–1947," in Ther and Siljak, *Redrawing Nations*, 155–72.

69. Alexander V. Prusin, *The Lands Between: Conflict in the East European Borderlands, 1870–1992* (Oxford, 2010), 223.

CHAPTER 12. REAFFIRMING COMMUNIST IDEOLOGY

1. Doc. 33 in Andrei Artizov and Oleg Naumov, eds., *Vlast i khudozhestvennaia intelligentsia: Dokumenty Tsk RKP(b)-VKP(b), VChK-OGPU-NKVD o kulturnoi politike, 1917–1953* (Moscow, 1953), 532.

2. Leszek Kolakowski, *Main Currents of Marxism*, vol. 3, *The Breakdown* (New York, 1981), 121.

3. HIA, U.S. Department of State, External Research Staff, *The Soviet Union as Reported by Former Soviet Citizens*, Report 1, Aug. 1951, 3.

4. Doc. 5 in Artizov and Naumov, *Vlast i khudozhestvennaia intelligentsia*, 532.

5. Kees Boterbloem, *The Life and Times of Andrei Zhdanov, 1896–1948* (Montreal and Kingston, 2004), 255.

6. Yoram Gorlizki and Oleg Khlevniuk, *Cold Peace: Stalin and the Soviet Ruling Circle, 1945–1953* (New York, 2004), 31.

7. Doc. 5 in Artizov and Naumov, *Vlast i khudozhestvennaia intelligentsia*, 550.

8. Doc. 13, Aug. 7, 1946, ibid., 563.

9. Meeting, Sept. 18, 1947, in Dmitrii T. Shepilov, *Neprimknushii* (Moscow, 2001), 87–90.

10. Andrei Zhdanov, "Report on the Journals 'Zvezda' and 'Leningrad' " in Zhdanov, *On Literature, Music and Philosophy* (London, 1950), 39–51.

11. Doc. 14 in Artizov and Naumov, *Vlast i khudozhestvennaia intelligentsia*, 565–81.

12. Doc. 19, ibid., 589.

13. See, e.g., *Pravda*, Sept. 18, 1946.

14. Nancy K. Anderson, *Anna Akhmatova: The Word That Causes Death's Defeat, Poems of Memory* (New Haven, Conn., 2004), 107–14, 135–42.

15. Leonid Koslov, "The Artist and the Shadow of Ivan," in Richard Taylor and Derek Spring, eds., *Stalinism and Soviet Cinema* (London, 1993), 109–11.

16. See the controversial Solomon Volkov, *Shostakovich and Stalin: The Extraordinary Relationship Between the Great Composer and the Brutal Dictator* (New York, 2004), 201.

17. Doc. 34 in Artizov and Naumov, *Vlast i khudozhestvennaia intelligentsia*, 613; also for what follows.

18. Konstantin M. Simonov, *Glazami cheloveka moego pokkoleniia: razmyshleniya o J. V. Staline* (Moscow, 1990), 162–63.

19. Maureen Perrie, *The Cult of Ivan the Terrible in Stalin's Russia* (New York, 2001), 163–79; Koslov, "Artist and the Shadow of Ivan," 129; Volkov, *Shostakovich and Stalin*, 202.

20. Doc. 34 in Artizov and Naumov, *Vlast i khudozhestvennaia intelligentsia*, 618.

21. Statements of Soviet Writers Union, meeting May 13, 1947, in G. V. Kostyrchenko, *Tainaia politikika Stalina: Vlast i antisemitizm* (Moscow, 2001), 310–14.

22. Kevin M. F. Platt, *Terror and Greatness: Ivan and Peter as Russian Myths* (Ithaca, N.Y., 2011), 248–52.

23. Boterbloem, *Zhdanov*, 303.

24. Shepilov, *Neprimknushii*, 105–8; *Pravda*, Feb. 11, 1948; Volkov, *Shostakovich and Stalin*, 215–31; Boterbloem, *Zhdanov*, 317–19.

25. Andrei Zhdanov, "On Music," in *On Literature, Music and Philosophy*, 52–75.

26. Shepilov, *Neprimknushii*, 127–36; Ethan Pollock, *Stalin and the Soviet Science Wars* (Princeton, N.J., 2006), 1–14, 47–56.

27. Nikolai Kremenstov, *The Cure: A Story of Cancer and Politics in the Annals of the Cold War* (Chicago, 2002), 84–89.

28. Ibid., 112–13.

29. RGASPI, f. 17, op. 3, d. 1064, l. 32.

30. Nikolai Kremenstov, *Stalinist Science* (Princeton, N.J., 1997), 137–38.

31. Kremenstov, *Cure*, 127.

32. Walter Bedell Smith, *My Three Years in Moscow* (New York, 1950), 290.

33. M. M. Wolff, "Some Aspects of Marriage and Divorce Laws in Soviet Russia," *Modern Law Review* (1949), 290–96.

34. Robert C. Tucker, "A Stalin Biographer's Memoir," in Samuel H. Baron and Carl Pletsch, eds., *Introspection in Biography: The Biographers' Quest for Self-Awareness* (London, 1985), 249–71; Robert C. Tucker, *Stalin in Power: The Revolution from Above, 1928–1941* (New York, 1990), 474–78.

35. Galina Mikhailovna Ivanova, *Istoriia GULAGa, 1918–1958: sotsialno-ekonomicheskii i politiko-pravovoi aspekty* (Moscow, 2006), 268–69; Boterbloem, *Zhdanov*, 302.

36. Doc. 40 in D. G. Nadzhafov and Z. S. Belousova, eds., *Stalin i kosmopolitizm : dokumenty Agitpropa TSK KPSS, 1945–1953* (Moscow, 2005).

37. Memo, Central Committee Agitprop, Jan. 28, 1948, doc. 58, ibid.

38. Simonov, *Glazami cheloveka moego pokoliniia*, 112–35.

39. Doc. 100 in Nadzhafov and Belousova, *Stalin i kosmopolitizm*.

40. V. L. Malkov, "Igra bez myacha: sotsialno-psikhologicheskii kontekst sovetskoi atomnoi diplomatii," in N. I. Egorova and A. O. Chubarian, eds., *Kholodnaia voina, 1945–1963 gg.: Istoricheskaia retrospektiva. Sbornik statei* (Moscow, 2003), 281–320.

41. Tucker, "Stalin Biographer's Memoir," 251.

42. Stalin, *Sochineniia*, vol. 8. The book, combined with reminiscences of Lenin, was translated into English as Joseph Stalin, *The Foundations of Leninism* (New York, 1932).

43. *Pravda*, May 6, 1937, in Stalin, *Sochineniia*, 14:209–12.

44. David Brandenburger, *National Bolshevism: Stalin Mass Culture and the Formation of Modern Russian National Identity, 1931–1956* (Cambridge, Mass., 2002), 47.

45. *Istoriia Vsesoiuznoe kommunisticheskoi partii (bolshevikov): Kratkii kurs* (Moscow, 1938), available as *The History of the Communist Party of the Soviet Union (Bolsheviks): Short Course* (Moscow, 1939).

46. Roy Medvedev, "How the *Short Course* Was Created," *Russian Politics and Law* (2005), 69–95.

47. For an example from war-torn Hungary, see János Kornai, *By Force of Thought: Irregular Memoirs of an Intellectual Journey* (Cambridge, Mass., 2006), 31.

48. Hua-yu Li, *Mao and the Economic Stalinization of China, 1948–1953* (New York, 2006); William J. Duiker, *Ho Chi Minh: A Life* (New York, 2000), 220–31; Philip Short, *Pol Pot: The Anatomy of a Nightmare* (New York, 2004), 66–67.

49. For a Russian perspective, see T. V. Volokitina et al., *Moskva i Vostochnaia Evropa: stanovlenie politicheskikh rezhimov sovetskogo tipa, 1949–1953: ocherki istorii* (Moscow, 2002), 1–30.

CHAPTER 13. NEW COMMUNIST REGIMES IN POLAND AND CZECHOSLOVAKIA

1. T. V. Volokitina et al., *Narodnaja demokratija: Mif ili realnost? Obchchestvenno-politicheskie processy v Vostochnoi Evrope: 1944–1948 gg.* (Moscow, 1993), 314; Norman Naimark, "Post-Soviet Russian Historiography on the Emergence of the Soviet Bloc," *Kritika: Explorations in Russian and Eurasian History* (2004), 561–80.

2. Krystyna Kersten, *The Establishment of Communist Rule in Poland, 1943–1948* (Berkeley, Calif., 1991), 63–65.

3. Stanisław Mikołajczyk, *The Rape of Poland: Pattern of Soviet Aggression* (New York, 1948), 100.

4. Report, Dec. 25, 1944, doc. 43a in *Russkii Arkhiv: Velikaya Otechestvennaya Voina: T 14 (3-1): SSSR i Polsha* (Moscow, 1994), 389–92, henceforth *SSSR i Polsha*.

5. Jan C. Behrends, *Die erfundene Freundschaft: Propaganda für die Sowjetunion in Polen und in der DDR* (Cologne, 2006), 101–6.

6. See, e.g., Beria report, Sept. 18, 1944, doc. 15, and Beria-Stalin, Oct. 13, doc. 18, in T. V. Volokitina et al., eds., *Sovetskii faktor v Vostochnoi Evrope 1944–1953* (Moscow, 1999), 1:96–98, 102–3.

7. Kersten, *Establishment of Communist Rule*, 118–56.

8. Treaty signed on April 21, published the next day in *Pravda*: see Stalin, *Sochineniia*, 15:214–15.

9. Kersten, *Establishment of Communist Rule*, 166.

10. Docs. 39–59, Nov. 1944–March 1945, in *SSSR i Polsha*, 383–419.

11. Marek Jan Chodakiewicz, *Between Nazis and Soviets: Occupation Politics in Poland, 1939–1947* (Oxford, U.K., 2004), 265–87.

12. Docs. 53 and 54, Feb. 17, 1945, in *SSSR i Polsha*, 407–9.

13. Doc. 44, March 17, 1945, in Volokitina et al., *Sovetskii faktor*, 1:165–66.

14. Doc. 112 in T. V. Volokitina et al., eds., *Vostochnaya Evropa v dokumentakh rossiiskikh arkhivov* (Moscow, 1997–98), 1:301–3.

15. Antoni Dudek and Andrzej Paczkowski, "Polen," in Łukasz Kamiński, Krzysztof Persak, and Jens Gieseke, eds., *Handbuch der kommunistischen Geheimdienste in Osteuropa, 1944–1991* (Göttingen, 2009), 265–89.

16. Włodzimierz Borodziej and Hans Lemberg, eds., *Die Deutschen östlich von Oder und Neisse 1945–1950: Dokumente aus polnischen Archiven* (Marburg, 2000), 2:55, 1:87, henceforth *Dokumente aus polnischen Archiven*.

17. Ibid., 3:311.

18. Andrzej Paczkowski, *The Spring Will Be Ours: Poland and the Poles from Occupation to Freedom* (University Park, Pa., 2003), 178–85; Kersten, *Establishment of Communist Rule*, 279–81.

19. Message from Warsaw, June 30, 1946, doc. 102 in Volokitina et al., *Sovetskii faktor*, 1:311–13.

20. Doc. 169 in Volokitina et al., *Vostochnaya Evropa*, 1:505; Soviet adviser report to Moscow, July 22, 1946, doc. 110 in Volokitina et al., *Sovetskii faktor*, 1:326–27.

21. Doc. 169 in Volokitina et al., *Vostochnaya Evropa*, 1:510–11.

22. Kersten, *Establishment of Communist Rule*, 331, 335.

23. Behrends, *Die erfundene Freundschaft*, 100, 115–16.

24. Maciej Korkuć, "Wybory 1947—mit założycielski komunizmu," *Biuletynie Instytutu Pamięci Narodowej* 1–2 (2007), 106–15.

25. V. F. Zima, *Golod v SSSR 1946–1947 godov: Proiskhozdenie i posledstviia* (Moscow, 1996), 149, 179.

26. Mikołajczyk, *Rape of Poland*, 230–50.

27. Andrzej Werblan, "Władysław Gomułka and the Dilemma of Polish Communism," *International Political Science Review/Revue internationale de science politique* (1988), 143–58.

28. Detlev Brandes, *Der Weg zur Vertreibung 1938–1945: Pläne und Entscheidungen zum "Transfer" der Deutschen aus der Tschechoslowakei und Polen*, 2nd ed. (Munich, 2005), 88.

29. Edvard Beneš, "The Organization of Postwar Europe," *Foreign Affairs* (Jan. 1942), 226–42.

30. July 6, 1942, in Brandes, *Der Weg zur Vertreibung*, 168.

31. May 12, 1942, ibid., 217–18.

32. Ibid., 226–27.

33. Record of the talks reprinted in Vojtech Mastny, ed., "The Beneš-Stalin-Molotov Conversations in December 1943: New Documents," in *Jahrbücher für Geschichte Osteuropas* (1972), 367–402.

34. Georgi Dimitrov, *Dnevnik: mart 1933–fevruari 1949: izbrano* (Sofia, 2003), 195.

35. Gusev talk with Beneš, March 17, 1945, doc. 46 in Volokitina et al., *Sovetskii faktor*, 1:173–74.

36. Quoted in Karel Kaplan, *The Short March: The Communist Takeover in Czechoslovakia, 1945–1948* (London, 1987), 11.

37. Hubert Ripka, *Czechoslovakia Enslaved: The Story of the Communist Coup d'état* (London, 1950), 30–31.

38. Chad Black, *Prague in Black: Nazi Rule and Czech Nationalism* (Cambridge, Mass., 2007), 235.

39. Report 29 in *Dokumentation der Vertreibung der Deutschen aus Ost-Mitteleuropa*, vol. 4, *Tschechoslowakei* (reprint, Munich, 2004), part 2, 159, henceforth *Dokumentation der Vertreibung*.

40. Report 25, ibid., 4:2:132–38.

41. Brandes, *Der Weg zur Vertreibung*, 412; Benjamin Frommer, *National Cleansing: Retribution Against Nazi Collaborators in Postwar Czechoslovakia* (Cambridge, U.K., 2005), 40–41.

42. Jiři Petráš and František Svátek, "Transport über die Grenze: Geschichte und Vorgeschichte der Aussiedlung der Deutschen Bevölkerung aus Südböhmen, 1945–1947," http://www.demokratiezentrum.org.

43. Report 29 in *Dokumentation der Vertreibung* 4:2:161–63.

44. Jeremy King, *Budweisers into Czechs and Germans: A Local History of Bohemian Politics, 1848–1948* (Princeton, N.J., 2002), 192.

45. Tomáš Staněk, *Internierung und Zwangsarbeit: Das Lagersystem in den böhmischen Ländern, 1945–1948* (Munich, 2007), 41–47, 66.

46. Ibid., 137, 164, 225.

47. Doc. 59 in Volokitina et al., *Sovetskii faktor*, 1:205–8; Norman M. Naimark, *Fires of Hatred: Ethnic Cleansing in Twentieth-Century Europe* (Princeton, N.J., 2001), 109.

48. Doc. 62 in Volokitina et al., *Sovetskii faktor*, 1:212–13.

49. Brandes, *Der Weg zur Vertreibung*, 438, 414.

50. Eagle Glassheim, "The Mechanics of Ethnic Cleansing: The Expulsion of Germans from Czechoslovakia, 1945–1947," in Philipp Ther and Ana Siljak, eds., *Redrawing Nations: Ethnic Cleansing in East-Central Europe, 1944–1948* (New York, 2001), 204.

51. Bradley F. Abrams, *The Struggle for the Soul of the Nation: Czech Culture and the Rise of Communism* (Lanham, Md., 2005), 53–68.

52. Heda Margolius Kovály, *Under a Cruel Star: A Life in Prague, 1941–1968* (New York, 1997), 67–70.

53. An activist from 1968 quoted in Abrams, *Struggle for the Soul,* 56; see also Kaplan, *Short March,* 34–37.

54. Czech CP report, July 16, 1946, doc. 108 in Volokitina et al., *Sovetskii faktor,* 1:318–22.

55. Petr Blažek and Pavel Žáček, "Tschechoslowakei," in Kamiński, Persak, and Gieseke, *Handbuch,* 395–413; Ripka, *Czechoslovakia Enslaved,* 150–52.

56. Kaplan, *Short March,* 133–44; Ripka, *Czechoslovakia Enslaved,* 154–55.

57. Zdeněk Radvanovský, "The Social and Economic Consequences of Resettling Czechs into Northwestern Bohemia, 1945–1947," in Ther and Siljak, *Redrawing Nations,* 251.

58. Petráš and Svátek, "Transport über die Grenze." See also Martin Broszat, *Nach Hitler: Der schwierige Umgang mit unserer Geschichte* (Munich, 1988), 185–88; 242–44.

59. Doc. 147 in Volokitina et al., *Sovetskii faktor,* 1:408–12; also doc. 141 in Volokitina et al., *Vostochnaya Evropa,* 402–6.

60. Czech CP report, not later than Nov. 2, 1946, doc. 127 in Volokitina et al., *Vostochnaya Evropa, v dokumentakh rossiiskikh arkhivov,* 363–65.

61. Speech, Jan. 12, 1942, and government declaration, Feb. 24, 1942, quoted in Brandes, *Der Weg zur Vertreibung,* 177–78.

62. John Colville, conversation: Dec. 12, 1940, in Rainer A. Blasius, ed., *Dokumente zur Deutschlandpolitik, 1:3, September bis 31. Dezember 1941. Britische Deutschlandpolitik* (Frankfurt am Main, 1984), 255–56.

63. Quoted in Naimark, *Fires of Hatred,* 54.

64. *Dokumente aus polnischen Archiven,* 1:481–83.

65. Harriman to Secretary of State, Apr. 10, 1945, in *FRUS, 1945,* 5:208. Kennan to Secretary of State, Apr. 18, 1945, in *FRUS, 1945,* 5:229–31.

66. *Dokumente aus polnischen Archiven,* 1:64.

67. Ibid., 3:77.

68. Report (2nd quarter 1945), military court, First Polish Army, doc. 48, ibid., 1:180–81.

69. Ibid., 1:69.

70. T. David Curp, *A Clean Sweep? The Politics of Ethnic Cleansing in Western Poland, 1945–1960* (Rochester, N.Y., 2006), 47–53.

71. Report beginning June 1945, doc. 163, and report, June 14, 1945, doc. 165, in *Dokumente aus polnischen Archiven,* 4:448–49, 452–55.

72. Curp, *Clean Sweep,* 44–45.

73. Doc. 219, *Dokumente aus polnischen Archiven,* 2:408.

74. Doc. 258, Sept. 7, 1945, ibid., 470–72.

75. Protocol of the meeting, in *FRUS, Potsdam Conference,* 2:1495.

76. *Dokumente aus polnischen Archiven,* 1:101.

77. Doc. 1, from the Gomułka papers, in Andrzej Werblan, "The Conversation Between Władysław Gomułka and Josef Stalin on 14 November 1945," *CWIHP Bulletin* 11 (Winter 1998), 134–38.

78. Matthew Frank, *Expelling the Germans: British Opinion and Post-1945 Population Transfer in Context* (Oxford, U.K., 2007), 227–73.

79. Bernard Linek, " 'De-Germanization' and 'Re-Polonization' in Upper Silesia, 1945–1905," in Ther and Siljak, *Redrawing Nations,* 121–34.

80. *Dokumente aus polnischen Archiven,* 2:385.

81. Czesław Miłosz, *The Captive Mind* (New York, 1951), 164–65.

82. Ilya Ehrenburg, *Liudi, gody, zhizn: vospominaniia, v trekh tomakh* (Moscow, 2005), vol. 3, kniga 6, chap. 2.

83. Michael Schwartz, *Vertriebene und "Umsiedlerpolitik": SBZ/DDR 1945 bis 1961* (Munich, 2004), 49–55, tables.

84. Hans-Ulrich Wehler, *Deutsche Gesellschaftsgeschichte*, vol. 4, *1914–1949* (Munich, 2004), cites 1.71 million and a total of 14.16 million expellees (944); Naimark, *Fires of Hatred*, gives 2.5 million for the death toll (14); Heinz Nawratil, *Schwarzbuch der Vertreibung 1945 bis 1948: Das letzte Kapitel unbewältigter Vergangenheit*, 12th ed. (Munich, 2005), cites the Statistisches Bundesamt, *Die deutschen Vertreibungsverluste* (Wiesbaden, 1958), as giving 2.23 million dead, but he adopts the figure of 2.8 million (75).

85. Rüdiger Overmans, *Deutsche militärische Verluste im Zweiten Weltkrieg*, 3rd ed. (Munich, 2004), 298–300; and Overmans, "Personelle Verluste der deutschen Bevölkerung durch Flucht und Vertreibung," in *Dzieje Najnowsze Rocznik* (1994), 51–63. For a critique of the literature, see Ingo Haar, "Die deutschen 'Vertreibungsverluste': Forschungsstand, Kontexte, und Probleme," in Josef Ehmer, Jürgen Reulecke, and Rainer Mackensen, eds., *Ursprünge, Arten und Folgen des Konstrukts "Bevölkerung" vor, im und nach dem "Dritten Reich:" Zur Geschichte der deutschen Bevölkerungswissenschaft* (Wiesbaden, 2008), 363–81.

86. Doc. 71, Aug. 11, 1945, and doc. 107, July 4, 1946, in Volokitina et al., *Sovetskii faktor*, 1:229–31, 317–18.

87. Anita J. Prażmowska, *Civil War in Poland, 1942–1948* (New York, 2004), 172.

88. Jan T. Gross, *Fear: Anti-Semitism in Poland after Auschwitz: An Essay in Historical Interpretation* (New York, 2006), 258–60; for a Soviet report on the situation of the Jews, see doc. 119, Sept. 24, 1946, in Volokitina et al., *Sovetskii faktor*, 1:340–45.

89. Joanna Beate Michlic, *Poland's Threatening Other: The Image of the Jew from 1880 to the Present* (Lincoln, Neb., 2006), 196–98.

90. Gomułka to Stalin, Dec. 14, 1948, doc. 307 in Volokitina et al., *Vostochnaya Evropa*, 1:937–44.

91. Quoted in Bradley F. Abrams, "Morality, Wisdom and Revision: The Czech Opposition of the 1970s and the Expulsion of the Sudeten Germans," *East European Politics and Societies* (1995), 248, 250.

92. Krystyna Kersten, "Forced Migration and the Transformation of Polish Society in the Postwar Period," in Ther and Siljak, *Redrawing Nations*, 75–86.

93. Recognition came in the two-plus-four agreement (1989–1990) and the German-Polish Border Treaty (1990). See Thomasz Kamusella, "The Expulsion of the Population Categorized as 'Germans' from the Post-1945 Poland," in Steffen Prauser and Arfon Rees, eds., *The Expulsion of the "German" Communities from Eastern Europe at the End of the Second World War*, EUI Working Paper HEC No. 2004/1, 21–30.

94. For the extensive literature and references of contemporary sources, see Sven Eliason, ed., *Building Democracy and Civil Society East of the Elbe: Essays in Honour of Edmund Mokrzycki* (New York, 2006).

CHAPTER 14. THE PATTERN OF DICTATORSHIPS: BULGARIA, ROMANIA, AND HUNGARY

1. L. Y. Gibiansky, "Problemii Vostochnoi Evropii i nachalo formiprovania miprovania sovetskogo bloka," in N. I. Egorova and A. O. Chubarian, eds., *Kholodnaia voina, 1945–1963 gg.: Istoricheskaia retrospektiva. Sbornik statei* (Moscow, 2003), 130–31.

2. Georgi K. Zhukov, *Vospominaniya i razmyshleniya* (Moscow, 2002), 2:246–49.

3. Jordan Baev and Kostadin Grozev, "Bulgarien: Organisation, Aufbau und Personal," in Łukasz Kamiński, Krzysztof Persak, und Jens Gieseke, eds., *Handbuch der kommunistischen Geheimdienste in Osteuropa 1944–1991* (Göttingen, 2009), 143–97.

4. Vesselin Dimitrov, *Stalin's Cold War: Soviet Foreign Policy, Democracy and Communism in Bulgaria, 1941–48* (New York, 2008), 72; R. J. Crampton, *Eastern Europe in the Twentieth Century—And After,* 2nd ed. (London, 2003), 225–26.

5. Ekaterina Nikova, "Bulgarian Stalinism Revisited," in Vladimir Tismăneanu, ed., *Stalinism Revisited: The Establishment of Communist Regimes in East-Central Europe* (Budapest–New York, 2009), 289; Marietta Stankova, "Das parteipolitische System in Bulgarien 1944–1949: Äussere Einflüsse und innere Faktoren," in Stefan Creuzberger and Manfred Görtemaker, eds., *Gleichschaltung unter Stalin? Die Entwicklung der Parteien im östlichen Europa, 1944–1949* (Paderborn, 2002), 185.

6. Ilya Ehrenburg, *Liudi, gody, zhizn: vospominaniia, v trekh tomakh* (Moscow, 2005), 6:26.

7. Entry for Sept. 24, in Ivo Banac, ed., *The Diary of Georgi Dimitrov, 1933–1949* (New Haven, Conn., 2003), 336–37.

8. Nikova, "Bulgarian Stalinism Revisited," 291–92. For slightly different numbers, see Stankova, "Das parteipolitische System in Bulgarien," 186–87, and E. L. Valeva, "Politicheskiye protsessy v Bolgarii 1944–1948 gg," *Mezhdunarodnyi istoricheskii zhurnal* (2000), http://history.machaon.ru/all/number_07/analiti4/total/valeva/index.html.

9. Tzvetan Todorov, *Voices from the Gulag: Life and Death in Communist Bulgaria* (University Park, Pa., 1999), 38–39.

10. Dimitrov, *Stalin's Cold War,* 80.

11. Meeting, Jan. 28, 1945, in Georgi Dimitrov, *Dnevnik: mart 1933–fevruari 1949: izbrano* (Sofia, 2003), 240–41.

12. Report, end Dec. 1944, in Stankova, "Das parteipolitische System in Bulgarien," 189.

13. Letter from Public Figures to King Boris, May 26, 1943, in Tzvetan Todorov, *The Fragility of Goodness: Why Bulgaria's Jews Survived the Holocaust* (Princeton, N.J., 2001), 106–7.

14. Docs. 72 and 73 in T. V. Volokitina et al., eds., *Sovetskii faktor v Vostochnoi Evrope, 1944–1953* (Moscow, 1999), 1:231–33; Stankova, "Das parteipolitische System in Bulgarien," 197–98.

15. Quoted in Dimitrov, *Stalin's Cold War,* 125.

16. Stankova, "Das parteipolitische System in Bulgarien," 200.

17. *FRUS, 1945,* 2:822.

18. Quoted in Stankova, "Das parteipolitische System in Bulgarien," 202; see also Dimitrov, *Dnevnik,* 287–88.

19. Doc. 90 in Volokitina et al., *Sovetskii faktor,* 1:267–69; also doc. 128, in T. V. Volokitina et al., eds., *Vostochnaya Evropa v dokumentakh rossiiskikh arkhivov* (Moscow, 1997–98), 1:355–61; Dimitrov, *Stalin's Cold War,* 140; Stankova, "Das parteipolitische System in Bulgarien," 204.

20. Entry for June 7, 1946, in Dimitrov, *Dnevnik,* 298–99.

21. Ibid., 304–6.

22. Stankova, "Das parteipolitische System in Bulgarien," 211.

23. Doc. 121 in Volokitina et al., *Sovetskii faktor,* 1:348–50.

24. Valeva, "Politicheskiye protsessy v Bolgarii 1944–1948 gg."

25. Ehrenburg, *Liudi, gody, zhizn,* 6:24.

26. Vladimir Solonari, *Purifying the Nation: Population Exchange and Ethnic Cleansing in Nazi-Allied Romania* (Baltimore, Md., 2010), 340–41.

27. Vladimir Tismăneanu, *Stalinism for all Seasons: A Political History of Romanian Communism* (London, 2003), 87–90, 120–24; Robert Levy, *Ana Pauker: The Rise and Fall of a Jewish Communist* (London, 2001), 79–80; Dennis Deletant, *Romania Under Communist Rule,* rev. ed. (Portland, Ore., 1999), 30–39.

28. TASS interview with Lucrețiu Pătrășcanu, Jan. 10, 1945, doc. 31 in Volokitina et al., *Sovetskii faktor*, 1:126–30.

29. Ulrich Burger, "Die Strategie der Kommunisten in Rumänien zur Gleichschaltung des Parteiensystems zwischen 1944 und 1948," in Creuzberger and Görtemaker, *Gleichschaltung unter Stalin*, 138–39; Levy, *Ana Pauker*, 78.

30. Doc. 40, Mar. 3, 1945, in Volokitina et al., *Sovetskii faktor*, 1:156–59.

31. Tismăneanu, *Stalinism for All Seasons*, 90–91; Deletant, *Romania Under Communist Rule*, 42.

32. Florian Banu, "Calamități ale secolului al XX-lea: foametea care a devastat Moldova în 1946–1947," http://www.comunism.ro/images/banu.pdf.

33. Vladimir Tismăneanu et al., *Comisia Prezidențială Pentru Analiza Dictaturii Comuniste din România: Raport Final* (Bucharest, 2006), 199–200.

34. Excerpts of transcripts in Eduard Mark, "Stalin's National-Front Strategy for Europe, 1941–1947," CWIHP, Working Paper no. 31 (2001), 26–30. These documents have since been closed to use.

35. Tismăneanu et al., *Comisia Prezidențială*, 200; Levy, *Pauker*, 75.

36. Tuvia Friling, Radu Ioanid, and Mihail E. Ionescu, eds., *Final Report, International Commission on the Holocaust in Romania* (Iași, 2004), 179, 313–14.

37. Burger, "Strategie der Kommunisten," 153–54.

38. Tismăneanu, *Stalinism for All Seasons*, 287–88; Burger, "Strategie der Kommunisten," 154, 158.

39. Tismăneanu, *Stalinism for All Seasons*, 91–94.

40. Quoted in Stejărel Olaru and Georg Herbstritt, eds., *Vademekum, Contemporary History Romania: A Guide Through Archives, Research Institutions, Libraries, Societies, Museums and Memorial Places* (Berlin–Bucharest, 2004), 20.

41. Tismăneanu, *Stalinism for All Seasons*, 20; 85–106; Dennis Deletant, *Communist Terror in Romania: Gheorghiu-Dej and the Police State, 1948–1965* (New York, 1999), 114–45, 195–224.

42. *Recensământul populației concentraționare 1945–1989*, www.memorialsighet.ro.

43. Alice Mocanescu, "Surviving 1956: Gheorghe Gheorghiu-Dej and the Cult of Personality in Romania," in Balázs Apor, Jan C. Behrends, Polly Jones, and E. A. Rees, eds., *The Leader Cult in Communist Dictatorships: Stalin and the Eastern Bloc* (New York, 2004), 246–50.

44. Charles Gati, *Hungary and the Soviet Bloc* (Durham, N.C., 1988), 31.

45. Krisztián Ungváry, *The Siege of Budapest: 100 Days in World War II* (New Haven, Conn., 2005), 40–43.

46. Ernő Gerő's notes, reprinted in William O. McCagg, Jr., *Stalin Embattled, 1943–1948* (Detroit, 1978), 314–16. The author ignores the last sentence, as pointed out in László Borhi, *Hungary in the Cold War, 1945–1956: Between the United States and the Soviet Union* (New York, 2004), 35.

47. Volokitina et al., *Sovetskii faktor*, 1:109–13; Gati, *Hungary and the Soviet Bloc*, 33–39, 67; Borhi, *Hungary in the Cold War*, 35.

48. Peter Kenez, *Hungary from the Nazis to the Soviets: The Establishment of the Communist Regime in Hungary, 1944–1948* (New York, 2006), 120.

49. G. F. Krivosheev, *Rossiia i SSSR v voinakh XX veka: poteri vooruzhennykh sil: statisticheskoe issledovanie* (Moscow, 2001), tables in chap. 5.

50. Ungváry, *Siege of Budapest*, 348–63.

51. Borhi, *Hungary in the Cold War*, 66.

52. Conversations, doc. 57 in Volokitina et al., *Sovetskii faktor*, 1:195–204.

53. Doc. 82 in Volokitina et al., *Vostochnaya Evropa*, 1:242–43.

54. László Karsai, "The People's Courts and Revolutionary Justice in Hungary, 1945–46," in

István Deák, Jan T. Gross, and Tony Judt, eds., *The Politics of Retribution: World War II and Its Aftermath* (Princeton, N.J., 2000), 233–51.

55. Kerenz, *Hungary*, 141–43.

56. Doc. 98 in Volokitina et al., *Vostochnaya Evropa*, 1:271–74.

57. Doc. 100, ibid., 276–77.

58. Susan Glanz, "Economic Platforms of the Various Parties in the Elections of 1945," in Nándor Dreisziger, ed., *Hungary in the Age of Total War* (New York, 1998), 179.

59. Telephone message to Stalin and Molotov, doc. 81, and Nov. 11, 1945, doc. 116, in Volokitina et al., *Sovetskii faktor*, 1:243–45; Borhi, *Hungary in the Cold War*, 77–78.

60. Kenez, *Hungary*, 149–62; Borhi, *Hungary in the Cold War*, 83.

61. Csaba Békés, "Soviet Plans to Establish the Cominform in Early 1946: New Evidence from the Hungarian Archives," CWIHP *Bulletin* 10 (Mar. 1998), 135–36.

62. Borhi, *Hungary in the Cold War*, 94–96.

63. Michael Korda, *Journey to a Revolution: A Personal Memoir and History of the Hungarian Revolution of 1956* (New York, 2006), 71.

64. János M. Rainer, "Der Weg der ungarischen Volksdemokratie: Das Mehrparteiensystem und seine Beseitigung 1944–1949," in Creuzberger and Görtemaker, *Gleichschaltung unter Stalin*, 333–42.

65. A. A. Chernobaev et al., eds., *Na prieme u Stalina: Tetradi (zhurnaly) zapisei lits, priniatykh I. V. Stalinym, 1924–1953* (Moscow, 2008).

66. Rainer, "Der Weg der ungarischen Volksdemokratie," 343–45.

CHAPTER 15. COMMUNISM IN YUGOSLAVIA, ALBANIA, AND GREECE

1. The ethnic figures are for 1921. See John R. Lampe, *Balkans into Southeastern Europe* (New York, 2006), 71 and 217, tables 3.1 and 7.1.

2. Note to Dimitrov, Feb. 3, 1943, in Georgi Dimitrov, *Dnevnik: mart 1933–fevruari 1949: izbrano* (Sofia, 2003), 171.

3. Edvard Kardelj, *Reminiscences: The Struggle for Recognition and Independence: The New Yugoslavia, 1944–1957* (London, 1982), 37–40.

4. Milovan Djilas, *Wartime* (New York, 1977), 120, 359–61.

5. Jerca Vodušk Starič, "Stalinismus und Selbst-Stalinismus in Yugoslawien: Von der kommunistischen Partisanenbewegung zu Tito's Einparteisystem," in Stefan Creuzberger and Manfred Görtemaker, eds., *Gleichschaltung unter Stalin? Die Entwicklung der Parteien im östlichen Europa 1944–1949* (Paderborn, 2002), 228–29; Djilas, *Wartime*, 361.

6. Doc. 13 in T. V. Volokitina et al., eds., *Sovetskii faktor v Vostochnoi Evrope, 1944–1953* (Moscow, 1999), 1:91–94; Stevan K. Pavlowitch, *Hitler's New Disorder: The Second World War in Yugoslavia* (New York, 2008), 237.

7. For the Stalin-Tito exchange, see Vladimir Dedijer, *Tito Speaks: His Self-Portrait and Struggle with Stalin* (London, 1953), 232–37.

8. Entry for Sept. 27, in Dimitrov, *Dnevnik*, 223–24.

9. For visits to Stalin in Nov. 1944, see Kardelj, *Reminiscences*, 41, 61.

10. S. I. Lavrenov and I. M. Popov, *Sovetskii Soiuz v lokalnykh voinakh i konfliktakh* (Moscow, 2003), 70–72.

11. Milovan Djilas, *Conversations with Stalin* (New York, 1962), 102.

12. Entry for April 8, 1945, in Dimitrov, *Dnevnik*, 247.

13. Kardelj, *Reminiscences*, 50–52.

14. Nora Beloff, *Tito's Flawed Legacy: Yugoslavia and the West Since 1939* (Boulder, Colo., 1985), 125.

15. Stephen Dorril, *MI6: Inside the Covert World of Her Majesty's Intelligence Service* (New York, 2002), 336.

16. The first figure is from Vladimir Žerjavić, cited in Pavlowitch, *Hitler's New Disorder*, 262. Janusz Piekalkiewicz, *Krieg auf dem Balkan, 1940–1945* (Munich, 1984), says that "50,000 Croat soldiers and about 30,000 refugees, mainly women and children, were executed over a five-day period" (309); cited in Misha Glenny, *The Balkans: Nationalism, War and the Great Powers, 1904–1999* (New York, 2000), 530.

17. Sabrina P. Ramet, *The Three Yugoslavias: State-Building and Legitimation, 1918–2005* (Washington, D.C., 2006), 159–60.

18. *Dokumentation der Vertreibung der Deutschen aus Ost-Mitteleuropa,* vol. 5, *Jugoslawien* (reprint, Munich, 2004), 180E–84E.

19. Aleksa Djilas, *The Contested Country: Yugoslav Unity and Communist Revolution, 1919–1953* (Cambridge, Mass., 1991), 170.

20. Ramet, *Three Yugoslavias*, 159.

21. Edvard Kardelj, list of requests, Feb. 5, 1945, doc. 35 in Volokitina et al., *Sovetskii faktor,* 1:138.

22. Milovan Djilas, *Rise and Fall* (New York, 1983), 82.

23. Starič, "Stalinismus und Selbst-Stalinismus in Yugoslawien," 233–36.

24. Djilas, *Contested Country,* 159.

25. Report, Jan. 19, 1946, doc. 91 in Volokitina et al., *Sovetskii faktor,* 1:269–76.

26. Letter, not later than Sept. 15, 1946, doc. 117, ibid, 338–39.

27. Quoted in Ramet, *Three Yugoslavias,* 169.

28. Starič, "Stalinismus und Selbst-Stalinismus in Yugoslawien," 229–31.

29. Quoted in Beloff, *Tito's Flawed Legacy,* 102, 132.

30. Glenny, *Balkans,* 531–32.

31. The first figure is from John R. Lampe, *Yugoslavia as History: Twice There Was a Country,* 2nd ed. (New York, 2000), 227, and the second is from Bor. M. Karapandžić, *The Bloodiest Yugoslav Spring, 1945—Tito's Katyns and Gulags* (New York, 1980), 20. See also in Oskar Gruenwald, "Yugoslav Camp Literature: Rediscovering the Ghost of a Nation's Past-Present-Future," *Slavic Review* (1987), 517.

32. See Arnold Suppan, "Between Hitler, Beneš, and Tito: Czechoslovak-German and Yugoslav-German Confrontations in World War II," paper, Stanford University, Mar. 6, 2008, http://iis-db.stanford.edu/evnts/5112/Between_Hitler,_Benes_and_Tito.pdf.

33. Jozo Tomasevich, *War and Revolution in Yugoslavia, 1941–1945: Occupation and Collaboration* (Stanford, Calif., 2001), 766.

34. Waddams's report quoted in Beloff, *Tito's Flawed Legacy,* 133–34.

35. Lampe, *Balkans into Southeastern Europe,* 188.

36. For an account from a former prisoner, see Josip Zoretić, *Goli Otok: Hell in the Adriatic* (College Station, Tex., 2007).

37. Report, *New York Herald Tribune,* Nov. 7, 1952, in T. V. Volokitina et al., *Moskva i Vostochnaia Evropa: stanovlenie politicheskikh rezhimov sovetskogo tipa, 1949–1953: ocherki istorii* (Moscow, 2002), 585–86.

38. For comments by a British officer who worked with the partisans, see Michael Lees, *The Rape of Serbia: The British Role in Tito's Grab for Power, 1943–1944* (London, 1990), 295–312.

39. Memorandum, Aug. 31, 1945, in *FRUS, 1945,* 5:1252–53

40. Glenny, *Balkans,* 562–63.

41. Ilya Ehrenburg, *Liudi, gody, zhizn: vospominaniia, v trekh tomakh* (Moscow, 2005), vol. 6, chap. 2.

42. Report (not earlier than Mar. 1, 1947), doc. 150 in Volokitina et al., *Sovetskii faktor,* 1:415–19.

43. Jon Halliday, ed., *The Artful Albanian: Memoirs of Enver Hoxha* (London, 1986), 62–71.

44. Ibid., 87–89.

45. Peter Danylow, "Sieg und Niederlage der Internationale: Die Sowjetizierung der Kommunistischen Partei in Albanien," in Creuzberger and Görtemaker, *Gleichschaltung unter Stalin*, 242–46.

46. Entry for Jan. 10, 1945, in Dimitrov, *Dnevnik*, 237–38.

47. Quoted in Vladimir Volkov, "The Soviet Leadership and Southeastern Europe," in Norman Naimark and Leonid Gibianskii, eds., *The Establishment of Communist Regimes in Eastern Europe, 1944–1949* (Boulder, Colo., 1997), 66.

48. Danylow, "Sieg und Niederlage der Internationale," 248–49.

49. Djilas, *Rise and Fall*, 111.

50. Speech quoted in ibid., 91.

51. Note cited in ibid., 92.

52. Meeting with Molotov, July 15, doc. 229, in T. V. Volokitina et al., eds., *Vostochnaya Evropa v dokumentakh rossiiskikh arkhivov* (Moscow, 1997–98), 1:677–81.

53. Doc. 150 in Volokitina et al., *Sovetskii faktor*, 1:417.

54. Enver Hoxha, *With Stalin: Memoirs* (Tirana, 1979), 53–86.

55. Minutes of meeting, July 23, 1947, doc. 170 in Volokitina et al., *Sovetskii faktor*, 1:474–77.

56. Mark Mazower, *Inside Hitler's Greece: The Experience of Occupation, 1941–44* (New Haven, Conn., 1993), 268, 296.

57. Violetta Hionidou, "Famine in Occupied Greece: Causes and Consequences," in Richard Clogg, ed., *Bearing Gifts to Greeks: Humanitarian Aid to Greece in the 1940s* (New York, 2008), 26.

58. André Gerolymatos, *Red Acropolis: The Greek Civil War and the Origins of Soviet-American Rivalry, 1943–1949* (New York, 2004), 149–85; Philip B. Minehan, *Civil War and World War in Europe: Spain, Yugoslavia, and Greece, 1936–1949* (New York, 2006), 212.

59. Entry for Dec. 8, 1944, in Dimitrov, *Dnevnik*, 231.

60. Doc. 37 in Volokitina et al., *Vostochnaya Evropa v dokumentakh rossiiskikh arkhivov*, 1:118–33.

61. Entry for Jan. 10, 1945, in Dimitrov, *Dnevnik*, 237–38.

62. Letter, Jan. 15, 1945, in John O. Iatrides, ed., *Ambassador MacVeagh Reports: Greece, 1933–1947* (Princeton, N.J., 1980), 670.

63. Mark Mazower, "The Cold War and the Appropriation of Memory: Greece After Liberation," in István Deák, Jan T. Gross, and Tony Judt, eds., *The Politics of Retribution: World War II and Its Aftermath* (Princeton, N.J., 2000), 213–15.

64. Ole L. Smith, "Communist Perceptions, Strategy, and Tactics, 1945–1949," in John O. Iatrides and Linda Wrigley, eds., *Greece at the Crossroads: Civil War and Its Legacy* (University Park, Pa., 1995), 92–98.

65. Joseph M. Jones, *The Fifteen Weeks (February 11–June 5, 1947)* (New York, 1955), 3–13.

66. Clark Clifford with Richard Holbrooke, *Counsel to the President: A Memoir* (New York, 1991), 108.

67. Wilson D. Miscamble, *From Roosevelt to Truman: Potsdam, Hiroshima, and the Cold War* (Cambridge, U.K., 2007), 285–86.

68. Dean Acheson, *Present at the Creation: My Years in the State Department* (New York, 1969), 217–25.

69. Address to House of Representatives, http://www.trumanlibrary.org.

70. Peter J. Stavrakis, "Soviet Policy in Areas of Limited Control: The Case of Greece, 1944–1949," in Iatrides and Wrigley, *Greece at the Crossroads*, 251.

71. A. A. Danilov and A. V. Pyzhikov, *Rozhdenie sverkhderzhavy: SSSR v pervye poslevoennye gody* (Moscow, 2001), 28–32.

72. V. K. Volkov and L. Ia. Gibianskii, "Na poroge pervogo raskola v sotsialiteches-

kom lagere: Peregovori rykovodiashikh deiatelei SSSR, Bolgarii i Iogoslavii 1948 r.," *Istoricheskii arkhiv* (1997), 92–123; Dimitrov, *Dnevnik*, 360–68.

CHAPTER 16. THE PASSING OF THE COMMUNIST MOMENT IN WESTERN EUROPE

1. For other plans, see Maxim Litvinov, Oct. 9, 1943, doc. 62 in G. P. Kynin and Jochen Laufer eds., *SSSR i germanskii vopros, 1941–1949: dokumenty iz arkhiva vneshnei politiki Rossiiskoi Federastsii* (Moscow, 1996), 1:277–86.
2. Doc. 79, Jan. 11, 1944, in Kynin and Laufer, *SSSR i germanskii vopros*, 1:333–60, here sections 3d and 17.
3. Doc. 114, July 28, 1944, ibid., 425–36, here 14h.
4. *FRUS, Conference at Quebec, 1944*, 467.
5. Gromyko to Molotov, Nov. 13, 1944, doc. 135 in Kynin and Laufer, *SSSR i germanskii vopros*, 1:571–75.
6. Secretary of War to the President, Sept. 15, 1944, in *FRUS, Conference at Quebec, 1944*, 482–85.
7. "Anglichanye i Amerikantziy xotyat vezde sozdat reakzionnyiye pravitlctva," *Istochnik* 4 (1995), 152–58; Georgi Dimitrov, *Dnevnik: mart 1933–fevruari 1949: izbrano* (Sofia, 2003), 229–30.
8. Dimitrov to Stalin, July 1, Oct. 6, 1934, and Stalin to Dimitrov, Oct. 25, 1934, in Alexander Dallin and F. I. Firsov, eds., *Dimitrov and Stalin, 1934–1943: Letters from the Soviet Archives* (New Haven, Conn., 2000), 13–22.
9. This was the conception since mid-1941. See entry for July 7, in Dimitrov, *Dnevnik*, 122.
10. Alfred J. Rieber, *Stalin and the French Communist Party, 1941–1947* (New York, 1962), 169, 189. On party memberships, see Thomas H. Greene, "The Communist Parties of Italy and France: A Study in Comparative Communism," *World Politics* (1968), 1–38; Joan Barth Urban, *Moscow and the Italian Communist Party: From Togliatti to Berlinguer* (London, 1986), 148.
11. Tony Judt, *Past Imperfect: French Intellectuals, 1944–1956* (Berkeley, Calif., 1992), 58–60.
12. Jean-Pierre Rioux, *The Fourth Republic, 1944–1958* (Cambridge, U.K., 1989), 54–55.
13. Charles de Gaulle, *The Complete War Memoirs of Charles de Gaulle* (New York, 1972), 978–94.
14. Memo, Norris B. Chipman, U.S. Embassy Paris, Nov. 23, 1946, *FRUS, 1947, British Commonwealth; Europe*. vol. 5, 471–77; Rioux, *The Fourth Republic*, 106–11; William I. Hitchcock, *France Restored: Cold War Diplomacy and the Quest for Leadership in Europe, 1944–1954* (Chapel Hill, N.C., 1998), 12–22.
15. Rioux, *Fourth Republic*, 125–26; also for what follows.
16. Barry Machado, *In Search of a Usable Past: The Marshall Plan and Postwar Reconstruction Today* (Washington, D.C., 2007), 11; Melvyn P. Leffler, *A Preponderance of Power: National Security, the Truman Administration, and the Cold War* (Stanford, Calif., 1992), 158.
17. Caffery to Secretary of State, May 12, 1947, in *FRUS, 1947, British Commonwealth; Europe*, 3:709–13.
18. Department of State, press release, June 4, 1947, ibid., 3:237–39.
19. Hitchcock, *France Restored*, 72–73; Rioux, *Fourth Republic*, 126–27.
20. Harry Bayard Price, *The Marshall Plan and Its Meaning* (Ithaca, N.Y., 1955), 47–48.
21. Entry for Mar. 5, 1944, in Dimitrov, *Dnevnik*, 204–5.
22. Hans Woller, *Die Abrechnung mit dem Faschismus in Italien 1943 bis 1948* (Munich, 1996), 115–17, 304–5.
23. James Holland, *Italy's Sorrow: A Year of War, 1944–1945* (New York, 2008), 398.

24. William I. Hitchcock, *The Bitter Road to Freedom: A New History of the Liberation of Europe* (New York, 2008), 235–36.

25. De Gasperi to Truman, Jan. 8, 1947, in *FRUS, 1947, British Commonwealth; Europe*, 3:850–51; Aldo Agosti, *Palmiro Togliatti: A Biography* (London, 2008), 184.

26. Tarchiani to De Gasperi, May 14, 1947, cited in Elena Agarossi and Victor Zaslavsky, *Stalin and Togliatti: Italy and the Origins of the Cold War* (Washington, D.C., 2011), 229–30. No American record of the conversation has been found.

27. Memorandum on Marshall-Tarchiani conversation, May 16, 1947, in *FRUS, 1947, British Commonwealth; Europe*, 3:904–8.

28. Richard J. Barnet, *The Alliance: America-Europe-Japan, Makers of the Postwar World* (New York, 1983), 140.

29. Agarossi and Zaslavsky, *Stalin and Togliatti*, 220–31.

30. See http://cronologia.leonardo.it/elezio2.htm.

31. Visit of Dec. 1947, in Agarossi and Zaslavsky, *Stalin and Togliatti*, 283–84.

32. Ibid., 285–88.

33. *New York Times*, Feb. 26 and March 11, 1947.

34. Molotov and Vyshinsky to Stalin, Aug. 20, 1945, doc. 31 in Kynin and Laufer, *SSSR i germanskii vopros* 2:218–20.

35. Wolfgang Leonhard, *Die Revolution entlässt ihre Kinder* (1955; Cologne, 2010), 503–9.

36. See doc. in *American Journal of International Law* 39, no. 3 (July 1945), supp. 171–78.

37. Report on the Tripartite Conference of Berlin, Aug. 2, 1945, in *FRUS, Potsdam Conference*, 2:1501–2.

38. Norman M. Naimark, *The Russians in Germany: A History of the Soviet Zone of Occupation, 1945–1949* (Cambridge, U.K., 1995), 20; Stefan Creuzberger, *Die sowjetische Besatzungsmacht und das politische System der SBZ* (Weimar, 1996), 27–28.

39. Richard Bessel, *Germany 1945: From War to Peace* (New York, 2009), 296–97.

40. Dwight D. Eisenhower, *Crusade in Europe* (Garden City, N.Y., 1948), 291–97; De Gaulle, *The Complete War Memoirs*, 431, 434.

41. The directive was slightly revised and issued on Apr. 26, 1945. See *FRUS, European Advisory Commission, Austria, Germany* (1945), 3:471–73, 484–503.

42. Robert Murphy, *Diplomat Among Warriors* (New York, 1964), 284.

43. Bessel, *Germany 1945*, 182–203.

44. "The Political and Economic Principles to Govern the Treatment of Germany in the Initial Control Period," in *FRUS, Potsdam Conference*, 2:1505–6.

45. Georgi K. Zhukov, *Vospominaniya i razmyshleniya* (Moscow, 2002), 2:338–40.

46. BAB, SAPMO, 629, Nachlass Pieck, 62–64. Some but not all the documents have been printed in Rolf Badstübner and Wilfried Loth, eds., *Wilhelm Pieck—Aufzeichnungen zur Deutschlandpolitik, 1945–1953* (Berlin, 1994), 50–52.

47. Quoted in V. K. Volkov, *Uzlovye problemy noveishei istorii stran Tsentralnoi i Iugo-Vostochnoi Evropy*, rev. and expanded as *Stalin wollte ein anderes Europa: Moskaus Aussenpolitik 1940 bis 1968 und die Folgen, eine Dokumentation*, Harald Neubert, ed. (Berlin, 2003), 168.

48. Ivo Banac, ed., *The Diary of Georgi Dimitrov, 1933–1949* (New Haven, Conn., 2003), 372–73.

49. Leonhard, *Die Revolution entlässt ihre Kinder*, 479–82.

50. Hermann Weber, ed., *Der deutsche Kommunismus: Dokumente* (Cologne, 1963), 431–38. Catherine Epstein, *The Last Revolutionaries: German Communists and Their Century* (Cambridge, Mass., 2003), 102–3.

51. Doc. 66, Dec. 15, 1945, in Kynin and Laufer, *SSSR i germanskii vopros*, 2:305–8.

52. Leonhard, *Die Revolution entlässt ihre Kinder*, 518–21.

53. Oliver Rathkolb, "Sonderfall Österreich? Ein peripherer Kleinstaat in der sowjetischen Nachkriegsstrategie 1945-1947," in Stefan Creuzberger and Manfred Görtemaker, eds.,

Gleichschaltung unter Stalin? Die Entwicklung der Parteien im östlichen Europa 1944–1949 (Paderborn, 2002), 368.

54. Bericht Ulbricht, BAB, SAPMO, 631, Nachlass Pieck, 33–34.

55. Open letter, May 7, 1946, in *Dokumente des Sozialistischen Einheitspartei Deutschlands: Beschlüsse und Erklärungen des Zentralkommittees und des Parteivorstandes* (Berlin, 1951), 1:32–33.

56. Patrick Major, *The Death of the KPD: Communism and Anti-Communism in West Germany, 1945–1956* (Oxford, U.K., 1997), 50–54.

57. Monika Kaiser, " 'Es muss demokratisch aussehen . . . ' Moskau und die Gleichschaltung des Parteiensystems in der sowjetischen Besatzungszone Deutschlands 1944–45 1948–49," in Creuzberger and Görtemaker, *Gleichschaltung unter Stalin,* 278–79.

58. Bericht Ulbricht, BAB, SAPMO, 631, Nachlass Pieck, 33–34.

59. Dirk Spilker, *The East German Leadership and the Division of Germany: Patriotism and Propaganda, 1945–1953* (Oxford, U.K., 2006), 84–85.

60. Memorandum, July 9, 1946, in Bernd Bonwetsch, Gennadij Bordjugov, and Norman M. Naimark, eds., *Sowjetische Politik in der SBZ 1945–1949: Dokumente zur Tätigkeit der Propagandaverwaltung* (Bonn, 1997), 49–50.

61. "The Principles of Newspeak," in George Orwell, *Nineteen Eighty-Four* (1949; New York, 2003), 309–23.

62. Creuzberger, *Die sowjetische Besatzungsmacht,* 93n266. All results can also be found at http://www.wahlen-in-deutschland.de/abundalg.htm.

63. Meeting, Oct. 24–25, 1946, cited in Spilker, *East German Leadership,* 103.

64. Lucius D. Clay, *Decision in Germany* (New York, 1950), 139.

65. Natalja Lebedeva, "Österreichische Kommunisten im Moskauer Exil: Die Komintern, die Abteilung für Information des ZK der VKP(b) und Österreich," in Stefan Karner et al., eds., *Die Rote Armee in Österreich: Sowjetische Besatzung 1945–1955: Beiträge* (Vienna, 2005), 39–60. See docs. 2–12, Apr. 1945, for Soviet and Austrian Communists' first steps, in G. A. Bordiugov, et al., eds., *Sovetskaia politika v Avstrii, 1945–1955 gg.: sbornik dokumentov* (Moscow, 2006), 46–67.

66. Günter Bischof, *Austria in the First Cold War, 1945–55: The Leverage of the Weak* (New York, 1999), 88–98.

67. Peter Ruggenthaler, "Warum Österreich nicht sowjetisiert werden sollte," in Karner et al., *Die Rote Armee in Österreich,* 61–87.

68. Wolfgang Mueller, *Die sowjetische Besatzung in Österreich 1945–1955 und ihre politische Mission* (Vienna, 2005), 172, 233–38.

69. Allan Bullock, *Ernest Bevin, Foreign Secretary, 1945–1951* (London, 1983), 286–89.

70. George F. Kennan, *Memoirs, 1925–1950* (Boston, 1967), 287.

71. James F. Byrnes, *Speaking Frankly* (New York, 1947), 172; for the Soviet record, see doc. 71 in Kynin and Laufer, *SSSR i germanskii vopros,* 2:335–36.

72. Byrnes, *Speaking Frankly,* 173–76, 194.

73. Spilker, *East German Leadership,* 88.

74. Meeting of Council of Foreign Ministers, July 10, 1946, in *FRUS, 1946. Council of Foreign Ministers,* 2:872–73.

75. Bullock, *Bevin,* 284.

76. *FRUS, 1946, Council of Foreign Ministers,* 2: 897; Byrnes, *Speaking Frankly,* 179–81.

77. Clay, *Decision in Germany,* 165; Spilker, *East German Leadership,* 90.

78. Georges Bidault, *Resistance: The Political Autobiography of Georges Bidault* (New York, 1965), 147–48.

79. Charles P. Kindleberger's reflections for the record, July 22, 1948, in *FRUS, 1947. Council of Foreign Ministers,* 2:241–43.

CHAPTER 17. STALIN'S CHOICES AND THE FUTURE OF EUROPE

1. L. Y. Gibiansky, "Forsirovanie sovetskoi blokovoi politiki," in N. I. Egorova and A. O. Chubarian, eds., *Kholodnaia voina, 1945–1963 gg: Istoricheskaia retrospektiva. Sbornik statei* (Moscow, 2003), 137–40.

2. Truman, State of the Union message, Jan. 6, 1947, at http://www.trumanlibrary.org/whistlestop/tap/1647.htm.

3. Andrew Roberts, *Masters and Commanders: How Four Titans Won the War in the West, 1941–1945* (New York, 2009), 10–12.

4. David McCullough, *Truman* (New York, 1992), 525–39.

5. Doc. 185 in *Sovetsko-Amerikanskie Otnosheniya, 1945–1948* (Moscow, 2004); Nikolai V. Novikov, *Vospominanya diplomata: zapiski, 1938–1947* (Moscow, 1989), 383.

6. Allan Bullock, *Ernest Bevin, Foreign Secretary, 1945–1951* (London, 1983), 393–94.

7. V. F. Zima, *Golod v SSSR 1946–1947 godov: proiskhozdenie i posledstviia* (Moscow, 1996), 179.

8. Georges Bidault, *Resistance: The Political Autobiography of Georges Bidault* (New York, 1965), 143.

9. Ibid., 142.

10. Michael Creswell, *A Question of Balance: How France and the United States Created Cold War Europe* (Cambridge, Mass., 2006), 10–11, and Marc Trachtenberg, *A Constructed Peace: The Making of the European Settlement, 1945–1963* (Princeton, N.J., 1999), 66–70.

11. Charles E. Bohlen, *Witness to History, 1929–1969* (New York, 1973), 263.

12. Secretary Marshall, Fourth Meeting of the Council of Foreign Ministers, report, Apr. 28, 1947, at http://avalon.law.yale.edu/20th_century/decade23.asp.

13. George F. Kennan, *Memoirs, 1925–1950* (Boston, 1967), 325–26.

14. Kennan to Acheson, May 23, 1947, in *FRUS 1947, British Commonwealth; Europe*, 3:223–30. For reflections, see Kennan, *Memoirs*, 325–37.

15. Dean Acheson, *Present at the Creation: My Years in the State Department* (New York, 1969), 226–35; Gregory A. Fossedal, *Our Finest Hour: Will Clayton, the Marshall Plan, and the Triumph of Democracy* (Stanford, Calif., 1993), 212–34.

16. Marshall, remarks, June 5, 1947, in *FRUS 1947, British Commonwealth; Europe*, 3:237–39.

17. Quoted in Trachtenberg, *Constructed Peace*, 56.

18. Bohlen, *Witness to History*, 264.

19. Doc. 35, Jan. 31, 1947, in G. P. Kynin and Jochen Laufer, eds., *SSSR i germanskii vopros, 1941–1949: dokumenty iz arkhiva vneshnei politiki Rossiiskoi Federastsii* (Moscow, 2003), 3:244–64.

20. Bevin quoted in Bullock, *Ernest Bevin*, 405, and with a slight variation in Bidault, *Resistance*, 151.

21. Caffery to Marshall, June 18, 1947, in *FRUS 1947, British Commonwealth; Europe*, 3:258.

22. Scott D. Parrish and Mikhail M. Narinsky, "New Evidence on the Soviet Rejection of the Marshall Plan, 1947: Two Reports," CWIHP Working Paper no. 9 (Mar. 1994), 46; hereafter Narinsky, "Soviet Union and Marshall Plan."

23. Vladislav Zubok and Constantine Pleshakov, *Inside the Kremlin's Cold War: From Stalin to Khrushchev* (Cambridge, Mass., 1996), 276.

24. Novikov, *Vospominanya diplomata: zapiski*, 394; also Novikov letter, June 9, 1947, doc. 198 in *Sovetsko-Amerikanskie Otnosheniya, 1945–1948*.

25. Narinsky, "Soviet Union and Marshall Plan," 47.

26. Alan S. Milward, *The Reconstruction of Western Europe, 1945–1951* (Berkeley, Calif., 1984), 64.

27. Scott D. Parrish, "The Turn Toward Confrontation: The Soviet Reaction to the Marshall Plan, 1947," CWIHP Working Paper no. 9 (1994), 24–25.

28. Galina Takhnenko, "Anatomy of the Political Decision: Notes on the Marshall Plan," *International Affairs* (Moscow and Minneapolis) (July 1992), 111–27.

29. Caffery to Marshall, June 29, 1947, in *FRUS 1947, British Commonwealth; Europe,* 3:301.

30. Doc. 203 in *Sovetsko-Amerikanskie Otnosheniya, 1945–1948.*

31. A recent example is Michael Cox and Caroline Kennedy-Pope, "The Tragedy of American Diplomacy? Rethinking the Marshall Plan," *Journal of Cold War Studies* (2005), 97–134. The classic account is Melvyn P. Leffler, *A Preponderance of Power: National Security, the Truman Administration, and the Cold War* (Stanford, Calif., 1992), 513–15.

32. Greg Behrman, *The Most Noble Adventure: The Marshall Plan and the Time When America Helped Save Europe* (New York, 2007), 86–87.

33. William Appelman Williams, *The Tragedy of American Diplomacy* (New York, 1959), 206.

34. *Sto sorok besed s Molotovym: iz dnevnika F. Chueva* (Moscow, 1991), 87–88.

35. For an overview, see Nicolaus Mills, *Winning the Peace: The Marshall Plan and America's Coming of Age as a Superpower* (Hoboken, N.J., 2008), 155–68.

36. Milward, *Reconstruction of Western Europe,* 125.

37. Barry Eichengreen, *The European Economy Since 1945: Coordinated Capitalism and Beyond* (Princeton, N.J., 2007), 65.

38. Wolfgang Leonhard, *Die Revolution entlässt ihre Kinder* (1955; Cologne, 2010), 564–69, 576–78.

39. Vladimir Tismăneanu, *Stalinism for All Seasons: A Political History of Romanian Communism* (London, 2003), 91–94.

40. Marietta Stankova, "Das parteipolitische System in Bulgarien 1944–1949: Äussere Einflüsse und innere Faktoren," in Stefan Creuzberger and Manfred Görtemaker, eds., *Gleichschaltung unter Stalin? Die Entwicklung der Parteien im östlichen Europa 1944–1949* (Paderborn, 2002), 200.

41. Dimitrov to Stalin, doc. 175 in T. V. Volokitina et al., eds., *Sovetskii faktor v Vostochnoi Evrope, 1944–1953* (Moscow, 1999), 1:491–92.

42. Ibid., 1:15.

43. László Borhi, *Hungary in the Cold War, 1945–1956: Between the United States and the Soviet Union* (New York, 2004), 123.

44. János M. Rainer, "Revisiting Hungarian Communism," in Vladimir Tismăneanu, ed., *Stalinism Revisited: The Establishment of Communist Regimes in East-Central Europe* (Budapest and New York, 2009), 231–54.

45. János M. Rainer, "Der Weg der ungarischen Volksdemokratie: Das Mehrparteiensystem und seine Beseitigung 1944–1949," in Creuzberger and Görtemaker, *Gleichschaltung unter Stalin,* 348; Peter Kenez, *Hungary from the Nazis to the Soviets: The Establishment of the Communist Regime in Hungary, 1944–1948* (New York, 2006), 262–65.

46. Doc. 127, Czech CP report, not later than Nov. 2, 1946, in Volokitina et al., *Sovetskii faktor v Vostochnoi Evrope,* 1: 363–65.

47. Parrish, "Turn Toward Confrontation," 25–26; Zubok and Pleshakov, *Inside the Kremlin's Cold War,* 106.

48. Narinsky, "Soviet Union and Marshall Plan," 49–50.

49. Doc. 166 in Volokitina et al., *Sovetskii faktor,* 1:462–65. For Gottwald's leaked telegram, see Steinhardt to Secretary of State, July 10, 1947, in *FRUS 1947, British Commonwealth; Europe,* 3:319–20.

50. Quoted in R. H. Bruce Lockhart, *Jan Masaryk: A Personal Memoir* (New York, 1951), 66.

51. Bradley Abrams, "Hope Died Last: The Czechoslovak Road to Stalinism," in Tismăneanu, *Stalinism Revisited,* 351.

52. Smith to Secretary of State, July 11, 1947, in *FRUS 1947, British Commonwealth; Europe,* 3:327.

53. Doc. 169 in Volokitina et al., *Vostochnaya Evropa*, 1:505–13.

54. Keith to Secretary of State, July 7, 1947, in *FRUS 1947, British Commonwealth; Europe*, 3:313.

55. Griffis to Secretary of State, report of the meeting the previous day, July 10, 1947, in *FRUS 1947, British Commonwealth; Europe*, 3:320–22.

CHAPTER 18. STALINIST FAILURES: YUGOSLAVIA AND GERMANY

1. A. A. Chernobaev et al., eds., *Na prieme u Stalina: Tetradi (zhurnaly) zapisei lits, priniatykh I. V. Stalinym, 1924–1953* (Moscow, 2008), 21–554; V. K. Volkov, *Uzlovye problemy noveishei istorii stran Tsentralnoi i Iugo-Vostochnoi Evropy*, rev. and expanded as *Stalin wollte ein anderes Europa: Moskaus Aussenpolitik 1940 bis 1968 und die Folgen, eine Dokumentation*, Harald Neubert, ed. (Berlin, 2003), 163–65.

2. That image was reflected in how participant parties were listed at the first Cominform conference.

3. See T. V. Volokitina et al., *Moskva i Vostochnaia Evropa: stanovlenie politicheskikh rezhimov sovetskogo tipa, 1949–1953: ocherki istorii* (Moscow, 2002), 1–30.

4. Doc. 116 in T. V. Volokitina et al., eds., *Sovetskii faktor v Vostochnoi Evrope, 1944–1953* (Moscow, 1999), 1:337–38.

5. George Orwell, preface to the Ukrainian edition of *Animal Farm*, 1947, at http://www.netcharles.com/orwell/articles/ukrainian-af-pref.htm.

6. Csaba Békés, "Soviet Plans to Establish the Cominform in Early 1946: New Evidence from the Hungarian Archives," *CWIHP Bulletin* 10 (Mar. 1998), 135–36.

7. Vladislav Zubok and Constantine Pleshakov, *Inside the Kremlin's Cold War: From Stalin to Khrushchev* (Cambridge, Mass., 1996), 125.

8. Grant Adibekov, "How the First Conference of the Cominform Came About," in Giuliano Procacci et al., eds., *The Cominform: Minutes of the Three Conferences, 1947, 1948, 1949* (Milan, 1994), 3–9.

9. For this speech and complete record in Russian and English, see Procacci et al., *Cominform*, 84–95.

10. Complete minutes, ibid., 217–49.

11. For their reflections, see Edvard Kardelj, *Reminiscences: The Struggle for Recognition and Independence: The New Yugoslavia, 1944–1957* (London, 1982), 98–102, and Milovan Djilas, *Rise and Fall* (New York, 1983), 134–36.

12. Minutes, Procacci et al., *Cominform*, 43.

13. Andrzej Werblan, "Władysław Gomułka and the Dilemma of Polish Communism," *International Political Science Review/Revue internationale de science politique* (1988), 151–52.

14. Vladimir Volkov, "The Soviet Leadership and Southeastern Europe," in Norman Naimark and Leonid Gibianskii, eds., *The Establishment of Communist Regimes in Eastern Europe, 1944–1949* (Boulder, Colo., 1997), 66; Ivo Banac, *With Stalin Against Tito: Cominformist Splits in Yugoslav Communism* (Ithaca, N.Y., 1988), 29–31.

15. Letter, not later than Sept. 15, 1946, doc. 117 in Volokitina et al., *Sovetskii faktor*, 1:338–39.

16. S. I. Lavrenov and I. M. Popov, *Sovetskii Soiuz v lokalnykh voinakh i konfliktakh* (Moscow, 2003), 72–75; Russian and Serbo-Croatian minutes, May 27–28, 1946, reprinted in Leonid Gibianskii, "The Soviet Bloc and the Initial State of the Cold War: Archival Documents on Stalin's Meetings with Communist Leaders of Yugoslavia and Bulgaria, 1946–1948," *CWIHP Bulletin* 10 (Mar. 1998), 119–28.

17. Djilas, *Rise and Fall*, 152.

18. V. K. Volkov and L. Ia. Gibianskii, "Na poroge pervogo raskola v sotsialisticheskom lagere: Peregovori rykovodiashikh deiatelei SSSR, Bolgarii i Iogoslavii 1948 r.,"

Istoricheskii arkhiv (1997), 92–123; Georgi Dimitrov, *Dnevnik: mart 1933–fevruari 1949: izbrano* (Sofia, 2003), 360–68; Vladimir Dedijer, *Tito Speaks: His Self-Portrait and Struggle with Stalin* (London, 1953), 320–22; Djilas, *Rise and Fall*, 152–53.

19. Dedijer, *Tito Speaks*, 310.

20. For the trade negotiations and Kardelj's visit with Stalin in Mar. 1947, see ibid., 285–93, 294–96.

21. Entry, with Stalin's note, for Jan. 24, 1948, and apology, in Dimitrov, *Dnevnik*, 357–58; Dedijer, *Tito Speaks*, 323–24.

22. Kardelj, *Reminiscences*, 104–7; Djilas, *Rise and Fall*, 166–67; Dedijer, *Tito Speaks*, 325–27.

23. Kardelj, *Reminiscences*, 110.

24. Mark Kramer, "Stalin, Soviet Policy, and the Consolidation of a Communist Bloc in Eastern Europe, 1944–53," in Vladimir Tismăneanu, ed., *Stalinism Revisited: The Establishment of Communist Regimes in East-Central Europe* (Budapest and New York, 2009), 83.

25. Docs. 117 and 118 in Stephen Clissold, ed., *Yugoslavia and the Soviet Union, 1939–1973: A Documentary Survey* (London, 1975), 169–74.

26. Quoted in Leonid Gibianskii, "The Beginning of the Soviet-Yugoslav Conflict and the Cominform," in Procacci et al., *Cominform*, 480.

27. Zhdanov, "On the Situation in the Communist Party of Yugoslavia," in Procacci et al., *Cominform*, 523–41.

28. Svetozar Stojanović, "Varieties of Stalinism in Light of the Yugoslav Case, in Tismăneanu, *Stalinism Revisited*, 394.

29. *New York Herald Tribune*, Nov. 7, 1952; T. V. Volokitina et al., *Moskva i Vostochnaia Evropa*, 585–86.

30. Robert Murphy, *Diplomat Among Warriors* (Garden City, N.Y., 1964), 309–10.

31. Lucius D. Clay, *Decision in Germany* (New York, 1950), 211; Murphy, *Diplomat Among Warriors*, 312.

32. Doc. 147 in G. P. Kynin and Jochen Laufer, eds., *SSSR i germanskii vopros, 1941–1949: dokumenty iz arkhiva vneshnei politiki Rossiiskoi Federastsii* (Moscow, 2003), 3:616–32.

33. Ibid. and BAB, SAPMO, 695, Nachlass Pieck.

34. Jochen Laufer, "Die UdSSR und die deutsche Währungsfrage 1944–1948," *Vierteljahrshefte für Zeitgeschichte* (1998), 483; doc. 160 in Kynin and Laufer, *SSSR i germanskii vopros*, 3:677–80.

35. Memorandum, June 4, 1948, in *FRUS, 1948, Germany and Austria*, 2:907–8.

36. Laufer, "Die UdSSR und Währungsfrage," 455.

37. Clay, *Decision in Germany*, 358–63.

38. Murphy, *Diplomat Among Warriors*, 298.

39. Derek Watson, *Molotov: A Biography* (New York, 2005), 240–41.

40. Gerhard Wettig, *Stalin and the Cold War in Europe: The Emergence and Development of East-West Conflict, 1939–1953* (Lanham, Md., 2008), 173–74.

41. See Stalin to Pieck, Oct. 13, 1949, in Stalin, *Sochineniia*, 16: 100–101; for the positive German responses, see Jan C. Behrends, *Die erfundene Freundschaft: Propaganda für die Sowjetunion in Polen und in der DDR* (Cologne, 2006), 198–217; Silke Satjukow, *Besatzer: "Die Russen" in Deutschland 1945–1994* (Göttingen, 2008), 63–67.

42. Doc. 50 in Peter Ruggenthaler, ed., *Stalins grosser Bluff: Die Geschichte der Stalin-Note in Dokumenten der sowjetischen Führung* (Munich, 2007), 111–13; Wettig, *Stalin and the Cold War*, 197–228. For a persistent opponent of this thesis, see Wilfried Loth, *Die Sowjetunion und die deutsche Frage: Studien zur sowjetischen Deutschlandpolitik* (Göttingen, 2007).

43. Acheson to U.S. High Commissioner, Bonn, Mar. 22, 1952, in *FRUS, 1952–1954, Germany and Austria*, 189–90; Dean Acheson, *Present at the Creation: My Years in the State Depart-*

ment (New York, 1987), 629–33. Acheson gives March 26 as the date of the handover; Vyshinsky's calendar gives March 25.

44. For analysis of the second note, see Ruggenthaler, *Stalins grosser Bluff*, 158–63.

45. The Russian minutes of SED conversations with Stalin, in Bernd Bonwetsch and Sergej Kudrjasov, "Stalin und die II. Parteikonferenz der SED: Ein Besuch der SED Führung in Moskau, 31. März–8. April 1952, und seine Folgen. Dokumentation" in Jürgen Zarusky, ed., *Stalin und die Deutschen: Neue Beiträge der Forschung* (Munich, 2006), 173–206. The German record is in BAB, SAPMO, NY 4036: Nachlass Pieck, 696, 12–25.

46. Ibid.-

CHAPTER 19. LOOKING AT ASIA FROM THE KREMLIN

1. Erik van Ree, *Socialism in One Zone: Stalin's Policy in Korea, 1945–1947* (Oxford, U.K., 1989), 108–74; Jongsoo Lee, *The Partition of Korea After World War II* (New York, 2006), 93, 143.

2. S. N. Goncharov interview with Ivan Kovalev, "Stalin's Dialogue with Mao Zedong," *Journal of Northeast Asian Studies* (Winter 1991), 15. Stalin conversation with Liu Shaoqi, July 1949, doc. 6 in Sergei N. Goncharow, John W. Lewis, and Xue Litai, *Uncertain Partners: Stalin, Mao, and the Korean War* (Stanford, Calif., 1993), 232.

3. Dieter Heinzig, *The Soviet Union and Communist China, 1945–1950: The Arduous Road to the Alliance* (New York, 2004), 255–56.

4. Stalin–Mao Zedong, Dec. 16, 1949, in "New Documents on Stalin's Conversations," CWIHP *Bulletin* 6/7 (Winter 1995–96), 5.

5. For the documents, see Odd Arne Westad, "Fighting for Friendship: Mao, Stalin, and the Sino-Soviet Treaty of 1950," in CWIHP *Bulletin* 8/9 (Winter 1996–97), 224–42; Jung Chang and Jon Halliday, *Mao: The Unknown Story* (London, 2005), 351–67; and Jonathan Haslam, *Russia's Cold War: From the October Revolution to the Fall of the Berlin Wall* (New Haven, Conn., 2011), 112–16.

6. Stalin–Mao Zedong, Jan. 22, 1950, "New Documents," 5–7.

7. Nikita Khrushchev, *Memoirs*, vol. 3, *Statesman, 1953–1964* (University Park, Pa., 2007), 415–16.

8. Westad, "Fighting for Friendship," 225; Chang and Halliday, *Mao*, 369.

9. Kathryn Weathersby, "Soviet Aims in Korea and the Origins of the Korean War, 1945–1950: New Evidence from Russian Archives," CWIHP Working Paper no. 8 (1993). Kim conversations with Stalin, doc. 1, Mar. 5, 1949, AVPRF, f. 059a, o. 5a, d. 3, p. 11, l. 10–20, in CWIHP, virtual archive, Korean War.

10. Telegram from Soviet representative to Moscow, Sept. 14, 1949, in AVPRF, f. 059a, op. 5a, d. 3, p. 11, l. 46–53, in CWIHP, virtual archive, Korean War.

11. Shtykov to Vyshinsky, Jan. 19, 1950, in AVPRF, f. 059a, op. 5a, d. 3, p. 11, l. 87–91, in CWIHP, virtual archive, Korean War.

12. Mao and Zhou Enlai to Liu Shaoqi, Feb. 1, 1950, doc. 24 in Westad, "Fighting for Friendship," 235.

13. Heinzig, *Soviet Union and Communist China*, 306.

14. Stalin to Shtykov, Jan. 30, 1950, in AVPRF, f. 059a, op. 5a, d. 3, p. 11, l. 92; Shtykov to Stalin, Jan. 31, 1950, in APRF, l. 123–124, fond and opis not given; and AVPRF, f. 059a, op. 5a, d. 3, p. 11, l. 92–93, in CWIHP, virtual archive, Korean War.

15. Heinzig, *Soviet Union and Communist China*, 277–79.

16. *Voina v Koree, 1950–1953* (Moscow, 2003), 11–14.

17. Document cited in full in Katheryn Weathersby, "Should We Fear This? Stalin and

the Danger of War with America," CWIHP Working Paper (July 2002), 9–11. See also A. Torkunov, *Zagadochnaya Voina: Koreiskii konflikt 1950–1953 godov* (Moscow, 2000), 58–64.

18. Docs. 1 and 2 in James G. Hershberg, "Russian Documents on the Korean War, 1950–53," CWIHP *Bulletin* 14/15 (2003–4), 372–73.

19. Muccio to Secretary of State, *FRUS, 1950, Korea,* 125–26.

20. Kirk to Secretary of State, ibid., 139–40.

21. Andrei A. Gromyko, *Pamiatnoe* (Moscow, 1990), 1:248–50.

22. UN Security Council Resolutions, at http://www.un.org/documents/sc/res/1950/scres50.htm.

23. Stalin to Klement Gottwald, Aug. 27, 1950, in A. V. Ledovsky, "Stalin, Mao Tsedun i koreiskaia voina 1950–1953 godov," *Novaia i noveishaia istoriia* (Sept.–Oct. 2005), 96–97.

24. For an alternative view, see Shen Zhihua, "Sino-Soviet Relations and the Origins of the Korean War: Stalin's Strategic Goals in the Far East," *Journal of Cold War Studies* (2000), 44–68.

25. David McCullough, *Truman* (New York, 1992), 799–800.

26. Kim Il Sung and Pak Heonyeong to Stalin (via Shtykov), sent on Sept. 30, 1950, in APRF, f. 45, op. 1, d. 347, l. 41–45, in CWIHP, virtual archive, Korean War.

27. Stalin to Mao, July 5 and Oct. 1, 1950, in APRF, f. 45, op. 1, d. 331, l. 79 and l. 97–98, in CWIHP, virtual archive, Korean War.

28. Mao to Stalin, Oct. 2, 1950, in APRF, f. 45, op. 1, d. 334, l. 105–10, in CWIHP, virtual archive, Korean War.

29. Stalin to Mao, Oct. 5, 1950, doc. 6 in CWIHP *Bulletin* 14/15 (2003–4), 376–77.

30. Mao, via Soviet ambassador in China, to Stalin, Oct. 7, 1950, doc. 7, ibid., 377–78.

31. Telegram, Fyn Si (Stalin) to Kim Il Sung (via Shtykov), Oct. 13, 1950, in APRF, f. 45, op. 1, d. 347, l. 74–75, in CWIHP, virtual archive, Korean War.

32. Quoted in Goncharow, Lewis, and Litai, *Uncertain Partners,* 197.

33. For a critique of this literature, see Chen Jian, *China's Road to the Korean War: The Making of the Sino-American Confrontation* (New York, 1994), 1–6.

34. Heinzig, *Soviet Union and Communist China,* 391.

35. Jian, *Mao's China,* 59–61.

36. Chang and Halliday, *Mao,* 377–78; Jian, *Mao's China,* 88–91.

37. *Voina v Koree, 1950–1953* (Moscow, 2003), 41–42; Chang and Halliday, *Mao,* 381–82.

38. Stalin to Zhou Enlai, Dec. 1 and 7, 1950, in APRF, f. 45, op. 1, d. 336, l. 20–21, and AVPRF, f. 059a, op. 5a, d. 3, p. 11, l. 196–97, in CWIHP, virtual archive, Sino-Soviet relations.

39. Jian, *Mao's China,* 93–95.

40. Stalin to Mao Zedong, June 5, 1951, in APRF, f. 45, op. 1, d. 339, l. 17–18, in CWIHP, virtual archive, Sino-Soviet relations.

41. Stalin and Zhou Enlai conversation, Sept. 3, 1952, in APRF, f. 45, op. 1, d. 329, ll. 75–87, in CWIHP virtual archive, Sino-Soviet relations.

42. Stalin and Zhou Enlai conversation, Aug. 20, 1952, in APRF, f. 45, op. 1, d. 329, l. 54–72, in CWIHP virtual archive, Sino-Soviet relations.

43. Stalin and Zhou Enlai, conversation, Sept. 19, 1952, in APRF, f. 45, op. 1, d. 343, ll. 97–103, in CWIHP virtual archive, Korean War.

44. Doc. 6 in Goncharov, Lewis, and Litai, *Uncertain Partners,* 232.

45. Chang and Halliday, *Mao,* 388–89.

46. Michael D. Gordon, *Red Cloud at Dawn: Truman, Stalin, and the End of the Atomic Monopoly* (New York, 2009), 203–13, 242–42.

47. Kirk to Acheson, Oct. 5, 1949, in *FRUS, 1949,* 5:664.

48. V. L. Malkov, "Igra bez myacha: sotsialno-psikhologicheskii kontekst sovetskoi atomnoi diplomatii," in N. I. Egorova and A. O. Chubarian, eds., *Kholodnaia voina, 1945–1963 gg.: Istoricheskaia retrospektiva. Sbornik statei* (Moscow, 2003), 281–320.

49. Dean Acheson, *Present at the Creation: My Years in the State Department* (New York, 1969), 420–21; Melvyn P. Leffler, *A Preponderance of Power: National Security, the Truman Administration, and the Cold War* (Stanford, Calif., 1992), 402; Walter Isaacson and Evan Thomas, *Wise Men: Six Friends and the World They Made* (New York, 1986), 513.

50. David Holloway, *Stalin and the Bomb* (New Haven, Conn., 1994), 94–319.

51. Cited in ibid., 318.

52. N. I. Egorova, "Voenno-politicheskaya integratsia stran Zapada i reaktsiya SSSR (1947–1953)," in Egorova and Chubarian, *Kholodnaia voina*, 200–2.

53. János M. Rainer, "Stalin and Rákosi, Stalin and Hungary," Oct. 4, 1997, paper at the workshop "European Archival Evidence. Stalin and the Cold War in Europe, Budapest, 1956." http://www.rev.hu/history_of_45/szerviz/bibliogr/rmj5.html.

54. Mark Kramer, "Stalin, Soviet Policy, and the Consolidation of a Communist Bloc in Eastern Europe, 1944–53," in Vladimir Tismăneanu, ed., *Stalinism Revisited: The Establishment of Communist Regimes in East-Central Europe* (Budapest and New York, 2009), 93.

55. Jian, *Mao's China*, 116.

56. Stalin to Mao, Dec. 27, 1952, in APRF, f. 45, op. 1, d. 343, l. 115–16, in CWIHP, virtual archive, Sino-Soviet relations.

57. Chang and Halliday, *Mao*, 390–91.

58. *Voina v Koree, 1950–1953*, 17–19.

59. G. F. Krivosheev, ed., *Rossiia i SSSR v voinakh XX veka: poteri vooruzhennykh sil: statisticheskoe issledovanie* (Moscow, 2001), 525.

60. Acheson, *Present at the Creation*, 652.

61. Max Hastings, *The Korean War* (New York, 1988), 329.

62. Ibid., 10–11.

63. See David Priestland, *The Red Flag: A History of Communism* (New York, 2009), 266–69, 302–3.

CHAPTER 20. NEW WAVES OF STALINIZATION

1. G. V. Kostychenko, *Tainaia politikika Stalina: Vlast i antisemitizm* (Moscow, 2001), 388–94.

2. Stalin, *Sochineniia*, 12:28.

3. Doc. 31 in D. G. Nadzhafov and Z. S. Belousova, eds., *Stalin i kosmopolitizm: dokumenty Agitpropa TSK KPSS, 1945–1953* (Moscow, 2005).

4. Arno Lustiger, *Rotbuch: Stalin und die Juden. Die tragische Geschichte des jüdischen Antifaschistischen Komitees und der sowetischen Juden* (Berlin, 1998), 123.

5. Anastas I. Mikoyan, *Tak bylo: Razmyshleniya o minushem* (Moscow, 1999), chap. 30; Simon Sebag Montefiore, *Stalin: The Court of the Red Tsar* (New York, 2004), chap. 50.

6. Kostyrchenko, *Tainaia politikika Stalina*, 388–94.

7. Doc. 83 in Nadzhafov and Belousova, *Stalin i kosmopolitizm*.

8. Doc. 124 in G. V. Kostyrchenko, ed., *Gosudarstvennyi antisemitizm v SSSR ot nachala do kulminatsii: 1938–1953* (Moscow, 2005).

9. Quoted in G. V. Kostyrchenko, *V plenu u krasnogo faraona* (Moscow, 1994), 203–4.

10. Ilya Ehrenburg, *Liudi, gody, zhizn: vospominaniia, v trekh tomakh* (Moscow, 2005), 6, part 15; Joshua Rubenstein, *Tangled Loyalties: The Life and Times of Ilya Ehrenburg* (New York, 1996), 240–65.

11. Yuri Slezkine, *The Jewish Century* (Princeton, N.J., 2004), 405n147.

12. T. V. Volokitina et al., *Moskva i Vostochnaia Evropa: stanovlenie politicheskikh rezhimov sovetskogo tipa, 1949–1953: ocherki istorii* (Moscow, 2002), 505–10.

13. Antoni Dudek and Andrzej Paczkowski, "Polen," in Łukasz Kamiński, Krzysztof Persak, and Jens Gieseke, eds., *Handbuch der kommunistischen Geheimdienste in Osteuropa 1944–1991* (Göttingen, 2009), 324–26.

14. Andrzej Paczkowski, *The Spring Will Be Ours: Poland and Poles from Occupation to Freedom* (University Park, Pa., 2003), 198–278.

15. Svetozar Sretenoviń and Artan Puto, "Leader Cults in the Western Balkans, 1945–90: Josip Broz Tito and Enver Hoxha," in Balázs Apor, Jan C. Behrends, Polly Jones, and E. A. Rees, eds., *The Leader Cult in Communist Dictatorships: Stalin and the Eastern Bloc* (New York, 2004), 216–18.

16. See Robert C. Austin, "Purge and Counter-Purge in Stalinist Albania, 1944–1956," in Kevin McDermott and Matthew Stibbe, eds., *Stalinist Terror in Eastern Europe: Elite Purges and Mass Repression* (New York, 2010), 206. Peter Danylow, "Sieg und Niederlage der Internationale: Die Sowjetizierung der Kommunistischen Partei in Albanien," in Stefan Creuzberger and Manfred Görtemaker, eds., *Gleichschaltung unter Stalin? Die Entwicklung der Parteien im östlichen Europa 1944–1949* (Paderborn, 2002), 259–60.

17. Enver Hoxha, *With Stalin: Memoirs* (Tirana, 1979), 205–6.

18. Peter Kenez, *Hungary from the Nazis to the Soviets: The Establishment of the Communist Regime in Hungary, 1944–1948* (New York, 2006), 278–88.

19. Martin Mevius, *Agents of Moscow: The Hungarian Communist Party and the Origins of Socialist Patriotism, 1941–1953* (Oxford, U.K., 2004), 242–46.

20. Volokitina et al., *Moskva i Vostochnaia Evropa*, 526–27.

21. László Borhi, *Hungary in the Cold War, 1945–1956: Between the United States and the Soviet Union* (New York, 2004), 207–13; George H. Hodos, *Show Trials: Stalinist Purges in Eastern Europe, 1948–1954* (New York, 1987), 64–65.

22. Mevius, *Agents of Moscow,* 245–57.

23. Transcript of conversations, June 13–16, 1953: Hungarian National Archives, Budapest, 276.f 102/65, in CWIHP, virtual archive. Miklós Molnár, *A Concise History of Hungary* (Cambridge, U.K., 1996), 303; Kristián Ungváry and Gabor Tabajdi, "Ungarn," in Kamiński, Persak, and Gieseke, *Handbuch,* 546–49.

24. George Konrád, *A Guest in My Own Country: A Hungarian Life* (New York, 2007), 194–197.

25. János Kornai, *By Force of Thought: Irregular Memoirs of an Intellectual Journey* (Cambridge, Mass., 2006), 44.

26. Charles Gati, *Failed Illusions: Moscow, Washington, Budapest, and the 1956 Hungarian Revolution* (Washington, D.C., 2006), 49n49.

27. V. G. Grigoryan to Stalin, Jan. 17, 1950, in T. V. Volokitina et al., eds., *Sovetskii factor v Vostochnoi Evrope, 1944–1953* (Moscow, 2002), 2:244–45.

28. Volokitina et al., *Moskva i Vostochnaia Evropa,* 530–40; Archie Brown, *The Rise and Fall of Communism* (New York, 2009), 212.

29. Georgi Dimitrov, *Dnevnik: mart 1933–fevruari 1949: izbrano* (Sofia, 2003), 417.

30. Report, Jan. 7, 1949, doc. 1 in Volokitina et al., *Sovetskii factor,* 2:11–12.

31. Letter cited in Karel Kaplan, *Report on the Murder of the General Secretary* (Columbus, Ohio, 1990), 34.

32. Frederick B. Chary, *History of Bulgaria* (Santa Barbara, Calif., 2011), 129–31.

33. Jordan Baev and Kostadin Grozev, "Bulgarien: Organisation, Aufbau und Personal," in Kamiński, Persak, and Gieseke, *Handbuch,* 181–87.

34. Georgi Markov, *The Truth That Killed* (New York, 1984), 12.

35. Robert Levy, *Ana Pauker: The Rise and Fall of a Jewish Communist* (Berkeley, Calif., 2001),

144–52; Dennis Deletant, *Communist Terror in Romania: Georghiu-Dej and the Police State* (New York, 1999), 84–85, 170–94.

36. MGB to Molotov, May 13, 1950, doc. 115 in Volokitina et al., *Sovetskii factor*, 2:325–26.

37. Vladimir Tismăneanu, *Stalinism for All Seasons: A Political History of Romanian Communism* (Berkeley, Calif., 2003), 132–35.

38. Interrogation notes cited in Levy, *Ana Pauker*, 157.

39. Denis Deletant, "Rumänien," in Kamiński, Persak, and Gieseke, *Handbuch*, 378–81.

40. Docs. 97 and 105 in T. V. Volokitina et al., eds., *Vostochnaya Evropa v dokumentakh rossiiskikh arkhivov* (Moscow, 1997–98), 2:298, 317.

41. Igor Lukes, "Rudolf Slánský: His Trials and Trial," CWIHP Working Paper no. 50, 14.

42. See Kaplan, *Report*, 16–17.

43. Ibid., 47–48.

44. Minutes, Slánský's address in Giuliano Procacci et al., *The Cominform: Minutes of the Three Conferences, 1947, 1948, 1949* (Milan, 1994), 727–37.

45. Lukes, "Rudolf Slánský," 26–27.

46. Cited in ibid., 31.

47. Kaplan, *Report*, 125–51; Lukes, "Rudolf Slánský," 47–51.

48. Marian Šlingová, *Truth Will Prevail* (London, 1968), 84–87.

49. Quoted in Lukes, "Rudolf Slánský," 54.

50. Jiří Pelikán, ed., *The Czechoslovak Political Trials, 1950–1954: The Suppressed Report of the Dubček Government's Commission of Inquiry, 1968* (Stanford, Calif., 1971), 110.

51. Kevin McDermott, "Stalinist Terror in Czechoslovakia: Origins, Processes, Responses," in McDermott and Stibbe, eds., *Stalinist Terror*, 98–113.

52. Ulrich Mählert, " 'Die Partei hat immer Recht!' Parteisäuberungen als Kaderpolitik in der SED (1948–1953)," in Hermann Weber and Ulrich Mählert, eds., *Terror: Stalinistische Parteisäuberungen 1936–1953* (Paderborn, 1998), 418.

53. Russian minutes of SED conversations with Stalin, Apr. 7, 1952, in Dmitri Volkogonov Collection, Hoover Institution. The German record is in BAB, SAPMO, NY 4036, Nachlass Pieck, 696, 12–25.

54. Hodos, *Show Trials*, xiii.

55. Jens Gieseke, "Deutsche Demokratische Republik," in Kamiński, Persak, and Gieseke, *Handbuch*, 199–260.

56. Dierk Hoffmann, *Otto Grotewohl (1894–1964): Eine politische Biographie* (Munich, 2009), 530–33.

57. Beria memorandum, May 6, 1953, in CWIHP, virtual archive, Germany in the Cold War.

58. Order, Soviet Council of Ministers, APRF, f. 3, op. 64, d. 802, l. 153–61, in CWIHP, virtual archive, Germany in the Cold War.

59. Docs. 292–301, Volokitina et al., *Sovetskii factor* 2:757–74.

60. Doc. 60, "On the Events of 17–19 June in Berlin and the GDR," June 24, 1953, in Christian F. Ostermann, ed., *Uprising in East Germany 1953* (New York, 2001), 257–85.

61. P. Naumov report, June 22, 1953, to D. T. Shepilov, in CWIHP, virtual archive, Germany in the Cold War.

62. Transcript of conversations, June 13–16, 1953, Hungarian National Archives, Budapest, 276.f 102/65, in CWIHP, virtual archive.

63. Michael Korda, *Journey to a Revolution: A Personal Memoir and History of the Hungarian Revolution of 1956* (New York, 2006), 80.

64. Mark Kramer, "The Early Post-Stalin Succession Struggle and Upheavals in East-Central Europe," *Journal of Cold War Studies* (1999), 3–66.

65. David E. Murphy, Sergei A. Kondrashev, and George Baily, *Battleground Berlin: CIA vs. KGB in the Cold War* (New Haven, Conn., 1997), 170.

66. Edith Sheffer, *Burned Bridge: How East and West Germans Made the Iron Curtain* (New York, 2011), 163.

67. Joachim Gauck, *Winter im Sommer—Frühling im Herbst* (Berlin, 2009), 78.

68. Sheffer, *Burned Bridge*, 167.

69. Gauck, *Winter im Sommer*, 33–52.

CHAPTER 21. STALIN'S LAST WILL AND TESTAMENT

1. Dmitrii T. Shepilov, *Neprimknushii* (Moscow, 2001), 181–97.

2. Ethan Pollock, *Stalin and the Soviet Science Wars* (Princeton, N.J., 2006), 168–82.

3. Stalin, *Sochineniia*, 16:184–86.

4. Nikita S. Khrushchev, *Doklad na zakrytom zasedanii XX Sezda KPSS: o kulte lichnosti i ego posledstviiakh* (Moscow, 1959).

5. Janet G. Chapman, *Real Wages in Soviet Russia Since 1928* (Cambridge, Mass., 1963), 166, 176, tables 27 and 28.

6. G. F. Kostyrchenko, *Tainaia politikika Stalina, Vlast i antisemitizm* (Moscow, 2001), 629–30.

7. RGASPI, f. 17, op. 162, d. 46, l. 19–21.

8. Kostyrchenko, *Tainaia politikika Stalina*, 422–74.

9. V. P. Naumov et al., eds., *Nepravednyi sud. Poslednii stanlinskii rasstrel; stenogramma sudebnogo protsessa nad chlenami Evreiskogo antifashistskogo komiteta* (Moscow, 1994), 375–83.

10. Jonathan Brent and Vladimir P. Naumov, *Stalin's Last Crime: The Plot Against Jewish Doctors, 1948–1953* (New York, 2003), 218–19.

11. CPSU CC resolution, Dec. 4, 1952, doc. 167 in G. V. Kostyrchenko, ed., *Gosudarstvennyi antisemitizm v SSSR ot nachala do kulminatsii: 1938–1953* (Moscow, 2005).

12. V. A. Malyshev, diary entry for Dec. 1, 1952, doc. 166, ibid.

13. Doc. 262 in Nadzhafov and Belousova, *Stalin i kosmopolitizm*; Kostyrchenko, *Tainaia politikika Stalina*, 654–56.

14. Lev Kopelev, *Ease My Sorrows: A Memoir* (New York, 1983), 185.

15. Gennady Kostyrchenko, "Deportatsia—Mistifikatsia: proshanie c mifom stalinskoi-epokhi," *Lekhaim* (2002), http://www.lechaim.ru/ARHIV/125/kost.htm. See also David Brandenburger, "Stalin's Last Crime? Recent Scholarship on Postwar Soviet Anti-semitism and the Doctors' Plot," *Kritika: Explorations in Russian and Eurasian History* (2005), 187–204.

16. See the ruminations in Vasily Grossman, *Vse technet* (Frankfurt am Main, 1970), 25.

17. Yoram Gorlizki and Oleg Khlevniuk, *Cold Peace: Stalin and the Soviet Ruling Circle, 1945–1953* (New York, 2004), 158–59.

18. See the interview (2004) in Cathy A. Frierson and Semyon S. Vilensky, eds., *Children of the Gulag* (New Haven, Conn., 2010), 349–50.

19. Alexander N. Yakovlev, *A Century of Violence in Soviet Russia* (New Haven, Conn., 2002), 207–8.

20. Ibid., 209–10.

21. Svetlana Alliluyeva, *Dvadtsat pisem k drugu* (New York, 1967), 182–83.

22. Politburo decision, Jan. 18, 1949, doc. 8 in Kostyrchenko, *Gosudarstvennyi antisemitizm*.

23. Simon Sebag Montefiore, *Stalin: The Court of the Red Tsar* (New York, 2004), 585–91.

24. Molotov to Stalin, Jan. 20, 1949, in Gorlizki and Khlevniuk, *Cold Peace*, 76.

25. Felix I. Chuev, *Molotov: Poluderzhavnyi vlastelin* (Moscow, 2000), 548–51.

26. Orlando Figes, *The Whisperers: Private Life in Stalin's Russia* (New York, 2007), 518–19.

27. Yuri Slezkine, *Jewish Century* (Princeton, N.J., 2004), 313.

28. Shepilov, *Neprimknushii*, 223; Konstantin M. Simonov, *Glazami cheloveka moego pokkoleniia: razmyshleniya o J. V. Staline* (Moscow, 1990), 206–7.

29. Stalin, *Sochineniia*, 16:227–29.

30. Ibid., 16:74–79.

31. Ibid., 16:194.

32. Ibid., 16:584–87.

33. Gorlizki and Khlevniuk, *Cold Peace*, 148–49.

34. Simonov, *Glazami cheloveka moego pokkoleniia*, 209–12.

35. Nikita Khrushchev, *Memoirs*, vol. 2, *Reformer* (University Park, Pa., 2006), 113; Kostyrchenko, *Tainaia politikika Stalina*, 654–63.

36. Stalin, *Sochineniia*, 18:588–90; Simonov, *Glazami cheloveka moego pokkoleniia*, 209–14.

37. David Holloway, *Stalin and the Bomb* (New Haven, Conn., 1994), 292–93, 431n126.

38. "Istoriya bolezin I. V. Stalina" is analyzed in Brent and Naumov, *Stalin's Last Crime*, 312–21.

39. Myasnikov is listed as one of the authors of "Istoriya bolezin I. V. Stalina." See his *Ya lechil Stalina: is sekretnikh arkhivov SSSR* (Moscow, 2011), chap. 9; also *Moskovskii Komsomolets*, Apr. 21, 2011.

40. Kitchlu's remarks are in Harrison E. Salisbury, *Moscow Journal: The End of Stalin* (Chicago, 1961), 327, 332.

41. Alliluyeva, *Dvadtsat pisem k drugu*, 10, 182.

42. Anne Applebaum, *Gulag: A History* (New York, 2003), 476–77.

43. Doc. 547, in *FRUS, 1952–1954. Eastern Europe; Soviet Union; Eastern Mediterranean*, 7:1083–85.

44. Doc. 554, ibid., 7:1099.

45. Doc. 557, ibid., 7:1102–3.

46. Salisbury, *Moscow Journal*, 340–49.

47. Grossman, *Vse technet*, 28–29.

48. Quoted in Irina Paperno, *Stories of the Soviet Experience: Memoirs, Diaries, Dreams* (Ithaca, N.Y., 2009), 28.

49. Their joint memoir is R. D. Orlova and Lev Kopelev, *My zhile v Moskve: 1956–1980* (Ann Arbor, Mich., 1988).

50. Catherine Merridale, *Night of Stone: Death and Memory in Twentieth-Century Russia* (New York, 2001), 257–69.

51. Quoted in Frierson and Vilensky, *Children of the Gulag*, 354.

52. See Vladimir Koslov, Sergei V. Mironenko, eds., *Kramola—inakomyslie v SSSR pri Khrushcheve i Brezhneve, 1953–1982 gg.* (Moscow, 2005), 65–98. Juliane Fürst, *Stalin's Last Generation: Soviet Post-War Youth and the Emergence of Mature Socialism* (Oxford, U.K., 2010), 122–23.

53. Alexander Solzhenitsyn, *The Gulag Archipelago, 1918–1956: An Experiment in Literary Investigation* (New York, 1978), 3:406–22.

54. Note 561, Mar. 10, 1953, in *FRUS, 1952–1954. Eastern Europe; Soviet Union; Eastern Mediterranean*, 7:1108–9.

55. Georgi Markov, *The Truth That Killed* (New York, 1984), 57.

56. Vladimir Tismăneanu, "Diabolical Pedagogy and the (Il)logic of Stalinism in Eastern Europe," in Vladimir Tismăneanu, ed., *Stalinism Revisited: The Establishment of Communist Regimes in East-Central Europe* (New York, 2009), 47.

57. E. A. Rees, "Introduction: The Sovietization of Eastern Europe," in Balázs Apor, Péter Apor, and E. A. Rees, eds., *The Sovietization of Eastern Europe: New Perspectives on the Postwar Period* (Washington, D.C., 2008), 13. Zhihua Shen and Yafeng Xia, "Between Aid and Restriction: Changing Soviet Policies Toward China's Nuclear Weapons Program: 1954–1960," Nuclear Proliferation History Project, Working Paper 2 (2012).

EPILOGUE

1. Odd Arne Westad, *The Global Cold War: Third World Interventions and the Making of Our Times* (New York, 2005), 67–69.
2. Noel E. Firth and James H. Noren, *Soviet Defense Spending: A History of CIA Estimates* (College Station, Tex., 1998); Vladislav M. Zubok, *A Failed Empire: The Soviet Union in the Cold War from Stalin to Gorbachev* (Chapel Hill, N.C., 2007), 299.
3. Amy Knight, *Beria: Stalin's First Lieutenant* (Princeton, N.J., 1993), 180–91.
4. Doc. 4 in V. Naumov and Y. Sigachev, eds., *Laverenty Beria. 1953. Stenogramma iiulskogo plenuma TsK CPSS i drugie dokumenty* (Moscow, 1999), 21–23.
5. *Pravda*, April 4, 6, 7, 1953.
6. Alexander Solzhenitsyn, *The Gulag Archipelago, 1918–1956: An Experiment in Literary Investigation* (New York, 1978), 3:285–331.
7. Anne Applebaum, *Gulag: A History* (New York, 2003), 506–13.
8. Nikita S. Khrushchev, *Doklad na zakrytom zasedanii XX Sezda KPSS: o kulte lichnosti i ego posledstviiakh* (Moscow, 1959), 9.
9. Ibid., 28.
10. Albert P. Van Goudoever, *The Limits of Destalinization in the Soviet Union: Political Rehabilitation in the Soviet Union Since Stalin* (New York, 1986), 8.
11. Applebaum, *Gulag*, 580.
12. Solzhenitsyn, *Gulag Archipelago*, 3:451.
13. Nanci Adler, *The Gulag Survivor: Beyond the Soviet System* (New Brunswick, N.J., 2002), 31–33.
14. Stephen F. Cohen, *The Victims Return: Survivors of the Gulag After Stalin* (Exeter, N.H., 2010), 4.
15. Pavel Polian, *Ne po svoyey vole. Istoriya i geografiya prinuditel'nykh migratsii v SSSR* (Moscow, 2001), 143–56.
16. For the complete story, see Y. Afiani and N. G. Tomilina, eds., *A za mnoiu shum pogoni: Boris Pasternak i vlast: dokumenty 1956–1972* (Moscow, 2001).
17. Zubok, *Failed Empire*, 342.
18. Alexander Yakovlev, "Doklad Komissii pri Prezidente Rossiiskoi Federatsii po reabilitatsii zertv polititseskikh repressii," report, Feb. 2, 2000, at http://www.alexanderyakov lev.org/personal-archive/articles/7141.
19. Measures are in 1990 U.S. dollars; findings of Angus N. Maddison, *Monitoring the World Economy* (Paris, 1995), recomputed as table 1.1 in Robert C. Allen, *Farm to Factory: A Reinterpretation of the Soviet Industrial Revolution* (Princeton, N.J., 2003), 5.
20. Tina Rosenberg, *The Haunted Land: Facing Europe's Ghosts After Communism* (New York, 1995).
21. For the OECD figures from 1990 to 1998, see Angus Maddison, *The World Economy: A Millennial Perspective* (Paris, 2001), 184–85, table A1-b.
22. "The Economist Intelligence Unit's Quality-of-Life Index," *Economist*, Sept. 5, 2007: http://www.economist.com/media/pdf/QUALITY_OF_LIFE.pdf.
23. E. A. Rees, "Conclusion: Crisis of the Soviet Model and De-Sovietization," in Balázs Apor, Péter Apor, and E. A. Rees, eds., *The Sovietization of Eastern Europe: New Perspectives on the Postwar Period* (Washington, D.C., 2008), 288–89.
24. Scott Shane, *Dismantling Utopia: How Information Ended the Soviet Union* (Chicago, 1994), 75–98.
25. Cohen, *Victims Return*, 174.

Illustration Credits

Police photos taken of Stalin after his arrest in Baku, Azerbaijan, 1908. Courtesy of Rue des Archives / The Granger Collection, New York.

Stalin and Khrushchev with members of the Communist Young Pioneers, c. 1935. Courtesy of Rue des Archives / The Granger Collection, New York.

Stalin with George C. Marshall, Archibald Clark Kerr, Harry Hopkins, and others at the Tehran Conference, 1943. Courtesy of The Granger Collection, New York.

Truman, Stalin, and others at the Potsdam Conference, 1945. Courtesy of ullstein bild / The Granger Collection, New York.

Roosevelt and Churchill, New Year's Day, 1942, in Alexandria, Virginia. Courtesy of The Granger Collection, New York.

Bernard Montgomery, Georgi Zhukov, and Konstantin Rokossovsky at a military ceremony, 1945. Courtesy of ullstein bild / The Granger Collection, New York.

Celebration of Stalin's seventieth birthday, 1949. Courtesy of ullstein bild / The Granger Collection, New York.

Theater production in honor of Stalin's life, Bolshoi Theater, 1951. Courtesy of ullstein bild / The Granger Collection, New York.

Propaganda poster of Stalin, 1952. Courtesy of ullstein bild / The Granger Collection, New York.

Seventh World Congress of the Communist International in Moscow, 1935. Courtesy of ullstein bild / The Granger Collection, New York.

Yugoslav Communist Partisan guerrilla leadership at Vis, Yugoslavia, 1944. Courtesy of ullstein bild / The Granger Collection, New York.

Communist leaders of Hungary, c. 1935. Courtesy of ullstein bild / The Granger Collection, New York.

Polish leader Władisław Gomułka. Courtesy of Rue des Archives / The Granger Collection, New York.

Newly appointed Czechoslovakian cabinet, 1948. Courtesy of ullstein bild / The Granger Collection, New York.

Romanian leaders in 1950. Courtesy of Fototeca (Romanian Online communism photo).

Berlin Airlift, 1948. Courtesy of The Granger Collection, New York.

Index

Page numbers in *italics* refer to maps.

Robert Gellately is the Earl Ray Beck Professor of History at Florida State University and recently was the Bertelsmann Visiting Professor of Twentieth-Century Jewish Politics and History at Oxford University. He is the author of *Lenin, Stalin, and Hitler: The Age of Social Catastrophe; The Gestapo and German Society: Enforcing Racial Policy, 1933–1945;* and *Backing Hitler: Consent and Coercion in Nazi Germany.* His work has been translated into more than twenty languages. He was born in St. John's, Newfoundland, and lives in Tallahassee, Florida.

A NOTE ON THE TYPE

This book was set in Monotype Dante, a typeface designed by Giovanni Mardersteig (1892–1977). Conceived as a private type for the Officina Bodoni in Verona, Italy, Dante was originally cut only for hand composition by Charles Malin, the famous Parisian punch cutter, between 1946 and 1952. Its first use was in an edition of Boccaccio's *Trattatello in laude di Dante* that appeared in 1954. The Monotype Corporation's version of Dante followed in 1957. Although modeled on the Aldine type used for Pietro Cardinal Bembo's treatise *De Aetna* in 1495, Dante is a thoroughly modern interpretation of the venerable face.

Composed by North Market Street Graphics,
Lancaster, Pennsylvania

Printed and bound by Berryville Graphics,
Berryville, Virginia

Designed by Soonyoung Kwon

DATE DUE